T0183199

Lecture Notes in Computer Science 9170

Commenced Publication in 1973
Founding and Former Series Editors:
Gerhard Goos, Juris Hartmanis, and Jan van Leeuwen

More information about this series at http://www.springer.com/series/7409

Masaaki Kurosu (Ed.)

Human-Computer Interaction

Interaction Technologies

17th International Conference,
HCI International 2015
Los Angeles, CA, USA, August 2–7, 2015
Proceedings, Part II

 Springer

Editor
Masaaki Kurosu
The Open University of Japan
Chiba-shi, Chiba
Japan

ISSN 0302-9743   ISSN 1611-3349 (electronic)
Lecture Notes in Computer Science
ISBN 978-3-319-20915-9   ISBN 978-3-319-20916-6 (eBook)
DOI 10.1007/978-3-319-20916-6

Library of Congress Control Number: 2015943050

LNCS Sublibrary: SL3 – Information Systems and Applications, incl. Internet/Web, and HCI

Printed on acid-free paper

Springer International Publishing AG Switzerland is part of Springer Science+Business Media
(www.springer.com)

Foreword

The 17th International Conference on Human-Computer Interaction, HCI International 2015, was held in Los Angeles, CA, USA, during 2–7 August 2015. The event incorporated the 15 conferences/thematic areas listed on the following page.

A total of 4843 individuals from academia, research institutes, industry, and governmental agencies from 73 countries submitted contributions, and 1462 papers and 246 posters have been included in the proceedings. These papers address the latest research and development efforts and highlight the human aspects of design and use of computing systems. The papers thoroughly cover the entire field of Human-Computer Interaction, addressing major advances in knowledge and effective use of computers in a variety of application areas. The volumes constituting the full 28-volume set of the conference proceedings are listed on pages VII and VIII.

I would like to thank the Program Board Chairs and the members of the Program Boards of all thematic areas and affiliated conferences for their contribution to the highest scientific quality and the overall success of the HCI International 2015 conference.

This conference could not have been possible without the continuous and unwavering support and advice of the founder, Conference General Chair Emeritus and Conference Scientific Advisor, Prof. Gavriel Salvendy. For their outstanding efforts, I would like to express my appreciation to the Communications Chair and Editor of HCI International News, Dr. Abbas Moallem, and the Student Volunteer Chair, Prof. Kim-Phuong L. Vu. Finally, for their dedicated contribution towards the smooth organization of HCI International 2015, I would like to express my gratitude to Maria Pitsoulaki and George Paparoulis, General Chair Assistants.

May 2015

Constantine Stephanidis
General Chair, HCI International 2015

HCI International 2015 Thematic Areas
and Affiliated Conferences

Thematic areas:

- Human-Computer Interaction (HCI 2015)
- Human Interface and the Management of Information (HIMI 2015)

Affiliated conferences:

- 12th International Conference on Engineering Psychology and Cognitive Ergonomics (EPCE 2015)
- 9th International Conference on Universal Access in Human-Computer Interaction (UAHCI 2015)
- 7th International Conference on Virtual, Augmented and Mixed Reality (VAMR 2015)
- 7th International Conference on Cross-Cultural Design (CCD 2015)
- 7th International Conference on Social Computing and Social Media (SCSM 2015)
- 9th International Conference on Augmented Cognition (AC 2015)
- 6th International Conference on Digital Human Modeling and Applications in Health, Safety, Ergonomics and Risk Management (DHM 2015)
- 4th International Conference on Design, User Experience and Usability (DUXU 2015)
- 3rd International Conference on Distributed, Ambient and Pervasive Interactions (DAPI 2015)
- 3rd International Conference on Human Aspects of Information Security, Privacy and Trust (HAS 2015)
- 2nd International Conference on HCI in Business (HCIB 2015)
- 2nd International Conference on Learning and Collaboration Technologies (LCT 2015)
- 1st International Conference on Human Aspects of IT for the Aged Population (ITAP 2015)

Conference Proceedings Volumes Full List

Human-Computer Interaction

Program Board Chair: Masaaki Kurosu, Japan

- Jose Abdelnour-Nocera, UK
- Sebastiano Bagnara, Italy
- Simone Barbosa, Brazil
- Kaveh Bazargan, Iran
- Thomas Berns, Sweden
- Adriana Betiol, Brazil
- Simone Borsci, UK
- Apala Lahiri Chavan, India
- Sherry Chen, Taiwan
- Kevin Clark, USA
- Torkil Clemmensen, Denmark
- Michael Craven, UK
- Henry Duh, Australia
- Achim Ebert, Germany
- Xiaowen Fang, USA
- Stefano Federici, Italy
- Sheue-Ling Hwang, Taiwan
- Wonil Hwang, Korea
- Yong Gu Ji, Korea
- Esther Jun Kim, USA
- Mitsuhiko Karashima, Japan
- Heidi Krömker, Germany
- Cecília Sík Lányi, Hungary
- Glyn Lawson, UK
- Cristiano Maciel, Brazil
- Chang S. Nam, USA
- Naoko Okuizumi, Japan
- Philippe Palanque, France
- Alberto Raposo, Brazil
- Ling Rothrock, USA
- Eunice Sari, Indonesia
- Dominique Scapin, France
- Milene Selbach Silveira, Brazil
- Guangfeng Song, USA
- Hiroshi Ujita, Japan
- Anna Wichansky, USA
- Chui Yin Wong, Malaysia
- Toshiki Yamaoka, Japan
- Kazuhiko Yamazaki, Japan
- Alvin W. Yeo, Malaysia

The full list with the Program Board Chairs and the members of the Program Boards of all thematic areas and affiliated conferences is available online at:

http://www.hci.international/2015/

Human-Computer Interaction

Program Board Chair: Masaaki Kurosu, Japan

- Jose Abdelnour-Nocera, UK
- Sebastiano Bagnara, Italy
- Simone Barbosa, Brazil
- Kaveh Bazargan, Iran
- Thomas Berns, Sweden
- Adriana Betiol, Brazil
- Simone Borsci, UK
- Apala Lahiri Chavan, India
- Sherry Chen, Taiwan
- Kevin Clark, USA
- Torkil Clemmensen, Denmark
- Michael Craven, UK
- Henry Duh, Australia
- Achim Ebert, Germany
- Xiaowen Fang, USA
- Stefano Federici, Italy
- Sheue-Ling Hwang, Taiwan
- Wonil Hwang, Korea
- Yong Gu Ji, Korea
- Esther Jun Kim, USA
- Mitsuhiko Karashima, Japan
- Heidi Krömker, Germany
- Cecília Sík Lányi, Hungary
- Glyn Lawson, UK
- Cristiano Maciel, Brazil
- Chang S. Nam, USA
- Naoko Okuizumi, Japan
- Philippe Palanque, France
- Alberto Raposo, Brazil
- Ling Rothrock, USA
- Eunice Sari, Indonesia
- Dominique Scapin, France
- Milene Selbach Silveira, Brazil
- Guangfeng Song, USA
- Hiroshi Ujita, Japan
- Anna Wichansky, USA
- Chui Yin Wong, Malaysia
- Toshiki Yamaoka, Japan
- Kazuhiko Yamazaki, Japan
- Alvin W. Yeo, Malaysia

The full list with the Program Board Chairs and the members of the Program Boards of all thematic areas and affiliated conferences is available online at:

http://www.hci.international/2015/

Human-Computer Interaction

Program Board Chair: Masaaki Kurosu, Japan

- Jose Abdelnour-Nocera, UK
- Sebastiano Bagnara, Italy
- Simone Barbosa, Brazil
- Kaveh Bazargan, Iran
- Thomas Berns, Sweden
- Adriana Betiol, Brazil
- Simone Borsci, UK
- Apala Lahiri Chavan, India
- Sherry Chen, Taiwan
- Kevin Clark, USA
- Torkil Clemmensen, Denmark
- Michael Craven, UK
- Henry Duh, Australia
- Achim Ebert, Germany
- Xiaowen Fang, USA
- Stefano Federici, Italy
- Sheue-Ling Hwang, Taiwan
- Wonil Hwang, Korea
- Yong Gu Ji, Korea
- Esther Jun Kim, USA
- Mitsuhiko Karashima, Japan
- Heidi Krömker, Germany
- Cecília Sík Lányi, Hungary
- Glyn Lawson, UK
- Cristiano Maciel, Brazil
- Chang S. Nam, USA
- Naoko Okuizumi, Japan
- Philippe Palanque, France
- Alberto Raposo, Brazil
- Ling Rothrock, USA
- Eunice Sari, Indonesia
- Dominique Scapin, France
- Milene Selbach Silveira, Brazil
- Guangfeng Song, USA
- Hiroshi Ujita, Japan
- Anna Wichansky, USA
- Chui Yin Wong, Malaysia
- Toshiki Yamaoka, Japan
- Kazuhiko Yamazaki, Japan
- Alvin W. Yeo, Malaysia

The full list with the Program Board Chairs and the members of the Program Boards of all thematic areas and affiliated conferences is available online at:

http://www.hci.international/2015/

HCI International 2016

The 18th International Conference on Human-Computer Interaction, HCI International 2016, will be held jointly with the affiliated conferences in Toronto, Canada, at the Westin Harbour Castle Hotel, 17–22 July 2016. It will cover a broad spectrum of themes related to Human-Computer Interaction, including theoretical issues, methods, tools, processes, and case studies in HCI design, as well as novel interaction techniques, interfaces, and applications. The proceedings will be published by Springer. More information will be available on the conference website: http://2016.hci.international/.

General Chair
Prof. Constantine Stephanidis
University of Crete and ICS-FORTH
Heraklion, Crete, Greece
Email: general_chair@hcii2016.org

http://2016.hci.international/

Contents – Part II

Gesture and Eye-Gaze Based Interaction

Natural User Interfaces

Adaptive and Personalized Interfaces

Distributed, Migratory and Multi-screen User Interfaces

Games and Gamification

HCI in Smart and Intelligent Environments

Gesture and Eye-gaze
Based Interaction

Using Gesture-Based Interfaces to Control Robots

Gabriel M. Bandeira[1]([✉]), Michaela Carmo[2], Bianca Ximenes[1],
and Judith Kelner[1]

[1] Centro de Informática (CIn) - Universidade Federal de Pernambuco (UFPE),
Recife, Pernambuco, Brazil
{gmb,bxhmm,jk}@cin.ufpe.br
[2] Universidade de Pernambuco (UPE), Recife, Pernambuco, Brazil
michaela.carmo@gprt.ufpe.br

Abstract. This paper analyzes human-robot interaction (HRI) to evaluate whether the use of a gesture-based interface is viable for robot control. An experiment was conducted with 19 volunteers. Using a body tracking device, they had to perform gestural commands to remotely control a mobile robot and complete a path marked on the floor. After the experiment, volunteers answered a questionnaire assessing aspects such as system's responsiveness, precision, and triggers to possible physical and psychological discomforts.

The results achieved validated the research aim partially, as it was determined that this control method is viable but only for short-term operations, pointing a necessity to create a more suitable control, less prone to cause user fatigue during long-term use. The developed system was designed not only for the analysis of HRI factors, but also for applications in remote operation contexts, such as industrial maintenance and exploration of inhospitable environments.

Keywords: Human-robot interaction · Human-computer interaction · Natural interfaces · Gestural interfaces · Remote operated robotics · Validation

1 Introduction

In the last few years, a wide range of researches explored usability in the fields of human-computer interaction (HCI) and human-robot interaction (HRI). Usability in this field comprehends several aspects, such as different kinds of command control, information feedback, communicability and its applicability on robotic systems [1–5].

To analyse the usability of a system, the way the interface decodes the commands must be considered. In the HRI field, a robot is usually controlled via classic interaction devices such as keyboards, mice and joysticks [6]. These devices may not be the most suited options for some applications because they work with complex software systems that commonly require prior training, which can be

M. Kurosu (Ed.): Human-Computer Interaction, Part II, HCII 2015, LNCS 9170, pp. 3–12, 2015.
DOI: 10.1007/978-3-319-20916-6_1

unpleasant and time consuming. These systems can be simplified with the use of an interface that requires less learning time, thereby improving user experience. Such simplification is made possible with the use of natural interfaces [7]. One option is to operate robots by using gestures, for instance, programming a body tracking device to capture movements the user performs, which correspond to commands recognized by the robot.

Having understood the types of interface currently available, this article analyzes the viability of human-robot interaction (HRI) via gesture-based interfaces [7] using a body tracking device to control a mobile robot. To do this, we built a system with a robot that sends images captured by a camera attached to its structure and is guided remotely by an user, who, in addition to the video stream, also counts on a graphical interface that contains auxiliary information to control the robot.

The aim of this research is to investigate whether the use of a gesture-based natural interface is viable for robot control. A viable interface for robot controlling in this study was considered to be a technically feasible interface that enables the user to control the robot accurately. Beyond that, an ideal gesture-based interface should depend on commands that are both easy to learn and execute, as well as that generate little to no physical or psychological discomfort. Those aspects were assessed via questionnaire with 19 volunteers that were willing to participate in the study controlling the robot and testing the working interface.

The implemented solution was designed not only for the analysis of HRI factors, but also has applications in remote operation contexts. Environments of industrial maintenance and exploration of inhospitable environments are good examples of possible operation fields for this system.

On the next section, we explained the related works that supported this study, containing works related to the interface chosen and the device we used to capture the movements. The following section, divided in two subsections, encloses the methodology followed to make the systems we made to validate this study and the experiment made to validate the same. The last two sections consists of the results achieved and the conclusion we made from this research.

2   Related Work

The development of the robot system and the gesture-based interface was based on a number of works addressing interfaces in HRI that were presented in forms other than the classical mice-keyboard combination. They are not necessarily studies on natural user interfaces, being instead evaluations of desirable aspects of HRI interfaces, and what may render them a higher usability.

The first group of works studied concerned human-robot interaction interfaces that did not use only classic interaction devices. Concerning the interface, a few researches were studied to base our choice. Initially, paper [3] analyzes controlling a robot using a Graphical User Interface (GUI). The lessons learned are deepened in [1], which performed an analysis of interfaces for a remote robot control that reduces task load and fatigue. [2] evaluated a human-machine interface where a combination of visual and haptic interactions was established to investigate the performance and viability of the proposed solution. Having studied these works, we could understand how each of the solutions could be explored and how a combination of GUI and another types of interface could be integrated. Finally, we found an example of natural user interfaces in the HRI field - an analysis of a semi-autonomous robot control using voice commands [4]. In this case, the robot accepts the commands and then analyzes its vicinity to recognise obstacles and possibly avoid them. This work analyzes the use of natural interface operated exclusively by voice command. As the use of a gesture-based natural interface had not been explored as far as we could find, we approach this aspect in our study. Users' attitude while they are interacting with robots is also a point of interest in the literature, as seen in [8,9]. For that reason, we also assessed this facet in our research.

Having defined how the interface would function, it was then necessary to determine how to track users' gestures. A common device used in HCI and HRI to recognise gestural commands is the camera. That happens because the camera can provide plenty of information about the scene, so developers can extract from the environment the exact information needed for their specific aims. That can be seen in an experiment where a hand-shape was recognised using an artificial neural network [10]. Based on this, we decided to use a camera based device, a RGB-D sensor. The RGB-D sensor can be understood in short as a device that captures images and the depth of each pixel of the image.

A research was performed to analyze how effective would be to read gesture commands tracking the user's body. Such a choice and its implications were presented in [10,11], being part of their analysis of user experience when interacting with a machine. Having understood the implications of the reading gestures choice, we could notice a few good aspects on adopting this approach and also some bad ones. In [11], for example, it was pointed some challenges like environmental noise including illumination changes and self occlusion - when one body part is occluded by another one - and how effective would it be to use multiple camera to reduce this last problem.

3   Methodology

The methodology is divided in two parts. The first contains an explanation of the technical aspects of the experiment, covering which modules were necessary to implement the system, why they were necessary, and the components used to build them. The next subsection contains a description of the experiment performed, including details of the interface and metrics used.

3.1   Technique

We adopted a gesture-based natural user interface [6] and analyzed the usability [6,12,13] of the user-robot interaction through a body tracking device. Such a choice was due to the fact that it is important that robot commands are intuitive and simple, as that provides an easier way to interact with robots. An easier way to operate is consequently more appropriate for people of different ages and skill levels and, moreover, enables robot interaction and interface operation without the need of exhaustive training of the user.

After the theoretical analysis of control interfaces, a prototype that allowed to conduct a practical assessment of gestural interaction was developed. For that, the team implemented two subunits responsible for complemental parts of the system architecture. The first one was called Control sub-system and it ran a software that detected the commands of the user in form of gestures and sent it to the second sub-system, called the Mobile sub-system. The Mobile entity comprehended a robot that executed actions corresponding to the user's commands, received from the Control. The Mobile unit also sent some information about its surroundings to the user by the Control's GUI, as it will be explained later.

The Control sub-system consisted in a personal computer (PC) connected to a Microsoft Kinect platform. The Microsoft Kinect platform was chosen due to its ease of use with to a PC - plenty of APIs and tools are available and both environments are compatible. Besides, Kinect's precision on body tracking and affordability were also considered to settle the choice. The Control sub-system was responsible for analysing the pose of the user and comparing that pose to the ones stored in the memory of the software. During this pose match, if a match occurred, the Control sub-system would send a command to the Mobile sub-system corresponding to the matched pose. On the Control's PC there was also a window on the screen with a few pieces of information sent by the robot from the Mobile sub-system. After that process, the Mobile unit received the command and executed the action related to it. During this execution process, the Mobile also captured images from the environment where it is currently located and sent it to the user.

On the Control unit, there were four available poses that represented four different commands. These poses were defined by different arm positions, which followed the same movement logic of those performed to operate tractor's levers. To move forward, both arms should stay in front of the person, outstretched as in Fig. 1a. To move backwards, both arms should also stay in front of the user's body, but bent, bringing hands closer in as shown in Fig. 1b. Turning right or left was triggered by keeping both arms in front of the user, one of them close to the body and the other stretched out. On the turning commands, if the user's right arm was outstretched and the left was close, the turn would be to the left side as in Fig. 1c. Equivalently, the opposite arm order, the right one close and the left one outstretched as in Fig. 1d, would make the robot perform a right turn.

The Mobile sub-system was composed by a robot that acted according to the commands sent by the Control. To build a suitable robot, it was necessary to have a movement or action module, a perception module and a communication module, beyond the robot's structure. The necessity of the movement or action module was due to the kind of experiment we were performing. Our experiment required that because we wanted a system where the user could control a robot to explore places where (s)he could not go but the robot could. Another necessary

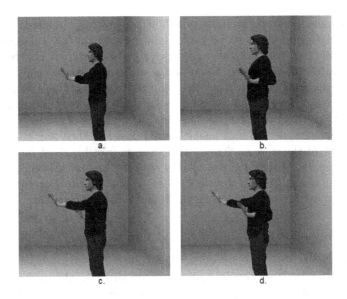

Fig. 1. Avatar performing the four available commands.

module, the perceptive one, was due to the fact that if the robot moves into places where humans cannot go, the human could not directly see the robot nor know how its surroundings are or what the robot could do there. To make the user aware of the robot's environment, (s)he must have some information about it in order to make informed decisions and command it. Finally, the communication module requirement was due to the constant exchange of information taking place between the Control and the Mobile subsystems.

The movement or action module consisted of a LEGO Mindstorms NXT 2.0 set, using its electric motors, wheels and structure components. To make the perception module, a camera was attached to the robot so the user could see exactly what was in front of the robot and make informed decisions. To build a communication module, we needed a fast enough system that allowed the robot to receive commands and also send images of the scene to the user as close as possible to real time. For these reasons, the team chose to use a dedicated wifi network, for a faster connection speed and less latency and packets loss, when compared to a communal use wifi network. The structure of the robot was also constructed with LEGO Mindstorms NXT 2.0 components, using its structure components and connectors. That choice was made to keep the modules of the robot easy to be assembled.

Considering the three modules that compose the robot on the Mobile subsystem, the platform chosen to connect these modules was the Raspberry Pi Model A. The Raspberry Pi was chosen due to its USB interface, programming possibilities for a C++ developer, processor speed and capacity, besides its size and weight. The USB interface was necessary to communicate with the LEGO Mindstorms NXT via USB cable and to connect the platform to the wifi network via a wifi dongle. The programming possibilities previously pointed out are the availability of the platform to be programmed using the C++ language and the compatibility of the compiler and processor with external libraries. Those external libraries were necessary to do things such as communicating with other modules or capturing images from the camera, while the C++ language was chosen just as a project option selected by the team, since our developers were already used to writing code on that language. The processor speed and capacity were important considering that images were taken and then sent constantly to make the view of the user as close to real time as possible. Last but not least, the size and weight of the platform used in that module integration was crucial because it was a small mobile robot, so none of the platforms could be too big nor too heavy, or the robot's motors could not perform movement.

3.2 Experiment

To test HRI via gesture-based interface, the team conducted an experiment with 19 randomly chosen volunteers from diverse areas of knowledge and an age span of 18 to 35 years old. One third of the volunteers were female and two thirds were male. In the test, the volunteers were required to control the robot aiming to complete a path marked on the floor and then answer a questionnaire to evaluate their experience.

The volunteers were selected randomly in the proximity of the laboratory of the research team, by being offered the chance to take part in a study with a robot. The ones who participated gave their spoken consent. They were from a variety of work areas such as Biology, Secretarial Studies and Physical Education. Regarding their ages, they were between eighteen and thirty-five years old. After chosen, all of them were conducted to the laboratory to perform the test.

To control the robot, the volunteers were presented to the four available commands: moving forward or backwards and turning left or right. The Fig. 1 above consists of parts of a video tutorial shown to volunteers to familiarize them with the system's commands. The complete video lasted less than 20 s, and presented an avatar controlling the robot and indicating the commands being executed so the user could identify and repeat the movements. The video was shown right before the beginning of the test, on the screen of the computer running the Control sub-system, where the user would see the robot informations later, when the test started.

As soon as the tutorial was over, the user started the experiment trying to control the robot, moving it through the complete path (Fig. 2). The path marked on the floor with delimiting lines was shaped so that volunteers had to use at least three of the four available commands to complete the task. The length of the path was defined considering a 1-min inferior time limit based on the time development team's members themselves took to arrive at the end of the path with the robot. Figure 3 depicts one of the tests executed by the team to analyze the time necessary to get to the end of the path. The path length and complexity also aimed to spark feelings in the user, such as exhaustion, frustration, accomplishment, relaxation or pleasure, and serve as extra indicators

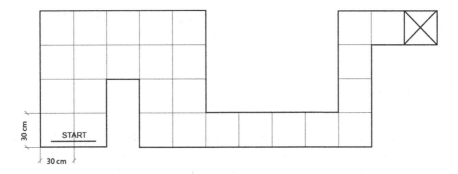

Fig. 2. Representation of the demarked path on the floor.

Fig. 3. One test executed by the team to analyze the necessary time to get the robot to the end of the path.

of the interaction validity. Objective metrics regarding system's precision and ease of operation included registering the number of times the robot was driven outside the marked path, as well as an overall average of the time volunteers needed to complete the path.

After having the robot complete the path, the volunteers answered a questionnaire evaluating their experience. On this evaluation, volunteers shared not only the amount of time needed to finish the experiment or how many times the robot got out of the delimiting path lines, but also their degree of difficulty to learn the movements and to perform them. They were also encouraged to talk about their impression of the robot's movement precision and the time for the actions to be executed by the robot after the commands were performed, which measure the system's responsiveness. We also tried to analyse the feelings the volunteers had during the experiment, be them related to controlling a robot or to the user control interface. Considering the feelings related to the interface, we asked the user to explain the ergonomic and psychological discomforts that may have arose from the experiment so that we could analyse their experience, identifying points of improvement for the experiment.

4   Results

The results of this research are a synthesis of the experiment's validation analysis. They were interpreted as positive in general, since 84 % of the volunteers considered that natural control commands were indeed easy to both learn and perform, one of this study's main goals when analysing the usability of the system.

At the beginning of the validation, before controlling the robot through the designated track, all volunteers watched a tutorial and 78,9 % of them have considered it reasonably easy, easy or very easy to learn the movements. After that, 94,7 % volunteers managed to finish the 5,4 meters path, having done so in an average time of 3 min. Figure 4 shows the time spent by users to complete the course in reference to the group average and the time spent by developers.

Concerning the control of the robot vehicle, 84,2 % of the interviewed considered it easy to perform the command movements and the same percentage found that the robot operation with this type of control was accurate or very accurate, with no negative considerations from the users concerning lack of precision due to the technical limitations of the body tracking device.

On the feelings experienced during the trial, 85 % of the participants considered the activity not physically tiresome. It was also perceived that, in general, there was no psychological discomfort, with 79 % of participants stating that the

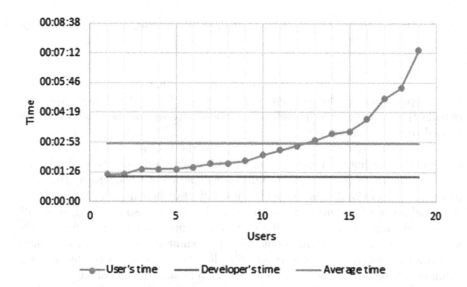

Fig. 4. Time spent by users to complete the course.

experience was pleasant, reporting feelings like amusement, relaxation and satisfaction. Some of them also described emotions related to the technical aspect, such as feeling innovative and immersed.

However, approximately 63 % of the volunteers claimed that even though they considered the activity pleasant or neutral and not tiresome during the experiment, they would not consider viable to operate the robot for long periods of time. That consideration was due to some degree of physical fatigue or ergonomic discomfort caused by the movements chosen to trigger the actions on the robot.

5   Conclusion

Our research assessed human-robot interaction through a gesture-based natural interface which worked with a body tracking device. It made possible for users to control a remote robot car in order to complete a path marked on the floor. The results allowed us to conclude that an improvement on users' experience and control intuitiveness occurs when using gestural interfaces. They also indicated that the loss of external command devices (keyboard, mice) had no effect on user's ability to learn or reproduce the movements that served as controls to the robot.

Despite the expected loss of precision in control due to the inherent inaccuracy of present-day body tracking devices, robot operation was not compromised by these limitations. The users found the sensor readings accurate and fast. The system also did not present any delays while processing, reading or interpreting the commands declared by the volunteers through gestures.

Additionally, the potential physical fatigue after long periods of operation highlighted by the users indicates that there is a fine line between the feasibility and infeasibility of gesture-based interfaces in the robot control field. This suggests there is a need to deepen the knowledge about the ergonomics of gestural commands in order to refine the movements used to control the robot.

The achievement of part of the research's aims, including intuitiveness on the use of gestural control and the precision on the control expressed by the volunteers, supports the use of gestural interface on the HRI field. With these results, the next steps of this study will focus on finding interaction methods in which users feel comfortable and that also minimize physical fatigue caused by the command movements, thus making the operation of machines using natural gesture-based interfaces for long periods viable.

References

1. Singh, A., Seo, S.H., Hashish, Y., Nakane, M., Young, J.E., Bunt, A.: An interface for remote robotic manipulator control that reduces task load and fatigue. In: Proceedings IEEE International Work. Robot Hum. Interact. Commun., pp.738–743 (2013)

2. Tanzini, M., Tripicchio, P., Ruffaldi, E., Galgani, G., Lutzemberger, G., Avizzano, C.A.: A novel human-machine interface for working machines operation. In: Proceedings IEEE International Workshop on Robot Human Communication, pp. 744–750 (2013)

3. Mayora-Ibarra, O., Sucar, E., Aviles, H., Miranda-Palma, C.: From HCI to HRI - Usability inspection in multimodal human - Robot interactions. In: Proceedings IEEE International Workshop on Robot and Human Interactive Communication, pp. 37–41 (2003)

4. Rao, A., Kumar, S., Renu, A., Nandi, G.C.: MILO - mobile intelligent Linux robot. In: Proceedings IEEE INDICON 2004. First India Annual Conference 2004 (2004)

5. Shackel, B., Richardson, S.J.: Human Factors for Informatics Usability. Cambridge UP, Cambridge (1991). Print

6. de Souza, C.S., Leite, J.C., Prates, R.O., Barbosa, S.D.J.: Interação Humano-Computador: Perspectivas Cognitivas e Semióticas. In: Fuks, H. (Org.) Anais das Jornadas de Atualização em Informática. Rio de Janeiro: Edições EntreLugar, 1999, pp. 420–470 (1999)

7. Wigdor, D., Wixon, D.: Brave NUI World: Designing Natural User Interfaces for Touch and Gesture. Elsevier Science, USA (2011)

8. Walker, R., Bartneck, C.: The pleasure of receiving a head massage from a robot. In: Proceedings IEEE International Workshop on Robot and Human Interactive Communication, pp. 807–813 (2013)

9. De Graaf, M.M.A., Ben Allouch, S.: The relation between peoples attitude and anxiety towards robots in human-robot interaction. In: Proceedings International Workshop on Robot and Human Interactive Communication, pp. 632–637 (2013)

10. Wei, J.W.J., Qin, H.Q.H., Guo, J.G.J., Chen, Y.C.Y.: The hand shape recognition of Human Computer Interaction with Artificial Neural Network. In: 2009 IEEE International Conference Human-Computer Interfaces, and Measurement System 04 (2009)

11. Cho, N.-G., Lee, S.-W.: Incorporating global and local observation models for human pose tracking. RO-MAN, 2013 IEEE, pp. 25–30 (2013)

12. Prates, R., Barbosa, S.: Avaliação de Interfaces de UsuárioConceitos e Métodos. An. do XXIII Congress, p. 14 (2003)

13. Prates, R.O., Barbosa, S.D.J.: Introdução Teoria e Prática da Interação Humano Computador fundamentada na Engenharia Semiótica. Jornadas de Atualização em Informática, JAI 2007, pp. 263–326 (2007)

Improvement of Accuracy in Remote Gaze Detection for User Wearing Eyeglasses Using Relative Position Between Centers of Pupil and Corneal Sphere

Kiyotaka Fukumoto$^{(\boxtimes)}$, Takumi Tsuzuki, and Yoshinobu Ebisawa

Graduate School of Engineering, Shizuoka University, Shizuoka 432-8561,
Japan
{fukumoto.kiyotaka,ebisawa.yoshinobu}@shizuoka.ac.jp

Abstract. One of the general problems of the pupil-corneal reflection-based gaze detection systems is that the frames and lens of eyeglasses produce reflection images of the light sources in the camera image when a user wears eyeglasses. The glass reflections tend to be misdetected as the pupil and corneal reflections. In the present paper, we propose a novel geometrical methodology based on the optical structure of the eyeball to detect a true pair of the pupil and corneal reflection. The experimental results show that the proposed method improved the precision of gaze detection when the subjects wore glasses or when disturbance light sources existed.

Keywords: Pupil · Corneal reflection · Corneal sphere center · Gaze detection

1 Introduction

Video-based gaze detection systems are about to be used in various fields such as the entertainment [1], medicine [2], and safety driving support [3]. In our previous study, we have developed a pupil-corneal reflection-based robust and precise gaze detection system using the two light sources and the image difference method, which allows large head movements and easy user calibration [4, 5]. In this system, an optical system for detecting the pupils and corneal reflections consists of a camera and two concentric near-infrared LED rings (inner and outer rings) light source attached to the camera. The inner and outer LED rings generate bright and dark pupil images, respectively. The pupils are detected from a difference image created by subtracting the bright and dark pupil images. In the difference image, a threshold for binarization to detect the pupils is easily determined automatically because the pupils are embossed from the relatively flat background image. However, when the users move their head, the pupil position differs between the bright and dark pupil images because of the acquisition time difference of both pupil images. As a result, the pupil position is not detected accurately. Therefore, in our system, the image difference processing is performed after shifting the small areas (small windows) including each pupil in the dark pupil image so that the corneal reflection in this dark pupil image may coincide with that in the bright pupil image. We call this method *the image difference method with positional*

© Springer International Publishing Switzerland 2015
M. Kurosu (Ed.): Human-Computer Interaction, Part II, HCII 2015, LNCS 9170, pp. 13–23, 2015.
DOI: 10.1007/978-3-319-20916-6_2

compensation based on the corneal reflection (the positionally compensated image difference (PCID) method) [6]. In addition, we proposed the easy gaze calibration methods: the automatic, one-point, and two-point calibration methods [4]. In the one-point calibration method, the user has only to fixate on one target having known coordinates presented at the center of the PC screen. By this procedure, the gaze points on the whole of the PC screen can be detected almost exactly.

However, when the user wears eyeglasses, their frames and lens produce various size, shape and intense of areas in the camera image as so-called glass reflections. The reflections often show image features similar to the pupil and the corneal reflection and tend to be misdetected as the pupil or the corneal reflection. The reflections of tears and disturbance light sources also cause the misdetection. In the present paper, we propose a novel geometrical methodology based on the optical structure of the eyeball to detect a true pair of the pupil and corneal reflection for accurate gaze detection even if the user wears glasses.

2 Our Gaze Detection System

2.1 System Configuration

Figure 1(a) shows an overview of the gaze detection system which we developed. This system has two optical systems (Fig. 1(b)), each of which consists of a digital video camera having near-infrared sensitivity, a 16-mm lens, an infrared filter (IR80), and a light source. Each of the two optical systems was placed under a 19-in. liquid crystal display (screen size: 376.3 × 301.1 mm, 1,280 × 1,024 pixels). The light source consisting of near-infrared 3ϕ LEDs which are arranged in a double concentric circle ring form is attached to the camera. The wavelengths of the inner and outer rings were 850 and 940 nm, respectively. The pupil becomes brighter in the 850 nm ring than the 940 nm ring because the transmissivity of the eyeball medium is different. The distance between the LEDs and the aperture of the camera also varies the pupil brightness. The combined effects of the differences of the distance and transmissivity were applied to the light source. In order to reduce the effect of an ambient light, it is desirable that the LEDs irradiation power on the user's face becomes as strong as possible compared with the ambient light. Therefore, the LEDs were flashed while the camera shutter opened (shutter speed 500 μs). The current flow was approximately one ampere during LED flashing. The two cameras were driven with a slight synchronization difference (670 μs) for avoiding mutual light interference of the optical systems. By this, basically, only one corneal reflection appears for each eye in an image.

An 8-bit gray scale image (640 × 480 pixels) of the user's face was input into a personal computer (PC, Intel Core i7 3.20 GHz CPU and 12 GB RAM) at 60 fps.

2.2 Detection of Centers of Pupils and Corneal

Our Conventional Method for Detection of Pupils and Corneal Reflections. First, the pupils are searched for and detected from the difference image generated from the

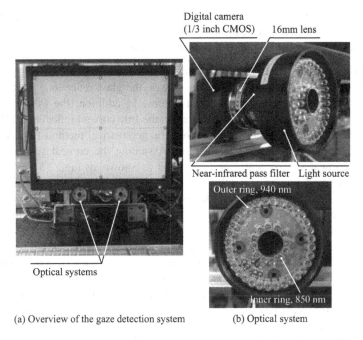

(a) Overview of the gaze detection system   (b) Optical system

Fig. 1. (a) Our gaze detection system. (b) Optical system for detecting pupil and corneal reflection.

bright and dark pupil images. The image is processed in the following order: binarization, removal of isolated pixels, noise reduction using mathematical morphology operations, and labeling. The largest and second largest labeled regions are detected as the two pupils.

When the pupil is undetected in the prior difference image (e.g., when the pupil is covered with the glass reflection), the pupils are searched for in the whole of the current difference image again. When two consecutive pupil detections occur, in order to perform *the PCID method*, the pupil positions in the current images are predicted using the linear Kalman filter, and the small window (70 × 70 pixels) is then applied around the predicted pupil positions, respectively. The image within the small window is transformed into the double-resolution (DR) image (140 × 140 pixels). An intense and tiny region closest to a center of the DR images is extracted and then the center of gravity considering the values of the pixels in the region is determined as the center of the corneal reflection. As described before, when the user's head is moving, the pupils cannot be obtained correctly because the pupil position differs between the bright and dark pupil images. Therefore, the DR difference image is generated after shifting the DR dark pupil image so that the corneal reflection in the DR dark pupil image coincides with that of the DR bright pupil image (*the PCID method*). When the corneal reflection is not detected in either one of the bright and dark pupil image, the difference image is generated without *the positional compensation*. After the image areas whose image feature similar to the pupil are labeled in the binarized DR difference image, the nearest area to the predicted pupil position is determined as the pupil in the current DR difference image. In this image, the ellipse-fitting of the contour of the pupil is performed. The center of the ellipse is determined as the pupil center.

Proposal Geometrical Method for Determining a True Pair of the Pupil and the Corneal Reflection. When the user wears glasses, the glass reflections are tend to be misdetected as the pupils and corneal reflections. In addition, the false images of disturbance light sources may be misdetected as the true corneal reflection of the light sources of the system. Therefore, we propose the geometrical method for detecting a true pair of the pupil and corneal reflection. Assuming the corneal surface to be a sphere, the corneal sphere center is determined as shown in Fig. 2(a). We use the pinhole camera model and assume that the light source is located at the same position as the pinhole. Therefore, the corneal sphere center exists on the line connecting the pinhole and the corneal reflection in the image sensor. The 3D position of the corneal sphere center can be determined by stereo-matching the corneal reflections obtained from the two cameras. However, when one or both corneal reflections (Fig. 2(b) and (c)) obtained from the two cameras are misdetected due to the glass reflection or the disturbance light source, the corneal sphere center is detected at wrong positions.

In the proposed method, m and n corneal reflection candidates for each camera and each eye are extracted from the bright and dark pupil images, respectively, which include the true and false corneal reflections. *The PCID method* is performed for all $m \times n$ combinations of the candidates. When the pupil is not detected, it is judged that at least one of the paired two candidates used for performing the method was not the true corneal reflection. When the pupil is detected, the pupil and corneal reflection pair used in the method is retained as one of the pair candidates. The 3D positions of the pupil and corneal sphere centers are detected by stereo-matching the pupils and the corneal reflections, respectively, of the remaining pair candidates obtained from two cameras. One true pair of the pupil and corneal sphere centers is chosen by the following two conditions:

Condition I: the angle between the vector from the corneal sphere center to the pupil center and the vector from the pupil center to the middle point between the two cameras is within 40°. This is because we thought that the gaze detection system suffices gaze detection of only PC screen area. So, considering the unknown angle difference between the visual and optical axes, we gave 40° so as to include the screen area.

Condition II: the distance d between the corneal sphere center and the pupil center satisfies $D_{C\text{-}P} - 1.5$ [mm] $< d < D_{C\text{-}P} + 1.5$ [mm], where $D_{C\text{-}P}$ is the distance obtained beforehand from the individual users.

Based on the chosen pair, the 3D pupil position and the coordinates of the pupil and corneal reflection in the camera image are obtained and are used for the gaze detection [5].

2.3   Gaze Detection Theory and Calibration Method [5]

In Fig. 3, O'_1 and O'_2 indicate the pinholes of the two camera-calibrated cameras. The 3D pupil position P is obtained by stereo-matching. As mentioned before, we assume

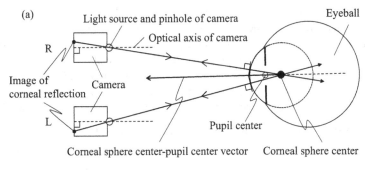

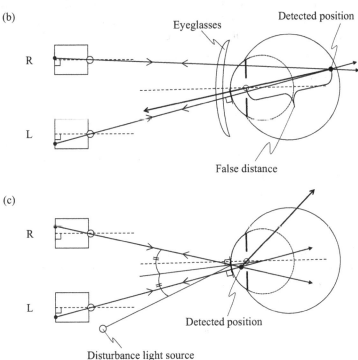

Fig. 2. (a) When two cameras detect a true corneal reflection of the light source attached to the corresponding camera, respectively. (b) When the left and right cameras detect a true corneal reflection and a false reflection of a glass reflection, respectively. (c) When the left camera detects a true corneal reflections produced by the light source attached to the left camera and the right camera detects a false reflection of the disturbance light .source, respectively.

that the light source attached to each camera is located at the same position as the corresponding camera. The line of sight (visual axis of the eyeball) passes through the fovea on the retina, the pupil center P and gaze point Q on the screen plane of the PC display. Now we define the virtual gaze planes H_1 and H_2 of the cameras for one eyeball. These planes are perpendicular to the line passing through P and O'_1 and the line passing through P and O_2, respectively, and they include O'_1 and O'_2, respectively. The X-axis (X_1 and X_2) of planes H_1 and H_2 is the intersection between the corresponding plane and the horizontal plane in the global coordinate system (x – y – z). H_1 and H_2 rotate according to the displacements of the pupil position.

Next, we define the virtual gaze sphere S whose center is P and whose radius is arbitrary. The visual axis PQ has intersection points with sphere S and planes H_1 and H_2. The intersection points are denoted as G, G'_1 and G'_2, respectively. Here, we define angular vectors $\boldsymbol{\theta}_1$ and $\boldsymbol{\theta}_2$ on sphere S as the projections of ordinary vectors $\overrightarrow{O'_1G'_1}$ and $\overrightarrow{O'_2G'_2}$ on planes H_1 and H_2 to sphere S. By projecting the horizontal axes X_1 and X_2 on planes H_1 and H_2 to sphere S, orientations ϕ_1 and ϕ_2 of vectors $\overrightarrow{O'_1G'_1}$ and $\overrightarrow{O'_2G'_2}$ can be also projected to sphere S and can be defined. According to these projections, you can see that angular vectors $\boldsymbol{\theta}_1$ and $\boldsymbol{\theta}_2$ can be determined by using ϕ_1 and $\angle O_1PG$ and by using ϕ_2 and $\angle O_2PG$, respectively. Here, angular vector $\overrightarrow{O_1O_2}(\left|\overrightarrow{O_1O_2}\right| = \angle O_1PO_2)$ is expressed as follows:

$$\overrightarrow{O_1O_2} = \boldsymbol{\theta}_1 - \boldsymbol{\theta}_2 \tag{1}$$

We assume a linear relationship between the actual size vector $\boldsymbol{r}$ from the corneal reflection to the pupil center and the angle θ between the visual axis of the eyeball and the line connecting the pupil and the camera as follows:

$$\boldsymbol{\theta} = k\boldsymbol{r} \tag{2}$$

where $\boldsymbol{r}$ is converted from the vector from the corneal reflection center to the pupil center, which is obtained from the camera image, using the pinhole model. k is a constant. Actually, in general, there is a difference between the optical and visual axes of the eyeball. So, $\boldsymbol{r}$ is calculated by compensating a measured vector $\boldsymbol{r}'$ using an offset vector $\boldsymbol{r}_0$ as the following equation:

$$\boldsymbol{r} = \boldsymbol{r}' - \boldsymbol{r}_0 \tag{3}$$

From Eqs. (2) and (3), the following equations are given for cameras 1 and 2.

$$\boldsymbol{\theta}_1 = k\boldsymbol{r}_1 = k(\boldsymbol{r}'_1 - \boldsymbol{r}_0) \tag{4}$$

$$\boldsymbol{\theta}_2 = k\boldsymbol{r}_2 = k(\boldsymbol{r}'_2 - \boldsymbol{r}_0) \tag{5}$$

From the above equations, k is calculated by the following equation:

$$k = \frac{\left|\boldsymbol{\theta}_1 - \boldsymbol{\theta}_2\right|}{\left|\boldsymbol{r}'_1 - \boldsymbol{r}'_2\right|} = \frac{\angle O_1PO_2}{\left|\boldsymbol{r}'_1 - \boldsymbol{r}'_2\right|} \tag{6}$$

Using the value of k, $\boldsymbol{r}_0$ is determined from Eqs. (4) and (5). Determining k and $\boldsymbol{r}_0$ mean the user calibration.

In the gaze detection procedure, first, the pupil-corneal reflection vectors r'_1 and r'_2 are obtained from the images of the two cameras. By using Eqs. (4) and (5), θ_1 and θ_2 are calculated. Next, the visual axis is determined for each eye from pupil position P, θ_1 and θ_2. Finally, the gaze point on the screen is estimated as the intersection point between the screen plane and the visual axis.

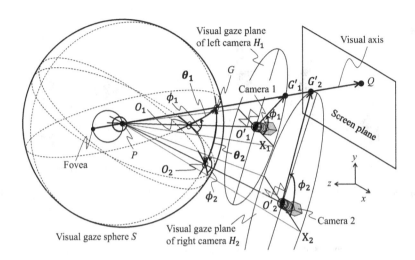

Fig. 3. Gaze detection theory using visual gaze sphere

3 Experiments

3.1 Experiment 1: Measurement of Distance Between Corneal Sphere Center and Pupil Center

Method. In order to examine and determine the distance D_{C-P} shown in Condition II, the 3D corneal sphere and pupil center positions of three university students who did not wear glasses were measured. In the calibration procedure, the subjects were asked to fixate on a calibration target presented at the center of the PC screen (the one-point calibration method). The distance between the eyes and the screen was approximately 80 cm. After the calibration procedure, the subjects fixated on a stationary target presented at the center of the screen and a slowly moving target between the right and left edges of the screen. Using a chinrest stand, the subjects' heads were positioned at the following five positions: approximately 75, 80, and 85 cm from the PC screen, and 5 cm to the left and 5 cm to the right at 80 cm. In addition, subject A wore glasses and participated in the same experiment again.

Results. Figure 4(a) and (b) show the averages and SDs of the distance d between the pupil and corneal sphere centers at the five head positions when the subjects fixated on the stationary target and the moving target, respectively. Although the distance d was different among the subjects, it did not depend on the head positions and the gaze directions for each subject. Figure 5 shows the results when subject A wore and did not wear glasses, respectively. Almost the same values were obtained by whether the subject wore glasses or not.

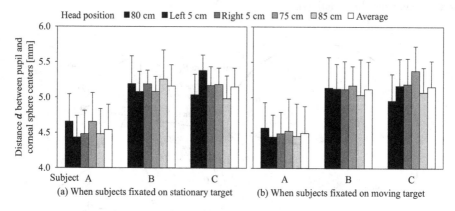

Fig. 4. Averages and SDs of the distance d between the pupil and corneal sphere centers at the five head positions for each subject.

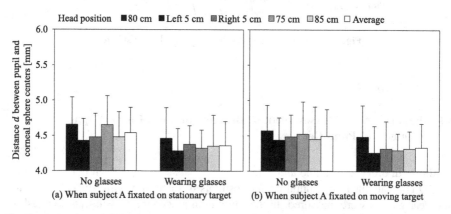

Fig. 5. Averages and SDs of the distance d between the pupil and corneal sphere centers at the five head positions when subject A wore glasses and when he did not wear glasses.

3.2 Experiment 2: Gaze Detection When Subjects Wear Glasses

Method. This experiment was conducted in order to compare the precision of gaze detection between the proposed and our previous methods when subjects wore glasses. In the previous method, the corneal reflection nearest to the predicted pupil center was chosen for *the PCID method*. The values of m and n were both three. The subjects were three university students. In the one-point calibration procedure, the head direction of the subjects was adjusted so that the lens reflections did not appear in the camera image. After the procedure, the subjects wearing glasses fixated on 25 (5 by 5) visual targets equally arranged on the PC screen one by one. The values of $D_{C\text{-}P}$ were obtained from each subject when they did not wear glasses before this experiment.

Results and Discussion. Figure 6(a) and (b) show the gaze point distributions of the left eye for the subject A in the proposed and our previous methods, respectively. In the previous method, the dispersion of the gaze points was large compared to the proposed method, especially when the subject fixated on the lower targets. This was caused by misdetection of the pupil and/or the corneal reflection due to the glass reflections. Especially, the subject fixated on the targets 17 and 22, the glass reflection had covered the left pupil. In the proposed method, no gaze point was detected. These results mean that the pupil and/or the corneal reflection were misdetected in the previous method, whereas the proposed method prevented these misdetections. Furthermore, 1.0 % gaze points outside of the region presented in Fig. 6 existed in the previous method while 0 % in the proposed method. The average and SD of the gaze error in visual angle for the subject A were 1.24 ± 1.61 [deg] in the previous method, whereas those of the proposed method were 1.08 ± 1.23 [deg]. The results of the other two subjects showed the similar results. The average gaze error for all the three subjects was 1.26 ± 1.62 [deg] in the previous method and $1.14 \perp 1.99$ [deg] in the proposed method. These results indicate that the proposed method functioned to prevent the misdetection of the pupil and corneal reflection and to select a true pair of the pupil and corneal reflection.

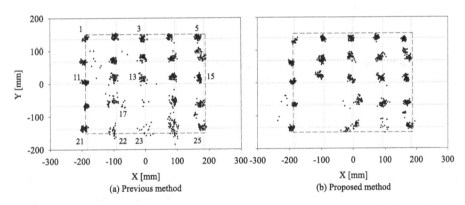

(a) Previous method   (b) Proposed method

Fig. 6. Detected gaze point distributions in the previous and proposed methods when subject A wore glasses. Dots and intersections of dotted lines indicate the gaze points and visual target positions, respectively. The rectangular area enclosed by the broken lines indicates the PC screen.

3.3 Experiment 3: Gaze Detection When Disturbance Light Sources Generated False Corneal Reflection

Method. Four small disturbance light sources were installed at the four corners of the PC screen, respectively, and they generated the false corneal reflections. Subjects were two university students who wore glasses. The calibration and gaze detection procedures were the same as in experiment 2, where the distance between the eyes and the screen was approximately 80 cm.

Results and Discussion. Figure 7(a) and (b) compare the averaged gaze points of the left and right eyes for subject A between the previous and proposed methods. In the previous method, the gaze point dispersions were large for many of the 25 targets. Whereas the proposed method showed the smaller dispersion for almost all targets. The gaze error in the previous method for subject A was 3.08 ± 5.62 [deg], whereas that of the proposed method was 1.23 ± 2.55 [deg]. Subject B showed the error of 5.31 ± 10.61 [deg] in the previous method and 2.43 ± 5.52 [deg] in the proposed method, respectively. These results indicate that the proposed method functioned to prevent the misdetection of the false corneal reflections produced by the disturbance light sources.

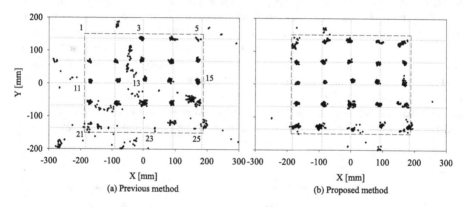

(a) Previous method   (b) Proposed method

Fig. 7. Detected gaze points (average of right and left eyes) in the previous and proposed methods when four disturbance light sources were installed at four corners of PC screen and generated false corneal reflections.

4   Conclusions

In our remote gaze detection system, in order to prevent the misdetection of the pupil and corneal reflection when a user wears glasses and/or when the disturbance light sources exist, the novel geometrical method based on the optical structure of the eyeball was proposed. The experimental results showed that the proposed method detects a true pair of the pupil and corneal reflection and improves the accuracy of the gaze detection when the glass reflections or the false corneal reflections of the disturbance light sources appear in the camera image. The proposed method would function well also in the other pupil-corneal reflection-based gaze detection systems.

References

1. Tobii Technology. http://www.tobii.com/
2. Bakker, N.M., Lenseigne, B.A.J., Schutte, S., Geukers, E.B.M., Jonker, P.P., van der Helm, F.C.T., Simonsz, H.J.: Accurate gaze direction measurements with free head movement for strabismus angle estimation. IEEE Trans. Biomed. Eng. **60**(11), 3028–3035 (2013)
3. Tawari, A., Martin, S., Trivedi, M.M.: Continuous head movement estimator for driver assistance: issues, algorithms, and on-road evaluations. IEEE Trans. Intell. Transp. Syst. **15**(2), 818–830 (2014)
4. Ebisawa, Y., Fukumoto, K.: Head-freeremote eye-gaze detection system based on pupil-corneal reflection method with easy calibration using two stereo-calibrated video cameras. IEEE Trans. Biomed. Eng. **60**(10), 2952–2960 (2013)
5. Ebisawa, Y., Fukumoto, K.: Head-free, remote gaze detection system based on pupil-corneal reflection method with using two video cameras – one-point and nonlinear Calibrations. In: Kurosu, M. (ed.) HCII/HCI 2013, Part IV. LNCS, vol. 8007, pp. 205–214. Springer, Heidelberg (2013)
6. Nakashima, A., Ebisawa, Y., Nurikabe, Y.: Pupil detection using light sources of different wavelengths. J. Inst. Image Inf. Telev. Eng. **60**(12), 2019–2025 (2006)

Designing Touchless Gestural Interactions
for Public Displays In-the-Wild

Vito Gentile[1], Alessio Malizia[2(✉)], Salvatore Sorce[1],
and Antonio Gentile[1]

[1] Dipartimento di Ingegneria Chimica, Gestionale, Informatica e Meccanica
(DICGIM), Universitá degli Studi di Palermo, 90128 Palermo, Italy
{vito.gentile,salvatore.sorce,antonio.gentile}@unipa.it
[2] Computer Science Department, Brunel University London,
Uxbridge, Middlesex UB8 3PH, UK
Alessio.Malizia@brunel.ac.uk

Abstract. Public displays, typically equipped with touchscreens, are used for interactions in public spaces, such as streets or fairs. Currently low-cost visual sensing technologies, such as Kinect-like devices and high quality cameras, allow to easily implement touchless interfaces. Nevertheless, the arising interactions have not yet been fully investigated for public displays in-the-wild (i.e. in appropriate social contexts where public displays are typically deployed). Different audiences, cultures and social settings strongly affect users and their interactions. Besides gestures for public displays must be guessable to be easy to use for a wide audience. Issues like these could be solved with user-centered design: gestures must be chosen by users in different social settings, and then selected to be resilient to cultural bias and provide a good level of guessability. Therefore the main challenge is to define touchless gestures in-the-wild by using novel UCD methods applied out of controlled environments, and evaluating their effectiveness.

Keywords: Public display · User-centered design · In-the-wild experiment · Gestural interaction · Natural user interaction · Kinect-like devices · Ubiquitous computing

1 Introduction

In the last twenty years, after the visionary ideas of Weiser [1] about ubiquitous computing, a lot of research contributions have been implemented and transformed in real products, deployed and used outside of controlled environments, such as laboratories or ad hoc experimental test beds. This led to augmented environments to interact with, and to related research issues [28]. Moreover, technological innovations have allowed for installations of interactive displays in private, semi-public and (more interesting for us) public places, like fairs, shop windows, malls, workspaces, and public institutions. Interactivity is usually implemented by equipping displays with touchscreens, whereas cameras are less often used. This means that new technologies, e.g. Kinect-like devices [2] and the related features, are still not commonly adopted,

M. Kurosu (Ed.): Human-Computer Interaction, Part II, HCII 2015, LNCS 9170, pp. 24–34, 2015.
DOI: 10.1007/978-3-319-20916-6_3

especially in integration with public displays. As a consequence, interactive displays often don't exploit all the interaction possibilities provided by cutting-edge technologies available today. Nowadays we have the opportunity to integrate Kinect-like devices, as well as other new technologies, in artifacts like public displays in order to explore touchless gestural interactions.

By using novel interaction techniques like touchless gestures, we can design for new scenarios: users will interact with wall-sized displays, and independently from their abilities (e.g. impairments, such as wheelchairs) they will be able to use gestures to get information from a public display. However, the main problem to be solved is to find a valid design methodology for gestures and interaction modalities. In order to make a product deployable in a wide range of social settings, studies cannot be conducted only in controlled environments, but rather they should take place directly "in-the-wild" (i.e. in appropriate social contexts where public displays are typically deployed). This is one of the few ways in which users' behavior can be observed by taking into account different audiences and contexts, and how they influence users' attitudes.

Moreover, different cultural backgrounds can affect the gestures used in order to achieve a particular goal. Therefore, a useful and robust gesture set for interaction with public displays should be also cultural-resilient. At last, gesture should be guessable to be easy to use for a wide audience. For these reasons, user-centered design appears to be the natural choice to define and test a proper method to obtain touchless gesture sets for public displays: gestures must be chosen by observing those adopted by users for various tasks and in different social settings. These observations and the subsequent selection of gestures can produce a cultural-resilient and guessable gesture set, as well as tips to improve the public display itself.

In the following sections of this paper, we will explain the main challenges to be faced with in order to develop a design methodology for touchless gestural interactions for public displays in-the-wild. These challenges will be explained in the next section. In Sect. 3 we suggest some solution to be tackled in order to solve the issues explained in Sect. 2. Finally, we will draw the conclusions in terms of indications to set up useful test beds for the design of suitable and resilient gesture sets.

2   Main Challenges

In this section we will describe the main challenges to be taken into account to define a robust methodology for designing touchless gestural interactions. Many works have been published in the area of gestural interaction design, and up to our knowledge, the majority of them were focused on touch-based interactions. However, some approaches can be inspiring for our goal, and the main challenges will be presented using these works as a starting point.

2.1   Touchless Gestural Interactions with Public Displays

Our work is mainly focused on the definition of a methodology for the design of touchless gestural interaction with public displays. There are many authors who have investigated the adoption of some gesture sets in public contexts. Müller et al. [3] and Zhai et al. [4] have combined touchless gestures and touch interactions in order to create a multimodal interface for public displays. This approach is interesting because it represents a real transition from the more common touch interactions to the novel touchless ones. However, touchless-only examples are more rare in literature. Hardy et al. [5] have deployed an interactive public display in a busy foyer at Lancaster University in UK. By using a coarse gesture set, they analyze the behavior of passers-by, and how their attention level varies with respect to the displayed content and to the social settings. In their work, the authors figured out that users were more interested in interacting with the display when other people did it rather than when nobody was in front of the display. This result confirms what Brignull and Rogers defined as *honeypot effect*, which means "the progressive increase in the number of people in the immediate vicinity" of the public display [26]. Hardy et al. also noticed that gestures defined by experimenters were slightly different from ones actually used by passers-by. Moreover, the display position affected how users decided to interact with it: if they could see the display from distance, users had more time to decide if watch, glance or totally ignore its content.

Hardy et al.'s work highlights two of the main problems of public displays: (1) users' attention is not simple to attract; (2) touchless gestures defined by experimenters are often unsuitable. In the following sections, we investigate how these issues may be solved.

2.2 User-Derived Gestural Interface

One of the most interesting approach for designing a gesture set is to base it on users' preferences. This idea, that is strictly related to the user-centered design research area, has been interestingly put in practice by Wobbrock et al. [6] for developing a touch gesture set for surface computing. In their work, authors presented a method executed in a controlled environment. According to this method, users were able to see the effect of an action on the display (what they called *referent*) and to propose a gesture (or a *symbol*) that, in the users' opinion, should be the most suitable to achieve the same effect. In this way, they collected, classified and selected 48 user-defined gestures. By comparing this set with another one made - before the experiments - by the authors (all experts in HCI and theoretically able to design suitable gestures), they discovered that only 60.9 % of their gestures matched with the user-defined ones.

This is only one application of the so-called *gesture elicitation studies* [7]. Such kind of approach has the advantage of capturing user preferences in a very direct way. However, it also has one main drawback: in order to maximize the results, it should be carried out in a real life environment, instead of a controlled environment. In fact, since users' behavior (and their preferences) is affected by the social context in which they operate [5, 8], and in order to define a gesture set for public displays, a valid social context for eliciting gestures is a real place, outside of any kind of laboratory, in which public displays are typically deployed. The main challenge in using a touchless gesture elicitation methodology is then to be able to collect a wide amount of data from users' behavior, minimizing any bias due to experimenters intervention. For this reason, we think that an implementation in-the-wild of gesture elicitation must be adopted.

2.3   Experiments In-the-Wild

In 2005, Sharp and Rehman coordinated the UbiApp Workshop [9], which had the aim to define new practices for application-led research in the area of ubiquitous computing. In particular, experts in this research field agreed on how to evaluate ubiquitous applications, "arguing that the only way to evaluate an application against the ideals of ubiquitous computing [...] is through long-term deployment in the wild. [...] Small-scale lab studies still have a place - everyone agreed that they're very useful in the early stages of user-centered design", but "once researchers have performed lab-scale trials, they [...] should use this data to continue to design, deploy, and evaluate similar applications on a larger scale" [9]. In other words, a fundamental result of the UbiApp Workshop was the need to evaluate applications outside of controlled environments, i.e. *in-the-wild*. This is particularly important in evaluating applications for public displays, because of the strong difference between a laboratory and the real settings in which these systems are deployed.

The necessity to execute longitudinal studies in-the-wild has been underlined by various authors after 2005 [10–12]. Ojala et al. [12] have been deployed various displays in public places, and published results from a three years-long study. During this period, they continuously observed behavioral changes in users, and collected new insights for improving display functionalities and contents. Such kind of findings demonstrate how important are longitudinal studies in order to follow users' preferences. This is particularly true when studying public displays, because of their implicit "wild" nature.

In order to correctly acquire users' preferences while interacting with public displays, the possible presence of researchers or experimenters should be taken into account. In real situations, users are not invited to interact by anyone, and they don't know which is the interaction modality. The presence of an experimenter that ask users to interact and explain how to do it, allow him to collect much more data than a totally uncontrolled situation. However, the intervention of an external agent on the users' behavior introduce a bias (what we refer as *experimenter bias*). Solutions to this problem fall in two categories: (1) allow experimenter intervention, and study the arising bias; (2) avoid experimenter intervention and keep the environment uncontrolled.

Johnson et al. [13], who participated in the activities to be evaluated with the users, investigated the first option. They derived several dimensions in which the role of researcher can be described, in terms of the abilities to facilitating or encouraging users, explaining the system, but also the level of authority and familiarity with participants, and the experimenter's relationship with the research. They concluded that participating and building a friendship with users can improve knowledge about how they see the system or the prototype object of the study. Another class of approaches that require experimenter intervention are the ones in which users are asked to fill up questionnaires directly provided by the researcher during the experiment. In [14] questionnaires are provided to users before and after interactions, in order to evaluate their expectations and experience. In this way, the behavior is biased, but there is a margin to evaluate this bias, by comparing expectations (questionnaires provided before the experiment) with experience (questionnaires provided after the experiment). Furthermore, it is possible to collect much more data and it is relatively easy to analyze them based on the answers to the questionnaires.

According to [13, 14], allowing experimenter intervention provides researchers with several advantages. However, this approach inevitably introduces biases in users' behavior. This is the main reason why avoid experimenter intervention should be the preferred option. With their three years-long deployment, Oyala et al. [12] have demonstrated how many information is available without the experimenter's intervention. They explicitly assessed that laboratory, single-location and campus-wide deployment cannot capture location influence, and so it is important to reproduce experiments and evaluation in a wider area, and in different locations. They are still continuing to evaluate their public displays, trying to solve the users' hesitancy to use technology in public (indeed, it is another finding which can be only discovered and studied with no experimenter intervention). Non-intrusive methods were used also by Messeter and Molenaar [15] in order to evaluate non-interactive ambient displays, basing all observation on data gathered from cameras and a Wizard-of-Oz approach to edit the displayed content. They also directly interviewed users, but only at the end of the experiment, when their intervention did not constitute a bias anymore. In [16], researchers evaluated gestures used to interact with a tabletop computer. They blended themselves in the crowd by using casual clothes, and collect data using cameras.

However, the main drawback of experiments in which researcher's intervention is not allowed is the requirement of long-term studies, which usually implies high costs. This is probably the main reason why public displays are often not evaluated using this approach, but usually with explicit researcher's intervention. The main challenge here is to find methods to reduce costs and time, or imitate the "experimenter blending in the crowd" [16] and the use of cameras. Such methods are not simple as they seem, because of ethical issues like privacy of users or the need to inform them before executing any personal information gathering.

2.4 Display and Interaction Blindness

Evaluations in-the-wild depend on the applications or systems to be studied, but some issues of this evaluation approach are clearly related to the specific research topic. In particular, when investigating interaction with public displays, some phenomena can strongly affect the level of difficulty in gathering enough information. One of these issues has been called *display blindness* by Müller et al. [17], and it - similarly to the *banner blindness* in web pages – causes users not to look at the displays because of their prejudice about the content, which is expected to be advertisement. They investigated which factors were related to this issue, and proposed possible solutions to the problem. According to Müller et al., factors that can mitigate display blindness are: colorfulness or attractiveness, amount of time the display is potentially visible to passers-by, and display size. However this problem is not simple to solve, and can require to apply some techniques from the persuasive computing area.

As noted by Ojala et al. in their longitudinal study, even when users notice the display they often do not interact with it "because they simply do not know that they can" [12]. This means that the interactivity of a public display is not intuitive as expected, and there is the need to explicitly entice the interactions. *Interaction blindness* (as this phenomenon has been called) was noticed also by other authors working on interactive public displays [5], and without any solutions it is impossible to experiment any kind of gesture elicitation method, even less if in-the-wild. Ojala et al. suggest that "one way to overcome interaction blindness and entice interaction is make the interface more natural. Proxemic interactions are emerging as a potential paradigm for realizing natural interfaces [...], but our simple visual proxemic cue [...] (the "Touch me!" animation) did not noticeably increase user interaction" [12]. *Proxemic interactions* were introduced by Ballendat et al. [18], and they are very related to (and actually based on) a previous work by Vogel and Balakrishnan [19]. In [17, 18] author propose systems that react on user's position and orientation, i.e. without any implicit interaction. Such idea seems promising in solving interaction blindness, because users can easily see the interactivity of the display if its contents change in correspondence with users' movements. Indeed, proxemic interactions allow the implementation of more sophisticated solutions than a simple "Touch me!" animation, and there is the need to better investigate how they can help to solve interaction blindness.

Moreover, proxemic interactions can help users to understand the features of an interactive public display, by modeling it as a sort of mirror (i.e. one of the four mental models proposed in [20]). The mirror mental model has been shown to have a strong potential to catch users' attention [20, 21], which suggest to use it also as a partial solution to display blindness, in addition to interaction blindness.

2.5 Gesture Characteristics

By keeping in mind display and interaction blindness, an approach based on gesture elicitation in-the-wild should allow for the design of a gesture set that can capture users' preferences and expectations. In order to study and validate an elicited gesture set, it is mandatory to know and define which characteristics a gesture should incorporate. In their work on developing gestural interfaces, Nielsen et al. [22] investigate some features of gesture vocabularies, by distinguishing *technology based vocabularies* and *human based vocabularies*. Gestures in the first set are easy to recognize technically, but they are often stressing, sometimes impossible to perform for some people, and illogical if compared with the functionality to activate. On the other hand, a human based vocabulary (often developed with a user-centered design technique) should be easy to perform and remember, intuitive (this feature is also known as guessability [6, 7]), metaphorically and iconically logical towards functionality and ergonomics [22].

Furthermore, gestures should be usable in the social context in which they will be performed. In other words, during the design of gestures, *social acceptability* [8] must be strongly taken into account. As stated by Rico and Brewster in [8], "with respect to gesture-based interfaces, users must evaluate if their motivation to use the technology outweighs the risk of looking strange or making a social blunder. In the face of such issues, gesture-based interfaces must be designed with an awareness of social context and social acceptability". Investigating social acceptability of a gesture is implicitly included in any evaluation of public displays in-the-wild without any experimenter's intervention. If users decide to interact by gestures, they implicitly categorize this interface as socially acceptable. With this in mind, the next challenge is the evaluation of gesture sets in a real social context, overcoming any experimenter's intervention, but taking into account ethical and privacy issues, which can easily become a primary obstacle.

3   Designing a User-Derived Gestural Interface In-the-Wild

As stated in the introduction of this paper, the main problem we aim to tackle is to find a valid methodology for designing touchless gestural interfaces in-the-wild. To this end, in this section we briefly summarize different approaches that might be suitable to address problems and opportunities related to the previously described challenges.

3.1   User-Derived Touchless Gestural Interface

We believe that a Wizard-of-Oz – based methodology can be effective to study users' interactions with public display. In particular, by means of a GUI (Graphical User Interface), Wizard-of-Oz approaches are tipically deployed in a two-step process: in the first one, users are implicitly suggested to interact with gestures, thus overcoming interaction blindness. Users could be quietly observed via cameras, and their gestures can be collected and used in real-time by experimenters to opportunely animate the GUI and making it reactive from the user's point of view. After collecting data about gestures, these can be analyzed to define a basic gesture set. In a second step, the evaluation in-the-wild of the defined gesture set will take place to get users' feedbacks and improve the set.

This idea has been inspired by a technique used by Good et al. [23] to develop a user-derived CLI (Command Line Interface). Basically, users had to interact with a console, using their words as commands, in order to write and send an email. The same approach could be extended to create a gesture set as above described, but its deployment is expected to be much more complicated to implement. On the other hand, this kind of approach is exactly what studies on gesture elicitation have exploited, although their experiments have been mainly deployed in controlled environments. Our goal is to extend the original idea proposed by Good et al. in the wild and without any experimenters intervention.

The main problem with an unsupervised and uncontrolled approach, is to catch users' attention, and to convince them to interact with the display. In other words, display and interaction blindness still need to be overcome. However, we don't focus on display blindness here. We suppose to reuse persuasive computing methods [27] to reduce the occurrence of this phenomenon. In the following section, we discuss some principles aimed to reduce interaction blindness and make gestural interactions more natural for novel users.

3.2   GUI for Touchless Gestural Interactions

In 1997, Andries van Dam introduced the notion of "post-WIMP user interfaces. These interfaces don't use menus, forms, or toolbars, but rely on, for example, gesture and speech recognition for operand and operation specification" [24]. This notion became common in the area of GUI design, but hitherto there are no standards as strong as the WIMP paradigm. Only in the main mobile operating systems for smartphones and tablets (e.g. Android or iOS), we can see some coherent approaches in the main components of GUIs. However, touchless gestural interaction is different, and it requires new ideas.

The definition of a new model for a touchless gestural-oriented GUI for public displays should follow four principles:

1. the GUI should implicitly suggest its interactivity (i.e. implicitly avoid interaction blindness);
2. the GUI should implicitly suggest the touchless and gestural nature of the interactions;
3. the GUI should make interactions natural[1] and guessable;
4. the GUI should minimize the effect of legacy bias [7] (i.e. GUI components should not have any relations with WIMP, leaving users free to guess the right gestures, without biases due to their previous experiences in using WIMP interfaces).

A possible solution to the first principle is the adoption of a proxemic interactive GUI, in which one or more components react to the implicit user movements. In this way, anyone moving in front of the GUI can guess its interactive nature. The fourth principle can also be implemented by suggesting new paradigms, removing typical WIMP signs (c.g. the "X" for closing windows) and components (e.g. windows and pointer) of GUIs. The main issue consists of complying with the second and third principles. Indeed their validity needs to be evaluated with suitable experiments, but some element can be used for any GUI prototype as a good starting point. A promising approach to suggest the touchless and gestural nature of the interactions, consists in using explicit tips in the interface. Furthermore, the affordance of some new technologies can be used to the same end (e.g. the presence of a visible Kinect-like device may suggest the interaction modality to anyone recognize the device).

The naturality and guessability of the interactions are more complicated topics. The naturality of an interface is strictly related to the meaning of natural interface, and can be evaluated by users but cannot be easily measured. On the other hand, guessability might be investigated with a long-term study, in which the trend of user gestures can be analyzed: gestures are guessable if many users use them repeatedly.

---

[1] As stated in [25], "today the word *natural*, as in "natural user interfaces" (NUI), is mainly used to highlight the contrast with classical computer interfaces that employ artificial control devices whose operation has to be learned". In this context, interactions should be *natural* in the sense they allow users to communicate with the same familiarity they have in interacting with objects in everyday life.

3.3   Ease of Use, Social Acceptability and Cultural Resiliency of Gestures

A Wizard-of-Oz approach might ensure that gestures are thought up by users. This means that their *preferences* are incorporated in the final gesture set. With the word "preferences", we are not only talking about the personal strategy that each user prefers to adopt in order to interact with a display. Everyone can prefer certain gestures for a specific action, and it is impossible to uniform users' preferences. However, as we stated in Sect. 2.5, there are some characteristics that should be shared in a gesture set: in addition to the previously cited guessability, gestures must be also socially acceptable and easy to perform (and use). Interestingly a Wizard-of-Oz approach implies that social acceptability and ease of use are part of the users' preferences: users will unlikely choose to perform a gesture if they are not motivated to use it or if the gesture is amiss; furthermore, it is very unlikely that several users think up a common gesture that is difficult to use.

Another reason why the Wizard-of-Oz approach may be an interesting approach is the possibility to incorporate the way in which users' preferences change in relation to different social contexts and users' cultural backgrounds. Without an unsupervised experiment, in which users are not biased by researchers, it is more difficult to make a cultural-resilient gesture set. Instead, valid and interesting results can be collected by multiple deployments in multiple places, such as different countries and locations. In this way it could be possible to analyze data and infer cultural similarities in the used gestures. These similarities may become a strong knowledge base for researchers, that can be used in the selection of gestures to include in the final set.

4   Conclusions

In this paper we presented the main challenges in designing methodologies to implement and investigate touchless gestural interactions with public displays. By definition, these are deployed "in-the-wild", i.e. outside controlled environments. This implies to study such interactions with novel approaches, in uncontrolled situations and without the explicit (or perceived) presence of experimenters. Factors such as social context, audience behavior and cultural differences can be primarily taken in account.

Furthermore, the novelty of touchless gestural interactions poses new challenges to the HCI community: the goal is to offer new instruments and paradigms, by which users can easily and naturally interact with the public display.

We proposed the use of a Wizard-of-Oz – based approach to collect users' preferences on gestures to be adopted in order to interact with a public display. We propose to use a suitable GUI inspired by the four given principles to make it usable and to avoid phenomena such as interaction blindness. Following these ideas, we believe it will be possible to create a valid gesture set, that will be socially acceptable, easy to use and cultural resilient. The latter property can be achieved by deploying several Wizard-of-Oz experiments in different places, countries and social contexts. Moreover, we are convinced that experimenters intervention should be minimized as much as possible, to avoid biases in users' behavior.

References

1. Weiser, M.: The computer for the 21st century. Sci. Am. **265**(3), 94–104 (1991)
2. Gentile, V., Sorce, S., Gentile, A.: Continuous hand openness detection using a kinect-like device. In: 2014 Eighth International Conference on Complex, Intelligent and Software Intensive Systems, pp. 553–557. IEEE Press, Birmingham (2014)
3. Müller, J., Bailly, G., Bossuyt, T., Hillgreen, N.: MirrorTouch: combining touch and mid-air gestures for public displays. In: Proceedings of the 16th International Conference on Human-Computer Interaction with Mobile Devices and Services, pp. 319–328. ACM Press, New York (2014)
4. Zhai, Y., Zhao, G., Alatalo, T., Heikkilä, J., Ojala, T., Huang, X.: Gesture interaction for wall-sized touchscreen display. In: Proceedings of the 2013 ACM Conference on Pervasive and Ubiquitous Computing Adjunct Publication, pp. 175–178. ACM Press, New York (2013)
5. Hardy, J., Rukzio, E., Davies, N.: Real world responses to interactive gesture based public displays. In: Proceedings of the 10th International Conference on Mobile and Ubiquitous Multimedia, pp. 33–39. ACM Press, New York (2011)
6. Wobbrock, J. O., Morris, M. R., Wilson, A.D.: User-defined gestures for surface computing. In: Proceedings of the 27th International Conference on Human Factors in Computing Systems, pp. 1083–1092. ACM Press, New York (2009)
7. Morris, M.R., Danielescu, A., Drucker, S., Fisher, D., Lee, B., Schraefel, M.C., Wobbrock, J.O.: Reducing legacy bias in gesture elicitation studies. Interactions **21**(3), 40–45 (2014)
8. Rico, J., Brewster, S.: Usable gestures for mobile interfaces: evaluating social acceptability. In: Proceedings of the 28th International Conference on Human Factors in Computing Systems, pp. 887–896. ACM Press, New York (2010)
9. Sharp, R., Rehman, K.: The 2005 UbiApp workshop: what makes good application-led research? IEEE Pervasive Comput. **4**(3), 80–82 (2005)
10. Jurmu, M.: Towards engaging multipurpose public displays, Ph.D. Thesis, University of Oulu (2014). http://www.oulu.fi/cse/node/27856
11. Chamberlain, A., Crabtree, A., Rodden, T., Jones, M., Rogers, Y.: Research in the wild: understanding "in the wild" approaches to design and development. In: Proceedings of Conference on Designing Interactive Systems Conference - DIS 2012, pp. 795–796. ACM Press, New York (2012)
12. Ojala, T., Kostakos, V., Kukka, H., Heikkinen, T., Linden, T., Jurmu, M., Hosio, S., Kruger, F., Zanni, D.: Multipurpose interactive public displays in the wild: three years later. Computer **45**(5), 42–49 (2012)
13. Johnson, R., Rogers, Y., van der Linden, J., Bianchi-Berthouze, N.: Being in the thick of in-the-wild studies: the challenges and insights of researcher participation. In: Proceedings of the 2012 ACM Annual Conference on Human Factors in Computing Systems CHI 2012, pp. 1135–1144. ACM Press, New York (2012)
14. Keskinen, T., Hakulinen, J., Heimonen, T., Turunen, M., Sharma, S., Miettinen, T., Luhtala, M.: Evaluating the experiential user experience of public display applications in the wild. In: Proceedings of the 12th International Conference on Mobile and Ubiquitous Multimedia MUM 2013, pp. 1–10. ACM Press, New York (2013)
15. Messeter, J., Molenaar, D.: Evaluating ambient displays in the wild: highlighting social aspects of use in public settings. In: Proceedings of the Conference on Designing Interactive Systems DIS 2012, pp. 478–481. ACM Press, New York (2012)

16. Hinrichs, U., Carpendale, S.: Gestures in the wild: studying multi-touch gesture sequences on interactive tabletop exhibits. In: Proceedings of the 2011 Annual Conference on Human Factors in Computing Systems - CHI 2011, pp. 3023–3032. ACM Press, New York (2011)

17. Müller, J., Wilmsmann, D., Exeler, J., Buzeck, M., Schmidt, A., Jay, T., Krüger, A.: Display blindness: the effect of expectations on attention towards digital signage. In: Tokuda, H., Beigl, M., Friday, A., Brush, A., Tobe, Y. (eds.) Pervasive 2009. LNCS, vol. 5538, pp. 1–8. Springer, Heidelberg (2009)

18. Ballendat, T., Marquardt, N., Greenberg, S.: Proxemic interaction: designing for a proximity and orientation-aware environment. In: ACM International Conference on Interactive Tabletops and Surfaces ITS 2010, pp. 121–130. ACM Press, New York (2010)

19. Vogel, D., Balakrishnan, R.: Interactive public ambient displays: transitioning from implicit to explicit, public to personal, interaction with multiple users. In: Proceedings of the 17th Annual ACM Symposium on User Interface Software and Technology - UIST 2004, pp. 137–146. ACM Press, New York (2004)

20. Müller, J., Alt, F., Michelis, D., Schmidt, A.: Requirements and design space for interactive public displays. In: Proceedings of the International Conference on Multimedia - MM 2010, pp. 1285–1294. ACM Press, New York (2010)

21. Schönböck, J., König, F., Kotsis, G., Gruber, D., Zaim, E., Schmidt, A.: MirrorBoard – an interactive billboard. In: Proceedings of Mensch und Computer 2008, pp. 207–216. Oldenbourg Verlag, Lübeck (2008)

22. Nielsen, M., Störring, M., Moeslund, T.B., Granum, E.: A procedure for developing intuitive and ergonomic gesture interfaces for HCI. In: Camurri, A., Volpe, G. (eds.) GW 2003. LNCS (LNAI), vol. 2915, pp. 409–420. Springer, Heidelberg (2004)

23. Good, M.D., Whiteside, J.A., Wixon, D.R., Jones, S.J.: Building a user-derived interface. Commun. ACM 27(10), 1032–1043 (1984)

24. Van Dam, A.: Post-WIMP user interfaces. Commun. ACM 40(2), 63–67 (1997)

25. Malizia, A., Bellucci, A.: The artificiality of natural user interfaces. Commun. ACM 55(3), 36–38 (2012)

26. Brignull, H., Rogers, Y.: Enticing people to interact with large public displays in public spaces. In: Rauterberg, M., Menozzi, M., Wesson, J. (eds.) Proceedings of the IFIP International Conference on Human-Computer Interaction - INTERACT 2003, pp. 17–24. IOS Press, Amsterdam (2003)

27. Fogg, B.J.: Persuasive Technology: Using Computers to Change What We Think and Do. Morgan Kauffman, San Francisco (2002)

28. Sorce, S., Augello, A., Santangelo, A., Gentile, A., Genco, A., Gaglio, S., Pilato, G.: Interacting with augmented environments. IEEE Pervasive Comput. 9(2), 57–58 (2010). doi:10.1109/MPRV.2010.34. ISSN 1536-1268

To Write not Select, a New Text Entry Method Using Joystick

Zhenyu Gu[(⊠)], Xinya Xu, Chen Chu, and Yuchen Zhang

Shanghai Jiao Tong University, Shanghai, China
{zygu,fireon7,cc060705}@sjtu.edu.cn, yczhang@gmail.com

Abstract. Existing joystick text entry methods for game and TV boxes are curser-based selections on virtual keyboards. In this paper we present a new text entry method using joysticks as tangible devices to capture users' freehand writing gestures. The method has considerable accuracy to accomplish English text entry. On the prediction model, we introduced HMM algorithm so users can enter text assisted with automatic correcting. We conducted a pairwise usability test on the keyboard selection method and writing-with-joystick method. The result shows that both of them are very easier to learn and writing-with-joystick is faster than the keyboard selection method both on the prediction model or none-prediction model. Subjects also report that using the keyboard selection method to enter text can be boring when using handwriting is somehow natural. This result indicates that writing with joystick may be another text entry option for game console or Smart TV users.

Keywords: Text entry · Joystick writing · Online recognition

1 Introduction

It's very common for a user sitting in the couch, input several letters like a user name or movie title on an Xbox or Smart TV. There is a long demonstrated need for people to entry text on the game console or Smart TV with joysticks. New technologies like voice recognition has been an alternative text entry method but still can't replace physical interfaces such as keyboards or joysticks in many situations. Ubiquitous connections to the net increase the need for text entry in register, search, instant messaging (IM), and email and so on from TV or game consoles. An effective text entry method would greatly enhance all of these applications and it is a fundamental requirement for extended use of IM and email [1].

The most common text entry method with joysticks is using joystick to select characters from an onscreen keyboard. Entering lots of text this way can be very slow and tedious [2]. Onscreen keyboards occupy more screen real-estate, exacerbating the need for frequent window management, and impose a secondary focus of attention [3].However, it's still very popular for everyday TV Box text entry because users can enter text immediately without learning. Some new key layouts [4, 5] were proposed to reduce selection time. The novices, however, have to visually search for characters and remember the location of them. Andrew D. Wilson(2006) presented a bimanual text entry technique designed for today's dual-joystick game controllers [1].

© Springer International Publishing Switzerland 2015
M. Kurosu (Ed.): Human-Computer Interaction, Part II, HCII 2015, LNCS 9170, pp. 35–43, 2015.
DOI: 10.1007/978-3-319-20916-6_4

While this approach increases entry speed, it needs users to pay more attention resources and possess more motion control ability. Early joystick writing approaches are alphabetical text entry methods without an onscreen keyboard. Users could write with a joystick according to a gesture alphabet [3, 7],which is designed to be simple and easy to recognize. The idea is from touch-typing on PDAs with stylus dating back to 1990 s [6].

In this paper we present a new text entry method allow users to write with joystick free of the gesture alphabet. Instead of making users learn the gesture alphabet, the approach uses an online handwriting recognition system [8] to learn users' freehand writing gestures. Discriminant features are extracted from users' handwriting samples to train a SVG [9] model. Then the model will be used to recognize user's handwriting trajectory in runtime. Online learning enables improvement of the input performance, the accuracy will increase when users enter more letters. The usability test shows that, our system is fast to learn and increases the entry speed by 2.65 characters per minute over the selection keyboard.

2 Related Work

Joystick-based text entry methods still play important roles in cases to input a short text on the game consoles, smart TVs or in-car navigation systems. There's vast body of research work on this topic, which generally consists of two main branches: selection-based and gesture-based techniques.

Selection-based text entry techniques allow users to select characters from an onscreen keyboard. Alphabetical layout and Qwerty layout are the most popular keyboard layouts. Some other layouts [4, 5] modify the layout of keys, making frequently used keys easy to access. MacKenzie, I. S., Soukoreff, R. W., & Helga, J. (2011) also proposed a zone based text entry method for joystick called H4-Writer [10]. It splits the items of keyboard into 4 sections and uses a joystick to select until only one is left. With H4-Writer, users can enter 20 words per minute, using only 1 thumb and 4 buttons.

Gesture-based text entry techniques use joystick to write, usually referring to a gesture alphabet. As the joystick is physically constrained to "write" an accurate trajectory of character, the gesture alphabets usually simplify the characters to make them easy to write. Graffiti and Unistrokes are handwriting text entry methods with stylus introduced in 1990 s [7]. Each of them designed a single stroke alphabet, easy to write and well recognized. EdgeWrite [3] places a square frame around the joystick to assist people writing along the physical edges. The trajectory of the joystick can be simplified to a sequence of touched edges and corners, which is relatively easy to recognize. The Edgewrite alphabet is shown in Fig. 1. Compared to selection-based methods, gesture-based methods need less screen real estate. Users however have to learn the gesture alphabet, and therefore the input speed is slow at the beginning.

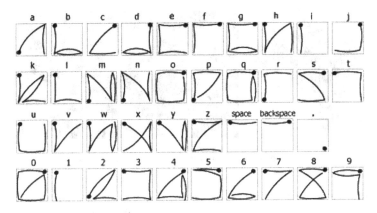

Fig. 1. The EdgeWrite gesture alphabet

3 Design

In this paper we present a new text entry method using joysticks as tangible devices to capture users' freehand writing gestures. First of all, the users' handwriting samples are collected to train a SVG (Scalable Vector Graphics) model, which will be used to recognize the users' handwriting trajectories. For sample providers, the system is considerable accurate even at the beginning. For new users other than the sample providers, we have found that the variety of samples have significant impact on the accuracy of the system. Besides samples covering more possible handwriting styles, online learning can improve the system performance as the users enter more text. Interactive feedback is also designed to guide the users to write more recognizable letters. We offered prediction input mode and non-prediction input mode as well. In the prediction mode, users entry text word by word while in the non-prediction mode, users entry text letter by letter.

3.1 Hardware & Interface

We test the prototype system on an Xbox game controller. A C ++ program was developed to deal with the signal in real time. We also designed an interactive interface including the input box and the prediction box (Fig. 2).

3.2 Online Handwriting Recognition

Handwriting recognition is the task of transforming a language represented in its spatial form of graphical marks into its symbolic representation [8]. Handwriting data can be converted to digital form either by scanning the writing on paper or by writing on an electronic surface. The two approaches are distinguished as off-line and on-line handwriting.

Fig. 2. The Xbox game controller and the interactive interface

The writing with joystick is an online handwriting recognition system referring a lot from that of touchpad. However, writing with joystick is quite different from the writing on touchpad. The trajectories of writing on touchpad spread on the plane and are often separated strokes while the trajectories of writing with joystick are continuous and most strokes are usually overlapped on the boundary, as swaging against the physical edge is natural and efficient for joystick writing. To segment the trajectories, we utilize state information of the stick on/off the boundary, bouncing back to the center or reversing its direction along the boundary. A character is generally segmented into on-boundary stokes and off-boundary strokes. And it also takes into account the sharp changes of directions (Fig. 3).

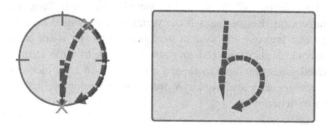

Fig. 3. Letter 'b' writing with joystick (left) and touchpad (right)

Feature extraction is one of the important cornerstone of any pattern classification system [11]. After a character is segmented into several strokes, each of the strokes will be transformed into a feature vector further. Seven kinds of features are extracted from their sequential and geometric information: distance, degree, absolute position, absolute degree, absolute distance and diff.

Feature vectors extracted from users' handwriting samples will be used to train a SVG (Scalable Vector Graphics) model. Then the model will be used to recognize user's handwriting trajectory in runtime.

Online learning enables improvement of the input performance. Though at the beginning extra selections are necessary to correct a few possible misrecognitions, online learning mechanism can increase the accuracy when users enter more letters. The mechanism is that when users confirm the entry result, the letters and trajectories will be added to the model. Considering most of times joysticks are very personal devices, the system will finally be customized.

In the prediction model, we use the HMM (Hidden Markov Model) to help increase accuracy and efficiency according to the word corpus. Though each gesture may get some letters misrecognized, with this model users can entry word without interrupting to correct. The model assesses each letter's recognition result—a series of possible letters and their joint probabilities, and in conjunction with the weights of the words in the word corpus, to give a best guess. This will also help when there is a mistyping or misrecognition in the input word.

One challenge of writing with joystick is that the trajectories of some letters could be too similar to distinguish. Restricted by the moving range of joystick, for instances, the trajectories of h and b, r and n, a and d, are easy to miswrite and hard to recognize even by human being. An interactive feedback animation of real-time recognition results was designed to guide users to write more recognizable letters. For example, when users move the joystick down, turn it right to hit the edge and then keep move down along the round edge, it will show "i", "r", "h" in a sequence. If users move more distance along the round edge, it will show a "b" instead (Fig. 4).

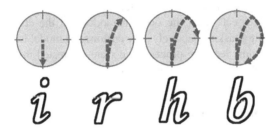

Fig. 4. The letter showed in the text box changes with the joystick's movement

4   Laboratory User Study

In order to evaluate the performance of the system, we have 15 subjects wrote each letter 10 times to get basic writing data. System training was controlled using a cross-validation procedure where 75 % of the training set was used for training and 25 % for validation. The model is not mature enough for more widely use but enough for a test.

We conducted a pairwise usability test on the keyboard selection method and writing-with-joystick method, both using an Xbox game controller and without prediction. Subjects were asked to enter text phrases as quickly as they could using both methods. It should be note that the system will keep capturing subjects' handwritings and prompting recognition results. After the test we retrained a model that was customized for the 20 subjects. The same subjects conducted another test on the writing–with-joystick method with prediction one day later. In this test, the original model and the customized model were both used (Fig. 5).

Fig. 5. The test interface of writing-with-joystick (left), keyboard selection (middle) and writing-with-joystick with prediction (right).

20 subjects were recruited for the test, aged from 20 to 24 years old. Each subject will take ten continuous sessions of tests using both two methods in an interlaced order. In each session, users needed to enter continuously for 3 min. To ensure the subjects not being disturbed, we also designed an automatic test system for both methods. Subjects could complete all ten sessions with themselves. Figure 6 shows the interfaces of the system. Polacek, O. and Sporka, A. J. (2013) proposed that the relative position of the presented phrase and the transcribed text could also affect the test results [12]. So in the test, the position of the target phrases and the input box are all the same. The phrases are randomly selected from a collection of 500 phrases for evaluations of text entry methods published by MacKenzie and Soukoreff (2003) [13], which contain no numbers or punctuation symbols but only letters.

In the next test, subjects used the original model and the customized model to accomplish the text entry task respectively. The customized model is used to imitate the system after a long online learning process. We were interested in how the text entry performance improved with the adaptive system.

5 Results and Discussions

5.1 Writing-with-Joysitck and Keyboard Delection

Speed. Table 1 shows the average input speed across all subjects during ten sessions, measured with characters per minute (CPM). The average input speed across all sessions and subjects of writing-with-joystick is 22.73 CPM, and that of keyboard selection is 20.08 CPM (also seen in Table 1), which means writing-with-joystick is 13.2 % faster than keyboard selection method. The variance of writing-with-joystick is 1.85 when the variance of keyboard selection is 0.12, indicating the input speed of keyboard selection is more stable than that of writing-with-joystick. In fact, Fig. 6 shows that the input speed of writing-with-joystick is increasing when that of keyboard selection is stable.

Error. Soukoreff and MacKenzie (2003) divided the input error into two categories: corrected errors (errors committed but corrected) and uncorrected errors (errors left in the transcribed text) [14]. As Table 1 shows, the uncorrected error rate of both methods are very low, indicating subjects tend to correct the errors. The total error rate of writing-with-joystick is 5.94 % when that of keyboard selection is 3.49 %. We calculated the average corrected error rate of the first three sessions and the last three

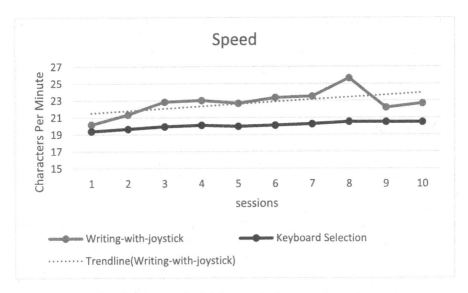

Fig. 6. Input speed of the two methods across ten sessions

sessions, and found that the session had a significant effect on the error rate of writing-with-joystick ($F_{1,38}$ = 5.325, p < 0.05). In other words, the error rate has a significant decease after several sessions. In fact, the total error rate of the first three sessions is 9.72 % when that of the last three sessions is 4.17 %. As online learning is not activated, it proves that interactive animations we designed play an important role in guiding subjects and making their handwritings more recognizable.

5.2   Writing-with-Joystick with Two Models

We compared the performance of the customized model and the original model. The average input speed using the customized model is 30.15 wpm (words per minute), higher than 28.76 wpm that using the original model. We found that using the retrained model had a significant effect on the input speed ($F_{1,38}$ = 5.724, p < 0.05),which indicated that online learning did help increase the input speed.

Compared to input speed, improvement of error rate is more remarkable. By using the customized model, total error rate drops from 7.59 % to 3.8 %. F-test also shows

Table 1. Results of tests, W is writing-with-joystick and K is keyboard selection

Methods	Prediction	Model	Speed	Corrected error rate	Uncorrected error rate	Total error rate
W	×	original	22.73 cpm	5.65	0.29	5.94
K	×	original	20.08 cpm	3.28	0.21	3.49
W	√	original	28.76 wpm	4.67	2.92	7.59
W	√	customized	30.15 wpm	1.94	1.86	3.8

that the customized model has a significant effect on total error rate. Corrected error rate drops from 4.67 % to 1.94 % sharply, the reason may be that corrected errors are mostly produced by misrecognitions, which are significant fewer when using the customized model. Relatively uncorrected errors are mostly produced by personal errors, so have no big change.

6 Discussion

Text entry on game consoles, smart TVs or other platforms have two types: letters entry and words entry. We compared the performance of writing-with-joystick and keyboard selection when entered letter by letter, found that the input speed of writing-with-joystick was faster and gone up sharply. Keyboard selection is an easy-to-learn method which means there's little difference between novices and experts. This means that writing-with-joystick is more efficient than keyboard selection ever for novices or experts. The error rate of writing-with-joystick was higher at the first, but decreased a lot after several sessions. We found interactive animations played an important role in improve the performance when online learning was not activated.

Words entry is usual when fill a form or write an email. Using a retrained customized model, we found both input speed and error rate had a remarkable promotion, indicating that online learning was an effective way to improve the system. There are still much room for improvement though. In fact, when figured out the reasons for errors, we found that many errors were caused by misoperations such as an unmeant 'OK'. If we can cut down misoperations, the error rate will have a significant decrease.

7 Conclusion and Future Works

In this paper we have presented a new text entry method that allows users to write with joystick freely without a preset gesture alphabet. The approach uses an online handwriting recognition system to extract features from users' handwritings and train a SVG model. Then the model will be used to recognize user's handwriting in runtime. Interactive animations we designed help users figure out how it works and avoid miswriting. Online learning keeps collecting users' handwritings and confirmed recognition results and retraining new models, makes it an adaptive and customizable system.

Our prototype and user study demonstrate that writing-with-joystick is technologically practical and efficient in terms of usability. We have suggested a relatively simple way to extract features from the segmented joystick writing trajectories. The pairwise usability test shows that the writing-with-joystick system is more efficient than keyboard selection method as the base line even for novices or experts. With more samples of writing accumulated on line, the customized model of recognition has a significant promotion in both input speed and accuracy comparing to its initial unused state. That means online learning can improve the performance of the method further in a long run. In conclusion, writing-with-joystick is an efficient and promotable system that can be an alternative text entry method in platform like a game console or smart TV.

References

1. Wilson, A.D., Agrawala., M.: Text entry using a dual joystick game controller. In: Proceedings of the SIGCHI conference on Human Factors in computing systems. ACM (2006)
2. Wobbrock, J.O., Myers, B.A., Aung, H.H.: Writing with a joystick: a comparison of date stamp, selection keyboard, and EdgeWrite. In: Proceedings of Graphics Interface 2004. Canadian Human-Computer Communications Society (2004)
3. Wobbrock, J.O., et al.: Integrated text entry from power wheelchairs. Behav. Inf. Technol. **24**(3), 187–203 (2005)
4. Rash, C.E.: Analysis and Design of Keyboards for the AH-64D Helicopter, DTIC Document (2005)
5. MacKenzie, I.S., Zhang, S.X.: The design and evaluation of a high-performance soft keyboard. In: Proceedings of the SIGCHI conference on Human Factors in Computing Systems, pp. 25–31. ACM, Pittsburgh (1999)
6. Goldberg, D., Richardson, C.: Touch-typing with a stylus. In: Proceedings of the INTERACT 1993 and CHI 1993 Conference on Human Factors in Computing Systems, pp. 80–87. ACM Amsterdam, The Netherlands (1993)
7. Castellucci, S.J., MacKenzie, I.S.: Graffiti vs. unistrokes: an empirical comparison. In: Proceedings of the SIGCHI Conference on Human Factors in Computing Systems, pp. 305–308. ACM, Florence (2008)
8. Plamondon, R., Srihari, S.N.: Online and off-line handwriting recognition: a comprehensive survey. IEEE Trans. Pattern Anal. Mach. Intell. **22**(1), 63–84 (2000)
9. Bahlmann, C., Haasdonk, B., Burkhardt, H.: Online handwriting recognition with support vector machines-a kernel approach. In: Proceedings. Eighth International Workshop on Frontiers in Handwriting Recognition. IEEE (2002)
10. MacKenzie, I.S., Soukoreff, R.W., Helga, J.: 1 thumb, 4 buttons, 20 words per minute: Design and evaluation of H4-Writer. In: Proceedings of the 24th annual ACM symposium on User interface software and technology. ACM (2011)
11. Parizeau, M., Lemieux, A., Gagne, C.: Character recognition experiments using Unipen data. In: Proceedings. Sixth International Conference on Document Analysis and Recognition (2001)
12. Polacek, O., Sporka, A.J., Butler, B.: Improving the methodology of text entry experiments. In: IEEE 4th International Conference on Cognitive Infocommunications (CogInfoCom), pp. 155–160 (2013)
13. MacKenzie, I.S., Soukoreff, R.W.: Phrase sets for evaluating text entry techniques. In: CHI 2003 Extended Abstracts on Human Factors in Computing Systems, pp. 754–755. ACM, Fort Lauderdale, Florida (2003)
14. Soukoreff, R.W., MacKenzie, I.S.: Metrics for text entry research: an evaluation of MSD and KSPC, and a new unified error metric. In: Proceedings of the SIGCHI conference on Human factors in computing systems. ACM (2003)

AirFlip: A Double Crossing In-Air Gesture using Boundary Surfaces of Hover Zone for Mobile Devices

Hiroyuki Hakoda[✉], Takuro Kuribara, Keigo Shima,
Buntarou Shizuki, and Jiro Tanaka

University of Tsukuba, Tsukuba, Japan
{hakoda,kuribara,keigo,shizuki,jiro}@iplab.cs.tsukuba.ac.jp

Abstract. Hover sensing capability provides richer interactions on mobile devices. For one such exploration, we show a quick double crossing in-air gesture for mobile devices, called *AirFlip*. In this gesture, users move their thumb into the hover zone from the side, and then move it out of the hover zone. Since this gesture does not conflict with any touch gestures that can be performed on mobile devices, it will serve as another gesture on mobile devices with touchscreens where only a limited input vocabulary is available. We implemented two applications based on Air-Flip. In this paper, we show the results of a comparative user study that we conducted to identify the performance of AirFlip. We also discuss the characteristics of AirFlip on the basis of the results.

Keywords: Hover gesture · Mobile · Input method · In-air gesture

1 Introduction

Mobile devices with hover sensing capability have recently emerged such as ELUGA P P-03E and AQUOS PHONE ZETA SH-06E. This capability provides richer interactions on mobile devices. For example, it allows users to unlock a pattern lock without touching the touchscreen, accordingly enabling secure authentication because users do not leave their fingerprints on the touchscreen. Moreover, the capability can be used to detect a finger's movement above the touchscreen, i.e., in-air gestures on mobile devices. However, few studies have explored in-air gestures in comparison with touch gestures on mobile devices.

For one such exploration, we show a quick double crossing in-air gesture for mobile devices, called *AirFlip*, which uses side boundary surfaces of the hover zone. In this gesture, users move their thumb into the hover zone from the side, and then move it out of the hover zone (Fig. 1). Since this gesture does not conflict with any touch gestures that can be performed on mobile devices, it will serve as another gesture on mobile devices with touchscreens where only a limited input vocabulary is available. In this study, we conducted a comparative user study with only touch and Bezel Swipe [1] to identify the performance of AirFlip.

© Springer International Publishing Switzerland 2015
M. Kurosu (Ed.): Human-Computer Interaction, Part II, HCII 2015, LNCS 9170, pp. 44–53, 2015.
DOI: 10.1007/978-3-319-20916-6_5

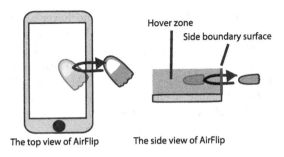

The top view of AirFlip   The side view of AirFlip

Fig. 1. Overview of AirFlip.

2 Related Work

In-air gestures on various input devices have been explored. For example, ThickPad [2] is a touchpad that can sense hover gestures with proximity-sensors. Similarly, Taylor et al. [3] presented a keyboard that senses in-air gestures on the keyboard. These studies presented in-air gestures on conventional input devices such as a touchpad and a keyboard. In contrast, we explore in-air gestures above the touchscreen of mobile devices.

In-air gestures above tabletops have been explored. Interactions in the Air [4] and Continuous Interaction Space [5] focused on the space above tabletops. Han and Park [6] proposed hover based zooming interaction above tabletops. Pointable [7] is an in-air pointing technique on tabletops. Pyryeskin et al. [8] proposed a system that senses a user's hand above multi-touch surfaces using only a diffused surface illumination device. In contrast, we focus on the space above mobile devices.

In-air gestures above mobile devices have also been explored. Air+Touch [9] is a synthesis of touch and in-air gestures using an additional depth camera. Kratz et al. [10] showed a detection algorithm for in-air gestures and the design space. While these studies utilized hovering in the hover zone, AirFlip utilizes boundary surfaces of the hover zone. Han et al. [11] proposed Push-Push utilizing the pressed state and the hover state that does not conflict with a drag operation. Hover Widgets [12] utilizes movements of a pen above a screen. In contrast, AirFlip utilizes movements of a finger above a screen.

Crossing has been explored intensively especially to enrich interactions [13–18]. For example, Bezel Swipe [1] is a drag gesture starting from the bezel of mobile devices. Nakamura et al. [19,20] proposed a double crossing gesture for hand gesture interfaces that crosses a target twice. In contrast, AirFlip is a double crossing in-air gesture that crosses a side boundary surface of the hover zone twice.

3 Design of AirFlip

AirFlip is a quick double crossing gesture using the boundary surfaces of the hover zone, and users perform it with the thumb of their holding hand. Fig. 1

illustrates AirFlip. Users move the thumb into the hover zone from the side, and then move it out of the hover zone quickly. While current in-air gestures on mobile devices with hover sensing capability utilize motions such as keeping or moving their finger *within* the hover zone, AirFlip utilizes the motion that crosses the boundary surfaces of the hover zone. Moreover, AirFlip adopts a double crossing gesture because a single crossing gesture may be incorrectly recognized when users touch the screen. Due to these designs, AirFlip does not conflict with conventional touch and in-air gestures.

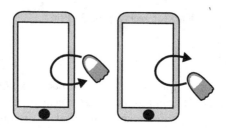

Fig. 2. Rotation gesture by twirling user's thumb.

AirFlip has two variations: just flipping the thumb (Fig. 1) and twirling the thumb (Fig. 2). The former is suitable as a trigger of a single action and thus can be used as a button; the latter is suitable to adjust a continuous value such as a rotational angle of a map.

4　Implementation

We implemented AirFlip as an Android application that monitors hover events. Currently, sensing capability in Android devices begins to generate hover events when a user's finger enters the hover zone and continues to generate them until the user's finger leaves the zone. Therefore, AirFlip is recognized when hover events begin to appear and then disappear quickly (600 ms in our current implementation).

However, AirFlip is incorrectly recognized in naïve implementation for the following two reasons. First, AirFlip is recognized when users tap the screen because hover events occur before and after a tap. To address this problem, AirFlip is ignored when a touch event occurs within 50 ms after hover events disappear. Second, AirFlip is recognized when users are searching for a target to touch because their thumb tends to enter and leave the top boundary of the hover zone frequently in this context. To address this problem, AirFlip is ignored when their thumb leaves the hover zone more than 600 ms after their thumb has entered it. These realize stable recognition of both AirFlip and conventional touch gestures.

5 Application

We present two applications of AirFlip. To test these application, we used ELUGA P P-03E (Android 4.2.2) as a mobile device with hover sensing capability.

5.1 Rotating a Map in Map Applications

We implemented a map viewer that adopts AirFlip. In this application, users can rotate a map by using AirFlip (Fig. 3); users can change the direction of rotation by changing the direction of twirl. Note that in conventional map applications, users touch an area of a map with two fingers and drag both fingers in a circular motion to rotate it. In contrast, users can rotate a map by using only one hand: i.e., users hold a device with one hand and perform AirFlip using the thumb of that hand.

5.2 Switching Tabs in Web Browsers

Users can use AirFlip to switch tabs to the next (Fig. 4). In conventional web browsers, users need to open a list and choose a tab from it. In contrast, users can switch tabs (i.e., go to the next tab and go back to the previous tab) quickly in this application, because AirFlip is only a double crossing gesture. Users can change the direction of switching by changing the direction of twirl.

6 Evaluation

We conducted a user study to measure the speed and usability of AirFlip. The user study is designed to measure the above metrics under the assumption that users browse web pages by selecting links and switch tabs in a web browser repeatedly.

6.1 Participants

Fourteen participants took part in the experiment as volunteers. However, we eliminated the data of two participants because we failed to collect their experimental data correctly. As the result, we used the data of 12 participants (eight males and four females) aged from 20 to 25 (mean = 22.7; SD = 1.29). They all used their mobile devices on a daily basis and were all right-handed. They had been using mobile devices for 11 to 99 months (mean = 34.8; SD = 24.9).

6.2 Apparatus

We used a mobile device (ELUGA P P-03E, OS: Android 4.2.2, size: height 132 mm × width 65 mm × thick 10.9 mm) with an approximately 4.7 in. touchscreen (resolution: 1080 × 1920 pixels).

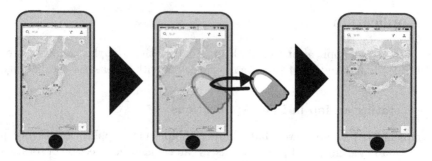

Fig. 3. Rotating a map in map applications.

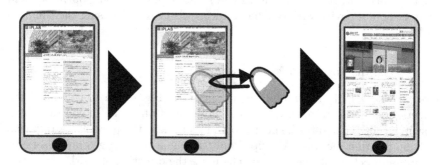

Fig. 4. Switching tabs in web browsers.

6.3 Methods

We compared the performance of the following three methods for switching tabs:

AirFlip. The participants switch tabs by AirFlip. They move their thumb into the hover zone from the right side, and then move it out of the hover zone quickly. A hover trajectory is displayed on the display of the device as visual feedback when users perform AirFlip.

Bezel Swipe. [1] The participants switch tabs by Bezel Swipe. They start a swipe gesture from the right bezel to the left. A touch trajectory is displayed on the display of the device as visual feedback when users perform Bezel Swipe.

Touch. The participants switch tabs by tapping one of the tabs.

6.4 Procedure

We asked the participants to sit on a chair and hold a mobile device in their right hand. To control the experimental conditions between participants, we also asked the participants to hold the device without supporting it by using a desk or their bodies. We asked the participants to perform this user study as accurately and rapidly as possible.

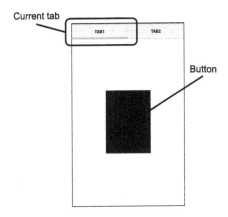

Fig. 5. Overview of the application for the user study. In this user study, there are two tabs in the web browser.

Each participant was told the goals of the user study. We also explained how to perform the three methods. Then a participant practiced each method for more than one minute. The user study started when the participant pressed the "Start" button displayed on the device's touchscreen. First, she touched a button randomly displayed on a cell in the 3 × 3 grid (Fig. 5). After that, she switched tabs by using one of the methods. In each session, she performed 18 trials (9 places × 2 tabs). She completed three sessions for each method. Thus, she performed 162 trials (3 sessions × 3 methods × 9 places × 2 tabs) in this user study.

The order of methods was counter-balanced across participants. After all trials were finished, we asked the participants to complete a questionnaire: they answered four five-point Likert scale questions (1 = strongly disagree, 5 = strongly agree) and gave reasons for their scores. The participants took about 20 min to complete this user study.

6.5   Results and Analysis

Figure 6 shows task completion time of all methods, which is defined as the elapsed time between pressing a button and switching tabs. As this figure shows, the fastest method was Touch (476 ms) and the second fastest was Bezel Swipe (479 ms). AirFlip was 912 ms, approximately 1.9 times slower than the other methods.

Figure 7 shows the results of questionnaires. Interestingly, while the accuracy of AirFlip is subjectively evaluated as the lowest, the participants felt AirFlip to be a quick gesture because its quickness is evaluated positively (4.0). On the other hand, by taking into account that AirFlip is rated the same as Touch in terms of easiness and preference, the participants were not considered to be satisfied with AirFlip. We analyzed the comments from the participants and found that this was due to too much incorrect recognition of AirFlip (that is, the system failed to recognize AirFlip while users believed they performed the

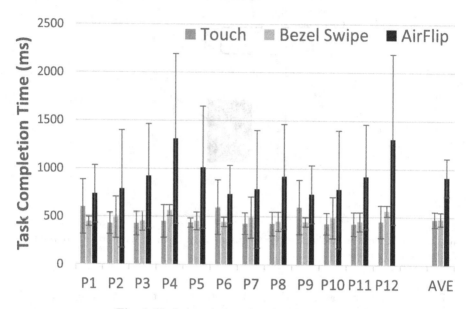

Fig. 6. Task completion time for all methods.

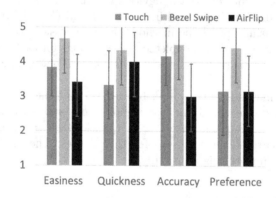

Fig. 7. The questionnaire results for the three methods (5-point Likert scale).

gesture correctly). Eleven participants mentioned this problem. Moreover, high variance of task completion time would be caused by this problem. Consequently, if we can reduce such errors of AirFlip, its performance may improve.

7   Discussion

While we found much incorrect recognition lowered the performance of AirFlip in the evaluation, we considered that two factors of this problem can be addressed to improve the performance.

7.1   Accidental Touching

We observed that participants often touched the touchscreen accidentally while performing AirFlip. This problem may have been caused by the hover zone being too narrow: hover zone is so low that hovering a finger above the screen may be difficult for users because they need to keep hovering their thumb in the hover zone when they perform AirFlip. In the questionnaire, the participants commented that the height of the hover zone is difficult to determine, and too low to perform AirFlip. Therefore, the performance of AirFlip will be improved if the hover sensing capability of mobile devices is improved to sense user's fingers at higher positions.

Moreover, we plan to attach a protective case to a mobile device shown in Fig. 9. This case is designed so that its side is higher than the surface of the device. With this case, users will be able to use AirFlip by flipping the side of the case.

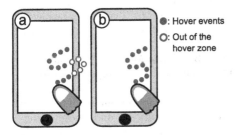

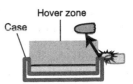

Fig. 8. Incorrect perception of thumb's position. Red circles show positions of hover events when users incorrectly thought that they had moved their thumb out of the hover zone; red rings show required trajectory to perform AirFlip (Color figure online).

Fig. 9. A mobile device in a protective case. Users move their thumb into the hover zone by flipping the side of the case.

7.2   Incorrectly Thinking One's Thumb Has Moved Out of the Hover Zone

We also observed that participants incorrectly perceived that they had moved their thumb out of the hover zone (Fig. 8a) to perform AirFlip although the thumb stayed within the hover zone (Fig. 8b). In this case, AirFlip was not recognized because hover events continued to occur. To address this problem, we plan to provide users with feedback such as vibration when users move their thumb out of the hover zone. Accordingly, users can be made aware of the boundary surfaces of the hover zone and thus can perform AirFlip stably.

8   Conclusion

We presented a quick double crossing in-air gesture for mobile devices called Air-Flip. We conducted a user study to measure its performance. From the results,

AirFlip is slower than the other methods. The data and the participants' comments suggest this result is caused by incorrect recognition of AirFlip due to an inability to sense user's fingers in high positions. For immediate future work, we plan to incorporate a haptic feedback and measure the performance of Air-Flip using a protective case whose side is higher than the surface of the device. Furthermore, we also plan to implement a mobile device with hover sensing capability that can sense user's fingers in higher positions by using a vision-based approach.

References

1. Roth, V., Turner, T.: Bezel swipe: conflict-free scrollingand multiple selection on mobile touch screen devices. In: Proceedings of CHI 2009, pp. 1523–1526 (2009)
2. Choi, S., Gu, J., Han, J., Lee, G.: Area gestures for a laptop computer enabled by a hover-tracking touchpad. In: Proceedings of APCHI 2012, pp. 119–124 (2012)
3. Taylor, S., Keskin, C., Hilliges, O., zadi, S.,Helmes, J.: Type-hover-swipe in 96 bytes: a motion sensing mechanical keyboard. In: Proceedings of CHI 2014, pp. 1695–1704 (2014)
4. Hilliges, O., Izadi, S., Wilson, A.D., Hodges, S., Garcia-Mendoza, A., Butz, A.: Interactions in the air: adding further depth to interactive tabletops. In: Proceedings of UIST 2009, pp. 139–148 (2009)
5. Marquardt, N., Jota, R., Greenberg, S., Jorge, J.A.: The continuous interaction space: interaction techniques unifying touch and gesture on and above a digital surface. In: Campos, P., Graham, N., Jorge, J., Nunes, N., Palanque, P., Winckler, M. (eds.) INTERACT 2011, Part III. LNCS, vol. 6948, pp. 461–476. Springer, Heidelberg (2011)
6. Han, S., Park, J.: A study on touch and hover based interaction for zooming. In: CHI EA 2012, pp. 2183–2188 (2012)
7. Banerjee, A., Burstyn, J., Girouard, A., Vertegaal, R.: Pointable: an in-air pointing technique to manipulate out-of-reach targets on tabletops. In: Proceedings of ITS 2011, pp. 11–20 (2011)
8. Pyryeskin, D., Hancock, M., Hoey, J.: Comparing elicited gestures to designer-created gestures for selection above a multitouch surface. In: Proceedings of ITS 2012, pp. 1–10 (2012)
9. Chen, X.A., Schwarz, J., Harrison, C., Mankoff, J., Hudson, S.E.: Air+Touch: interweaving touch and in-air gestures. In: Proceedings of UIST 2014, pp. 519–525 (2014)
10. Kratz, S., Rohs, M.: HoverFlow: expanding the design space of around-device interaction. In: Proceedings of MobileHCI 2009, pp. 4:1–4:8 (2009)
11. Han, J., Ahn, S., Lee, G.: Push-Push: a two-point touchscreen operation utilizing the pressed state and the hover state. In: Proceedings of UIST 2014 Adjunct, pp. 103–104 (2014)
12. Grossman, T., Hinckley, K., Baudisch, P., Agrawala, M., Balakrishnan, R.: Hover widgets: using the tracking state to extend the capabilities of pen-operated devices. In: Proeedings of CHI 2006, pp. 861–870 (2006)
13. Pook, S., Lecolinet, E., Vaysseix, G., Barillot, E.: Control menus: excecution and control in a single interactor. In: Proceedings of CHI EA 2000, pp. 263–264 (2000)
14. Guimbretiére, F., Winograd, T.: FlowMenu: combining command, text, and data entry. In: Proceedings of UIST 2000, pp. 213–216 (2000)

15. Accot, J., Zhai, S.: More than dotting the i's — foundations for crossing-based interfaces. In: Proceedings of CHI 2002, pp. 73–80 (2002)
16. Dragicevic, P.: Combining crossing-based and paper-based interaction paradigms for dragging and dropping between overlapping windows. In: Proceedings of UIST 2004, pp. 193–196 (2004)
17. Luo, Y., Vogel, D.: Crossing-based selection with direct touch input. In: Proceedings of CHI 2014, pp. 2627–2636 (2014)
18. Chen, C., Perrault, S.T., Zhao, S., Ooi, W.T.: BezelCopy: an efficient cross-application copy-paste technique for touchscreen smartphones. In: Proceedings of AVI 2014, pp. 185–192 (2014)
19. Nakamura, T., Takahashi, S., Tanaka, J.: Double-crossing: a new interaction technique for hand gesture interfaces. In: Lee, S., Choo, H., Ha, S., Shin, I.C. (eds.) APCHI 2008. LNCS, vol. 5068, pp. 292–300. Springer, Heidelberg (2008)
20. Nakamura, T., Takahashi, S., Tanaka, J.: The selection technique of hand gesture in large screen environment: proposal of double-crossing and comparison with other techniques. Inst. Electron. Inf. Commun. Eng. Trans. J96-D(4), 978–988 (2013) (in Japanese)

Design and Evaluation of Freehand Gesture Interaction for Light Field Display

Vamsi Kiran Adhikarla[1,2], Grega Jakus[3(✉)], and Jaka Sodnik[3]

[1] Holografika, Budapest, Hungary
[2] Pazmany Peter Catholic University, Budapest, Hungary
[3] University of Ljubljana, Ljubljana, Slovenia
{grega.jakus, jaka.sodnik}@fe.uni-lj.si

Abstract. The paper reports on a user study of freehand gesture interaction with a prototype of autostereoscopic 3D light field display. The interaction was based on a direct touch selection of simple objects rendered at different positions in space. The main goal of our experiment was to evaluate the overall user experience and perceived cognitive workload of such freehand interaction in 3D environment and compare it to the simplified touch-based interaction in 2D environment. The results of the experiment confirmed the hypothesis that significantly more time is required for the interaction in 3D than the interaction in 2D. Surprisingly, no significant difference was found in the results of the assessment of cognitive workload when comparing 3D and 2D. We believe the interaction scenario proposed and evaluated in this study could represent an efficient and intuitive future interaction technique for the selection and manipulation of content rendered on autostereoscopic 3D displays

Keywords: 3D display · Light field display · Free-hand interaction · Direct touch · Leap Motion Controller · Human-machine interface (HMI) · Human-computer interface (HCI)

1 Introduction

Projection-based light field displays [1] represent a novel technology in the field of 3D rendering, which provides a more sophisticated solution for visualizing 3D content than any other glasses-free 3D technology. The illusion of 3D perception is generally created by providing two slightly offset views of a scene, one for each eye. Figure 1 illustrates how different views are delivered in traditional stereoscopic 3D technology (S3D), multiview 3D and light field technologies. In S3D, the two views are captured by two cameras simultaneously and synchronized to the left and right eye of the viewer respectively (Fig. 1a). View isolation is achieved by using special eyewear.

In a glasses-free system, the process of view separation is generally achieved by producing light beams with directionally-dependent colour and intensity of emitted light from each pixel on the display, which enables a more realistic 3D visualization compared to S3D technology. As opposed to S3D, view separation is inherent to the hardware itself, which is why such displays are often called *autostereoscopic displays*.

© Springer International Publishing Switzerland 2015
M. Kurosu (Ed.): Human-Computer Interaction, Part II, HCII 2015, LNCS 9170, pp. 54–65, 2015.
DOI: 10.1007/978-3-319-20916-6_6

The view separation in the existing autostereoscopic displays is often achieved by directing the light using lenticular lenses and parallax barriers. Such approach enables the projection of multiple views of a scene (Fig. 1b). However, due to its discrete nature, it requires the user to be located at certain predefined positions in order to perceive 3D comfortably. Any user entering the space between the views can see the light barrier, which can impair the overall 3D quality perception. The limited number of available views directly affects the angular resolution and the effective field of view (FOV) of the multiview autostereoscopic display.

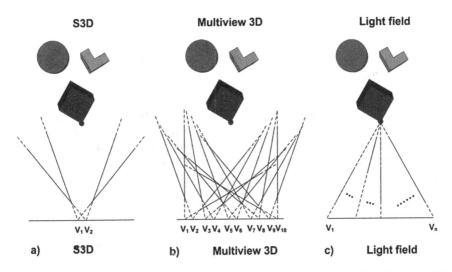

Fig. 1. Displaying a sample scene and a point in the scene (shown in red) in 3D using S3D, multiview 3D and light field technologies (Color figure online).

Additionally, S3D and multiview autostereoscopic displays do not take into account the positions of 3D scene points and display only a limited number of perspectives. These perspectives are actually 2D projections of the 3D image, which, when combined, define the scene. Light field displays, in contrast, treat each scene point differently resulting in a much more realistic and accurate 3D visualization. This is achieved by defining the scene by using a set of direction-dependent light rays emitted from various optical modules as if they were emitted from real scene points (Fig. 1c). A scene point is created at the point of crossing of two light rays emitted from two optical modules.

A light field display consists of a holographic screen, a group of optical modules and two mirrors along the sidewalls of the display (see Fig. 2). The screen is a flat hologram while the optical modules are arranged densely and equidistantly from the screen. The so-called *light field* is created when the light beams emitted from the optical modules hit the holographic screen and disperse in different directions. The separation of views created by the holographic screen provides a continuous-like horizontal motion parallax without blocking zones in the FOV of the display [2].

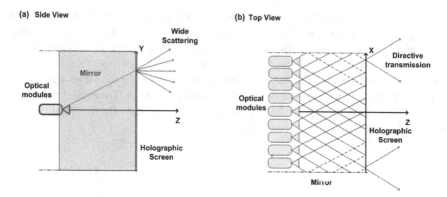

Fig. 2. Main components of a light field display: geometrically aligned multiple optical modules, a holographic screen and side mirrors.

The possibility of manipulating virtual objects in 3D environment through natural interfaces, such as freehand gestures, brings new opportunities for more useful 3D applications. As light field displays represent an innovative technology in the field, novel interaction technologies and techniques need to be designed and evaluated in order to enable such interaction. The main goal of the experiment described in this paper was to evaluate the performance, perceived user experience and cognitive workload while interacting with 3D content on a light field display. The interaction was based on the selection of objects by touching their virtual position. Leap Motion Controller (LMC) was used as the tracking device as it enables continuous tracking of hands with millimetre accuracy [3], thus allowing the interaction with individual 3D voxels of a light field display.

The remainder of this paper is organized as follows: the following section presents the related work on free-hand interaction with 3D content. The study design is described in Sect. 3, while the results of the study are presented and analysed in Sect. 4. The paper concludes with discussion and key conclusions.

2   Related Work

The input devices that enable free-hand interaction can be categorized into wearable and hands-free devices. As traditional wearable devices generally obstruct the use of hands while performing activities, it is more suitable to track hand movement visually, for example, by means of optical tracking systems. Such systems operate by tracking reflective markers attached to the user's hand and were used as the tracking device for the interaction with the 3D content in various experiments, including [4] and [5].

Optical tracking can also be applied for true hands-free tracking where users do not need to wear markers. However, as body surface reflects less light compared to highly-reflective markers, this generally results in a smaller interaction space. A number of studies with hands-free tracking for 3D interaction have been conducted using various input devices and setups (e.g. [6–8]) including Microsoft Kinect sensor, one of the commercially most successful hands-free tracking devices in the market (7, 9–11).

Another important contribution to the affordable desktop hands-free motion tracking devices was the release of Leap Motion Controller [12] in 2013. The device uses three LED emitters to illuminate the surrounding space with infra-red (IR) light which is reflected back to the device from the nearby objects and captured by two IR cameras. The determined positions of recognized hands, fingers and other objects as well as detected gestures can be obtained through API (Application Programming Interface). The device and its coordinate system are shown in Fig. 3.

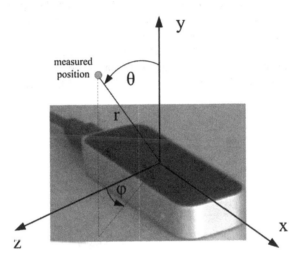

Fig. 3. Leap Motion Controller and the coordinate system used to describe positions of recognized objects.

A study on the LMC performance [3] revealed that the effective range of the device extends from approximately 3 to 30 cm above the device (y axis), approximately 0 to 20 cm behind the device (negative z axis) and 20 cm in each direction along the device (x axis). Standard deviation of the measured position of a static object was shown to be less than 0.5 mm.

A variety of studies on interaction involving LMC have been performed including studies with 3D gestures [13, 14] and pointing tasks [15, 16]. However, to our knowledge, we report on the first study involving LMC and a 3D display.

3 User Study

The main goal of the user study was to evaluate the performance, perceived user experience and cognitive workload while interacting with 3D content. The interaction consisted of selecting the tile-like objects using the "direct touch" method.

3.1 Study Design

The interaction with the light field display was evaluated through a comparison of 2D and 3D displaying modes representing two different experimental conditions:

- in 2D mode, the displayed tiles were distributed on a plane in close proximity of the display surface;
- in 3D mode, the displayed tiles were distributed in a space in front of the display (the distance between the tiles and the screen surface varied from 0 to 7 cm).

The 2D mode provided a control environment which was used to evaluate the specifics of this particular interaction design: the performance and properties of the input device, display dimensions, specific interaction scenario (e.g. touching the tiles), etc.

The study design was within-subject. Each participant was asked to perform 11 trials within each condition. In each trial, three tiles of the same size were displayed simultaneously and the participant was asked to touch the surface of the red tile as perceived in space (Fig. 4). The positions of the tiles varied from trial to trial to cover the FOV of the display.

Fig. 4. The interaction with the content rendered on the light field display (Color figure online).

The main variables measured in the experiment were:

- task completion times;
- cognitive workload (measured through NASA TLX questionnaire);
- UEQ (User Experience Questionnaire) on the perceived user experience.

3.2 Test Subjects and Groups

A total of 12 test subjects (5 female and 7 male) participated in the study. The average age of the participants was 27 years and ranged from 20 to 36 years. All participants reported to have normal or corrected to normal sight.

To avoid learning effects, the participants were equally distributed among two experimental groups which differed in the order of the two conditions.

3.3 Technical Setup

A small-scale prototype light field display developed by Holografika was used for the study. The FOV of the display was comparable to the tracking volume of the LMC. The light field display was placed at the participants' eye-level at a distance of approximately 50 cm from the viewer. The gesture input was tracked by LMC placed on the table in front of the display.

Figure 5 shows the technical setup. The controlling PC hosts two applications. The frontend OpenGL application renders content for 2D LCD display and also communicates with LMC in real-time in order to receive and process user interaction commands. The second application (backend wrapper) generates a modified stream for light field rendering and tracks the commands in the current instance of OpenGL (frontend application).

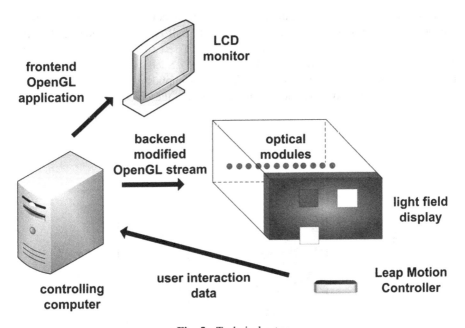

Fig. 5. Technical setup

3.4 Procedure

Prior to the experiment, the participants were informed about the nature and structure of the study. They were then asked to complete a pre-study questionnaire (age, gender, sight disabilities, and prior experience with LMC and autostereoscopic 3D displays). The participants were then thoroughly introduced to their tasks, the interaction scenario and methods. Finally, they were given five minutes to familiarize themselves with their tasks and the interaction.

Participants were asked to perform the given tasks as quickly as possible. Task completion times and interaction activity were recorded automatically for each task. The measurements started automatically when the participants reached the distance of 15 cm from the display. After successfully completing the task, the participants had to remove their hand from this area and place it on their knee before proceeding with the next task. For the purpose of post-evaluation of the interaction performance, the entire user study was recorded with a digital video camera.

After completing each of the experimental conditions, the participants were asked to fill the NASA TLX [16] and UEQ questionnaires [17] to evaluate their perceived workload and user experience. After both conditions, the participants were asked to fill in a short post-study questionnaire on their overall perception of the interfaces, the design and realism of the display, and the complexity of the given tasks.

4 Results and Discussion

Figure 6 shows mean task completion times in both conditions. The mean object selection time in 3D condition was approximately half of a second longer than the selection time in 2D condition. The results of the T-test ($t(22) = 2.521$, $p = 0.019$) showed this time difference to be significant ($p < 0.05$). Such results of task completion times were expected since the additional dimension implies extra time to cognitively process the visual information and to physically locate the object.

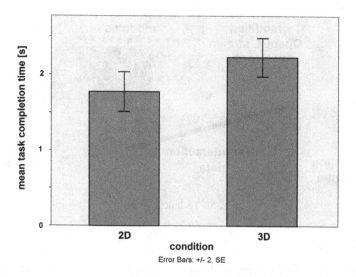

Fig. 6. Mean task completion times

When analysing the approach path of the finger towards the rendered object, some typical patterns of finger movement can be observed. Figure 7, for example, displays the fingertip positions measured along the z-axis (i.e. the depth; see Fig. 2 or Fig. 3 for coordinate system orientation). In 2D selection (Fig. 7a), the pattern is generally straightforward with direct approach towards the object (rendered just in front of the display in 2D) and then holding the finger still to trigger the selection. On the other hand, the trajectory of the finger in 3D typically includes a confident initial move towards the perceived position of the object, followed by a set of small corrections. Finally, the selection is triggered, often while still slowly moving the finger (Fig. 7b).

Figure 8 displays the results of the NASA TLX test. The T-test analysis ($t(22) = -0.452$, $p = 0.655$) revealed no significant difference in total cognitive workload between the conditions ($p > 0.05$) as well as no significant difference on any of the subscales.

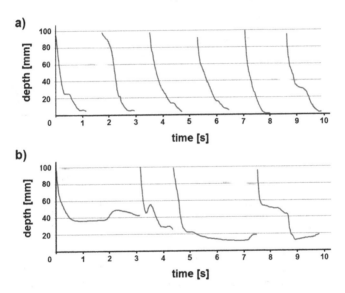

Fig. 7. Typical traces of fingertip positions in (a) 2D and (b) 3D conditions measured along z-axis (depth).

Similarly, the results of the UEQ (Fig. 9) also did not reveal any significant difference between both conditions ($t(22) = -0.708$, $p = 0.486$), except for the "novelty" subscale where a tendency towards higher preferences for the 3D mode can be observed.

When asked about their preference, two thirds of the participants chose the 3D mode as their favourite. The participants generally found the objects rendered on the light field display more realistic and reported that all the objects were seen clearly. The tasks were also found realistic and the participants reported they could be solved in a very straight-forward manner. The input device was also reported to be easy to use in the combination with the 3D display.

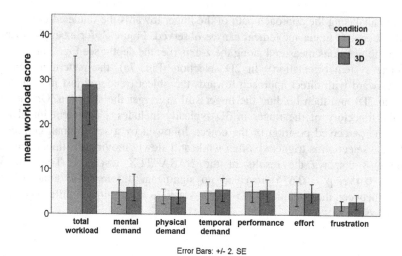

Fig. 8. Mean workload scores

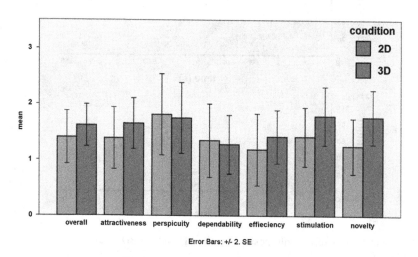

Fig. 9. Mean user experience scores

5   Discussion and Conclusions

The statistical analysis of the selection times revealed that less time is needed to select the object in 2D than in 3D condition. Such result was, in fact, expected, as the interaction in an additional dimension undoubtedly requires extra time needed to cognitively process the visual information and then to physically locate the object in space.

When analysing the time course of the selection gesture, some interesting observations are also worth mentioning. The depth component of the gesture (the distance from the display surface) can, in both conditions, be generally divided into two sections: the initial direct and relatively confident approach towards the target and the final ("triggering") part of the gesture. While the pattern of the first section is similar in both conditions, this is generally not true for the "triggering" part of the gesture. In 2D condition, the targeted tile was always displayed directly in front of the display with a permanent depth component of its location. Therefore, after identifying the longitudinal and transverse components of the tile location, all the users were required to do was to simply hold their finger at constant distance for a certain amount of time in order to trigger the tile selection. On the other hand, in 3D condition the users were not entirely certain of the exact displaying depth of the tile as it varied from trial to trial. Therefore, when they reached the approximate depth at which they perceived the tile, the participants began locating it more precisely by making small and slow corrections in order to trigger the selection. Longer task completion times in 3D condition can, therefore, be contributed precisely to such triggering attempts, which were based more or less on trial and error.

The somewhat longer and uncertain last stage of the selection gesture can be attributed to the lack of a tactile feedback due to the intangibility of the tiles that are being displayed and selected. The problem of object intangibility in 3D interaction is not insignificant and has already been addressed in similar studies (see for example [8]). A logical solution (and also the probable subject of our future experiments in the field) would be to provide the user with some sort of feedback when the selection gesture reaches close proximity of the targeted object.

In the present study, we have addressed the problem of human-computer interaction in 3D environment and also the transition between 2D and 3D modalities. As the old-fashioned but very effective computer mouse has been successfully replaced by various direct-input mechanisms in touch-screen environment, a similar evolutionary step will be required when upgrading displaying technologies with an additional dimension. We believe the freehand interaction setup proposed in this study could represent the next logical step in this transition as it enables very intuitive selection and manipulation of content in 3D environment. Simple and affordable tracking devices such as LMC will play a key role in the future human-machine interaction, either as primary input devices or as a part of a complex multi-modal interface. The results of UEQ questionnaires in our study revealed a high preference of users for freehand interaction setups resulting in a fast and straightforward adoption process of such technologies. Additionally, the NASA TLX test revealed a relatively low cognitive demand comparable to a simplified 2D environment. We believe this reflects the efficiency and the intuitiveness of the proposed interaction setup and the freehand interaction with 3D content in general.

In the future, we are planning on extending the freehand interaction paradigm in 3D environment by including both hands and more complex gestures. The "selecting" scenario should additionally be upgraded to free manipulation of objects in 3D space by changing their positions and orientations. Additionally, some form of audio or tactile feedback should also be considered offering a more realistic perception of 3D space and an even better user experience.

Acknowledgements. The research leading to these results has received funding from the DIVA Marie Curie Action of the People programme of the European Union's Seventh Framework Programme FP7/2007–2013/ under REA grant agreement 290227.

References

1. Agocs, T., Balogh, T., Forgacs, T., Bettio, F., Gobbetti, E., Zanetti, G., Bouvier, E.: A large scale interactive holographic display. In: IEEE Virtual Reality Conference (VR 2006), p. 57. Washington, DC, USA (2006)
2. Balogh, T., Kovács, P.T., Megyesi, Z., Barsi, A.: HoloVizio – true 3D display system. In: 3DTV Conference, pp. 1–4 (2007)
3. Guna, J., Jakus, G., Pogačnik, M., Tomažič, S., Sodnik, J.: An analysis of the precision and reliability of the leap motion sensor and its suitability for static and dynamic tracking. Sensors **14**, 3702–3720 (2014)
4. Bruder, G., Steinicke, F., Sturzlinger, W.: To touch or not to touch?: Comparing 2D touch and 3D mid-air interaction on stereoscopic tabletop surfaces. In: Proceedings of the 1st Symposium on Spatial User Interaction, pp. 9–16. ACM (2013)
5. Grossman, T., Wigdor, D., Balakrishnan, R.: Multi-finger gestural interaction with 3D volumetric displays. In: Proceedings of the 17th Annual ACM Symposium on User Interface Software and Technology, pp. 61 – 70. ACM, New York (2004)
6. Wang, R., Paris, S., Popović, J.: 6D hands: markerless hand-tracking for computer aided design. In: Proceedings of the 24th Annual ACM Symposium on User Interface Software and Technology, pp. 549–558. ACM (2011)
7. Butler, A., Hilliges, O., Izadi, S., Hodges, S., Molyneaux, D., Kim, D., Kong, D.: Vermeer: direct interaction with a 360 viewable 3D display. In: Proceedings of the 24th Annual ACM Symposium on User Interface Software and Technology, pp. 569–576. ACM (2011)
8. Chan, L.W., Kao, H.S., Chen, M.Y., Lee, M.S., Hsu, J., Hung, Y.P.: Touching the void: direct-touch interaction for intangible displays. In: Proceedings of the SIGCHI Conference on Human Factors in Computing Systems, pp. 2625–2634. ACM (2010)
9. Vogel, D., Balakrishnan, R.: Distant free hand pointing and clicking on very large, high resolution displays. In: Proceedings of the 18th Annual ACM Symposium on User Interface Software and Technology, UIST 2005, pp. 33–42. ACM, New York (2005)
10. Hilliges, O., Kim, D., Izadi, S., Weiss, M., Wilson, A.: HoloDesk: direct 3D interactions with a situated see-through display. In: Proceedings of the SIGCHI Conference on Human Factors in Computing Systems, pp. 2421–2430. ACM (2012)
11. Ren, Z., Yuan, J., Meng, J., Zhang, Z.: Robust part-based hand gesture recognition using kinect sensor. IEEE Trans. Multimedia **15**, 1110–1120 (2013)
12. Leap Motion Controller. https://www.leapmotion.com
13. Fanini, B.: A 3D interface to explore and manipulate multi-scale virtual scenes using the leap motion controller. In: Proceedings of ACHI 2014, the Seventh International Conference on Advances in Computer-Human Interactions, pp. 258–263 (2014)
14. Apostolellis, P., Bortz, B., Peng, M., Polys, N., Hoegh, A.: Poster: exploring the integrality and separability of the leap motion controller for direct manipulation 3D interaction. In: IEEE Symposium on 3D User Interfaces (3DUI), pp. 153–154. IEEE (2014)
15. Coelho, J. C., Verbeek, F. J.: Pointing task evaluation of leap motion controller in 3d virtual environment. In: Creating the Difference: Proceedings of the Chisparks 2014 Conference, pp. 78–85. The Hague, The Netherlands (2014)

16. Hart, S.G., Staveland, L.E.: Development of a multi-dimensional workload rating scale: results of empirical and theoretical research. In: Hancock, P.A., Meshkati, N. (eds.) Human Mental Workload, pp. 139–183. Elsevier, Amsterdam (1988)
17. Laugwitz, B., Held, T., Schrepp, M.: Construction and Evaluation of a User Experience Questionnaire. Springer, Heidelberg (2008)

Beyond Direct Gaze Typing: A Predictive Graphic User Interface for Writing and Communicating by Gaze

Maria Laura Mele[1,2(✉)], Damon Millar[2],
and Christiaan Erik Rijnders[2]

[1] ECONA, Interuniversity Centre for Research on Cognitive Processing in
Natural and Artificial Systems, Sapienza University of Rome, Rome, Italy
marialaura.mele@gmail.com, marialaura@cogisen.com
[2] COGISEN Engineering Company, Rome, Italy
{damon, chris}@cogisen.com

Abstract. This paper introduces a new gaze-based Graphic User Interface
(GUI) for Augmentative and Alternative Communication (AAC). In the state of
the art, prediction methods to accelerate the production of textual, iconic and
pictorial communication only by gaze control are still needed. The proposed
GUI translates gaze inputs into words, phrases or symbols by the following
methods and techniques: (i) a gaze-based information visualization technique,
(ii) a prediction technique combining concurrent and retrospective methods, and
(iii) an alternative prediction method based either on the recognition or morph-
hing of spatial features. The system is designed for extending the communication function of individuals with severe motor disabilities, with the aim to allow
end-users to independently hold a conversation without needing a human
interpreter.

Keywords: Augmentative and alternative communication · Graphical user
interfaces for disabled users · Gaze based interaction · Assistive technologies

1 Introduction

Many assistive technologies have been proposed to provide disabled people with
means of communicating that enhance speech and language production, called Augmentative and Alternative Communication (AAC) methods. AAC methods include aids
for language, speech and/or writing difficulties, and they are suited for different use
cases, environments and contexts. AAC systems are not strictly related to a health
condition, but they are addressed to a wide variety of functional needs of people of all
ages and health conditions, such as learning difficulties, cerebral palsy, cognitive disabilities, head injury, multiple sclerosis, spinal cord injury, autism and more [1].

The term AAC refers to both low-tech and high-tech aided communication systems.
Low-tech AAC systems are based on non-electronic devices that may use body gestures, expression or signs as communication media, for example, tangible boards and
gaze communication boards such as the E-Tran (eye transfer) communication frame,
which is a transparent board showing pictures, symbols or letters that can be selected

© Springer International Publishing Switzerland 2015
M. Kurosu (Ed.): Human-Computer Interaction, Part II, HCII 2015, LNCS 9170, pp. 66–77, 2015.
DOI: 10.1007/978-3-319-20916-6_7

by using gaze pointing and which must be placed between two people –one communicator and one translator. Hi-tech AAC systems are based on electronic devices such selection switches or gaze-based pointing boards [2].

Unless low-tech AAC systems are very inexpensive and simple to use, they often require a human interpreter that translates the user's inputs into verbal commands and requests. Differently from low-tech assistive systems, hi-tech AAC systems can be easily suited for input by minimal movements (such as eye movements) and may increase users' independence and autonomy from a human interpreter, thus increasing the quality of life to disabled persons. However, individuals with severe motor disabilities (e.g., locked-in syndrome, cerebral palsy, motor neuron disease, or spinal cord injury) are still prevented from enjoying the full benefits of AAC systems due to usability issues [3–6] and the constant need for support and assistance [7–10], often leading to the assistive technology non-use and abandonment [11].

As the COGAIN (COmmunication by GAze INteraction) network points out, most severe motor disabilities could take advantage of gaze-based communication technologies [12] since the eye movement control is usually the least affected by peripheral injuries or disorders, being directly controlled by the brain [13]. The muscles of the eyes are able to produce the fastest movements of the body, therefore they can be used as an efficient method to control user interfaces as alternative to a mouse pointer, touch-screen or voice-user interfaces. Moreover, eye gaze is an innate form of pointing since the first months of life, and natural eye movements are related to low levels of fatigue [14].

The term "gaze control" commonly refers to systems measuring the points of regard and wherein eye movements are used to control a device. Gaze control systems differ from each other by the user requirement that they aim to address, and the expertise that is asked to use gaze as an input device. Usually, gaze control is performed by pointing and dwelling on a graphic user-interface. When involuntary movements prevent eye fixations, blinks or simple eye gestures are used as switches.

In the state of the art, the most proposed gaze-based communication method is direct gaze typing, which uses direct gaze pointing to choose single letters on a keyboard displayed on a screen. In direct gaze typing, once a user selects a letter, the system returns a visual or an acoustic related feedback and the typed letter is then shown in the text field. Direct gaze typing communication can be very slow since human speech has high-speed entry rates (150–250 words per minute–wpm) compared to gaze typing on on-screen keyboards (10–15 wpm) [15]. Methods to speed-up the production of phrases and sentences are therefore needed. Different systems based on methods predicting words or/and phrases are proposed in the field to provide more efficient gaze text entry. However, the current prediction techniques force users to frequently shift gaze from the on-screen keyboard to the predicted word/phrases list, thus reducing the text entry efficiency and increasing cognitive load [15].

The aim of this paper is to propose a graphic user interface (GUI) that translates gaze inputs into communication words, phrases and symbols by new methods and techniques overcoming the limitations of currently used prediction methods for direct gaze speech communication. The GUI is an AAC system for both face-to-face and distance communication. The paper focuses on describing the following methods and techniques for writing and communicating by gaze control: (i) a gaze based information visualization technique, (ii) a prediction technique combining concurrent and retrospective methods, and (iii) an alternative prediction method based on the recognition of spatial features.

2 Design Methodology

2.1 Objectives

The AAC system here proposed is a gaze based GUI aiming to (i) avoid that the user's gaze frequently shifts from the keyboard field to a separated text field (usually above the on-screen keyboard in traditional AAC systems) (ii) increase both efficiency and ease of use; and (iii) facilitate the selection of words or icons when a very high numbers of items have to be shown (e.g., a dictionary). Evaluating the usability and the user experience of the GUI with end-users is planned for future work.

2.2 Methods and Techniques

The GUI belongs to AAC systems that use gaze tracking for text entry for both face-to-face and distance communication. The GUI also provides users with both pictorial and iconic stimuli for people who are not able to read or write.

The system is designed by the following methods and techniques:

(i) *A gaze-based branched decision tree visualization technique*, which arrays successive rounds of alphabetic letters to the right-hand side of the last choice, and depicts the choice, thus creating a directional path of all the choices made, until a word is formed.

(ii) *A retrospective and concurrent word prediction technique.* The system may operate in two ways: (1) prospectively, to make it easier for the user to select the most likely next decision among the others and (2) retrospectively, to predict what a user would have meant to type, given a certain gaze input.

(iii) *A prediction method called Directed Discovery,* which is based on the recognition of the spatial structures constituting items.

3 Results

A gaze-based keyboard has been developed. The keyboard GUI navigation is based on three modules: (i) a branched decision-tree module, (ii) a word prediction module, and (iii) a direct discovery module.

3.1 Branched Decision Tree Module

The branched decision tree module prevents gaze shifting from an on-screen keyboard to predicted lists of words, and provides users with a navigable trail back through the history of choices made, so the user can easily look back, thus effectively undoing decisions made in error.

A branched decision tree is a bifurcation tree in which the next rounds of choices are arranged to one side of the last choice. The tree arrays the next round of choices to one side of the last choice, creating a directional depiction of the choices that have been made (Fig. 1).

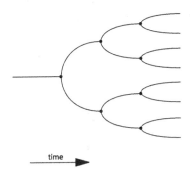

time

Fig. 1. Figure shows a bifurcation tree in which rounds of choices are arranged to the right side of the last choice, allowing users to easily undo their decisions made by looking back to previous choices.

The directionality allows simple navigation back up the tree, by looking towards the original choice. The directionality also provides momentum, because when making choices the user's eyes always move in one direction (e.g., left to right), allowing the user to chase the solution. If a bifurcation tree has more choices than fit into the screen width, then the screen can scroll to the right.

3.2 Word Prediction Module

In branched decision trees, not all choices are equally likely to be selected. One example of an unequal likelihood decision tree is a gaze-based keyboard that presents a range of letters at each round, with every round selecting one letter until a word is formed (Fig. 2).

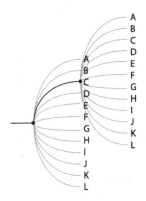

Fig. 2. Figure shows a gaze-based keyboard based on an unequal likelihood decision tree

When typing a word, given that certain letters have been selected before, there is a higher likelihood that some other choices will be selected next. To make it easier for the user's eyes to select the most likely next decision, but not preclude other less likely decisions, more likely choices may be emphasized. In the proposed GUI, emphasis is given by changing the visual properties of graphic elements (e.g., color, contrast) or drawing lines from the middle to the choices that are weighted by likelihood (Fig. 3).

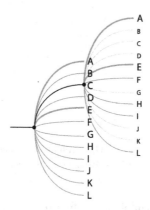

Fig. 3. Figure shows a method of visually weighting likely choices by drawing lines from the middle to the choices that are weighted by likelihood on a gaze-based keyboard.

Rather than only prospectively predict what a user will decide, the system is also able to retrospectively predict what a user did decide given an input. Given a path traversed by the eyes, it is possible to calculate all the possible meanings (including a degree of error) and choose the most likely choice intended. For example, if the user

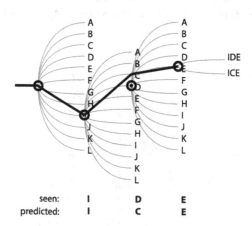

Fig. 4. Figure shows a post prediction technique that calculates all the possible words (including a degree of error) that a user could want to select given a certain gaze path on the branched decision tree keyboard.

quickly sweeps their eyes through a gaze-based branch keyboard and selects an impossible combination of letters, then similar trajectories can be analyzed to see if they produce likely words, and all of these selections presented to the user at the final round to choose from (Fig. 4).

The system combines post-predictions with forward-predictions to present complete decisions as choices before reaching the final round (Fig. 5). For example in a keyboard, before a word is complete, one choice may be a complete phrase of words rather than a single letter.

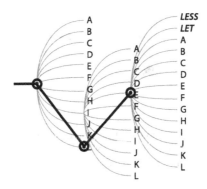

Fig. 5. Figure shows a branched decision tree keyboard showing predicted complete decisions in a non-final round.

3.3   Direct Discovery Module

A new selection method called Directed Discovery has been proposed to accommodate situations where selection from pre-existing objects is not appropriate, such as when there are so many choices that selection by sight would be inefficient (e.g., selecting words from a dictionary), when pictorial work is being created (e.g., drawing), or when abstract non-textual elements such as iconic objects are shown (e.g., peace).

Because gaze is particularly suited to make visual decisions, the Directed Discovery module shows to users' eyes a range of graphic possibilities. However, differently from the word prediction module, the direct discovery method involves the user in directly creating the range of possibilities that (s)he will decide on, from sub-sequential rounds of shapes, and deciding which features change until the last choice is selected. The method is based on the theory that visual overt attention is guided by both task-related needs (top-down process) [16] and the visual saliency of certain features of an object (bottom-up processes), e.g., edge, orientation or termination of edges [17].

Different techniques using the Directed Discovery method have been created to allows users to make gaze-based discovery of non-pre-existing choices: (1) the Evolution technique; (2) the Directed Morph technique; (3) the Sculpture technique. Each technique uses blob-like graphic elements as nodes of the branched decision tree which are sub-sequentially linked to other children nodes, and final choices as leaves of the tree, i.e., elements with no children.

(1) *Evolution technique.* The technique randomly mutates the graphic element and lets the user's visual overt attention evolve the product towards the desired result, through cycles of mutation and selection. These cycles of selection of the fittest would evolve the element towards the desired result, even if that result had never been seen before. Eye fixations last only fractions of a second (usually 200 ms), so preference selection may happen quickly, allowing many iterations of evolution to occur in a short time. In the Evolution technique, a text entry system is proposed whereby blob-like graphic elements are gradually mutated into the shape of the word required. At some point, the blob will unambiguously match a single word (Fig. 6).

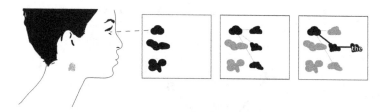

Fig. 6. Figure shows a branched decision tree using the Evolution technique for communication. In the example, the user directly creates range of elements starting from groups of different shapes which features change until the last choice is selected.

Selecting a word from its outline makes text entry more similar to the way humans recognize words when reading, i.e. by the shape of the word not by the individual letters as current keyboards do [18]. Humans perceive words by their first, middle and last letters, which spatial relation gives them a peculiar shape, commonly called Bouma shape [19, 20]. Word recognition is based on visual *gestalten*, i.e. structured spatial wholes, which help the perceiver to rapidly recognize words among many others. The Evolution technique allows users to recognize words by the gradual mutation or the directed morph of a range of Bouma shapes, until one of them unambiguously matches to a single word.

(2) *Directed Morph technique.* In some circumstances the Evolution technique can take too long to produce the result needed. An alternative technique called Directed Morph has been designed to allow non-random mutation to occur, based on prediction of the desired result through cycles of mutation and selection over discrete rounds. These predictions may present choices that are completely resolved decisions (e.g., "this blob looks like the word 'hello', so the word 'hello' will present as a choice"), or it may result in presenting families of choices (Fig. 7), based on some defining characteristics of predictions (e.g., "if a blob looks like the Eiffel tower, then thin struts may be added to it"). The predictions may be offered alongside other non-predicted choices, so the user is not restricted by incorrect predictions.

Prediction can occur more effectively if the prediction system has knowledge of context. A categorical search tree is offered to users to work within a known sphere of knowledge chosen from a master list of conceptual or semantic domains (e.g. emotions, activities, tasks, etc.) rather than only perceptual categories. The prediction system may use the knowledge of the context to predict the shape/object that is being selected.

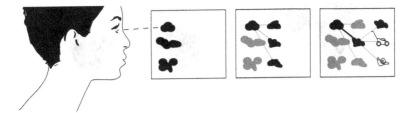

Fig. 7. Figure shows a branched decision tree using the Directed Morph technique for communication. In the example, the user directly creates range of elements starting from families of choices, based on some defining characteristics of predictions of the desired result.

In one example of Directed Morph, a text entry system is proposed that whereby blob-like graphic elements are gradually resolved into words (Fig. 8). Using prediction and context, a range of possible words may be offered alongside other mutated blobs, allowing the correct word to be selected using fewer choices.

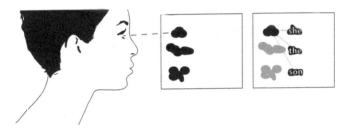

Fig. 8. Figure shows a branched decision tree using the Directed Morph technique for communication. In the example, the user directly creates two and three letter-sized blob-like graphic elements starting from knowledge-based predictions of choices rather than random shapes.

(3) *Sculpture technique.* A different type of Directed Discovery GUI is not based on separate choices over discrete rounds, but constructs the solution continuously and in-place. The Sculpture technique is particularly suited for people who are not able to read or write and need to use pictorial and iconic stimuli to communicate. Instead of the sites for modification being randomly selected, they can be chosen by the user's gaze. One simple form of sculpting is for the user's eyes as form guidance, to locate an area of discrepancy. If a particular feature is missing or incorrect, it will attract the user's visual overt attention and that area can be selectively mutated (Fig. 9).

Rather than use mutation, a more controlled form of sculpture is possible by parametric modification of the element. With parametric modification, the attributes of the object are modified (e.g., offset, curve diameter), until they no longer provoke the user's eye(s) fixation (Fig. 10). For example, if the object was an animal, and the user was attending to the head, the parametric search might change the size of the head until it no longer provoked fixation. Because parametric sculpture is not based on generating options for selection, there is no need to present multiple choices to the user. Changes

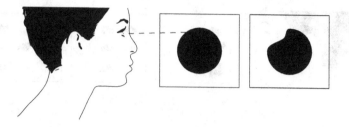

Fig. 9. Figure shows the Sculpture technique for communication. In the example, the user directly performs the in-place selective mutation with the gaze.

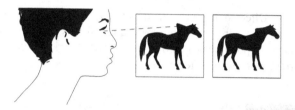

Fig. 10. Figure shows the Sculpture technique for communication. In the example, the user directly performs the mutation of the graphic element sculpting it by eye fixation.

may be presented in-place, with the object modified according to the user's sculpting eye fixation.

Most parts of shapes have more than one attribute, so the user needs to be able to select which attribute to modify. One technique is to modify each attribute in turn, while observing the user's attention, to discover which attribute causes the user's fixation to increase or decrease, indicating that the shape is closer to that expected (Fig. 11).

Fig. 11. Figure shows the Sculpture technique for communication. In the example, the technique performs parametric modification to discover which attribute reduces the user's eye(s) fixations.

Modifying one attribute at a time would be very slow when creating complex graphic elements, and the modification causes changes that may attract the user's attention thus causing incorrect sculpting. A more efficient technique consists in modifying many attributes at once, over the entire object, and tracking which of the modifications is increasing or decreasing user's visual overt attention. By a process of combinations, the sensitive parameters and their preferred directions can be identified while the element evolves its way towards the wanted result (Fig. 12).

Fig. 12. Figure the Sculpture technique for communication. In the example, many parameters of many parts are altered simultaneously.

The parametric modifications to the shape do not need to be in the spatial domain. Frequency-domain changes may be performed on the shape, so large parts vary at once. Frequency domain modification allows a complex image to be constructed, first with low-frequency fundamental shapes, then later with details (Fig. 13).

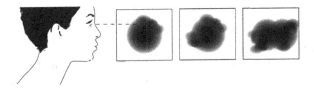

Fig. 13. Figure shows the Sculpture technique for communication. In the example, frequency-domain modifications produce basic shape, then details.

Prediction can be used with sculpture, but because sculpture shapes one graphic element rather than display a range of choices, predictive features are presented in a different way: The presentation of the object is optimized to weight the user's visual attention towards the predicted result (Fig. 14). This weighting may be performed in a variety of ways, including modifying the brightness, color or position of parts of the displayed object.

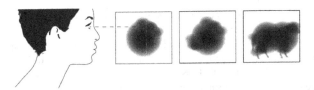

Fig. 14. Figure shows the Sculpture technique for communication. In the example, elements are optimized to weight the user's eye(s) fixations towards the predicted result.

4 Conclusion

One challenge of assistive technologies for communication is reaching effective word prediction methods for increasing the autonomy of people with severe motor disabilities. The main objective of the proposed Augmentative and Alternative Communication system is to empower the sensorimotor users' abilities and allow end-users to independently communicate without needing a human interpreter. The system proposed follows new information visualization methods and techniques to prevent gaze shifting from a display keyboard to lists of graphic elements and facilitates the selection of items among complex data sets. The system is specifically designed for users whose residual abilities and functions include: (1) eye motor abilities, (2) language comprehension, decoding and production, (3) symbolic communication abilities. In future experimental work, the usability and the user experience of end-users will be evaluated.

References

1. Millar, S., Scott, J.: What is augmentative and alternative communication? An introduction. Augmentative communication in practice 2. University of Edinburgh CALL Centre, Edinburgh (1998)
2. Lancioni, G.E., Singh, N.N., O'Reilly, M.F., Sigafoos, J., Oliva, D., Basili, G.: New rehabilitation opportunities for persons with multiple disabilities through the use of microswitch technology. In: Federici, S., Scherer, M.J. (eds.) Assistive Technology Assessment Handbook, pp. 399–419. CRC Press, New York (2012)
3. Borsci, S., Kurosu, M., Federici, S., Mele, M.L.: Computer Systems Experiences Of Users With And Without Disabilities: An Evaluation Guide For Professionals. CRC Press, Boca Raton (2013)
4. Borsci, S., Kurosu, M., Federici, S., Mele, M.L.: Systemic User Experience. In: Federici, S., Scherer, M.J. (eds.) Assistive Technology Assessment Handbook, pp. 337–359. CRC Press, Boca Raton (2012)
5. Federici, S., Scherer, M.J.: The Assistive Technology Assessment Model and Basic Definitions. In: Federici, S., Scherer, M.J. (eds.) Assistive Technology Assessment Handbook, pp. 1–10. CRC Press, Boca Raton (2012)
6. Federici, S., Corradi, F., Mele, M.L., Miesenberger, K.: From cognitive ergonomist to psychotechnologist: a new professional profile in a multidisciplinary team in a centre for technical aids. In: Gelderblom, G.J., Soede, M., Adriaens, L., Miesenberger, K. (eds.) Everyday Technology for Independence and Care: AAATE 2011, vol. 29, pp. 1178–1184. IOS Press, Amsterdam (2011)
7. Mele, M.L., Federici, S.: Gaze and eye-tracking solutions for psychological research. Cogn. Process. **13**(1), 261–265 (2012)
8. Mele, M.L., Federici, S.: A psychotechnological review on eye-tracking systems: towards user experience. Disabil. Rehabil. Assist. Technol. **7**(4), 261–281 (2012)
9. Federici, S., Corradi, F., Meloni, F., Borsci, S., Mele, M.L., Dandini de Sylva, S., Scherer, M.J.: A person-centered assistive technology service delivery model: a framework for device selection and assignment. Life Span Disabil. **17**(2), 175–198 (2014)
10. Federci, S., Borsci, S., Mele, M.L.: Environmental evaluation of a rehabilitation aid interaction under the framework of the ideal model of assistive technology assessment process. In: Kurosu, M. (ed.) HCII/HCI 2013, Part I. LNCS, vol. 8004, pp. 203–210. Springer, Heidelberg (2013)
11. Federici, S., Borsci, S.: Providing assistive technology in Italy: the perceived delivery process quality as affecting abandonment. Disabil. Rehabil. Assist. Technol. 1–10 (2014)
12. Bates, R., Donegan, M., Istance, H.O., Hansen, J.P., Räihä, K.J.: Introducing COGAIN: communication by gaze interaction. Universal Access Inf. **6**(2), 159–166 (2007)

13. Leigh, R.J., Zee, D.S.: The Neurology of Eye Movements, vol. 90. Oxford University Press, New York (1999)
14. Saito, S.: Does fatigue exist in a quantitative measurement of eye movements? Ergonomics **35**(5/6), 607–615 (1992)
15. Majaranta, P.: Communication and text entry by gaze. In: Majaranta, P., Aoki, H., Donegan, M., Hansen, D.W., Hansen, J.P., Hyrskykari, A., Räihä, K.J. (eds.) Gaze Interaction and Applications of Eye Tracking: Advances in Assistive Technologies, pp. 63–77. IGI Global, Hershey (2012)
16. Yarbus, A.L.: Eye Movements and Vision. Plenum Press, New York (1967)
17. Itti, L., Koch, C., Niebur, E.: A model of saliency based visual attention for rapid scene analysis. IEEE Trans. Pattern Anal. Mach. Intell. **20**(11), 1254–1259 (1998)
18. Kintsch, W.: Models for Free Recall and Recognition. Models of Human Memory, vol. 124. Academic Press, New York (1970)
19. Bouma, H.: Visual interference in the parafoveal recognition of initial and final letters of words. Vision. Res. **13**, 762–782 (1973)
20. Bouwhuis, D., Bouma, H.: Visual word recognition of three letter words as derived from the recognition of the constituent letters. Percept. Psychophys. **25**, 12–22 (1979)

Nonlinear Dynamical Analysis of Eye Movement Characteristics Using Attractor Plot and First Lyapunov Exponent

Atsuo Murata$^{(\boxtimes)}$ and Tomoya Matsuura

Department of Intelligent Mechanical Systems, Graduate School of Natural Science and Technology, Okayama University, Okayama, Japan
murata@iims.sys.okayama-u.ac.jp

Abstract. The purpose of this study was to clarify eye movement characteristics during a visual search using nonlinear dynamics (chaos analysis). More concretely, the first Lyapunov exponent and the attractor plot were obtained for the time series data of x- and y-directional eye-gaze locations. An attempt was made to compare the first Lyapunov exponent and the attractor plot during a visual search task as a function of layout complexity of the display and to verify whether chaotic properties existed in the fluctuation of eye-gaze locations, and to examine how the scaling properties change as a function of the layout complexity. First Lyapunov exponent of the time series of eye-gaze locations took positive values, and tended to increase with the increase of search task difficulty (layout complexity). The attractor plot drew a trajectory like an ellipse, and the variation in attractor plots tended to be more complicated with the increase of task difficulty.

Keywords: Nonlinear dynamics · Eye movement · Attractor plot · First Lyapunov exponent · Layout complexity of display

1 Introduction

It has been widely known that nonlinear chaotic dynamics are ubiquitous in many biological systems such as Electroencephalography (EEG), body sway, and hear rate [1, 2]. Fairbanks and Taylor [3] proposed a method for measuring the scaling properties of temporal and spatial patterns of eye movements. Eye movements are classified into saccade, fixation, and micro-saccade. Micro-saccades generally occur over an angular range of typically 0.5° called dwell region. The characteristics of saccades are represented by ballistic jumps. It is regarded that saccades and micro-saccades are produced by different physiological mechanisms. Therefore, the nonlinear behaviors of these eye movements are expected to be different. It has not become clear whether the nonlinear characteristics are helpful for understanding eye movement further, and provide us with new information which the traditional analysis of eye movements cannot produce.

We look at some object to obtain information from it, and comprehend the situation around the object. Although eye gaze is relatively simple as compared with other communication means such as gesture or speech, it can provide us with abundant information on our perception and cognition so that we can conjecture our internal cognitive state.

© Springer International Publishing Switzerland 2015
M. Kurosu (Ed.): Human-Computer Interaction, Part II, HCII 2015, LNCS 9170, pp. 78–85, 2015.
DOI: 10.1007/978-3-319-20916-6_8

There are four types of eye movement. Eye gaze is typically directed to one location on a display for about 200–300 ms (this is called fixation), and then moves to another location extremely rapidly (in about 20–30 ms) (this is termed saccade). The angular rotation of saccade is about 600 deg/s. We are momentarily and effectively blind during the saccadic eye movement. Saccade jumps automatically to the location predetermined by the brain's visual system during the preceding fixations. If the movement is more than 15°, our head rotates automatically. Nystagmus is explained by reference to a common experience that of looking out of the window of a moving train and attempting to keep up with the view rather than find out some feature within the view. Nystagmus is a response to rapidly moving objects. The last eye movement is smooth pursuit to smoothly follow an object. However, it must be noted that there is a limit to the speed of such a movement.

The question of how people select fixation point as they move their eyes around a display in front of them might be addressed with reference to specific activities necessary for cognition. In daily life, nothing can be performed without the retrieval of information. The evaluation of eye movement characteristics and performance measures provides us with an important knowledge on the information strategy used in search tasks. Many studies on eye movement characteristics are conducted to clarify a variety of cognitive processes [5–14].

Murata et al. [4] investigated eye movement characteristics during a visual search using nonlinear dynamics (scaling properties) using the fractal dimensional analysis for the time series data of x- and y-directional gaze-locations. For both x- and y-directional eye movements, the scaling property represented by the fractal dimension tended to increase with the increase of difficulty Layout complexity) of a search task. The fractal dimension also tended to be smaller for the wide display than for the narrow display. On the basis of the result that the search time and the x- and y-directional fractal dimensions were not so strongly related, they conjectured that the search time and the fractal dimension stem from the different mechanism underlying a variety of search activities. However, they did not discuss whether chaotic behavior is observed in the fluctuation of time series of eye-gaze location.

The purpose of this study was to clarify eye movement characteristics during a visual search using nonlinear dynamics (chaos analysis). More concretely, the first Lyapunov exponent and attractor plot were obtained for the time series data of x- and y-directional gaze-locations. An attempt was made to compare the first Lyapunov exponent and attractor plot during a visual search task as a function of layout complexity of the display and to verify whether chaotic properties existed in the fluctuation of eye-gaze location, and to examine how the scaling properties change as a function of the layout complexity.

2 Method

2.1 Participants

Ten male undergraduate or graduate students from 22 to 24 years old took part in the experiment. All signed the document on informed consent after receiving a brief explanation of the aim and the contents of the experiment.

2.2 Apparatus

The eye movement during a search task was measured using an eye-tracker equipment (ViewTracker, DITECT). This eye-gaze measurement system makes use of infrared and visual camera technologies to determine the eye-gaze locations. The resolution of the computer display was 640 by 480 pixel. The sampling frequency of the eye-tracker equipment was 60 Hz.

2.3 Task, Design, and Procedure

The search task was to search for a target stimulus that consisted of three random letters. The layout complexity LC (Murata and Furukawa [15]) was calculated according to Eq. (1)

$$LC = -N \sum_{i=1}^{n} p_i \log_2 p_i \tag{1}$$

(a) LC=50bit

	1	2	3	4	5	6	7
1	IOB		ULK				
2	RTJ					DRX	
3		XOG					
4					JGV		
5							
6		PBE			EOA		BCX
7			MTH				

(b) LC=100bit

	1	2	3	4	5	6	7
1	IEU	EXC			YGH		RHG
2					HJI		
3	PBE				GAH		SZD
4		FAR	IZS	UAM			
5	LJW			BCX			
6		WZH		KTA			XOG
7		CQF	OTB	MYI			

(c) LC=150bit

	1	2	3	4	5	6	7
1		AJB	NYI		HNM	LJW	MRY
2		IOB		VZA	JWI		
3	RWV	YRJ				XJI	
4			DKV	FXT	ULK	QHJ	EFN
5		GIO			UXP	WAF	
6	TLA		OAC		BKL		KLU
7	CWJ		PBE	ZSP			SYT

(d) LC=200bit

	1	2	3	4	5	6	7
1	EOA	RTJ		OJY	IBG	GJK	HVT
2	ZNL		RHG	FTJ	UAM	BZN	
3	NUA				JGV		BCX
4	SRF	CDK	KTA	QZN		VWY	OTB
5	ALR	IEU	XOG	LKC		MHJ	
6	GAH		EXC	NDV	QRU	YTP	XSO
7	WUQ	PYR		LNA	DUK		TJM

Fig. 1. Display used in the search task. Each display (a)–(d) subtended vertically and horizontally 14.4° and 22.6°, respectively.

in which N is the number of objects on the display, n is the number of groups of similar objects, and p_i is the probability of selecting an object from group i. *LC*s for the horizontal and the vertical directions are calculated separately. In this study, four kinds of *LC*s (50 bits, 100 bits, 150 bits, and 200 bits) were used. The displays for *LC* of 50 bits, 100 bits, 150 bits, and 200 bits subtended vertically and horizontally 14.4° and 22.6°, respectively (For more detail, see Murata et al. [4]). In Fig. 1, the displays for *LC* = 50, 100, 150, and 200 bits are exemplified.

In this experiment, *LC* was a within-subject factor. The order of performance of four conditions of *LC* was randomized across the participants. Eye movements during the search task of each condition were recorded ten times for each participant.

The time series data were linearly interpolated so that data length is larger than 1000, and entered into R language package (tseries Chaos) in order to obtain first Lyapunov exponent and attractor plot.

3   Results

Figure 2 shows first Lyapunov exponent compared among *LC* conditions for embedding dimensions 3, 4, and 5. Figure 3 shows first Lyapunov exponent compared among embedding dimensions for each *LC* conditions. Here, the time series of x-directional eye gaze locations were used to calculate first Lyapunov exponent. The attractor plots for *LC* = 50, 100, 150, and 200 bits are shown in Figs. 4, 5, 6, and 7, respectively. As for the y-directional eye-gaze locations, similar results were obtained.

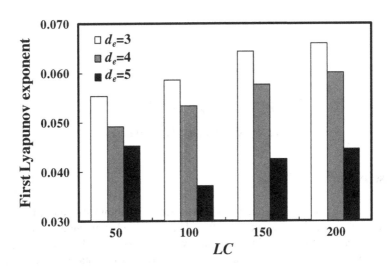

Fig. 2. First Lyapunov exponent compared among *LC* conditions for each embedding dimension.

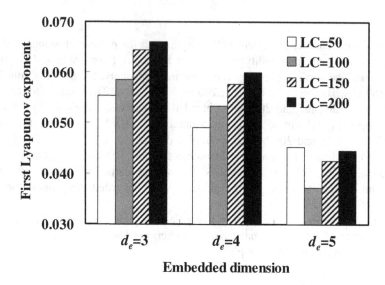

Fig. 3. First Lyapunov exponent compared among embedding dimensions for each *LC* conditions.

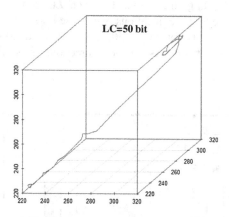

Fig. 4. Attractor plot (*LC* = 50 bits)

4 Discussion

The positive value of first Lyapunov exponent generally shows that the time series of eye-gaze locations include chaotic property. The chaotic phenomenon is characterized by two properties, that is, orbital instability and unpredictability. The larger first Lyapunov exponent is, the larger the width of variation of data gets larger. It was clarified that the search time, the x-directional and the y-directional first Lyapunov exponents tended to increase with the increase of search task difficulty (layout

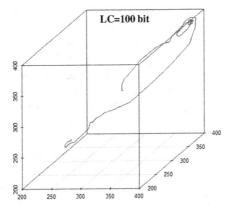

Fig. 5. Attractor plot (*LC* = 100 bits)

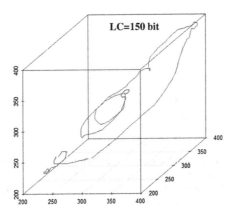

Fig. 6. Attractor plot (LC = 150 bits)

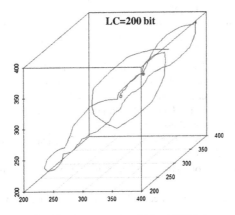

Fig. 7. Attractor plot (LC = 200 bits)

complexity). Therefore, it was investigated how the search time was related to the x- and y-directional first Lyanunov exponent.

The search time and the first Lyapunov exponent were not so strongly correlated. This must mean that the first Lyapunov exponent is variable based on different mechanism from the search time. The x- and y-directional first Lyapunov exponents were strongly correlated. Like the fractal dimension in Murata et al. [4], the variation behind the first Lyapunov exponent must be different from that of the search time, which means that the first Lyapunov exponent must be one of the important indices to get further insight into human's eye movement.

As for the attractor plot, in accordance with the tendencies of first Lyapinov exponent above, the width of variation in attractor plots tended to be wider and more complicated with the increase of task difficulty. As a whole, it seems that the attractor plot draws a trajectory like an ellipse as in Figs. 4, 5, 6, and 7. The ellipse-like trajectory got more and more complicated with the increase of LC.

Future research should examine the scaling properties of more practical visual activities such as Web search and conjunction search in order to generalize the scaling properties in eye movements.

References

1. Murata, A., Iwase, H.: Chaotic analysis of body sway. In: 20th Annual International Conference - IEEE/EMBS, pp. 1557–1560 (1998)
2. Murata, A., Iwase, H.: Application of chaotic dynamics in EEG to assessment of mental workload. IEICE Trans. Inf. Syst. 84(8), 1112–1119 (2001)
3. Fairbanks, M.S., Taylor, R.P.: Measuring the scaling properties of temporal and spatial patterns: from the human eye to foraging albatross. In: Guastello, S.J., Gregson, R.A.M. (eds.) Nonlinear Dynamical Systems Analysis for the Behavioral Science Using Real Data, pp. 341–366. CRC Press, London (2010)
4. Murata, A., Matsyuura, T., Moriwaka, M.: Nonlinear dynamical analysis of eye movement characteristics. In: AHFE 2014, pp. 4041–4052 (2014)
5. Chekaluk, E., Llewelly, K.R.: The Role of Eye Movements in Perceptual Process. North-Holland, Amsterdam (1992)
6. Findlay, J.M., Walker, R., Kentridge, R.W.: Eye Movement Research: Mechanisms, Processes and Applications. Studies in Visual Information Processing, vol. 6. North-Holland, Amsterdam (1995)
7. Hung, G.K.: Models of Oculomotor Control. World Scientific Pub., Singapore (2001)
8. Hyönä, J., Radach, R., Deubel, H.: The Mind's Eye: Cognitive and Applied Aspects of Eye Movement research. North-Holland, Amsterdam (2003)
9. Land, M.F., Tatler, B.W.: Looking and Acting: Vision and Eye Movements in Natural Behavior. Oxford University Press, Oxford (2009)
10. Spence, R., Witkowski, M.: Rapid Serial Visual Presentation: Design for Cognition. Springer, Heidelberg (2013)
11. Tovée, M.J.: An Introduction to the Visual System. Cambridge University Press, Cambridge (2008)
12. Underwood, G.: Cognitive Processes in Eye Guidance. Oxford University Press, Oxford (2005)

13. Wade, N.J., Tatler, B.W.: The Moving Tablet of the Eye: The Origins of Modern Eye Movement Research. Oxford University Press, Oxford (2005)
14. Wartburg, R.V.: Eye Movements and Scene Perception: An Investigation of Basic Effects. Südwesteutscher Verlag für Hochschulschriften, Saarbrücken (2009)
15. Murata, A., Furukawa, N.: Relationship between display features, eye movement characteristics, and reaction time in visual search. Hum. Factors **47**(3), 598–612 (2005)

Optimal Scroll Method for Eye-Gaze Input System

Comparison of R-E and R-S Compatibility

Atsuo Murata[✉], Makoto Moriwaka, and Yusuke Takagishi

Department of Intelligent Mechanical System,
Graduate School of Natural Science and Technology, Okayama University,
Okayama, Japan
murata@iims.sys.okayama-u.ac.jp

Abstract. It is not clear which of the R-E and the S-R compatibility principles is proper for the eye-gaze input. This issue should be addressed for the development of more usable eye-gaze input system. The aim of this study was to explore which of the two compatibility principles was proper for the eye-gaze input system. For all scroll methods, the task completion time did not differ between R-E and S-R compatibility conditions (see Fig. 4). In other words, the speed of scroll did not differ between two compatibility conditions for all of three scroll methods. The number of errors per 90 trials significantly differed among scroll conditions and between R-E and S-R compatibility conditions. Judging from the accuracy of scroll, the error was less when the S-R compatibility like non-touch screen Microsoft Windows was applied than when the R-E compatibility like iPod or iPad was applied. In the range of this study, it seems that the S-R compatibility is dominant from the viewpoints of scroll accuracy for all of three scroll methods. The subjective rating on both usability and fatigue also supported the superiority of S-R compatibility over the R-E compatibility condition. In conclusion, the S-R compatibility was found to be superior for the eye-gaze input system.

Keywords: Eye-gaze input · Scroll · Auto scroll · Scroll icon · S-R compatibility · R-E compatibility

1 Introduction

The technology for measuring a user's visual line of gaze in real time has been advancing [1–9]. Appropriate human-computer interaction techniques that incorporate eye movements into a human-computer dialogue have been developed. It has also not been explored how the scroll location on Web browsers affects the performance. Although a few scroll methods have been proposed, these are not assumed to be used on Web pages. Murata et al. [9] made an attempt to determine empirically the optimal scroll method among the scroll methods (improved scroll-icon, auto-scroll, improved auto-scroll methods). The scroll-icon method was found to be not proper for use in an eye-gaze input system on the basis of the results of the task completion time, the error rate, and the subjective rating on usability. It was found that the improved auto-scroll

M. Kurosu (Ed.): Human-Computer Interaction, Part II, HCII 2015, LNCS 9170, pp. 86–93, 2015.
DOI: 10.1007/978-3-319-20916-6_9

method (quadratic and quadratic combination) with nonlinear relationship between the vertical scroll location and the scroll velocity was optimal from the viewpoints of the task completion time, the error rate and the subjective evaluation on usability.

Scrolling methods are mainly based on either R-E (Response-Effect) compatibility or S-R (Stimulus- Response) compatibility. The R-E compatibility a natural scrolling, and the responses are congruent with their forthcoming effects or consequences. This compatibility principle is used in iPod, iPad, and a variety of smart phones. The S-R compatibility is mainly used in Microsoft Windows. When the scrolling control goes one direction, the display content goes the other. The computer task by a mouse on Windows System adopts the R-S compatibility principle.

Chen and Proctor [10] compared the performance between two scrolling methods (R-E and S-R compatibility) on non-touch screen computer operating system using a keyboard, and showed that the responses were facilitated when the response direction was compatible with the forthcoming display-content movement direction (R-E compatibility). However, it is not clear which of the R-E and the S-R compatibility principles is proper for the eye-gaze input. This issue should be addressed for the development of more usable eye-gaze input system. The aim of this study was to explore which of the two compatibility principles was proper for the eye-gaze input system.

2 Method

2.1 Participants

Eight male undergraduate students aged from 21 to 23 years (average: 21.8 years) took part in the experiment. The visual acuity of the participants in both young and older groups was matched and more than 20/20. They had no orthopedic or neurological diseases.

2.2 Apparatus

An eye-tracking device (EMR-AT VOXER, Mac Image Technology) was used to measure eye movement characteristics during the experimental task. The eye-tracker was connected with a personal computer (HP, DX5150MT) with a 15-in. (303 mm × 231 mm) CRT. The resolution was 1024 × 768 pixels. Another personal computer was also connected to the eye-tracker via a RS232C port to develop an eye-gaze input system. The line of gaze, via a RS232C port, is output to this computer with a sampling frequency of 60 Hz.

2.3 Task

The task was to scroll and select a pre-specified item by scrolling up or down the display in Figs. 1, 2, and 3. The following scroll methods were used: (1) scroll icon method (see Fig. 2), and (2) auto scroll method (see Fig. 3) with nonlinear relationship

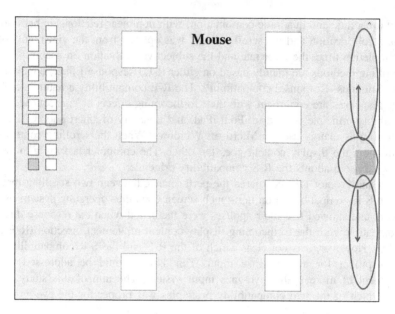

Fig. 1. Display for scrolling using a mouse

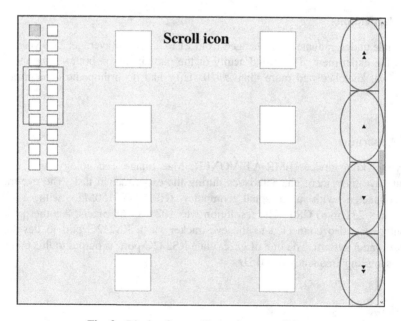

Fig. 2. Display for scrolling using a scroll icon

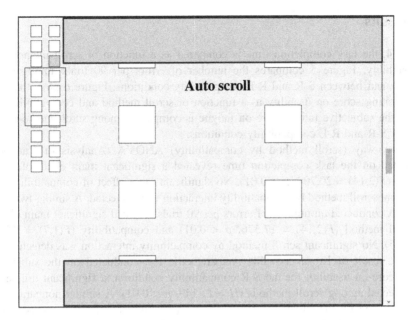

Fig. 3. Display for scrolling using a auto scroll method

between vertical scroll location and scroll velocity. For each scroll method, both of R-E and S-R compatibility principles were applied (a total of four combination), and it was examined what combination of scroll method and compatibility principle facilitate scrolling responses. Both scroll method (scroll icon and auto scroll) and compatibility principle (R-E and S-R compatibility) were within-subject factors.

2.4 Design and Procedure

The experimental factors were a scroll method (mouse, scroll icon method, and auto scroll method) and compatibility (S-R compatibility and R-E compatibility). Both were within-subject factors. There were six combinations of scroll method and compatibility.

The order of performance of six combinations (conditions) was randomized across the participants. For each condition, the participants were required to click a predetermined target using an eye-gaze input or mouse input 90 times. In the scroll conditions (scroll icon method, or auto scroll method), the participants were required to scroll the display to find a predetermined target using an eye-gaze input, and to click the target using a mouse. The performance measures were the task completion time, the number of errors (failure to click a predetermined target), and the subjective rating on usability (5-point scale: 1 = not usable at all, 5 = very usable) and the fatigue induced during the task (5-point scale: 1 = much fatigued, 5 = not fatigued at all).

The performance measures above were compared among the scroll methods and between S-R compatibility and R-E compatibility conditions).

3   Results

In Fig. 4, the task completion time is compared as a function of scroll method and compatibility. Figure 5 compares the number of errors per 90 trials among scroll methods and between S-R and R-E compatibility conditions. Figure 6 plots the subjective rating score on usability as a function of scroll method and compatibility. In Fig. 7, the subjective rating score on fatigue is compared among scroll methods and between S-R and R-E compatibility conditions.

A two-way (scroll method by compatibility) ANOVA (Analysis of Variance) conducted on the task completion time revealed a significant main effect of scroll method ($F(2,14) = 20.709$, $p < 0.01$). No significant main effect of compatibility and significant scroll method by compatibility interaction were detected. A similar two-way ANOVA conducted on number of errors per 90 trials revealed significant main effects of scroll method ($F(2,14) = 17.576$, $p < 0.01$) and compatibility ($F(1,7) = 8.710$, $p < 0.05$). No significant scroll method by compatibility interaction was detected.

As a result of Krusakal-Wallis nonparametric test conducted on the subjective rating score on usability for the S-R compatibility condition, a significant difference was detected among scroll methods ($H = 11.149$, $p < 0.01$). A similar nonparametric test conducted on the subjective rating score on usability for the R-E compatibility condition revealed a significant main effect of scroll method ($H = 9.084$, $p < 0.01$).

As a result of Krusakal-Wallis nonparametric test conducted on the subjective rating score on fatigue for the S-R compatibility condition, a significant difference was detected among scroll methods ($H = 15.365$, $p < 0.01$). A similar nonparametric test conducted on the subjective rating score on usability for the R-E compatibility condition revealed a significant main effect of scroll method ($H = 12.414$, $p < 0.01$).

As a result of Man-Whitney nonparametric test conducted on the subjective rating scores on both usability and fatigue for the mouse scroll condition, no significant

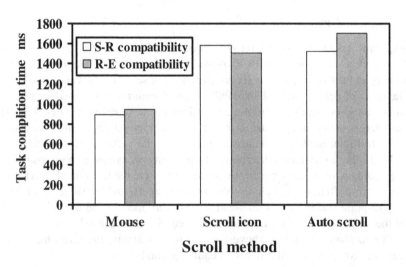

Fig. 4. Task completion time as a function of scroll method and compatibility

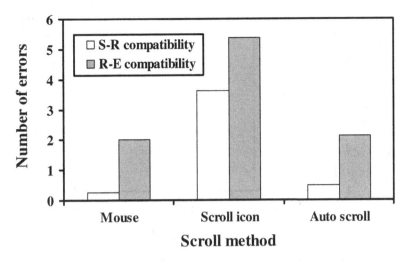

Fig. 5. Number of error per 90 trials as a function of scroll method and compatibility

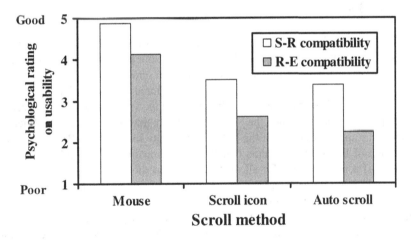

Fig. 6. Psychological rating on usability as a function of scroll method and compatibility

differences were detected between S-R and R-E compatibility conditions. As a result of Man-Whitney nonparametric test conducted on the subjective rating scores on both usability and fatigue for the scroll icon, no significant differences were detected between S-R and R-E compatibility conditions. A similar Man-Whitney nonparametric test conducted on the subjective rating scores on usability revealed a significant difference between S-R and R-E compatibility conditions ($z = -2.836$, $p < 0.01$). As a result of a similar test conducted on the subjective rating scores on usability, no significant main effect of compatibility condition was detected.

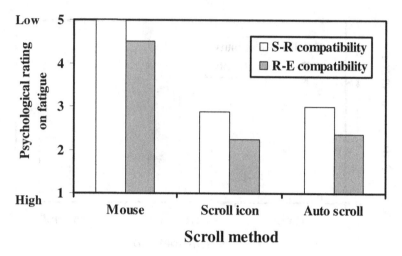

Fig. 7. Psychological rating on fatigue as a function of scroll method and compatibility

4 Discussion

For all scroll methods, the task completion time did not differ between R-E and S-R compatibility conditions (see Fig. 4). In other words, the speed of scroll did not differ between two compatibility conditions for all of three scroll methods.

The number of errors per 90 trials significantly differed among scroll conditions and between R-E and S-R compatibility conditions (see Fig. 5). Judging from the accuracy of scroll, the error was less when the S-R compatibility like non-touch screen Microsoft Windows was applied than when the R-E compatibility like iPod or iPad was applied. In the range of this study, it seems that the S-R compatibility is dominant from the viewpoints of scroll accuracy for all of three scroll methods.

The subjective rating on both usability and fatigue (see Figs. 6 and 7) also supported the superiority of S-R compatibility over the R-E compatibility condition. These results did not agree with the results by Chen and Proctor [10] who showed that R-E compatibility was desirable for the scrolling on PCs. This shows that the desirable scroll method for the traditional interaction using a keyboard and a mouse does not necessarily apply to the scroll method using an eye-gaze input system. In future work, the validity of this study should be verified by collecting more data or observing the learning process to each compatibility and each scroll method.

References

1. Jacob, R.J.K., Sibert, L.E., Mcfarlanes, D.C., Mullen, M.P.: Integrality and reparability of input devices. ACM Trans. Comput. Hum. Inter. 1(1), 2–26 (1994)
2. Sibert, L.E., Jacob, R.J.K.: Evaluation of eye gaze interaction. In: CHI 2000, pp. 281–288. Hague (2000)

3. Murata, A.: Eye-gaze input versus mouse: cursor control as a function of age. Int. J. Hum. Comput. Inter. **21**, 1–14 (2006)
4. Murata, A., Moriwaka, M.: Effectiveness of the menu selection method for eye-gaze input system - comparison between young and older adults. In: 5th International Workshop on Computational Intelligence and Applications, pp. 306–311. Hiroshima (2009)
5. Murata, A., Miyake, T.: Effectiveness of eye-gaze input system - identification of conditions that assures high pointing accuracy and movement directional effect. In: 4th International Workshop on Computational Intelligence and Applications, pp. 127–132. Hiroshima (2008)
6. Murata, A., Moriwaka, M.: Basic study for development of web browser suitable for eye-gaze input system -identification of optimal click method. In: 5th International Workshop on Computational Intelligence and Applications, pp. 302–305. Hiroshima (2009)
7. Murata, A., Hayashi, K., Moriwaka, M., Hayami, T.: Optimal scroll method to browse web pages using an eye-gaze input system. In: AHFE2012, pp. 7106–7115. San Francisco (2012)
8. Murata, A., Uetsugi, R., Hayami, T.: Study on cursor shape suitable for eye-gaze input system. In: SICE2012, pp. 926–931. Akita (2012)
9. Murata, A., Hayashi, K., Moriwaka, M., Hayami, T.: Study on character input methods using eye-gaze input interface. In: Kurosu, M. (ed.) HCII/HCI 2013, Part IV. LNCS, vol. 8007, pp. 320–329. Springer, Heidelberg (2013)
10. Chen, J., Proctor, R.W.: Response-effect compatibility defines the natural scrolling direction. Hum. Factors **55**(6), 1112–1129 (2013)

Effects of Target Shape and Display Location on Pointing Performance by Eye-Gaze Input System

Modeling of Pointing Time by Extended Fitts' Law

Atsuo Murata[✉], Makoto Moriwaka, and Daichi Fukunaga

Department of Intelligent Mechanical System, Graduate School of Natural Science and Technology, Okayama University, Okayama, Japan
murata@iims.sys.okayama-u.ac.jp

Abstract. This study aimed at investigating the effects of the target shape, the movement distance, the target size, and the direction of target presentation on the pointing performance using an eye-gaze input system. The target shape, the target size, the movement distance, and the direction of target presentation were within-subject experimental variables. The target shape included: diamond, circle, rectangle, and square. The direction of target presentation included eight directions: upper, lower, left, right, upper left, upper right, lower left, and lower right. As a result, the pointing time of the rectangle tended to be longer. The upper directional movement also tended to prolong the pointing time. Such results would be effective for designing an eye-gaze-input HCI (Human-Computer Interaction). Moreover, as a result of modeling the pointing time by Fitts' modeling, it was suggested that the index of difficulty in Fitts' modeling for the rectangle should be defined separately from the circle, the diamond, and the square.

Keywords: Eye-gaze input · Target shape · Display location · HCI

1 Introduction

The opportunities to use PCs or internets daily and in workplaces are increasing more and more irrespective of sex, age, and educational level. In other words, PCs or internets are widespread universally. Although a mouse input is mostly widespread among PC and internet users, this device is not usable for older adults and disabled people. For such a user population, an eye-gaze input system is paid more and more attention as an alternative of a mouse input.

The technology for measuring a user's visual line of gaze in real time has been advancing. Appropriate human-computer interaction techniques that incorporate eye movements into a human-computer dialogue have been developed [1–9]. These studies have found the advantage of eye-gaze input system. However, few studies except Murata [8] have examined the effectiveness of such systems with older adults. Murata [8] discussed the usability of an eye-gaze input system to aid interactions with computers for older adults. Systematically manipulating experimental conditions such as

© Springer International Publishing Switzerland 2015
M. Kurosu (Ed.): Human-Computer Interaction, Part II, HCII 2015, LNCS 9170, pp. 94–106, 2015.
DOI: 10.1007/978-3-319-20916-6_10

the movement distance, target size, and direction of movement, an eye-gaze input system was found to lead to faster pointing time as compared with mouse input especially for older adults.

As eye-gaze input interfaces enable us to interact with PC by making use of eye movements, it is expected that even disables persons with deficiency on the upper limb can easily use it. A lot of studies [10–14] are reported on eye-gaze input interfaces as an alternative to a mouse. In these studies, an optimal click method, menu selection method, dragging method, and character input method have been discussed. However, there are still a lot of problems we must overcome so that such an input system can be put into practical use. For example, the shape of mouse cursor suitable for general human-computer interactions (HCI) except for eye-gaze interfaces is discussed, for example, by Pastel [15], Lecuier [16], and Phillips [17]. Like general HCI, we should use a proper cursor shape which enhances the usability of eye-gaze input system. As the eye-gaze input system differs from the mouse input in input mechanism, and has a lower resolution as compared with the mouse input, it is natural and reasonable to predict that the cursor shape proper for the mouse input does not necessarily lead to the high usability of eye-gaze interfaces. Although a conventional arrow-type cursor is used even in eye-gaze input interface, there seems to be no definite reason to use such a conventional cursor shape in eye-gaze input interfaces. It has been explored what type of cursor shape is suitable for eye-gaze input interfaces [13].

As compared with a lot of usability studies on mouse input, the usability of eye-gaze input system has not been systematically explored. More concretely, the effects of the target form (figure), the movement distance, the target size, and the direction of target presentation on the pointing performance by an eye-gaze input system has not been examined until now.

Therefore, this study aimed at investigating the effects of the target shape, the movement distance, the target size, and the direction of target presentation on the pointing performance by an eye-gaze input system. The target form (figure), the target size, the movement distance, and the direction of target presentation were within-subject experimental variables. The target shape included: diamond, circle, rectangle, and square. The direction of target presentation included eight directions: upper, lower, left, right, upper left, upper right, lower left, and lower right. On the basis of the experiment above, an attempt was made to model the pointing time in an eye-gaze input interface using Fitts' modeling.

2 Method

2.1 Participant

Ten healthy young adults aged from 21 to 24 years old took part in the experiment. All participants had an experience of personal computer with an average of 5.5 years (6-7 years). The visual acuity of the participants in both young and older groups was matched and more than 20/20. They had no orthopedic or neurological diseases.

2.2 Apparatus

Using EMR-AT VOXER (Nac Image Technology) (See Fig. 1), an eye-gaze input interface was developed. Visual C# (Microsift) was used as a programming language. This apparatus enables us to determine eye movements and fixation by measuring the reflection of low-level infrared light (800 nm), and also admits the head movements within a predetermined range. The eye-tracker was connected with a personal computer (HP, DX5150MT) with a 15-in. (303 mm x 231 mm) CRT. The resolution was 1024 × 768 pixel. Another personal computer was also connected to the eye-tracker via a RS232C port to develop an eye-gaze input system. The line of gaze, via a RS232C port, is output to this computer with a sampling frequency of 60 Hz. The illumination on the keyboard of a personal was about 200 lx, and the mean brightness of 5 points (four edges and a center) on CRT was about 100 cd/m^2. The viewing distance was about 70 cm. The experimental situation is shown in Fig. 1.

Fig. 1. Photo of experimental setting

2.3 Task, Design, and Procedure

The task was to point to a target presented either of eight directions in Fig. 2 by moving fixation from the initial fixation point to the target, and fixate it for 300 ms. The experimental conditions are summarized in Fig. 3. As well as the movement direction, the movement distance (210 pixel and 290 pixel), the target shape (square, diamond, circle, and rectangle), and the size of target (100 X 100 pixel^2, 75 X 75 pixel^2, and 50 X 50 pixel^2) were within-subject experimental factors. For each combinations of the movement distance, the target shape, and the size of target (there were a total of 24 conditions), the participant was required to carry out pointing task 10 times for each direction in Fig. 2. The eight kinds of directions were randomly presented to the participant. The order of performance of 24 conditions was also randomized across the participants.

After the calibration of eye camera and the practice session, the participants began the experimental session. First, the participants were ordered to fixate the center of the display. After the fixation to the center area, the target to be pointed to is presented on one of the eight directions in Fig. 2. The participants move their fixation from the central area to the target, and fixate there for the predetermined duration (in this study, 300 ms). This corresponds to one pointing trial.

The evaluation measure was the pointing time for the correct trial. The size of each form (square, diamond, circle, and rectangle) when the size corresponded to 100 X 100 pixel^2 is shown in Fig. 4.

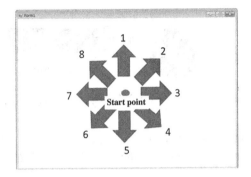

Fig. 2. Movement directions used in the experiment

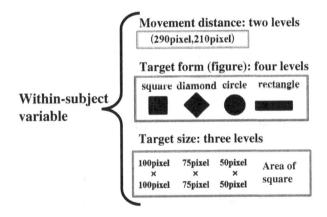

Fig. 3. Three factors other than movement direction used in the experiment

3 Results

In Fig. 5, the mean pointing time is compared between the two movement distance conditions (210 pixel and 290 pixel). The pointing time is compared among target shapes ((square, diamond, circle, and rectangle) in Fig. 6. In Fig. 7, the pointing time is compared among three levels of target size (100 X 100 pixel^2, 75 X 75 pixel^2, and 50 X 50 pixel^2). In Fig. 8, the pointing time is plotted as a function of target shape and target size. A three-way (size by shape by distance) ANOVA (Analysis of Variance) conducted on the pointing time revealed main effects of distance ($F(1,9) = 14.818$,

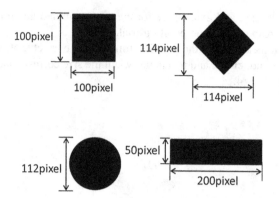

Fig. 4. Four shapes (100 X 100 pixel^2) used in the experiment

$p < 0.01$), size ($F(2,18) = 206.360, p < 0.01$), and shape ($F(3,27) = 538.883, p < 0.01$). A shape by size interaction was also significant ($F(6,54) = 12.712, p < 0.01$).

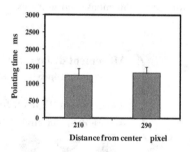

Fig. 5. Pointing time compared between two movement distances

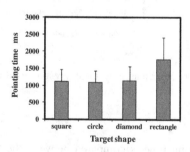

Fig. 6. Pointing time compared between four shape conditions

For each movement distance, a three-way (direction by shape by size) ANOVA was conducted on the pointing time. First, the result of movement distance of 210 pixels is mentioned. Significant main effects of size ($F(2,18) = 92.942, p < 0.01$), shape ($F(3,27) = 294.368, p < 0.01$), and direction ($F(7,63) = 12.996, p < 0.01$) were detected.

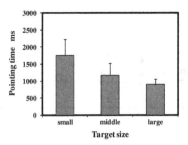

Fig. 7. Pointing time compared among three size conditions

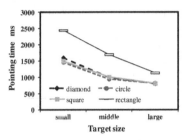

Fig. 8. Pointing time as a function of target shape and target size

A shape by size interaction ($F(6,54) = 6.913, p < 0.01$) and a size by direction interaction were also significant ($F(14,126) = 3.182, p < 0.01$). In Fig. 9, the pointing time is plotted as a function of target shape and target size. In Fig. 10, the pointing time is plotted as a function of movement direction and target size. Figure 11 compares the pointing time among three levels of target size (100×100 pixel^2, 75×75 pixel^2, and 50×50 pixel^2). In Fig. 12, the pointing time is shown as a function of target shape. In Fig. 13, the pointing time is compared among eight movement directions.

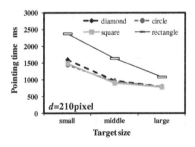

Fig. 9. Pointing time as a function of target size and target shape ($d = 210$ pixel)

Next, the results for the movement distance of 290 pixel are described. A three-way (direction by shape by size) ANOVA was conducted on the pointing time. Significant main effects of size ($F(2,18) = 249.927, p < 0.01$), shape ($F(3,27) = 117.269, p < 0.01$),

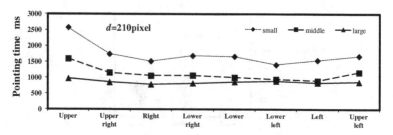

Fig. 10. Pointing time as a function of movement direction and target size (d = 210 pixel)

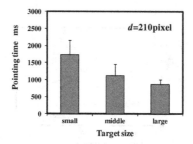

Fig. 11. Pointing time compared among target size conditions (d = 210 pixel)

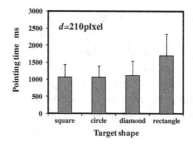

Fig. 12. Pointing time compared among target shape conditions (d = 210 pixel)

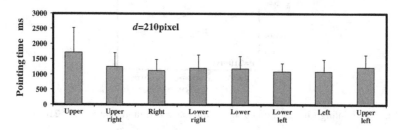

Fig. 13. Pointing time compared among movement direction conditions (d = 210 pixel)

and direction ($F(7,63) = 13.948$, $p < 0.01$) were detected. A shape by size interaction ($F(6,54) = 6.558$, $p < 0.01$) and a size by direction interaction were also significant ($F(14,126) = 4.088$, $p < 0.01$). In Fig. 14, the pointing time is plotted as a function of target size and target shape. In Fig. 15, the pointing time is plotted as a function of movement direction and target size. In Fig. 16, the pointing time is plotted as a function of movement direction and target shape. Figure 17 compares the pointing time among three levels of target size (100 X 100 pixel^2, 75 X 75 pixel^2, and 50 X 50 pixel^2). In Fig. 18, the pointing time is shown as a function of target shape. In Fig. 19, the pointing time is compared among eight movement directions.

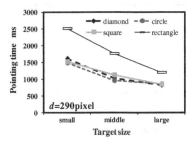

Fig. 14. Pointing time as a function of target size and target shape ($d = 290$ pixel)

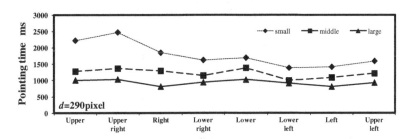

Fig. 15. Pointing time as a function of movement direction and target size ($d = 290$ pixel)

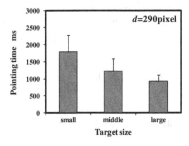

Fig. 16. Pointing time compared among target size conditions ($d = 290$ pixel)

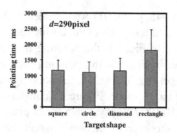

Fig. 17. Pointing time compared among target shape conditions (d = 290 pixel)

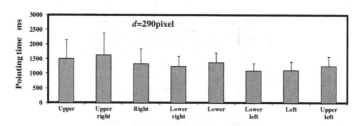

Fig. 18. Pointing time compared among movement direction conditions (d = 290 pixel)

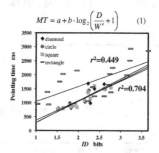

Fig. 19. Fitts' modeling (Eq. (1)) for the rectangle group and the diamond, circle, and square group

The results of modeling the relationship between the index of difficulty and the pointing time by means of Fitts' law are shown in Figs. 19 and 20. The indices of difficulty in Figs. 19 and 20 are given by Eqs. (1) and (2), respectively.

$$MT = a + b \cdot \log_2\left(\frac{D}{W'} + 1\right) \tag{1}$$

$$MT = a + b \cdot \log_2\left(\frac{D}{S} + 1\right) \tag{2}$$

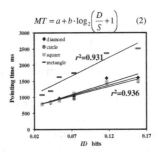

Fig. 20. Fitts' modeling (Eq. (2)) for the rectangle group and the diamond, circle, and square group

MT is the pointing time, D is the movement distance, S is the size of the target, and W is the depth of the target along the movement direction. The parameters a and b are empirically determined.

4   Discussion

Figure 5 shows that the movement distance affected the pointing time as expected. As shown in Fig. 6, the target shape affected the pointing time, and the pointing time of the rectangle was by far longer than that of other target shapes. As expected, the target size affected the pointing time (see Fig. 7). As shown in Fig. 8, the size by shape interaction shows that the effects of target size on the pointing time are similar for circle, square, and diamond, although the effects of target size on the pointing time is not similar to those of circle, square, and diamond. As no interactions were detected between the movement distance and other factors, a three-way (shape by size by movement direction) ANOVA was carried out on the pointing time for each movement distance.

As shown in Figs. 9-13 and Figs. 14-18, similar results (effect of shape, size, and movement direction on pointing time) were observed for both movement distances. An attempt was made to model the pointing time using Fitts' model (Murata et al. [18]). The results are shown in Figs. 19 and 20. The fit to the data is better in Fig. 20 (Eq. (2)) than in Fig. 19 (Eq. (1)). This indicates that the area of the target should be used as the size parameter in Fitts' law modeling. Moreover, Fig. 20 indicates that the circle, the diamond, and the square can be modeled using the same equation, although the Fitts' equation for the rectangle is different from that for the circle, the diamond, and the square. This means that the index of difficulty ($\log_2(D/S + 1)$) does not apply to the rectangle. Therefore, the indices of difficulty for these two types of shapes (the circle, the diamond, and the square (Eq. (3)) and the rectangle (Eq. (4))) were defined as follows separately.

$$ID = \log_2\left\{\left(\frac{D}{S}+1\right)\right\} \tag{3}$$

$$ID = \log_2\left\{ \alpha\left(\frac{D}{S}+1\right)\right\} \tag{4}$$

In Eq. (4), α is empirically determined parameter. When α is one, this coincides with Eq. (3). The results of separate definition of index of difficulty are shown in Figs. 21 and 22. As compared with Fig. 21, the separate definition of index of difficulty improved the fit to the data (Fig. 22), and made the contribution r^2 increase from 0.539 to 0.702. The difficulty of pointing to the rectangle target like a Web menu item can be well expressed by the model (Eq. (4)) proposed in this study.

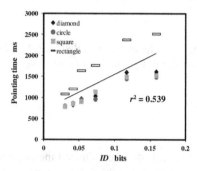

Fig. 21. Fitts' modeling (Eq. (3)) for all of the shape conditions

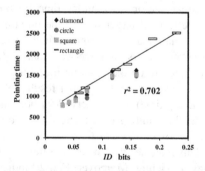

Fig. 22. Fitts' modeling (Eq. (4)) for all of the shape conditions

5 Conclusions

The pointing time of the rectangle tended to be longer than that of the square, the diamond, and the circle. The pointing time of the square, diamond, and the circle was similar even when the movement direction, the movement distance, and the target size changed. This property was not true for the rectangle. The upper directional movement also tended to prolong the pointing time. Moreover, as a result of modeling the pointing time by Fitts' modeling, it was suggested that the index of difficulty in Fitts' modeling for the rectangle should be defined separately from the circle, the diamond, and the square.Such results would be effective for designing an eye-gaze-input HCI (Human-Computer Interaction).

Future research should verify the effectiveness of this study under more realistic HCI such as a Web search.

References

1. Jacob, R.J.K.: What you look at is what you get: Eye movement- based interaction technique. In: Proceedings of the ACM CHI 1990 Human Factors in Computing Systems Conference, pp. 11–18. ACM, Seattle (1990)
2. Jacob, R.J.K.: The use of eye movements in human-computer interaction techniques: What you look at is what you get. ACM Trans. Inf. Syst. **9**, 152–169 (1991)
3. Jacob, R.J.K.: Eye-movement-based human-computer interaction techniques: Towards non-command interfaces. In: Harston, H.R., Hix, D. (eds.) Advances in human-computer interaction, vol. 4, pp.151–190. Ablex, Norwood (1993)
4. Jacob, R.J.K.: What you look at is what you get: Using eye movements as computer input. In: Proceedings CHI 1990, pp.11–18. ACM, Seattle (1990)
5. Jacob, R.J.K.: Eye tracking in advanced interface design. In: Baefield, W., Furness, T. (eds.) Advanced Interface Design and Virtual Environments, pp. 212–231. Oxford University Press, Oxford (1994)
6. Jacob, R.J.K., Sibert, L.E., Mcfarlanes, D.C., Mullen, M.P.: Integrality and reparability of input devices. ACM Trans. Comput. Hum. Interact. **1**(1), 3–26 (1994)
7. Sibert, L.E., Jacob, R.J.K.: Evaluation of eye gaze interaction. In: Proceedings CHI 2000, pp. 281–288, Hague (2000)
8. Murata, A.: Eye-gaze input versus mouse: cursor control as a function of age. Int. J. Hum. Comput. Interact. **21**, 1–14 (2006)
9. Murata, A., Moriwaka, M., Effectiveness of the menu selection method for eye-gaze input system -Comparison between young and older adults. In: 5th International Workshop on Computational Intelligence and Applications, pp.306–311, Hiroshima (2009)
10. Murata, A., Miyake, T.: Effectiveness of eye-gaze input system -Identification of conditions that assures high pointing accuracy and movement directional effect. In: 4th International Workshop on Computational Intelligence & Applications, pp. 127–132, Hiroshima (2008)
11. Murata, A., Moriwaka, M.: Basic study for development of web browser suitable for eye-gaze input system -Identification of optimal click method. In: 5th International Workshop on Computational Intelligence & Applications, pp. 302–305, Hiroshima (2009)
12. Murata, A., Hayashi, K., Moriwaka, M., Hayami, T.: Optimal scroll method to browse web pages using an eye-gaze input system. In: AHFE 2012, pp. 7106–7115, San Francisco (2012)
13. Murata, A., Uetsugi, R., Hayami, T.: Study on cursor shape suitable for eye-gaze input system. In: SICE 2012, pp. 926–931, Akita (2012)
14. Murata, A., Hayashi, K., Moriwaka, M., Hayami, T.: Study on Character Input Methods Using Eye-gaze Input Interface. In: Kurosu, M. (ed.) HCII/HCI 2013, Part IV. LNCS, vol. 8007, pp. 320–329. Springer, Heidelberg (2013)
15. Pastel, R.: Positioning graphical objects on computer screens: A three-phase model. Hum. Factors **53**(1), 22–37 (2011)
16. Lecuier, A.: A study of the modification of the speed and size of the cursor for simulating pseudo-haptic bumps and holes. ACM Trans. Appl. Percept. **5**(3), 1–21 (2008)

17. Phillips, G.: Conflicting directional and locational cues afforded by arrowhead cursors in graphical user interfaces. J. Exp. Psychol. Appl. **9**(2), 75–87 (2003)
18. Murata, A.: Empirical Evaluation of Performance Models of Pointing Accuracy and Speed with a PC Mouse. Int. J. Hum. Comput. Interact. **8**(4), 457–469 (1996)

Analysis of Eye Hand Interaction in Drawing Figure and Letter

For the Development of Handwrite-Training Device

Yumiko Muto[1] and Takeshi Muto[2(✉)]

[1] Department of Information Processing, Interdisciplinary Graduate School of Science and Engineering, Tokyo Institute of Technology, 4259 G2-1, Nagatsuta, Midoriku, Yokohama, Kanagawa 226-8503, Japan
muto.yumiko@gmail.com
[2] Faculty of Information and Communications, Bunkyo University, 1100, Namegaya, Chigasaki, Kanagawa 253-8550, Japan
muto@shonan.bunkyo.ac.jp

Abstract. We investigated the eye hand interaction by focusing on the position of fixation, in order to clarify the role of eye in drawing. In the experiment, participants were asked to draw the simple circle and popular Chinese letters under the three different conditions; drawing by using the pen which is out of ink, tracing and drawing. The result showed that three modes of eye-hand behaviour were observed. We suggested that these three modes should be considered to develop the training device to realize more effective handwrite-training.

Keywords: Handwriting · Handwrite training · Eye-hand interaction · Motor control

1 Introduction

Human beings can express their individualities or sensibilities through drawing of characters and figures. Handwriting training is for drawing figures and letters by using writing instruments in order to write or draw such hand-written letters or drawing accurately and beautifully. In conventional handwriting training, tracing of letters using a writing instrument such as a pen or a transcription while looking a copybook is a common method, based on the view point of motor learning.

On the other hand, in recent years, a technique to more effectively perform the handwriting training by providing sounds or images using computer technology has been proposed (e.g., a handwrite-training device for training in visually exchanging a model draw-stroke motion with another person [1]). The above-mentioned studies were different from the handwriting training based on the motor learning conventionally used and reported that effective handwriting training could be achieved by providing controlled sensory information to a trainee.

According to the above-mentioned backgrounds, in this study, authors focused on the point that the draw-stoke of handwriting was principally performed based on the

M. Kurosu (Ed.): Human-Computer Interaction, Part II, HCII 2015, LNCS 9170, pp. 107–117, 2015.
DOI: 10.1007/978-3-319-20916-6_11

sensory information from eyes, we investigate the relationship between eye information and motion control in handwriting, aiming at developing the handwrite-training device in consideration of the position of fixation. Specifically, we analyze time variation processes of spatial positions of tips of a position of fixation and a pen in handwriting by using an eye mark recorder and extract patterns of positional relationship of the pen tip and the position of fixation.

2 Related Study

Few studies on the sight line during drawing letters or figures had been performed by the year 2000, and early studies were conducted by measuring the sight line of a professional painter [2, 3]. However, in recent years, studies of the role of the sight line in drawing of simple lines or figures are gradually conducted with average test subjects. As a result, the study revealed that the sight line and the hand movements had a bilateral relationship [4]. In addition, Tchalenko measured the sight line in drawing of simple straight line, curve, and square and reported two types of signature sight lines (1. a sight line following a pen tip and 2. a sight line for watching a target point such as an endpoint of a line prior to the movements of the hand) [5]. In the studies of the reaching movements and the holding movements, it has been reported that the coordination of the sight line and the hand movements becomes strong when the sight line moves following a moving object [6, 7].

3 Experimental Approach

3.1 Experiment Device

In this study, we created an experiment environment as shown in Fig. 1 in order to measure the movements of the position of fixation during the draw-stroke motion. A test subject wore an eye mark recorder (EMR-8B, NAC Image Technology, Inc.) and wrote, with a ballpoint pen, on a B4-size white plain paper attached on a 19" LCD monitor (LCD-AD195 GB, I-O DATA DEVICE, Inc.) placed in front of the subject at a distance of 47 cm from a subject's eye. All experiments were conducted in a quiet room with sufficient illumination.

3.2 Experiment Condition

This experiment was started after the test subject wore the eye mark recorder and then the recorder was sufficiently calibrated. The test subject was asked to see a sample of a perfect circle (with a 0.5 mm thick black solid line having a diameter of 10 cm) drawn in a center of the B4-size white plain paper for a few seconds in order to recognize a task figure. From prior studies, it had been known that the position of fixation of the subject moved to the corners in each time figures with corners were presented and therefore the movements of the position of fixation become complex in whole [4, 5]. In addition, if small figures were presented, drawing time become short, and the basic

Fig. 1. Experiment environment

movements of the position of fixation were hardly captured. For the above reasons, this study adopted a slightly large perfect circle with the diameter of 10 cm as the task in the Experiment #1 in order to clearly investigate the basic movements of the position of fixation during the draw-stroke motion. As the task in the Experiment #2, drawing relatively simple Chinese letters "田", "永" for Japanese inside of 10 × 10 cm square were adopted.

In the experiment, the following three different conditions were prepared, and the test subject drew the perfect circle as the task figure clockwise in one stroke (Experiment #1) or the target letter in usual stroke order (Experiment #2) on the white plain paper attached of the LCD monitor once in each condition. Only in the Experiment #1, in order not to arise variations in the starting point of writing among all test subjects, a red "+" symbol in 1 cm square size was presented on the LCD monitor (at a position of 5 cm above the center of the paper) for only one second after the start of the experiment.

(a) **No Ink Condition:** Draw a circle with a pen which did not leave the handwriting.
(b) **Normal Condition:** Draw a circle with a pen (black).
(c) **Tracing Condition:** Trace a task figure drawn on a paper; use a pen without ink as the condition (a).

3.3 Analysis

Acquisition of Coordinate Data of Position of fixation and Pen Tip. The movements of the position of fixation and the pen tip for each test subject were recorded with a CCD camera of the position of the eye mark recorder mounted on a head of the subject as video of 29.97 fps with superimposed position of fixation pointers. The video data was processed as follows by using a motion capture software (PV-studio 2D, L.A. B Inc.) and converted into coordinate data in time series. After correcting the lens curvature, we used tracking functions of the software to extract the time series data of the coordinates of both the position of fixation pointer and the movements of the pen tip. After that, we converted the time series data into the absolute coordinate system in which a yellow marker point attached on an upper section of the monitor was determined to be a reference point. Furthermore, we calculated draw-stroke time in each condition through the method.

Analysis on Position of Fixation Point. First, we calculated the distance $d_{(t)}$ between the fixation point and the pen tip from the fixation point $(x_{e(t)}, y_{e(t)})$ and the coordinate of the pen tip $(x_{p(t)}, y_{p(t)})$ at a given point in time $d_{(t)}$ based on the following Eq. (1).

$$d_{(t)} = \sqrt{\left(x_{e(t)} - x_{p(t)}\right)^2 + \left(y_{e(t)} - y_{p(t)}\right)^2} \tag{1}$$

Also, in order to investigate the movement of the position of fixation in which the subject watches the endpoint prior to the hand movement, we determined min $d_{(t)}$. newly calculated with the Eq. (2) in this study.

$$\mathrm{min}d_{(t)} = \sqrt{\left(x_{e(t)} - x_{p(\tilde{t})}\right)^2 + \left(y_{e(t)} - y_{(\tilde{t})}\right)^2} \tag{2}$$

where min $d_{(t)}$ is the shortest distance between the fixation point $(x_{e(t)}, y_{e(t)})$ at time t and the path of the draw-stroke, and the $(x_{p(\tilde{t})}, y_{p(\tilde{t})})$ is the coordinates on the path of the draw-stroke indicating the shortest distance. At this time, the fixation point is in a position ahead of the pen tip, and $t \leq \tilde{t}$ is obtained.

By conducting the above analysis, it is considered possible to quantitatively separate two kinds of the phenomenon on the positional relationship between the position of fixation and pen tip that has already been reported in the prior study.

Classification Method of Movements of Position of fixation and Pen Tip. In a case where a human captures an object in the center of the retina, it is generally known that the viewing angle is physiologically within the range of 2.5 deg. This is referred to as central vision, and it is also known that the central vision is conscious and the response to the moving object is weak. From the facts described above, in this study, we defined that the range within 2.0 cm was the position of fixation in proximity of the pen tip; because the distance between the eye and the monitor was 47 cm ($47 \cdot tan\ 2.5$[deg] $\fallingdotseq 2.0$ cm).

4   Experiment #1

4.1   Movements of Position of Fixation and Pent Tip on Each Condition

With the analysis method described in the above Sect. 3.3 and DFT analysis of time series data of the fixation point and the pen tip, the distance $d_{(t)}$ between the fixation point and the pen tip and the time series data of the shortest distance min $d_{(t)}$ between the fixation point and the path of the draw-stroke are shown in Figs. 2 and 3. The eye gaze data shows significant difference between the conditions, more than the data of pen tips .

In addition, the values of $d_{(t)}$ and min $d_{(t)}$ averaged over the test subjects are listed on Table 1. The result of one-way analysis of variance revealed that the mean values of

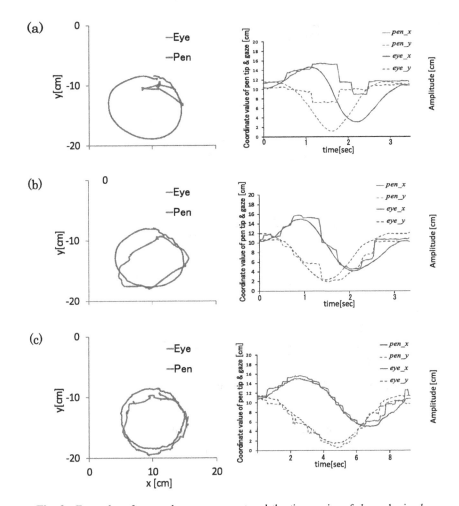

Fig. 2. Examples of eye and pen movement and the time series of $d_{(t)}$ and min $d_{(t)}$

$d_{(t)}$ and min $d_{(t)}$ had significant differences under the conditions (a) through (c) ($d_{(t)}$: $F(2, 33) = 17.31$, $p < 0.01$; min $d_{(t)}$: $F(2, 33) = 7.95$, $p < 0.01$). Furthermore, it is found that the distance $d_{(t)}$ between the fixation point and the pen tip is 1.7 cm in the tracing on the condition (c). The result shows that the position of fixation tends to correspond in proximity to the pen tip (c.f., Sect. 3.3).

4.2   Detection of Position of Fixation Following Pen Tip

In order to investigate the proximity state of the fixation point and the pen tip, we focused on the distance $d_{(t)}$ between the fixation point and the pen tip and determined the rate of the state where $d_{(t)}$ at draw-stroke time is 2 cm or less (Fig. 4 ①).

As a result, it has been found that the condition (c) maintains significantly higher rate than the condition (a) or (b) ($F(2, 33) = 10.90$, $p < 0.01$; Post hoc comparisons:

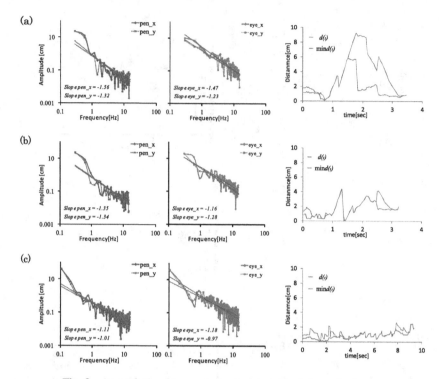

Fig. 3. An analysis of eye and pen movement and $d_{(t)}$ and min $d_{(t)}$.

Table 1. Average (S.D.) of $d_{(t)}$ and *min* $d_{(t)}$

Condition	$d_{(t)}$ [cm]	min $d_{(t)}$ [cm]
(a)	4.0 (0.8)	2.3 (1.0)
(b)	3.6 (1.4)	1.9 (0.8)
(c)	1.7 (0.6)	1.0 (0.4)

$p < 0.05$). That is, in a case of the tracing on the condition (c), it can be found that the fixation point is positioned in proximity of the pen tip in comparison with the other conditions, and the position of fixation follows the pen tip.

4.3   Detection of Position of Fixation Prior to Movements of Hand

The results of the experiment in the Sect. 4.2 showed that the position of fixation is not only following the pen tip. Therefore, we determined, other than the fixation point in proximity of the pen tip, the fixation point where the shortest distance min $d_{(t)}$ between the fixation point and the path of the draw-stroke became 2 cm or less (*c.f.*, Sect. 3.3). Accordingly, we investigated the phenomenon in which the position of fixation was fixed on a position in proximity of the path ahead of the position of the pen tip. The

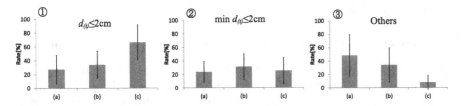

Fig. 4. The rates of $d_{(t)} \leq 2$ cm, min $d_{(t)} \leq 2$ cm and others in each experimental conditions

results of determination of the rate for all fixation point are shown in Fig. 4 ②. As a result, it was revealed that there were no differences among the conditions (a) through (c) ($F(2, 33) = 0.59$, $p = 0.56$). That is, it is found that such movements of the position of fixation prior to the pen tip were observed irrespective of the condition.

4.4   Other Fixation Point

We determined the rate of the fixation point that could not explain in the experiments of Sects. 4.2 and 4.3 (the fixation point located in the position away from the pen tip or the path of the draw-stroke) among all fixation points (Fig. 4 ③). The result showed that, under all the conditions, there were the fixation points which could not explain in the experiments of Sects. 4.2 and 4.3. Furthermore, in a case of drawing with a pen without ink on the condition (a) which does not leave the handwriting, the result showed that the rate of the fixation point in the position away from the pen tip and the path of the draw-stroke was higher than that on the other conditions (b) and (c) ($F(2, 33) = 8.62$, $p < 0.01$; Post hoc comparisons: $p < 0.05$)).

4.5   Roles of Eye Movements

Under the condition (b), similar to the condition (a) in which the handwriting is not left the position of fixation in the position away from the pen tip or the path of the draw-stroke was revealed in addition to two categories (a position of fixation following the pen tip and a position of fixation indicating the goal point prior to the movements of the hand). From the result, it is suggested that the position of fixation has at least three roles in the draw-stroke motion.

It has been revealed that the first role of the position of fixation following the pen tip is principally observed in the draw-stroke for adjusting to the sample already drawn as the tracing or immediately after the starting of the drawing, named **Close Pursuit (CP) mode**. The second role of the position of fixation which serves as the role of an attainment target prior to the pen tip has been performed in the same rate on all the conditions, named **Target Locking (TL) mode**. The third role is considered to be a role for perceiving the overall draw-stroke motion since the position of fixation is principally positioned in the center part away from the pen tip or the path of the draw-stroke, named **Overlooking (OL) mode**.

5 Experiment #2

5.1 Movements of Position of Fixation and Pent Tip on Each Condition

Figure 5 shows the typical examples of the movements of the position of fixation and the pen tip in each conditions of the letters "永" and "田". It has been found that the position of fixation has moved inside of smaller area than the area of the pen tip, in the condition (a). On the other hand, in condition (b), the area of the movements of the position of fixation has been larger than the area in the condition (a), becoming to more similar shape of the movements of pen tip. Additionally, in the condition (c), the movements of the position of fixation has tended to be longer than other conditions, becoming to the most similar shape of the movements of pen tip.

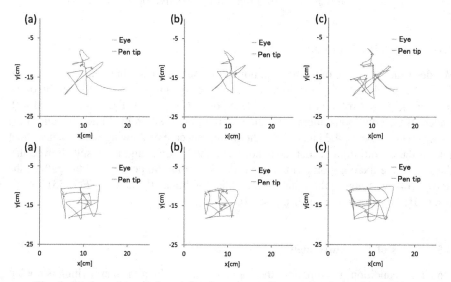

Fig. 5. Motion of pen tip's and fixation x-y coordinate value during handwriting

Figure 6 shows the average of time rate among the all 3 roles of eye movement in the experiments, classified to the data of time series of the distance of each time (min d (t)) and the minimum distance (min d(t)) between the fixation and the pen tip, during handwriting of "永", by the method named at last Sect. 4.5.

Then, in the condition (c), the rate of Close pursuit mode (CP) has been significant larger than the other modes ($F(8,72) = 18.24$, $p < 0.001$; Post hoc comparisons: $p < 0.05$). However in the other conditions, such tendency has not been observed. Additionally, the rate of OL has been significantly smaller (Post hoc comparisons: $p < 0.001$) than CP, except in the freehand condition.

When the letter "田" has been written, the rate of OL has been significantly smaller than TL in the all 3 conditions, also smaller than CP in the condition (b) & (c), as shown in Fig. 5. ($F(8,72) = 15.22$, $p < 0.001$; Post hoc comparisons: $p < 0.001$).

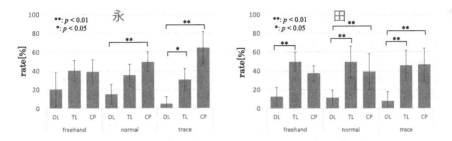

Fig. 6. Classification of position of fixation motion during writing "永"&"田"

5.2 Difference of Movements of the Position of Fixation from Target Letters

In the conditions (b) & (c), it has been observed that the rate of OL was significantly smaller than the rate of CP when they wrote "永" and "田", then the result is as same as the results in experiment #1.

Especially the rate of OL is also significantly smaller than the rate of TL when they wrote "田". The letter "田" has relatively simpler structure than the letter "永". Accordingly delicate curve line required delicate motion control or complicated stroke like "harai" (sweeping stroke) or "hane" (upward stroke) are not so necessary when they write the letter "田". Therefore they can achieve the drawing task, even if controlling pen tip just following simple straight line, watching the pen tips or the target point, then the rate of OL has been smaller than also TL. On the other hand, the tendency that the rete of OL has been smaller than the rate of TL when they draw the letter "田", in the freehand condition. This result may say that they draw the target letter by TL or CP mainly even in the freehand condition they cannot visually recognize the stroke because the structure of "田" is simple which already mentioned.

On the other hand, there have not observed significant difference between the 3 modes when they draw "永". So the draw stroke of "永" has been realized by not only TL or CP but also all 3 modes which involve OL, properly. Already mentioned, the draw control when they draw the letter "永", contain the 3 basic draw strokes; "*tome*" (stop stroke), "*hane*" (upward stroke), "*Harai*" (sweeping stroke). Therefore it may be more difficult to recognize the error information with the target for controlling pen tip or to anticipate the target point, than drawing more simple figures. So they draw the target figure, perceiving and overlooking the whole motion of pen tip by peripheral vision, focusing their eyes on far point from the pen tip and stroke lines. Also it has been known that the peripheral vision is superior in perception of movement to the central vision that partially captures the object [8].

It is suggested that the role of the sight line on the condition (a) is to perceive overall draw-stroke motion with the peripheral vision in addition to two basic roles. It might be inferred from the suggestion that, in the case of drawing "永", the rate of OL was not significantly smaller than the rates of other 2 modes, being different from the case of drawing "田". Therefore we suggest that they use 3 kinds of the model properly to control the motion of pen tip dexterously in case of drawing more complicated letter than drawing simple figure.

6 Conclusion

In this study, we investigated the relationship between eye information and motion control in handwriting, aiming at developing the handwrite-training device in consideration of the position of fixation. In the experiment #1, we adapted the drawing of a circle that was the simplest figure without corners as a task, analyzed time variation processes of spatial positions of tips of a position of fixation and a pen, and extracted patterns of positional relationship of the pen tip and the position of fixation. As a result, we revealed three basic roles of the position of fixation in the draw-stroke motion.

In the Experiment #2, we adapted the drawing of two kinds of popular Chinese letters, analyzed time variation extracted patterns of positional relationship of the pen tip and the position of fixation, by the three basic roles of the position of fixation suggested in Experiment #1. As the results, it has been observed that the eye control mode of CP and TL were used mainly in case of drawing the letter "田" which is relatively simple figure but the mode of OL were not. However in case of drawing more complicated letter "永", it have been suggested that not only TL and CP but also OL have been used, which means all 3 eye control mode were applied properly for drawing figures.

Although additional investigation is needed about how the motion control with the peripheral vision is conducted, we can presume that the overall draw-stroke motion is perceived with the peripheral vision, the control target is internally created, and the balance of the whole figures can be maintained. Thus, it is considered that such roles are necessary functions for maintaining good appearances of letters and figures.

Acknowledgements. We thank to Mr. Syun Yamasaki (Aoyama Gakuin University), who supported the analysis of handwriting data, and all the participants in our study.

References

1. Muto, T., Komiyama, S., Ishikawa, R.: Inter-personal interaction for handwrite training: a study for development of handwrite skill training robot. In: Proceedings of Robot and Human Interactive Communication 2009 (RO-MAN 2009), Toyama, Japan, pp.1173–1178, 27 September – 2 October, 2009
2. Miall, R.C., Tchalenko, J.: A painter's eye move-ments: a study of eye and hand movement during portrait drawing. Leonardo **34**(1), 35–40 (2001)
3. Tchalenko, J.S., Dempere-Marco, L., Hu, X.P., Yang, G.Z.: Eye movements and voluntary control in portrait drawing. In: Hyona, J., Radach, R., Deubel, H. (eds.) The Mind's Eye, Cognitive and Applied Aspects of Eye Movement Research, pp. 705–727. Elsevier, Amsterdam (2003)
4. Gowen, E., Miall, R.C.: Eye-hand interactions in tracing and drawing tasks. Hum. Mov. Sci. **25**(4-5), 568–585 (2006)
5. Tchalenko, J.: Eye movements in drawing simple lines. Perception **36**, 1152–1167 (2007)

6. Neggers, S.F., Bekkering, H.: Coordinated control of eye and hand movements in dynamic reaching. Hum. Mov. Sci. **21**(3), 349–376 (2002)
7. Johansson, R.S., Westling, G., Backstrom, A., Flana-gan, J.R.: Eye-hand coordination in object manipulation. J. Neurosci. **21**(17), 6917–6932 (2001)
8. Finlay, D.: Motion perception in the peripheral visual field. Perception **11**(4), 457–462 (1982)

Swift Gestures: Seamless Bend Gestures Using Graphics Framework Capabilities

Samudrala Nagaraju[✉]

Web and Services Team, Samsung R&D Institute Bangalore, Bangalore, India
raju.sn@samsung.com

Abstract. With the advent of bendable devices, Lahey et al. [1], explored bend gestures for mobile phone applications. Considering **millions of applications present on app stores** [2], it would be a challenge to modify source code to handle bend gestures. We propose a novel approach to assign bend gestures *using graphics framework capabilities, which does not require application source code changes*. Because of the ease in use of the proposed approach, bend gestures get acceptance from research community and industry.

Keywords: Bendable devices · Rendering engine · Graphics event processing · Bend gestures · Tangible interaction · Usability study · Rendering tree

1 Introduction

Various types of gestures like air gestures, shake gestures and write gestures are developed for hands-free input or partial-hands-free input to ease device interaction [3, 4]. With the advent of bendable devices, bend gestures [1] are being researched for technical feasibility and usability factors. Modern device platforms support downloadable applications for installation on the device. In this paper, we focus on practical issues in assigning bend gestures to applications in a uniform way by introducing logic in graphics framework without changing application code.

1.1 Definition of Terms

Definitions used in this paper are detailed based on [5]. Device platform – A software stack which includes operating system and middleware. Graphics Framework – Widgets and layouts are the primary elements for creating user interfaces using a graphics framework. Graphics Layout - A layout defines the visual structure for an activity or application widget. Widget - A graphical control element for interaction in a graphical user interface (GUI), such as a button or a scroll bar. View - A View is an object that draws something on the screen that the user can interact with. Graphics Event - Events are objects sent to an app to inform it of user actions e.g. multi-touch. Render Tree - This is generated from application UI and is responsible for the layout and subsequent rendering. Application Packaging - containers for application binaries, based on build settings e.g. apk file for each app. User - A smartphone or tablet user.

© Springer International Publishing Switzerland 2015
M. Kurosu (Ed.): Human-Computer Interaction, Part II, HCII 2015, LNCS 9170, pp. 118–129, 2015.
DOI: 10.1007/978-3-319-20916-6_12

1.2   Types of Applications

An application is classified based on the application shipment type along with the device and development ownership. *Pre-embed applications* are present in limited number and are shipped along with the device. *Downloadable applications* are developed by 3rd party companies and are hosted on app stores [2].

1.3   Graphics Frameworks for Application Development

State of the art device platforms provide at least 3 types of graphics capabilities for application development. (1) Native graphics framework (iOS UIKit, Android native widgets and layouts, etc.). (2) Web framework (HTML, CSS, JavaScript) and (3) Advanced graphics framework (OpenGL ES) [5]. Application developers make use of one or more of above mentioned graphics capabilities for application development. In this paper, we work with native graphics framework in Android platform.

1.4   Bendable Device

Bendable device research and development is in full swing from both academic and commercial fronts. Announcements from device manufacturers about the launch of these devices in market created lot of buzz around [6]. Numerous challenges are waiting with hardware, software, electro mechanical, battery and usability domains [7]. In parallel, this calls for taking the existing research needs to be accommodated into commercial setup to get acceptance in main stream development. This is one of the main goals of this paper for bendable device gestures.

2   Background

Background of this paper is focused in explaining the ongoing research in bendable devices and device frameworks essential for the topics discussed in further sections. Along with these topics, this section also focuses on how research teams are prototyping the bendable device concepts.

2.1   Bendable Devices and Gestures

Research is ongoing in multiple areas that are essential in developing the base technologies for bendable devices [8], e.g. user interactions, bend gestures and physical materials. These technologies are essential to make a significant shift in approaching and solving the problem space of bendable device products. Among the whole set of topics available for research, bendable gesture is a topic actively researched by both academic and industry because of the unique problem space not available earlier when flexibility in device physical characteristics is not thought of. In bendable gesture space, researchers are focusing on gesture interactions, gestures classification and usability factors [9] for detailed study. Role of bend sensors in identifying the bend gesture parameters is also studied [10].

2.2 Bendable Device Prototypes

Researchers substantiated bendable device concepts with various types of prototypes which are classified as follows based on the material used for prototype development. (1) Low fidelity are developed using materials like paper and cloth [11]. (2) Near high fidelity emulations are developed using projected displays and software emulations [12]. (3) High fidelity are developed using device hardware. The scope of prototype emulation for Point (2) encompasses one or all of following. (1) Emulation of the proposed concept implementation. E.g. gestures classification. (2) Emulation of the device hardware. e.g. bendable mobile phone and bendable watch. (3) Emulation of the device sensors. E.g. bend sensors. In this paper, a software implementation of the proposed approach on android graphics framework using mobile phone hardware is used for implementation of "Swift Gestures". Emulation of bend sensors is achieved using a software based implementation on mobile phone hardware.

2.3 Device Platform

Some researchers extend the device capabilities by adding logic in one or more frameworks of device [13] without changing the API. But, some implementations require change in the API structure based on the extent to which control is exposed to 3rd party developers. In this paper, we use the earlier methodology which does not require changes in device platform API on Android.

3 Problem Statement

Focused research is ongoing with bendable device interactions and gesture assignment [10–12]. Even though this research is interesting and productive, bend gesture assignment procedures mentioned in these papers talk about changing application code for handling bend gestures. Second problem is the dependence of bend gestures on device bend physical parameters.

3.1 Source Code Changes

With introduction of bend gestures, application developers face unique problem adapting the legacy downloadable applications to handle these gestures, as it may not be feasible to change the application source code. Figure 1 (a) is Android sample application used to explain the source code changes required to handle bend gestures. Figure 1 (b) shows corresponding source code to Fig. 1(a) to display a dialog 'Dialog Title' on clicking a button titled 'Click Me'. Figure 1(c) shows source code changes required on top of Fig. 1(b) to handle bend gesture for the same action performed on the button 'Click Me'. A source code change needs <u>compile, package</u> (APK generation in case of Android) <u>and upload stages</u> to upload a new version of the downloadable application to app store, which is not feasible for all apps on app store.

3.2   Device Bend Physical Parameters

Bend gestures depend on the physical properties of a device to the extent it is flexible and provide response to application. The role of physical parameters like stiffness, deformable range and feedback is studied [14]. Device size and aspect ratio also play an important role. In this paper, we focus to assign and use a bend gesture to an application in a uniform way with addition of additional logic to graphics frameworks of device platform. This is achieved by mapping the bend gestures to actions already registered by the application.

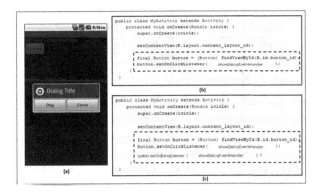

Fig. 1. (a) Sample application with clickable button and dialog (b) Action registration for click event (c) Same action registration extended for bend gesture

4   Proposed Approach

4.1   User Experience (UX) Flow

User experience flow for bend gesture assign and bend gesture invoke procedures is explained in detail in this section. Scope of a bend gesture can either be per application or for the entire device.

4.2   Bend Gesture Assign Procedure

Steps to assign bend gesture are as follows. (1) Select a subset of widgets from application layout at native graphics framework based on the render tree of application. (2) Selected widgets from application layout are highlighted as in Fig. 2 (c). Visual highlighting is done by native graphics framework. (3) User selects a widget from the highlighted list to assign gesture as in Fig. 2 (d). Let's call this as <u>target widget</u>. User does the selection by interacting with highlighted widgets. All interactions at this stage are taken care by native graphics framework and no control is given to application. (4) Visual indication is given to target widget selected as in Fig. 2 (e) by native graphics framework. (5) User does a physical bend of the device and holds it for a short span of time as in Fig. 2 (e). At this stage, native graphics framework registers the bend gesture and assigns to target widget. This step makes bend gesture assignment independent of device physical parameters as in Sect. 3.2 (6) Visual indication is changed for the target widget post gesture assignment, as in Fig. 2 (f).

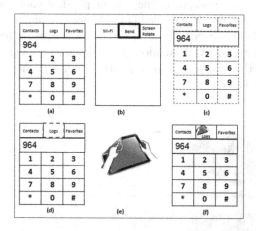

Fig. 2. UX Flow for Gesture Assign (a) Open target application view (b) Drop down notification bar, select 'bend gesture' assignment mode and drop back notification bar (c) Highlight widgets in target application layout (d) Select target widget for gesture assignment (e) Do actual device bend and hold (f) Target widget icon changed based on physical bend parameters

4.3   Bend Gesture Invoke Procedure

As we scoped the bend gesture to the entire mobile, same gesture cannot be duplicated at other applications and this check point is taken care by native graphics framework at bend gesture assign procedure. Post bend gesture assignment, device user needs to invoke the mapped action by physically bending the device as shown in Fig. 3 (d) from any application as shown in Figs. 3 (a) (b) (c).

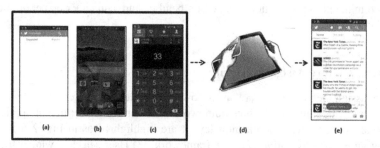

Fig. 3. UX Flow for gesture invoke (a)(b)(c) Invoke from any application (d) Physically bend device and hold (e) Invoke target application and registered action

4.4   Realization Using Android Device Platform

As described in the previous sub-sections of this section, device platform takes care of the following architectural changes for user experience procedures detailed. (1) Identify the subset of widgets from target application layout. (2) Highlight the subset of widgets in target application. (3) Accept the user click of target widget. (4) Highlight the target widget. (5) Capture the physical parameters of device bend. (6) Assignment of device bend gesture to target widget. (7) Changing the visual indication of target widget. (8) Handle gesture invoke trigger.

4.5   Modules Affected in Android Device Platform

Figure 4 highlights the modules affected in android device platform for implementing "Swift gestures". Key responsibility of each module for bend assign and bend invoke procedures is listed in Fig. 5. (1) Quick Setting Panel: This panel is a tiled pane on notification bar to access common settings and can be modified at device platform (2) View System: View occupies a rectangular area on the screen and is responsible for drawing and event handling used to create interactive UI components (buttons, text fields, etc.) (3) Activity Manager: An activity is a focused part of the visible application that the user can interact. Activity takes care of creating a window for application in which it can place a user interface. This is also used to interact with other Activities running in the system. (4) Window Manger: This is a software component that controls the placement and appearance of windows within a windowing system [5].

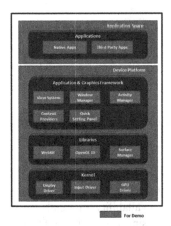

Fig. 4. Modules affected in device platform

4.6   State Transition Flow

Figure 6 shows states introduced at Activity Manger and Window Manger to distinguish among normal application interaction, gesture assign procedure and gesture invoke procedure. Description of each state is as follows (1) NO_BEND: Used for

Module	Responsibility
Quick Panel Setting	• Display notification panel button • Initiate Register Bend Session
View System	• Highlight Clickable widgets • Highlight Selected widget
Activity Manager	• Bend Gesture Callback Handle • State Change Initiation
Window Manager	• State Management • Differentiated Event Handling • Store Bend Gesture Assignment • Invoke mapped action to Bend Gesture

Fig. 5. Module responsibilities for handling bend assign and invoke procedure

normal user interaction with device. (2) HIGHLIGHT_WIDGETS: Used for highlighting the shortlisted widgets and providing visual indication as in Fig. 2(c) (3) ASSIGN_BEND: This state is active from selection of target widget till the physical bend as in Figs. 2 (d) (e) (4) BEND_GESTURE_ASSIGNED: This state is active post bend assignment procedure as in Fig. 2 (f).

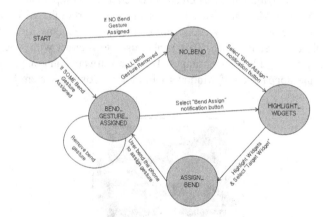

Fig. 6. State transition flow for handling bend assign and invoke procedures

5   Prototype Setup

'Swift gestures' explained in this paper is software driven and hardware dependence is on mobile hardware and the availability of bend sensors with the hardware. We developed the implementation using two mobile phones. First device is demo prototype, which has changes implemented to handle bend gesture assign and invoke procedures on device platform as shown in Fig. 8. Second mobile is bend emulator, on which bend emulation application is developed. Bend emulator is developed on Samsung galaxy S3 on Android ICS platform and is connected to demo prototype over Wi-Fi. Gestures from [1] are reused for bend emulation as shown in Fig. 7 (b).

Dialer is a preloaded application on the mobile phone and ChatON is a downloadable application from app store. We chose these two applications to work with

Fig. 7. BEND EMULATOR APPLICATION (a) Input peer ip address and port no on bend emulator application (b) Select bend gesture from the gesture list on bend emulator application (c) Send bend gesture application to peer demo prototype device.

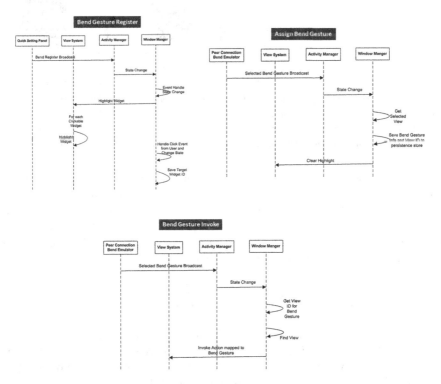

Fig. 8. Call sequence on demo prototype device (a) Bend gesture assign procedure – involves peer connection bend gesture receive, selection of quick settings panel and handling at device platform (b) Bend gesture invoke procedure.

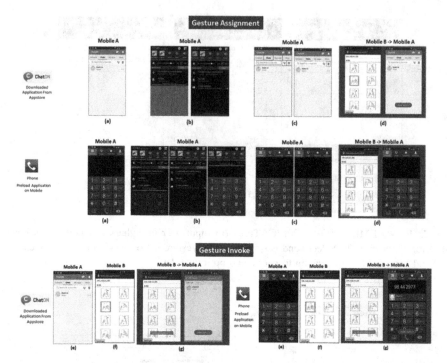

Fig. 9. GESTURE ASSIGN (a) Open Target Screen (b) Drop down notification bar and select bend register (c) Highlight selectable widgets and select target widget (d) Select bend type from bend emulator and assign gesture on demo prototype. GESTURE INVOKE (e) optionally open the desired screen (f) Select bend type from 'Bend gesture emulator' (g) This triggers the action registered on the target widget (Delete chat action for ChatON& Last call action for Dialer).

'Swift gestures' as bend assign and invoke procedures need to work with both preload and downloadable applications. These applications are installed on demo prototype mobile, a Samsung Galaxy S5 running on Android Kitkat platform. ChatON version used is v3.5 downloaded from Google play store [2]. Steps to connect both the mobiles are as follows (1) Launch connection app in both mobile phones (2) Input peer ip address and port no (3) Establish the connection.

6   Bend Emulation and Prototype Usage

The demo prototype mobile is referred as "Mobile A" and bend emulator is referred to as "Mobile B" in Fig. 10. Procedure to work with the setup post connection establishment is as follows. (1) Launch Dialer or ChatON application on demo prototype device (2) Select a bend gesture from the predefined list (3) Send the selected bend gesture parameters – bend position, bend angle, direction of bend, bend extent - to demo prototype mobile. *Bend position* parameter are – top, bottom, left, right – based on the position at which device is bent. *Bend angle* gives the angle at which device is bent between 0 and 90. *Bend direction* is either inward or outward. *Bend extent* is the distance from edge where bend angle is calculated. Figure 9 gives the screen shots of bend assign and invoke procedures. Based on the definitions given in Sect. 4, target widget for ChatON is "Delete Chats" button and "Initiate Call" button for Dialer application. Figure 8 gives the sequence flow of the implementation.

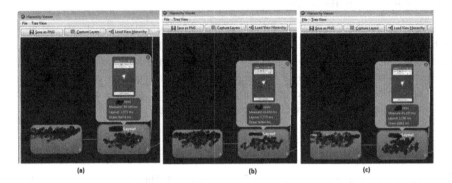

Fig. 10. Hierarchy Viewer for ChatON application (a) Screen without any highlighting (b) Selected widgets highlight (c) Target widget highlight

7 Performance Overhead

As overall rendering time is an important consideration for graphics framework, we captured rendering time using hierarchical viewer debug tool provided by Android, which provides total screen render time in terms of Measure, Layout and Draw parameters [5]. As shown in Fig. 10, rendering time of a screen for is measured for (a) Original screen when opening target application (b) Highlight widgets in target application and (c) Select target widget for gesture assignment. The average total rendering time is (a) 55.144 ms (b) 57.107 ms (c) 56.181 ms. Overhead for (b) is 1.963 ms (c) is 1.037 ms, which are minimal considering gesture procedures are not used frequently.

8 Usability Study

"Swift gestures" work with legacy applications available in market and so user evaluation is required to gain acceptance. We divided the users to two sets in the age group of 23 and 28 years. First set consist of 7 users aware of developing 3rd party applications. Second set consist of 5 novice users who use smart phones.

8.1 Usability Evaluation Sessions

Usability evaluation sessions are conducted for both the user sets as follows. (1) Moderator introduced "Swift gestures" as a presentation to the participants (2) Bend sensor emulation using mobile application is briefed. (3) Prototype setup using the two mobiles connected over Wi-Fi is introduced. (4) Users perform the bend gesture assign and invoke procedures with Dialer and ChatON applications. (5) Capture feedback from user using feedback forms. (6) Discussion based on feedback.

8.2 Feedback Questionnaire

Feedback involved answering quantitative rating as follows - between 1 and 5, 1 being highly usable - (1) Ease of using the bend assign task (2) Ease of identifying the widget for which a bend gesture is assigned (3) Ease of using the bend gesture invoke task. These are followed by descriptive questions as follows users can provide comments for these questions. (1) Improvements suggested for bend gesture assign procedure (2) Improvements suggested for bend gesture invoke procedure.

8.3 Evaluation Results

Average rating for quantitative tasks is 2.2, 3.1 and 2.4. Based on the feedback, bend assign gesture task is relatively usable when compared to other two tasks. Comments provided for the descriptive questions are consolidated as follows. (1) Seven participants felt that there needs a limit to the number of target widgets highlighted as sometimes screen looks cluttered. (2) Six participants felt that a preview of the widget action e.g. button click, is helpful. (3) Majority of participants (10 totals) felt a need to list the assigned bend gestures at a common place for latter reference. (4) Users expressed satisfaction as preload and download app interaction is uniform. Based on the comments, recommendations are (1) Widget highlighting can be controlled by graphics framework or user. (2) Assigned bend gestures are listed at a common place like settings.

9 Conclusion

In this paper, bend gestures are assigned to applications without changing source code based on graphics framework capabilities. User experience design and implementation details in device platform are described which give minimal performance overhead and validated based on a usability study. "Swift gestures" takes care of problems caused by device stiffness and deformation parameters as device bend parameters are collected dynamically while assigning.

One limitation of this work is that it doesn't take into consideration if 'associated data with gesture' is relevant at bend gesture invoke time. Swift gestures' can be extended to scroll, swipe, etc. giving due importance to user experience. We thank G Purushothama Chowdari and C Krishna Bharadwaj for their inputs in implementation and demo.

References

1. Lahey, B., Girouard, A., Burleson, W., Vertegaal, R.: Paper-phone: understanding the use of bend gestures in mobile devices with flexible electronic paper displays. In: CHI 2011 (2011)

2. App Stores: play.google.com, itunes.apple.com. www.samsungapps.com
3. Suarez, J., Murphy, R.R.: Hand gesture recognition with depth images: a review. In: 2012 IEEE RO-MAN (2012)
4. Gesture Play. www.panasonic.com
5. Developer API. https://developer.apple.com, http://developer.android.com
6. www.samsung.com/sec/galaxyround
7. Nagaraju, S.: Novel user interaction styles with flexible/rollable screens. In: CHItaly 2013, Article No. 20 (2013)
8. Samsung Graphene Structure. http://www.sait.samsung.co.kr/saithome/AboutView.do?method=get&newSeq=1091
9. Khalilbeigi, M. Lissermann, R., Mühlhäuser, M., Steimle, J.: Xpaaand: interaction techniques for rollable displays. In: CHI 2011 (2011)
10. Warren, K., Lo, J., Vadgama, V., Girouard, A.: Bending the rules: bend gesture classification for flexible displays. In: CHI 2013 (2013)
11. Wolf, K., Müller-Tomfelde, C., Cheng, K., Wechsung, I.: PinchPad: performance of touch-based gestures while grasping devices. In: Proceedings of TEI 2012, pp. 103–110 (2012)
12. Steimle, J., Jordt, A., Maes, P.: Flexpad: highly flexible bending interactions for projected handheld displays. In: Proceedings of CHI 2013 (2013)
13. Machiry, A., Tahiliani, R., Naik, M.: Dynodroid: an input generation system for Android apps. In: proceedings ESEC/FSE 2013, pp. 224–234 (2013)
14. Johan, K., Graham, W.: Feeling It: The roles of stiffness, deformation range and feedback in the control of deformable UI. In: Proceedings of ICMI 2012 (2012)

Phases of Technical Gesture Recognition

Tobias Nowack[1](✉), Nuha Suzaly[1], Stefan Lutherdt[2],
Kirsten Schürger[1], Stefan Jehring[1], Hartmut Witte[2], and Peter Kurtz[1]

[1] Ergonomics Group, Technische Universität Ilmenau, Ilmenau, Germany
{tobias.nowack,nuha.suzaly,kirsten.schuerger,
stefan.jehring,peter.kurtz}@tu-ilmenau.de
[2] Biomechatronics Group, Technische Universität Ilmenau, Ilmenau, Germany
{stefan.lutherdt,hartmut.witte}@tu-ilmenau.de

Abstract. To realize a hands-free controlled system by recognition of mid-air gestures still a bundle of serious problems exists. It is not really clarified how commands have to be interpreted by gestures because it is possible to understand the stroke phases as static as well as dynamic. But depending on which meaning will be used the gesture itself has to be executed in different manners. With video sequences of different interpretations and an online questionnaire this question was examined. The results and also pending problems led to a first solution of a mobile and hands-free controlled transportation system (for picking, lifting and transportation of small boxes) in logistic domains.

Keywords: Mid-air-gestures · Technical gesture recognition · Gesture phases · Hands-free control of robotic systems

1 Introduction

Which kind of input devices may be used in industrial environments? A lot of devices exist, like touchscreens, buttons, keyboards or remote control devices, depending on the task the user has to fulfill. But are these different devices necessary? During communication people (mostly) do not touch each other, but they of course have interaction. The main type of this interaction between people of course are spoken words. But as already Austin [1] wrote: "The third division of the external port or oratory, or of delivery, is gesture." Human beings use gestures to enhance their speech.

In industrial environments certain difficulties do exist to use speech for communication between worker and machine. Technical speech recognition needs a signal (nearly) clear from noise. German laws limit noise levels to 85 dB(A) in production areas [2]. Taking these limitations into account, for proper speech recognition a microphone has to be located directly in front of the mouth. This is in contradiction to most usual working conditions.

2 Propaedeutics

Preferring interactions without additional handheld or body mounted devices, an alternative method to interact with a machine is discussed here: the usage of mid-air gestures instead of voice commands. McNeill [3] "classif[ies] gesture movements into

M. Kurosu (Ed.): Human-Computer Interaction, Part II, HCII 2015, LNCS 9170, pp. 130–139, 2015.
DOI: 10.1007/978-3-319-20916-6_13

four major categories: iconic, metaphoric, deictic (pointing) and beat gestures". In the technical approach we propose, only iconic and pointing gestures are regarded.

To define a gesture which is not combined with speech, the technical system requires a specific hint in order to classify a certain action as a gesture. Comparing mid-air gestures with speech recognition, Wigdor [4] identifies that this "live mic problem" is similar in both interaction techniques.

Kendon [5] divided gestures into three parts called preparation (1), stroke (2) and recovery (3). Using a gesture for Human-Machine-Interface (HMI) part one and two are necessary. In most cases the preparation part has to act as a wakeup event (see "live mic problem"). This preparation must be equal even if the command and the following stroke will be different. Depending on "the live mic problem" in [6] three phases were defined: "(1) registration…, (2) continuation […] and (3) termination". Alternatively Pavlovic [7] defined that during "the preparation phase […] the hand […moves] from some resting position" to starting point. The stroke will be the interaction command.

Although a plenty of 3D recognition systems like Microsoft$^\circledR$ Kinect™ with as well a lot of libraries available for the public exist, they all do not have special algorithms to detect, whether a body movement is part of a preparation phase entering the interaction area (see Fig. 1), or if it is only a spontaneously movement. So it is necessary to newly define a wake up event during the preparation phase.

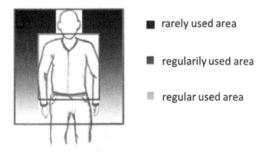

Fig. 1. Areas for human interaction (own image based on [3], modification based on [8, 9])

McNeill [3] identified that iconic gestures will be performed in the center region, and deictic gestures will be performed in more peripheral areas.

Our technical approach with vision based system uses OPEN NI (NITE) libraries to identify the "joints" corresponding to Fig. 2. These joints could be recognized easily in peripheral areas, but in the center area the vision based approach will lead to an erroneous capture of a lot of points (see Fig. 3, wrong identifications of both arms). It is obvious that a pointing gesture towards the camera system cannot be identified by this system setup.

Pavlovic [7] mentioned that "human gestures are a dynamic process, it is important to consider the temporal characteristics of gestures". He discussed the temporal aspect in order to characterize the "preparation and reaction […] by rapid change in position of the hand while the stroke […] exhibits relatively slower hand motion."

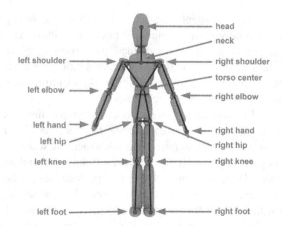

Fig. 2. Joints used for identification by OPEN NI (NITE) (modified, based on [10])

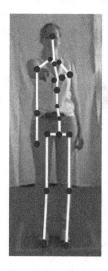

Fig. 3. Wrong identification of arm joints (vision based with OPEN NI libraries)

The discussion of the temporal aspect might also be interesting for the definition of the stroke phase. The question might be if the stroke phase of a deictic (pointing) gesture is more static, like a body posture, and the stroke phase of an iconic (in case of an action) is more dynamic? For an iconic gesture in case of a concrete event or object this question might be answered without discussion.

The model of McNeill [3] uses even five phases for one gesture-phrase (see Fig. 4). He added a pre-stroke hold (1a) and a post-stroke hold (2a). "The pre-stroke hold (optional) is the position and hand posture [...] held [...] until the stroke begins." This hold is necessary to sync speech and gesture, but is this hold also necessary for the HMI-use of gesture?

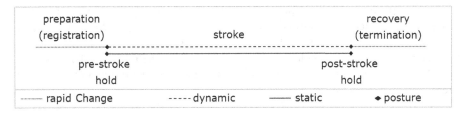

Fig. 4. Gesture phases based on [3, 5–7]

If the stroke phase (2) should be defined as dynamically, then it is necessary to regard as well as on temporal aspect as on spatial (the necessity to first enter the interaction area). Under this conditions it is possibly necessary to have a pre- or post-stroke hold or sometimes both.

3   Method

The general question of using gestures in human computer interaction has to be divided into at least two single aspects:

- The human users' comprehension and application of gestures (what does influence the user acceptance).
- How could such an intuitive gesture be recognized by a technical system?

To analyze the first aspect, we developed and applied an online questionnaire. The main questions were the following:

- Will a user accept to command a technical system, e.g. a personal assisting robot, with gestures?
- Is there a direct relationship between intended commands and preferred gestures? For example in the case the user wants to force the system to approach himself, we predict that he will use a dynamic stroke phase, like beckoning.
- Will be a pre- or post-stroke hold or both necessary if the stroke phase is dynamic?

To answer these questions a set of video sequences were recorded. To limit the amount of possible commands, six commands were selected and rated as static or dynamic. The three predicted dynamic commands were "come over", "lift up" and "turn around", and the three predicted static commands were "register", "stop" and "select a (certain) object". For each of these commands two dynamic and two static gestures were presented. According to the definition of Pavlovic [7], each of the gestures starts and ends outside the interaction area, and all video sequences start with the rapid move into the interaction area (preparation phase).

Depending on the above mentioned definition the question could still not be answered clearly, when (at which time) and/or where (at which position) the stroke phase does start. The answer to this question leads to the necessity of an explicit description of gestures, which finally is useable in identification algorithms of technical systems.

An example to explain this approach could be the pointing gesture, which could be defined as to be static (posture) at an shoulder angle of more than 20° and an elbow angle of more than 160°(gained during the stroke phase (2) and hold for a time of minimally 5 s. (post-stroke hold (2a), see Fig. 5). During the recovery phase the user can release his arm and return to the resting position, the gesture recognition is finished already.

Fig. 5. Static post-stroke hold phase of pointing gesture

To fulfil requirements of the online survey to give two opportunities of each command a second video, presenting a dynamic stroke phase, was necessary. This pointing gesture could also be described only as dynamic stroke with following procedure: move the hand up to the shoulder, and direct it from the shoulder to the object chosen. After the arm reaches its fully stretched position, the interaction area directly has to be left (without post-stroke hold) to the resting position with hands on the hips (see Fig. 5).

If this dynamic definition of gestures shall be used for recognition in technical systems it will provide some additional problems. An explanation will be given by pointing gesture like above. Like shown in Fig. 6 it is generally difficult to recognize the current position of hand-arm during a pointing gesture. As a dynamic gesture the hand has to be observed the whole time, and online the algorithm has to recognize this as the movement of the hand joint. Because the aim is to detect that one certain object was pointed to continuously, a resulting pointing vector (which matches the mean point where the desired object is placed) has to be calculated. By the use of static gesture approach it is much easier to calculate this vector only by following the line from shoulder joint over hand joint to an object after the post-stroke hold was performed.

Fig. 6. Dynamic stroke phase of pointing gesture

In dynamic gesture case the vector changes all the time, and additionally the elbow angle has to be monitored. Only if the elbow angle is larger than 160° and after this, the arm left the calculated vector, the desired gesture was confirmed to have been performed. But the thresholds and criteria for this moment of leaving the calculated vector still have to be defined.

The online questionnaire was created to investigate only the first aspect. The usability definition exposes the parameters effectiveness, efficiency and satisfaction to measure how a user will achieve specific goals in particular environments [11]. To evaluate *effectiveness* and *efficiency*, a first prototype of the technical gesture recognition system has to be available. If it would be available [12] we propose to measure *fatigue, naturalness, gesture duration* and *accuracy* as indicators for the quality of a gesture. This method only could be used if the person under analysis could be observed optically. So in this early morning of the study and with an online questionnaire only the satisfaction could be analyzed. The dimensions for the *satisfaction* are *acceptance* and *intuitiveness* of gestures shown. As *intuitiveness* is an abstract term it is not as easy to evaluate as *acceptance*. With the online questionnaire *acceptance* will be evaluated by the following questions:

- Can I imagine that I interact with a mid-air gesture?
- Do I feel really strange when I'm interacting with mid-air gestures?
- Do I think that interacting with gestures is complicated?
- Do I have fun when I'm interacting with gestures?

Another research question was to examine, how *intuitiveness of gestures* could be identified and what does *intuitiveness* of a gesture generally mean.

As indicators to answer these questions three criteria were used: *awareness level, authenticity* and *comprehensibility*. The participants had to rate the gestures with a four-stage scale (it fits, it quite fits, it doesn't rather fit, it doesn't fit). The following questions had to be answered:

- Do I know the gesture from my daily conversation?
- Do I find the gesture to be authentic?
- If I cannot talk, would I use this gesture?
- Do I feel strange/uncomfortable when I have to perform this gestures?
- Can I understand why this gesture should be used for this command?
- Are the steps to perform the gesture easy?

To compare dynamic and static stroke phases of a gesture with the user understanding of the type of command (dynamic or static) the following items had been used:

- Rate the gestures with a four-stage scale (static, rather static, rather dynamic, and dynamic) about your understanding of the command.
- List the gestures presented in accordance to your understanding of the command.

4 Results

The survey was finished by 90 participants, mostly students from Technische Universität Ilmenau, 73 % of these in age between 21 years and 30 years.

Figure 7 shows the main results of the acceptance test. About 70 % of participants could accept to perform a mid-air gesture to interact with a technical system in their workspace.

Fig. 7. Assessment order results of general acceptance of mid-air gestures

For test of intuitiveness it first was necessary to review the chosen items. As Table 1 shows relations between all items are significant at the 5 % level, but only between the four items "gesture is known", "gesture is authentic", "if speaking is impossible using this gesture instead" and "understanding gesture in connection with command" the interrelation is significantly positive at 5 % level. To describe intuitiveness with only one consolidated value the average rating of the six items is used. To raise the weight of the items with best interrelation and highest correlation, the items "gesture is authentic" and "understanding gesture in connection with command" were weighted double.

Table 1. Relation between the items to measure the intuitiveness (as example the command "register").

r_{SP} / p-Wert	gesture is known	gesture is authentic	if speeking is impossible using this gesture instead	understanding gesture in connection with command	not feeling strange performing this gesture	gesture is easy to perform	whole scale
gesture is known	1	0,562	0,676	0,569	0,082	0,156	0,782
		<0,0001	<0,0001	<0,0001	0,446	0,156	<0,0001
gesture is authentic	0,562	1	0,626	0,55	0,327	0,286	0,743
	<0,0001		<0,0001	<0,0001	0,002	0,007	<0,0001
if speeking is impossible using this gesture instead	0,676	0,626	1	0,545	0,25	0,329	0,83
	<0,0001	<0,0001		<0,0001	0,019	0,002	<0,0001
understanding gesture in connection with command	0,569	0,55	0,545	1	0,243	0,243	0,769
	<0,0001	<0,0001	<0,0001		0,023	0,023	<0,0001
not feeling strange performing this gesture	0,082	0,327	0,25	0,243	1	0,306	0,486
	0,446	0,002	0,019	0,023		0,004	<0,0001
gesture is easy to perform	0,156	0,286	0,329	0,243	0,306	1	0,451
	0,147	0,007	0,002	0,023	0,004		<0,0001
whole scale	0,782	0,743	0,83	0,769	0,486	0,451	1
	<0,0001	<0,0001	<0,0001	<0,0001	<0,0001	<0,0001	

The participants had to give an explicit order of all gestures for one command. The corresponding values have been compared. The results shown in Table 2 demonstrate

Table 2. Preference to dynamic and static commands

	dynamic commands			static commands		
	come over	lift up	turn around	register	stop	select
user preference by order (place 1)	dynamically	dynamically	dynamically	dynamically	statically	statically
	79%	37%	72%	50%	91%	79%
user preference by intuitiveness value	dynamic	static / static	dynamic	dynamic	static	static
	(1.4)	(2.0)	(2.2)	(1.4)	(1.2)	(1.3)
significant relation between command specification and user interpretation	yes	no	yes	yes	no	yes
user understanding of command	dynamically	dynamically	dynamically	statically	statically	dynamically

that the predicted understanding of the type of a gesture is mostly equal to the intuitive understanding of a gesture.

But as shown at the command lift up, it is sometimes difficult (for probands and probably for later potential users) to define what makes a gesture to be statical or dynamic. As an example the value of intuitiveness of three gestures for command "lift up" was equal 2.0. These gestures were listed at first place for this command by 24 % up to 37 % of probands. That means that half of the probands understand this command as statical (but with two different gestures), and another third as dynamic. Additionally the second dynamic gesture was not accepted as intuitive (value of intuitiveness of 2.8) and was classified as not qualified for the command by 50 % of the probands (Fig. 8).

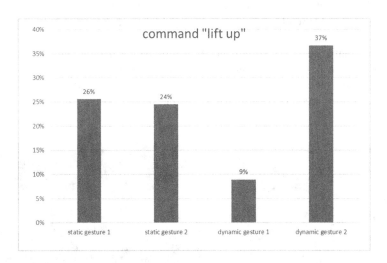

Fig. 8. Order of user preference (for command "lift up" at position 1)

This part of research shows that it is probably impossible to find a definite type of gesture for all commands, which implies that it is better to have two or more implementations. Thus the later users are able to choose which one fits best at their own, and the system can be designed as a self-learning system for these gesture implementations.

5 Summary and Outlook

As shown by the example of only one command ("lift up") it is not easy to exactly predefine if a gesture will be accepted by the user in a special dynamic or static version. Even as has been demonstrated with the pointing gesture in chapter three it is not even easy to define what a dynamic or a static gesture is. Even as McNeill defines that the preparation phase is used to enter the interaction area the stroke phase has a dynamic part, and so it is only possible to define or determine the difference(s) between a static and a dynamic gesture as time during the pre- or post-stroke hold.

The two definitions of gestures described (cp. Chapter 3) show how many parameters have to be calculated during gesture recognition. But in most setups not only two gestures are needed to use for interaction with a technical systems. Additional algorithms to distinguish different commands are necessary to solve this problem of complexity.

The next step of the development of robust mid-air gestures for human machine interaction is to define more parameters to describe a gesture (and its phases). This description of a gesture to humans in the best manner will be a real presenter, showing how the gesture will be performed. Only the second best way is showing a good performed and recorded video sequence which shows all the desired details.

For the recognition by a technical system all the general parameters like joints, angels or time aspects need to be identified and described. These parameters must fit for a set of gestures. Currently a first test system was created with only one pointing gesture.

In the current state of that system a combination between a pointing gesture for the estimated position (see Fig. 9 a) and an image based touch confirmation for the fine position (see Fig. 9 b) is used. This combination is necessary due to the multiple problems of robust recognition, to have a safe and proper system for use in industrial

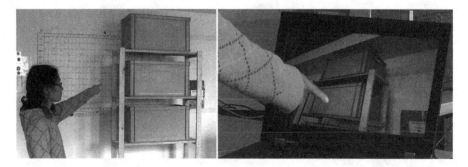

Fig. 9. (a) Pointing gesture towards a box (left); (b) confirm selection with support of an image on a touch screen (right).

environments. Using this recognition algorithm a personal assisting system for lifting and carrying of small boxes (project called KLARA) will execute the lifting and carrying process. For this system the described principles of execution and detection of mid-air-gestures are used. Currently only the static pointing gesture, described in chapter 3, is used to select a certain box. Even to physically restricted persons this solution will give the ability to handle these boxes, because the system can pick boxes from the floor or from above users head only by using the pointing gesture.

References

1. Austin, G.: Chironomia; or a Treatise on rethorical delivery. Printed for T. Cadell & W. Davies in the Strand; by Bulmer, Cleveland-Row, St. Jame's, London (1806)
2. LärmVibrationsArbSchV: Verordnung zum Schutz der Beschäftigten vor Gefährdungen durch Lärm und Vibrationen (Lärm- und Vibrations- Arbeitsschutzverordnung - LärmVibrationsArbSchV), 06 March 2007 . http://bundesrecht.juris.de/bundesrecht/l_rmvibrationsarbschv/gesamt.pdf. Accessed January 2015
3. McNeill, D.: Hand and Mind. What Gestures Reveal About Thought. University of Chicago Press, Chicago (1992)
4. Wigdor, D., Wixon, D.: Brave Nui World Designing Natural User Interfaces for Touch and Gesture. Morgan Kaufmann/Elsevier, Burlington (2011)
5. Kendon, A.: Gesture Visible Action as Utterance. Cambridge University Press, Cambridge (2004)
6. Walter, R., Bailly, G., Müller, J.: StrikeAPose: revealing mid-air gestures on public displays. In: Mackay, W.E. und A. Special Interest Group on Computer-Human Interaction (Hg.) Proceedings of the SIGCHI Conference on Human Factors in Computing Systems, pp. 841–850. ACM (2013)
7. Pavlovic, V.I., Sharma, R., Huang, T.S.: Visual interpretation of hand gestures for human-computer interaction: a review. IEEE Trans. Pattern Anal. Mach. Intell. 19(7), 677–695 (1997)
8. MICROSOFT: Human Interface Guidelines V1.8 (HIG). https://msdn.microsoft.com/en-us/library/jj663791.aspx and http://go.microsoft.com/fwlink/?LinkID=247735. Accessed February 2015
9. Deutsche Gesetzliche Unfallversicherung (DGUV) (Hg.), Ergonomische Maschinengestaltung. von Werkzeugmaschinen der Metallbearbeitung. Berlin (2010). http://publikationen.dguv.de/dguv/pdf/10002/i-5048-1.pdf
10. thearmagamer. Wooden dummy (rigged). Blend Swap, LLC (2014). http://www.blendswap.com/blends/view/72452. Accessed January 2015
11. DIN EN ISO 9241-11, Ergonomische Anforderungen für Bürotätigkeiten mit Bildschirmgeräten Teil 11: Anforderungen an die Gebrauchstauglichkeit – Leitsätze, Beuth Verlag GmbH, Berlin (1999)
12. Barclay, K., Wei, D., Lutteroth, C., Sheehan, R.: A quantitative quality model for gesture based user interfaces. In: Proceedings of the 23rd Australian Computer-Human Interaction Conference (OzCHI 2011), pp. S.31–S.39. ACM, New York (2011). http://doi.acm.org/10.1145/2071536.2071540

Automatic Classification Between Involuntary and Two Types of Voluntary Blinks Based on an Image Analysis

Hironobu Sato[1(✉)], Kiyohiko Abe[1], Shoichi Ohi[2],
and Minoru Ohyama[2]

[1] College of Engineering, Kanto Gakuin University, 1-50-1 Mutsuura-Higashi,
Kanazawa-Ku, Yokohama-Shi, Kanagawa 236-8501, Japan
{hsato,abe}@kanto-gakuin.ac.jp
[2] School of Information Environment, Tokyo Denki University,
2-1200, Muzaigakuendai, Inzai-Shi, Chiba 270-1382, Japan

Abstract. Several input systems using eye blinking for communication with the severely disabled have been proposed. Eye blinking is either voluntary or involuntary. Previously, we developed an image analysis method yielding an open-eye area as a measurement value. We can extract a blinking wave pattern using statistical parameters yielded from the measurement values. Based on this method, we also proposed an automatic classification method for both involuntary blinking and one type of voluntary blinking. In this paper, we aim to classify a new type of voluntary blinking in addition to the two previous known types. For classifying these three blinking types, a new feature parameter is proposed. In addition, we propose a new classification method based on the measurement results. Our experimental results indicate a successful classification rate of approximately 95 % for a sample of seven subjects using our new classification method between involuntary blinking and two types of voluntary blinking.

Keywords: Eye blink detection · Input interface · Automatic classification · Voluntary eye blink · Involuntary eye blink

1 Introduction

Several input systems using eye blinking have been proposed [1–7], one of the purposes of which is communication for the severely disabled. Eye blinking is either voluntary or involuntary [8]. A system employing a human-computer interface based on eye-blink information is used to distinguish a user's input requests based on the classification of voluntary blinks. For application to human-computer interfaces, we previously proposed an automatic classification method for both involuntary blinking and one type of voluntary blinking [9]. However, if the types of classifiable voluntary blinking increase, we can assign an individual command to each type. Applying this to a human-computer interface will significantly improve the efficiency when inputting commands.

© Springer International Publishing Switzerland 2015
M. Kurosu (Ed.): Human-Computer Interaction, Part II, HCII 2015, LNCS 9170, pp. 140–149, 2015.
DOI: 10.1007/978-3-319-20916-6_14

In previous studies, several measurement methods using an image analysis for eye blinking were proposed. Based on these measurement methods, several classification methods for voluntary blinking using a special pattern of eye blinks were proposed [1–5]. As a special pattern of eye blinks, some systems employ a blinking duration of several seconds [1–4]. For one of these systems, multiple levels of thresholds in duration were set to distinguish additional input requests in addition to standard inputs [4]. A classification system for voluntary blinking using multiple blinks was also proposed [5]. In this system, a sequence of multiple blinks is assigned to a command that emulates a mouse click. By performing many more voluntary blinks, users can input a multiple click command along with standard click commands into the system. However, employing such special blinking types may be a burden to users.

Previously, we developed a classification method for both involuntary blinking and one type of voluntary blinking, i.e., blinking firmly. The purpose of this paper is to classify a new type of voluntary blinking in addition to our proposed classification between involuntary blinking and one type of voluntary blinking. To achieve this purpose, we introduce a new blinking parameter. Based on this parameter, we also propose a new classification method for involuntary blinking and the two types of voluntary blinking.

2   Eye Blinking Measurement Based on an Image Analysis

Several measurement methods for eye blinking have been traditionally proposed. One of these measurement methods is the electro-oculogram (EOG) [6], [8], which measures the difference in potential between the retina and cornea from electrodes placed near the user's eye. On the other hand, a detection method using an infrared sensor is proposed [7]. In a system employing this method, infrared LEDs or other lighting equipment emit light to the user's eyelid. A variation of the reflected light is measured using an infrared sensor. These measurement methods require some specific equipment for eye-blink detection. Hence, we employ a method based on an image analysis for measuring eye blinking [9]. This method can be set up with a PC and a video camera for home use.

Typically, a high-speed video camera has been required for measuring eye blinking in detail [10]. However, we developed a method for measuring eye blinking using field images from interlaced images [9], which we refer to as a "frame-splitting method." This developed method yields a time resolution double that of a standard NTSC or 1080i Hi-Vision camera, i.e., 60 fps. Using field images split through this method, our measurement system calculates the pixels of an open-eye area as a measurement value. A detailed eye-blinking wave pattern is then obtained by recording these values in a time series.

We then employ an automatic extraction method using statistical parameters calculated from this pattern [9]. The thresholds for this extraction are determined by the following equations:

$$Th_1 = \overline{E} + 2\sigma \qquad (1)$$

$$Th_2 = \overline{E} - 2\sigma, \qquad (2)$$

where $\overline{E}$ is the average difference value when the eye is open, and σ (sigma) is its standard deviation. The difference value is defined as the difference in measurement values yielded from a sample point and the immediately previous point. If the difference value is larger than Th_1, the sample point indicates that the eye is opening. Similarly, if the difference value is smaller than Th_2, the sample point indicates that the eye is closing. The part between the closing sample points and the opening sample points is extracted as a wave pattern of an eye blink.

3 Classification of Blink Types

Previously, our classification method was able to classify blinking types between involuntary blinking and one type of voluntary blinking when performed firmly. To increase the classifiable type of voluntary blinking, we need to introduce a new type of voluntary blinking. In this chapter, we introduce two types of voluntary blinking in which a new blinking type is added. We also show a new parameter for classifying these types of eye blinks.

3.1 Two Types of Voluntary Blinking

In addition to standard voluntary blinking, blinks of several seconds in duration, as well as multiple blinks, can be employed as additional blinking types. However, a system using blinking of several seconds in duration can make users feel that their time is being wasted [5]. This type of voluntary blinking may burden users. If multiple blinks are employed as additional voluntary blinking, the user needs to count the number of voluntary blinks while performing voluntary blinking. This parallel operation may place a cognitive burden on users more than simple blinking, which may cause user fatigue. Psychological burden, such as fatigue, may affect the wave patterns of eye blinks [8]. Thus, our new classification method employs two types of voluntary blinking, i.e., "blinking firmly" and "blinking firmly for a brief time." Figure 1 shows the wave patterns of eye blinks measured during our experiments.

The x-axis in Fig. 1 indicates the sampling point, and the y-axis indicates the open-eye area pixels. These plots were normalized based on the estimated value of the first field image. The black line is a wave pattern from blinking firmly, and the gray line is a wave pattern from blinking firmly for a brief time. Finally, the dashed line is a wave pattern for involuntary blinking. From Fig. 1, we can see that the difference in duration between blinking firmly, which we proposed previously, and blinking firmly for a brief time, is significant. However, the difference in duration between blinking firmly for a brief time and involuntary blinking may be small.

In our previous studies, we used the duration of eye blinking as a parameter for classifying between involuntary blinking and blinking firmly, which is one type of

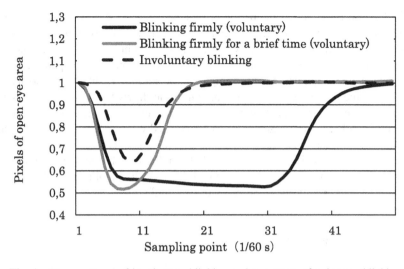

Fig. 1. Wave patterns of involuntary blinking and two types of voluntary blinking

voluntary blinking. However, from Fig. 1, we can estimate that the duration for blinking firmly for a brief time and that for involuntary blinking are similar. Thus, classifying these three types of eye blinks with a high degree of accuracy using only this parameter is difficult to achieve. We therefore propose an integrated value of the amplitude as a new parameter for this type of classification.

3.2 New Parameter for Classification of Blinking Types

Previously, we investigated the feature values of an eye blink based on employing the duration and maximum amplitude as parameters. Figure 2 shows the feature parameters of an eye blink.

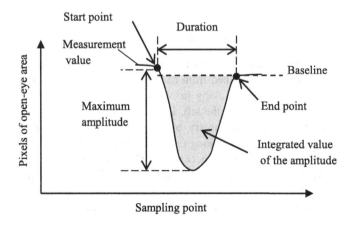

Fig. 2. Wave pattern parameter definitions

The duration is defined as the period of time between the start point and end point of an extracted wave pattern. The maximum amplitude is defined as the difference in amplitude between the measurement value of the start point and that of the point that changes the most from the start point. In this paper, we propose a new parameter, i.e., an integrated value (summation) of the amplitude, in addition to the parameters used in our previous studies. We define the summation of the difference between the baseline and measurement values as an integrated value of the amplitude, which is shown in the shaded region in Fig. 2. The baseline for each extracted wave pattern is set individually as the smaller of the start and end points. This new parameter is calculated based on the time integration (summation) of the amplitude from the start point to the end point. We expect that this new parameter, the integrated value of the amplitude, will show significant differences among the three types of eye blinks.

4   Metering Experiments

To extract two types of voluntary blinks, we conducted two 30-s long experiments. Before the start of each experiment, the subjects were asked to keep their eyes open for 3 s to estimate the thresholds, Th_1 and Th_2, of our extraction method, which utilizes Eqs. (1) and (2) described in chapter 2. During the measurements, beeping sounds were generated at random intervals of 5 to 7 s. For experiment 1, we detected their voluntary blinks after asking the subjects to close their eyes firmly upon hearing a beep. For experiment 2, we instructed them to briefly close their eyes firmly. We also detected their involuntary blinks through the same experiments.

Our measurement system includes a Hi-vision video camera (Sony HDR-HC9, for home use) and a PC (OS, Microsoft Windows 7; CPU, 2.8 GHz Intel(R) CoreTM i7). In each of our experiments, an image sequence of each subject's eye blinking was recorded and stored on the PC. We used the PC to analyze these recorded image sequences. In this chapter, we describe the measurement results for the parameters obtained from successfully extracted blinks using Eqs. (1) and (2). We also discuss the measurement results.

4.1   Measurement Results of Parameters

Figure 3 shows the measurement results for the eye-blinking duration. In Fig. 3, the y-axis indicates the duration obtained from each type of eye blinking. The bar graphs indicate the average values for blinking firmly, blinking firmly for a brief time, and involuntary blinking in order, from the left. Figure 3 makes it clear that the difference between blinking firmly and involuntary blinking was significant for each subject. Similarly, the difference between blinking firmly and blinking firmly for a brief time is also large. However, the difference between blinking firmly for a brief time and involuntary blinking was slight for several of the subjects, including subjects A and G.

Figure 4 shows the measurement results for the maximum amplitude parameter. In Fig. 4, the y-axis indicates the normalized maximum amplitude of an eye blink. The bar

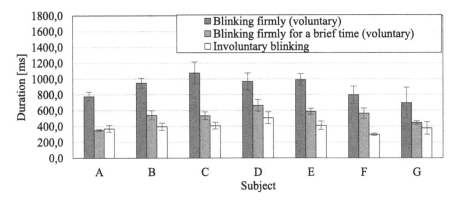

Fig. 3. Measurement results of the duration

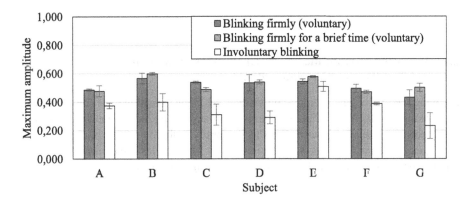

Fig. 4. Measurement results of the maximum amplitude

graphs in Fig. 4 indicate the average values of this parameter, which were obtained from each type of eye blinking in the same way as shown in Fig. 3.

In the comparison of this parameter, the difference between the two types of voluntary blinking is slight, and the difference between each type of voluntary blinking and involuntary blinking is significant for many of the subjects. However, the differences among the three blinking types are slight in certain cases, such as subject E. Additionally, there are significant individual differences in the relations based on the magnitudes of this parameter when obtained from the three types of blinking.

Figure 5 shows the measurement results based on the integrated value of the amplitude. In Fig. 5, the y-axis indicates this parameter, and the bar graphs indicate the average values of the parameter obtained from each type of eye blinking in the same way as in Fig. 3.

The results shown in Fig. 5 make it clear that blinking firmly has the largest integrated value of the amplitude, followed by blinking firmly for a brief time, and involuntary blinking. In addition, the differences between each blinking type are significant. Based on this tendency, we propose a new classification method between involuntary blinking and the two types of voluntary blinking.

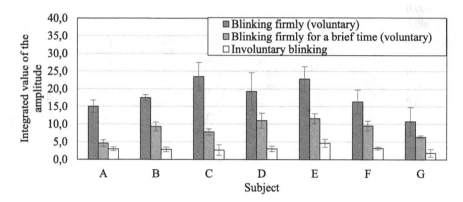

Fig. 5. Measurement results of the integrated value of the amplitude

4.2 Automatic Classification Between Involuntary Blinking and Two Types of Voluntary Blinking

The integrated value of the amplitude tends to be largest for blinking firmly, followed by blinking firmly for a brief time and involuntary blinking. A new classification method based on this tendency enables us to classify both involuntary blinking and the two types of voluntary blinking. The thresholds for the classification of these three blinking types are determined through the following equations:

$$\mathrm{Th}_{ia1} = \frac{\overline{\mathrm{Ia}_{v1}} + \overline{\mathrm{Ia}_{v2}}}{2} \tag{3}$$

$$\mathrm{Th}_{ia2} = \frac{\overline{\mathrm{Ia}_{v2}} + \overline{\mathrm{Ia}_{iv}}}{2}, \tag{4}$$

where $\overline{\mathrm{Ia}_{v1}}$, $\overline{\mathrm{Ia}_{v2}}$, and $\overline{\mathrm{Ia}_{iv}}$ are the average integrated values of the amplitude obtained from blinking firmly, blinking firmly for a brief time, and involuntary blinking, respectively.

Our new classification method compares each threshold and the integrated value of the amplitude obtained from the extracted blinks. If the value of this parameter is larger than threshold Th_{ia1}, the blinking type is classified as blinking firmly. Otherwise, if the value is larger than threshold Th_{ia2}, the blinking type is classified as blinking firmly for a brief time. Finally, if the value is not larger than threshold Th_{ia2}, the blinking type is classified as involuntary blinking. These thresholds were determined for each of the subjects and using the same experimental data as the estimation of the classification rates. The classification results of the blinking types using our proposing method are shown in Table 1.

Table 1 shows the number of extracted blinks that were classified into the three blinking types for each subject. This table also shows the number of classification errors that occurred during these experiments using our proposing method. Table 2 shows the results of the classification rates calculated using the numbers of classified blinks and classification errors listed in Table 1.

Table 1. Classification results for involuntary blinking and two types of voluntary blinking

Subject	Number of extracted blinks			Number of classification errors		
	Blinking firmly	Blinking firmly for a brief time	Involuntary blinking	Blinking firmly	Blinking firmly for a brief time	Involuntary blinking
A	5	5	18	0	1	2
B	5	5	29	0	0	0
C	4	4	20	0	0	0
D	4	5	21	1	0	0
E	4	5	9	0	0	0
F	5	5	5	1	0	0
G	4	4	16	1	0	0

Table 2. Classification rates between involuntary blinking and two types of voluntary blinking [%]

Subject	Blinking firmly	Blinking firmly for a brief time	Involuntary blinking	Total
A	100	80.0	88.9	89.6
B	100	100	100	100
C	100	100	100	100
D	75.0	100	100	91.7
E	100	100	100	100
F	80.0	100	100	93.3
G	75.0	100	100	91.7
Average	90.0	97.1	98.4	95.2

The results of the total classification rate in Table 2 show that the average rate of successful classification is approximately 95 % for the experimental sample of seven subjects using our new method for classification between involuntary blinking and the two types of voluntary blinking. Previously, several methods for classification between long and short voluntary blinks were proposed [1], [3]. These methods employed an image analysis, which calculates the correlation coefficients of the template matching as an eye-blinking wave pattern. This definition of the wave pattern is different from that used in our measurement method. However, these methods classify the blinking types based on the duration parameter, which is the same as in our method. Grauman et al. conducted an experiment to investigate the classification rate using long and short voluntary blinks for 15 subjects [1]. The results of this experiment show a successful classification rate of 93.0 %. On the other hand, Królak et al. reported a classification rate of 98.31 % [3] using these types of voluntary blinking. However, in each experiment described in these studies, a short voluntary blink and an involuntary blink are treated as equal. In other words, these types of blinks are not classified. Our experimental results show similar classification rates as these previous experiments. In addition, our experimental results also show that our proposed method can properly classify between involuntary blinking and the two types of voluntary blinking.

5 Conclusions

In previous studies, we developed a measurement method using an image analysis to yield variations in an open-eye area as a wave pattern. This measurement method enables us to extract wave patterns of eye blinks. Using this measurement method, our experimental system can classify between involuntary blinking and one type of voluntary blinking, i.e., blinking firmly.

In this paper, we added a new type of voluntary blinking, and measured three types of eye blinking: blinking firmly, blinking firmly for a brief time, and involuntary blinking. For classifying these blinking types with a high degree of accuracy, we introduced a new blinking parameter, i.e., the integrated value of the amplitude. This parameter was compared for each blinking type, and other parameters that we previously proposed, i.e., the duration and maximum amplitude, were also compared. Based on the results obtained from this comparison, we proposed a new method for classifying these three blinking types. Using our proposed method, we yielded an average classification rate of approximately 95 % for seven subjects.

In the future, we plan to investigate the efficiency of our proposed method experimentally using additional subjects. The classification method proposed in this paper was designed on the basis of a single parameter, the integrated value of the amplitude. To yield a higher degree of accuracy, we also plan to consider a better method using the multiple parameters described herein.

Acknowledgements. This work was supported by JSPS KAKENHI Grant Number 24700598. We would like to thank Mr. Shogo Matsuno, a doctoral student at the University of Electro-Communications, for helpful discussions.

References

1. Grauman, K., Betke, M., Lombardi, J., Gips, J., Bradski, G.R.: Communication via eye blinks and eyebrow raises: video-based human-computer interfaces. Univ. Access Inf. Soc. **2** (4), 359–373 (2003)
2. Missimer, E., Betke, M.: Blink and wink detection for mouse pointer control. In: 3rd International Conference on Pervasive Technologies Related to Assistive Environments (PETRA 2010). Article 23, pp. 1–8. ACM, New York (2010)
3. Królak, A., Paweł, S.: Eye-blink detection system for human-computer interaction. Univ. Access Inf. Soc. **11**(4), 409–419 (2012)

4. MacKenzie, I.S., Behrooz, A.: BlinkWrite: efficient text entry using eye blinks. Univ. Access Inf. Soc. **10**(1), 69–80 (2011)
5. Krapic, L., Kristijan, L., Sandi, L.: Integrating blink click interaction into a head tracking system: implementation and usability issues. Univ. Access Inf. Soc. **14**(2), 247–264 (2013)
6. Hori, J., Sakano, K., Saitoh, Y.: Development of a communication support device controlled by eye movements and voluntary eye blink. Trans. Inf. Syst. IEICE **89**(6), 1790–1797 (2006)
7. Lim, H., Vinay, K.S.: Design of healthcare system for disable person using eye blinking. In: 4th Annual ACIS International. Conference on Computer and Information Science (ICIS 2005), pp. 551–555. IEEE, New York (2005)
8. Stern, J.A., Walrath, L.C., Goldstein, R.: The endogenous eyeblink. Psychophysiology **21** (1), 22–33 (1984)
9. Abe, K., Sato, H., Matsuno, S., Ohi, S., Ohyama, M.: Automatic classification of eye blink types using a frame-splitting method. In: Harris, D. (ed.) EPCE 2013, Part I. LNCS, vol. 8019, pp. 117–124. Springer, Heidelberg (2013)
10. Ohzeki, K., Ryo, B.: Video analysis for detecting eye blinking using a high-speed camera. In: 40th Asilomar Conference on Signals, Systems and Computers, pp. 1081–1085. IEEE, New York (2006)

Touch-based and Haptic Interaction

GUIs with Haptic Interfaces

M. Arda Aydin[1], Nergiz Ercil Cagiltay[2(✉)], Erol Ozcelik[1],
Emre Tuner[2], Hilal Sahin[2], and Gul Tokdemir[3]

[1] Department of Computer Engineering, Atilim University, Ankara, Turkey
ardaaydin@outlook.com, erol.ozcelik@atilim.edu.tr
[2] Department of Software Engineering, Atilim University, Ankara, Turkey
{necagiltay, tuneremre, hilal91sahin}@gmail.com
[3] Department of Computer Engineering, Cankaya University, Ankara, Turkey
gtokdemir@gmail.com

Abstract. While there are many studies regarding utilization of haptic feedback to enhance desktop GUIs and utilizing haptic devices as additional interfaces to improve performance in current interaction techniques, there are not many studies that uses haptic device as a primary input device. In this study, we present an experimentation conducted with 30 students, comparing performance of a haptic device with mouse to use a GUI elements commonly used with mouse gestures. This study is inspired by a system that utilizes both mouse and a haptic device, thus also taking task switching into consideration. We conclude that it is possible to achieve an acceptable performance with a haptic device in a desktop-like GUI but further study and experimentation is necessary.

Keywords: Human-computer interaction · Haptic devices · GUI

1 Introduction

The term haptic relates to or proceeds from the sense of touch, and with developments in technology, and haptic interfaces were developed to allow a user to receive tactile feedback via movement of a limb or the head [1]. There are two primary types of haptic devices as follows: force feedback devices and tactile displays, where the former provides reacting forces to our movements in space, and the latter targets the skin [2]. In force feedback haptic devices, movements of user are measured and a force is generated in response as a virtual representation of the displayed physical environment. These devices have degrees of freedom that corresponds to axes where the touched end of the haptic device can move along, ranging from 1 to many (e.g. 3 matches to graphical three-dimensional space) [2]. Sensable Devices' PHANToM is noteworthy due to it being the first commercially available force feedback display with 3 degrees of freedom [2]. As haptic technologies have advanced, haptic interfaces became more affordable and accessible. Sensory stimuli became more believable [3] which enables users to interact with computers in a more "realistic" way with the feedback provided, guiding the user through the task in a non-visual way. Haptic devices are now being used in different areas, from professional areas such as surgery simulation and animation to more consumer-focused markets such as gaming [3].

© Springer International Publishing Switzerland 2015
M. Kurosu (Ed.): Human-Computer Interaction, Part II, HCII 2015, LNCS 9170, pp. 153–164, 2015.
DOI: 10.1007/978-3-319-20916-6_15

One way to utilize haptic devices is to use it as an input device to manipulate desktop GUIs on computers. Certainly, mouse is the most widespread input device, along with keyboard, and there have been attempts to enhance it with haptic feedback to improve user performance. Studies exploring the effects of haptically enhanced mouse resulted in reduced error rates but similar speed, which are later described in this paper.

There are studies which incorporate haptic devices to control desktop like GUIs. A study incorporating a new technique enabled it as a secondary input device with only haptic feedback to control a palette-like toolbox that is mostly seen in graphic manipulation software such as Adobe Photoshop, and mouse in dominant hand to apply the selected tool, showed that similar performance was obtained, but traditional interface was faster and more preferred [4]. Another study used a haptic device to control a desktop GUI to solve multi-target haptic interaction problems and results showed that although haptic enhancements did reduce error rates, the speed was not improved [5].

In this paper, we show it is possible to manipulate desktop like GUIs with haptic devices, while taking task switching paradigm into consideration for both switching between tasks and also the input devices, mouse and haptic device.

On the following sections of this paper, we present the background study consisting of mouse as input device, haptic interfaces and previous studies on utilizing haptic enhancements and interfaces for manipulation of desktop-like GUIs, in addition to task-switching paradigm, followed by experimentation details and tasks. Later, we present the analysis of obtained results and finally, we present conclusions and discussions of this study.

2 Background of Study

2.1 Mouse as Input Device

As an input device, mouse has some advantages over other input devices; its widespread availability and acceptance, and it being non-obstructive to user's view despite the requirement of hand-eye coordination, as movements of cursor needs to be projected on the movements of user [6].

Mouse can be used to point at an object, to move it or click it. It can be stated that pointing actually consists of three stages which is going towards target, reducing the speed and then aiming the target, respectively. Clicking adds an additional stage where pressing/releasing mouse button is necessary whilst mouse is kept stationary. Lastly, moving an object would require repetition of those four stages to be done twice, as the steps needed to move an object consists of hovering mouse over the target, clicking the mouse button to select and holding the button pressed during the movement, and releasing the mouse button when object has been positioned at the desired spot [6].

Fitts' law predicts that the time to acquire a target is logarithmically related to the distance over the target size [7]. It has been used prevalently to study and compare input devices such as mouse and trackball [8–10] in addition to predicting user performance in some tasks such as point-select and point-drag using those input devices.

Although Fitts' Law can be used to compare mouse movements, on the basis of target variables and movements speed, it only applies to error-free movement [6]. Moreover, there are cases where Fitts Law results in incorrect predictions such when the input device is not suited to Fitts' law, such as isometric joysticks that are force sensing and endure negligible human limb motion [11]. Fitts Law has also some limitations such as not covering the performance difference between preferred and non-preferred hands [12] and the observation that subjects were uniformly more accurate when arm motions were towards the body than when they were away from the body movements [7]. In addition, Fitts Law doesn't not work for trajectory based activities such as drawing, writing and steering [13]. Lastly, it does not address parameters such as system response time, mental preparation time for user, home timing, etc. [11].

2.2 Haptic Feedback with Current Interaction Techniques

Haptics have been added to interaction techniques previously, especially with mouse featuring haptic feedback to indicate certain occasions to user such as when a cursor reaches a certain point, or when they enter a certain target, such as a study by Akamatsu, Mackenzie and Hasbroucq [14]. However, results did not prove to be significant, as although the error rates have been reduced, overall pointing time was not improved [4]. Even though Dennerlein, Martin and Hasser [15] achieved an improved performance where the cursor was to be moved down in a "tunnel" to a target, it must be noted that the path was more restricted than general pointing.

There have been attempts to add haptic effects to GUI features such as window borders, buttons and checkboxes; forces being used to pull pointer towards a target or keep it on target once reached [16], but in [4], it is suggested that neither of those studies report empirical evaluation of their designs.

Haptic devices have been around for a while and as the technology advances, their costs have been drastically reduced, making them widely available and more accessible. In addition to studies that uses force-feedback mouse to provide haptic interaction, there are attempts to utilize a haptic device, such as PHANToM,[1] to manipulate desktop-like GUIs. An interaction technique called Pokespace [4] uses a Sensable PHANToM device which is to be used with non-dominant hand, while mouse is used with the dominant hand. On that technique, haptic device was used to select tool and alter its parameters (e.g. font style), and mouse was used to point on where the selected tool was to be applied. The technique featured a haptic wall to act as a backstop to indicate that cursor moved enough to select desired command (out of 8 possible commands). The results indicated that although haptics can provide strong enough feedback to perform selection without visual feedback, users were able to do it faster with traditional interface. However, it must be noted that Pokespace is an important technique that showed haptic interfaces can be used without visual attention in order to let users focus on their primary goals.

---

[1] PHANToM haptic interface is a device which measures a user's fingertip position and exerts a precisely controlled force vector on the fingertip [17].

Another study utilized a haptic interface, PHANToM, for cursor control on a menu system that is similar to Microsoft Windows Start Menu where three conditions were tested, namely Visual, Haptic and Adjusted; visual condition not featuring any haptic enhancement, other conditions incorporating haptic feedback for menu items, lining them with walls to produce a tunnel-like feedback, with adjusted compromising reduced forces having an effect of providing weak forces to oppose user's motion and strong forces supporting it [5]. Users were to click a start button and select a menu item. Results showed that adjusted condition produced "best of both worlds" with less target selection errors as in haptic condition whilst maintaining the speed when compared to visual condition [5].

Based on the results of previous attempts mentioned earlier, in [4], it is suggested that new interaction techniques must be designed from scratch with taking strengths and weaknesses of haptic and motor systems into consideration, stating that those previously stated techniques were simply haptic decorations of existing interaction techniques.

2.3   Task Switching

In task switching occurs when one has to switch between different tasks, although the generic explanation of the term "task" is rather debatable [18]. In practice, tasks to be performed within those experiments need to provide some specified mental operation or action as a response to a stimulus input [18]. Switch cost, preparation effect, residual cost and mixing cost are the four phenomena directly associated with the task switching.

Switch Cost. Usually, it takes longer for initiation of responses on a switch trial than on a non-switch trial, where error-rate is also usually higher after a task switch.

Preparation Effect. The average switch cost is often reduced when advance knowledge about upcoming task is given.

Residual Cost. Although preparation reduces switch cost, it does not completely eliminate the switch cost. A substantial asymptote that reduction in switch cost seems to have reached to where substantial residual costs have been reported even when more than 5 s of preparation has been allowed [19].

Mixing Cost. Although performance recovers quickly after a switch, responses remain slower than when just one task is needed to be performed.

Process or processes of task-set reconfiguration (TSR) must occur to change tasks. This can consist of shifting attention between stimulus attributes or elements, or between conceptual criteria, acquiring what to do and how to do it into procedural working memory, enabling a different response set [19].

There are different paradigms regarding task-switching experimental methods such as predictable task switching, task cueing, intermittent instructions, voluntary task selection, and comparing mixed-task blocks vs. single-block tasks, although the latter one is rarely used due to criticism it received [18].

In predictable task sequences, also known as alternating-runs paradigm, task switch is in a regular manner after a fixed number of trials (or runs), involving the same task, tasks switches occurring in every second trial such as AABBAABB sequence [16]. This paradigm revealed that switch trials had increased reaction time and error rates when compared to repetition trials [18].

Task-cueing paradigm with unpredictable sequences has been developed as an alternative to predictable sequences. In this paradigm, order of the tasks are random, hence the order of task switches and repetitions, too. Performance is usually worse in switch trials compared to repetition trials, as in predictable runs paradigm; but it differs regarding further reduced response times when the same task is repeated for several times [18]. Performance in this paradigm also relies on the type of cues given, transparent (e.g. word cues) or non-transparent (cues are needed to be learned by participants). Several studies have shown that switch costs are smaller with transparent cues than with non-transparent cues [18].

In intermittent instruction paradigms, participants are required to perform a sequence of trials with the same task. A cue to inform participants about what to do on the following trial sequence usually interrupts the sequence of trials, where the order of the task cues are also random, ensuring that the tasks either repeat or switch in sequential runs [18].

In voluntary task selection, participants decide between two tasks on each trial to perform. Responses for the two tasks are given on separate and non-overlapping sets of keys to allow experimenter to deduce the chosen task. Despite the free-choice, robust switch costs emerge in this paradigm [18].

An important diary study analyzing task switches found the interruptions participants encountered over a week and discussed designs to support task-switching and recovery [20]. This study focuses on multitasking of information workers and causes of task interruptions and proposes some design prototypes to support multitasking. In [20], it is suggested that "*methods for capturing and remembering representations of tasks may be valuable in both reminding users about suspended tasks, and in assisting users to switch among the tasks*". Although the study is important, it focuses on interruptions caused by systems, and tools to help workers remember the tasks to be done by providing ways to organize, and group them in addition to visual cues.

3   Research Procedure

For this study, a user interface is developed to better understand the behaviors of the participants while performing some tasks that need to be conducted by a mouse or haptic interface. As seen from Fig. 1, participants can start the experiment by entering their name ("*isim*") and last name ("*soyisim*") information. However, the participants' names are not stored; instead, an ID is assigned to them for the records.

The experiment is organized in two groups of tasks. The first group of tasks are organized for better understanding the task switching process between mouse and haptic interfaces. Accordingly, as seen from Table 1, the participants clicked different but-tons shown in different locations in the screen.

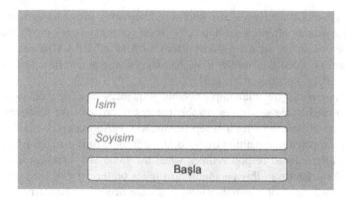

Fig. 1. Entering to the system

Table 1. Task switching between haptic device and mouse

Task Type	Interface									Total tries
Click the button	H	H	M	M	H	H	M	M	...	48
Drag and Drop the shape	H	H	M	M	H	H	M	M	...	48

As seen from Fig. 2, the button was to be clicked using haptic device (H) for two times. When the haptic cursor is on the button, it turns green to guide the participant to click on it. For the clicking process, the buttons on the haptic device were used.

After the participant clicks two buttons on the screen by haptic, other two buttons are asked to be clicked by mouse as seen in Fig. 3.

The second group of tasks are organized for better understanding the task switching process between tasks "drag & drop" and "click on the button" by using haptic device and mouse. In this group of experiments, as seen from Table 2, the participants used haptic interface first to perform Click on Button (B) task or Drag & Drop (D) task.

As seen in Fig. 4, for the Drag & Drop tasks, the participants were asked to drag the circle to the dashed circle area, either by using mouse or haptic device. Input device to be used for the task was shown on the top of the screen.

As seen in Fig. 5, when the haptic or mouse is on the circle to be dragged and dropped, the color of the circle changes to blue.

However, during performing the tasks with only haptic interface, because of the limitations of the haptic movements since a calibration is required at some points the haptic operation is stuck. This happened in average of 5 times out of 48 tries of haptic tasks. At these stages the application is stopped and re-started from previous two tasks. Because of the technical limitations, this calibration problem could not be solved in this experiment.

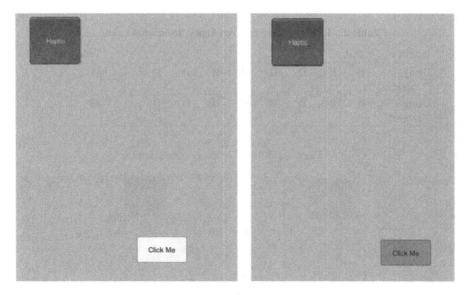

Fig. 2. Clicking buttons with haptic device

Fig. 3. Clicking buttons with haptic device and mouse

4 Results

A two-way repeated measures analysis of variance (ANOVA) was conducted to examine the effect of task type and task switching on reaction time. The within-subjects variables were task type with two levels (i.e., click, drag-and-drop) and task switching with two levels (i.e., no switching, and switching). There was a significant main effect for task type, $F(1, 29) = 96.46$, $p < .001$, partial $\eta^2 = .77$, with a very large effect size. The main effect of task switching was also significant, $F(1, 29) = 418.41$, $p < .001$, partial $\eta^2 = .94$, with a very large effect size. The interaction between task type and task switching was significant, $F(1, 29) = 12.81$, $p = .001$, partial $\eta^2 = .31$, with also a very large effect size. Planned comparisons were carried out between the switching and no switching trials for each task type. Separate paired-samples t tests showed that

Table 2. Task switching between haptic device and mouse

Interface	Task									Total tries
Using haptic	B	B	D	D	B	B	D	D	...	48
Using mouse	B	B	D	D	B	B	D	D	...	48

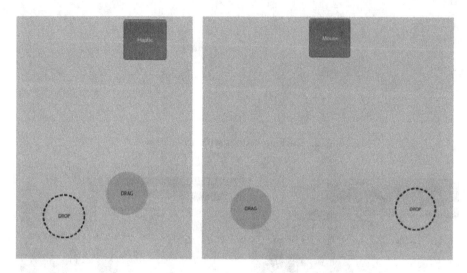

Fig. 4. Drag & drop task by using haptic device and mouse

Fig. 5. Drag & drop by using haptic device

participants spent more time on the switching condition compared to the no switching condition in the click task, $t(29) = 18.01$, $p < .001$, and in the drag-and-drop task, t $(29) = 20.32$, $p < .001$, (see Fig. 6).

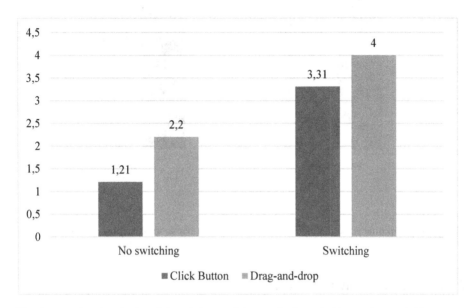

Fig. 6. Reaction time in the click and drag-and-drop tasks for switching and no switching trials

A separate two-way repeated measures ANOVA was run to examine the effect of input device and task switching on reaction time. The within-subjects variables were input device with two levels (i.e., mouse, haptic) and task switching with two levels (i.e., no switching, and switching). There was a significant main effect for input device, $F(1, 29) = 92.35$, $p < .001$, partial $\eta^2 = .76$, with a very large effect size. The main effect of task switching was also significant, $F(1, 29) = 13.96$, $p = .001$, partial $\eta^2 = .33$, with a very large effect size. The interaction between input device and task switching was significant, $F(1, 29) = 77.52$, $p < .001$, partial $\eta^2 = .73$, with also a very large effect size. Planned comparisons were carried out between the switching and no switching trials for each input device. Separate paired-samples t tests indicated that participants spent more time on the switching condition compared to the no switching condition when the input device was mouse, $t(29) = 12.16$, $p < .001$, (see Fig. 7). However, the effect of task switching approached to significance when the input device was haptic, $t(29) = -1.96$, $p = .06$. In contrast to the expectations, there was a tendency of higher reaction time in the no switching trials than in the switching trials (see Fig. 7).

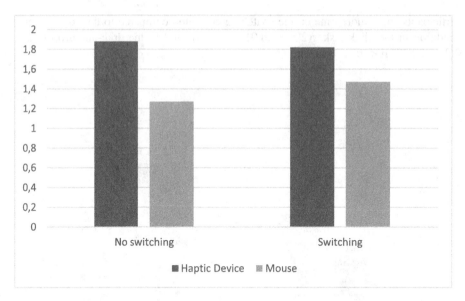

Fig. 7. Reaction time when the input device is mouse and haptic for switching and no switching trials.

5 Discussions and Conclusion

There are variety of input devices that can be used to manipulate desktop GUIs, from mouse to joysticks and haptic devices such as PHANToM. Although mouse is a widely used input device and desktop GUIs are made to be used with them, interaction techniques available in desktop GUIs such as drag-and-drop, point, click and move, can also be used with other devices such as stylus and tablet, and there are studies showing that those devices can have a similar performance to mouse [10].

Although there have been attempts to incorporate haptic interfaces for the manipulation of GUIs, decreasing visual clues did not help the performance and using traditional interface observed to be quicker than using haptic-only interaction [4]. Nevertheless, the study showed it is possible to get similar performance without visual attention. Another attempt of operation of desktop GUIs with haptic devices showed that haptic enhancements did reduce the error rates, however there was not significant improvements on speed rates [5]. The study is noteworthy, but limited in terms of its scope as it aimed to provide an alternative solution to multi-target menu interaction problems by designing a haptically enhanced menu.

It is important to note that haptic interfaces have not been accepted as an input device in a similar way of computer mouse. Although there are studies, some covered within this study, on manipulating GUIs with haptic interfaces, they are either not used as a primary input device or focus on limited GUI areas.

This study compares mouse and haptic interfaces, utilizing both as only input device in tests and with GUIs in both cases rather than depending on solely haptic feedback when using haptic interfaces for the manipulation of GUIs. Our experiment showed the significant impact of task switching for both devices, where reaction times varied across different types of tasks. Switch conditions required more time. We showed that it is possible to obtain acceptable performance results when using the GUI with a haptic device but further study and experimentation is necessary to include more participants who have more experience with haptic devices. Another important point is that desktop like GUIs as well as the GUI used within this study was 2-D and we believe that with the development of 3-D GUIs for haptic devices will provide much better performance results, forming need for even further studies on the topic.

It must be taken into consideration that this study is inspired from a surgical education system where both devices need to be used in different parts of the GUI and we believe showing this possibility is important to eliminate split attention that occurs due to switching those input devices.

Acknowledgements. The idea of utilizing a haptic interface as an input device came from another project, "E.C.E." (TUBITAK; 112K287), that incorporates them for medical education where they are used for surgical simulation purposes. As the software contains much more than just the simulation, we questioned the possibility of eliminating separate input devices to control that GUI, i.e. the rest of the system, with the haptic interface, in a way to have a similar comfort and performance to those input devices, mouse, in our case. The research team would like to thank the TUBITAK support for realizing this research study.

References

1. Tan, H.: Perceptual user interfaces: haptic interfaces. Commun. ACM **43**(3), 40–41 (2000)
2. MacLean, K.E.: Haptic interaction design for everyday interfaces. Rev. Hum. Factors Ergon. **4**, 149–194 (2008)
3. Stone, R.J.: Haptic feedback: a brief history from telepresence to virtual reality. In: Brewster, S., Murray-Smith, R. (eds.) Haptic HCI 2000. LNCS, vol. 2058, pp. 1–16. Springer, Heidelberg (2001)
4. Smyth, T.N., Kirkpatrick, A.E.: A new approach to haptic augmentation of the GUI. In: ICMI 2006 Proceedings of the 8th International Conference on Multimodal Interfaces, pp. 372–379 (2006)
5. Oakley, I., Brewster S., Gray, P.: Solving multi-target haptic problems in menu interaction. In: CHI 2001 Extended Abstracts on Human Factors in Computing Systems, pp. 357–358. ACM, New York (2001)
6. Donker, A., Reitsma, P.: Young children's ability to use a computer mouse. Comput. Educ. **48**, 602–617 (2007)
7. Fitts, P.M.: The information capacity of the human motor system in controlling the amplitude of movement. J. Exp. Psychol. **47**, 381–391 (1954)
8. Card, S.K., English, W.K., Burr, B.J.: Evaluation of mouse, rate-controlled isometric joystick, step keys and text keys for text selection on a CRT. Ergonomics **21**, 601–613 (1978)
9. Gillan, D.J., Holden, K., Adam, S., Rudisill, M., Magee, L.: How does Fitts' Law fit pointing and dragging? In: CHI 1990 Human Factors in Computing Systems Conference, pp. 227–234. ACM Press, Seattle (1990)

10. MacKenzie, I.S., Sellen, A., Buxton, W.: A comparison of input devices in elemental pointing and dragging tasks. In: CHI 1991 Conference on Human Factors in Computing Systems, pp. 161–166. ACM Press, New York (1991)
11. MacKenzie, I.: Fitts' Law as a Performance Model in Human-Computer Interaction, Ph.D. thesis. University of Toronto (1991)
12. Kabbash, P., MacKenzie I.S., Buxton W.: Human performance using computer input devices in the preferred and non-preferred hands. In: CHI 1993 Human Factors in Computing Systems, pp. 474–481. ACM Press (1993)
13. Accot, J., Zhai, S.: Beyond Fitts' Law: models for trajectory-based HCI tasks. In: ACM CHI 1997 Human Factors in Computing Systems Conference. ACM Press, Atlanta (1997)
14. Akamatsu, M., MacKenzie, I.S., Hasbrouq, T.: A comparison of tactile, auditory, and visual feedback in a pointing task using a mouse-type device. Ergonomics **38**, 816–827 (1995)
15. Dennerlein, J.T., Martin, D.B., Hasser, C.: Force-feedback improves performance for steering and combined steering-targeting tasks. In: CHI 2000 Human Factors in Computing Systems Conference, pp. 423–429. ACM Press (2000)
16. Rogers, R.D., Monsell, S.: Costs of a predictable switch between simple cognitive tasks. J. Exp. Psychol. Gen. **124**, 207–231 (1995)
17. Massie, T.H., Salisbury, K.J.: The PHANToM haptic interface: a device for probing virtual objects. In: DSC-Dynamic Systems and Control (1994)
18. Kiesel, A., Steinhauser, M., Wendt, M., Falkenstein, M., Jost, K., Philipp, A.M., Koch, I.: Control and interference in task switching—a review. Psychol. Bull. **136**, 849–874 (2010)
19. Monsell, S.: Task switching. Trends Cogn. Sci. **7**, 134–140 (2003)
20. Czerwinski, M., Horvitz, E., Wilhite, S.: A diary study of task switching and interruptions. In: CHI 2004 Conference on Human Factors in Computing Systems, pp. 175–182. ACM Press (2004)

Effect of Button Size and Location When Pointing with Index Finger on Smartwatch

Kiyotaka Hara[✉], Takeshi Umezawa, and Noritaka Osawa

Graduate School of Advanced Integration Science, Chiba University,
Chiba, Japan
x0tl567@students.chiba-u.jp, ume@chiba-u.jp,
n.osawa@faculty.chiba-u.jp

Abstract. Users control smartwatches through touch screen interfaces such as smartphones. However, because smartwatches are very small and users' postures differ depending on the device, control using touch screens needs to be adapted for smartwatches. Users tap buttons on the touch screen to control the smartwatch, so speed and accuracy of button input are required. Users' button input speed and accuracy are affected by displayed button size and location. In this study, we investigated the effects of button size and location when pointing with the index finger on a smartwatch. The results suggest that the pointing error rate is significantly affected by button size and location. The error rates became lower as the buttons became larger and when the buttons were located near the center of the screen.

Keywords: Smartwatch · Touch input · Pointing performance

1 Introduction

Smartwatches provide users with access to various smartphone applications directly from their wrists without using their smartphones. While applications such as email and social networking clients display text and images on the watch, no text entry is supported, and text and image transmission functions are limited. To efficiently use smartwatches, text entry support on smartwatches is needed.

Users control smartwatches through touch screen interfaces like smartphones. However, because the smartwatch display is very small, it severely limits users' behaviors. Moreover, because users wear smartwatches on their wrists, their hand postures when controlling smartwatches are different from those when controlling smartphones. Text entry methods on touch screens need to be adapted for smartwatches.

Users tap buttons on the touch screen for text entry, so speed and accuracy of button input are important factors. Users' button input speed and accuracy are called pointing performance. Pointing performance on touch screens depends on displayed button size and location. There have been studies on pointing performance on many kinds of devices, but pointing performance on smartwatches has not been fully investigated. Therefore, we investigated the effects of button size and location when tapping with the index finger on a smartwatch. The results suggest that the pointing

© Springer International Publishing Switzerland 2015
M. Kurosu (Ed.): Human-Computer Interaction, Part II, HCII 2015, LNCS 9170, pp. 165–174, 2015.
DOI: 10.1007/978-3-319-20916-6_16

error rate was significantly affected by button size and location. We obtained basic data to optimize text-entry time.

2 Related Work

The size and location of buttons are known as important factors for pointing performance on touch screens. Pointing performance is measured using task completion time and error rate. Higher pointing performance is achieved when task completion time and error rate are lower. Text entry methods that utilize high pointing performance are easy to use because users can control the devices quickly without having to correct errors.

2.1 Effect of Button Size on Touch Screen

Colle and Hiszem [3] conducted research on pointing performance and preference for index finger input with different button size and space between buttons on a 12.1-inch touch screen. The results showed that button size had a significant effect on pointing performance. Task completion times and error rates were high for smaller keys. Similar results were shown in studies about pointing performance with one-handed thumb input on small devices like smartphones [10, 11]. Moreover, users' fingers occlude the buttons when they tap small buttons, and finger movement accuracy is limited, so users have difficulty in touching the buttons accurately (fat finger problem [7]).

Fitts' law model, which was originally published in 1954 [4], is used to estimate time to complete a targeting task. Fitts' law model has proven to be one of the most robust and successful models of human motor behavior and is defined by the following equation [8].

$$T = a + bID \tag{1}$$

$$ID = \log_2\left(\frac{A}{W} + 1\right) \tag{2}$$

T is the average time taken to complete the movement, ID is the index of difficulty, A is the distance from the starting point to the center of the target, W is the width of the target, and a and b are constants reflecting the efficiency of the pointing system. Furthermore, FFitts' law model [2], which is applied to pointing to a small target by finger touch input, has been derived. FFitts' law model's index of difficulty validates the dual-distribution hypothesis, which provides a more logical and reasonable interpretation of the distribution of touch points than the target width interpretation. In accordance with Fitts' law model and FFitts' law model, the task completion time becomes low when the distance from the starting point to the center of the target is low or the width of the target is high.

In addition to the above research, there have been studies about relationships between pointing performance and button size on various devices. However, the effects of button sizes on smartwatches have not been fully investigated.

2.2   Effect of Button Location and Hand Posture on Touch Screen

Park and Han [10] investigated pointing performance of one-handed thumb input using only the right hand thumb on different button locations of a PDA. The results showed that task completion time was generally low in the left areas on the touch screen when the one-side length of a button was 4 mm while the task completion time was generally low in the center and right areas when the one-side length of a button was 7 mm and 10 mm. The error rates tend to be low in the left areas. Hwangbo et al. [6] studied the pointing performance of elderly smartphone users using their thumbs of right hands. The results showed that pointing performance was low when tapping on buttons in the four corners.

Moreover, it is known that the distribution of touch points depends on button location. Henze et al. [5] conducted research on pointing performance of one-handed thumb input when tapping on different button locations of smartphone. The results showed that touch points skewed towards the lower-right of the screen. The direction of the skew suggests that touches shift towards the base of his/her thumb when the phone is held in his/her right hand. In Azenkot and Zhai's study [1] about soft QWERTY keyboards on smartphones, hand postures (two thumbs, one thumb, and one index finger) affected the distribution of touch points.

Related work shows that pointing performance is affected by button location and hand postures. However, pointing performance has not been investigated in smartwatch control where button locations and hand postures are different from smartphone control. Therefore, pointing performance needs to be investigated.

3   Method

3.1   Participants

Fifteen university students (9 males and 6 females) participated in our experiment. The age of the participants ranged from 19 to 21 years old. There were 13 right-handed participants and 2 left-handed participants. No participants had used smartwatches, but 14 participants routinely used their smartphones, so they were used to controlling touch screen devices.

3.2   Apparatus

We used a SONY SmartWatch 2 SW2 for our experiment. The smartwatch has a display size of 32 × 26 mm and a resolution of 220 × 176 pixels.

We investigated the touch screen pointing performance of three square button sizes whose one-side lengths were 5, 7, and 10 mm (38, 49, 68 pixels) and spacing was 1 mm (7 pixels). The one-side length of buttons of a QWERTY keyboard on a smartphone is 5 mm; the recommended minimum and maximum sizes are 7 mm and 10 mm, respectively, for Android developers [9].

The number of buttons on a display depends on its size (Fig. 1). When the one-side length of buttons was 5, 7, and 10 mm, the display had 20, 12, and 6 buttons in 5 lines by 4 rows, 4 lines by 3 rows, and 3 lines by 2 rows, respectively. There were gaps between the buttons and the screen frame because the total size of the button arrays was smaller than the display size.

In this experiment, a participant was requested to tap designated buttons. When the participant touched on the smartwatch's screen, the time and touch points were recorded, and auditory feedback that differed depending on whether the tapping was on target or off target was sounded. The auditory feedback was played from an ASUS Nexus 7 connected to the smartwatch by Bluetooth. Moreover, to analyze participants' behaviors, videos of their upper bodies and hands were captured by a camera mounted on a control PC (NEC NS PC-LS700NS) and a web camera (Microsoft LifeCam HD-3000), respectively.

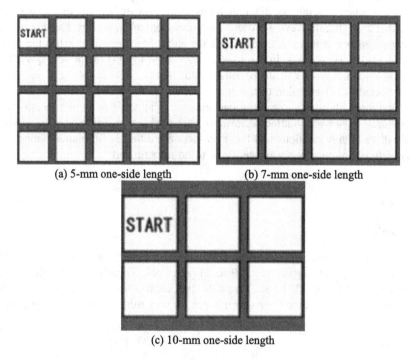

(a) 5-mm one-side length   (b) 7-mm one-side length

(c) 10-mm one-side length

Fig. 1. Button layouts used in experiment

3.3   Experimental Procedure

The participant wore the smartwatch on his/her non-dominant wrist and used his/her dominant index finger for pointing while sitting on a chair. In one trial of button size, the participant tapped each button once. The buttons to be tapped were designated in a sequence. One set has a trial for each button size (three trials), and the participant repeated each set three times. Each participant was randomly assigned to an order of button sizes and buttons to be tapped.

The experiment and how the obtained data will be used were explained to all participants, and they gave their consent to participate in this study. The participants were requested to tap precisely without caring about tapping speed. The participant started a set by tapping the set start button. After that, the trial start button was displayed at the upper left corner. The participant started a trial by tapping the trial start button. The participant was requested to tap the button that was designated with a red circle. The next target button to be tapped was indicated with a blue ring. When the participant tapped on the display, the next target button was designated, that is, the blue ring changed to a red circle, the next blue ring was displayed on another button (Fig. 2), and sound feedback was played. After all buttons were designated, the trial finished, and the trial finish button was displayed at the upper left corner. After the trial finish button has been tapped, the participant proceeded to the next trial. After the set was complete, the set finish button was displayed. The pointing performance measurements were determined from the button tapping intervals (the time between tapping buttons) and error rates (rates of tapping outside the area of the designated button). After finishing all sets, participants answered a questionnaire to evaluate usability on a 5-point Likert scale.

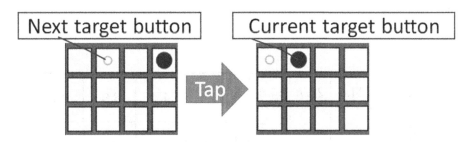

Fig. 2. Examples of displayed buttons in trial (Color figure online)

4 Results

Figure 3 shows the averages of button tapping intervals and error rates against button sizes. The averages of button tapping intervals are 0.91, 0.88, and 0.85 s for 5, 7, and 10 mm one-side length buttons, respectively. The averages of button tapping error rates were 25.22, 12.96, and 2.22 % for 5, 7, and 10 mm one-side length buttons, respectively. Performance was best (the shortest button tapping interval and lowest error rate) when the button size was a one-side length of 10 mm. Generally, participants performed better as the buttons became larger. Figure 4 shows the button tapping error rates on button locations. Figure 5 shows scatter plots of the tap positions. The circle, triangle, and broken line show the tap position, centroid of tap positions, and button frame, respectively. In Figs. 4 and 5, left-handed participants' data are flipped horizontally. For all button sizes, the error rates of tapping on buttons near the right side of the screen frame tend to be high, and for buttons near the center of the screen, the error rates tend to be low.

Figure 6 shows participants' answers to the question "operation was easy". The participants evaluated it using a 5-point Likert scale (5: strongly agree, 4: agree, 3: neutral, 2: disagree, 1: strongly disagree). The evaluation averages are 2.27, 3.87, and 4.73 for 5, 7, and 10 mm one-side length buttons, respectively.

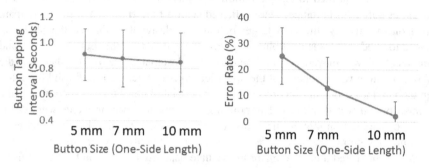

Fig. 3. Average of button tapping interval and error rate by button size (with standard deviation bars).

31.1	33.3	24.4	26.7	64.4
22.2	6.6	2.2	2.2	73.3
17.2	2.2	2.2	2.2	73.3
22.2	2.2	6.7	4.4	80.0

(a) 5-mm one-side length

11.1	4.4	8.9	48.9
4.4	0.0	0.0	35.6
0.0	0.0	2.2	42.2

(b) 7-mm one-side length

0.0	0.0	6.7
2.2	0.0	4.4

(c) 10-mm one-side length

Fig. 4. Button tapping error rate by buttons (%)

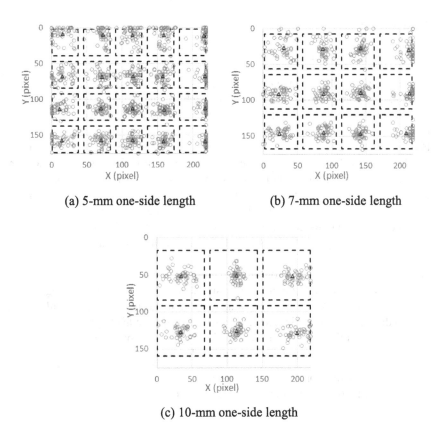

(a) 5-mm one-side length   (b) 7-mm one-side length

(c) 10-mm one-side length

Fig. 5. Plot of tap position (circle: tap position, triangle: centroid of tap positions, broken line: button frame).

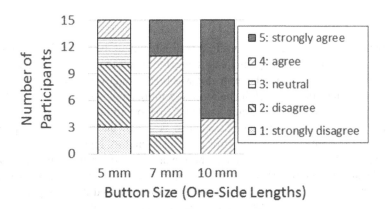

Fig. 6. Questionnaire results: operation was easy

5 Discussion

5.1 Effect of Button Size

The results show that the average of button tapping intervals did not vary largely with button size. The participants were able to comprehend the whole screen and find the designated button easily because the screen was small and was kept within their visual field.

However, the average of the error rates was significantly different. The error rate became lower as the buttons became larger. The analysis of variance showed that there were statistically significant differences between the error rates of the button sizes (F (2, 132) = 59.97, $p < .0001$), and the least significant difference multiple comparison test showed that there were statistically significant differences between each average of error rates of every combination of two button sizes (all $p < .0001$). We think that these results were affected by the fat finger problem in the same way as discussed in the related work.

We observed that the errors on small button sizes changed some subjects' hand postures. When he or she felt that the button size was small or he tapped wrong buttons frequently, he bents his dominant index finger so that it was nearly perpendicular to the screen to reduce errors by minimizing a contact area between his finger and the screen. The tendency is particularly strong among high error rate participants. We got the following comments for buttons of 5-mm one-side length.

- "I felt fatigue of my dominant index finger."
- "It was hard to tap buttons because my dominant index finger became perpendicular."

The hand posture that makes dominant index fingers perpendicular did not reduce the error rate, but it placed an extra load on the participants' hands.

5.2 Effect of Button Location

For all button sizes, tapping on buttons near the right side of the screen frame tended to be off to the right (left-handed participants tended to be off to the left when tapping on buttons near the left side), and the error rate was high. Moreover, when the button size was small (the one-side length of the button was 5 mm), tapping on buttons near the left and upper side of the screen frame tended to be off to the left and upper side, respectively (left-handed participants tended to be off to the right when tapping on buttons near the right side), and the error rate was high, too. Figure 7 shows a plot of tap positions on the 5-mm one-side length button at the bottom-right corner. The circle, X, triangle, and broken line show the correct tapping, errors, centroid of tap positions, and the button frame, respectively. Most of the errors occurred due to tapping on the gaps between the button and the screen frame. Errors when tapping on other buttons near the screen frame showed a similar tendency. Therefore, we think error rates can be reduced by having a button layout with no gaps between buttons and the screen frame. The error rates when tapping on buttons near the lower side of the screen are lower than those of buttons near the other sides of the screen. We think this result was caused by the button layout where functional keys, such as the Back key, Home key, and Action keys, are placed between displayed buttons and the lower screen frame. Participants tried to avoid tapping on the functional keys.

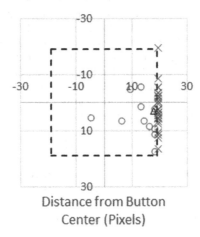

Fig. 7. Plot of tap positions on 5-mm one-side length button at bottom-right corner (circle: correct tapping, X: errors, triangle: centroid of tap positions, broken line: button frame).

6 Conclusion

Our study investigated the relationships between pointing performance and button layouts when tapping with the index finger on a smartwatch. The results show button sizes and button layouts have significant effects on pointing errors. Like pointing on larger devices, the error rates became lower as the buttons became larger. However, button tapping speed did not vary largely with button sizes. Regardless of button size, error rates when tapping on buttons near the right side of the screen frame tended to be high because the tap positions were off to the right (for left-handed participants, right and left are reversed), and on buttons near the center of the screen, the error rates tended to be low. For small buttons whose one-side length is 5 mm, tapping on buttons near the left and upper side of the screen frame tended to be off to the left and upper side, respectively, (for left-handed participants, the same as above), and the error rate was high.

We believe that these results contribute to determining appropriate button sizes for precise and efficient text entry for smartwatch applications.

References

1. Azenkot, S., Zhai, S.: Touch behavior with different postures on soft smartphone keyboards. In: MobileHCI 2012, pp. 251–260. ACM (2012)

2. Bi, X., Li, Y., Zhai, S.: FFitts law: modeling finger touch with fitts' law. In: CHI 2013, pp. 1363–1372 (2013)
3. Colle, H., Hiszem, K.: Standing at a kiosk: effects of key size and spacing on touch screen numeric keypad performance and user preference. Ergonom. **47**, 1406–1423 (2004)
4. Fitts, P.M.: The information capacity of the human motor system in controlling the amplitude of movement. J. Exp. Psychol. **47**, 381–391 (1954)
5. Henze, N., Rukzio, E., Boll, S.: 100000000 taps: analysis and improvement of touch performance in the large. In: MobileHCI 2011, pp. 133–142 (2011)
6. Hwangbo, H., Yoon, S.H., Jin, B.S., Han, Y.S., Ji, Y.G.: A study of pointing performance of elderly users on smartphones. Int. J. Hum. Comput. Interact. **29**(9), 604–618 (2013)
7. Siek, K.A., Rogers, Y., Connelly, K.H.: Fat finger worries: how older and younger users physically interact with PDAs. In: Costabile, M.F., Paternó, F. (eds.) INTERACT 2005. LNCS, vol. 3585, pp. 267–280. Springer, Heidelberg (2005)
8. MacKenzie, I.S.: Fitts' law as a research and design tool in human-computer interaction. Hum. Comput. Interact. **7**(1), 91–139 (1992)
9. Metrics and Grids Android Developers. http://developer.android.com/design/style/metrics-grids.html
10. Parhi, P., Karlson, A.K., Bederson, B.B.: Target size study for one-handed thumb use on small touchscreen devices. In: MobileHCI 2006, pp. 203–210. ACM (2006)
11. Park, Y.S., Han, S.H.: Touch key design for one-handed thumb interaction with a mobile phone: effects of touch key size and touch key location. Int. J. Ind. Ergon. **40**(1), 68–76 (2010)

Preliminary Study to Determine a "User-Friendly" Bending Method: Comparison Between Bending and Touch Interaction

BoKyung Huh, HaeYoun Joung, SeungHyeon Im, Hee Sun Kim,
GyuHyun Kwon, and JiHyung Park[✉]

Korea Institute of Science and Technology (KIST), Hwarangno 14-Gil 5,
Seongbuk-Gu, Seoul 136-791, Korea
{090748,090615,jhpark}@kist.re.kr, haey.
joung@gmail.com, ishl21@hanmail.net

Abstract. We suggest "User-Friendly" bending methods applied in a suitable context to flexible displays by a comparative analysis of touch interaction (TI). To determine appropriate method, we selected video and eBook applications for our experiment tasks. In the experiment, participants executed application commands through touch or bending interaction (BI) to determine the appropriate interaction method between two comparative interactions: flexibility and touch-based interaction. From the experiment, we found that BI does not apply to all commands in a flexible display. In both applications, users preferred BI for infrequently or continuously used commands: bookmarking, fast-forwarding, and rewinding. When users executed these commands, they intuitively used an "analog metaphor" as the BI. However, in both applications, users did not prefer BI for commands that required detailed and quantitative control. Based on the results of this study, we expect to discover new interactions for flexible displays and to suggest utilization direction of bending interaction.

Keywords: Flexible display · Bending interaction · Touch interaction · Bendable display · Flexible paper-like display · Bend input

1 Introduction

Many studies on flexible displays have been conducted as the consumer device market demands greater portability and durability. Flexible displays are thin, pliable, and yielding; they do not break easily [4]. Such displays are highly portable and durable. Flexible displays can be divided into various hardware types by the development flow shown in Fig. 1. Currently, second-generation bendable displays, such as curved displays, are being released into the device market. When displays have more freedom of flexibility, they can achieve a disposable property, such as paper-like thin displays.

The paper-like thin displays are more portable. However, the displays do have certain disadvantages. For example, display with higher flexibility can be bent unintentionally, because it is relatively difficult to prop up a paper-thin display. Thus, the

© Springer International Publishing Switzerland 2015
M. Kurosu (Ed.): Human-Computer Interaction, Part II, HCII 2015, LNCS 9170, pp. 175–183, 2015.
DOI: 10.1007/978-3-319-20916-6_17

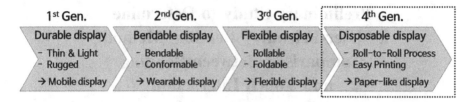

Fig. 1. Flexible display roadmap [9] (adapted from Displaybank: flexible display technology and market (2007–2017) report).

user might not be able to accurately touch an appropriate target on the display, because TI in paper-like thin display can induce an unintentional bending.

Consequently, the use of bending interactions (BIs) on flexible displays is being developed to allow users to interact with applications using methods other than touch. However, BIs cannot completely replace touch because there are strengths and weaknesses for each interaction type [5]. Thus, BIs and TIs have to be used for complementary use between those two interactions.

The majority of previous BI studies analyzed the performance [6] or user preference [2, 3] and [7] for BIs by comparing various flexible shapes. However, it is difficult to be certain that the extracted bending interaction can be applied to flexible displays with touch interface, because they did not compare the preference of BIs with existing touch-based interactions. Thus, results can change when the defined interactions applied to flexible displays are compared with familiar TIs currently used on many different devices.

There was study that BI was more effective in specific command by comparing TI [1, 10]. However, it is hard to know that the effective BIs are intuitively chosen in flexible display, because the study did not observe an intuitive choice between BI and TI. Moreover, in the TT Ahmaniemi et al. study, a mobile-size display was used and the display was not thin like a paper. The properties are different from properties of paper-like display which have high flexibility. Therefore, in order to suggest utilization directions of BI, it is necessary to find out why users intuitively choice TI or BI in each command when they use the paper-like tablet prototype.

We have questions regarding effective use of the BI on flexible displays along with commonly used TIs in current displays: in flexible display, can BI be used as an intuitive interaction for all commands? Is the preference for BI higher than for TI? What are the implications of a preference for familiar TI being higher than for unfamiliar BI?

2   Methods

2.1   Focus Group Interview and Pilot Test

From focus group interview (FGI), we extracted appropriate applications for comparison of preference between BI and TI. And we provided interaction options that contains BIs and TIs based on previous studies and pilot test.

Applications. To understand the preference for TI or BI, we considered BI unfamiliarity because there is a familiarity difference between TI and BI. Thus, we extracted applications where we could find a potential for BI use. Through FGI, we considered the posture of the "Lap hand" [11] among various use postures for tablet devices. The "Lap hand" is the way in which users hold a tablet in their lap supported by their hand. We decided that holding a display with both hands (display-holding posture) offers a higher degree of flexibility than placing the display on a desk. Thus, we selected applications that could be used in the display-holding posture for most of the applications' commands. Based on our consideration factors, we chose applications for watching contents by the FGI. Moreover, in order to understand the similarities and differences in the interaction patterns according to the application, we divided the applications into a dynamic application of video contents and a static application of eBook content.

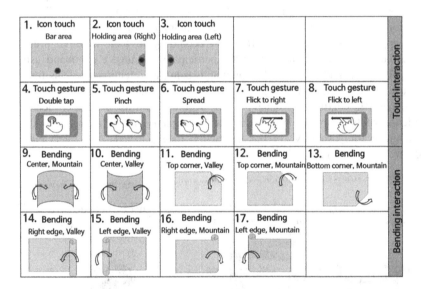

Fig. 2. Interaction options: eight for TI and ten for BI

Interaction Options. In our experiment, we provided 18 possible interactions for executing commands, as shown in Fig. 2. To extract the interactions, we considered a common feature of the input method between BI and TI, and selected interactions that required only two hands without an additional tool, such as a touch pen. Thus, we selected "icon touch" and "touch-gesture" as the TIs. The icon TI was divided into three interactions, numbered 1 to 3 in Fig. 2, by considering the display-holding posture. Based on our FGI, the five most common touch gestures, numbered 4 to 8 in Fig. 2, were extracted in reference to the touch-gesture reference guide [8]. Further, eight BIs, numbered 9 to 16 in Fig. 2, were selected based on the experiment results of Lee et al. [7] and Lahey et al. [2]. We extracted BIs with a high preference rating in these studies, and then conducted a pilot test to analyze these BIs. We added additional BIs, numbered 17 and 18 in Fig. 2, based on our participants' opinions from the pilot test.

2.2   Experiment

Experiment Design. The experiment had a within-participants design factor of TI and BI and a between-participants factor of video and eBook applications. 10 out 20 participants invoked the commands in the video application by choosing TI or BI. And remaining 10 participants invoked the commands in the eBook application by choosing TI or BI.

Experiment Procedure. The experiment participants viewed an instruction video that illustrated the 18 interactions. We allowed time for the participants to adapt to these interactions. The participants attempted to control the paper prototype. Following the adaptation time, the participants invoked the commands specified on the video and eBook applications using either BI or TI according to their intuitive preference. A secondary task was required when the participant executed a command using TI. These participants had to repeat the commands using BI intentionally. This time, they could use other bending shapes as well as the offered BIs. We called this interaction "intentional BI." Participant behavior was recorded during the experiment. Upon completion of the experiment process, the participants completed a five-point-scale questionnaire for "usability" of the interaction they selected. And interviews were conducted as shown in Fig. 3.

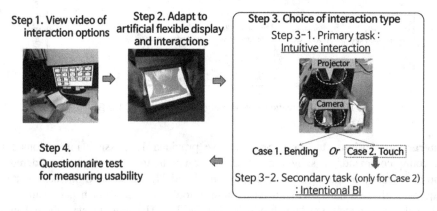

Fig. 3. Experiment procedure

Materials and Participants. A total of 40 participants between the ages of 20 to 35 years were invited to participate in the experiment. The experiment proceeded after KIST institutional review board approval (IRB number: 2014–012) and the task-completion time per participant took about 30 min. In experiment, a low-fidelity prototype was used. The prototype made by putting an OHP film and a paper together in order to have a similar curvature to a bendable display currently in development. The prototype was about the size of a fifth generation iPad (240 * 170). Moreover, in order to give a feeling of working prototype, we provided the visual feedbacks for each command using animation function of PowerPoint presentations. When the participants performed certain command, the visual feedback was provided at the same time by researcher.

3 Results and Discussion

To analyze preference and usability between TI and BI, we performed the Wilcoxon's signed rank test of nonparametric statistics because the data did not assume normality.

3.1 Frequency of BI Use

The frequency of BI use for the video application was significantly lower than that of TI ($Z = -2.742$, $p < 0.05$, $N = 20$): TIs were mostly used for executing seven commands in the video contents. However, for the eBook content application, there were no significant differences between frequency of use of the two interaction types ($Z = -1.064$, $p = 0.287$, $N = 20$): When the participants executed seven commands for the eBook content application, BI and TI were distributed among the commands at an almost equal frequency.

3.2 Commands with Potential BI Use

In both applications, the frequency of BI use was not significantly higher than TI. However, we found potential BI use for certain commands through frequency analysis, as shown in Table 1.

Command 1 for User Friendly Bending: *'Infrequently'* Used Command. Participants preferred BI use for bookmark command included in both applications. The participants indicated that BI felt more intuitive, but required more muscle movement because BI is a direct physical movement compared with touch. Thus, participants wanted to use BIs for infrequently used bookmark commands.

Command 2 for User Friendly Bending: *'Continuously'* Used Command. In addition, for fast-forward and rewind commands included in both applications, the participants preferred BI, or used BI at nearly the same rate at TI. The commands were

Table 1. Interaction frequency in each application

(a) Video content   (b) eBook content

Commands		Choice ratio (% of total subjects)	
		FBI	TI
	Play	10%	90%
	Temporary pause	10%	90%
	Bookmark	75%	25%
	Fast forward	55%	45%
	Rewind	50%	50%
	Volume up	30%	70%
	Volume down	30%	70%
	Total rate	37%	63%

Commands		Choice ratio (% of total subjects	
		FBI	TI
	Turn to next page	25%	75%
	Turn to previous page	25%	75%
	Bookmark	70%	30%
	Fast forward	70%	30%
	Rewind	70%	30%
	Zoom in	30%	70%
	Zoom out	30%	70%
	Total rate	46%	54%

required for moving a considerable range in whole range of data. BI allowed the participants continuous control with one movement. However, the participants did not recognize volume control as a continuous command, although volume ranged from high to low. Rather, the participants preferred to control the volume quantitatively with several movements using TI.

3.3   Property of Preferred BIs

To understand detailed use context for BIs, we analyzed the preferred bending shape and area for bookmark, fast-forward, and rewind commands as indicated in Table 2.

Table 2. Bending shape with high preference rate

	Fast-forward	Rewind	Bookmark	
Video-contents	45%	60%	67%	
eBook-contents	79%	79%	50%	43%

(Bending shape with concordance rate of over forty percent)

User Friendly Bending Method 1: BI Applying "Analog Metaphor". The preferred bending shapes were similar for both applications. When the participants executed the bookmark, fast-forward, and rewind commands, they used BIs with appropriate "analog metaphors" for the commands: an analog metaphor of page tagging was applied to the bookmark command. And an analog metaphor of leafing through the pages was applied to forward and rewind commands. In particular, the preference rates for BIs in the fast-forward/rewind commands were higher for eBook contents than for video contents. The participants indicated that analog metaphors for leafing through the pages were easier to fit into the commands for eBook contents because the paper prototype felt similar to a page in a book.

User Friendly Bending Method 2: BI in Corner and Edge area. The shapes in edge and corner area were mostly used for the commands: for the fast-forward/rewind commands, BIs in edge areas, numbered 16 and 17 in Fig. 2, were used most frequently. For the bookmark command, BI in a top corner area, numbered 11 in Fig. 2, was used most frequently. Through an interview, the participants indicated that they preferred BIs in corner and edge area to avoid screen distortion by bending.

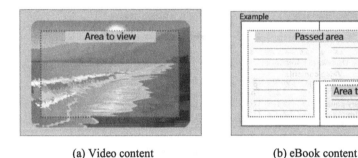

(a) Video content   (b) eBook content

Fig. 4. Focus area (red dotted square) (Color figure online)

However, in bookmark command of the eBook contents, BI in a center area, numbered 10 in Fig. 2, was preferred, as well as BI in a top corner area, numbered 11 in Fig. 2. In the case of the center area, the participants folded the paper prototype in half, as if closing a book. The participants indicated that the static application of eBook contents was less affected by screen distortion, compared with the dynamic application of video contents. The reason is that the focus area for eBook contents is smaller than for video contents, as indicated in Fig. 4 (b): when users read eBook contents, they only need to focus on the "reading area", with the exception of the "passed area." Therefore the range of flexibility use was wider in static application than in dynamic application.

3.4 User Experience of TI and BI

Intuitive TI vs. Intuitive BI. We analyzed the usability difference between intuitive BI and intuitive TI. For both applications, there were no significant differences (video application: $Z = -1.680$, $p = 0.093$, $N = 20$; eBook application: $Z = -0.311$, $p = 0.756$, $N = 20$). The participants were comfortable with both intuitive TI and BI (Usability average values of TI and BI in video contents: 4.307 and 4.007, respectively; Usability average values of TI and BI in eBook contents: 4.28 and 4.335, respectively).

Intuitive TI vs. Intentional BI. For the commands where TI was used more often than BI, we compared the "usability levels" between intuitive TI and intentional BI obtained by the secondary task. Our analysis results indicate that the usability levels for intuitive TI were statistically higher than for intentional BI in both applications, as listed in Fig. 5. The participants indicated that BI for these commands was not accepted as an intuitive interaction because it is hard to apply an analog metaphor into the commands.

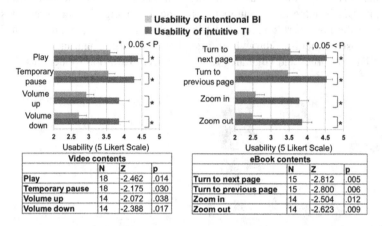

Fig. 5. Usability comparison between intuitive TI and intentional BI

In particular, we found from the participant interview a common reason for not using BI with zoom in/out commands. When the participants executed these commands using BI, they could not accurately control the zoom because of difficulties selecting a target on the display. Interestingly, the participants indicated that TI was also uncomfortable for these commands. For the commands, the touch gestures numbered 6 and 5 in Fig. 2 were used most frequently. However, when the participants used the TIs, the paper prototype was bent unintentionally because of its high flexibility. Thus, the participants wanted a combined use of both BI and TI for zoom commands.

4 Conclusion and Future Works

In this study, we found a "User-Friendly" bending method for video and eBook applications through comparative analysis of TI. Through observation, we found the reason that BI does not apply to all commands in a flexible display. BI can give intuitive feeling, but it can induce screen distortion and requires significant muscle movement. Thus, the following conditions are required in order to become "User-Friendly" BI.

- Which of commands in application are used *'infrequently'* or *'continuously'*?
- Is there a BI applied an *analog metaphor* for the commands? Or is it easy to apply an analog metaphor into the commands?
- Is the BI in *corner or edge area*?

Of these conditions, influence of the third condition can become weak depending on application. Thus, we propose BI using analog metaphors when users execute a "saving task" that is used less frequently, but that is important, and for executing a "moving task" in a wide range of data. There was also an opinion that combined interaction between BI and TI is suitable for commands that require detailed control. Thus, we will propose a new interaction that uses TI for target selection and BI for target control. And it is necessary to verify the optimum conditions using a working prototype in future work.

Acknowledgements. This work was supported by the IT R&D program of MOTIE/KEIT. [10042418, UI and User Interaction Technology for more than 60 HD-level Transparent Flexible Display Applied Product Using Eye-tracking and Space Recognition].

References

1. Ahmaniemi, T.T., Kildal, J., Haveri, M.: What is a device bend gesture really good for? In: Proceedings of the 32nd Annual ACM Conference on Human Factors in Computing Systems, pp. 3503–3512. ACM, April 2014
2. Lahey, B., Girouard, A., Burleson, W., Vertegaal, R.: PaperPhone: understanding the use of bend gestures in mobile devices with flexible electronic paper displays. In: Proceedings of CHI 2011, pp. 1303–1312. ACM Press (2011)
3. Schwesig, C., Poupyrev, I., Mori, E.: Gummi: a bendable computer. In: Proceedings of CHI 2004, pp. 263–270. ACM Press (2004)
4. Crawford, G.P.: Flexible Flat Panel Display, Flexible Flat Panel Display Technology. Wiley, New York (2005)
5. Kildal, J., Paasovaara, S., Aaltonen, V.: Kinetic device: designing interactions with a deformable mobile interface. In: CHI 2012 Extended Abstracts on Human Factors in Computing Systems, pp. 1871–1876. ACM (2012)
6. Steimle, J., Jordt, A., Maes, P.: Flexpad: highly flexible bending interactions for projected handheld displays. In: Proceedings of CHI 2013, pp. 237–246. ACM Press (2013)
7. Lee, S.S., Kim, S., Jin, B., Choi, E., Kim, B., Jia, X., Kim, D., Lee, K P.: How users manipulate deformable displays as input devices. In: Proceedings of CHI 2010, pp. 1647–1656. ACM Press (2010)
8. Villamor, C., Willis, D., Wroblewski, L.: Touch Gesture Reference Guide, 15 April 2010. http://www.lukew.com/touch/
9. When Will Flexible Display Push into Market? Displaybank, 26 March 2007. http://www.displaybank.com/_eng/research/print_contents_m.html?cate=column&id=2312
10. Watanabe, J.I., Mochizuki, A., Horry, Y.: Bookisheet: bendable device for browsing content using the metaphor of leafing through the pages. In: Proceedings of the 10th International Conference on Ubiquitous Computing, pp. 360–369. ACM, September 2008
11. Young, J.G., Trudeau, M., Odell, D., Marinelli, K., Dennerlein, J.T.: Touch-screen tablet user configurations and case-supported tilt affect head and neck flexion angles. Work: J. Prev. Assess. Rehabil. **41**(1), 81–91 (2012)

Musician Fantasies of Dialectical Interaction: Mixed-Initiative Interaction and the Open Work

Leonardo Impett[1]([✉]), Isak Herman[2], Patrick K. A. Wollner[1], and Alan F. Blackwell[2]

[1] Department of Engineering, University of Cambridge, Cambridge, England
leoimpett@googlemail.com
[2] Computer Laboratory, University of Cambridge, Cambridge, England

Abstract. We compare some recent trends in mixed-initiative HCI and interactive electronic music, and consider what useful knowledge can be shared between them. We then present two novel principles for understanding the nature of this common trend: $spaces of co-agency$ and $dialectical interaction$; and discuss some of the philosophical and technical challenges they present in relation to musical interaction. A technically advanced prototype, the Mephistophone, is discussed as a case-study for understanding these design principles, concluding with some more general points for creative mixed-initiative interaction.

Keywords: HCI · Interactive music · Haptic control · Mixed-initiative interaction · Augmented cognition

1 Introduction

This paper seeks to re-assess some of the principles of computer-human collaboration, particularly for creative goals. Although we later discuss current trends in mixed-initiative interaction, human-computer collaboration and co-creation has been a dream since the start of the digital revolution. Early (1950s) attempts at imagining a collaborative man-machine relationship moved between two models of interaction: prosthesis (the 'Mechanically Extended Man' [22]) and symbiosis (where, by analogy to biological systems, computers and humans provide for each other). In 1960, Licklider provided perhaps the most elegant summary of this hope for computer-human cooperation, in an age when computer occupied whole rooms and had to be booked in advance [19]:

> The hope is that, in not too many years, human brains and computing machines will be coupled together very tightly, and that the resulting partnership will think as no human brain has ever thought and process data in a way not approached by the information-handling machines we know today

© Springer International Publishing Switzerland 2015
M. Kurosu (Ed.): Human-Computer Interaction, Part II, HCII 2015, LNCS 9170, pp. 184–195, 2015.
DOI: 10.1007/978-3-319-20916-6_18

2 Background

2.1 Mixed-Initiative Interaction

In 1997, a series of debates between Ben Shneiderman and Pattie Maes at the IUI and CHI conferences dichotomised the division in HCI between *direct manipulation* and *interface agents* [27]. Two years later, Horvitz argued for a resolution of this debate through the paradigm of *mixed-initiative interaction*. Horvitz proposes to unite the advantages of both intelligent-interface agents, which predict the activity of a user and take action automatically, and direct manipulation interfaces, which - often through the intelligent use of metaphor - allow the user to control the system fluidly and directly [2].

Mixed-initiative interaction involves direct collaboration between computer and human towards a one goal. Psychological principles of *grounding* and *joint activity* are evoked [17] - models originally meant to explain human-human collaboration and communication. Implicit in this model of interaction is a sort of implicit equality between the heterogenous human and computer agents, working together towards a single goal. The principle is not dissimilar to Licklider's symbiotics three decades earlier - diverse organisms working together, where the result is greater than the sum of the parts. In the hierarchy of control, the computer is neither below nor above the human - neither an unimaginative tool of direct control, nor a master-agent working only on its own predictions of the user's behaviour.

The role of the computer in mixed-initiative interaction is explicitly different to that of the prosthetic, which seeks to make itself invisible by becoming an extension of the body. Non-hierarchical collaboration with another agent (human or computer) relies, to some extent, on the limited externality of that agent. A book, for instance, is seldom seen as the collaborative work of a pen and an author, any more than this article can be attributed to my laptop keyboard. To return to Horvitz, mixed-initiative interaction is instead: [17]

> Quick-paced sensing, reasoning, and reacting support an elegant problem-solving dance among parties, where the nature and timing of human and machine contributions are coordinated carefully.

The computer, then, is no longer a tool but a performer, dancing alongside the human towards some common goal. The prosthetic pen interacts so fluidly and predictably that the human is hardly notices any interaction. In mixed-initiative interaction, on the other hand, the externality is obvious to the user - they are continually conscious of the process of interaction.

2.2 Interactive Musical Instruments

The musical instrument, at least in a pre-electronic age, has popularly been considered a prosthetic - not just in the sense that all melodic instruments ultimately imitate the human voice (as the first instrument), but also in the sense that technical virtuosity is often described as prosthesis - the instrument becomes an extension of the self. In his discussion of the Faustian violin virtuoso Niccolò Paganini, David Palmer writes: 'Everyone in the hall... became keenly aware that the violin was for Paganini not merely a musical instrument, but an integral part of his body' [23]. Prosthetics are also found explicitly in electronic musical instruments [20] - but in this case, their relationship becomes more complex.

In recent decades, digital interfaces for musical interaction have moved from metaphors of the instrument-as-tool (John Cage's musical ideal is using instruments as though they were tools, i.e. so that 'they leave no traces' [18]) to the instrument-as-participant, in many ways following (and sometimes pre-empting) the HCI concept of mixed-initiative interaction.

Precision and predictability in digital instruments is seen as reactive, not interactive [12] - to quote Bert Bongers [6]:

> Note that in some cases only parts of the loop can occur, for instance when the cognition is left out on one side or the other this part rather *reacts* than *interacts*. Many interactive systems in new media arts are in fact reactive systems. Ideally, interaction between a human and a system should be mutually influential

Bown compares the *acoustic paradigm* of European musical history, in which the composer, performer and instrument have clearly defined (and separate) roles, to interactive electronic music [7]:

> In recent years there have been calls for new interactive metaphors that take the *active* nature of the computational medium into account. The dominant metaphor of instrumental interaction emphasises a one-way reactivity that many feel is inappropriate... Hankering after a more collaborative form of interaction, we see discussion of *conversation models* or systems with a degree of *cognition*

Both Bongers and Bown urge us to move towards mutually influential humans and systems, interactivity that goes both ways, and machines with cognition - that is, where both humans and machines have agency. When the machine becomes a performer (Horvitz' *dancer*), an agent in the same space as the human, we have musical interaction that is mixed-initiative in the strictest sense.

2.3 Predictive, Suggestive and Oppositional Systems

We have thus far identified similar trends in mixed-mode interaction design and electronic interactive music. The shift is from a technology of direct control, of prosthetics and of inanimate tools, to a technology which focuses on equal collaboration, co-creation, and the machine as an external critic.

A non-trivial question in all these fields becomes: what does an external critic look like? In Bongers' terms, a truly *interactive* system implies cognition on behalf of the machine.

Formal definitions of computational *cognition*, *intelligence* and *agency* are beyond the scope of this work - but as we observed with traditional-musical interaction above, the important characteristic of such a system is the human perception of cognition. One could imagine a sort of mixed-initiative Turing-test here: the important question is not whether the technology really has intelligence or agency, but whether humans interact with it in a way that ascribes it that agency.

But can we talk about co-creation with an agent that exists only through human experience? In other words: if a human experiences a dialogue with an inanimate machine, have we really produced human-machine collaoration (in the sense of mixed-initiative interaction)? Much recent work in mixed-initiative HCI (cite) can be seen as *reactive* on some level - the computer gives the human something already inherent in their own actions. Many implementations [2] use the computer for prediction or suggestion of human behaviour based on previous use. Pre-empting human actions - is this co-creation, or a labour-saving device?

Mixed-initiative systems that focus on suggestions [28] tend to leave all fitness functions (value judgements) with the human user - by leaving all the agency with the human, we return to the simple appropriation of computational resources which is the instrument/software-as-tool paradigm.

An interesting musical alternative to predictive or suggestive systems is Nick Collins' oppositional system, Contrary Motion. The rationale for his system is similar to Bongers' critique, and is as descriptive of musical systems as it is of mixed-initiative HCI generally [10]:

> Computational agents as musical interlocutants have been extensively studied, though the degree to which they can comfortably demonstrate independent but appropriate musical action in real contexts reflects the deep challenges in machine listening technology and music generation. Many interactive systems turn out to be directly reactive slaves, or even if exhibiting some autonomy, lag behind human auditory and cognitive capabilities

Collins' solution is to use the machine to usefully contradict the performer: *'opposition can be a temporary state on the path to new musical awareness'* [ibid.]. From a strict information-theory point of view, we have the same state of affairs: we present a computational reaction which is already entirely intrinsic to the human action (in photography, a negative gives you no more information than the positive). As Collins himself writes: 'A surprising finding for the author was that the system proved more deterministic than expected'. Though the degree of autonomy or cognition hasn't formally increased, the *experience of interaction* has changed completely.

3   The Instrument-as-Critic

3.1   Externalisation

The paradigms for digital musical interaction discussed above mark out a distinction between traditional instruments, which are prosthetic and passive, and new digital instruments, which are external and intelligent. We question this.

Heidegger's notion of *Zuhandenheit* (readiness-to-hand) is a way of understanding the difference between the prosthetic and the external. In his example, a hammer is such a functional object that it only has *Zuhandenheit* - so predictable and close, that it becomes invisible. Only when the hammer behaves unpredictably - the head shatters - does it acquire *Vorhandenheit* (presence-at-hand), where we approach it theoretically and critically [15]. A similar idea is playwright Bertol Brecht's *Verfremdungseffekt* (alienation effect), where actors in a play behave so strangely that the audience cannot identify with the characters or lose themselves in the narrative - forcing the audience to interact with the work on a conscious, critical plane.

Another useful comparison is the legend of the Golem, as the archetypal artefact coming to life through the power of code. Medieval traditions of the Kabbalah ascribe code components in which the Golem is separately provided with vitality (hiyyut) and soul (neshamah) [25]. Previous technically-advanced musical instruments, such as Vaucanson's flute-playing automaton, fascinated observers with their life-force of *pneuma*. Sophisticated contempoary observers should be less disturbed by the implications of a machine that breathes, but the addition of *soul* still appears to be implicit in the dialectic agency of an instrument.

Clearly, violins do not exhibit advanced cognition. But it is an immensely unpredictable, nonlinear mechanical instrument - the constant, dynamic unpredictability gives it *Vorhandenheit*. These unpredictabilities make interaction with such an instrument conscious and critical - instead of a prosthesis, we can understand violin-playing as a collaboration between man and machine. Though the violin has no independent cognition, this unpredictability creates a subjectivity in the musician's experience of performance. In extreme cases, this imagined subjectivity might be great enough to attribute the instrument with human traits - quite a common phenomenon, from African traditional instruments [24] to 70 s analogue synthesisers [11].

3.2   Spaces of Co-Agency

This fantastical agency of the machine, whether or not in an explicitly anthropomorphic fashion, forms part of the musicians experience of interaction. Traditional musical instruments direct the player acoustically and haptically in new directions based on dynamic acoustic-mechanical interactions: a trumpet split-note acoustically-haptically invites the player to blow harder, just as audial and vibrational cues tell the violinist to change the bowing force and achieve better resonance. In some sense, these interactions result in a path which traverses a timbral space (the space of all possible sounds of that instrument) - a space in which musician and instrument both share agency, that is to say, a *space of co-agency*.

Under the Heidiggerian notion of interacting with *Vorhandenheit*, the instrument's imagined agency derives from its unpredictability. It should come as no surprise that instruments with perfectly predictable characteristics - such as early digital samplers - are refered to as '*cold*', that is to say inanimate, dead, in full contrast with the rich nonlinearity of the human voice. An analysis of musicians' discussions and judgements of violin sounds shows the frequent use of similar terms, relating to the percieved vitality and animation of the instrument: 'lively', 'alive', 'dead', 'cold' and 'unresponsive' [14]

In traditional musical instruments, the musician's control is most often mechanical - the force on a piano-key, for instance. In terms of user interfaces, we can think of this as tangible control. The collaborative output of the system, the eventual performance, can be thought of as audio. The feedback from the instrument to the musician, however, lies somewhere in-between - part micro-haptic ('feeling' the instrument), part audial (hearing the instrument). The chin-rest of a violin, for instance, connects the vibrations of the violin body to the musician's jaw, providing important vibrational feedback. If it is possible for musicians to collaborate with traditional instruments, it must be in this shared physical-audial space - where the human and the instrument are co-agent.

Schelleng's diagram of violin dynamics, in Fig. 1, is an example of such a space. While the dimensions are entirely mechanical (the musician's input: force and position), the space explored by these two variables is both physical and audial - it relates to both the haptic feedback in playing a note, and to the sound produced. While the axes are completely controlled by the musician, the complex nonlinear mechanics of sound production are completely controlled by the instrument - the eventual sound produced is as a result of a continuous feedback-loop between these two agencies, similar to Nash's *performance loop* [21]. During the technological development of musical instruments, complexity and unpredictability are often added to this space - such as the keyed trumpet of the 18th century.

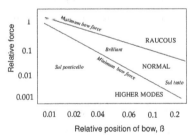

Fig. 1. The Schelleng diagram - the axes are the musician's major degrees of control, and are related to the sounds produced through complex nonlinear dynamics. Reproduced from [26]

Mixed-mode interaction design proposes a balance of agency between a human and a machine. Similarly, these spaces of co-agency rely on a balance of agency between musician and instrument - a tension between the directness of human control and the unpredictability of instrumental response. We arrive at our first principle of mixed-mode instrument design, the *instrument-as-critic*:

First. The space of co-agency should be at once physical, haptic and audial. A co-agent space will always be a balance between controllability and unpredictability.

3.3   Dialectical Interaction

Much of the rhetoric presented above in musical interaction has presented a dichotomy betwen the prosthetic machine-as-tool, the old order of doing things, and the external machine-as-critic. Mixed-mode interaction design allows us to develop a more sophisticated view: the emphasis is not only on creating intrinsic computational intelligence (Bongers' *cognition*, Collins' *autonomy*), but rather on seeking to achieve a balance between the agency of the human and the machine. The agency of the human within the system is considered explicitly.

One way of considering this *balance of agency* is to look at the human-machine system as a dialectic - the human action, the dialectical *thesis*, is confronted by the first negation, the computational *antithesis*. In a process of interaction and conflict between thesis and antithesis, knowledge emerges in the *synthesis*. As with Licklider's computational symbiotics, the synthesis is greater than the sum of its parts.

Cacciari's key philosophical critique of dialectics [9] is an important consideration for the nature of this antithetical system: for him, the dialectic cannot produce new meaning because the antithesis (the behaviour of our computational system) is fully intrinsic to the thesis (a deterministic consequence of human action): mathematically, no new information has been added. Cacciari's view seems consistent with the rhetoric of interactive musical instruments presented above - where meaningful collaboration can only occur with a computer that is fundamentally independent, with its own *cognition*. Under this view, meaningful content cannot emerge from an interaction with a deterministic machine.

This conclusion, present in much of the musical literature presented above, ignores the important distinction between *information* and *meaning*. In Collins' Oppositional System, the antithesis is mathematically inherent in the thesis; but this same information is inverted to produce new meaning. In this case, we move closer to an Adornian interpretation of *negative dialectics* [3]; where negation (or opposition) is itself an emancipatory process - one which adds meaning.

Classical music gives us a useful analogy. Sonata form can be seen as a dialectical interaction between the exposition (thesis) and the development (antithesis), resolving in the recapitulation (synthesis) [8, p.63]. The first subject group, the main melodic structure presented in the exposition, re-appears unaltered in the recapitulation - the same information, but with a completely new and different meaning. Situated, contextual knowledge allows an entirely deterministic system (a time delay) to produce different musical understanding.

Our second principle of the instrument-as-critic becomes:

Second. The instrument should be *critical* - that is, unpredictably and dialectically opposed to the musician - in order to produce new musical knowledge. Where this is the case, musician-instrument collaboration can occur even without complex artificial cognition; instead, it requires a balance of agency between instrument and musician.

3.4   The Open Work

Eco's *Opera Aperta* predates the pursuit of autonomous electronic musical systems, but speaks very clearly of the dialectic between musician and musical work [13, p.3]:

> It must be observed, for the avoidance of terminological doubt, that the definition of "open" given to these works[1] - although it is of excellent use in outlining a new dialectic between work and musician - must be taken in such a way that, by virtue of a [new] convention, allows us to abstract from other possible and legitimate meanings of this phrase.

Eco's idea of *open* is rooted in the interpretability and freedom inherent in the musical work itself - the musical works he discusses, such as Stockhausen's *Klavierstück XI*, subvert the traditional separation between work and performance and allow for a dialectical openness between them.

In a later chapter, Eco's analysis of the difference between (Shannonian) information and meaning gives us an understanding of the nature of poetics and interpretation in relation to the musician-work dialectic. Blackwell [4] has highlighted the importance of these notions in relation to HCI, and identifies a conflict between 'open' interpretative understanding and the 'simplicity, transparency and ease of learning' that is sought after in user interface design. As we have seen with the *spaces of co-agency*, the balance between human controllability and instrumental unpredictability is key to the design of traditional instruments.

As noted by Bown [7], the distinction between instrument and musical work in interactive music is being dismantled - in digital interactive music, the work is often simply the instrument. Eco's musician-work dialectic, under these conditions, is consistent with our musician-instrument interactive dialectic.

Our final principle of the instrument-as-critic describes this openness:

Third. Interaction with the instrument should be open: interpretable, ambiguous, unpredictable, non-repeatable, non-deterministic.

4   The Mephistophone

As a case-study for our principles of mixed-initiative instrument design, we use the Mephistophone, a haptic interaction device created to question the dynamics of modern music composition, production and performance.

Our technically advanced prototype was built to demonstrate mixed initiative design [1], and many of the ideas and considerations presented above have emerged from its design and development. As the Mephistophone itself is an ongoing project, we aim both to understand its current behaviour and to suggest future directions using the principles presented above.

---

[1] He is discussing four pieces by Stockhausen, Berio, Pousseur and Boulez, where each performance is an open interpretation of the work.

The Mephistophone consists of a deformable control surface (a large latex sheet) and a set of live machine-learning algorithms on a local computer: processing the surface depth-data, and controlling actuators to deform the surface electromechanically. The machine-learning algorithms learn directly from experience and observation of human performances. During training, the computer pre-learns sound representations of the audio space, linking the two inseparably [5].

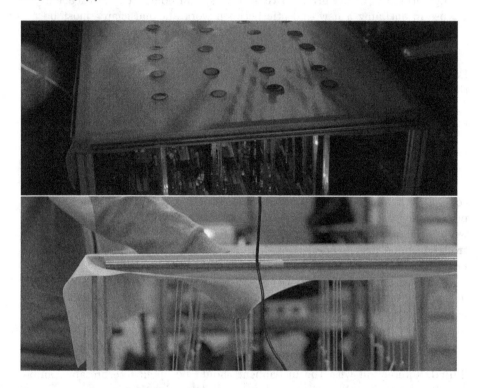

Fig. 2. Top: the Mephistophone's control surface, with sensors and actuators underneath. Bottom: deformations of audio representations during training

4.1   Haptic Spaces of Co-Agency

The latex control surface of the Mephistophone has displacement sensors and actuators throughout the controllable area (Fig. 2), allowing for machine and human collaboration over a restricted physical domain. This corresponds closely to our notion of the *space of co-agency*.

Audially, the Mephistophone is theoretically capable to sense sounds by using the control surface as a large microphone[2]. This physical space is explicitly and non-linearly linked to an audial representation, as discussed elsewhere [16]. The

---

[2] It is also fitted with a small onboard audio microphone.

instrument both listens 'to itself' (to the sounds produced by the actuators and by onboard speakers), and to its human collaborator.

In terms of the requirements discussed above, the control surface of the Mephistophone - its space of co-agency - is concurrently physical and audial. Haptic, vibrational and audio information (mechanical motion at various scales) are inseparable in the instrument, and travel in both directions between performer and machine.

Agency over the space is explicitly shared: the machine can physically oppose or interact with a human using its powerful actuation, giving haptic feedback in an ergonomically relevant way. By deforming the surface, it can play itself (physically explore a region of co-agent space) - by doing this, it makes a set of other physical deformations impossible, dynamically interfering with the agency of the musician.

4.2   Antithetical System and the Open Synthesis

How might we program or control the Mephistophone to use the spaces of co-agency that it presents in an antithetical way? For this, the instrument's reactions must respond to the musician's input dialectically, and in an open way. As discussed, this concept of 'open' relates both to the unpredictability of behaviour and to the flexibility of interpretation. The Mephistophone is also open-source - both the physical design and algorithmic control are freely accessible and modifiable. This is quite close to Eco's original example of 'openness' - a composition which can be freely tampered with or modified by the performer.

Our early-prototype antithetical system utilises performance data analysis - building a generative model of movement through the space of co-agency from its training phase, and potentially from datasets of traditional-instrument performances of violins. Having learned a physical representation of the audio-space, the machine can respond to sound by trying to deform out of the shape linked to the live audio signal. This can be seen as a development of the Oppositional System, where opposition to the musician is not just through sound, but through all the mechanical properties (haptic-vibrational-audial) in the space of co-agency.

The uncanny nature of the physical unpredictability of the machine, however, does lend itself to Heidegger's *Vorhandenheit*. We might describe the acquisition of soul through code, over and above the vitality of the machine, as *noomorphism* - a term that we coin by analogy to anthropomorphism, and in acknowledgement of the neomystical tradition through which the actuators of the Internet of Things partake in the digital soul of Teilhard de Chardin's *noosphere*.

A key subject of ongoing research and experimentation is the algorithmic implementation of open interaction - the antithetical system is only open in a very restricted sense. Though unpredictable, it does not explicitly lend itself to openness of interpretation. In line with our understanding of spaces of co-agency, the noomorphism of the machine must also exhibit symmetric openness - a reciprocal interpretability on behalf of both human and machine.

5   Concluding Remarks

The Mephistophone's physical design and software setup represents an important prototype for the *instrument-as-critic*, as the deformable/self-deforming surface is perhaps the most simple instance of an instrumental space of co-agency. Traditional musical instruments follow this pattern more subtley - we have presented a brief analysis of how the violin can be seen to exhibit such a space, but clearly there are some exceptions and limit-cases (such as the harpsichord). Notwithstanding these caveats, an explicit consideration of the space of co-agency is relevant not only in the analysis of traditional musical instruments, but especially as a design tool for interactive electronic instruments.

Although there is some clear overlap, in our prototype the space of co-agency can be thought of as primarily a hardware consideration, where dialectical interaction and the open synthesis are mostly important in the machine-learning software and control of the instrument. In this simplified light, and to return to outdated - but useful - distinctions between the musical (hardware) *instrument* and the (software) *work*, the Mephistophone's physical setup provides a useful testing-bed for the open musical work.

Mixed-initiative interaction is a popular paradigm for the (co-)creative use of computers, such as in game design [28]. It is hoped that this specific consideration of mixed-initiative interaction in musical performance could be of use to human-computer interaction more generally. In particular, a consideration of openness and interpretability between human and machine for non-artistic purposes could provide an interesting topic for further research.

References

1. The mephistophone. Accessed: 19 March 2015. http://mephistophone.com/
2. Allen, J.E., Guinn, C.I., Horvtz, E.: Mixed-initiative interaction. IEEE Intell. Syst. Appl. **14**(5), 14–23 (1999)
3. Badiou, A., Spitzer, S.: Five lessons on Wagner. Verso, London (2010)
4. Blackwell, A.F.: What does Digital Content Mean? Umberto Eco and The Open Work (2015)
5. Blackwell, A.F., Impett, L., Wollner, P.K.A., Herman, I., Pribadi, H.: The mephistophone. Technical report 855, Computer Lab, University of Cambridge (2014)
6. Bongers, B.: Physical interfaces in the electronic arts. In: Wanderley, M.M., Battier, M. (eds.) Trends in Gestural Control of Music, pp. 41–70. IRCAM Pompidou, Paris (2000)
7. Bown, O., Eldridge, A., Mccormack, J.: Understanding interaction in contemporary digital music: from instruments to behavioural objects. Organ. Sound **14**(02), 188–196 (2009)
8. Buchanan, I., Swiboda, M.: Deleuze and Music. Oxford University Press, New York (2004)
9. Cacciari, M.: Krisis: saggio sulla crisi del pensiero negativo da Nietzsche a Wittgenstein, vol. 332. Feltrinelli, Milan (1977)

10. Collins, N.: Contrary motion: an oppositional interactive music system. In: The Conference on New Interfaces for Musical Expression (2010)
11. Collins, N.: Improvisation. Leonardo Music J. **20**, 7–9 (2010)
12. Drummond, J.: Understanding interactive systems. Organ. Sound **14**(02), 124–133 (2009)
13. Umberto Eco. Opera aperta: Forma e indeterminazione nelle poetiche contemparanee, vol. 3. Tascabili Bompiani, Milan (1962)
14. Fritz, C., Blackwell, A.F., Cross, I., Woodhouse, J., Moore, B.C.J.: Exploring violin sound quality: investigating english timbre descriptors and correlating resynthesized acoustical modifications with perceptual properties. J. Acoust. Soc. Am. **131**(1), 783–794 (2012)
15. Harman, G., et al.: Technology, objects and things in heidegger. Camb. J. Econ. **34**(1), 17–25 (2010)
16. Herman, I., Impett, L., Woller, P.K.A., Blackwell, A.: Augmenting bioacoustic cognition with tangible user interfaces (2015)
17. Horvitz, E.J.: Reflections on challenges and promises of mixed-initiative interaction. AI Mag. **28**(2), 3 (2007)
18. Impett, J.: The identification and transposition of authentic instruments: musical practice and technology. Leonardo Music J. **8**, 21–26 (1998)
19. Licklider, J.C.R.: Man-computer symbiosis. IRE Trans. Hum. Factors Electron. **1**, 4–11 (1960)
20. McNutt, E.: Performing electroacoustic music: a wider view of interactivity. Organ. Sound **8**(03), 297–304 (2003)
21. Nash, C., Blackwell, A.: Liveness and flow in notation use. In: Proceedings of the International Conference on New Interfaces for Musical Expression (NIME), Ann Arbor, Michigan (2012)
22. North, J.D.: The Rational Behavior of Mechanically Extended Man. Boulton Paul Aircraft Ltd., Wolverhampton (1954)
23. Palmer, D.L.: Virtuosity as rhetoric. agency and transformation in paganini's mastery of the violin. Q. J. Speech **84**(3), 341–357 (1998)
24. Peek, P.M.: The sounds of silence: cross-world communication and the auditory arts in african societies. Am. Ethnol. **21**(3), 474–494 (1994)
25. Segol, M.: Word and Image in Medieval Kabbalah. Palgrave Macmillan, New York (2012)
26. Serafin, S., Smith, J.O., Woodhouse, J.: An investigation of the impact of torsion waves and friction characteristics on the playability of virtual bowed strings. In: 1999 IEEE Workshop on Applications of Signal Processing to Audio and Acoustics, pp. 87–90. IEEE (1999)
27. Shneiderman, B., Maes, P.: Direct manipulation vs. interface agents. Interact. **4**(6), 42–61 (1997)
28. Yannakakis, G.N., Liapis, A., Alexopoulos, C.: Mixed-initiative cocreativity. In: Proceedings of the 9th Conference on the Foundations of Digital Games (2014)

RICHIE: A Step-by-step Navigation Widget to Enhance Broad Hierarchy Exploration on Handheld Tactile Devices

Alexandre Kabil and Sébastien Kubicki[✉]

ENI Brest, Lab-STICC UMR6285, 29200 Brest, France
{kabil,kubicki}@enib.fr

Abstract. Exploring large hierarchies is still a challenging task, especially for handheld tactile devices, due to the lack of visualization space and finger's occlusion. In this paper, we propose the RICHIE (Radial InCremental HIerarchy Exploration) tool, a new radial widget that allows step-by-step navigation through large hierarchies. We designed it to fit handheld tactile requirements such as target reaching and space optimization. Depth exploration is made by shifting two levels of hierarchy at the same time, for reducing the screen occupation. This widget was implemented in order to adapt a Command and Control (C2) system to mobile tactile devices, as these systems require the on-screen presence of an important unit's hierarchy (the ORder of BATtle). Nevertheless, we are convinced that RICHIE could be used on several systems that require hierarchical data exploration, such as phylogenetic trees or file browsing.

Keywords: Multi-touch · Information visualization · Hierarchy

1 Introduction

Various existing interaction and visualization techniques for large datasets aim at displaying all linked items, using node-link or space-filling approaches [1]. Enhanced node-link approaches give the opportunity to visualize and select elements from various datasets, whereas radial space-filling ones are centered on hierarchical data [2]. These approaches have drawbacks when used on mobile devices, especially when datasets are substantial. To overcome these limitations, we propose RICHIE, a Radial InCremental Hierarchy Exploration widget composed of two concentric quadrant shapes, which are placed at a bottom corner of the screen, facilitating thumb usability. The first arc contains a first level selected item and its siblings, whereas the second arc contains its children.

Our approach is inspired by ControlTree [3], which defines three zones for a selected item: a sibling zone, a children zone and a parent zone. However, for minimizing occupation space, we display only few items at once from sibling and children zones; circular dragging gesture on quadrants allow navigation through hidden items. Moreover, depth exploration is made selecting an item on the

© Springer International Publishing Switzerland 2015
M. Kurosu (Ed.): Human-Computer Interaction, Part II, HCII 2015, LNCS 9170, pp. 196–207, 2015.
DOI: 10.1007/978-3-319-20916-6_19

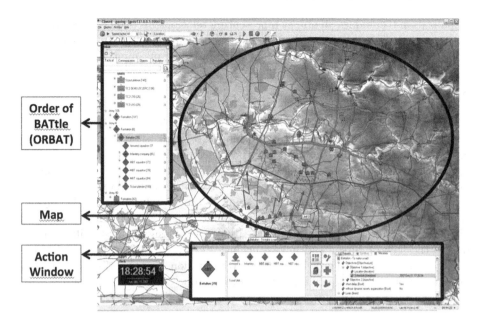

Fig. 1. View of the existing C2 system.

second quadrant and by shifting itself and its siblings to the first quadrant (forward navigation) or by shifting items from the first quadrant to the second one, allowing items from the parent zone to appear on the first arc (backward navigation).

We choose this specific design because we do not want our widget to occupy the whole screen area, like Radial Edgeless Tree [4] or Radial Space Filling [5] methods, as we implemented it in a C2 (Command and Control) system [6], in which users interact mainly on a map but also need to control a large number of hierarchical units (Fig. 1).

Finally, we think that our widget can be used in different domains, such as files browsing or phylogenetic trees exploration, which requires exploration of large hierarchical datasets.

This paper is organized as follows. First, we will give a review of the current hierarchy exploration techniques and especially those that can be used on tactile devices. Then we will present our RICHIE widget, designed to overcome broad hierarchy navigation issues on mobile tactile devices. The next section will describe in details the functioning of the widget, and the different interaction techniques that we are developing in order to evaluate them from a user's point of view. Finally, some considerations on the usability of our widget in different domains will be exposed.

2   Related Work

There exists numerous hierarchy visualization and navigation techniques, but we can classify them into two categories [1,4]: (1) node-link, connection or explicit visualization techniques [4] aim at representing relations between connected data with semantic links whereas (2) space-filling, enclosure or implicit techniques [7] use positions and sizes of nodes to convey hierarchical meaning.

2.1 Node-Edge Approaches

Hao *et al.* [4] show that major issues for node-link displaying approaches are the location and the connection of the nodes. Visualization's optimization of graphs and especially hierarchical ones have been exhaustively researched, and approaches like H-Tree or Radial trees [8] (Fig. 2) are convenient for simple desktop usages. But, when users want to interact with graphs, they need adapted interaction techniques. ControlTree [3], for instance, helps user by displaying siblings and children of selected item in specific spaces (Fig. 3). However, these visualization and interaction techniques are not well designed for tactile devices, due to the lack of cursor and fingers occlusion, which limit precise interaction. That is why there is a growing need in Information Visualization domain for novel interaction techniques that enables multi-touch graph interaction [9].

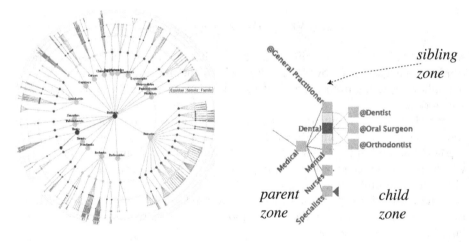

Fig. 2. Radial tree visualization [8]   **Fig. 3.** ControlTree zones [3]

More recently, Holzinger *et al.* [10] made a multi-touch graph-based interaction review that highlights the techniques used and the challenges new devices offers for information visualization. Yet, for hierarchical graphs, where links between nodes are quite implicit (parents-children or siblings semantic relationships), the space-filling approach seems more adapted to mobile devices, even if some mixed techniques such as SpaceTree [11] or EnCon [12] tried to take advantage of both approaches by adapting a graph to a specified size.

2.2 Space-Filling Approaches

Links in enclosure visualization techniques are implicit, and the geometric positions and sizes of nodes reveals the nature of their connections. Treemap [13] is the most simple space-filling approach, but lacks clarity regarding the hierarchy (Fig. 4). That is why, radial or concentric techniques were developed [2], such as InterRing [5] (Fig. 5). RELT (Radial EdgeLess Tree), developed by Hao *et al.* is a visualization technique that aims at maximizing the space used by data and providing a clear hierarchy view [4]. These techniques are less convenient when hierarchies are imbalanced (when items have very different number of siblings or children). To curb this issue, Chhetri *et al.* proposed ERELT (Enhanced RELT) [7] which allows users to perform a drag gesture in order to display hidden items, allowing the visualization of large hierarchies without reducing node sizes (Fig. 6).

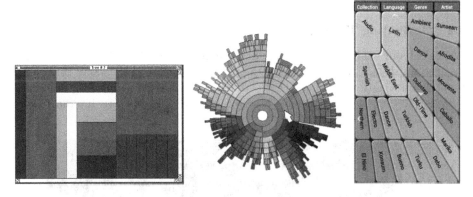

Fig. 4. TreeMap [13]   **Fig. 5.** InterRing [5]   **Fig. 6.** ERELT [7]

All of approaches made for mobile devices tends to maximize the utilization of screen area, which sometimes is not required, when for example you do not want to lose the view of an application while browsing some data hierarchy. Moreover, the size-changing of items could limit finger interaction, if their number is too important.

In the next section we will introduce RICHIE, a step-by-step widget that tends to curb these issues.

3 Design

We designed the RICHIE technique with the constraints that it should not take whole screen space, items size should be finger-adapted, and the interaction should be easy on mobile tactile devices, such as tablets or smartphones.

3.1 Concentric Shape

The radial concentric shape was proved efficient for displaying hierarchical data [7]. Moreover, putting the center of widget in a bottom corner of the device facilitates thumb [14] or two-hands interaction [15], due to the grasping position and the physiology of hands [16]. By taking inspiration from the wheel metaphor [14], we decided to consider a quadrant radial design, similar to a corner menu [17]. But, we do not want all items of the same hierarchy level to be visible, so, as ERELT [7], we display only a part of items and user can access hidden ones by dragging them on the active view. This design allows us to make all items the same size (Fig. 7), which can fit through tactile guidelines [18], and not to limit the broadness of hierarchy datasets.

Moreover, to facilitate lisibility of hierarchical links between items, selection of a first quadrant's item puts it at 45°, in a highlight zone (Fig. 7), whereas its children appears on second arc.

3.2 Navigating Through Hierarchy

We called our widget RICHIE (Radial InCremental HIerarchy Exploration) because we do not want to display the whole hierarchy at the same time. We propose a navigation technique that is different from Moire graph [19], Stacked-half-pie [20] and wavelet menus [21], because we only want to interact with

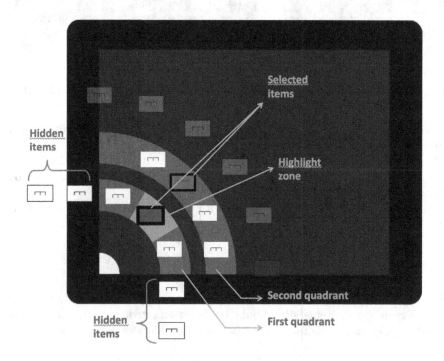

Fig. 7. Prototype view of item's positionning.

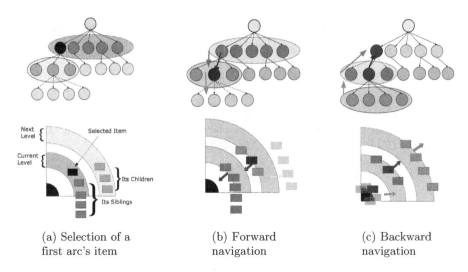

(a) Selection of a first arc's item

(b) Forward navigation

(c) Backward navigation

Fig. 8. Different states of the widget compared to a hierarchical view

two levels of hierarchy, for limiting screen occupation (Fig. 8). The first quadrant contains selected item and its siblings whereas second one contains selected items children (Fig. 8a). We took inspiration from ControlTree [3] zones, namely sibling zone, children zone and parent zone which is hidden in our widget. Forward navigation (Fig. 8b) is made by dragging second quadrant s selected item to the first quadrant and backward navigation (Fig. 8c) by dragging first arc 's selected item to the second one. Drag and tap gestures used in this navigation technique are considered direct manipulation gestures, and are proved effective for selection tasks [22,23].

The next section will provide information about development issues and choices.

4 Implementation and Development

We developed our widget with Unity3D, a real-time game engine. This choice was made because this software allowed us to design the shapes and behaviors we wanted, in a framework that takes into account tactile events and which is more evolutive than sketching or prototyping tools, partly because of its multiplatform capabilities.

4.1 Display and Interaction with Items

We designed a unique function that allows positioning of same level hierarchy items. Let U being a list of M items and N the number of visible elements we want on our widget's quadrants ($N > 1$). By taking the center of widget, horizontal and vertical axes of device for geometrical frame, position $\overrightarrow{U_i}$ of $U[i]$

item will depends on two coordinates and its angle θ_i with abscissa axis, given the radius R of the display circle (Eq. 1):

$$\theta_i = \frac{i \times \pi}{2(N - 1)} + C \qquad (1)$$

where C is a variable controlled by dragging: dragging to the upper side of the widget increases C whereas dragging to the bottom side decreases it. Initial positions of U's items are, for $i \in [0, M - 1]$ (Eqs. 2, 3, 4):

$$\text{If} \quad \theta_i < 0: \qquad \overrightarrow{U_i} \cdot \overrightarrow{x} = R; \qquad \overrightarrow{U_i} \cdot \overrightarrow{y} = -\theta_i \times K \qquad (2)$$

$$\text{If} \quad \theta_i < \frac{\pi}{2}: \qquad \overrightarrow{U_i} \cdot \overrightarrow{x} = R \times \cos(\theta_i); \qquad \overrightarrow{U_i} \cdot \overrightarrow{y} = R \times \sin(\theta_i) \qquad (3)$$

$$\text{Else}: \qquad \overrightarrow{U_i} \cdot \overrightarrow{x} = (\frac{\pi}{2} - \theta_i) \times K; \qquad \overrightarrow{U_i} \cdot \overrightarrow{y} = R \qquad (4)$$

where $K > 1$ is a constant that spreads out-the-screen items.

This function allows us to move all items correctly, and by defining a number of visible objects we can adapt the visualization to the device.

4.2   Step-by-step Navigation

One major issue raised by HCI researchers is the importance of animations or animated transitions for user's understanding of interface behavior [24] or decision-making [25]. These animations should therefore be cancellable if user stops interacting, allowing him to undo his action in a fluid way [26]. That is why we modeled a Behavioral State Machine for each of our widget's items which describes items states and transitions (Fig. 9).

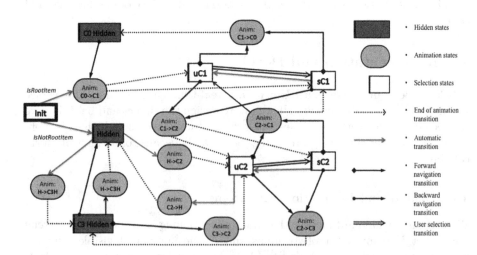

Fig. 9. Item's behavior

On the Fig. 9, one can notice that **Anim** states represent animated transitions from one circle to another, allowing the cancellation of actions and the understanding of interaction. All items are initially on the **Init** state, and depending if they are at the first level of hierarchy, they go either on the first circle or hidden below their fathers. In Unity3D, we put children at the same position of fathers, but we deactivate their sprite renderer and box collider, disabling their interactive capabilities. **uC1**, **sC1**, **uC2** and **sC2** corresponds respectively to unselected state on circle one, selected state on circle one and the same for circle two. **C0** and **C3 Hidden** states correspond to specific hidden states which represents non-interactive states displayed respectively at the origin of the widget and above the second circle, as represented on Fig. 7.

When a user selects an item on the first circle for the first time (Double arrow), this item goes from **uC1** to **sC1**, and its children goes from **Hidden** to **uC2**. If user selects another item from the first circle, formerly selected item goes from **sC1** to **uC1**, its children from **uC2** to **Hidden** and the newly selected item and its children behaves as previously described. When a user selects an item on the second circle, it goes from **uC2** to **sC2** and its children goes from **Hidden** to **C3 Hidden**. Selecting another item from second circle acts as previously said for circle one. When a user perform a forward navigation (square-beginning arrows), items from circle one disappeared and goes to **C0**, origin of the widget, but we are saving their status (selected, unselected) for backward navigation. Items from second circles goes on the first one, according to their selected statuses, and items from third hidden circle goes all unselected on the second one.

Backward navigation (round-beginning arrows) makes items hidden in circle zero to move to circle one, items in circle one to circle two with same statuses and items from circle three to **Hidden** state, under their parent.

We also add a global state machine for the widget, for controlling the global behavior and saving statuses of items (if an item is selected, its siblings should be deselected and so on).

This section described the implementation and development of RICHIE, a step-by-step hierarchy exploration widget. The following one will present shortly the Command and Control application in which we implemented and tested it, and other domains we think it can be used for. We will describe also our on-going efforts to evaluate usability of our system.

5 Tests and Perspectives

C2 systems usually deal with large and imbalanced hierarchies of units displayed within a map and in a linear classic way [27]. These constraints limits the screen space used by the hierarchy visualization and its interaction, that is why existing multitouch C2 systems were developed usually for interactive tabletops [28,29]. As we want to adapt an existing C2 system showed in Fig. 7 to handheld tactile devices, we are currently testing a C2-tactile prototype which embeds our RICHIE widget (Fig. 10). Our widget might be used in every domain that need browsing through large hierarchies without displaying the whole dataset.

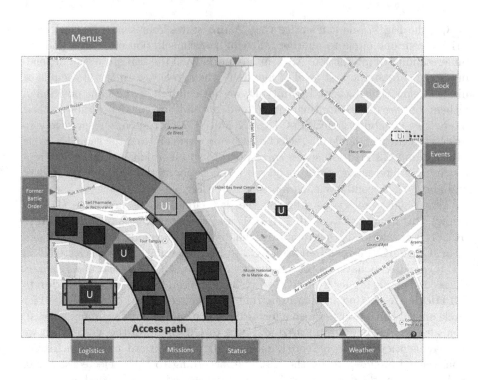

Fig. 10. Sketch of our adaptation.

Genomic data visualization systems such as those proposed by Shaer *et al.* [30] could, for example, benefit from our solution. Semantic relationships between elements could also be explored, such as with the MASCARET Virtual Environment meta-model [31]; our widget could facilitate the exploration of information towards a simulation.

We will perform experimentations in order to test different ways of interaction (for example adding a breadcrumb trail will allow users to jump from one level of hierarchy to a previous one, as in file systems or websites [32,33]). Simultaneous map interaction and hierarchy exploration will be evaluated too [34]. Performance comparisons between RICHIE and existing exploration techniques for item retrieval or other specific tasks would bring cues of user's preferences [35].

6   Conclusion

This paper has presented RICHIE, a step-by-step widget that allows the exploration through larges data hierarchies on tactile handheld devices. Unlike other approaches, it uses minimal on-screen space, enabling the interaction with distinct tools, such as interactive maps. Users do not dispose of a global view of data, but instead they navigate level after level through hierarchy. Our immediate future work is to made experimentations in order to explore RICHIE's capabilities and usages in different applications and on different devices.

Acknowledgments. This research work was partially funded by the "Ministère de l'Enseignement Supérieur et de la Recherche", the "Conseil Général du Finistère", the "Brest Métropole Océane", and especially the "Agence Nationale de la Recherche" (TACTIC ANR Project, ANR-12-ASTR-0020).

References

1. Herman, I., Melançon, G., Marshall, M.S.: Graph visualization and navigation in information visualization: a survey. IEEE Trans. Visual Comput. Graphics **6**, 24–43 (2000)
2. Draper, G., Livnat, Y., Riesenfeld, R.: A survey of radial methods for information visualization. IEEE Trans. Visual. Comput. Graph. **15**, 759–776 (2009)
3. Appert, C., Fekete, J.-D. et al.: Controltree: navigating and selecting in a large tree. In: ACM Symposium on User Interface Software and Technology (2006)
4. Hao, J., Gabrysch, C.A., Zhao, C., Zhu, Q., Zhang, K.: Visualizing and navigating hierarchical information on mobile user interfaces. Int. J. Adv. Intell. **2**(1), 81–103 (2010)
5. Yang, J., Ward, M.O., Rundensteiner, E.A.: Interring: an interactive tool for visually navigating and manipulating hierarchical structures. In: Proceedings of the IEEE Symposium on Information Visualization (InfoVis 2002), INFOVIS 2002, Washington, DC, USA, pp. 77–84. IEEE Computer Society (2002)
6. McCann, C., Pigeau, R.: Clarifying the concepts of control and of command. In: Proceedings of the 1999 Command and Control Research and Technology Symposium, vol. 29 (1999)
7. Chhetri, A.P., Zhang, K., Jain, E.: Erelt: a faster alternative to the list-based interfaces for tree exploration and searching in mobile devices. In: Proceedings of the 6th International Symposium on Visual Information Communication and Interaction, VINCI 2013, New York, NY, USA, pp. 54–63. ACM (2013)
8. Sheth, N., Borner, K., Baumgartner, J., Mane, K., Wernert, E.: Treemap, radial tree, and 3d tree visualizations. IEEE InfoVis Poster Compendium **1**, 128–129 (2003)
9. Schmidt, M.A., Nacenta, S., Dachselt, R., Carpendale, S.: A set of multi-touch graph interaction techniques. In: ACM International Conference on Interactive Tabletops and Surfaces, ITS 2010, New York, NY, USA, pp. 113–116. ACM (2010)
10. Holzinger, A., Ofner, B., Dehmer, M.: Multi-touch graph-based interaction for knowledge discovery on mobile devices: state-of-the-art and future challenges. In: Holzinger, A., Jurisica, I. (eds.) Interactive Knowledge Discovery and Data Mining in Biomedical Informatics. LNCS, vol. 8401, pp. 241–254. Springer, Heidelberg (2014)
11. Plaisant, C., Grosjean, J., Bederson, B.B.: Spacetree: supporting exploration in large node link tree, design evolution and empirical evaluation. In: Proceedings of the IEEE Symposium on Information Visualization (InfoVis 2002), INFOVIS 2002, Washington, DC, USA, p. 57. IEEE Computer Society (2002)
12. Nguyen, Q.V., Huang, M.L.: Enccon: an approach to constructing interactive visualization of large hierarchical data. Inf. Visual. **4**(1), 1–21 (2005)

13. Johnson, B., Shneiderman, B.: Tree-maps: a space-filling approach to the visualization of hierarchical information structures. In: Proceedings of the 2Nd Conference on Visualization 1991, VIS 1991, Los Alamitos, CA, USA, pp. 284–291. IEEE Computer Society Press (1991)
14. Seipp, K., Devlin, K.: The one hand wonder: A framework for enhancing one-handed website operation on touchscreen smartphones. In: Proceedings of the 10th International Conference on Web Information Systems and Technologies, WEBIST 2014, Barcelona. Goldsmiths Research Online (2014)
15. Wagner, J., Huot, S., Mackay, W.: Bitouch and bipad: designing bimanual interaction for hand-held tablets. In: Proceedings of the SIGCHI Conference on Human Factors in Computing Systems, CHI 2012, New York, NY, USA, pp. 2317–2326. ACM (2012)
16. Wolf, K., Henze, N.: Comparing pointing techniques for grasping hands on tablets. In: Proceedings of the 16th International Conference on Human-computer Interaction with Mobile Devices & #38; Services, MobileHCI 2014, New York, NY, USA, pp. 53–62. ACM (2014)
17. Huot, S., Lecolinet, E.: Focus+context visualization techniques for displaying large lists with multiple points of interest on small tactile screens. In: Baranauskas, C., Abascal, J., Barbosa, S.D.J. (eds.) INTERACT 2007. LNCS, vol. 4663, pp. 219–233. Springer, Heidelberg (2007)
18. Park, Y.S., Han, S.H., Park, J., Cho, Y.: Touch key design for target selection on a mobile phone. In: Proceedings of the 10th International Conference on Human Computer Interaction with Mobile Devices and Services, MobileHCI 2008, New York, NY, USA, pp. 423–426. ACM (2008)
19. Jankun-Kelly, T.J., Ma, K.-L.: Moiregraphs: radial focus+context visualization and interaction for graphs with visual nodes. In: Proceedings of the Ninth Annual IEEE Conference on Information Visualization, INFOVIS 2003, Washington, DC, USA, pp. 59–66. IEEE Computer Society (2003)
20. Hesselmann, T., Flöring, S., Schmitt, M.: Stacked half-pie menus: navigating nested menus on interactive tabletops. In: Proceedings of the ACM International Conference on Interactive Tabletops and Surfaces, ITS 2009, New York, NY, USA, pp. 173–180. ACM (2009)
21. Francone, J., Bailly, G., Lecolinet, E., Mandran, N., Nigay, L.: Wavelet menus on handheld devices: stacking metaphor for novice mode and eyes-free selection for expert mode. In: Proceedings of the International Conference on Advanced Visual Interfaces, AVI 2010, New York, NY, USA, pp. 173–180. ACM (2010)
22. Kin, K., Agrawala, M., DeRose, T.: Determining the benefits of direct-touch, bimanual, and multifinger input on a multitouch workstation. In: Proceedings of Graphics Interface 2009, GI 2009, Toronto, Ont., Canada, Canada, pp. 119–124. Canadian Information Processing Society (2009)
23. Cockburn, A., Ahlström, D., Gutwin, C.: Understanding performance in touch selections: tap, drag and radial pointing drag with finger, stylus and mouse. Int. J. Hum.-Comput. Stud. **70**, 218–233 (2012)
24. Chang, B.-W., Ungar, D.: Animation: from cartoons to the user interface. In: Proceedings of the 6th Annual ACM Symposium on User Interface Software and Technology, UIST 1993, New York, NY, USA, pp. 45–55. ACM (1993)
25. Gonzalez, C.: Does animation in user interfaces improve decision making?. In: Proceedings of the SIGCHI Conference on Human Factors in Computing Systems, CHI 1996, New York, NY, USA, pp. 27–34. ACM (1996)
26. Elmqvist, N., Vande, A., Moere, H.-C., Jetter, D., Cernea, H., Jankun-Kelly, T.J.: Fluid interaction for information visualization. Inf. Visual. **10**, 327–340 (2011)

27. Ucuzal, L., Kopar, A.: GIS (geographic information systems) in CCIS (command & control systems). Geogr. Inf. Convers. Manage. Syst. **30**, 6 (2010)

28. Bortolaso, C., Oskamp, M., Graham, T.N., Brown, D.: Ormis: a tabletop interface for simulation-based training. In Proceedings of the 2013 ACM International Conference on Interactive Tabletops and Surfaces, ITS 2013, New York, NY, USA, pp. 145–154. ACM (2013)

29. Szymanski, R., Goldin, M., Palmer, N., Beckinger, R., Gilday, J., Chase, T.: Command and control in a multitouch environment. In: 26th Army Science Conference (2008)

30. Shaer, O., Strait, M., Valdes, C., Wang, H., Feng, T., Lintz, M., Ferreirae, M., Grote, C., Tempel, K., Liu, S.: The design, development, and deployment of a tabletop interface for collaborative exploration of genomic data. Int. J. Hum.-Comput. Stud. **70**, 746–764 (2012)

31. Buche, C., Querrec, R., De Loor, P., Chevaillier, P.: Mascaret: pedagogical multi-agents systems for virtual environment for training. In: 2003 Proceedings of International Conference on Cyberworlds, pp. 423–430, December 2003

32. Hudson, W.: Breadcrumb navigation: there's more to hansel and gretel than meets the eye. Interactions **11**, 79–80 (2004)

33. Smith, A., Hawes, T., Myers, M.: Hiérarchie: interactive visualization for hierarchical topic models. In: Proceedings of the Workshop on Interactive Language Learning, Visualization, and Interfaces, pp. 71–78. Association for Computational Linguistics (2014)

34. Pietriga, E., Appert, C., Beaudouin-Lafon, M.: Pointing and beyond: an operationalization and preliminary evaluation of multi-scale searching. In: Proceedings of the SIGCHI Conference on Human Factors in Computing Systems, CHI 2007, New York, NY, USA, pp. 1215–1224. ACM (2007)

35. Stasko, J.: An evaluation of space-filling information visualizations for depicting hierarchical structures. Int. J. Hum.-Comput. Stud. **53**, 663–694 (2000)

Information Select and Transfer Between Touch Panel and Wearable Devices Using Human Body Communication

Yuto Kondo[✉], Shin Takahashi, and Jiro Tanaka

Department of Computer Science, University of Tsukuba,
1-1-1 Tennodai, Tsukuba, Ibaraki, Japan
kondoy@iplab.cs.tsukuba.ac.jp, {shin,jiro}@cs.tsukuba.ac.jp

Abstract. This paper proposes a technique to enable the simple transfer of information between a computer with a large touch-panel display, such as a tabletop PC, and another computer, typically one worn by the user. With our technique, the user touches an intended item displayed on the panel to select and transfer it to his or her device. We describe some illustrative usage scenarios and outline a prototype system that can communicate image data between a tabletop PC and a wearable device. We conducted preliminary experiments to evaluate this system's user interface and performed interviews with test subjects regarding the prototype.

1 Introduction

With the drop in the cost of computers, people now often have the opportunity to use multiple devices simultaneously. Users typically own and operate various types of PCs, tablets, and smart phones. In addition, they occasionally encounter public access terminals such as information kiosks, ATMs, and digital signages. It is desirable to establish communication between such devices, but enabling them to function cooperatively is often difficult and requires tedious configuration. It is necessary to provide more user-friendly interfaces for connecting and using multiple devices in cooperation.

This paper proposes a method to enable the straightforward transfer of information between a computer with a large touch-panel display, such as a tabletop PC, and another device, typically one worn by the user. The technique uses human body communication protocols proposed by Zimmerman [1], which utilize the human body as part of an electronic circuit. With our technique, the user touches an item on the display to select and transfer it to his or her computer. Upon touching the panel, the two devices are automatically connected, and the selected information is transmitted directly through the user's body. The user does not need to configure the connections between devices in advance, and can easily transfer data between devices.

M. Kurosu (Ed.): Human-Computer Interaction, Part II, HCII 2015, LNCS 9170, pp. 208–216, 2015.
DOI: 10.1007/978-3-319-20916-6_20

2   Selection and Transfer by Touch

2.1   Basic Interaction Technique

We propose a method for information transfer between multiple devices with a touch panel, utilizing human body communication. Figure 1 illustrates our proposed technique. Icons that represent information such as a file or an image are displayed on the large touch screen of a tabletop PC. The user has a wearable device on his or her wrist and the device has a small touch screen, much like a smartphone. To transfer information from the tabletop PC to the user's wearable, he or she selects an icon and touches it with his or her finger. The system automatically connects the two devices, and transmits the data represented by the selected icon. Alternatively, to transfer information from the wearable device to the tabletop PC, the user first selects an icon on the wearable, and then touches the screen of the tabletop PC.

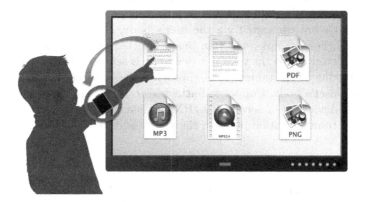

Fig. 1. Overview of our proposed method: transfer by touching the interactive screen.

2.2   Example Use of the Interaction Technique

Combining with Multitouch and Gesture Operations. Various types of touch interaction can be used with our technique. For example, multiple pieces of information can be selected and transferred simultaneously by touching multiple icons. In addition, multi-touch operations can be used. The user designates the range with his or her fingers and items within the range are selected and transferred simultaneously. Images transferred to a device can also be scaled with multi-touch gestures.

Receiving Streaming Data. In our method, devices can communicate only while the user is touching the screen. We can take advantage of this characteristic. For example, it is only possible to stream video while the user is touching the screen. This may be useful when presenting promotional material to specific customers, or offering coupons corresponding to the time the visitor watched the video.

Transferring a User's Profile to Customize Interactions. With our technique, a touch operation can be used to transfer user profiles from a consumer
device to a public terminal, and vice versa, enabling customized interaction.
Information can be recommended based on the user's personal preferences.
For example, if a user is searching for a restaurant from an information kiosk,
he or she can provide his or her preference by touching the screen. When a
restaurant is decided upon, a map can be transferred to the user's device by
touching the restaurant's icon.

3   Prototype Implementation

3.1   Overview

Figure 2 shows an overview of a prototype implementation. The system consists
of two parts: a device worn by the user (Fig. 2 (right)) and a tabletop PC with a
touch panel screen (Fig. 2 (left)). When the user interacts with the tabletop PC,
these two parts are connected via the user's body, and a communication link
is established. For example, when an image selected by the user is transferred
from the tabletop PC to the wearable device, it is sent via the transmit/receive
(TX/RX) module of the tabletop PC, through the transparent conductive sheet,
and into the user's body. Copper foil attached to the wearable couples the signal into the device via a second TX/RX module. This path can be used for
bidirectional communication between the wearable device and the tabletop PC.

3.2   Wearable Devices

Figure 3 shows a prototype wearable device designed to be worn on the wrist
(Fig. 3 (a)). A smartphone (Samsung Galaxy S II LTE) was used for interaction

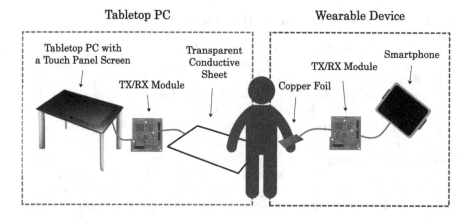

Fig. 2. Overview of the data communication path established when a user touches the
tabletop PC display.

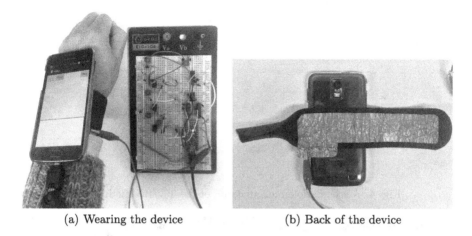

(a) Wearing the device   (b) Back of the device

Fig. 3. The prototype wearable device.

with the user. An external TX/RX circuit was connected to the smartphone via copper foil fitted to the back of the wearable device that allowed signals to be coupled into the human body (Fig. 3 (b)).

3.3   TX/RX Circuit Board

Figure 4 shows a schematic of the TX/RX circuit board that was used for both the tabletop PC and the wearable device. The transmission (TX) circuit comprised a crystal oscillator and an AND logic circuit. Data were sent using amplitude shift keying (ASK) modulation. A carrier wave of 1 MHz was generated by the crystal oscillator. The receive (RX) circuit comprised a band-pass filter, two operational amplifiers, an envelope-detection circuit, and a comparator. Received signals were amplified, demodulated and read by an Arduino microcontroller. The signal path was half-duplex and therefore only one circuit could operate in TX mode at any one time, a condition satisfied by using relays. For example, when data were transmitted from the tabletop PC to the wearable device, the TX module of the PC and the RX module of the wearable were activated. The prototype implementation of the TX/RX circuits used a breadboard. Printed circuit boards are being fabricated at the time of writing.

3.4   Tabletop PC with a Touch Panel

The tabletop PC, fitted with a touch panel screen (Fig. 5), communicated with the wearable device via the screen's surface while the user was touching it. The touch panel screen was covered with a transparent conductive sheet, connected to the PC via the TX/RX circuit board.

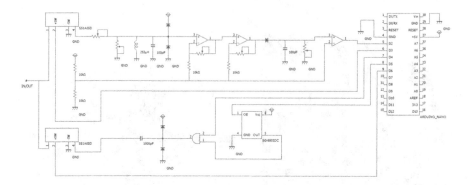

Fig. 4. A schematic circuit diagram of the TX/RX modules.

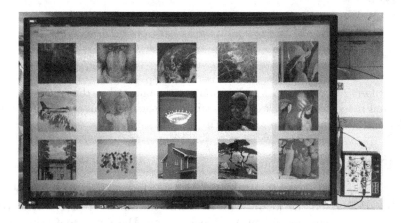

Fig. 5. A tabletop PC with a touch panel screen, and the TX/RX circuit board.

A PQ Labs multitouch sensor frame[1] was used to detect the user's touch gestures on the 60″ display. Since infrared sensors were used to detect the point at which contact was made, interference between the display unit and the touch operation was avoided.

3.5 Data Transmission Protocol

Upon user contact with the screen, an electrical connection between the tabletop PC and wearable device was established. At this moment, the system attempted to establish a logical data connection using the following handshake method (Fig. 6 (a)).

First, a synchronization packet (SYN) was sent by the TX module. Upon reception of the SYN packet, the RX module returned a synchronization acknowledgement packet (SYN/ACK), which the TX module replied to with an ACK

---

[1] http://multitouch.com.

packet. Upon receiving the ACK at the RX module, a logical connection was established and the TX module began transmission.

If the TX module did not receive a SYN/ACK after transmission of a SYN packet, the SYN was resent several times. This situation was typically caused by insufficient contact between the user and the screen. Transmission was successful in most cases where a firm contact was achieved.

The protocol for termination of the communication link was similar to the initiation protocol (Fig. 6 (b)). First, the TX module sent a final packet (FIN). When the RX module received the FIN packet, it returned a FIN/ACK packet, to which the TX module replied with an ACK. Upon receiving the ACK packet at the RX module, the data transmission was complete and the connection was closed.

The above sequence assumes that the TX module knows when the user has touched the screen, making transmission possible. The tabletop PC can sense contact via the touch panel, however the wearable device did not have this information. Therefore, when user input was detected at the tabletop PC without data to be transmitted, a connection packet (CNT) was sent to the wearable device. When a CNT packet was detected by the wearable, the transmission protocol described above was initiated.

3.6 An Application Example: Exchanging Image Data

Software was written and installed on a tabletop PC and a wearable device to enable the exchange of image data.

To transfer the image data from the tabletop PC to the wearable device, the user was required to touch the image file icon on the screen. This operation was recognized by the touch panel sensor, triggering transmission of the selected file. The user was required to maintain contact until the transmission process was completed. During transmission, a progress indicator was displayed on the screen

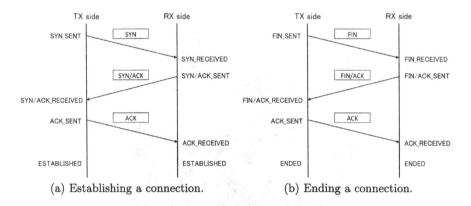

(a) Establishing a connection.   (b) Ending a connection.

Fig. 6. The data transmission protocol.

of the wearable device. After transmission had been completed, the received image was displayed on the screen of the wearable device.

To send the image data from the wearable device to the tabletop PC, the user first selected an image by touching the relevant icon on the screen of the wearable. The device waited until a connection with the tabletop PC had been established to transmit the data. Then, the user touched the screen of the tabletop PC; if he or she touched the background area rather than an image icon, the wearable device sent the selected image data to the PC. If he or she touched an image icon, the transmission from the wearable device was cancelled. If the user maintained contact and the transmission was successful, the transmitted image was displayed on the screen of the tabletop PC. In this case, a progress indicator was also displayed on the screen of the wearable device.

In Fig. 7, the user has downloaded image data from the tabletop PC. Since the transmission has been successfully completed, the image selected by the user is displayed on the screen of the device. The user can then browse the image on the wearable.

3.7   Preliminary Evaluation

We conducted a preliminary experiment to evaluate the system. We recruited four students, two undergraduates and two graduates, as subjects, and asked them to use our system. The system operated at a data rate of approximately 17 kbps. It took 4–6 s to transfer an image in this experiment. The transmission was generally successful, but failed in some cases because of insufficient contact between the user and the screen, or release of the user's finger before the transmission was complete.

Fig. 7. Transfer of an image file with our prototype system.

We conducted interviews about the usability of the system after each subject completed the experiment. Most subjects responded that they could easily transfer image data between the wearable device and the tabletop PC. For example, some of their positive comments were: *"The process of information transfer is very simple"*, *"It is intuitive because we can visually recognize a target image, and select it with a direct physical operation"*, *"It seems secure because information is not sent without touch"*. On the other hand, they made some negative comments: *"Maintaining touch during the transmission is troublesome"*, *"I felt the transmission time was too long"*, *"Sometimes, the transmission was not stable"*, *"The wearable device is a little large"*. Improvements to the speed and stability of the transmission, and reductions in the size of the device are therefore necessary. We are planning to improve these factors in future implementations.

4 Related Work

In Pick-and-Drop [2] systems, users can transfer files between computers. The user picks a file from one computer by touching its icon with a pen, and drops it on the other by touching on its display with the same pen. In Memory Stones [3], a user can 'pick up' a file displayed on a device screen, carry it to another device, and place the data by using his or her fingers. During this operation, the user is invited to pantomime the act of carrying a tangible object (the "stone") and to keep his or her fingertip positions unchanged. The system identifies the source and target devices by matching the shape of the polygon formed by the fingertips when touching the respective screens.

Using these techniques, a user can transfer information in an intuitive way, but since the actual data transmission is achieved via the wireless network, the user needs to configure the connection in advance. With our method, no configuration is necessary to communicate, even with public access terminals.

Hinckley [4] proposed interaction techniques to connect multiple computers by physically bumping them. A user can bump a tablet into another resting on a desk. The software recognizes the gesture by synchronizing the two accelerometers across a wireless network. The tablet moved by the user annexes the display of the stationary tablet, allowing a panoramic image to span both displays. Seifert et al. [5] presented a system that allowed users to extend the display of their mobile phones by using external screens. Users connected their mobile phone with a screen by holding it against the border. When the connection was established, the GUI of the active mobile application was distributed across the phone and the external display. Using our technique, the user only has to touch an item on the touch-panel display to select and transfer data between two devices.

DiamondTouch [6] is a multi-user touch technology that uses human body communication for tabletop front-projected displays. It works by transmitting a different electrical signal to each part of the table surface that is to be uniquely identified. When a user touches the table, signals are capacitively coupled from directly beneath the touch point, through the user, and into a receiver unit associated with that user. The receiver can then determine which parts of the table surface are being touched by the user. Our method also communicates between wearable devices and tabletop PCs using the human body. DiamondTouch technology is used to identify which person is touching where. On the other hand, our study is intended to transfer information easily from or to the user's device by automatically connecting it and a tabletop PC.

5 Conclusion

We proposed a technique for information transfer between multiple devices, utilizing human body communication with a touch-panel. We also developed a prototype system that could send and receive image data between a tabletop PC and a wearable device. We performed a preliminary experiment to evaluate this system. Users responded mostly positively, but some comments indicated that the prototype system should be refined so that the transmission speed and stability were improved and the size of the device was reduced. In future work, we aim to improve upon our design by developing a system that results in more stable information transfer between devices.

References

1. Zimmerman, T.G.: Personal area networks: near-field intrabody communication. IBM Syst. J. **35**(3–4), 609–617 (1996)
2. Rekimoto, J.: Pick-and-drop: a direct manipulation technique for multiple computer environments. In: Proccedings of the 10th Annual ACM Symposium on User Interface Software and Technology (UIST 1997), pp. 31–39 (1997)
3. Ikematsu, K., Siio, I.: Memory stones: an intuitive copy-and-paste method between multi-touch computers. In: CHI 2013 Extended Abstracts on Human Factors in Computing Systems (CHI EA 2013), pp. 1287–1292 (2013)
4. Hinckley, K.: Synchronous gestures for multiple persons and computers. In: Proceedings of the 16th Annual ACM Symposium on User Interface Software and Technology (UIST 2003), pp. 149–158 (2003)
5. Seifert, J., Schneider, D., Rukzio, E.: Extending mobile interfaces with external screens. In: Kotzé, P., Marsden, G., Lindgaard, G., Wesson, J., Winckler, M. (eds.) INTERACT 2013, Part II. LNCS, vol. 8118, pp. 722–729. Springer, Heidelberg (2013)
6. Dietz, P., Leigh, D: DiamondTouch: a multi-user touch technology. In: Proceedings of the 14th Annual ACM Symposium on User Interface Software and Technology (UIST 2001), pp. 219–226 (2001)

Mouse Augmentation Using a Malleable Mouse Pad

Takuro Kuribara$^{(\boxtimes)}$, Buntarou Shizuki, and Jiro Tanaka

University of Tsukuba, Tsukuba, Japan
{kuribara,shizuki,jiro}@iplab.cs.tsukuba.ac.jp

Abstract. We present mouse augmentation that uses a malleable mouse pad, which is named "Sinkpad". Sinkpad augments mouse functionalities by allowing a user to sink the mouse into the pad and tilt the mouse on the pad. In addition, the user is provided with haptic feedback via the mouse on the pad. Sinkpad allows the user to perform: sink, tilt, and sink+move actions. This paper describes Sinkpad, its applications, and its evaluation.

Keywords: Input device · Hybrid interaction device · Interaction technique · Malleable surface · Haptic feedback · Window management · Overlapping windows

1 Introduction

A computer mouse is an established input device for computer users. A conventional mouse, however, only allows simple actions such as clicking its buttons, rolling the wheel, and moving it. To enrich the input vocabulary of the mouse, many previous researches have tried to augment it with new sensing capabilities. As a different approach, we have augmented the mouse pad instead of the mouse.

In this paper, we present "Sinkpad", an augmented mouse pad that has a malleable surface consisting of an elastic material and that augments mouse functionalities by allowing the user to sink the mouse into the pad and tilt it on the pad (Fig. 1; a demonstration of Sinkpad is in [9]). It allows the user to perform interesting actions: sink, tilt, and sink+move. In addition, the pad provides the user with haptic feedback as the mouse deforms its surface. Moreover, the user can also use Sinkpad as a conventional mouse pad, because the pad serves as a flat surface unless the user sinks the mouse into it.

We conducted user evaluations on two-dimensional (2D) pointing and gathered feedback. First, we conducted a preliminary experiment to investigate the 2D pointing accuracy. The results show that users can perform 2D pointing as accurately on Sinkpad as on a regular pad and that Sinkpad had no effect on the accuracy of 2D mouse pointing. Second, we demonstrated Sinkpad at an academic workshop. We observed that all users could easily use their mice on the pad except for accidental clicks. The results of the experiment and the demonstration show that Sinkpad is usable as a conventional mouse pad and that users can get used to the new actions quickly.

© Springer International Publishing Switzerland 2015
M. Kurosu (Ed.): Human-Computer Interaction, Part II, HCII 2015, LNCS 9170, pp. 217–226, 2015.
DOI: 10.1007/978-3-319-20916-6_21

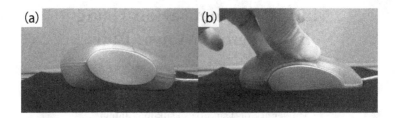

Fig. 1. (a) Using Sinkpad as a conventional mouse pad, (b) sinking a mouse into the pad.

2   Related Work

Sinkpad augments conventional mouse functionalities by using a malleable mouse pad that consists of an elastic material. Here, we summarize the work on augmenting the conventional mouse functionality and the input surfaces consisting of elastic materials.

Much research has gone into augmenting mice with diverse features, such as extending its degrees of freedom [1,7,10,14], supporting touch interactions [2,15,18], adding pressure input [3,12], providing actuated inflation and deflation [8], and making the buttons adapt to the user's fingers [13]. In contrast, we augmented the mouse pad so that users can use a conventional or augmented mouse on it.

There has been a lot of development of input surfaces made from elastic materials. GelForce [16] calculated the force vectors on a surface made of elastic material. PhotoelasticTouch [11] was a tabletop system using deformable transparent objects on its surface. deForm [5] was a 2.5D surface that combined a deformable surface with arbitrary physical objects and manual manipulations that can handle a wide variety of inputs. While these systems required large form factors because they used optical sensing, our system is small because we use pressure sensing.

There is other research on a malleable surfaces such as [6,17]. However, none of them focus on exploring the possibilities of a malleable mouse pad.

3   Sinkpad

Sinkpad is a malleable mouse pad, whose surface is smooth and soft, allowing the user to sink the mouse and tilt it into the pad, in addition to using conventional actions as shown in Fig. 2a. This design allows the user to perform three different techniques: sink, tilt, and sink+move.

Sink Sink the mouse downward vertically into the pad (Fig. 2b).
Tilt Tilt the mouse by sinking one side into the pad (Fig. 2c).
Sink+Move Move the mouse after sinking (Fig. 2d).

This design enables the user to perceive the depth of the mouse or the angle of tilt because of the deformation of the pad and haptic feedback provided by

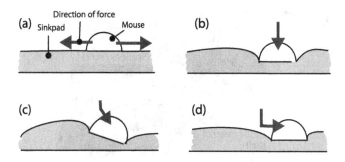

Fig. 2. (a) Conventional actions, (b) sink, (c) tilt, (d) sink+move.

the deformation. Moreover, we also expect that the sink+move action allows the user to perform precise pointing because the user has to move their mice slowly due to greater friction from the pad while performing sink+move.

4 System Configuration

We describe the implementation of our prototype system: its hardware and analysis software.

4.1 Hardware

The Sinkpad hardware consists of two parts: a pad that is made of an elastic material and a sensing module that senses the actions. Figure 3 shows the hardware setup of Sinkpad. We attached the sensing module to the bottom of the pad.

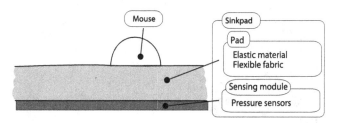

Fig. 3. Hardware.

The pad is made of an elastic material 1 cm thick, which has been cut into a square measuring 18 cm × 18 cm. The elastic material is Hitohada gel (Exseal Corporation, Asker-C 0). The gel is soft enough that the mouse sinks into it when the user pushes it. At the same time, the gel is stiff enough that it serves as a flat surface until the user sinks the mouse into it. Moreover, we covered the gel with spandex fabric, as shown in Fig. 4, which makes the surface flexible enough to allow the mouse to slide smoothly.

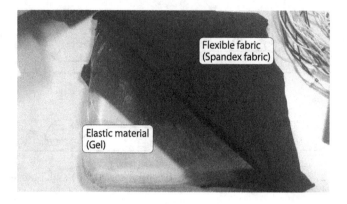

Fig. 4. The pad.

The sensing module uses a pressure-based approach to detect the actions. Figure 5 shows the sensing module. The sensing module consists of 64 pressure sensors, four multiplexers, and four microcontrollers. Our current prototype uses an FSR402 as a pressure sensor and mbed as a microcontroller. These 64 pressure sensors are arranged in an 8 × 8 matrix. Each set of 16 pressure sensors was connected to a microcontroller via a multiplexer. The four microcontrollers are connected to a PC and send data at 25 fps. The reason why we used four microcontrollers instead of one is to increase the frame rate.

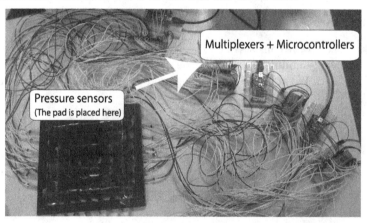

Fig. 5. The sensing module.

4.2 Analysis Software

The analysis software measures the centroid and average of pressures in each frame. The area of Sinkpad is divided into an 8 × 8 matrix. The value from each pressure sensor, which is sent to a microcontroller, is considered to be the pressure of the corresponding area in the matrix. The centroid (x_g, y_g) is expressed as follows:

$$x_g = \frac{\sum_{i=1}^{8} x_i \sum_{j=1}^{8} m_{(i,j)}}{\sum_{i=1}^{8} \sum_{j=1}^{8} m_{(i,j)}}, y_g = \frac{\sum_{i=1}^{8} y_i \sum_{j=1}^{8} m_{(i,j)}}{\sum_{i=1}^{8} \sum_{j=1}^{8} m_{(i,j)}}$$

where $m_{(i,j)}$ is the pressure of sensor (i,j), x_i is the x-coordinate of the i-th column where the sensor is placed, and y_i is the y-coordinate of the i-th row.

The depth to which the mouse sinks into the pad is calculated from the average pressure. The tilt angle is calculated from the variation between current and previous locations of the centroid (x_g, y_g) under the condition that the average pressure is less than a certain threshold.

5   Applications

We present three example applications to explore the possibilities of using the pad.

5.1   Bringing a Background Window to the Front Quickly

The user can bring a background window between overlapping windows to the front quickly by sinking the mouse into the pad, as shown in Fig. 6. When the user hovers the pointer over the overlapping windows and sinks the mouse into the pad, some windows under the pointer become translucent (the number of windows depends on how strongly the user sinks the mouse into the pad), allowing the user to examine the content of the windows underneath. When the user clicks a button while sinking the mouse into the pad, the window, which is at the front of the overlapping windows except the translucent ones, is brought to the front. At this time, the translucency ends.

5.2   Examining Hidden Windows Quickly

The user can quickly examine the windows that are hidden under the overlapping windows by tilting the mouse as shown in Fig. 7. When the pointer hovers over the overlapping windows and the user tilts, some background windows move in the direction of the tilt. The deeper the background window is, the more it moves. When the user finishes tilting the mouse, the windows return to the positions before the tilt. Thus, the user can quickly examine overlapping windows. When the user finishes tilting the mouse, the windows return to the positions before the tilt. Thus, the user can move background windows that are between overlapping windows in order to examine them quickly.

5.3   Changing C-D Ratio Dynamically and Magnifying the Area Around the Pointer

The user can change the C-D ratio dynamically and magnify the area around the pointer as shown in Fig. 8. When the user performs sink+move, the pointer moves with a small C-D ratio. At the same time, the area around the pointer is magnified so that it can be viewed in more detail. Thus, the user can selectively perform normal pointing or precise pointing.

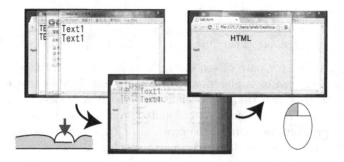

Fig. 6. Bringing a background window to the front quickly.

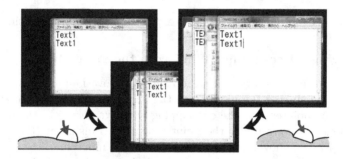

Fig. 7. Examining hidden windows quickly.

6   Evaluation 1

To examine how a user uses a mouse on Sinkpad in a 2D graphical user interface, we conducted a target acquisition experiment based on the ISO9241-9 standard for pointing evaluations [4]. We compared three cases: a mouse alone, a 3D mouse, and a mouse on Sinkpad.

6.1   Participants

Eighteen participants (14 males and 4 females) ranging in age from 21 to 32 took part in the experiment as volunteers. All participants were mice users on desktop computers.

6.2   Apparatus

The experiment was conducted on a desktop computer running Windows 7, with an Intel Core i3 540 CPU, and 2 GB of RAM. The monitor was 20.1 in. Dell E207WFP, with a resolution of 1680 × 1050 pixels with a viewable screen width and height of 27 cm and 44 cm, at a refresh rate of 60 Hz. The devices used in the experiment were:

Fig. 8. Changing the C-D ratio dynamically and magnifying the area around the pointer.

- A mouse (Dell MS111 3-Button Optical USB 2.0 Mouse).
- A 3D mouse (3Dconnexion SpaceNavigator 3DX-700028).
- A mouse on Sinkpad.

6.3   Procedure

Participants were presented with a randomized series of target rings with different indexes of difficulty (2.04–4.70), as determined by two amplitudes (300, 600 pixels) and three target widths (16, 32, 64 pixels). Each target ring had 16 circular targets arranged in a circular layout as shown in Fig. 9. We asked each participant to click on the illuminated target. Once the target was clicked, the opposite target would be illuminated. The first three selections were illustrated by lines (Fig. 9). All participants were instructed to select the targets as fast and accurately as possible.

6.4   Design

The experiment was a 3×2×3 within-subjects design. The factors and levels were as follows:

- Device {mouse, 3D mouse, mouse on Sinkpad}
- Amplitude {300 and 600 pixels (103, 206 mm)}
- Width {16, 32, and 64 pixels (4, 8, 12 mm)}

Participants were randomly assigned to one of six groups (three participants per group). The order of devices differed for each group for counter-balancing. With 18 participants and 15 selections, the total number of trials in the experiment was $18 \times 15 \times 3 \times 2 \times 3 = 4860$.

6.5   Results and Analysis

Table 1 shows the mean time, standard deviation, and mean error rate for each device. A paired t-test revealed that the 3D mouse was significantly slower than the mouse alone ($t_{17} = 12.279$, p = .000) and mouse on Sinkpad ($t_{17} = 12.078$,

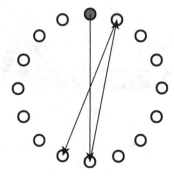

Fig. 9. Experimental task showing circular targets.

Table 1. Mean time, standard deviation, and mean error rate.

Pointing device	Mean time (s)	SD (s)	Mean error rate (%)
Mouse	0.914	0.076	3.8
3D mouse	2.950	0.721	9.0
Mouse on sinkpad	0.910	0.075	4.1

$p = .000$). The 3D mouse also had a significantly higher error rate than the mouse alone ($t_{17} = 4.341$, $p = .000$) and mouse on Sinkpad ($t_{17} = 4.025$, $p = .000$). On the other hand the mouse alone and mouse on Sinkpad showed no significant differences in error rate ($t_{17} = .327$, $p = .374$) and mean time ($t_{17} = .425$, $p = .338$). These results suggest that Sinkpad does not affect the speed and accuracy in 2D mouse pointing.

7   Evaluation 2

To investigate the usability of Sinkpad, we demonstrated a prototype at an academic workshop (20th Workshop on Interactive Systems and Software held in Japan). Approximately 50 participants used the system. We observed those participants and collected their feedback on the pad.

We found that users could easily sink their mice into the pad by using their palms. Some people commented that they could recognize the depth and angle of tilt from both the deformation of the pad and haptic feedback provided by the deformation, and they had to move their mice slowly because of friction when they performed the sink+move action. These comments suggest that users can use our techniques and point precisely.

We also found a problem: if there is a button on the mouse in the direction of tilting, some people clicked it accidentally. This is because the user has to push the mouse to tilt it: if the user's fingers are in contact with the mouse buttons, a mouse click could be accidentally triggered. To solve this problem, after this demonstration, we changed the analysis software so that it would ignore clicks during tilting.

8   Conclusions and Future Work

We presented Sinkpad, a mouse pad that has a malleable surface consisting of an elastic material. The user can perform three different actions by sinking the mouse into Sinkpad: sink, tilt, sink+move. Moreover, the user can also use Sinkpad as a conventional mouse pad. We presented three practical applications and presented the results of an evaluation showing that users could use the mouse on the pad as if it were a regular pad and could perform the sink, tilt, sink+move actions with fine control.

In the future, we plan to improve the system by adding more techniques such as ones utilizing z-axis angular motion of the mouse on Sinkpad. To this end, we will try a different hardware implementation, for example, using an array of photoreflectors for more precise sensing. We also plan to investigate the use of a 3D mouse on Sinkpad. Finally, we are interested in conducting user studies to measure the performance of Sinkpad in more realistic situations (e.g., in 3D applications such as 3D CAD).

References

1. Balakrishnan, R., Baudel, T., Kurtenbach, G., Fitzmaurice, G.: The rockin'mouse: integral 3D manipulation on a plane. In: Proceedings of CHI 1997, pp. 311–318 (1997)
2. Balakrishnan, R., Patel, P.: The PadMouse: facilitating selection and spatial positioning for the non-dominant hand. In: Proceedings of CHI 1998, pp. 9–16 (1998)
3. Cechanowicz, J., Irani, P., Subramanian, S.: Augmenting the mouse with pressure sensitive input. In: Proceedings of CHI 2007, pp. 1385–1394 (2007)
4. Douglas, S.A., Kirkpatrick, A.F., Scott MacKenzie, I.: Testing pointing device performance and user assessment with the ISO 9241, part 9 standard. In: Proceedings of CHI 1999, pp. 215–222 (1999)
5. Follmer, S., Johnson, M., Adelson, E., Ishii, H.: Deform: an interactive malleable surface for capturing 2.5D arbitrary objects, tools and touch. In: Proceedings of UIST 2011, pp. 527–536 (2011)
6. Follmer, S., Leithinger, D., Olwal, A., Cheng, N., Ishii, H.: Jamming user interfaces: programmable particle stiffness and sensing for malleable andshape-changing devices. In: Proceedings of UIST 2012, pp. 519–528 (2012)
7. Hinckley, K., Sinclair, M., Hanson, E., Szeliski, R., Conway, M.: The VideoMouse: a camera-based multi-degree-of-freedom input device. In: Proceedings of UIST 1999, pp. 103–112 (1999)
8. Kim, S., Kim, H., Lee, B., Nam, T.-J., Lee, W.: Inflatable mouse: volume-adjustable mouse with air-pressure-sensitive input and haptic feedback. In: Proceedings of CHI 2008, pp. 211–224 (2008)
9. Kuribara, T., Shizuki, B., Tanaka, J.: Sinkpad: a malleable mousepad consisted of an elastic material. In: CHI EA 2013, pp. 1251–1256 (2013)
10. Scott MacKenzie, I., Soukoreff, R.W., Pal, C.: A two-ball mouse affordsthree degrees of freedom. In: CHI EA 1997, pp. 303–304 (1997)
11. Sato, T., Mamiya, H., Koike, H., Fukuchi, K.: Photoelastic-Touch: transparent rubbery tangible interface using an lcd and photoelasticity. In: Proceedings of UIST 2009, pp. 43–50 (2009)

12. Shi, K., Irani, P., Gustafson, S., Subramanian, S.: PressureFish:a method to improve control of discrete pressure-based input. In: Proceedings of CHI 2008, pp. 1295–1298 (2008)
13. Tang, S.K., Tang, W.Y.: Adaptive mouse: a deformable computer mouse achieving form-function synchronization. In: CHI EA 2010, pp. 2785–2792 (2010)
14. Venolia, D.: Facile 3D direct manipulation. In: Proceedings of CHI 1993, pp. 31–36 (1993)
15. Villar, N., Izadi, S., Rosenfeld, D., Benko, H., Helmes, J., Westhues, J., Hodges, S., Ofek, E., Butler, A., Cao, X., Chen, B.: Mouse 2.0: multi-touch meets the mouse. In: Proceedings of UIST 2009, pp. 33–42 (2009)
16. Vlack, K., Mizota, T., Kawakami, N., Kamiyama, K., Kajimoto, H., Tachi, S.: GelForce: a vision-based traction field computer interface. In: CHI EA 2005, pp. 1154–1155 (2005)
17. Wimmer, R., Baudisch, P.: Modular and deformable touch-sensitive surfaces based on time domain reflectometry. In: Proceedings of UIST 2011, pp. 517–526 (2011)
18. Yang, X.-D., Mak, E., McCallum, D., Irani, P., Cao, X., Izadi, S.: LensMouse: augmenting the mouse with an interactive touch display. In: Proceedings of CHI 2010, pp. 2431–2440 (2010)

Spatial Arrangement of Data and Commands at Bezels of Mobile Touchscreen Devices

Toshifumi Kurosawa$^{(\boxtimes)}$, Buntarou Shizuki, and Jiro Tanaka

University of Tsukuba, Tsukuba, Japan
{kurosawa,shizuki,jiro}@iplab.cs.tsukuba.ac.jp

Abstract. We show a data and commands arrangement design on mobile touchscreen devices. In this design, a user can arrange any data, such as text and Web pages, *at the bezel* of the touchscreen by using a simple crossing gesture across the bezel. Our design has three main merits: data can be arranged while the small display area on mobile environment is kept open; the user can continuously execute multiple commands with the user's minimal visual attention; and memorizing the locations of the data is made easier by utilizing the user's spatial memory.

Keywords: Data placing · Data management · Touch gestures · Bezel gestures · Shortcuts · Menu · Crossing · Spatial memory

1 Introduction

Many designs of user interfaces enabling a user to arrange thumbnails of documents spatially in a manner that allows many documents held on computers to be managed, called *data arrangement designs*, have been explored. Prominent examples of such designs are DataMountain [1] and BumpTop [2]. A great advantage of such data-arrangement designs is that they allow the user to organize the documents by utilizing his or her spatial memory, thereby enabling the user to group related documents. While the efficacy of such designs in environments in which a large amount of screen real estate is available, such as desktop environments [1–3] and multiple displays environment [4,5], was demonstrated, data-arrangement designs in mobile environments in which the amount of screen real estate is limited are still open.

In this paper, we show a data arrangement design on mobile touchscreen devices. In the case of this design, a user can arrange any data, such as texts and Web pages, *at the bezels* of a touchscreen by using a simple double-crossing gesture across the bezels, named *bezel check*. After the user performs the bezel check, the system generates a virtual clipboard to store the datum, which is determined by the context. If the user wants to use a datum in a virtual clipboard, he or she selects an intended command from a marking menu, whose items depend on the context, displayed by swiping from the bezel to the corresponding virtual clipboard.

M. Kurosu (Ed.): Human-Computer Interaction, Part II, HCII 2015, LNCS 9170, pp. 227–237, 2015.
DOI: 10.1007/978-3-319-20916-6_22

Fig. 1. In the case of the proposed design, the user uses a double-crossing gesture, named a "bezel check," which is performed across the bezel of a touchscreen device, just like drawing a check mark. The yellow arrow indicates a swipe movement on the touchscreen and its bezels. (Left) When the user copies the selected text by a bezel check, (Center) the copied datum is stored in a virtual clipboard placed at the bezel where the gesture was given. The virtual clipboard then appears as a semi-translucent green rectangle. (Right) The user can use (e.g., paste or Web search) a copied datum by using a marking menu displayed by swiping from the bezel to the corresponding virtual clipboard (Color figure online).

Moreover, the user can also arrange commands such as text search at a bezel in the same way as the above-described data arrangement. To do this arrangement, a user firstly selects a command by using an ordinary method (e.g., select a "search" command from a menu bar of a text editor) and then performs a bezel check. After that, a virtual clipboard is generated, which serves as a *shortcut* to the command. Thereafter, the user can execute the command arranged at the bezel by swiping from the bezel. If the command needs an argument such as a text, the user firstly selects the text to be an argument of an intended command. The user then drags it to the bezel where the command was arranged and performs a double-crossing across the bezel.

In the proposed design, data and commands are arranged in physical space on a touchscreen; the design is thus helpful for memorizing the places storing the data and commands because it utilizes a user's spatial memory while keeping the small display area of a mobile touchscreen open. Moreover, the user can execute command(s) repeatedly and continuously with the user's minimal visual attention because a command arranged at the bezel is executed by a simple crossing gesture, which promotes the fluid composition of commands [6], and is easier than a pointing to select a target [7].

2   Related Work

Many data-arrangement designs have been proposed [1–3,5,8,9]. The "pile metaphor," a pioneering one of these designs, was proposed more than a few decades ago [3], and since then it has been applied to various uses (e.g., organizing files on a 3D desktop [2], organizing physical and digital documents on tabletops [9], and even organizing small displays showing digital documents [5]). Data Mountain [1], which allows a user to arrange digital documents at arbitrary positions on an inclined plane in a 3D desktop environment by using a simple 2D interaction technique. They showed that the spatial layout created by Data Mountain can utilize users' spatial memory. While the proposed design also adopts a spatial layout, it is different from the above-mentioned designs; namely, data and even commands are arranged only at bezels on a touchscreen. Thus, placing data and commands does not consume real estate of touchscreens, and it keeps the small display area of mobile touchscreen devices open.

Many bezel gestures have been proposed [10–13] and used [14–16]. Bragdon et al. found that bezel-initiated gestures were the fastest and the most preferred gestures in a mobile environment [17]. Serrano et al. proposed Bezel-Tap Gestures [12], which allows a user to immediately execute a command on a handheld tablet device regardless of whether the device is alive or in sleep mode. Roth et al. showed that a bezel-initiated swipe supports multiple selections, cut, copy, paste, and other operations without conflicting with pre-defined multi-touch gestures such as zooming, panning, and tapping [13]. Wagner et al. proposed a design space called BiTouch [18], which introduces support commands in a kinematic chain model for interacting with handheld tablet devices (including their bezels). In contrast, the design proposed in the current work uses bezel gestures to arrange data and apply commands to data. This design makes it possible to design bezel gestures that allow a user to arrange data spatially and to execute commands with the user's minimal visual attention.

Many researchers have explored crossing gestures on the touchscreen environment and revealed its efficacy [7, 13, 19–21]. Moreover, many crossing-based interaction techniques, such as Control Menu [22], FlowMenu [23], and CrossY [24], and Bezel Swipe [13], have been proposed. These crossing-based gestures and techniques allow the user to execute multiple commands continuously. In the case of the proposed design, the user also uses crossing gestures to execute multiple commands continuously.

3   A Design for Arranging Data and Commands

3.1   Arranging Data and Commands

In the proposed design, a user performs a double crossing gesture [25] across a bezel of a touchscreen, which is our own bezel-initiated gesture we named a *bezel check*. This gesture is designed to allow the user to arrange data and commands spatially with the destination being indicated by the simple gesture. First, the user selects a datum or a command by using an ordinary method (e.g., a long tap to select a text and select a "search" command in a menu bar). Next, the user performs a bezel check: swiping from the bezel across part of the display edge into the interior of the screen and returning the finger to the outside of the screen, just like drawing a check mark (Fig. 1 left). Then, the system generates a virtual clipboard (a semi-translucent green rectangle in the center of Fig. 1) at the bezel where the bezel check is completed, and it stores the selected datum or command in the virtual clipboard.

3.2   Using the Arranged Data and Commands

To use the datum in the virtual clipboard, the user begins with activating an application that uses the datum. The user then selects a command in the marking menu, whose items depend on the activated application, displayed by swiping from the bezel to the corresponding virtual clipboard (Fig. 1 right).

A command in the virtual clipboard can be executed in two ways. The first way is for the user to swipe from the bezel to the corresponding virtual clipboard to execute a command with no argument. In this case, the user selects the command in the marking menu displayed near the virtual clipboard. The second way is used when the user wants to give an argument to a command. For example, if the user wants to search a text in an Web page, the user firstly selects the text in the page (Fig. 2 left) or in another virtual clipboard by a gesture called "holding," which will be described later (Fig. 3). Next, the user drags the selected text to the virtual clipboard storing the searching command and performs a double crossing across the clipboard as shown in the center of Fig. 2. The search command is then executed with the selected text. The user also executes the command repeatedly by repeating bezel crossings in a manner just like drawing circles (Fig. 2 right).

Fig. 2. Executing a search command with an argument. (Left) Selecting a text. (Center) Dragging the selected text to the virtual clipboard that stores a searching command and performing a double crossing across the clipboard from the interior of the screen. (Right) Executing the command repeatedly by repeating bezel crossings in a manner just like drawing circles.

3.3   Organizing Virtual Clipboards

Users can organize virtual clipboards by moving, integrating, and deleting them.

Moving. A user can move a virtual clipboard to any part of a bezel of the screen. To do this, the user first "holds" the clipboard by swiping from the bezel to the clipboard and then tapping the clipboard with another finger (Fig. 3). Next, the user moves the clipboard by dragging it to the free parts of the bezels (i.e., parts of the bezels where no virtual clipboard is placed) using a finger. This procedure allows the user to easily edit positional relations among virtual clipboards. For example, the user can arrange the data in chronological order (Fig. 4).

Integrating. The user can integrate a virtual clipboard into another one. When the user moves the clipboard to another one, the stored data in the two clipboards are stored in the destination clipboard of dragging (Fig. 5). In addition, if the

Fig. 3. Holding a virtual clipboard by swiping from the bezel to the clipboard and then tapping the clipboard with another finger.

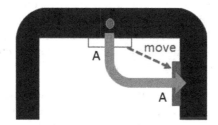

Fig. 4. If the user drags a virtual clipboard to a free space of a bezel, the clipboard moves there.

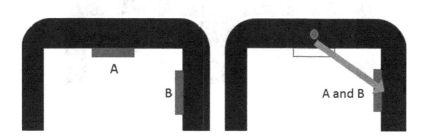

Fig. 5. If the user drags the clipboard containing A to the clipboard containing B, the two clipboards are integrated to have two contents, A and B.

user touches a clipboard that holds multiple data, the hierarchy of the data is expanded (left of Fig. 6). To use an object in the hierarchy, the user selects the object by swiping from the bezel to the object. This procedure allows the user to easily group many data, such as login data and mail addresses, into categories.

Deleting. The user can delete a virtual clipboard by moving it to a trash can displayed at the center of the screen. The trash can appears there when the user holds a virtual clipboard.

3.4   Merits

The proposed design allows the user to use the bezel of a touchscreen to arrange data and commands. It thereby leads to the following three merits.

Keeping the display area open. The user can store data and commands while keeping the (small) display area of a mobile touchscreen device open, because the proposed design only uses the bezel of a touchscreen. In addition, the marking menus displayed by a single swipe from the bezel are a kind of bezel menus, which enable interaction with a mobile touchscreen with the user's minimal visual attention and thus solve the occlusion problem [26].

Executing multiple commands continuously. The user can continuously execute multiple commands because the execution requires only simple crossing gestures, which promote fluid composition of commands [6] in the same manner as reported in [23,24,27]. Moreover, the user can execute a command repeatedly by performing a bezel check continuously across the virtual clipboard that stores the command, just like drawing circles on the bezel (Fig. 2 right).

Mapping data to place. The user can arrange data and commands spatially. For example, the user can arrange placed data in the order of priority or chronologically. This spatial layout of data might be helpful in memorizing the data's places by utilizing the user's spatial memory [1,3,4].

Fig. 6. (Left) Expanding the multi-objects-clipboard by swiping. (Right) Selecting the content.

4   Prototype Applications and their Use Cases

A prototype of the proposed design was developed as a system daemon running on a Dell 10.1-in. Windows 8 mobile touchscreen device. The daemon continuously monitors the active application, since the marking menu (displayed by swiping from the bezel) and the command executed when a user performs a bezel check depend on the active application, as shown in Table 1. These applications and their use cases are described in the following sections.

4.1 Data Arrangement

As for the prototype design, texts and Web pages can be the data to be stored at bezels. As a result, the user can use the bezel as a multiple clipboard or bookmark bar. A use case of such a data arrangement is described as follows. If the user wants to place a text at a bezel, he or she firstly selects the text and performs a bezel check. Then, the daemon generates a virtual clipboard where the bezel check is performed and copies the text to it. After that, if the user performs a swipe from the bezel across the virtual clipboard when the text editor is active, the daemon displays the "paste" and "text search" command in the marking menu, as shown in Fig. 7. Another use case is that if the user performs a bezel check when an Web browser is active, the opened URL is bookmarked at the virtual clipboard.

Table 1. Commands displayed in the marking menu at the time each application is active.

Application	On a bezel check	Commands
Text editor	Copy	Paste / Text Search
Web browser	Copy / Bookmark	Paste / URL open Web search / Text search
PDF viewer	Copy	Text search

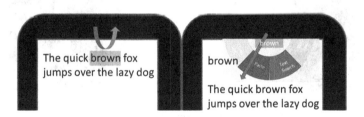

Fig. 7. Using a virtual clipboard with a text editor. (Left) Copying a text. (Right) Display a marking menu at the virtual clipboard.

4.2 Commands Arrangement

We implemented some arrangeable commands, namely, searching, changing volume, and page transition. Use cases of arranging commands by using a search command are described as follows. When an Web browser or a text editor is activated and the user executes a bezel check, the virtual clipboard that contains the search command is generated at the bezel where the bezel check is completed. If the user performs a swipe from the bezel and a crossing across the virtual clipboard when an application such as a text editor or an Web browser is activated, the daemon displays the "search" command in the marking menu. After the user selects the command, the daemon activates the search command, just like executing a keyboard shortcut *Ctrl + F*. Then, the user can execute the search by typing a search word or pasting a copied word.

The user can also execute such commands with an argument. For example, if a user selects a text in a text editor and drags it to a virtual clipboard storing a search command, and then performs a double-crossing across the clipboard, the user can execute the search command with the selected text as the argument, as shown in the center of Fig. 2. Moreover, in this case, the user can find occurrences of the text one by one (i.e., incrementally search the text) by executing the search command repeatedly by double crossing the bezel repeatedly, as shown in Fig. 2 right.

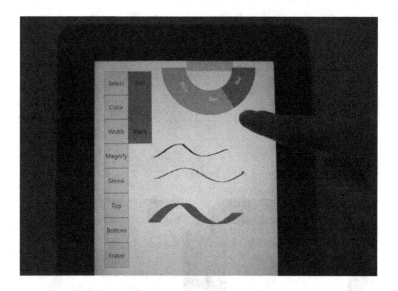

Fig. 8. A drawing tool which provides the user with our design.

In addition, we have also developed a drawing tool similar to CrossY [24] which provides the user with our design. This tool revealed that the continuous execution of commands is especially useful. For example, after selecting a drawing object, the user can continuously execute the commands "changing line width," "changing line color," and "swap to the top layer" with only one stroke gesture (Fig. 8). Moreover, the commands can be combined into one virtual clipboard by integrating multiple clipboards, each of which stores a command as described in the section "Organizing the Virtual Clipboards." The user can thus define a complicated command with two or more processes such as "Increase the line width while changing the line color of an argument object to red."

5   Implementation

The prototype system daemon was implemented as a separate program from the applications for providing application-independent services.

To detect double-crossing gestures across the bezel and swipes from the bezel, touch-sensitive transparent windows were placed near the four edges of the bezels, as shown in Fig. 9 left.

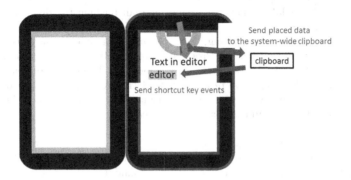

Fig. 9. (Left) Four touch-sensitive transparent windows (gray). (Right) Send data to an active application.

The daemon monitors an active application to transmit the data from it. The transmission process is illustrated on the right of Fig. 9. To transmit the data between an active application and the virtual clipboard, the daemon sends key events and uses the system-wide clipboard provided by the operating system as a relay point. For example, when the user activates a text editor and performs a bezel check, the daemon sends a *Ctrl + C* key event in order to copy the selected text to the system-wide clipboard. The daemon then retrieves the copied data from the clipboard. When the user selects a command in the marking menu displayed by swiping from the bezel, the daemon also sends the data contained in the virtual clipboard to the system-wide clipboard, and then it sends appropriate shortcut-key events on the active application (e.g., send *Ctrl + V* to paste).

6   Conclusion and Future Work

We show a data and commands arrangement design of mobile touchscreen devices. The design uses virtual clipboards, which are laid out along the bezel of the touchscreen (so they help in memorizing the contents by utilizing the user's spatial memory) and are generated by a simple crossing gesture across the bezels, bezel check. The data and commands are arranged at the bezel, so the display area of a mobile touchscreen is kept open. Moreover, users can execute command(s) repeatedly and continuously because a command displayed at the bezel is executed by a crossing gesture.

For future work, we will evaluate our design in terms of the effects of the spatial layout of the proposed design on the user's cognitive processing [1,3,4].

References

1. Robertson, G., Czerwinski, M., Larson, K., Robbins, D.C., Thiel, D., van Dantzich, M.: Data mountain: using spatial memory for document management. In: Proceedings of UIST 1998, pp. 153–162 (1998)
2. Agarawala, A., Balakrishnan, R.: Keepin' it real: pushing the desktop metaphor with physics, piles and the pen. In: Proceedings of CHI 2006, pp. 1283–1292 (2006)
3. Mander, R., Salomon, G., Wong, Y.Y.: A pile metaphor for supporting casual organization of information. In: Proceedings of CHI 1992, pp. 627–634 (1992)
4. Ragan, E.D., Endert, A., Bowman, D.A., Quek, F.: The effects of spatial layout and view control on cognitive processing. In: CHI EA 2011, pp. 2005–2010 (2011)
5. Girouard, A., Tarun, A., Vertegaal, R.: DisplayStacks: interaction techniques for stacks of flexible thin-film displays. In: Proceedings of CHI 2012, pp. 2431–2440 (2012)
6. Baudisch, P.: Don't click, paint! using toggle maps to manipulate sets of toggle switches. In: Proceedings of UIST 1998, pp. 65–66 (1998)
7. Accot, J., Zhai, S.: More than dotting the i's—foundations for crossing-based interfaces. In: Proceedings of CHI 2002, pp. 73–80 (2002)
8. Watanabe, N., Washida, M., Igarashi, T.: Bubble clusters: an interface for manipulating spatial aggregation of graphical objects. In: Proceedings of UIST 2007, pp. 173–182 (2007)
9. Steimle, J., Khalilbeigi, M., Mühlhäuser, M.: Hybrid groups of printed and digital documents on tabletops: a study. In: CHI EA 2010, pp. 3271–3276 (2010)
10. Hinckley, K., Pierce, J., Sinclair, M., Horvitz, E.: Sensing techniques for mobile interaction. In: Proceedings of UIST 2000, pp. 91–100 (2000)
11. Kim, S., Yu, J., Lee, G.: Interaction techniques for unreachable objects on the touchscreen. In: Proceedings of OzCHI 2012, pp. 295–298 (2012)
12. Serrano, M., Lecolinet, E., Guiard, Y.: Bezel-tap gestures: quick activation of commands from sleep mode on tablets. In: Proceedings of CHI 2013, pp. 3027–3036 (2013)
13. Roth, V., Turner, T.: Bezel swipe: conflict-free scrolling and multiple selection on mobile touch screen devices. In: Proceedings of CHI 2009, pp. 1523–1526 (2009)
14. Zeleznik, R., Bragdon, A., Adeputra, F., Ko, H.: Hands-on math: a page-based multi-touch and pen desktop for technical work and problem solving. In: Proceedings of UIST 2010, pp. 17–26 (2010)
15. Hinckley, K., Yatani, K., Pahud, M., Coddington, N., Rodenhouse, J., Wilson, A., Benko, H., Buxton, B.: Pen + touch = new tools. In: Proceedings of UIST 2010, pp. 27–36 (2010)
16. Yu, N., Huang, D., Hsu, J., Hung, Y.: Rapid selection of hard-to-access targets by thumb on mobile touch-screens. In: Proceedings of Mobile HCI 2013, pp. 400–403 (2013)
17. Bragdon, A., Nelson, E., Li, Y., Hinckley, K.: Experimental analysis of touch-screen gesture designs in mobile environments. In: Proceedings of CHI 2011, pp. 403–412 (2011)
18. Wagner, J., Huot, S., Mackay, W.: BiTouch and BiPad: designing bimanual interaction for hand-held tablets. In: Proceedings of CHI 2012, pp. 2317–2326 (2012)

19. Dragicevic, P.: Combining crossing-based and paper-based interaction paradigms for dragging and dropping between overlapping windows. In: Proceedings of UIST 2004, pp. 193–196 (2004)
20. Luo, Y., Vogel, D.: Crossing-based selection with direct touch input. In: Proceedings of CHI 2014, pp. 2627–2636 (2014)
21. Chen, C., Perrault, S.T., Zhao, S., Ooi, W.T.: BezelCopy: An efficient cross-application copy-paste technique for touchscreen smartphones. In: Proceedings of AVI 2014, pp. 185–192 (2014)
22. Pook, S., Lecolinet, E., Vaysseix, G., Barillot, E., Menus, C.: Excecution and control in a single interactor. In: CHI EA 2000, pp. 263–264 (2000)
23. Guimbretiére, F., Winograd, T.: FlowMenu: combining command, text, and data entry. In: Proceedings of UIST 2000, pp. 213–216 (2000)
24. Apitz, G., Guimbretière, F.: CrossY: a crossing-based drawing application. In: Proceedings of SIGGRAPH 2005, pp. 930–930 (2005)
25. Nakamura, T., Takahashi, S., Tanaka, J.: An object selection tecnique using hand gesture in large display -proposing double-crossing and comparing with other techniques. IEICE Trans., J96-D(4), 978–988 (In Japanese)
26. Jain, M., Balakrishnan, R.: User learning and performance with bezel menus. In: Proceedings of CHI 2012, pp. 2221–2230 (2012)
27. Shizuki, B., Hisamatsu, T., Takahashi, S., Tanaka, J.: Laser pointer interaction techniques using peripheral areas of screens. In: Proceedings of AVI 2006, pp. 95–98 (2006)

Fitts' Throughput and the Remarkable Case of Touch-Based Target Selection

I. Scott MacKenzie[✉]

Department of Electrical Engineering and Computer Science, York University,
Toronto, ON, Canada
mack@cse.yorku.ca

Abstract. The method of calculating Fitts' throughput is detailed, considering task characteristics, the speed-accuracy trade-off, data collection, and data aggregation. The goal is to bring consistency to the method of calculation and thereby strengthen between-study comparisons where throughput is used as a dependent measure. In addition, the distinction between indirect and direct pointing devices is elaborated using the examples of a mouse as an indirect pointing device and a finger as a direct pointing device. An experiment with 16 participants using a smart phone was conducted as an empirical test of direct touch-based target selection. Overall, the throughput was 6.95 bps. This is a remarkable figure – about 50 % higher than accepted values for a mouse. The experiment included task type (1D vs. 2D) and device position (supported vs. mobile) as independent variables. Throughput for the 1D task was 15 % higher than for the 2D task. No difference in throughput was observed between the supported and mobile conditions.

Keywords: Fitts' law · Throughput · Touch input

1 Background

The graphical user interface (GUI) first appeared in 1981 when Xerox Corp. introduced the *8100 Information Workstation*, better known as the *Star* [9, p. 11]. The Star was the first commercial system to use a mouse and point-and-click interaction. About the same time, Shneiderman coined the expression *direct manipulation* to reflect this promising new genre of interaction [13]. Instead of typing commands in a terminal window, users maneuver a mouse to directly manipulate on-screen graphical objects, such as icons, menus, and buttons.

While Shneiderman's broad insights were correct, a lower level of analysis reveals that mouse operation is an example of *indirect input*: Input actions occur on the desktop while output responses appear on the display. Because of the indirectness, a cursor is required as an intermediary. With *direct input*, the input and output spaces are merged. We will return to this point shortly.

In the 35 years since the GUI appeared, there has been considerable research on evaluating the mouse and comparing it with alternative devices or techniques (see [8, 15] for reviews). Most evaluations use target selection tasks modeled after Fitts' law [4, 5]. For the mouse and other indirect input devices, this involves manipulating the device to

© Springer International Publishing Switzerland 2015
M. Kurosu (Ed.): Human-Computer Interaction, Part II, HCII 2015, LNCS 9170, pp. 238–249, 2015.
DOI: 10.1007/978-3-319-20916-6_23

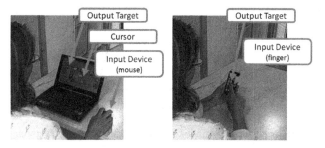

Fig. 1. Indirect input (left) requires a cursor as an intermediary. With direct input (right), actions occur directly on output targets

move an on-screen cursor over a specified amplitude (*A*) to acquire a target of a specified width (*W*). Selection involves a final button press.

Direct input is different: Targets appear on the display and the input device operates directly on the targets. Indirect input and direct input are contrasted in Fig. 1.

The primary dependent variable for a Fitts' law study is *throughput* in *bits/s*. In the next section, the calculation of throughput is detailed. Due to space limitations, the discussion is brief. Additional details are found in other sources (e.g. [4, 8, 15]).

Fitts' Law and Throughput. Fitts' motivation was to investigate whether human performance in target acquisition tasks could be measured or quantified using an information metaphor. He reasoned that a human operator that acquires targets over a certain amplitude (signal) and with variable success (noise) is demonstrating a "rate of information transfer" [4, p. 381]. Fitts' *index of performance*, now *throughput* (*TP*), is

$$TP = ID_e \ / \ MT \tag{1}$$

where ID_e is a task's effective *index of difficulty* (in bits) computed from the movement amplitude (*A*) and target width (*W*) and *MT* is the mean movement time (in seconds) recorded over a sequence of trials. The ID_e-term in Eq. 1 expands as follows:

$$ID_e = \log_2(A_e \ / \ W_e + 1) \tag{2}$$

Use of the effective values (subscript "e") is a change proposed by Crossman [2, 16, p. 146] and subsequently endorsed by Fitts [5] to include spatial variability or accuracy in the calculation. With this, W_e is computed as $4.133 \times SD_x$, where SD_x is the standard deviation in the selection coordinates and A_e is the mean of the actual movement amplitudes in the sequence of trials. Adjusted in this manner, throughput is a single human performance measure that embeds both the speed and accuracy in human responses. The trade-off is revealed in Fig. 2.

Throughput computed using Eq. 1 is a measure of human performance in the context of the task, device, and environmental conditions when the data were collected. If testing over, say, two or three separate test conditions, the differences in throughput can be used to assess performance differences between the conditions.

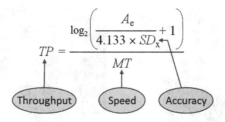

Fig. 2. The speed-accuracy trade-off in the calculation of Fitts' throughput

Since throughput includes speed and accuracy, the comparison is a composite, and bears no prejudice toward speed or accuracy as viewed alone [10]. This is clearly a useful property of throughput. However, inconsistencies in the method of collecting data and performing the calculation have exacerbated the use of throughput as a dependent variable in experimental research. One goal in this paper is to remedy this.

Data Collection and Calculation of Throughput. In this section, the best-practice method for calculating throughput is detailed.

Most Fitts' law experiments combine either serial or discrete responses with one-dimensional (1D) or two-dimensional (2D) movements. See Fig. 3. Example tasks are described in the ISO 9241-9 standard for evaluating non-keyboard devices and interaction techniques [7, 15].

Regardless of the task, the calculation of throughput requires Cartesian coordinate data for each trial for the starting position ("from"), the target position ("to"), and the select position. See Fig. 4.

The calculation begins by computing the length of the sides connecting the `from`, `to`, and `select` points in the figure. Using Java syntax,

```
double a = Math.hypot(x1 - x2, y1 - y2);
double b = Math.hypot(x - x2, y - y2);
double c = Math.hypot(x1 - x, y1 - y);
```

The x-y coordinates correspond to the `from` (x_1, y_1), `to` (x_2, y_2), and `select` (x, y) points in the figure. Given a, b, and c, as above, dx and ae are then calculated:

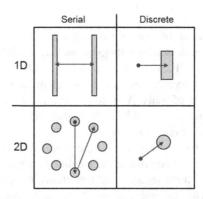

Fig. 3. Fitts' law tasks: 1D versus 2D. Serial versus discrete

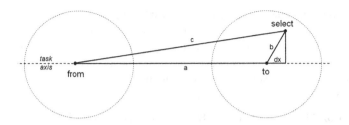

Fig. 4. Geometry for a trial

```
double dx = (c * c - b * b - a * a) / (2.0 * a);
double ae = a + dx;
```
Note that dx is 0 for a selection at the center of the target (as projected on the task axis), positive for a selection on the far side of center, and negative for a selection on the near side. It is an expected behaviour that some selections will miss the target.

The effective target amplitude (A_e) is ae in the code above. It is the actual movement distance for the trial, as projected on the task axis. For serial responses, an additional adjustment for A_e is to add dx from the previous trial (for all trials after the first). This is necessary since each trial begins at the selection point of the previous trial. For discrete responses, each task begins at the center of the from target.

Given arrays for the from, to, and select points in a sequence of trials, A_e is the mean of the ae values and SD_x is the standard deviation in the dx values. With these, ID_e is computed using Eq. 2 and throughput (*TP*) is computed using Eq. 1.

The use of the effective target amplitude (A_e) has little influence on *TP*, provided selections are distributed about the center of the targets. However, it is important to use A_e to prevent "gaming the system." For example, if all movements fall short and only traverse, say, ¾ of *A*, *TP* is artificially inflated if calculated using *A*. Using A_e prevents this. This is part of the overall premise in using "effective" values: Participants get credit for what they actually did, not for what they were asked to do.

Calculate Throughput on Each Sequence of Trials. The correct level of data aggregation for calculating Fitts' throughput is a *sequence of trials*. The premise for this is twofold:

1. Throughput cannot be calculated on a single trial.
2. A sequence of trials is the smallest unit of action for which throughput can be attributed as a measure of performance.

On the first point, the calculation of throughput includes the variability in selection coordinates (akin to "noise"). Thus, multiple selections are required and from these data the variability in the coordinates is computed.

The second point is of ecological concern. After a sequence of trials, the user pauses, stretches, adjusts the apparatus, has a sip of tea, adjusts her position on a chair, or something. There is a demarcation between sequences and for no particular purpose other than to provide a break or pause between sequences, or perhaps to change to a different test condition. It is reasonable to assert that once a sequence is over, it is over!

Behaviours were exhibited, observed, and measured and the next sequence is treated as a separate unit of action with separate performance measurements.

Related to the second point is the following: Throughput should not be calculated on larger sets of raw data. For example, if six participants each perform five sequences of trials under the same test condition, there are $6 \times 5 = 30$ calculations of throughput, rather than a single calculation on the pooled raw data.

Calculation of Throughput in the HCI Literature. A detailed review of the calculation of throughput in the HCI literature is beyond the scope of this paper. Inconsistency is common and this weakens between-study comparisons based on throughput. A few examples follow.[1]

Dijkstra et al. reported throughput in research on flexible displays [3]. The movement amplitude (A) differed from one trial to the next in a sequence. Furthermore, A was "freely determined by the participant" [3, p. 1300]. Pedersen and Hornbæk reported throughput in research on touch input with a tabletop surface [12, Table 1]. Error trials were excluded in the calculation. Wobbrock and Gajos reported throughput in research using participants with and without a motor impairment [17]. The calculation excluded accuracy, and used W instead of W_e. Forlines et al. reported throughput in a docking task on a tabletop display [6]. Throughput was calculated as $1/b$ – the slope reciprocal from the regression equation: $MT = a + b\ ID$. Provided the intercept a is 0, or close to 0, there is little difference between this value and that computed using Eq. 1. But, the intercept was large: 460 ms [6, Table 1]. Also, error trials were excluded.

Interpreting throughput as $1/b$ from the regression equation is a point of particular contention in the HCI literature. (For contrasting opinions, see [15, Sect. 3.5; 18]) Although $1/b$ has units "bits per second", this term cannot be used as a dependent variable in experimental research – because of the wavering influence of the intercept, a, which is absent in $1/b$. Besides, using $1/b$ as throughput is inconsistent with Fitts' original definition: "The average rate of information generated in a series of movements is the average information per movement divided by the time per movement" [4, p. 390].

It makes little sense to recite and compare the values for throughput in the studies just cited: They were computed in different ways. A goal herein is to remedy this by providing a clear articulation of the method of calculating Fitts' throughput.

2   Method

In this section, a user study is described that demonstrates the calculation of throughput for touch-based target selection. The study examined the effects of task type (1D vs. 2D) and device position (supported vs. mobile). For the supported condition, participants sat at a desk with the device positioned on the desktop. For the mobile condition, participants stood and held the device in one hand while selecting targets with the index finger on the opposite hand.

---

[1] To be clear, the examples are not necessarily wrong. They are given and distinguished only to reveal inconsistencies in the literature.

2.1   Participants

Participants were recruited from the local university campus. The only stipulation was that participants were regular users of a touchscreen phone, pad, or tablet. Sixteen participants were recruited from a wide range for disciplines. Six were female. The mean age was 24.3 years (*SD* = 3.0). Participants' average touchscreen experience was 22.9 months (*SD* = 15.8). All participants were right-handed.

As the experiment involved target selection using the finger on a small display, we also investigated the relationship between finger width and performance. The width of each participant's index finger was measured at the distal joint using the caliper in Fig. 5. The mean finger width was 14.0 mm (*SD* = 1.4).

2.2   Apparatus (Hardware and Software)

Testing was done on a LG *Nexus 4* touchscreen smartphone running Android OS version 4.2.2. The display was 61 × 102 mm (2.4 in. × 4.0 in.) with a resolution of 768 × 1184 px (pixels) and a px density of 320 dpi. All communication with the phone was disabled during testing.

Custom software called *FittsTouch* was developed using Java SDK 1.6. The software implemented the serial 1D and 2D tasks commonly used in Fitts' law experiments.

The same target amplitude and width conditions were used for both task types. The range was limited due to the small display and finger input. In all, six combinations were used: *A* = { 156, 312, 624 } px × *W* = { 78, 130 } px. These corresponded to task difficulties from *ID* = 1.14 bits to *ID* = 3.17 bits (see Eq. 2). A wider range is desirable but pilot testing at *W* = 30 was deemed untenable. The scale of target conditions was chosen such that the widest condition (largest *A*, largest *W*) spanned the width of the display (portrait orientation) minus 10 px on each side. Examples of target conditions are shown in Fig. 6.

The 2D conditions included 20 targets, which was the number of trials in a sequence. The target to select was highlighted. Upon selection, the highlight moved to the opposite target. Selections proceeded in a rotating pattern around the layout circle until all targets were selected. For the 1D task, selections were back and forth.

Fig. 5. Caliper used to measure the width of each participant's index finger

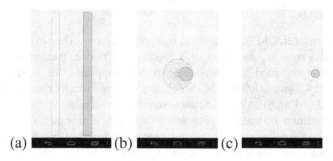

Fig. 6. Example target conditions: (a) 1D nominal (b) 2D easiest (c) 2D hardest

Block 3	Ae = 312.9 px
Sequence 1 of 6	We = 94.4 px
Number of trials = 20	IDe = 2.1 bits
A = 312 px (nominal)	MT = 256 ms (per trial)
W = 78 px	Misses = 2
ID = 2.3 bits	Throughput = 8.25 bps

Fig. 7. End-of-sequence dialog

Data collection for a sequence began on the first tap and ended after 20 target selections (21 taps). An auditory beep was sounded if a target was missed.

At the end of each sequence a dialog appeared showing summary results for the sequence. Figure 7 gives an example. The dialog is useful for demos and to help inform and motivate participants during testing.

2.3 Procedure

After signing a consent form, participants were briefed on the goals of the experiment. The experiment task was demonstrated to participants, after which they did a few practice sequences for each test condition. For the mobile condition, participants were asked to stand and hold the device in their non-dominant hand and select targets with the index finger on their dominant hand. For the supported condition, participants sat at a desk with the device positioned on the desktop. They were allowed to anchor the device with their non-dominant hand if desired. An example of a participant performing the 1D task with the device supported on the desktop is shown in Fig. 8.

Participants were asked to select targets as quickly and accurately as possible, at a comfortable pace. They were told that missing an occasional target was OK, but that if many targets were missed, they should slow down.

Fig. 8. A participant doing the experiment task in the 1D-supported condition

2.4   Design

The experiment was fully within-subjects with the following independent variables and levels:

Device position	mobile, supported
Task type	1D, 2D
Block	1, 2, 3, 4, 5
Amplitude	156, 312, 624
Width	78, 130

The primary independent variables were device position and task type. Block, amplitude, and width were included to gather a sufficient quantity of data over a reasonable range of task difficulties.

For each condition, participants performed a sequence of 20 trials. The 4 device position × task type conditions were assigned using a balanced Latin square with 4 participants per order. The amplitude and width conditions were randomized within blocks.

The dependent variables were throughput, movement time, and error rate. The relationship between participants' finger widths and performance was also examined.

Testing lasted about 45 min per participant. The total number of trials was 16 participants × 2 device positions × 2 task types × 5 blocks × 3 amplitudes × 2 widths × 20 trials = 38,400.

3   Results and Discussion

In this section, results are given for throughput, movement time, and error rate. As space is limited and the calculation and use of throughput is the primary theme in this paper, the results for movement time and error rate are abbreviated.

3.1   Throughput

The grand mean for throughput was 6.95 bps. This result, in itself, is remarkable. Here we see empirical and quantitative evidence underpinning the tremendous success of

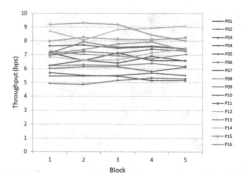

Fig. 9. Throughput by block for 16 participants

contemporary touch-based interaction. Not only is the touch *experience* appealing, touch *performance* is measurably superior compared to traditional interaction techniques. For desktop interaction the mouse is well-known to perform best for most point-select interaction tasks.[2] In a review of Fitts' law studies following the ISO 9241-9 standard, throughput values for the mouse ranged from 3.7 bps to 4.9 bps [15, Table 5]. The value observed in the present study for touch input reveals a performance advantage for touch in the range of 42 %–88 % compared to the mouse. The most likely reason lies in the distinguishing properties of *direct input* versus *indirect input*, as discussed earlier. With a mouse (and other traditional pointing devices), the user manipulates a device to indirectly control an on-screen tracking symbol. Selection requires pressing a button on the device. With touch input there is neither a tracking symbol nor a button: Input is direct!

Participant by block results for throughput are shown in Fig. 9. Each point in the figure is the mean of 24 separate calculations for throughput.

There was only a 0.2 % performance difference between the 1st block and the 5th block. Three reasons seem likely: participants had prior experience with touch input, the task was simple, and practice trials were given before testing. The means for individual participants ranged from 5.12 bps to 8.83 bps. For subsequent analyses the block data are pooled.

Throughput across the two main independent variables is shown in Fig. 10. The difference by device position was small – only 3 %, with values of 6.85 bps supported and 7.06 bps mobile. The difference was not statistically significant ($F_{1,3}$ = 2.80, p > .05). At first glance, this result seems surprising since a device is clearly more stable when positioned on a desktop than when held in the hand. However, several participants commented that they felt the supported condition was odd or awkward: *they wanted to hold the device!* Clearly, there is a culture around mobile device usage – an expectation that the device is operated in an unsupported position, such as holding it in one hand while touching with fingers on the opposite hand.

---

[2] A possible exception is the stylus. Performance with a stylus is generally as good as, or sometimes slightly better than, a mouse [11].

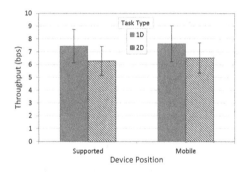

Fig. 10. Throughput (bps) by device position and task type. Error bars show ±1 *SD*

The difference in throughput by task type revealed a different story. Throughput for the 2D condition was 6.39 bps. At 7.52 bps, performance in the 1D condition was 15.0 % better. The difference was statistically significant ($F_{1,12} = 29.6, p < .0001$). With back-and-forth movement only, the 1D condition is clearly easier. Movements in the 2D condition are more complicated, since the direction of movement changes by 360°/20 = 18° with each trial. Furthermore, occlusion is unavoidable for some trials in a sequence. This does not occur for the 1D task.

3.2   Movement Time and Error Rate

The grand mean for movement time was 341 ms per trial. By task type, the means were 306 ms (1D) and 377 ms (2D). The difference was statistically significant ($F_{1,12} = 48.5, p < .0001$). By device position, the means were 343 ms (mobile) and 339 ms (supported) The difference was not statistically significant ($F_{1,12} = 0.35$, ns).

The grand mean for error rate was 7.4 % per sequence. By task type, the means were 7.3 % (1D) and 7.6 % (2D). The difference was not statistically significant ($F_{1,12} = 0.03$, ns). By device position, the means were 6.7 % (mobile) and 8.1 % (supported). The difference was not statistically significant ($F_{1,12} = 1.60, p > .05$).

The error rates cited are high compared to similar studies in desktop environments [15]. The reason is revealed by examining results by target width and participants' finger widths. By target width, the mean error rates were 2.7 % for the large targets ($W = 130$ px) and 12.2 % for the small targets ($W = 78$ px). Thus there were 4.6 × more errors for the small targets. Clearly, selecting small targets with the finger is a problem for touch input. The display width of the 78-px target was 6.2 mm (0.25 in.). As noted earlier, the mean width of the tip of participants' index finger was 14.0 mm, which is more than 2 × the target width!

Not only are small targets harder to select, the effect is more pronounced for users with wide fingers. This is evident in Fig. 11, which shows both the increase in error rate for the small targets as well as a pronounced positive trend by finger width for the smaller target. It is no surprise then, that a research theme in touch-based mobile computing is improving the techniques for selecting small targets (e.g. [1, 14]).

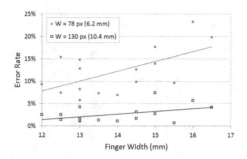

Fig. 11. Error rate by target width (*W*) and participants' finger width

It is worth noting that the trend in Fig. 11 for error rate does not appear in a similar chart for throughput (not shown). The scatter for throughput by finger width is essentially flat, demonstrating that participants' can achieve good performance (as indicated in measures for throughput) irrespective of finger width.

3.3   Distribution Measures and Normality Test

A software tool was also used to assess the distribution characteristics of the selection coordinates. The mean skewness of the distributions, over all 1920 sequences, was −0.038 (*SD* = 0.523). The mean kurtosis was −0.120 (*SD* = 1.198). Both of these figures are low, indicating no overall tendency toward a negative or positive skewness or toward a flat or peaked distribution. A normality test was conducted using the Lilliefors procedure at *alpha* = .05. In all, 93.2 % of the sequences were deemed to have selection coordinates conforming to the normal distribution, which is to say, the null hypothesis of normality was not rejected.

4   Conclusion

In this paper, the best-practice calculation for Fitts' throughput was demonstrated in a user study on touch-based target selection. During the experiment, throughput and other measures were calculated. The grand mean for throughput was 6.95 bps, which is 42 %–88 % higher than values typically reported for the mouse. The 1D condition yielded a throughput of 7.52 bps which was 15 % higher than the 6.39 bps observed for the 2D task.

References

1. Bi, X., Li, Y., Zhai, S.: FFitts law: modeling finger touch with Fitts' law. In: Proceedings of CHI 2013, pp. 1363–1372. ACM, New York (2013)
2. Crossman, E.R.F.W.: The information-capacity of the human motor-system in pursuit tracking. Q. J. Exp. Psychol. **12**, 1–16 (1960)

3. Dijkstra, R., Perez, C., Vertegaal, R.: Evaluating effects of structural holds on pointing and dragging performance with flexible displays. In: Proceedings of CHI 2011, pp. 1293–1302. ACM, New York (2011)

4. Fitts, P.M.: The information capacity of the human motor system in controlling the amplitude of movement. J. Exp. Psychol. **47**, 381–391 (1954)

5. Fitts, P.M., Peterson, J.R.: Information capacity of discrete motor responses. J. Exp. Psychol. **67**, 103–112 (1964)

6. Forlines, C., Wigdor, D., Shein, F., Balakrishnan, R.: Direct-touch vs. mouse input for tabletop displays. In: Proceedings of CHI 2007, pp. 847–856. ACM, New York (2007)

7. ISO: Ergonomic requirements for office work with visual display terminals (VDTs) - Part 9: requirements for non-keyboard input devices (ISO 9241-9). International Organisation for Standardisation. Report number ISO/TC 159/SC4/WG3 N147, 15 Feb 2000

8. MacKenzie, I.S.: Fitts' law as a research and design tool in human-computer interaction. Hum. Comput. Interact. **7**, 91–139 (1992)

9. MacKenzie, I.S.: Human-Computer Interaction: An Empirical Research Perspective. Morgan Kaufmann, Waltham (2013)

10. MacKenzie, I.S., Isokoski, P.: Fitts' throughput and the speed-accuracy tradeoff. In: Proceedings of CHI 2008, pp. 1633–1636. ACM, New York (2008)

11. MacKenzie, I.S., Sellen, A., Buxton, W.: A comparison of input devices in elemental pointing and dragging tasks. In: Proceedings of CHI 1991, pp. 161–166. ACM, New York (1991)

12. Pedersen, E.W., Hornbæk, K.: An experimental comparison of touch interaction on vertical and horizontal surfaces. In: Proceedings of Nordic CHI 2012, pp. 370–379. ACM, New York (2012)

13. Shneiderman, B.: Direct manipulation: A step beyond programming languages. In: IEEE Computer, pp. 57–69, Aug 1983

14. Song, H.T., Clawson, J., Radu, I.: Updating Fitts' law to account for small targets. Int. J. Hum. Comput. Interact. **28**, 433–444 (2012)

15. Soukoreff, R.W., MacKenzie, I.S.: Towards a standard for pointing device evaluation: perspectives on 27 years of Fitts' law research in HCI. Int. J. Hum. Comput. Stud. **61**, 751–789 (2004)

16. Welford, A.T.: Fundamentals of Skill. Methuen, London (1968)

17. Wobbrock, J.O., Gajos, K.Z.: A comparison of area pointing and goal crossing for people with and without motor impairments. In: Proceedings of ASSETS 2007, pp. 3–10. ACM, New York (2007)

18. Zhai, S.: Characterizing computer input with Fitts' law parameters: the information and non-information aspects of pointing. Int. J. Hum. Comput. Stud. **61**, 791–801 (2004)

Investigation of Transferring Touch Events for Controlling a Mobile Device with a Large Touchscreen

Kazusa Onishi[(✉)], Buntarou Shizuki, and Jiro Tanaka

University of Tsukuba, Tsukuba, Japan
{onishi,shizuki,jiro}@iplab.cs.tsukuba.ac.jp

Abstract. When users hold large mobile devices equipped with a large touchscreen in one hand, the region distant from the thumb is too distant for users to control. This forces users to change their hand posture so that their thumb can reach to the top half. To address this problem, we explore a technique that transfers touch events on the bottom half of a touchscreen to its top half. This technique may allow users to control all regions of a large touchscreen by using only the bottom half. Thus, users can control a mobile device without changing hand posture. We conducted a user study to investigate the feasibility of our technique. From the results, our technique is marginally faster than direct touch and thus, might be feasible.

Keywords: Large mobile device · Touch gesture · Single-handed control

1 Introduction

While the vast majority of users want single-handed interaction with mobile devices [9], *large mobile devices* equipped with a large touchscreen have been spreading widely. This trend presents a new problem that we call the *reachability problem*: when users hold such large mobile devices in one hand, the region distant from the thumb is too distant for users to control [15]. This forces users to change their hand posture so that their thumb can reach the top half.

In this research, we explore a technique for controlling a large device (Fig. 1) to address the reachability problem. This technique transfers touch events on the bottom half of a touchscreen to its top half. This design allows users to control the top half using only a bottom half. Therefore, the design may allow users to control all regions of a large touchscreen without changing hand posture and thus grip the device stably. We also report the user studies we conducted to investigate the feasibility of our technique.

2 Related Work

There have been many studies using a cursor controlled by dragging to address the reachability problem. MagStick [11] is a cursor that moves in the opposite direction of a thumb and sticks to a target. CornerSpace [15] uses a UI

© Springer International Publishing Switzerland 2015
M. Kurosu (Ed.): Human-Computer Interaction, Part II, HCII 2015, LNCS 9170, pp. 250–261, 2015.
DOI: 10.1007/978-3-319-20916-6_24

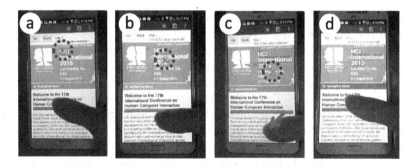

Fig. 1. Our technique allows users not only to point but also to perform touch gestures at the top half of a large mobile device without changing their hand posture. As an example, suppose that a user wants to select the text "HCI International 2015" in an Web browser. (a) In our technique, a *red X-shaped* cursor appears as visual feedback. The user selects the initial text "HCI" by long-tapping using our technique. (b) She points to the handle using our technique. (c) To adjust the handle to the end text "2015", she drags her thumb in the bottom half without removing it from the touchscreen. (d) She finishes the text selection by removing her thumb from the touchscreen after adjusting the handle (Color figure online).

shown by BezelSwipe [10] to determine the cursor's rough position. Extendible Cursor [6] is a cursor activated using BezelSwipe or a touch gesture using a wide area of the finger; users can point at a distant position by moving the cursor quickly (i.e., the control-display ratio is over one) by dragging. While these techniques are designed for pointing, our technique is designed to be used for not only pointing but also for other touch gestures (e.g., dragging or long tapping). ExtendedThumb [7] is activated with a double tap and shows a cursor moving in the direction of the thumb's movement. A touch event (e.g., tapping and dragging) following a user's touch up is transferred to the cursor position (e.g., tapping an icon at the top half of a touchscreen). Our technique also transfers touch events but does not require the position to which touch events are transferred to be determined.

Many studies have use indirect pointing techniques other than cursors to solve the problem of "fat fingers" [12]. When the user touches the screen, Shift [14] creates a callout showing a copy of the occluded screen area and places it in a non-occluded location. The callout also shows a pointer representing the selection point of the finger. LinearDragger [1] is the target acquisition technique for small and clustered targets. LinearDragger allows users to point at a target from a clustered group of selectable objects by scanning the objects one by one while continuously dragging.

ThumbSpace [5] was designed to improve access to the borders and corners of the screen. It uses an on-demand "radar view" that the user can trigger at the center of the screen. Interacting directly on this radar view allows the user to reach all locations on the screen. Thumbspace thus works as an absolute pointing touchpad superimposed on the standard touchscreen.

Other studies that have allowed users to move targets to near their thumb to make distant objects easily accessible. LoopTouch [13] provides a roll gesture, where a thumb moves on the front of the device and the same hand's index finger on the back of the device, close to each other. This gesture rolls the whole screen. Because users can make the whole screen roll by this gesture, they can move a target near to their thumb. To detect this gesture, LoopTouch requires a mobile device equipped with a touch panel on the back. Sliding Screen [6] is activated by BezelSwipe or a touch gesture using a wide area of the finger; this moves all objects on a whole screen to the touched position. In the study of Nagata et al. [8], users could pull all the objects near their thumb; among them, users could touch the target directly. Drag-and-Pop and Drag-and-Pick [2] allow users to pull icons on a desktop screen near to the cursor by dragging.

In contrast to these techniques, our technique is indirect. However, it incorporates the advantage of LoopTouch and Sliding Screen: the users can virtually bring a distant region of a screen near to their hand. This advantage gives us a chance to design a single-handed control technique for large mobile devices that allows the users to perform various touch gestures on the distant region, while still maintaining grip stability.

3   Transferring Touch Events from the Bottom to the Top

Our technique transfers touch events on the bottom half of a touchscreen to the top half (Fig. 1). This design leads to a stable single-handed grip because users can control a large mobile device without changing hand posture: users control the top half of a large touchscreen using only its bottom half. Our technique has a mode that transfers touch events on the bottom half to its top half. In this mode, our technique colors the bottom half red (Fig. 1) and displays a cursor at its corresponding point in the top half as visual feedback when somewhere on the bottom is touched.

As a use case of our technique, Fig. 1 shows a text selection. Suppose that a user wants to select the text "HCI International 2015" in an Web browser. First, the user long-taps the start of the target text while using our technique to transfer the touch event on the bottom half to the top half (Fig. 1a). Second, she points to (Fig. 1b) and moves (Fig. 1c) a handle to the end of the target text using our technique. Finally, she completes selection by removing her thumb from the touchscreen after moving the handle from the start to the end of the target text (Fig. 1d).

4   User Studies

To investigate the feasibility of our technique, we measured its performance in terms of two typical tasks on mobile devices: pointing and dragging. To clarify the pros and cons of our technique, we compared *our technique* (Transfer) with the existing *direct touch* (Touch) as the control condition.

The two controls were performed under the following two *dummy* conditions: *non dummy* (ND) and *with dummy* (WD). In the ND condition, only one target square or one target seek bar was displayed at a time on the screen as shown in Figs. 3a and 7a. On the other hand, in the WD condition, one target or one seek bar was displayed with 23 dummy targets or 5 dummy seek bars, as shown in Figs. 3b and 7b. These dummies were displayed to serve as hints to point out the place where events will be transferred. We explained this dummy design to participants and asked them to consider this hint positively. In the Transfer condition, we asked participants to use our technique to control all the targets in the top half, even if their thumb could reach the target, and to use direct touch to control all the targets in the bottom half.

4.1 Participants and Experimental Environment

The participants were 10 undergraduate and graduate students from the engineering department, one undergraduate student from the art department, and one professional designer of user interfaces aged from 22 to 26 (M = 22.5, SD = 0.5). Two were left-handed, and four were females. None had ever used our technique. All used their smartphones daily.

The user studies were conducted in the environment shown in Fig. 2. For the smartphone in this experiment, we used a Samsung GALAXY Note 3 SCL22 (79 × 151 × 8.4 mm, 5.7" display). We chose this device because it is almost the same size as the device used in the user study of Yu et al. [15], one of previous studis on the reachability problem. We asked the participants to sit on a chair and control the smartphone in one hand as they usually do. To control experimental conditions between participants, we also asked the participants to put their elbow on a desk and hold the smartphone without supporting it by using the desk or their bodies.

We asked the participants to perform the tasks as accurately as possible. This instruction is based on the design principle that focuses on accuracy rather than speed. If the participants could not reach the target (which they frequently could not under the Touch condition), we asked them to change the hand posture of the hand holding the smartphone. If participants could not change their hand posture in midair, we permitted them to touch the smartphone to the desk to support it.

Fig. 2. Experimental environment.

4.2 Task

We asked the participants to perform a pointing task and then a dragging task. In addition, the order of the two dummy conditions was ND and WD. We asked them to complete 12 sessions (4 learning sessions, 4 training sessions, and 4 real sessions) for each task in both techniques and both dummy conditions. We divided the participants into two groups to counterbalance the order effect between the two technique conditions: one group performed the tasks under the Transfer condition first; the other performed them under the Touch condition first.

We asked them to answer a questionnaire after they had finished all the tasks. The experiment lasted approximately two hours per participant, including the questionnaire. All participants were paid 1640 JPY (approximately 16 USD) for their participation.

4.3 Study 1: Pointing

In each trial, the participants pointed to a target square, which was blue (e.g., the blue square in Fig. 3b). The target square was the same size as the application icons displayed on the default home screen of this device. Participants had to successfully perform each trial before proceeding to the next trial.

A participant started each session by touching the touchscreen. A new target square was automatically presented by the experimental software when a trial was completed.

In this task, the independent variables were target position (24) and technique (Transfer and Touch). Each participant performed 12 sessions in each combination of positions, techniques, and dummy conditions, thus performing 1152 (24 × 2 × 12 × 2) trials in total. The target position was presented in randomized order.

Results

Trial-times for both conditions: We analyzed the time to complete a trial (trial-time) in real sessions. The two left and two right bars in Fig. 4 show the mean

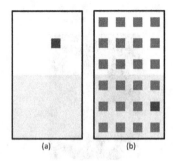

(a)   (b)

Fig. 3. Positions of target squares in (a) ND and (b) WD.

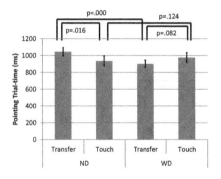
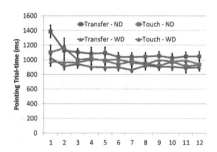

Fig. 4. Trial-times for each technique and dummy condition.

Fig. 5. Trial-times of all conditions for each session.

trial-times of both techniques in ND and WD, respectively. The mean times were 1044 ms in Transfer-ND and 935 ms in Touch-ND. In turn, the mean times were 901 ms in Transfer-WD and 976 ms in Touch-WD. Repeated measures analysis of variance showed a significant main effect on dummy condition ($p(11) = .045 < .05$). With pairwise t-tests, there was a significant effect on dummy condition in Transfer ($p(1) = .000 < .050$). In addition, there was a marginal significance on the technique condition in WD ($p(1) = .082 < .100$). This result suggests that pointing in Transfer was marginally significantly faster than that in Touch in WD.

Trial-time for each session: We show trial-times of all conditions in each session in Fig. 5. In ND, the trial-times in all the sessions after the second are faster than that in the first one ($p(11) = .000$). This result suggests that participants learned how to use our technique during the first session. Thus, our technique can be learned with little effort (approximately 0.55 min).

Error Rate: We analyzed the error rates in the real sessions. The two left and two right bars in Fig. 6 show the mean error rates of both techniques in ND and WD, respectively. Note that this study was designed such that participants had to successfully perform each trial before proceeding to the next trial, even if this required multiple trials. As such, all trials were ultimately "successful". However, we classified the cases where trials were not cleared on the first attempt as errors, and analyzed this error data. The mean error rates were 12.76 % in Transfer-ND and 6.51 % in Touch-ND. In turn, the mean error rates were 3.99 % in Transfer-WD and 5.99 % in Touch-WD. Repeated measures analysis of variance showed a significant main effect on dummy condition ($p(11) = .000 < .05$). With pairwise t-tests, there was a significant effect on dummy condition in Transfer ($p(1) = .000 < .050$). In WD, while Transfer is more accurate than Touch, we found no significant effect.

Considerations. Although, in WD, the trial-time in Transfer was marginally significantly faster than that in Touch, there was no significant or marginally

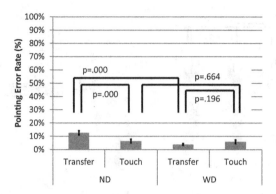

Fig. 6. Error rates for both techniques and both dummy conditions.

significant effect on the error rate. These results suggest that the trial-times are faster in Transfer-WD than in Touch-WD because our technique does not include time for changing the hand posture in Transfer. In the questionnaire, some participants said that it is easy to perform this task was easy to perform in Transfer because they did not need to change their hand posture.

To examine this hypothesis, we compare the trial-times of each region in Tables 1, 2, 3, and 4. We mirrored the data of the two left-handed regions (e.g., A1 and A4). Even in ND where no hint was displayed, the trial-time in Transfer in region A1 was shorter than that in Touch. Note that A1 is the most distant region from the thumb. Furthermore, in the dummy condition, the trial-times in Transfer in row F, which is the lowest region, were shorter than those in Touch. This result suggests that our technique does not require users to change hand posture.

These features are far more valid in WD where hints are displayed. In WD, the trial-times in Transfer in row A, which is the highest region, and rows D–F which are lower regions, are shorter than those in Touch. Because of this, the trial-time in Transfer are shorter than those Touch. Thus, our technique allows users to grip a smartphone stably (Tables 5 and 6).

In rows B and C, the trial-times were shorter in Touch than in Transfer, and the error rates were lower in Touch than in Transfer except Region B4. The possible cause of this derives from the fact that users were required to touch in rows E and F, which are the most difficult regions to touch, and to point to rows B and C using Transfer. However, this problem could be solved by allowing users to use Transfer and Touch arbitrarily by expanding touch vocabulary.

4.4   Study 2: Dragging

We asked the participants to adjust a seek bar by dragging its knob. We illustrate the seek bars in both dummy conditions in Fig. 7. Following the scroll experiment of Cockburn et al. [3], we displayed a target as a range of value (target range) whose center is determined randomly. The range is bounded by two red bars.

Table 1. Trial-times of each region in Transfer-ND.

	1	2	3	4
A	1121.75	1103.48	1223.65	1113.54
B	1528.10	1166.69	1292.50	1227.38
C	1976.29	1155.63	1134.29	1151.42
D	951.90	817.06	737.48	809.94
E	879.29	683.94	697.94	785.94
F	1116.63	838.02	738.65	802.54

Table 2. Trial-times of each region in Touch-ND.

	1	2	3	4
A	1292.48	988.17	934.96	920.77
B	975.71	744.10	841.08	866.73
C	947.06	759.13	744.56	822.92
D	927.98	796.08	755.00	827.96
E	1023.79	791.75	852.63	785.42
F	1841.63	1052.54	986.77	962.02

Table 3. Trial-times of each region in Transfer-WD.

	1	2	3	4
A	1049.19	891.21	836.42	873.00
B	1133.27	838.48	869.85	908.21
C	1301.54	1004.94	928.67	1049.19
D	830.19	736.04	759.85	766.17
E	944.67	696.85	696.19	773.46
F	1367.15	817.49	702.71	842.06

Table 4. Trial-times of each region in Touch-WD.

	1	2	3	4
A	1519.35	964.83	1060.65	937.79
B	1006.77	817.96	819.96	825.67
C	885.27	745.19	755.50	907.38
D	849.04	749.85	781.77	840.17
E	1202.98	883.71	782.48	894.94
F	1815.21	1361.73	960.50	1015.71

Table 5. Error rates of each region in Transfer-WD.

	1	2	3	4
A	6.25	2.08	2.08	4.17
B	2.0	4.17	4.17	2.08
C	6.25	6.25	6.25	14.58
D	0.00	2.08	0.00	0.00
E	0.00	2.08	2.08	2.08
F	14.58	4.17	0.00	8.33

Table 6. Error rates of each region in Touch-WD.

	1	2	3	4
A	18.75	2.08	6.25	4.17
B	2.08	4.17	0.00	10.42
C	4.17	2.08	4.17	14.58
D	0.00	0.00	6.25	8.33
E	2.08	6.25	2.08	4.17
F	16.67	12.50	4.17	10.42

The participants were instructed to drag the knob and release their hand from it when the knob was within the target range. The action to start the session was the same as that of the pointing task.

In this task, the independent variables were seek bar position (6) and technique (Transfer and Touch). Each participant performed 12 sessions in each combination of factors and dummy conditions, thus performing 288 ($6 \times 2 \times 12 \times 2$) trials in total. The seek bar position was presented in a randomized order.

Results

Trial-time for both conditions: We analyzed the trial-times in the real sessions. The two left and two right bars in Fig. 8 show the mean trial-times of both techniques in ND, respectively. The mean trial-times were 2235 ms in Transfer-ND and 2151 ms in Touch-ND. In turn, the mean times were 1900 ms in Transfer-WD and 1978 ms in Touch-WD. Repeated measures analysis of variance showed a significant main effect on dummy condition ($p(11) = .006 < .05$). With pairwise t-tests, there were significant effect on dummy condition in Transfer ($p(1) = .001 < .050$) and a marginal significance on dummy condition in Touch ($p(1) = .059 < .100$).

Trial-time for each session: There were no significant effects on the trial-times in 12th session in ND and the trial-time of 1st session in WD (Transfer: $p = .263 > .050$, Touch: $p = .186 > .050$) (Fig. 9). This result suggests that dummy does not significantly affect the trial-time (if there were significant effect, the trial-time of the first session in WD would have been shorter than that of the 12th session in ND). Moreover, the trial-time of each technique in WD was significantly shorter than ND, and the trial-time of Transfer is slightly shorter than that of Touch in WD. These results might be due to the learning effect. Therefore, after finishing learning, the trial-time of Transfer should become shorter than Touch in ND.

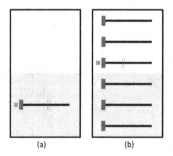

Fig. 7. Positions of the seek bars in (a) ND and (b) WD (Color figure online).

Error Rate: We calculated and analyzed the error rates in the real sessions in the same manner as in Study 1. The two left and two right bars in Fig. 10 show the mean error rates of both techniques in ND and WD, respectively. The mean error rates were 24.00 in Transfer-ND and 13.54 in Touch-ND. In turn, the mean error rates were 11.80 in Transfer-WD and 14.23 in Touch-WD. Repeated measures analysis of variance showed a significant main effect on dummy condition ($p(11) = .012 < .05$). With pairwise t-tests, there was a significant effect on dummy condition in Transfer ($p(1) = .002 < .050$). With pairwise t-test, there was a significant effect between the dummy condition in Transfer ($p(1) = .002 < .050$) and techniques in the ND condition ($p(1) = .007 < .050$).

Unlike trial-time, there is no significant error in dummy condition in Touch. Thus, in ND, participants could adjust the seek bars as accurately as in the WD condition, although they took longer to adjust that one. On the other hand, in the Transfer condition, the error rate in WD is lower than that in ND. Thus, our technique requires a hint in seek tasks, as well as in pointing tasks.

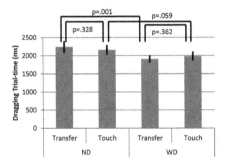

Fig. 8. Trial-times for both techniques and both dummy conditions.

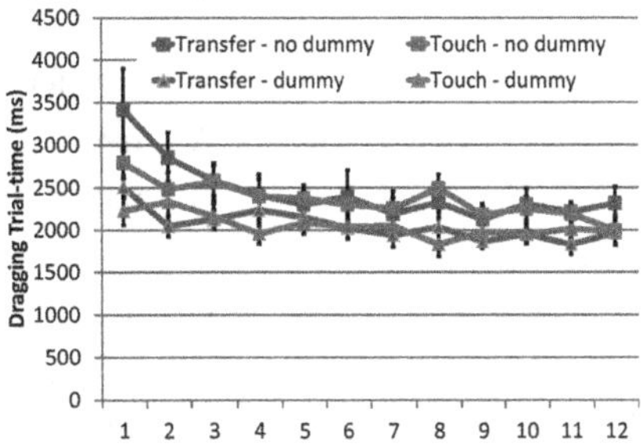

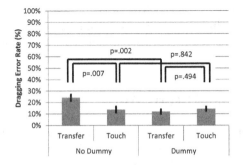

Fig. 9. Trial-times of all conditions for each session.

Fig. 10. Error rates for both techniques and both dummy conditions.

Table 7. Trial-times of each region

	Transfer-ND	Touch-ND	Transfer-WD	Touch-WD
A	2414.65	2550.67	2034.85	2386.15
B	2529.85	2025.77	1925.60	1976.63
C	2455.40	1971.77	2275.79	1726.69
D	2022.48	1896.85	1632.27	1675.93
E	1855.04	1965.63	1704.33	1854.88
F	2130.15	2423.25	1899.38	2245.40

Considerations. Table 7 compares the trial-times of each region. In the ND condition, the trial-time in region A, the upper-most, in Transfer is shorter than that in Touch. Furthermore, in WD, trial-times in the all regions except C are shorter in Transfer than in Touch, because the control is easier in Touch than in Transfer in region C.

Table 8. Error rates of each region

	Transfer-WD	Touch-WD
A	10.42	27.08
B	0.00	12.5
C	20.83	12.5
D	6.25	8.33
E	16.67	8.33
F	16.67	16.67

In WD, the error rates in Transfer in regions A and B are lower for over 10 % than those in Touch in Table 8. The possible cause of this derives from the fact that adjusting using Touch is difficult due to "fat fingers", although our technique is an indirect control and nothing hide the target range. In the questionnaire, one participant said that it was hard to see the target region in the bottom half.

5 Conclusion and Future Work

We proposed a technique for transferring touch events for controlling a large device. The studies using our technique revealed that it is marginally faster than direct touch and thus might be feasible.

However, we found two areas to be further explored in our technique. First, our technique requires a hint pointing out the place where a touch event will be transferred. To this end, we will implement visual feedback of the place using hover events that can be sensed in some smartphones. Second, to use our technique realistically, we must explore the interaction design for mode switching between the two modes: the mode where touch events on the bottom half are transferred to the top half and when they are used on the bottom half as usual. For a possible solution, we are testing using the strength of touch to classify them (similar to Forcetap [4]): users touch strongly to transfer touch events. Future work will need to explore more designs.

References

1. Au, O.K.C., Su, X., Lau, R.: LinearDragger: a linear selector for one-finger target acquisition. In: Proceedings of CHI EA 2014, pp. 487–490. ACM (2014)
2. Baudisch, P., Cutrell, E., Robbins, D., Czerwinski, M., Tandler, P., Bederson, B., Zierlinger, A.: Drag-and-pop and drag-and-pick: techniques for accessing remote screen content on touch- and pen-operated systems. In: Proceedings of Interact Conference, pp. 57–64 (2003)
3. Cockburn, A., Savage, J., Wallace, A.: Tuning and testing scrolling interfaces that automatically zoom. In: Proceedings of CHI 2005, pp. 71–80. ACM (2005)

4. Heo, S., Lee, G.: Forcetap: extending the input vocabulary of mobile touch screens by adding tap gestures. In: Proceedings of MobileHCI 2011, pp. 113–122. ACM (2011)

5. Karlson, A.K., Bederson, B.B.: One-handed touchscreen input for legacy applications. In: Proceedings of CHI 2008, pp. 1399–1408. ACM (2008)

6. Kim, S., Yu, J., Lee, G.: Interaction techniques for unreachable objects on the touchscreen. In: Proceedings of OzCHI 2012, pp. 295–298. ACM (2012)

7. Lai, J., Zhang, D.: ExtendedThumb: a motion-based virtual thumb for improving one-handed target acquisition on touch-screen mobile devices. In: Proceedings of CHI EA 2014, pp. 1825–1830. ACM (2014)

8. Nagata, K., Murata, K., Shibuya, Y.: A method for selecting unreachable objects on one-hand operated mobile device with drawing them close to user's thumb. In: Proceedings of Symposium on Mobile Interactions, pp. 35–40 (2012) (in Japanese)

9. Parhi, P., Karlson, A.K., Bederson, B.B.: Target size study for one-handed thumb use on small touchscreen devices. In: Proceedings of MobileHCI 2006, pp. 203–210. ACM (2006)

10. Roth, V., Turner, T.: Bezel Swipe: conflict-free scrolling and multiple selection on mobile touch screen devices. In: Proceedings of CHI 2009, pp. 1523–1526. ACM (2009)

11. Roudaut, A., Huot, S., Lecolinet, E.: TapTap and MagStick: improving one-handed target acquisition on small touch-screens. In: Proceedings of AVI 2008, pp. 146–153. ACM (2008)

12. Siek, K.A., Rogers, Y., Connelly, K.H.: Fat finger worries: how older and younger users physically interact with PDAs. In: Costabile, M.F., Paternó, F. (eds.) INTER-ACT 2005. LNCS, vol. 3585, pp. 267–280. Springer, Heidelberg (2005)

13. Tosa, S., Tanaka, J.: LoopTouch:one-handed operation technique using the screen looping on mobile devices. In: Proceedings of Interaction 2013. IPSJ (2013) (in Japanese)

14. Vogel, D., Baudisch, P.: Shift: a technique for operating pen-based interfaces using touch. In: Proceedings of CHI 2007, pp. 657–666. ACM (2007)

15. Yu, N.H., Huang, D.Y., Hsu, J.J., Hung, Y.P.: Rapid selection of hard-to-access targets by thumb on mobile touch-screens. In: Proceedings of MobileHCI 2013, pp. 400–403. ACM (2013)

GyroTouch: Wrist Gyroscope with a Multi-Touch Display

Francisco R. Ortega[✉], Armando Barreto, Naphtali Rishe,
Nonnarit O-larnnithipong, Malek Adjouadi, and Fatemeh Abyarjoo

Florida International University, Miami, FL 33199, USA
fort007@fiu.edu
http://www.franciscoraulortega.com/

Abstract. We present GyroTouch, a multi-modal approach to the use of a digital gyroscope in a watch form-factor and a multi-touch desktop display with the aim to find properties that can yield better navigation in 3D virtual environments. GyroTouch was created to augment multi-touch gestures with other devices. Our approach addressed 3D rotations and 3D Translation used in navigation of virtual environments. This work also includes an algorithm for estimating angular velocity for any given axis, using only one previous sample.

Keywords: Multi-touch · Gyroscope · Modern input devices · Multi-modal · Multimodal input

1 Introduction

The emergence of new widely accessible input technologies such as Microsoft Kinect, Leap Motion, and iPad, among others, in the past few years has created opportunities to improve user interaction. The introduction of digital smart watches has also allowed to find how multi-modal interaction can benefit different types of interaction between users and computer systems. In particular, our interest lies in 3D navigation in virtual environments.

When developing gestures to aid the navigation of 3D worlds, one can find several methods, including multi-touch interaction. However, one of the primary limitations of multi-touch displays is the 2D nature of their surface. This limitation can be circumvented by creating custom 2D gestures to map the 3D equivalent input actions. In pursuit of a more realistic 3D experience, augmenting or complementing the multi-touch display gives the users a more natural interaction. We have explored the development of a fast, natural and accurate real-time 3D navigation technique using multi-touch by augmenting (or complementing) it with commodity devices (e.g., Nintendo WiiMote, Leap Motion), in order to find a more intuitive user interaction. We also want to provide a simple algorithm in the spirit of the $1 algorithm [1] and the Rubine algorithm [2], which have shown that simple solutions using commodity devices can be as efficient as more complex algorithms. We showed an algorithm in [3] which

© Springer International Publishing Switzerland 2015
M. Kurosu (Ed.): Human-Computer Interaction, Part II, HCII 2015, LNCS 9170, pp. 262–270, 2015.
DOI: 10.1007/978-3-319-20916-6_25

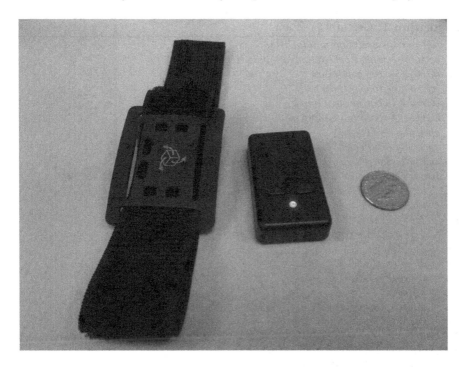

Fig. 1. 3 Space sensor and strap

demonstrated a simple approach to recognize some touch gestures, as shown in Algorithm 1. These efforts are is also aligned with recent work on multi modal touch and pen input [4].

The proposed solution uses standard multi-touch gestures (e.g., rotate with two fingers) and a Microelectromechanical System (MEMS) that has a 3-axis Accelerometer, a 3-axis Gyroscope and a 3-Axis Compass (YEI's "3 Space Sensor"). This approach can be used to complement the multi-touch displays which may lead to a better user experience.

The work is novel when it comes to complementing multi-touch devices with gyroscopes. The ability to use additional sensors in a watch wristband is realistic and not invasive. In addition, Algorithm 2 uses simple computations to estimate the rotation angle for any given axis using only two samples received from the MEMS module.

We are inspired by the quest of the ubiquitous computing as proposed by Weiser [5] and the vision of the ultimate display by Sutherland [6]:

> "The ultimate display would, of course, be a room within which the computer can control the existence of matter. A chair displayed in such a room would be good enough to sit in. Handcuffs displayed in such a room would be confining, and a bullet displayed in such a room would be fatal."

Algorithm 1. GestureDetection

1: $top \leftarrow traces.getTop(windowSize)$
2: $bottom \leftarrow traces.getBottom(windowSize)$
3: $tGrip.x \leftarrow top.getGrip.x$
4: $tGrip.y \leftarrow top.getGrip.y$
5: $bGrip.x \leftarrow bottom.getGrip.x$
6: $bGrip.y \leftarrow bottom.getGrip.y$
7: $spread.x \leftarrow iTrace[1].x - iGrip.x$
8: $spread.y \leftarrow iTrace[1].y - iGrip.y$
9: $swipeDistance \leftarrow sqrt(spread.x^2 + spread.y^2)$
10: **for** $t = 1$ to $traces.Count$ **do**
11:    $i.x \leftarrow tTrace[t].x - tGrip.x$
12:    $i.y \leftarrow tTrace[t].y - tGrip.y$
13:    $f.x \leftarrow bTrace[t].x - bGrip.x$
14:    $f.y \leftarrow bTrace[t].y - bGrip.y$
15:    $di \leftarrow sqrt(i.x^2 + i.y^2)$
16:    $df \leftarrow sqrt(f.x^2 + f.y^2)$
17:    $iSpread \leftarrow iSpread + di$
18:    $fSpread \leftarrow fSpread + df$
19:    $angle \leftarrow atan2(f.y - i.y, f.x - i.x)$
20:    $rotAngle \leftarrow rotAngle + angle$
21: **end for**
22: $iSpread \leftarrow iSpread/traces.Count$
23: $fSpread \leftarrow fSpread/traces.Count$
24: $rotAngle \leftarrow rotAngle/traces.Count$
25: $zoomDistance \leftarrow fSpread - iSpread$
26: $rotDistance \leftarrow rotAngle/360.0 * 2 * \pi * swipeDistance$
27: **return** Gesture With Highest Distance

Algorithm 2. Rotation Algorithm for a Gyroscope

Ensure: midLevel=0 & unitDegree = 1 for 3Space Sensor
1: $roll \leftarrow rawdata.roll - midLevel$
2: $rot.x[0] \leftarrow rot.x[1]$
3: $rot.x[1] \leftarrow roll$
4: $omega.x[0] \leftarrow omega.X[1]$
5: $omega.x[1] \leftarrow roll.x[1]/unitDegree$
6: $x \leftarrow angle.x[1]$
7: $angle.x[1] \leftarrow x + T * ((omega.x[1] + omega.x[0])/2)$
8: **return** angle.x[1] as roll

---

2   Related Work

Multi-touch interaction for 3D environments has been explored before for domain-specific applications (e.g., [7]). There have also been attempts to augment the multi-touch experience. For example, Z-Touch [8], developed by Takeoka et al., captures a depth map to add the z-axis to the touch display. However, the Z-Touch has limitations and it is not a commodity device. Augmenting the touch with a

Fig. 2. 3M multi-touch display and WiiMote motion plus

force sensor has also been tried [9]. Vision has also been used to complement touch with Microsoft Kinect [9]. Similarly there are Apple iOS or Android OS devices that allow users to combine touch with some MEMS components (e.g., Accelerometer). As stated in the introduction, there have been different efforts that us the bi-manual model [10–12] using pen and multi-touch [4,13–16]. Additional multi-modal efforts include free-air and multi-touch [17], gaze and touch [18], pen and touch for games [13], pen and touch for problem solving [19], among others [20,21].

3   GyroTouch

"We have developed **GyroTouch** using Visual Studio running on a Windows 7 platform with a 3M 22" multi-touch display and a MEMS module by YEI Technology (3 Space Sensor, shown in Fig. 1). The first iteration of **GyroTouch** was done with the WiiMote, as shown in Fig. 2. Currently, we are using the 3 Space Wireless Sensor in the non-dominant hand, as shown in Figs. 3 and 4. The dominant hand is used for the multi-touch interaction. For our 3D rendering, we have used OGRE3D. We believe that combining both devices gives the user the freedom to use the hands for some of the rotations and translations, while keeping the tactual feedback intact for other gestures.

Our approach is to use our multi-touch algorithm to detect swipe, zoom and rotate gestures on the display surface. This allows us to use the touch for

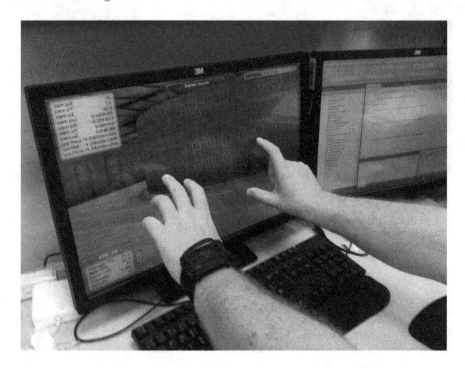

Fig. 3. 3M multi-touch display and gyroscope (left wrist)

translating in x and y (using two-finger swipe). For z translation, we map a one-finger swipe (same direction as the y-axis) to the z translation. For the rotation about the z-axis (yaw), we use the 2-finger touch rotation as it is commonly done with touch tablets. In order to keep the interaction as natural as possible, we complement the touch with the gyroscope for rotations about the x-axis (roll) and the y-axis (pitch) using the gyroscope.

Our touch detection method, described in [3], consists of finding certain characteristics for each gesture using a very fast and simple algorithm. The gyroscope found in the MEMS, shown in Figs. 3 and 4, is used only to indicate the roll and pitch rotations, whereas the third rotation is indicated via the touch interaction. Algorithm 2 shows the integration over time of the gyroscope signal, using the current and previous samples, required to obtain the angle of rotation about the x-axis. The same applies for each of the other two axes. The sensor already provides data processed by a Kalman Filter. In addition, we filter data within a threshold, calculated when the sensor is initialized, in an idle position. The sampling rate varies depending on the sensor. We are using a sampling rate of 160 Hz (with a possible maximum for this device of 800 Hz). This gives us the period T to be $1/FS$ or $1/160$. Since the data is already normalized, there is no need to use the *midLevel* and the *unitDegree* variables in Algorithm 2. Hence, we set them to 0 and 1 respectively. It is important to point out that this

Fig. 4. Gyroscope in idle state

is not always the case for all devices. For example, for the WiiMote (as shown in Fig. 2), it is necessary to set the midLovol at 2^{13} and the unitDegree at 8192/592.

4   Discussion

Our goal was to explorer the initial feasibility of combining both of theses devices. Preliminary trials we conducted showed that there is further work needed to accomplish this type of multi-modality but it is possible. An important challenge was to determined when the gyroscope is idle. The easiest way, yet not desirable, is to leave the handle idle, as shown in Fig. 4. Another option is to make the gyroscope only active when touch is not active, but that will remove the multi-modality that is desired. Adding a button to the watch to activate it, was not desirable on this type of design either. Therefore, the best way to overcome this still needs to be studied further. The other problem is that gyroscopes have noise, which yields a less stable indication of input devices. In the case of pen and touch [4], the action with the pen provided a more predictable input.

Multi-modal interaction it does have benefits. Smart watches may become more pervasive allowing the watch to become another input device for virtual environments and graphical interfaces. The main benefit of using a gyroscope (and other sensors such as accelerometer and compass) is that it provides a natural reading of rotations and translations for the third dimension. It is also expected that noise removal on these devices will keep improving, making it a viable option.

When developing multi-modal interactions, we adhere to the recommendation of Bowman and colleagues: "Match the interaction technique to the device" [22, p.179]. Each device has its complexity, its strengths and weakness. Also, a more formal study is needed to find out what gestures are appropriate for Gyro-Touch. An approach that seems reasonable to follow is finding a user-defined gesture set, as it was done for multi-touch in [23]. Finally, while formal quantitative evaluation is very important, initial trials are important to improve the interaction [24].

5   Conclusion and Future Work

We have shown a simple method for real-time 3D Navigation using multi-touch and gyroscope devices. Our next step is to provide additional gestures for new devices including multi-touch displays and inertial navigational systems. We will look at combining multiple devices to create a fusion algorithm to enhance the user experience. There are important questions to address. For example, how can the accelerometer, gyroscope and compass serve to improve the touch interaction? The next step is to find how the utilization of those sensors mentioned provides a better user interaction when combined with multi-touch. This should include the study of the properties of each of the devices, as done by [4] in his pen+touch study, as well as to find common gestures that work well with this interaction. Every incremental effort towards ubiquitous computing helps to get closer to vision of Mark Weiser [5]:

> "The most profound technologies are those that disappear. They weave themselves into the fabric of everyday life until they are indistinguishable from it."

Acknowledgments. This work was sponsored by NSF grants NSF-III-Large-MOD 800001483, HRD-0833093, CNS-0959985, CNS-0821345, and CNS-1126619. We would like to Acknowledge YEI Technologies, makers of the 3 Space Sensor for their support. Francisco Ortega is a GAANN fellow (US Department of Education) and McKnight Dissertation Fellow (Florida Education Fund).

References

1. Wobbrock, J.O., Wilson, A.D., Li, Y.: Gestures without libraries, toolkits or training: a $1 recognizer for user interface prototypes. In: Proceedings of the 20th Annual ACM Symposium on User Interface Software and Technology UIST 2007, October 2007
2. Rubine, D.: Specifying gestures by example. In: Proceedings of the 18th Annual Conference on Computer Graphics and Interactive Techniques SIGGRAPH 1991, pp. 329–337, July 1991

3. Ortega, F., Barreto, A., Rishe, N., Adjoudi, M., Abyarjoo, F.: Poster: real-time gesture detection for multi-touch devices. In: IEEE 8th Symposium on 3D User Interfaces, pp. 167–168 (2013)
4. Hinckley, K., Yatani, K., Pahud, M., Coddington, N., Rodenhouse, J., Wilson, A., Benko, H., Buxton, B.: Pen + touch = new tools. In: Proceedings of the 23nd Annual ACM Symposium on User Interface Software and Technology UIST 2010. ACM, New York, USA, October 2010
5. Weiser, M.: The computer for the 21st century. Sci. Am. **265**, 94–104 (1991)
6. Sutherland, I.E.: The Ultimate Display, invited lecture. In: IFIP Congress (1965)
7. Fu, C.W., Goh, W.B., Ng, J.A.: Multi-touch techniques for exploring large-scale 3D astrophysical simulations. In: Proceedings of the SIGCHI Conference on Human Factors in Computing Systems CHI 2010. ACM, April 2010
8. Takeoka, Y., Miyaki, T., Rekimoto, J.: Z-touch: an infrastructure for 3d gesture interaction in the proximity of tabletop surfaces. In: International Conference on Interactive Tabletops and Surfaces ITS 2010, November 2010
9. Lai, H.: Using commodity visual gesture recognition technology to replace or to augment touch interfaces. In: 15th Twente Student Conference on IT (2011)
10. Kelso, J.S., Southard, D.L., Goodman, D.: On the coordination of two-handed movements. J. Exp. Psychol. Hum. Percept. Perform. **5**(2), 229–238 (1979)
11. Peters, M.: Constraints in the performance of bimanual tasks and their expression in unskilled and skilled subjects. Q. J. Exp. Psychol. **37A**(2), 171–196 (1985)
12. Wing, A.M.: Timing and co-ordination of repetitive bimanual movements. Q. J. Exp. Psychol. **34**(3), 339–348 (1982)
13. Hamilton, W., Kerne, A., Robbins, T.: High-performance pen+ touch modality interactions: a real-time strategy game eSports context. In: UIST 2012, pp. 309–318 (2012)
14. Hinckley, K., Yatani, K., Pahud, M., Coddington, N., Rodenhouse, J., Wilson, A., Benko, H., Buxton, B.: Manual deskterity: an exploration of simultaneous pen + touch direct input. In: CHI 2010 Extended Abstracts on Human Factors in Computing Systems, vol. 2793, April 2010
15. Brandl, P., Forlines, C., Wigdor, D., Haller, M., Shen, C.: Combining and measuring the benefits of bimanual pen and direct-touch interaction on horizontal interfaces. In: Proceedings of the Working Conference on Advanced Visual Interfaces AVI 2008. ACM, May 2008
16. Hinckley, K., Pahud, M., Benko, H., Irani, P., Guimbretiere, F., Gavriliu, M., Anthony' Chen, X., Matulic, F., Buxton, W., Wilson, A.: Sensing techniques for tablet+stylus interaction. In: Proceedings of the 27th Annual ACM Symposium on User Interface Software and Technology UIST 2014. ACM, October 2014
17. Moeller, J., Kerne, A.: ZeroTouch: an optical multi-touch and free-air interaction architecture. In: Proceedings of the SIGCHI Conference on Human Factors in Computing Systems CHI 2012. ACM, May 2012
18. Pfeuffer, K., Alexander, J., Chong, M.K., Gellersen, H.: Gaze-touch: combining gaze with multi-touch for interaction on the same surface. In: Proceedings of the 27th Annual ACM Symposium on User Interface Software and Technology UIST 2014. ACM, October 2014
19. Zeleznik, R., Bragdon, A., Adeputra, F., Ko, H.S.: Hands-on math: a page-based multi-touch and pen desktop for technical work and problem solving. In: Proceedings of the 23nd Annual ACM Symposium on User Interface Software and Technology UIST 2010. ACM, New York, USA, October 2010

20. Hasan, K., Yang, X.D., Bunt, A., Irani, P.: A-coord input: coordinating auxiliary input streams for augmenting contextual pen-based interactions. In: Proceedings of the SIGCHI Conference on Human Factors in Computing Systems CHI 2012, pp. 805–814. ACM, New York, USA, May 2012

21. Ruffieux, S., Lalanne, D., Mugellini, E.: ChAirGest: a challenge for multimodal mid-air gesture recognition for close HCI. In: Proceedings of the 15th ACM on International Conference on Multimodal Interaction ICMI 2013. ACM, December 2013

22. Bowman, D.A., Kruijff, E., LaViola Jr, J.J., Poupyrev, I.: 3D User Interfaces: Theory and Practice. Addison-Wesley Professional, Boston (2004)

23. Wobbrock, J.O., Morris, M.R., Wilson, A.D.: User-defined gestures for surface computing. In: Proceedings of the SIGCHI Conference on Human Factors in Computing Systems CHI 2009 (2009)

24. Greenberg, S., Buxton, B.: Usability evaluation considered harmful (some of the time). In: Proceedings of the SIGCHI Conference on Human Factors in Computing Systems CHI 2008. ACM, April 2008

Natural User Interfaces

Giving Voices to Multimodal Applications

Nuno Almeida[1,2], António Teixeira[1,2(✉)], Ana Filipa Rosa[1],
Daniela Braga[3], João Freitas[4], Miguel Sales Dias[4,5], Samuel Silva[1,2],
Jairo Avelar[4], Cristiano Chesi[4], and Nuno Saldanha[4]

[1] Institute of Electronics and Telematics Engineering, University of Aveiro,
Aveiro, Portugal
[2] Department of Electronics, Telecommunications and Informatics Engineering,
University of Aveiro, Aveiro, Portugal
ajst@ua.pt
[3] Voicebox Technologies, Bellevue, WA, USA
[4] Microsoft Language Development Center, Lisbon, Portugal
[5] Instituto Universitário de Lisboa (ISCTE-IUL), ISTAR-IUL, Lisbon, Portugal

Abstract. The use of speech interaction is important and useful in a wide range of applications. It is a natural way of interaction and it is easy to use by people in general. The development of speech enabled applications is a big challenge that increases if several languages are required, a common scenario, for example, in Europe. Tackling this challenge requires the proposal of methods and tools that foster easier deployment of speech features, harnessing developers with versatile means to include speech interaction in their applications. Besides, only a reduced variety of voices are available (sometimes only one per language) which raises problems regarding the fulfillment of user preferences and hinders a deeper exploration regarding voices' adequacy to specific applications and users.

In this article, we present some of our contributions to these different issues: (a) our generic modality that encapsulates the technical details of using speech synthesis; (b) the process followed to create four new voices, including two young adult and two elderly voices; and (c) some initial results exploring user preferences regarding the created voices.

The preliminary studies carried out targeted groups including both young and older-adults and addressed: (a) evaluation of the intrinsic properties of each voice; (b) observation of users while using speech enabled interfaces and elicitation of qualitative impressions regarding the chosen voice and the impact of speech interaction on user satisfaction; and (c) ranking of voices according to preference.

The collected results, albeit preliminary, yield some evidence of the positive impact speech interaction has on users, at different levels. Additionally, results show interesting differences among the voice preferences expressed by both age groups and genders.

Keywords: Synthetic voices · Speech output · Multimodal interaction · Age effects

---

Daniela Braga — Work done while at Microsoft, now at Voicebox.

M. Kurosu (Ed.): Human-Computer Interaction, Part II, HCII 2015, LNCS 9170, pp. 273–283, 2015.
DOI: 10.1007/978-3-319-20916-6_26

1 Introduction

The use of speech in HCI is gaining more popularity [1]. Assistants such as Siri and Cortana are major examples of the success and user acceptance. Speech enabled applications should also offer the traditional ways of interaction. For example, in mobile phones the user should additionally be able to interact with touch and have visual feedback. So, developing such applications is more time consuming and implies some complex tasks. To add speech-based interaction to applications, developers use what the market offers in terms of speech engines. In this context, it is important to simplify the process of creating speech enabled applications, providing developers with easy methods and tools to embody speech into their application.

Another issue concerning the use of speech for interaction is the reduced variety of voices available. Most speech engines offer only one or, at most, two voices for each language, typically an adult male or female, and they do not support every language. This way, the user is forced to use that voice for all applications. For example, for European Portuguese, the language we adopt for this paper, there was only one female voice easily available, although it has been shown that the voice is an important factor of engagement [2], possibly leading to a stronger confidence in the application and improved comfort for the user. If multiple voices are made available, another problem that must be addressed is the selection of the more adequate voice for the user and application. In fact, choosing a particular voice might have different impacts depending on the target audience and on the context it is used. Sometimes, providing a gender match between the voice and the user might enable social-identification and enhance user engagement, but female voices that sound too masculine or vice versa, might have a negative impact [2]. The user might also be confused if a voice uses vocabulary that is inconsistent with its perceived age, e.g., a younger voice speaking as an older adult. Therefore, the available voices might influence what can be said and how it is said. There are issues that concern certain user groups. For example, if speech rate is too fast there is evidence that the elderly have problems in understanding it, which might constitute a strong barrier to its use [3–5]. Furthermore, when an application involves very different tasks or interface elements, using different voices for each might improve usability [6].

Considering all these aspects, the need for supporting multiple voices adapted to the HCI scenario, with different characteristics, is made clear. These voices will allow addressing, in a first instance, user preferences, and will serve as grounds for research to improve our understanding of the impact of individual voice characteristics on interaction and user experience, in a variety of applications and contexts.

In this paper we present contributions regarding: (a) our method to deliver speech interaction to applications, simplifying developers work and making available a simple way of choosing the voice (in Sect. 2); (b) the process that we have used to create new voices for Portuguese with different genders and ages (in Sect. 3); and (c) the results of three preliminary evaluations assessing voice preferences by adult and elderly users of both genders (Sect. 4). Conclusions are presented in Sect. 5.

2 Speech Modality – Generic Support to Multiple Languages and Voices

Taking into consideration the challenges identified in the previous section, it is important to foster ways to easily support speech output in different languages, with a rich set of voices, and enabling their selection both during development and runtime.

Our consideration of speech interfaces is inserted in the wider scope that encompasses the design and development of applications supporting multimodal interaction. In this context, speech is addressed as a modality, aligned with the concepts of the W3C recommendations for a multimodal architecture [7]. The speech modality communicates with the interaction manager (IM), responsible for managing all the modalities and their communication with the application, through standard markup messages. One of the major features provided by this architecture is that its different components can be developed as standalone modules [8] that communicate with the remaining architecture elements in a standard way. Therefore, developers do not need to master all the constantly evolving technologies considered in multimodal interaction scenario. Experts may be given specific tasks on that subject proposing a standalone module that is easily integrated. This also has a positive impact on how easily a modality can be improved, without need of changing the application core, and on how existing modalities can be reused in new applications adopting the same architecture.

Following this rationale, a generic modality was proposed [9] supporting speech input and output. Considering speech output, which has the most relevance to the subject matter of this paper, this modality uses the installed engines and language dependent language packs and voices, and provides a small set of simple methods for application developers to change/select voices and send texts for being synthesized and transmitted to sound output devices, such as speakers or headphones (Fig. 1).

It is in the context of this generic modality that the outcomes of the work described in the following section were considered and made available in different applications, in the scope of project AAL4ALL and PaeLife, resulting in a modality supporting a rich set of voices created for multiple languages in a unified way.

3 Development of New Voices

Until recently, for a given language, only one or two voices were available, as the methods to create voices for Speech Synthesis were complex, time consuming and very expensive. Recent technological developments and the work done in collaboration with Microsoft Language Development Center in Portugal, in projects such as Smartphones for Seniors[1] [10–12] and AAL Paelife[2] [13], allowed the creation of a set of new voices. More specifically, the application of robust stochastic training methods (e.g. Statistical Parameter Synthesis, SPS, or Voice Adaptation, VA), which are extensions of simpler methods based on Hidden-Markov-Models (HMM) applied to TTS [14, 15],

---

[1] http://www.smartphones4seniors.org/en-us/home.aspx.

[2] http://www.microsoft.com/portugal/mldc/paelife/.

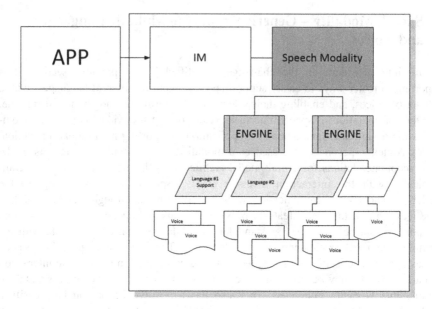

Fig. 1. The generic speech modality offers the means to add multilanguage support to an application, offering easy access to multiple languages and voices without changes to the core of the application.

required fewer recordings with respect to the ones required using classic approaches to speech synthesis (e.g. Units Selection based methods [16]) and permitted faster realizations of high-quality, flexible, personalized voices.

The methodology used for creating these new voices, one of the main contributions presented in this article, consists of a set of stages that can be summarized as follows:

1. The voice donors, providing the recordings to be used for training a personalized voice, need to be selected. Since recording voices is time consuming, a first selection, based on small samples of audio recorded from different individuals, is implemented using an online interface.
2. The collected recordings go through a two-stage evaluation procedure:

    (a) First, a group of speech experts rate the voices based on criteria such as pleasantness, intelligibility, expressiveness, attitude, accent and perceived age, as well as the adequacy of the voice profile with respect to the application scenario.
    (b) Second, a group of end-users listen to the shortlisted recordings and score them on a scale similar to the one used by experts (Mean Opinion Score, MOS [17]).
3. The higher ranked individuals record less than 2000 phonetically rich prompts. The recordings should be performed in a sound treated room to suppress noise.
4. These recordings get automatically chucked according to various acoustic features and aligned with a phonetically annotated version of the script used to elicit them.

5. The processed audio materials are used to train the artificial voice model using either a Statistical Parameter Synthesis approach or the Voice Adaptation approach (this is possible only if a rich acoustic language model already exists based on previous recordings).

With the increasing number of elderly and their involvement in the development of applications for seniors and/or AAL, it became relevant to explore if the availability of seniors' voices as an option would facilitate voice enabled applications' adoption by elderly users. Therefore, following this methodology, we have added two senior voices to the existing two adult voices.

4 Users' Preferences

To gather information regarding preferences – needed for guidelines for developers, to accompany the multimodal framework – it was decided to have information from users on their voice preferences. A first objective, reflected in the choice of users, was to understand whether the senior users prefer to have TTS systems interacting with them using young or senior voices. The second objective was to perform the evaluation in the context of applications we have developed using the generic speech modality and the new voices (the personal assistant AALFred [13] and the Medication Assistant for Windows Phone [10–12]). Due to practical constraints, our initial plan for evaluating the two applications with the same users was replaced by separate evaluations.

4.1 Evaluation of the Voices by Different Age Groups in AALFred

An online MOS evaluation was conducted with a paragraph of news and a sentence from the AALFred application produced with the 5 voices (4 new ones plus the existent female voice, Hélia).

Test Conditions. The evaluation started with an introductory text providing general information about the test. Before beginning, data pertaining the user profile and context was collected (gender, year of birth, loudspeakers/headphones, silent/noisy environment, and whether the speaker was native or not). During the test, the listener played a sound sample and, after that, answered 8 questions, all of which were on a 5 point scale (1–5). The questions of the test are listed in the following Table 1:

Listeners. Thirty-two **Portuguese** speaking listeners participated in the test (11 of them were elderly - above 60 years old - and 21 were young adults). The average age of the elderly listeners was 65 years old, whereas for the young listeners it was 29 years old. All of them except three were native speakers. Twenty-six of them were males and fourteen of them used loudspeakers, while 18 used headphones. Thirty of them listened to the test in a silent environment, and two users were in noisy conditions.

Results. The average values for each parameter were considered for analysis. As average performance of the voices is different, as a first step, scores were preprocessed by subtracting the average value for the parameter.

Table 1. Information on the parameters, questions and scales used in the evaluation of the voices.

ID	Parameter	Question	Scale
Q1	Pleasantness	How do you like this voice?	Not at all! (1) ... Yes, a lot! (5)
Q2	Intelligibility	How understandable is this voice?	I missed many words (1) ... Everything was crystal clear (5)
Q3	Expressiveness	How dynamic is this voice?	Do you feel the person speaking bored? (1) ... Is the person speaking exited and motivated while speaking? (5)
Q4	Attitude	Do you find the speaker charismatic?	Yes, a lot! (1) ... Not at all! (5)
Q5	Rhythm/speech rate	How do you like the pacing rate?	Not at all! (1) ... Yes, a lot! (5)
Q6	Accent	Do you hear an accent in the voice?	Yes, I perceive an accent and this is unacceptable (1) ... No, this is perfect Portuguese (5)
Q7	Perceived age	Is the person speaking matching the age range?	Not at all! (1) ... Yes, a lot! (5)
Q8	Artificiality	Do you feel the voice has an annoying artificial flavor?	Yes, this is extremely annoying (1) ... No, at all! (5)

The new scores were used in a MANOVA with listener age and voice age as factors. MANOVA results indicated as significant, for example, the effect of listeners age for Q3 and Q8. MANOVA results were also confirmed, in general, with an ANOVA made with the sum of the several evaluation parameters.

The identified significant differences were further investigated. As representative examples, the results for listeners' age and voice age interaction are presented in Fig. 2 and for listeners' age and voice's gender in Fig. 3.

It is noticeable, in Fig. 2, that the two groups of listeners (elderly and young adults) have very different preferences and perceptions regarding speech rate and artificiality. Elderly consider the elderly voices as having the best speech rate, while young listeners have an opposite opinion. Regarding artificiality, the elderly assigned a score above average to the voices for both age groups, contrasting to the below average scores attributed by young listeners

When looking at the results for each of the two tasks (AALFred and News), as presented in Fig. 3, it is again noticeable that elderly and young listeners have different preferences regarding attitude (Q4) and speech rate (Q5). Elderly listeners score male voices with higher values in the two tasks. The effect of the utterance type is also visible.

4.2   Evaluation of TTS in AALFred

As part of a broader evaluation of the PaeLife assistant, information was gathered on the TTS quality of the new voices.

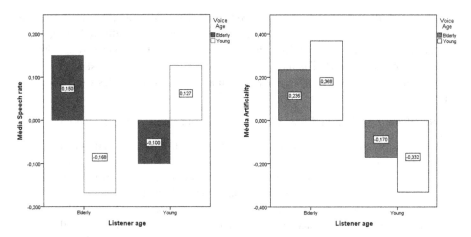

Fig. 2. - Results regarding speech rate (Q5) and artificiality (Q8) as function of listener and voice ages.

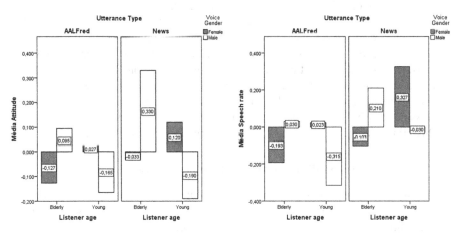

Fig. 3. - Results regarding attitude (Q4) and speech rate (Q5) as function of listener age, voice gender and utterance type.

Method and Users. The evaluation adopted a direct observational method, which involved a researcher observing users behavior and actions while taking notes.

Five users were recruited and had the opportunity to experience and use AALFred for a period of time. The field trials started in the beginning of November 2014 and are planned to be finished by the end of February 2015. The emphasis was placed on speech and touch usability evaluation. Regarding TTS voices, 5 were made available for selection by the users, 4 of them specifically developed for the Project, as described earlier.

The AALFred configuration process was performed individually for each one of the users and email and Facebook accounts where created for those who did not use these services before but were interested in trying them out in AALFred.

Users were then introduced to AALFred and a short demonstration was done for each one of the participants. A small instruction leaflet was also delivered to the users for them to consult if they had difficulties interacting with the tablet and/or with the AALFred application itself. The media diary (where participants were asked to register all interactions with AALFred) was then explained and a few examples were discussed and registered.

Results. Regarding TTS and the voices, the main outcomes of the evaluation were:

1. Output using synthetic speech was felt as important, necessary and very useful in some particular cases like messages and news;
2. Although there was a preference for the speech modality, most of the users found that speech and touch were noteworthy and complementary;
3. All the users enjoyed the fact that they could choose between 5 available voices;
4. The Microsoft standard voice "Hélia" was not chosen and used by any of the users;
5. Some of the users also stated that they had chosen a voice that somewhat resembled the researchers' own voice – in this study the researcher was also the one responsible for solving the existing problems and helping the elderly user whenever needed. Therefore, the researcher and the help topic seemed to be closely linked;
6. The importance of feedback by voice and the recognition that this somewhat filled the void that is present when users interact with technology. The possibility of having AALFred's reply seemed to be well appreciated by all seniors and was considered one of the most useful features of the application. Two users stated that this kind of interaction was an important help when they were feeling lonely as voice simulates presence, enabling the application to communicate with the user in the same way the user communicates with their family and friends: by using speech. This brings another meaning to "assistant applications for the elderly".

4.3   Evaluation in a Medication Assistant for Smartphones

The Medication Assistant application [10, 12] allows the user to manage his/her medication intakes by showing reminders, but it also aims to go beyond that by providing information and advice in case he/she forgets to take the medicine or feels side effects.

Method and Users. A set of 6 elderly with ages from 57 to 90, two male and four female, participated in this third evaluation. They were instructed to select one of the voices, and after this, they were asked to perform a task in the application consisting in navigating in the application through the different menus and obtain the information of any drug. While browsing, the application gives spoken feedback and at the end reads information about the drug. They repeated the process for all the voices available (only the 4 new ones were considered, leaving 'Hélia' out). After using the application, users were asked to rank the voices.

Results. The results obtained (ranks from 1 to 4, with 1 meaning first choice) were analyzed using repeated measures ANOVA, that showed as significant ($p < 0.05$) the effect of voice gender, the gender of the listener and the interaction between gender of the voice and gender of the listener. The interaction effect, the most relevant for this

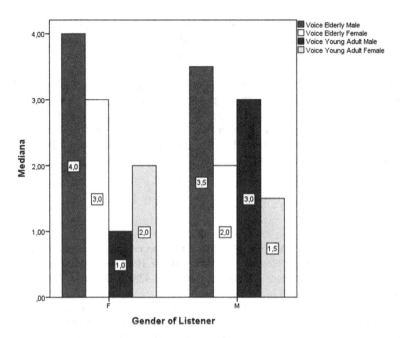

Fig. 4. Median voice ranks as function of the listener's gender. As bars represent ranks, smaller bars represent better positions, contrary to the most common interpretation.

paper objective, is depicted in Fig. 4, using the median of the ranks (considered more adequate than average values).

The figure shows that while female listeners prefer the voice of the young adult male (with a median rank of 1), male listeners prefer the two female voices, with some preference for the young one.

5   Conclusion

In this paper we report the three lines of work we are exploring to give more and better voices to HCI applications. First, we report on the generic/unified way we developed to ease the inclusion of voice output in applications, even by developers with a lack of knowledge in the area. We also describe how new voices are being created, profiting from recent advances in corpus based speech synthesis is also described. We regarded the inclusion of these additional voices as a very important addition to the proposed speech modality, particularly addressing both genders and young adult and senior voices.

Last, but not least, results on differences in preferences regarding two age groups (young adult and older-adult) and their correlation with applications are presented, providing very useful first insights and contribution for guidelines on how to select voices for certain applications and interaction models.

The results highlight the importance of giving the users the possibility of choice and also illustrates that sometimes the preferred TTS voice is not the voice with more quality (from the technical point of view) but a more familiar sounding voice.

Acknowledgments. Research partially funded by IEETA Research Unit funding (PEst-OE/EEI/UI0127/2014), project Cloud Thinking (funded by the QREN Mais Centro program, ref. CENTRO-07-ST24-FEDER-002031), Marie Curie Actions IRIS (ref. 610986, FP7-PEOPLE-2013-IAPP), project Smart Phones for Seniors (S4S), a QREN project (QREN 21541), co-funded by COMPETE and FEDER, project PaeLife (AAL-08-1-2001-0001) and project AAL4ALL (AAL/0015/2009).

References

1. Bijani, C., White, B.-K., Vilrokx, M.: Giving voice to enterprise mobile applications. In: Proceedings of the 15th International Conference on Human-Computer Interaction with Mobile Devices and Services - MobileHCI 2013, p. 428. ACM Press, New York, USA (2013)
2. Nass, C., Brave, S.: Wired for Speech: How Voice Activates and Advances the Human-Computer Relationship. MIT Press, Cambridge, MA, USA (2007)
3. McCoy, S.L., Tun, P., Cox, L., Wingate, A.: Aging in a fast-paced world: rapid speech and its effect on understanding. ASHA Lead. **12**, 30–31 (2005)
4. Gordon-Salant, S., et al.: Sources of age-related recognition difficulty for time-compressed speech. J. Speech Lang. Hear Res. **44**, 709–719 (2001)
5. Vipperla, R., Wolters, M., Renals, S.: Spoken dialogue interfaces for older people. Adv. Home Care Technol. **1**, 118–137 (2012)
6. Hale, K., Reeves, L., Stanney, K.: Design of systems for Improved Human Interaction (2006)
7. Bodell, M., Dahl, D., Kliche, I., Larson, J., Porter, B., Raggett, D., Raman, T., Rodriguez, B.H., Selvaraj, M., Tumuluri, R., Wahbe, A., Wiechno, P., Yudkowsky, M.: Multimodal architecture and interfaces: W3C recommendation. http://www.w3.org/TR/mmi-arch/
8. Dahl, D.A.: The W3C multimodal architecture and interfaces standard. J. Multimodal User Interfaces **7**, 171–182 (2013)
9. Almeida, N., Silva, S., Teixeira, A.: Design and Development of Speech Interaction: A Methodology. In: Kurosu, M. (ed.) HCI 2014, Part II. LNCS, vol. 8511, pp. 370–381. Springer, Heidelberg (2014)
10. Teixeira, A., Ferreira, F., Almeida, N., Rosa, A., Casimiro, J., Silva, S., Queirós, A., Oliveira, A.: Multimodality and adaptation for an enhanced mobile medication assistant for the elderly. In: Proceedings of the Third Mobile Accessibility Workshop (MOBACC), CHI 2013, France (2013)
11. Ferreira, F., Almeida, N., Rosa, A.F., Oliveira, A., Teixeira, A., Pereira, J.C.: Multimodal and adaptable medication assistant for the elderly: A prototype for interaction and usability in smartphones. In: 2013 8th Iberian Conference on Information Systems and Technologies (CISTI), pp. 1–6. IEEE, Lisboa (2013)
12. Ferreira, F., Almeida, N., Rosa, A.F., Oliveira, A., Casimiro, J., Silva, S., Teixeira, A.: Elderly centered design for interaction – the case of the S4S medication assistant. In: 5th International Conference on Software Development and Technologies for Enhancing Accessibility and Fighting Info-exclusion, DSAI (2013)

13. Teixeira, A., Hämäläinen, A., Avelar, J., Almeida, N., Németh, G., Fegyó, T., Zainkó, C., Csapó, T., Tóth, B., Oliveira, A., Dias, M.S.: Speech-centric multimodal interaction for easy-to-access online services: a personal life assistant for the elderly. In: Proceedings of the DSAI 2013, Procedia Computer Science, pp. 389–397 (2013)
14. Zen, H., Tokuda, K., Black, A.W.: Statistical parametric speech synthesis. Speech Commun. **51**, 1039–1064 (2009)
15. Zen, H., Nose, T., Yamagishi, J., Sako, S., Masuko, T., Black, A.W., Tokuda, K.: The HMM-based speech synthesis system version 2.0. In: Speech Synthesis Workshop, Bonn, Germany, pp. 294–299 (2007)
16. Hunt, A.J., Black, A.W.: Unit selection in a concatenative speech synthesis system using a large speech database. In: Proceedings of the IEEE International Conference on Acoustics, Speech, and Signal Processing Conference, pp. 373–376. IEEE (1996)
17. Viswanathan, M., Viswanathan, M.: Measuring speech quality for text-to-speech systems: development and assessment of a modified mean opinion score (MOS) scale. Comput. Speech Lang. **19**, 55–83 (2005)

It's not What It Speaks, but It's How It Speaks: A Study into Smartphone Voice-User Interfaces (VUI)

Jaeyeol Jeong and Dong-Hee Shin[✉]

Department of Interaction Science, Sungkyunkwan University, Seoul, Korea
{jael0,dshin}@skku.edu

Abstract. Since voice-user interfaces (VUI) are becoming an attractive tool for more intuitive user interactions, this study proposes a between-subject experiment in which variations in voice characteristics (i.e., voice gender and manner) of VUI are examined as key determinants of user perceptions. This study predicts that the voice gender (male vs. female) and manner (calm vs. exuberant) are likely to have significant effects on psychological and behavior outcomes, including credibility and trustworthiness of information delivered via VUI.

Keywords: Voice user interface · Voice gender · Voice manner · Smart device · Credibility · Trust

1 Introduction

As smart devices (e.g., smartphones, smartwatches, smart TVs) have become ubiquitous, an increasing emphasis is being placed on voice-user interfaces (VUI), such as Apple Siri and Google Voice Search, as an effective solution to providing greater interactivity and more positive user experience. VUI enables users to interact with computers through the voice recognition and command. It offers more convenient, safe, and user-friendly interfaces than the conventional touch-based interface, allowing seemingly hands-and-eyes-free interactions via the device.

Voice is an integral component of human-human interaction because it reflects and conveys emotions, intentions, and manners of the speaker. Judgments are often made simply based on how credible and believable the speaker's voice sounds [1]. But, does the voice also matter in human-computer interactions? Does it influence how users evaluate the credibility of the information delivered by digital media and its source? The Computers Are Social Actors (CASA) paradigm suggests that human-human and human-computer interactions share similar characteristics, such that users mindlessly apply the same social rules and expectations when using computers with social cues as they would in human-human interactions [2]. Given that voice is a humanlike attribute that functions as a strong social cue, the CASA paradigm is also likely to be applicable to investigating the role of voice characteristics in inducing greater credibility of information delivered via VUI.

Ample research on human-computer interaction has demonstrated that variations in voice characteristics lead to different user attitude and perception. For example,

© Springer International Publishing Switzerland 2015
M. Kurosu (Ed.): Human-Computer Interaction, Part II, HCII 2015, LNCS 9170, pp. 284–291, 2015.
DOI: 10.1007/978-3-319-20916-6_27

individuals are found to apply gender stereotypes to computers and machines. Product descriptions provided by male voice are perceived as more credible than those with female voice [3]. Women with masculine voice are perceived to be more rational and persuasive than those with feminine voice [4]. In addition, masculine voice is rated as more competent than feminine voice, regardless of the actual gender [5].

Given that such stereotypical vocal cues are found to affect the persuasiveness, credibility, and competence of the delivered messages [6], they are also likely to have notable effects on the ways in which users evaluate and perceive information conveyed via VUI. Therefore, this study intends to explore whether variations in voice gender (male vs. female) and voice manner (dynamic vs. calm) of VUI contribute to affecting psychological and behavioral outcomes.

2 Literature Review and Relative Works

Voice Interface. Popularity of voice interfaces on smartphones have been growing recently. As for most users typing on a phone is more laborious than typing on a full-size keyboard, voice interfaces serve a real practical purpose. Voice recognition technology is nothing new – having been around since the 1950 s when introduced by Bell Labs. However, it wasn't until the 1990 s when IVR systems (interactive voice response) systems became more widespread that the technology really began to solidify. A certain number of studies about audio technology in smart device have been conducted. This includes speech recognition [7], sound recognition [7, 8], speech synthesis [9] or dialogue [10–12].

Voice interfaces have gained public recognition since the release of Siri on iPhone. Siri's popularity is an exciting development for speech technologies. Many voice interfaces with functionalities similar to Siri's are also available on Android smartphones, including Google's Voice Search, SpeakToIt assistant, Vlingo Assistant, Jeannie, and Eva. Google Android Search interfaces that focus exclusively on search functions include Dragon and Bing search. An example of Apple's Siri, which can process a user's speech in natural language, reply the user within a reasonable period of time and perform routine tasks. iPhone users can make reservations at specific restaurants, buy movie tickets or call a taxi by dictating instructions in natural language to Siri. Users can also pose simple queries such as "What is the weather tomorrow?"

Why Voice makes Sense as a User Interface. As consumers grow more comfortable with voice recognition technology for everyday tasks, developers are putting speech into a variety of devices including remote controls, cars and wearable technology. Voice as a user interface makes sense because it is something that comes naturally to humans and is used on a daily basis. According to research conducted by Matthias Mehl, the average number of words spoken by an adult per day is 16,000, while the average number of words typed per day is 3,000 to 4,000 [13]. A key advantage is the fact that voice is not only hands-free, but eyes-free, making it suitable for use in a variety of environments, as well as for the visually-disabled. And unlike most written words, voice can communicate mood, gender, identity (such as recognizing a voice), emphasis and even personality.

Voice Interface Types. Voice interfaces help users perform functions such as sending an email or a text message, playing a song from a music library, accessing calendar, performing a web search, or checking weather forecast. The interfaces differ in the functions that they support, modality of communication, text-to-speech and recognition components, amount of initiative taken by the system, and dialogue handling methods. Virtual assistant voice interfaces take a role of a personal assistant. Siri, SpeakToIt assistant, and Eva/Evan apps speak back to a user. They address the user by name and exhibit emotions both in a choice of a spoken response and in a facial expression. SpeakToIt assistant shows happiness when it is turned on by saying "Good to see you again", apologizes when they do not understand or is unable to handle a command "I am sorry I'm not able to do that just yet but I will be soon". When iPhone loses network connection, Siri (which relies on the connection) responds with error messages, such as "There is something wrong", "I cannot answer you now". These responses sound very cute and human-like and give an impression that the app has a personality, however more helpful responses "Network is down, try again later" or "Try turning on your wireless connection", would reveal the problem to a user or suggest a solution.

Quality of TTS makes a big difference for the perceived quality of a voice app. Neither of the mechanical voices used by the free versions of Android systems compares to affective Siri's voice. SpeakToIt and Eva assistants also have a graphical persona. A character in SpeakToIt assistant app has a customizable appearance and displays subtle facial expressions during communication. However, it is not clear how much this adds to the system's functionality.

Voice Search Interfaces. Other types of apps, such as Dragon and Bing specialize on search only. These interfaces are not attempting to be 'can-do-all' assistants. Instead, they have a focused set of functions relevant to search. Bing has a pre-set list of search types: images, videos, maps, local, etc. We found this helpful because it suggests to a user which functionalities are supported by the system. Dragon, on the other hand, provides a speaking-only interface equivalent to 'how may I help you'. A user can guess by trial and error what the system capabilities are.

User Evaluation of Speech Output. User evaluation of speech output comprises three factors; the users' personal preferences; the operational context; and overall system functionality. These factors are not independent of each other and will integrate to inform the user in their evaluation of speech output. Personal preferences for speech are constructed through the application of the social representations held by the listener. Social representations are created by, for example, norms and stereotypes, and are employed to facilitate communication with in social groups. Simply based on the 'sound' of speech, social representations are formed in relation to, for example, geographical origin, gender and age [14].

A large amount of research has focused on the social representations generated by speech as 'human' output, but few studies consider those generated by speech as system output. The limited number of studies that have investigated social reactions to synthetic speech have discovered that synthetic speech, is often reacted to in similar ways to natural(human) speech [15]. For example, personality and gender are awarded to synthetic speech outputs and gender stereotypes may arise similarly for both natural and synthetic speech [4–14]. Given that speech output is evaluated on the basis of user preferences informed by social representations, it appears appropriate to consider the smartphone users' social representations of speech outputs to determine the spoken characteristics that provoke both positive and negative user evaluations.

Speech Gender. Even when a speaker is not present, speech is extremely useful in identifying the gender of a speaker and provokes associated social representations [15]. Additionally, Reeves and Nass [4] argue that everyone assigns gender to both natural and synthetic speech outputs. They found that even when the content of the speech output was identical, male speech outputs that praised the user were better received than female speech outputs; male speech output was evaluated as more friendly than female speech outputs; and male speech outputs were evaluated as better information providers on computers. Here, it would be interesting to investigate the current social representations of gender that are invoked in relation to speech as smart phone output and the impact that gender may have on smartphone user evaluations.

3 Research Question

In human-human interaction, gender bias affects credibility of agent. For example, male news casters are rated as more credible and competent than female casters [18]. Research in human-computer interaction has also demonstrated that users apply similar gender stereotypes when interacting with computers [19]. By extension, this gender bias is also likely to be discovered when exposed to VUI with either male or female voices and affect user experience with VUI and perception of information conveyed via VUI if the CASA paradigm is indeed applicable to the smartphone VUI context.

In addition to voice gender, voice manner is another critical vocal characteristic that contribute to shaping user perceptions. Voice manner is largely determined by variations in pitch, such that voice with calm manner is defined as having low pitch and monotone sounds while voice with dynamic manner is defined as having high pitch and wide range of varied tones. Researchers have demonstrated that voice with dynamic manner is generally perceived to be more enjoyable and useful [20]. Together, voice gender and manner are likely to serve as critical components of VUI and influence user experience and perception. The following research question is aimed at examining this possibility.

RQ: Does voice gender (male vs. female) and voice manner (dynamic vs. calm) of VUI affect credibility and trust in messages delivered via VUI and enjoyment of interacting with VUI?

4 Methodology and Analysis

A 2 (voice gender: male vs. female) × 2 (voice manner: dynamic vs. calm) factorial design experiment (Fig. 1) will be conducted. Participants will be recruited from a large private university in Seoul, Korea, and paid five dollars for their participation.

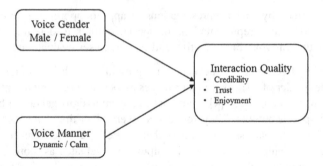

Fig. 1. Research model

4.1 Stimulus Material

The researcher will select 10 restaurants near the experiment site and create verbal descriptions of each restaurant. In order to select restaurants that do not elicit strong positive or negative reactions, 15 respondents will participate in a pretest that is designed to rate their familiarity and involvement in each restaurant (e.g., "this place is relevant/irrelevant," "important/unimportant," and means nothing/means a lot to me") [9]. Based on the result of this pretest, five restaurants rated as the most neutral will be selected. Next, professional voice actors will be hired to record the descriptions of the selected restaurants in the four different types (i.e., voice gender x voice manner) of VUI.

4.2 Procedure

80 undergraduate and graduate students will be recruited from a large university in Seoul, Korea. Upon arrival at the laboratory, participants will be randomly assigned to one of the four conditions and given a brief instruction on operating the VUI. Participants will then launch the VUI app and ask it to recommend a restaurant near the university. The VUI app will recommend one of the five selected restaurants. After receiving the recommendation from the VUI app, participants will complete a questionnaire with a paper and pencil measuring the following variables.

4.3 Dependent Variables

Participants will respond to the questionnaire by marking on 7-point Likert scales (1 = "strongly disagree/not at all," 7 = "strongly agree/very much so"). *Credibility* will be measured with 10 items adopted from [19]: believable, trustworthy, convincing, credible, reasonable, unquestionable, conclusive, authentic, honest, and likable. *Trust* will be assessed by two items adopted from [20]: "I have to be cautious about recommendation made by the smartphone because it is somewhat questionable (reversed)" and "The smartphone voice was warm and caring." *Enjoyment* will be measured with two items adopted from [19]: "Using the smartphone with VUI was exciting" and "I enjoyed using the smartphone with VUI" [20].

Participants will also respond to the manipulation check items that are designed to confirm that the independent variables are successfully manipulated: "The smartphone had male/female voice" and "The smartphone had dynamic/calm voice."

5 Discussions and Conclusion

What makes a user perceive system as intelligent? Subjective characteristics play an important role in user perception: such as witty and varied responses, personalized addressing to a user, quality of TTS and affective intonation. Objective characteristics that affect a user's perception, besides quality of speech recognition, include the ability of the system to communicate to a user what the system capabilities are, effective error detection and handling. Voice interfaces that take initiative can be perceived as more intelligent, however taking initiative also means taking a risk of annoying a user with an unnecessary question or request. The new popularity of voice interfaces on smartphones is an exciting opportunity that can drive advances in dialogue research.

The advantages of the voice-based interaction design have been highlighted as the following:

- It provides a simple, usable and interesting user interface and satisfies the need for more freedom in a human computer interaction environment.
- It provides people new experience and great pleasure which traditional interaction could not offer.
- It makes the interaction between human and computer more natural. It has been illustrated in science fiction movies that this technology can improve people's lives if it is applied rightly.
- It is widely used in various application areas since it gives the user a new experience of feeling.

In this paper we have study the trends in Voice User Interface and experimental design. Smart devices become more autonomous they also have become increasingly present in human world. More research can follow the upcoming trends. We also concluded that the biggest challenge will be to keep the user engaged and continually using the device. Voice is the most natural and easiest fit to keep consumers engaged and will become a necessity as most wearable devices will be in increasingly smaller form factors. For example, a number of smartphones such as Moto X are widely incorporating this technology via Google Now to deliver a "touchless" experience. A lot of the assistants have very robotic voices, but a few(e.g. Evi, assistant) have very nice/real voices. A few have their own voices (e.g. VoiceBrief), and SVOX has custom voices for android.

As speech synthesis and speech recognition technologies improve, applications requiring more complex and more natural human-computer interactions are becoming feasible. A well-designed user interface is critical to the success of these applications. A carefully crafted user interface can overcome many of the limitations of current technology to produce a successful outcome from the user's point of view, even when the technology works imperfectly. With further technological improvements, the primary role of the user interface will gradually shift from a focus on adapting the user's input to fit the limitations of the technology to facilitating interactive dialogue between human and computer by recognizing and providing appropriate conversational cues. Among the factors that must be considered in designing voice interfaces are the task requirements of the application, the capabilities and limitations of the technology, and the characteristics of the user population. This paper discussed how these factors influence voice user interface design and then describes components of voice user interfaces that can be used to facilitate efficient and effective human-computer voice-based interactions.

6   Contribution of This Study

This study intends to demonstrate whether variations in vocal characteristics of VUI influence user experience and perception. In doing so, this study will offer both theoretical and practical insights for manufacturers, designers, and communication scholars who are interested in the role of VUI in promoting adoption for emerging smart communication media such as smartphones and smartwatches.

Acknowledgment. This research was supported by the Ministry of Education, South Korea, under the Brain Korea 21 Plus Project (Grant No. 10Z20130000013).

References

1. Addington, D.W.: The effect of vocal variations on ratings of source credibility. Speech Monogr. **38**, 242–247 (1971)
2. Sundar, S.S., Nass, C.: Source orientation in human-computer interaction programmer, networker, or independent social actor. Commun. Res. **27**(6), 683–703 (2000)
3. Morishima, Y., Nass, C., Bennett, C., Lee, K.M.: Effects of 'gender' of computer-generated speech on credibility. Technical report of IEICE TL2001-16, 31(8), pp. 557-562 (2001)
4. Reeves, B., Nass, C.: How People Treat Computers, Television, and New Media Like Real People and Places. CSLI Publications and Cambridge University Press, New York (1996)
5. Ko, S.J., Judd, C.M., Blair, I.V.: What the voice reveals: within-and between-category stereotyping on the basis of voice. Pers. Soc. Psychol. Bull. **32**(6), 806–819 (2006)
6. Leigh, T.W., Summers, J.O.: An initial evaluation of industrial buyers' impressions of salespersons' nonverbal cues. J. Pers. Selling Sales Manage. **22**(1), 41–53 (2002)
7. Vacher, M., Fleury, A., Portet, F., Serignat, J.F., Noury, N.: Complete sound and speech recognition system for health smart homes: application to the recognition of activities of daily living. In: New Developments in Biomedical Engineering, pp. 645–673 (2010)
8. Rougui, J.E., Istrate, D., Souidene, W.: Audio sound event identification for distress situations and context awareness. In: Annual of the IEEE International Conference on Engineering in Medicine and Biology Society, EMBC 2009, pp. 3501–3504. IEEE (2009)
9. Lines, L., Hone, K.S.: Multiple voices, multiple choices: older adults' evaluation of speech output to support independent living. Gerontechnology **5**(2), 78–91 (2006)
10. Gödde, F., Möller, S., Engelbrecht, K.P., Kühnel, C., Schleicher, R., Naumann, A., Wolters, M.: Study of a speech-based smart home system with older users. In: International Workshop on Intelligent User Interfaces for Ambient Assisted Living, pp. 17–22 (2008)

11. Hamill, M., Young, V., Boger, J., Mihailidis, A.: Development of an automated speech recognition interface for personal emergency response systems. J. NeuroEngineering Rehabil. **6**(1), 26 (2009)

12. López-Cózar, R., Callejas, Z.: Multimodal dialogue for ambient intelligence and smart environments. In: Nakashima, H., Aghajan, H., Augusto, J.C. (eds.) Handbook of ambient intelligence and smart environments, pp. 559–579. Springer, Heidelberg (2010)

13. Stevens, C., Lees, N., Vonwiller, J., Burnham, D.: On-line experimental methods to evaluate text-to-speech (TTS) synthesis: effects of voice gender and signal quality on intelligibility, naturalness and preference. Comput. Speech Lang. **19**(2), 129–146 (2005)

14. Lines, L., Hone, K.S.: Multiple voices, multiple choices: older adults' evaluation of speech output to support independent living. Gerontechnology **5**(2), 78–91 (2006)

15. Mullennix, J.W., Stern, S.E., Wilson, S.J., Dyson, C.L.: Social perception of male and female computer synthesized speech. Comput. Hum. Behav. **19**(4), 407–424 (2003)

16. Mairesse, F., Walker, M.A., Mehl, M.R., Moore, R.K.: Using linguistic cues for the automatic recognition of personality in conversation and text. J. Artif. Intell. Res. **30**, 457–500 (2007)

17. Roe, D.B., Wilpon, J.G. (eds.): Voice Communication Between Humans and Machines. National Academies Press, Washington, DC (1994)

18. Brann, M., Himes, K.L.: Perceived credibility of male versus female television newscasters. Commun. Res. Rep. **27**(3), 243–252 (2010)

19. Niculescu, A., Van Dijk, B., Nijholt, A., See, S.L.: The influence of voice pitch on the evaluation of a social robot receptionist. In: 2011 International Conference on User Science and Engineering (i-USEr), pp. 18–23. IEEE (2011)

20. Nass, C., Lee, K.M.: Does computer-synthesized speech manifest personality? Experimental tests of recognition, similarity-attraction, and consistency-attraction. J. Exp. Psychol. Appl. **7** (3), 171 (2001)

StringWeaver: Research on a Framework with an Alterable Physical Interface for Generative Art

Yunshui Jin and Zhejun Liu[✉]

Tongji University, 4800 Cao an Road, Shanghai, China
{jinyunshui, wingeddreamer}@tongji.edu.cn

Abstract. In order to improve the input interface for generative art, the author was inspired by a traditional game called *string figure* to design a framework with an alterable physical input interface named StringWeaver. The input system of StringWeaver is consisted of strings (made of black conductive rubber tube) which can be customized physically by rearranging and blob tracking system that can track audience finger. The visual output is directly projected on the input interface with music and sound generated. StringWeaver was proved to be useful by three prototypes developed under the framework of it. Limitations and future work are introduced at the end of the paper.

Keywords: Physical interface · Traditional game · Generative art · Framework

1 Background

In recent years, there has been much active research on generative art. Contemporary research on generative art mainly focuses on several different levels, such as its history, principles, implications, its relationship with art and artists, ways of creation, fields of application, aesthetic evaluation and so forth. Among these levels, the studies on the ways of creating generative art put more emphasis on how to control the content generated by computers. Methods like *Genetic Algorithm*、*L-system*、*Catastrophe Theory* (from René Thom)、*Cellular Automaton*、*Fractal Generation* and *Chaos Simulation* were brought forward, while the human factors were ignored. Generative art was born and used, according to Professor Philip Galante's theory,[1] long before computers were invented. Famous examples include: W.A. Mozart, a famous musician, obtained inspirations for his composition by throwing dices into numbered grids; Ellsworth Kelly, an American artist, made randomly colorized collages with children's books; William Burroughs, an American writer, created visual artworks by blasting paint with shotguns. Generative art was born in the physical world with physical

---

[1] He explained that "Generative art refers to any art practice where the artist uses a system, such as a set of natural language rules, a computer program, a machine, or other procedural invention, which is set into motion with some degree of autonomy contributing to or resulting in a completed work of art." [1].

© Springer International Publishing Switzerland 2015
M. Kurosu (Ed.): Human-Computer Interaction, Part II, HCII 2015, LNCS 9170, pp. 292–304, 2015.
DOI: 10.1007/978-3-319-20916-6_28

operations, but when computer age came, physical operations were gradually forsaken and artists turned to regulated interfaces of computers, e.g. keyboards and mice. For art creation, however, keyboards and mice are so non-intuitive that they cannot encourage artists to release their passion and inspirations. Is there a more intuitive computer interface for art creation? The answer is yes.

Physical interface (PI in short) is also known as tangible media with roots in seminal work of Wellnerand Fitzmaurice, which uses physical forms to represent data. Instead of a generic screen, mouse, and keyboard capable of representing all types of data, PI uses specific physical forms to represent and manipulate the pieces of data in the system. PI often uses simple, transparent mechanical structures, so the user can use his or her existing knowledge of the physical world to figure out how to operate them and what they mean. A concept underlying these interaction styles is to build on the "natural" equipment and skills humans have acquired through evolution and experience and exploit these for communicating with the machine [2].

There are already many outcomes from PI research. It has been prototyped in several different areas. Computer will continue to play an important role in this field, but the constraints brought by its rigid input devices, such as keyboards and mice, must be broken to meet the tendencies of modern times. On the basis of PI research outcomes, this paper tries to put forward a framework for the creation of generative art using physical interfaces, so as to meet the requirements to create certain kinds of generative art, and to allow artists to create in more artistic, intuitive and friendly ways.

2   Related Work

Although different kinds of PI research were mostly done for pragmatic usages instead of artistic creation, it's difficult to differentiate art from practical design strictly. A small fraction of research projects even began to explore possible relations between physical interfaces and generative art. For this reason, the perspectives of much research are highly valuable as references. The following paragraphs include analysis of some typical cases and their contexts, from which the research direction of this paper was defined.

Project *PY-ROM* (2009) was a matchstick-like video recording and storage device concept that burned itself away after being used. Reference [3] This project was just a concept instead of an actualized product. This concept enabled users to trigger a virtual event, recording and playing a video clip, via an action uniquely bound to match sticks: striking. Project *Cord Uis* (2015) used sensorial augmented cords that allowed for simple metaphor-rich interactions to interface with their connected devices. Reference [4] A user might control brightness, direction and other properties of the light by twisting and pressing the cord as if it was a water hose. The design thinking behind these two projects was similar: the utilization of simple daily objects and the using habits behind them.

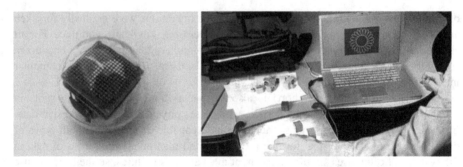

Fig. 1. Project Wavo (left) and project Trackmate (right)

Project *Wavo* (Fig. 1, 2010) was an interactive ball to express light waves with wave equation. Reference [5] A user might appreciate the beauty of wave equations with this device, and might also wave it to see the generation of different patterns. Project *Trackmate* (Fig. 1, 2009) was a customizable tangible system that allowed a computer to recognize (track) tagged objects and their corresponding position, rotation, and color information when placed on a surface. Reference [6] A user might move, rotate colorful cubes to control the changing shapes on the screen. The design thinking behind these two projects was: transplanting a person's basic cognition and intrinsic manipulation, such as moving and rotating, of physical objects to a tangible agent. The difference between them is that: in Project *Wavo*, the agent was a single man-made geometry in fixed shape, while in Project *Trackmate*, the agent was an alterable set of physical objects that might be redefined and combined according to certain rules.

Fig. 2. Project Andante (left) and project BiiliARt (right)

Project *Andante* (Fig. 2, 2014) visualized animated characters walking along the piano keyboard that appeared to be playing the physical keys with each step. Reference [7] An ordinary user might simply play with *Andante* for fun or for learning, and as for advanced users they might use their skills of playing a piano to make *Andante's* visual effects even more interesting and exciting. Project *BiiliARt* (Fig. 2, 2014) was a framework for processing visual and auditory textures in an augmented billiards environment that enabled real time artistic creativity without imposing predefined interaction rules or constraints. Reference [8] Users might use their skills of playing pool to interact with it. In fact, *Andante* and *BiiliARt* were both complex systems. To make them simple for end users, the key point was the props with embedded systems, piano and pool table. They transplanted objects or systems in the real world together with the complex behaviors behind them, rather than an instinctive action.

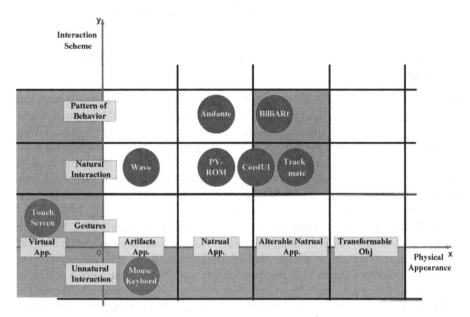

Fig. 3. Diagram of input modules (For transformable physical object, Professor Ishii pointed out a new trend of tangible median that takes a leap beyond tangible interfaces by assuming a hypothetical generation of materials that can change form and appearance dynamically [9].)

Based on the analysis above, various input modules are organized into a diagram as shown in Fig. 3, where X axis stands for physical appearance of input interfaces, Y axis stands for interaction scheme. The essence of this diagram is to relate interaction schemes (Y axis) to the input interfaces (X axis), and thus to clearly reveal the design rules of physical input interfaces. In this diagram, the grey areas either lack physical interfaces or natural interaction methods. Although most of the present approaches of generative art creation belong to these grey areas, it's what needs to be changed. On the Y axis, the difference between simple habitual manipulation and behavior pattern needs a second thought. If a simple habitual manipulation is mapped onto a fixed physical object, the resulting control mode is monotone or very limited, as in project *Wavo* or *PY-ROM*. Contrarily, if a behavior pattern, as in project *Andnate*, is mapped onto an alterable physical agent, as in project *Trackmate*, very rich control can be expected. It is evident that optimal interfaces for creating generative artworks shall provide rich controls, which graphically means that only green areas in Fig. 3 can possibly meet this criterion.

3 Design

It's still not easy to design a framework with alterable physical input interface, as Alessandro Valli pointed out in his paper that "the problem of natural interface appearance design is closer to the creative problem of film directors and artists than it is to usability engineering [10]." Although designing a natural interface seems like a rational job, the process is pretty close to artistic creation affected by accidental factors and personal inspirations. There is no fixed route leading to successful design.

3.1 Beginning with Interaction Scheme: Enlightenment from Children's Game

A 5 month old infant, with no rational knowledge of any object's appearance, has already got the impulse to interact. It's difficult and full of accidental factors to begin the design with interface appearance, and therefore the design issue may be solved from another staring point: the interaction scheme. Children's interaction scheme is an optimal study object. Where do children learn their behaviors? Besides some training of basic actions, a lot of their behaviors are usually learned via games, traditional ones instead of electronic ones.

This fact provided us with the most critical point of breakthrough: TCG (Traditional Children's Games). There are many benefits to start from TCGs: (1) Since children are normally weak in comprehension, TCGs are usually easy to understand and memorize; (2) There is a huge pool of TCGs to study. In the category "list of traditional children's games" of Wikipedia, there are 79 different games, which is obviously an incomplete collection with even more to be discovered. (3) The TCGs coming down the ages are proven to be effective and popular. In fact, some games have histories of thousands of years. (4) Thanks to the fact that certain TCGs are still popular regionally today, the learning cost is even lower because learning is unnecessary for some users.

The following two elements were selected and utilized: children's interaction scheme and physical toys in TCGs. Children's interaction scheme is especially interesting and useful in this case.

3.2 From the Initial Idea to the Final Concept

A number of TCGs have great potential to be redesigned. To narrow down the references, TCGs using no external media are neglected, such as finger-guessing game, clapping game and hide-and-seek game. (It doesn't mean that they are lower in value. They are removed from the list simply because they are not closely related to the topic of this paper.) There are many different TCGs using external media, and the popular ones can be categorized into 3 major types: card games, ball games and string games.

Among these three major types of TCGs, string games seemed to fit our needs better, because the output included aural elements while many musical instruments such as zither, guitar and violin have string parts. Among all those string games, the one named *string figure* stood out. The regulations of the *string figure* game are as follow: One player uses his/her fingers to create a string loop, and the other player takes it over with his/her own hands and changes it into a new loop. The game continues this way until someone fails to hold the string loop in his/her hands (Fig. 4).

Fig. 4. String figure (Fig. 6 comes from Baidu Encyclopedia, http://baike.baidu.com/.)

The behavioral regulations and physical interfaces of the string figure game were abstracted and developed into the initial concept: MRB (Melodic Rope Box). MRB was a 30 cm x 30 cm red box with a 4 × 4 matrix of round holes at top. A user might insert several sticks into the holes and wrap strings around these sticks so as to create his/her own pattern, as shown in Fig. 5. This personalized interface might be used to create music. A user may pluck, press and rub different sections of the string to play music. (A section is a string segment between two adjacent sticks.) Different from the fixed interfaces of traditional musical instruments, MRB is an alterable and programmable interface. Users might customize this interface to suit their own preferences, and play sound of different instruments, for example stringed instruments, wind instruments, percussion instruments and keyboard instruments.

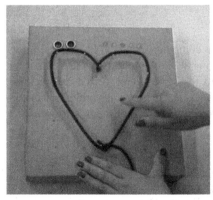

Fig. 5. Melodic Rope Box

Continuing from MRB, in order to make it more suitable for the generation of visual elements, the red box was replaced with white table so that projection was visible on the platform. The manipulation space expanded from 30 cm x 30 cm to 60 cm x 60 cm, offering more space and freedom to users and making visual effects more impressive. In previous design, it was noticed that users had difficulty warping strings around sticks and a string tend to be curvy all along its length if the strings are thicker ones. In the final design, strings were cut into predefined various lengths, and cap them with copper terminals, which might be easily hooked onto metal sticks. This modification provided more convenience to users and making the resulting shapes tidier and more modern with its straight segments (Fig. 6). When users "played" with the strings of the interfaces designed by themselves, the projected visual elements appeared exactly where the fingers touched the strings and changed together with the melodies. Similarly, users might also interact with visual elements using the interface, and generate corresponding aural effects simultaneously.

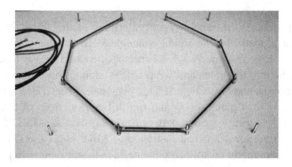

Fig. 6. Final design (In this case, there are altogether 12 holes along the edges of a rectangle. However, the number of holes in the platform can be customized.)

4   Input System

The feedback signals from this interface to the computer include: (1) Position information of a user's finger in that 60 cm x 60 cm area, working like a mouse cursor for visual art creation. (2) Triggering signals from the strings, categorized as plucking, pressing and rubbing (three commonest action taken when playing a musical instrument) (3) Index number of the strings so as to identify which of them is triggered.

4.1   Blob Tracking

It's a typical blob tracking task to obtain the finger position. There is much research and many solutions in this field, among which POT (Passive Optical Tracking) was finally chosen in this case. Compared with other solutions, POT has the advantages of low cost, high precision, reliable stability and convenience.

A POT system usually contains a projector, an infrared camera (i.e. a camera with infrared-pass filter), infrared lights and targets to track (i.e. objects with strong infrared reflectivity). In this case, the track target, namely the user's fingers, was wrapped in infrared reflective tapes. On the software side, CCV[2] was chosen because it not only supports keystone correction, lens calibration, multiple cameras and cross-platform usage, but also transfers tracking information, including the target's position, speed, acceleration and size, via TUIO protocol which is compatible with most platforms for generative art creation.

4.2   Input Detection

Unlike blob tracking, there is no standard solution for acquiring the triggering signals from the strings. The basic idea was that the physical signals of string triggering shall be converted to digital signals so that they may be processed by computers. SCMs (Single Chip Microcomputer) and sensors might be used to accomplish this task. After many trials, a largely reliable solution was found, which used conductive rubber tubes and Arduino based SCM. Conductive rubber tubes not only were used as strings in the interface, but also helped to convert physical signals to digital signals. This was because conductive rubber tubes were elastic and had a certain amount of electric resistance which would increase if they were stretched. When a user used his/her finger to touch a tube, its length changed together with its electric resistance value. In this way, the conversion from physical world to the digital world was done.

Detailed description of the scheme is as follows:

- Black conductive rubber tubes made of silicon and carbon were used.
- Outer diameter of the tubes equals 5 mm, and inner diameter equals 2 mm
- For tubes, each 10 cm has resistance of 1.5 KΩ, and their stretching after/before ratio is approximately 1.25.
- Arduino Uno was chosen as the SCM.

12 holes[3] were numbered sequentially from 0 to 11, and connected with different analog input pins[4] of Arduino. Arduino can apply a *HIGH* (refers to 5 V) or *LOW* (refers to 0 V) voltage to each hole, and might also perform *AnalogRead* function for each hole via analog input pins. When metal sticks, connected by strings, were inserted into these holes, each string was then connected into the circuit.

---

[2] Community Core Vision, CCV for short, is an open source/cross-platform solution for blob tracking with computer vision.

[3] In the author's example, 12 holes were used as shown in Fig. 6.

[4] The analog input pins have the *AnalogRead* function which means voltage between 0 and 5 volts can be read and a integer values between 0 and 1023 is returned. Arduino Uno only has 6 analog input pins which are not enough. To make it easier, the method to expand analog input pins is introduced later.

- Step 1: Confirm which pins were connected.[5] Perform the following operations one by one on all 12 pins: set all analog input pins to *input mode*, and set one of them to *HIGH* voltage while keep the other 11 pins to *LOW* voltage. Then read from the pin set to *HIGH* voltage. If the returned value was *HIGH*, the pin was not connected; otherwise, the pin was connected in the circuit. All the index number of the connected pins are put into an array named A.
- Step 2: Confirm the sequence of the how pins contained in *array A* were connected. (1) Find the first and last pins in the sequence. Perform the following operations on all pins belong to *array A*: pick two of them as a combination. Set one of them (*output mode*) to *HIGH* voltage, the other to *LOW* voltage. All the other pins were set to *input mode*, and their voltage values were read and recorded. After every possible combination is implemented, all the recorded values are compared to get the maximum one. The combination which generates the maximum value is the correct one. That is to say, either one of the combination is the first pin while the other is the last. (2) Resort array A. Set the first pin (*output mode*) to *HIGH* voltage, the last (*output mode*) to *LOW* voltage. All the other pins were set to *input mode*, and sorted (from high to low) by the values read from themselves. The resorting is done.
- Step 3: Dynamically detect changes in electric resistance. Perform the following operations for the resorted array A: for 3 consecutive pins, connected by two strings, of array A, give the 1st pin (*output mode*) *HIGH* voltage and 3rd pin (*output mode*) *LOW* voltage. Read and record the change of voltage from the 2nd pin (*input mode*). The increasing value from the 2nd pin indicates the string between 2nd and 3rd pins is triggered while the decreasing value suggests the string between 1st and 2nd pins is triggered. A rapid bounce of the value implies a quick trigger (pluck) and a gentle bounce intimates a slower trigger (press/rub). Combining the data from blob tracking module (speed of the target/finger), it's easy to distinguish between "press" and "rub".

In this way, it is possible to convert 3 different inputs (pluck, press, rub) together with the index of the triggered string as digital signals and sent them to the development platform via Serial port. There are several issues worth noticing:

- Conductive rubber tubes were not ideal electric resistors. They had some bizarre properties that might introduce strong noise to the feedback signals. It's important to maximize the variable range of a rubber tube's resistance value, and use filtering algorithms to smooth out the noise. In this case, media filter[6] was used and basically eliminated the negative influence of noise.
- A standard Arduino didn't have enough analog input pins. (Arduino Uno was used in this case.) But if a more complicated StringWeaver with more holes and sticks is expected, analog input pins must be extended with analog multiplexer and shift register. In this case, 74HCT4051 NXP semiconductors and 74HC595 NXP

---

[5] There is a limitation that all the strings must be connected end to end in this scheme, due to the technological reasons.

[6] In this case, the detailed algorithm of median filter is: record 5 coherent values from analog input pin, wipe off the maximum value together with the minimum and average the rest.

semiconductors was used. The first one expanded the number of analog input pins by 8 at the cost of 3 digital output pins and 1 analog input pins, while the second expanded the number of digital output pins by 8 at the cost of 3 digital output pins. (Please pay attention that analog multiplexers have internal resistance,[7] which would have influence on the value that analog input pin gets.)

4.3 Actuators

In order to manifest the pictures and make sound, a projector which projects image directly onto the physical input interface and a loudspeaker that generates sounds are used as actuators of StringWeaver.

On account of the popular protocol that input system adopts, it's simple to modify the source code to adapt the framework of StringWeaver. Thanks to the rich interaction scheme that input system offers, it's reasonable to believe StringWeaver can achieve better outcomes and give audience more pleasure as well.

Three prototype testaments are done as examples of StringWeaver:

- Case1: project *Silking*, modified from project *Painting Rectangles*[8] which was an exercise developed by Jeff Hendrickson using Processing. *Painting Rectangles* was a straightforward program that painted rectangles in random size and color following paths that affected by random factors. The original outcome (Fig. 7) looked like "worms" has a lot of ups and downs along the path. For project *Silking*, minor modifications were required to make it fit the StringWeaver framework. Input data were introduced instead of random parameters while sound module was added. The audience could play with the strings after weaving them in the input interface. The rectangles were painted along the strings that were triggered by audience fingers. Since the arc algorithm was kept, lines arced over the strings as the audience pulled strings at different parts. And the string interface could be changed dynamically without destroying the current visual creation during playing if the audiences want. The outcome (Fig. 7) was satisfied for its rhythm shape. Sound module was developed with Sonia (a library of Processing). Fundamental elements of music (do-re-mi-fa-sol-la-ti-do) were mapped on every string according to its position in the interface, as the scale of sound was determined by the index of sticks connected with strings. Some sort of melody was produced along with the painting process.
- Case2: project *Naughty Ball* (Fig. 8) was a new version of bouncing ball. Bouncing ball was a common and regular program that could generate balls (physical property) through keyboard and mouse. With the help of StringWeaver, much more fun was brought into this simple program. Faster and smaller balls were shot by pulling

---

[7] In our testing situation, the internal resistance is about 1 KΩ which can be found from the datasheet of 74HC595 NXP.

[8] An open source project could be download: http://www.openprocessing.org/sketch/4651.

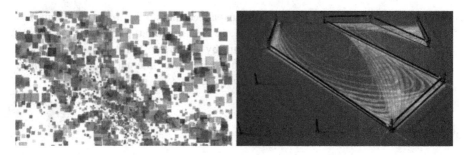

Fig. 7. Project Painting Rectangles (left) and Project Silking (right)

the strings as slower bigger ones were created by pressing. Meanwhile, the bouncing boundary is defined by these strings which could be reorganized. Sound module was developed with Sonia by mapping different musical instrument tones to sticks. When the strings were touched by audiences or hit with balls, drum, piano, trumpet sound effects come up.

- Case3: project *Palette* (Fig. 8) was another interesting simple program because of StringWeaver. Colorful dots were sprayed with sound effects by striking the strings.

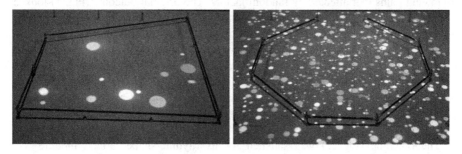

Fig. 8. Project Naughty Ball (left) and Project Palette (right)

5 Conclusion

In conclusion, we designed a system named StringWeaver that could generate visual and audible art simultaneously, via a physical interface inspired by traditional children's game named *String Figure*.

Our study explored the following new possibilities of generative art:

- Input modules could be designed basing on the interaction schemes of TCGS. In this case, the game *String Figure* served as the foundation of design. Finally a framework of physical interfaces suitable for generative art creation was conceived and three prototypes were made under the framework.

- In addition to the well-known advantages of PI, such as rapid and fluid manipulation, natural operation and less learning pressure, our alterable interface offers more variation and fun to the audience.
- The input and output ends of our interactive system are integrated as one. Their sharing the same space guarantees that the feedback is instant, direct and consistent. This mechanism gives improvisational performances more inspiration and makes it much easier.
- Our output contains motion pictures and sound, satisfying audience both visually and aurally. This cross modal outcome makes this piece of artwork an entertainment as well.

Future work: (1) Due to technological limits, all the strings are supposed to be connected end to end, which needs to be improved in the future. (2) In addition to the existing three input actions (i.e. plucking, pressing and rubbing), more need to be developed. (3) Signal noise may lead to misunderstanding of the actions, which means better filtering algorithms need to be developed. (4) It is possible to integrate String-Weaver into existing generative artworks so as to make them more friendly and interesting.

Acknowledgement. We show our sincere gratitude to Professor Jens Geelhaar (Bauhaus University Weimar) and Jie Wang (Tongji University) for their valuable suggestions, and Lecturer Martin Schied (Bauhaus University Weimar) for his technological support.

References

1. Galanter, P.: What is generative art? Complexity theory as a context for art theory. In: The 6th International Conference on Generative Art, Milan, Italy (2003)
2. Jacob, R.J., Ishii, H., Pangaro, G., Patten, J.: A tangible interface for organizing information using a grid. CHI 2002 Proceedings of the SIGCHI Conference on Human Factors in Computing Systems: Changing Our World Changing Ourselves, pp. 339–346. ACM Press, New York (2002)
3. Chi, P., Xiao, X., Chung, K., Chiu, C.: Burn your memory away: one-time use video capture and storage device to encourage memory appreciation. In: CHI 2009 Proceedings of the 27th International Conference Extended Abstracts on Human Factors in Computing Systems, pp. 2397–2406. ACM Press, New York (2009)
4. Schoessler, P., Leigh, S.-W., Ishii, H., Jagannath, K., van Hoof, P.: Cord UIs: controlling devices with augmented cables. In: TEI (2015)
5. Mukaiyama, K.: WAVO: an interactive ball to express light waves with wave equation. In: Taylor, R., Boulanger, P., Krüger, A., Olivier, P. (eds.) Smart Graphics. LNCS, vol. 6133, pp. 257–260. Springer, Heidelberg (2010)
6. Kumpf, A.: Trackmate: large-scale accessibility of tangible user interfaces. Thesis (M.S.)—Massachusetts Institute of Technology, Program in Media Arts and Sciences (2009)
7. Xiao, X., Tome, B., Ishii, H.: Andante: walking figures on the piano keyboard to visualize musical motion. In: Proceedings of the 14th International Conference on New Interfaces for Musical Expression (2014)

8. Saenen, I.P., De Bock, S., Abdou, E., Lambert, P., Van de Walle, R., Vets, T., Lesaffre, M., Demey, M., Leman, M.: BilliARt - AR carom billiards. In: Stephanidis, C. (ed.) HCI 2014, Part I. CCIS, vol. 434, pp. 636–641. Springer, Heidelberg (2014)
9. Ishii, H., Lakatos, D., Bonanni, L., Labrune, J.-B.: Radical atoms: beyond tangible bits, toward transformable materials. Interactions. **19**, 38–51 (2012)
10. Valli, A.: The design of natural interaction. Multimedia Tools Appl. **38**, 295–305 (2008)

Synchronization Between Utterance Rhythm and Body Movement in a Two-Person Greeting

Kenta Kinemuchi$^{(\boxtimes)}$, Hiroyuki Kobayashi, and Tomohito Yamamoto

Department of Information and Computer Science, College of Engineering,
Kanazawa Institute of Technology, 7-1 Oogigaoka,
Nonoichi, Ishikawa 921-8501, Japan
{b6400561,b6301321}@planet.kanazawa-it.ac.jp,
tyama@neptune.kanazawa-it.ac.jp

Abstract. In this study, designed to clarify the relationship between utterance rhythm and body movement in a greeting, two experiments were conducted to examine the greeting between persons of equal social standing and that between persons of different social standings. In both experiments, high synchronization between speakers was observed. In the analysis of the relationship between durations in subjects, synchronization was found between utterance rhythm and body movement for the greetings between social equals. However, for the greetings between persons of different social standings, there was little synchronization between utterance rhythm and body movement in subjects. These results are used to discuss the mechanism of the greeting, the starting point for communication.

Keywords: Communication · Synchronization · Greeting · Utterance rhythm · Body movement

1 Introduction

Communication robots have, to date, been treated primarily as entertainment systems. However, recently they have been receiving more attention in the fields of medicine and nursing care. One reason is that in the near future, Japan will be suffering the effects of its decreasing birthrate and aging population, and it is expected that robots of this kind may replace caregivers in some situations.

The communication robot of today has its own body and can move some of its joints. When developing the movement that is to accompany an utterance by a robot, the engineer designs it at his discretion, using the limited robot mechanisms available. As a result, the robot sometimes generates an unnatural movement, giving the user a feeling different from that created by actual human communication. In the future, this kind of robot will be used increasingly by the general public and by elderly users. Therefore, it is necessary to analyze in detail the relationship between utterances and their associated body movements in human communication and to systematize the results in order to attain more natural communication between users and robots.

Previous studies of utterance and body movement in human communication have focused on the synchronization of various communication elements. For example,

M. Kurosu (Ed.): Human-Computer Interaction, Part II, HCII 2015, LNCS 9170, pp. 305–316, 2015.
DOI: 10.1007/978-3-319-20916-6_29

Studies by Nagaoka and Komori have shown that in psychological counseling, the synchronization between body movements of counselor and client is closely related to the quality of the counseling [1]. Shintoku and Watanabe and Watanabe et al. have analyzed the synchronization between nodding and sound pressure changes of utterances and implemented the relationship into artificial communication systems [2, 3]. Yamamoto and Watanabe have analyzed the utterances and body movements of greetings and implemented the result into a communication robot; they found that a latency of 300 ms for an utterance after a body movement creates a natural impression, while longer latencies convey a polite impression to a user [4, 5].

In addition, our own research group has analyzed the synchronization of utterance rhythms in human dialogue. In this research, the relationship between explicit speed changes and temporal features of utterances was analyzed. The results showed a positive correlation between duration of instruction utterance and that of switching pause when the change in utterance speed was noticeably large [6]. Moreover, we have introduced these results into a communication robot and have evaluated the timing of utterance and body movement to optimize it from a user's perspective [7].

Besides this research into the relationship between utterances and body movements, artificial dialogue systems that are able to understand spoken words and respond in real time have recently been developed. In this context, we have developed a simple dialogue system and evaluated the proper response timing for such a system. Our findings show that a pause of duration 600 ms, or a pause duration synchronized to the utterance duration, is favorable [8].

In summary, the relationship between utterances and body movements in human communication has been analyzed, and dialogue systems that can understand spoken words and control response timing in real time have been developed. Given these advancements, a communication robot that is able to recognize spoken words at a deep level and to generate proper utterances and body movements in real time is likely to be developed in the near future. To accomplish the development of such a robot, the relationship between speakers' utterances and body movements needs to be clarified in detail. However, at present, even the most basic communication form, the greeting, has not been thoroughly studied.

In this study, therefore, we analyze the relationship between utterance rhythms and body movements in a greeting. In particular, we conduct an experiment in which a greeting between two persons of equal social standing is observed and their utterance rhythms and body movements are analyzed; then we do the same for a greeting between two persons of different social standings.

2 Method

2.1 Experiment 1: Greeting Between Two Persons of Equal Social Standing

Our first experiment (Experiment 1) was designed to study the greeting between two persons of equal social standing to analyze the relationship between their utterance rhythms and body movements. In this experiment, two persons say "Konnichiwa" (in English, "Hello") to each other, with the same body movements, as a greeting.

| (a) Deep bowing | (b) Bowing | (c) Raising a hand |

Fig. 1. The three types of greeting in Experiment 1

In the experiment, an experimenter acted as the first speaker, and subjects were asked to respond to this speaker's initial greeting. Moreover, the experimenter changed his greeting speed to be "fast," "natural," or "slow," and three types of greeting actions were performed, having different movement sizes (Fig. 1).

2.2 Experiment 2: Greeting Between Two Persons of Different Social Standings

In Experiment 1, we focused on greetings between two persons of equal social standing. However, in a typical greeting (especially in Japan), one speaker makes a formal greeting and the other speaker makes a casual greeting, such as raising a hand, when there is a difference of social position between them. In Experiment 2, we focus on this type of greeting to analyze the relationship between utterance rhythms and body movements.

In this experiment, two persons were designated as a senior person and a junior person, and they performed a greeting. Two greetings were prepared for carrying out a natural greeting procedure: "Konnichiwa" and "Otsukaresama" (used for "Goodbye" in Japanese business settings). For the greeting actions, raising a hand was used by the senior person and deep bowing was used by the junior person. In the experiment, an experimenter played the senior part and acted as the first speaker, and subjects were asked to respond to this senior person's greeting as a junior person (Fig. 2). The experimenter changed his greeting speed to be "fast," "natural," or "slow" and varied the size of his greeting action between "large" and "small".

Fig. 2. A greeting in Experiment 2

Experiments 1 and 2 were conducted as follows: An experimenter and a subject stood face to face 1.5 m apart, and the experimenter explained the outline of the experiment. Then, the subject practiced each greeting action at "natural" speed. After this practice run, the experimental trials began. Each trial was composed of three greeting speeds and two or three greeting actions. Experiment 1 had five trials per subject and Experiment 2 had three trials per subject. In Experiment 1, 10 subjects (mean age: 22.4) who knew the experimenter participated. In Experiment 2, another 10 subjects (mean age: 22.1) who were junior to the experimenter participated (i.e., there was a genuine difference in social level between the subjects and the experimenter).

2.3   Data Capture and Analysis

Audio data of the experimenter and subjects were recorded using headsets (Audio Technica PRO&HEW/P) and a video camera (Canon iVIS HF S21). Body movement was recorded using a motion capture system (OptiTrack Flex 3 with six cameras). The sampling rate of capture was 100 Hz, and markers were attached at main joints of the upper half of the body.

Figure 3 shows the durations used for analysis. Duration of precedence utterance (PU), duration of switching pause of utterance (SPU), and duration of response utterance (RU) were used for analyzing utterance rhythm. For analyzing body movement, duration of precedence motion (PM), duration of response motion (RM), and duration of switching pause of motion (SPM) were used. The duration of a body motion is the length of time from the start time of a head or hand movement to its stop time.

An analysis of the correlations between these durations was conducted. After that, a Kruskal–Wallis test was conducted on the mean values of the correlation coefficients. For Experiment 1, multiple comparisons were applied to the results as needed, using the Steel–Dwass method. For Experiment 2, ANOVA (2 levels and 2 factors) was applied to the mean values of the correlation coefficients.

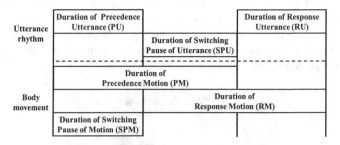

Fig. 3. Durations for analysis

3   Results of Experiment 1

3.1   Means and SDs of Durations of Greeting Components

Figure 4 shows the means and standard deviations (SDs) of the durations of the six components for the three different greeting actions. These are calculated from 50 data points [1 speed ("natural") × 5 trials × 10 subjects] for each of the three greeting actions.

It is confirmed that durations of the body movement components (PM, RM, and SPM) become longer from "raising a hand" through "bowing" to "deep bowing". For all three actions, the utterance is "Konnichiwa," but durations of the utterance, including the pause durations, generally become greater from "raising a hand" through "bowing" to "deep bowing". These results indicate that the longer the durations of the body movement become, the longer the durations of the utterance likewise become.

3.2   Relationship Between Durations in Experimenter

Figure 5 shows the means and SDs of PU and PM performed by the experimenter for each of the three greeting actions at each of three speeds. These are calculated from 50 data points (5 trials × 10 subjects) for each greeting action. It is confirmed that each duration becomes longer from "fast" through "natural" to "slow" and that there is a strong correlation between PU and PM.

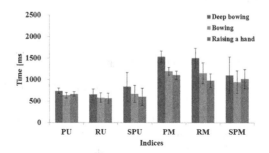

Fig. 4. Means and SDs of durations of greeting components

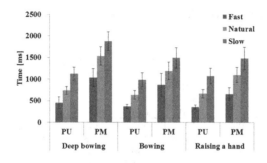

Fig. 5. Means and SDs of durations of the experimenter

In this experiment, the experimenter changed his greeting speed from "fast" through "natural" to "slow," but he did not separately change his utterance or body movement speed. As a result, his utterance and body movement durations strongly correlated. With these results in mind, in the following subsection we go on to explore the relationship between the durations of the utterance and motion performed by the experimenter and the other durations.

3.3   Relationship Between Durations Across Speakers in Greeter Pairs

Table 1 shows the means (across all 10 greeter pairs) of the correlation coefficients between PU or PM on the one hand and RU, RM, SPU, and SPM, respectively, on the other hand, for each of the three greeting actions. The 24 correlation coefficients for each greeter pair were first calculated, each using 15 data points (3 speeds × 5 trials), and then the mean of each correlation coefficient was taken across the 10 greeter pairs; these means are the values shown in the table. Colored cells indicate absolute values greater than or equal to 0.4.

As Table 1 shows, there is a high positive correlation between PU and each of RU, RM, and SPM for every greeting action. Moreover, there is a high positive correlation between PM and each of RU, RM, and SPM for every greeting action. In Subsect. 3.2, it was noted that there was a strong correlation observed between the utterance rhythm and the body movement of an experimenter. Therefore, it is likely that the results for PU and PM show the same tendency. On the other hand, the results of the correlation analysis indicate that a high degree of synchronization between greeters exists for all three greeting actions.

3.4   Relationship Between Durations in Subjects

Table 2 shows the means (across all 10 subjects) of the pairwise correlation coefficients between RU, RM, SPU, and SPM for each of the three greeting actions. The 18 correlation coefficients were first calculated, each using 15 data points (3 speeds × 5 trials), and then the mean of each correlation coefficient was taken across the 10 subjects; these means are the values shown in the table. Colored cells indicate absolute values greater than or equal to 0.4.

Table 1. Mean correlation coefficients between experimenter durations and other durations

		Deep bowing	Bowing	Raising a hand
PU	RU	0.77	0.84	0.85
	RM	0.53	0.66	0.74
	SPU	-0.11	-0.16	-0.10
	SPM	0.60	0.64	0.78
PM	RU	0.78	0.64	0.78
	RM	0.56	0.55	0.68
	SPU	-0.03	-0.11	-0.09
	SPM	0.57	0.61	0.75

Table 2. Mean correlation coefficients between durations in subjects

		Deep bowing	Bowing	Raising a hand
RU	RM	0.54	0.66	0.74
	SPU	-0.13	-0.12	-0.04
	SPM	0.47	0.54	0.75
RM	SPU	-0.10	-0.01	0.07
	SPM	0.18	0.32	0.59
SPU	SPM	0.40	0.28	0.25

As Table 2 shows, there is a positive correlation between RU and RM for every greeting action. Within these results, the value for "raising a hand" is the highest of all greeting actions, and the difference between the mean for "raising a hand" and that for "deep bowing" is marginally significant ($p < .10$). These results indicate that there is synchronization between utterance and body movement duration in subjects and that its degree is especially strong in "raising a hand".

We also observe that there is a positive correlation between RU and SPM for every greeting action. Within these results, the difference between the mean for "raising a hand" and that for "deep bowing" is also marginally significant ($p < .10$). These results indicate that the longer subjects wait to respond, the longer they speak, and that this correlation is especially strong in "raising a hand".

4 Results of Experiment 2

4.1 Means and SDs of Durations of Greeting Components

Figures 6 and 7 show the means and SDs of the durations of the six components for the two greeting actions. Figure 6 shows the results for "Konnichiwa," and Fig. 7 shows those for "Otsukaresama". These are calculated from 30 data points [1 speed ("natural") × 3 trials × 10 subjects] for each of the two greeting actions.

It is confirmed from the figures that durations of body movement for the "large" condition are longer than those for the "small" condition. In addition, durations of

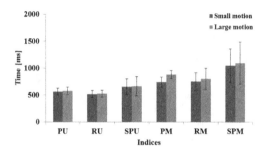

Fig. 6. Means and SDs of durations for "Konnichiwa"

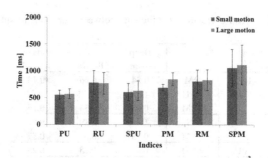

Fig. 7. Means and SDs of durations for "Otsukaresama"

utterance, including the pause duration, for the "large" condition are generally longer than those for the "small" condition. These results indicate that as in Experiment 1, the longer the durations of the body movement become, the longer the durations of the utterance likewise become.

4.2 Relationship Between Durations in Experimenter

Figures 8 and 9 show the means and SDs of PU and PM performed by the experimenter for each of the two greeting actions at each of three speeds. Figure 8 shows the results

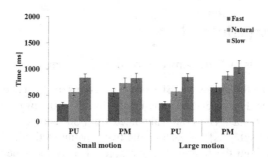

Fig. 8. Means and SDs of durations of the experimenter for "Konnichiwa"

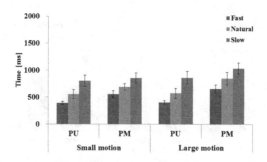

Fig. 9. Means and SDs of durations of the experimenter for "Otsukaresama"

for "Konnichiwa," and Fig. 9 shows those for "Otsukaresama." These are calculated from 30 data points (3 trials × 10 subjects) for each greeting action.

It is confirmed that each duration becomes longer from "fast" through "natural" to "slow" and that there is a strong correlation between PU and PM. As in Experiment 1, in this experiment the experimenter changed his greeting speed from "fast" through "natural" to "slow," but he did not separately change his utterance or body movement speed. As a result, his utterance and body movement durations strongly correlated. With these results in mind, in the following subsection we go on to explore the relationship between the durations of the utterance and motion performed by the experimenter and the other durations.

4.3   Relationship Between Durations Across Speakers in Greeter Pairs

Tables 3 and 4 show the means (across all greeter pairs) of correlation coefficients between PU or PM on the one hand and RU, RM, SPU, and SPM, respectively, on the other hand, for each of the two greeting actions. Table 3 shows the results for

Table 3. Mean correlation coefficients between experimenter durations and other durations for "Konnichiwa"

		Small motion	Large motion
PU	RU	0.60	0.64
	RM	0.49	0.49
	SPU	-0.33	-0.47
	SPM	0.68	0.72
PM	RU	0.52	0.60
	RM	0.40	0.49
	SPU	-0.12	-0.33
	SPM	0.70	0.67

Table 4. Mean correlation coefficients between experimenter durations and other durations for "Otsukaresama"

		Small motion	Large motion
PU	RU	0.55	0.56
	RM	0.41	0.42
	SPU	-0.38	-0.50
	SPM	0.68	0.67
PM	RU	0.52	0.55
	RM	0.36	0.42
	SPU	-0.34	-0.33
	SPM	0.59	0.66

"Konnichiwa," and Table 4 shows those for "Otsukaresama". The correlation coefficients for each greeter pair were first calculated, each using 9 data points (3 speeds × 3 trials), and then the mean of each correlation coefficient was taken across the 10 greeter pairs; these means are the values shown in the tables. Colored cells indicate absolute values greater than or equal to 0.4.

As Tables 3 And 4 show, there are positive correlations between PU and each of RU, RM, and SPM for both greeting actions. Moreover, there are positive correlations between PM and each of RU and SPM for both greeting actions. These results indicate that as in Experiment 1, synchronization between greeters often exists for both greeting actions and utterance contents.

4.4   Relationship Between Durations in Subjects

Tables 5 and 6 show the means of the pairwise correlation coefficients between RU, RM, SPU, and SPM for both greeting actions. Table 5 shows the results for "Konnichiwa," and Table 6 shows those for "Otsukaresama". The correlation coefficients were first calculated, each using 9 data points (3 speeds × 3 trials), and then the mean of each correlation coefficient was taken across the 10 subjects; these means are the values shown in the table. Colored cells indicate absolute values greater than or equal to 0.4.

Compared with the correlations between speakers, here there are no significant correlations between durations other than those for RU–SPM in the "small" condition and RM–SPM in the "large" condition. In this experiment, the experimenter raised a

Table 5. Mean correlation coefficients between durations in subjects for "Konnichiwa"

		Small motion	Large motion
RU	RM	0.35	0.46
	SPU	-0.06	-0.29
	SPM	0.38	0.43
RM	SPU	-0.08	-0.15
	SPM	0.31	0.21
SPU	SPM	-0.18	0.06

Table 6. Mean correlation coefficients between durations in subjects for "Otsukaresama"

		Small motion	Large motion
RU	RM	0.22	0.31
	SPU	-0.11	-0.32
	SPM	0.40	0.33
RM	SPU	0.02	-0.15
	SPM	0.02	0.45
SPU	SPM	0.01	-0.13

hand and subjects bowed as a greeting action. In such a situation, the correlation between speakers may weaken the synchronization between utterance and body movement duration in subjects, in contrast with the findings of Experiment 1.

5 Discussion

In this study, to clarify the relationship between utterance rhythm and body movement in a greeting, an experiment to study the greeting between two persons of equal social standing was conducted; a second experiment was conducted to study the greeting between two persons of different social standings. In the results for both experiments, high synchronization between speakers was observed for every greeting action. In the analysis of the relationship between durations in subjects, synchronization was found between utterance rhythm and body movement for the greetings between social equals. However, for the greetings between persons of different social standings, there was little synchronization between utterance rhythm and body movement in subjects.

The results of the two experiments show high synchronization between speakers. These results indicate that the greeting is a highly synchronous communication phenomenon. Given these results as background, we can conjecture that humans may synchronize various temporal elements unconsciously during a greeting, which is the starting point for communication. By means of this synchronization, communication following the greeting is smoothed and may thereby lead to greater agreement between speakers.

In the analysis of the relationship between durations in subjects, when speakers' social position and greeting action was the same, synchronization was observed between utterance rhythm and body movement. On the other hand, when speakers' social positions and greeting actions were different, the synchronization between them became weak. Given these results as background, we can make a conjecture about the mechanism at work in the speakers. In the first experiment (between persons having the same social position), both speakers performed the same greeting action. In this situation, synchronization between utterance rhythm and body movement of the experimenter was high, and synchronization between speakers was also high. As a result, synchronization between utterance rhythm and body movement in subjects was likewise high. On the other hand, in the greetings between persons of different social standings, although speakers synchronized their mutual durations about greeting, the body movements differed from each other. As a result, in the subjects, the cooperation between utterance and body movement was broken, and synchronization between utterance rhythm and body movement thus became weak. In other words, if there is a difference of social position between speakers, the junior person may sometimes synchronize to the senior person's greeting action by breaking his or her own synchronization. By this act, the junior person pays respect to the senior person.

It is believed that this kind of detailed analysis of utterance and body movement will lead to clarification of the complex mechanisms of communication. After that, it will be possible to achieve natural communication between humans and robots. In this study designed to clarify the relationship between utterance rhythm and body movement in greetings, two types of experiments were conducted. In future research, various communication forms that include a range of social factors will be analyzed, and the results will be systematized for the development of user-friendly communication robots.

6 Conclusions

In this study, designed to clarify the relationship between speakers' utterance rhythms and body movements in a greeting, experiments were conducted to study greetings between two persons of equal social standing and between two persons of different social standings. In both experiments, high synchronization between speakers was observed for every greeting action. Synchronization was found between utterance rhythm and body movement in subjects when greeting a person of equal social standing but not when greeting a person of higher social standing.

In future research, various communication forms that include a range of social factors (age, gender, and other social positions) will be analyzed, and the mechanisms of communication will thereby be more clearly established.

References

1. Nagaoka, C., Komori, M.: Body movement synchrony in psychotherapeutic counseling: a study using the video-based quantification method. IEICE Trans. Inf. Syst. **E91-D**(6), 1634–1640 (2008)
2. Shintoku, T., Watanabe, T.: An embodied virtual communication system for three human interaction support and analysis by synthesis. In: Proceedings of the 5th IEEE International Symposium on Computational Intelligence in Robotics and Automation (CIRA 2003), pp. 211–216 (2003)
3. Watanabe, T., Okubo, M., Nakashige, M., Danbara, R.: InterActor: speech-driven embodied interactive actor. Int. J. Hum. Comput. Interact. **17**(1), 43–60 (2004)
4. Yamamoto, M., Watanabe, T.: Time delay effects of utterance to communicative actions on greeting interaction by using a voice-driven embodied interaction system. In: Proceedings of the 5th IEEE International Symposium on Computational Intelligence in Robotics and Automation (CIRA 2003), pp. 217–222 (2003)
5. Yamamoto, M., Watanabe, T.: Time lag effects of utterance to communicative actions on robot-human greeting interaction. In: Proceedings of the 12th IEEE International Workshop on Robot-Human Interactive Communication (RO-MAN 2003), pp. 217–222 (2003)
6. Yamamoto, T., Kobayashi, Y., Muto, Y., Takano, K., Miyake, Y.: Hierarchical timing structure of utterance in human dialogue. In: Proceedings of the 2008 IEEE International Conference on Systems, Man and Cybernetics (SMC 2008), pp. 810–813 (2008)
7. Muto, Y., Takasugi, S., Yamamoto, T., Miyake, Y.: Timing control of utterance and gesture in interaction between human and humanoid robot. In: Proceedings of the IEEE International Symposium on Robot and Human Interactive Communication (RO-MAN 2009), pp. 1022–1028 (2009)
8. Kobayashi, H., Ohmura, T., Yamamoto, T.: Generation of proper utterance timing for dialogue system. Correspondences Hum. Interface **15**(9), 23–28 (2013). (in Japanese)

Heuristics for NUI Revisited and Put into Practice

Vanessa Regina Margareth Lima Maike[1(✉)], Laurindo de Sousa
Britto Neto[1,2], Siome Klein Goldenstein[1],
and Maria Cecília Calani Baranauskas[1]

[1] Instituto de Computação, Universidade Estadual de Campinas (UNICAMP),
Campinas, Brazil
{vanessa.maike,siome,cecilia}@ic.unicamp.br,
laurindoneto@ufpi.edu.br
[2] Departamento de Computação, Universidade Federal Do Piauí (UFPI),
Teresina, Brazil

Abstract. Natural User Interfaces (NUIs) represent a strong tendency for interaction with new computational technologies. They also represent a big challenge for designers, since delivering the promised feelings of naturalness is not trivial. In this paper, we revisit a set of 23 heuristics for NUI applications within the context of three experiments to evaluate the design of two scenarios of using NUI as assistive technology systems. While using the initial set of heuristics, they also were evaluated. Results of the experiments led to a leaner set of 13 NUI heuristics, with a compliance scale ranging from –4 to 4. The heuristics in the revisited set were defined, described and illustrated in the context of the experiments, so that they can be useful for designers and evaluators.

Keywords: Natural user interfaces · Design · Usability · Accessibility

1 Introduction

New technological devices have experimented input and output methods based on gestures, touch, and voice, considered more "natural" for interaction than the conventional mouse and keyboard. The new forms of interaction provided by Natural User Interfaces (NUIs) should evoke the feeling of naturalness in their users, by fitting the executed task to its context, and by meeting the user's capabilities [11]. This naturalness makes it possible to address a wide variety of contexts. For instance, Nebe et al. [5] propose using a multi-touch table for the management of disaster control, allowing several users to interact with a map at the same time. Renzi et al. [9] propose a serious game with a gesture-based interface to teach music concepts for children. Ringland et al. [10] show how a NUI to create paintings on a projected surface can help children with neurodevelopmental disorders. Finally, Bolton et al. [1] present an exergame that uses virtual reality goggles, a Kinect, and a stationary bicycle so that users can exercise while they play a game based on the concept of delivering newspapers with a bike.

© Springer International Publishing Switzerland 2015
M. Kurosu (Ed.): Human-Computer Interaction, Part II, HCII 2015, LNCS 9170, pp. 317–328, 2015.
DOI: 10.1007/978-3-319-20916-6_30

Each of these examples employ different input and output methods with distinct purposes and for varied types of users. They all try to make the interactions between users and computers more natural and seamless.

Despite the numerous examples in literature of studies involving NUIs, there is a debate [7, 8] around the use of the term "natural" and its implications in interaction design. We believe, however, that this is an indication that successfully designing a NUI is a challenge that involves more than considerations regarding input and output technologies. Therefore, to face this challenge, a set of 23 heuristics for NUIs were proposed [4]. These heuristics were the result of a systematic literature review that also aimed at finding the state of the art of the use of NUIs to assist people with disabilities. In this paper, we present the results of applying these heuristics in practical contexts of design and evaluation of different NUI applications scenarios. In Sect. 2 we present a description of the experiments we conducted and the main results obtained. In Sect. 3 we show how the original set of 23 heuristics was revisited based on analysis of their use, and we present for each new heuristic a description and an example of use. Finally, in Sect. 4 we present concluding remarks.

2   The Heuristics in Practice

The heuristics proposed by Maike et al. [4] were applied in three different experiments involving NUI scenarios; Table 1 presents a summary of each experiment. The three experiments also had a common feature: they were all preliminary studies with the goal of finding critical system bugs, technical issues and usability problems in their tested systems.

First, let us detail Experiment 1. It followed these steps:

1. Thirteen participants were registered in the database, with five pictures for each, from different angles and distances. Therefore, two participants were left out to act as unknown.
2. One of the participants volunteered to act as a blind user. Before being blindfolded, this person received instructions on how to access the GFR software through voice commands, and on how to aim the smartwatch to capture people's faces. He was also instructed that his goal was to find and recognize (by their name or as unknown) the people that would be in front of him.
3. In silence, other four participants were placed in front of the blindfolded user, and at least one of them was not registered in the database.
4. The timer started counting and the blindfolded user accessed the GFR application. For each person she found, she must say aloud who she believes that person is, based solely on the feedback received from GFR. Timer stops when the user signalizes she believes she has achieved her goal.
5. Steps 3 and 4 were repeated twice for the same blindfolded user and two different sets of four individuals to be recognized.
6. Steps 2 to 5 were repeated four more times with a different participant acting as the blind user and different sets of people to be recognized.

Table 1. Tested system and participants of each experiment

Experiment	Tested System	Participants
1	Gear Face Recognition (GFR) [2], a face recognition software installed in a first-generation Samsung Gear smartwatch. Developed especially for visually impaired users, this software application has the goal of helping them find and recognize people in their surroundings. The software offers several sound cues to help the user when framing a person's face (a voice says "recognizing") and identifying that person from the database (a voice says the recognized person's name) or identifying the person as unregistered (voice says "unknown").	15 Human-Computer Interaction (HCI) researchers from the University of Campinas, Brazil.
2	Gear Face Recognition (GFR) with a few improvements in the face framing audio instructions. In addition, the way to access the application was made easier.	23 graduate students from a Human Factors class in the University of Campinas.
3	A face recognition software that uses the Microsoft Kinect placed on top of a helmet to detect and recognize people in the surroundings of a visually impaired user. The system provides 3D auditory cues to indicate who someone is and where they are located in relation to the user. Besides the Kinect, the system also requires a laptop with high processing power to run the face recognition software. This laptop is placed inside a backpack so the user can carry it hands-free.	9 Human-Computer Interaction (HCI) researchers from the University of Campinas, Brazil.

At the end of Experiment 1, the set of 23 heuristics [4] was used during the debriefing session to discuss the design of the GFR system. Additionally, the heuristics themselves were discussed, so that we could figure out if their writing was clear, if they were understandable and if they actually made sense in the context of designing Natural User Interfaces (NUIs) applications. During this debriefing session, the participants reached a consensus regarding a grade for each heuristic; the scale used for the grade was the same proposed by Nielsen [6] for his usability heuristics: from 0 (not a problem) to 4 (meaning a catastrophic problem).

Regarding the GFR system, the main problem pointed out by the participants was that the audio cues to help the user in framing someone's face needed to be more helpful. Regarding the heuristics, participants suggested that the scale of grades could include, besides problems, a positive aspect, i.e., how much the system was in accordance with the heuristic. Additionally, some heuristics could be grouped together since they were understood as semantically similar.

As for Experiment 2, it followed these steps:

1. Students were divided into five groups of four or five participants. Each group was asked to elect a member to act as a blind user, and another to be "unknown" in the database. The remaining members of each group were then registered in the database: three pictures for each person, from different angles.
2. The participant elected to be blindfolded received instructions on how to operate the GFR system. A group of non-blind users was silently placed in front of her. Her task was to find and recognize all the people who are in front of her, assisted only by the GFR system.
3. The timer started counting and the blindfolded user accessed the GFR application. For each person she found, she must say aloud who she believed that person was, based solely on the feedback received from GFR. Timer stopped when user signalized she had achieved her goal.
4. Steps 2 and 3 were repeated four more times for a different blindfolded user and different groups of people to be recognized.

At the end of Experiment 2, the participants received the set of 23 heuristics [4] to analyze during the experiment. As an after class activity, they were asked to discuss the GFR in the context of the heuristics and reach a consensus for the grades of each heuristic. The applied scale of grades was the same as in Experiment 1, but it also included grading how much the system is adherent to the heuristic: from −1 (adheres the heuristic in a superficial manner) to −4 (completely adheres the heuristic). After the participants submitted their heuristic evaluations, a debriefing session was conducted. During this session, participants suggested that, for improving the heuristics, the option "not applicable" was included in the grading scale.

Finally, Experiment 3 followed these steps:

1. Verify which participants were and which were not registered in the database, since the registration process is time consuming and was made in advance.
2. One participant volunteered to act as a blind user. She received instructions on how the system works, and her main goal: finding and reaching a specific person amid a group of four people. The participant then was wearing the helmet, the backpack and was blindfolded.
3. In silence, other four participants were placed in front of the blindfolded user, and at least one of them was not registered in the database.
4. The timer started counting and the blindfolded user began walking towards the group of people to be recognized, moving her head sideways to scan the room. For each person she found, she had to say aloud who she believed that person was, based solely on the feedback received from the system. The timer stopped when the

user signalized she had achieved her goal (success), or when the time reached 2 min (fail).
5. Steps 3 and 4 were repeated once for the same blindfolded user and a different set of four individuals to be recognized.
6. Steps 2 to 5 were repeated eight more times with a different participant acting as the blind user.

After the experiment, a debriefing session was conducted. The participants discussed the experiment and the main problems found, trying to analyze them with the help of the set of 23 heuristics [4]. The heuristics themselves were also dis-cussed, aiming at to regroup and rewrite them to better support evaluation. To grade each heuristic, the participants had to reach a consensus using two concurrent scales: from 0 (not a problem) to 4 (catastrophic problem), and from −1 (follows the heuristic in a superficial manner) to −4 (completely follows the heuristic). Therefore, it is the same scale used in Experiment 2, but with the possibility of pointing out problems, and measure how much the system complies with the heuristic.

The main problems pointed out by the participants during the debriefing were the need for regrouping the heuristics, since many of them had very close meanings, and the need to change the grading scale, since having negative numbers representing something positive (following the heuristic) is counter-intuitive. Therefore, the suggested grading would represent the level of compliance with a heuristic and would range from −4 (does not follow the heuristic at all) to 4 (follows the heuristic completely). In this case, 0 would be a neutral evaluation, i.e. there are no indications of neither problems nor heuristic compliance.

3   The NUI Heuristics Revisited

The previous section described the use of the heuristics for NUI [4] in three different experiments; each experiment pointed out to improvements that were necessary in order to make the heuristics more understandable and useful. In this section we will present the regrouping and, in some cases, rewriting of the 23 original heuristics. First, we show our criteria in evaluating the need for change in a heuristic. Then, we will give a general view of before and after. Finally, we will present the new heuristics in detail, with practical examples of use.

3.1   Change Criteria

The changes in the heuristics were based on both quantitative and qualitative analysis of the experiments results. The quantitative analysis come from Experiments 1 and 2; since both experiments tested the same system but with distinct groups of participants, we decided to compare the grades from these experiments. Hence, we placed the grades from the HCI researchers (one grade for each heuristic) in a table, along with the grades from the Human Factors students (one grade for each group, five in total). Additionally, we colored the grades in a scale of gray: the smaller the number (i.e., the more the system followed the heuristic), the whiter the table cell; conversely, the higher the number (i.e., the more critical a problem was), the darker the cell. The result is in Fig. 1, where the grades of the HCI researchers are the bottom line of each table. It is important to note that the heuristics regarding "Multiple Users" are not shown in Fig. 1 because the tested system is not in that category.

Our main goal with the comparison in Fig. 1 was analyzing the interpretations given for each heuristic by finding divergence or convergence in the grades. This way, a column with a predominant tone of color (clear or dark) shows convergence in the grades, suggesting the heuristic had homogeneous interpretation. Likewise, a column with no color tone predominance indicates that there was divergence in the heuristics interpretation, suggesting possible problems with its writing.

Interaction								
Operation Modes	"Interactability"	Accuracy	Responsiveness	Identity	Metaphor Coherence	Distinction	Comfort	Device-Task Compatibility
-1	0	3	-2	-3	-4	-3	3	-3
0	0	3	2	-3	-3	-2	3	-3
0	0	3	2	3	-3	-2	4	-3
2	3	3	2	3	-2	0	4	-1
3	3	4	2	3	0	0	4	0
3	3	2	1	2	0	0	2	3

Navigation				User Adoption					
Guidance	Wayfinding	Active Exploration	Space	Engagement	Competition	Affordability	Familiarity	Social Acceptance	Learnability
-4	-2	-3	2	-4	-3	-2	-3	-1	-3
0	0	-2	2	0	-2	-2	-2	0	-3
0	0	0	2	0	-2	0	-2	0	-3
0	0	0	2	0	0	2	-2	0	-2
3	2	3	3	0	0	3	-2	3	0
2	3	3	0	2	0	2	1	0	0

Fig. 1. Specialists' evaluations in Experiments 1 (bottom row) and 2 (first five rows)

The qualitative analysis draws on the comments, suggestions and discussions from the debriefings of the three experiments. These data allowed deeper insights into how the specialists actually understood each heuristic, often corroborating with the quantitative data and possibly providing a reason for the divergence in interpretations. Some examples of this will be given in Sect. 3.3.

3.2   Before and After

Prior to detailing the new set of heuristics Fig. 2 illustrates the process of change. As shown in Fig. 2, the two heuristics Accuracy and Responsiveness (indicated by the number 1 in the image), were removed. Although both the quantitative and the qualitative analysis did not suggest any confusion related to the interpretation of these heuristics, in all three experiments they pointed to problems regarding algorithmic and technological issues only. For instance, in Experiment 2 many of the participants reported lack of precision in the face recognition software for the Accuracy heuristics (hence, the dark tone of its column in Fig. 1). Conversely, in Responsiveness, they reported delays in the audio feedback provided by the system.

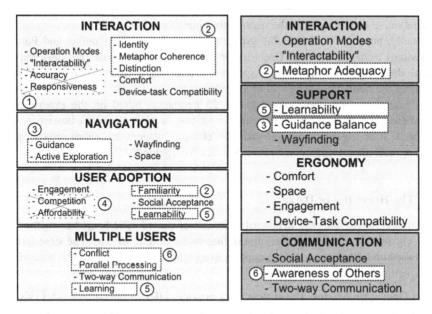

Fig. 2. To the left, the original set of heuristics and, to the right, the new set of heuristics

The four heuristics indicated by the number 2 in Fig. 2 (Identity, Metaphor Coherence, Distinction and Familiarity) were grouped together mainly because, during every debriefing, there was a clear confusion regarding their difference in meaning. Looking at Fig. 1, we can see that these heuristics seem to have the same scores, except for Identity, which seemed to be the representative of the system's interaction metaphor problems. However, the qualitative data shows that the four heuristics were used to analyze the same aspect (interaction metaphors). Therefore, they were grouped into one heuristic, Metaphor Adequacy.

Figure 2 also shows the grouping of the heuristics Guidance and Active Exploration (marked by the number 3) into one called Guidance Balance. Figure 1 suggests they both had similar scores, and the qualitative analysis reveals that both heuristics focus on the learning curve and on the balance between expert and novice users. The analysis of the HCI researchers for the Active Exploration heuristics even reads "as pointed in Guidance, there is free exploration of the system".

The number 4 in Fig. 2 points to the exclusion of the two heuristics Affordability and Competition. Figure 1 shows some divergence in Affordability, but that was because of the different views the participants had on how affordable the system was. Furthermore, the qualitative data showed that these two heuristics pointed to problems related to costs, market and technology.

The number 5 in Fig. 2 shows that the two heuristics Learnability and Learning were grouped as Learnability. Although originally one was meant for every type of system and the other was specific for interfaces with simultaneous multiple users, the way they were written was semantically very close. Furthermore, the quantitative and the qualitative data show that the users fully understood the heuristic.

Finally, number 6 indicates the grouping of two heuristics (Conflict and Parallel Processing) from the Multiple Users major group. Although we did not have experimental data about them, closer inspection reveals they were semantically close, becoming the heuristic Awareness of Others.

In summary, from the original set of 23 heuristics, based on the experimental quantitative and qualitative data regarding its use, a new set of 13 heuristics was generated. It is important to note that the changes made were either removing or grouping heuristics together; no new heuristics were added.

3.3   The Heuristics in Detail

This subsection presents the details of each one of the 13 NUI heuristics, within the following format: number, name, description and example of use. The descriptions were based on both the original description from Maike et al. [4] and on the analysis of the experimental data.

[NH1] Operation Modes. The system must provide different operation modes (visual, auditory, tactile, gestural, voice-based, etc.). In addition, the system must provide an explicit way for the user to switch between the modes, offering a smooth transition.

Example of Use: For the system tested in Experiments 1 and 2, the operation modes were: voice command (to run the application), pressing the smartwatch's physical button (also to run the application), dragging the screen (to close the application) and moving the arm to point the camera and frame someone's face. The evaluation for this heuristic pointed to problems related mostly to the transition between the modes. The experts concluded that the modes were competing with each other, since there was a delay to open the application, there was no sound feedback to inform the successful closing of the application, and the framing with the arm movement was difficult.

[NH2] "Interactability". In the system, the selectable and the "interactable" objects should be explicit and allow both their temporary and permanent selection.

Example of Use: In Experiments 1 and 2, participants pointed as "interactable" objects, the smartwatch's physical button, its camera and its screen. In Experiment 3, the HCI researchers said the people in front of the Kinect were the "interactable" objects.

[NH3] Metaphor Adequacy. The sets of interaction metaphors the system provides should make sense as a whole, so that it is possible to understand what the system can and cannot interpret. When applicable, there should be a visual grouping of semantic similar commands. In addition, the interaction metaphors should have a clear relationship with the functionalities they execute, requiring from the user a reduced mental load and providing a sense of familiarity. Finally, the metaphors should not be too similar to one another, to avoid confusion and facilitate recognition.

Example of Use: In Experiments 1 and 2, one of the interaction metaphors was the visual feedback the system provided while framing a person's face. When a face was detected, the system placed a rectangle around it and a voice said "framing". This audio clue did not translate completely the metaphor of the rectangle, which represents the focus functionality of a digital camera, which usually displays a rectangle in the screen to say that the image focus is being adjusted. Additionally, the evaluations also pointed that since the system is embedded in a smartwatch, a device that resembles a normal wristwatch, there is a natural sense of familiarity in using the system.

[NH4] Learnability. There has to be coherence between learning time and frequency of use. Therefore, if the task is performed frequently then it is acceptable to require some learning time; otherwise, the interface should be usable without much learning effort. In addition, the design must consider that users learn from each other by copying when they work together, so it is important to allow them to be aware of each other's actions and intentions.

Example of Use: In Experiment 1, the same person acted as a blind user more than once. This allowed us to measure the execution time of each iteration, and the results [2] showed that this time greatly decreased after the first round. Therefore, the system was easy to learn after a few minutes of use.

[NH5] Guidance Balance. There has to be a balance between exploration and guidance, to maintain a flow of interaction to both the expert and the novice users. To enhance transition from novice to expert usage, active exploration of the set of interaction metaphors should be encouraged by the system. Finally, it is important to provide shortcuts for the expert users.

Example of Use: The system tested in Experiments 1 and 2 provided both visual (rectangle around a face) and auditory guides (voice saying "framing", the name of the recognized person or "unknown"). In this sense, the user has freedom to explore freely, but to achieve her goal she will have to follow these feedbacks. In addition, the differentiation between novice and expert users is in how they interpret the feedbacks. For instance, it takes some time to understand that when the system says "framing" it is necessary to keep the arm still, so the system can finalize the recognition.

[NH6] Wayfinding. At any time, users should be able to know where they are from a big picture perspective and from a microscopic perception. This is important regardless of user proficiency with the system, i.e., novice and expert users need both views of the system.

Example of Use: In Experiments 1 and 2, the big picture perspective is the search for faces to scan, which also involves knowing how many people are in the environment and how big it is. The microscopic perception is the framing of one person's face, to find out who she is. In this sense, the feedbacks the system offers are more helpful to the microscopic perception than to the big picture.

[NH7] Comfort. Interacting with the system should not require much effort from the user and should not cause fatigue.

Example of Use: The system tested in Experiments 1 and 2, with the smartwatch, received several negative evaluations from the experts due to fatigue caused by keeping the arm raised for a long period. They noted, however, that there were the issues of lack of practice from the users and low compatibility between the experiment and the real use. In contrast, the system tested in Experiment 3, with the Kinect, did not present physical discomforts, neither from the helmet nor from the backpack.

[NH8] Space. The location where the system is expected to be used must be appropriate for the kinds of interactions it requires and for the number of simultaneous users it supports.

Example of Use: In Experiment 3, a problem that happened many times was that, when the blindfolded user came too close to someone (around 60 cm), the system would stop detecting that person. In this sense, to fully comply with the heuristic the system would have to emit a warning before the user left the ideal distance from the person (which is around 1,20 m).

[NH9] Engagement. The system should provide immersion during the interaction, at the same time allowing for easy information acquiring and integration.

Example of Use: For the system tested in Experiments 1 and 2, the task of framing people's faces and finding out who they are could be more fun once the fatigue issue is resolved.

[NH10] Device-Task Compatibility. The system has to offer kinds of interactions that are compatible with the task for which it is going to be used.

Example of Use: In Experiment 3, the task of using the Kinect for locating and recognizing people proved to be very compatible with this device, given the lack of comfort issues and satisfactory success rates. In literature, however, there are examples of bad task compatibility for the Kinect, such as those reported by Cox et al. [3] who used it as a mouse cursor to select objects in a screen. This way, the user had to keep the arm raised and control the cursor by moving the arm or the hand. In this case, compared to other devices the authors found the Kinect presented high fatigue, low efficiency and high error rates.

[NH11] Social Acceptance. Using the system should not cause embarrassment to the users.

Example of Use: For the system tested in Experiments 1 and 2, participants pointed out that the smartwatch should not cause embarrassment because it is very similar to a regular wristwatch. In fact, they noted that, given its novelty and cost, it can be seen as a symbol of status.

[NH12] Awareness of Others. If the system supports multiple users working in the same task at the same time, then it should handle and prevent conflicting inputs. Therefore, users must be able to work in parallel without disturbing each other, but having awareness of the others.

Example of Use: Nebe et al. [5] present the multi-touch table they have built and how it is used in a scenario of disaster control management. In that case study, multiple users work simultaneously on a map displayed on the table. Each user can have their own tangible object (a puck) to interact with the map. Placing the puck on the map can zoom in, make markings on the map or create a personal window for the user on the screen, so each person can execute their own tasks in parallel without disturbing the group view of the map.

[NH13] Two-way Communication. If multiple users are working on different activities through the same interface, and are not necessarily in the same vicinity, the system must provide ways for both sides to communicate with each other.

Example of Use: Yang et al. [12] present a study in which participants used a multi-touch screen interface to collaborate remotely. In a ludic activity, one participant shared what she was doing in the multi-touch screen and a group of other participants, in a remote location, had to guess what was the task being executed. The participants in the remote location could not communicate back to the person performing the task, so one of the reported results was that participants wished they could do that through the system's interface.

4   Conclusions

Natural User Interfaces (NUIs) represent a strong tendency for new computer systems, as well as a challenge for designers, since delivering the promised feelings of naturalness is not trivial. In this paper, we showed three practical experiments using a set of 23 NUI heuristics as a tool for evaluating the design of two distinct assistive technology systems. During the experiments, participants also evaluated the heuristics themselves. Results of the experiments led to a leaner set of 13 NUI heuristics, with a compliance level ranging from –4 to 4.

This new set of heuristics is result of revisiting the previous set with both quantitative and qualitative analysis. Since two experiments tested the same system but with completely different groups of participants, we were able to look for divergences in the interpretations of the heuristics, so we could find the ones that needed to be rewritten or regrouped. This quantitative analysis was supported by the qualitative evaluation of the participants' justifications for their grades, which gave insight into how they understood each heuristic and, hence, what improvements were necessary.

Therefore, the experiments provided us both with the view of the heuristics in practice and with the opportunity to improve them. They also allowed us to enhance the description of each heuristic by providing an example of use taken straight from the experiments, whenever possible. Some heuristics were not applicable to the experiments, so we see as necessary future work applying the new set of heuristics in systems that support multiple users working simultaneously on the same interface. Additionally, we also believe further experiments and empirical uses of the heuristics will point to design principles that can be helpful in guiding designers in early stages of NUI applications design.

Acknowledgements. We thank the volunteers who participated in the experiments, Samsung Research for the hardware equipment and Microsoft and FAPESP for the grant #2012/50468-6. We also thank CAPES (grant #01-P-04554/2013) and CNPq (grants #141254/2014-9, #308618/2014-9 and #308882/2013-0). Unicamp Institutional Review Board (CAAE 15641313.7.0000.5404 and 31818014.0.0000.5404) approved this work.

References

1. Bolton, J., Lambert, M., Lirette, D., Unsworth, B.: PaperDude: a virtual reality cycling exergame. In: Proceedings of Extended Abstracts on Human Factors in Computing Systems, CHI EA 2014, pp. 475–478. ACM, New York (2014)
2. Britto Neto, L.S., Maike, V.R.M.L., Koch, F.L., Baranauskas, M.C.C., Rocha, A.R., Goldenstein, S.K.: A wearable face recognition system built into a smartwatch and the visually impaired user. In: 17th International Conference on Enterprise Information Systems, ICEIS 2015, Barcelona (2015, to appear)
3. Cox, D., Wolford, J., Jensen, C., Beardsley, D.: An evaluation of game controllers and tab-lets as controllers for interactive tv applications. In: Proceedings of the 14th ACM International Conference on Multimodal Interaction, ICMI 2012, p. 181. ACM Press, New York (2012)
4. Maike, V.R.M.L., de Sousa Britto Neto, L., Baranauskas, M.C.C., Goldenstein, S.K.: Seeing through the Kinect: a survey on heuristics for building natural user interfaces environments. In: Stephanidis, C., Antona, M. (eds.) UAHCI 2014, Part I. LNCS, vol. 8513, pp. 407–418. Springer, Heidelberg (2014)
5. Nebe, K., Klompmaker, F., Jung, H., Fischer, H.: Exploiting new interaction techniques for disaster control management using multitouch-, tangible- and pen-based-interaction. In: Jacko, J.A. (ed.) Human-Computer Interaction, Part II, HCII 2011. LNCS, vol. 6762, pp. 100–109. Springer, Heidelberg (2011)
6. Nielsen, J.: Usability Engineering. (1994)
7. Norman, D.: Natural user interfaces are not natural. Interactions 17, 6–10 (2010)
8. O'Hara, K., Harper, R., Mentis, H., Sellen, A., Taylor, A.: On the naturalness of touchless: putting the "interaction" back into NUI. ACM Trans. Comput. Hum. Interact. 20, 1–25 (2013)
9. Renzi, M., Vassos, S., Catarci, T., Kimani, S.: Touching notes: a gesture-based game for teaching music to children. In: Proceedings of the 9th International Conference on Tangible, Embedded, and Embodied Interaction, TEI 2015, pp. 603–606. ACM, New York (2015)
10. Ringland, K.E., Zalapa, R., Neal, M., Escobedo, L.E., Tentori, M.E., Hayes, G.R.: SensoryPaint: a natural user interface supporting sensory integration in children with neurodevelopmental disorders. In: Proceedings of the Extended Abstracts on Human Factors in Computing Systems (CHI EA 2014), pp. 1681–1686. ACM, New York (2014)
11. Wigdor, D., Wixon, D.: Brave NUI World: Designing Natural User Interfaces for Touch and Gesture. Morgan Kaufmann Publishers Inc., San Francisco (2011)
12. Yang, J., Dekker, A., Muhlberger, R., Viller, S.: Exploring virtual representations of physical artefacts in a multi-touch clothing design collaboration system. In: Proceedings of the 21st Annual Conference of the Australian Computer-Human Interaction Special Interest Group, OZCHI 2009, pp. 353–356. ACM, Melbourne (2009)

Using Neural Networks for Data-Driven Backchannel Prediction: A Survey on Input Features and Training Techniques

Markus Mueller[(✉)], David Leuschner, Lars Briem, Maria Schmidt,
Kevin Kilgour, Sebastian Stueker, and Alex Waibel

Interactive Systems Lab, Institute for Anthropomatics and Robotics,
Karlsruhe Institute of Technology, Karlsruhe, Germany
m.mueller@kit.edu

Abstract. In order to make human computer interaction more social, the use of supporting backchannel cues can be beneficial. Such cues can be delivered in different channels like vision, speech or gestures. In this work, we focus on the prediction of acoustic backchannels in terms of speech. Previously, this prediction has been accomplished by using rule-based approaches. But like every rule-based implementation, it is dependent on a fixed set of handwritten rules which have to be changed every time the mechanism is adjusted or different data is used. In this paper we want to overcome these limitations by making use of recent advancements in the field of machine learning. We show that backchannel predictions can be generated by means of a neural network based approach. Such a method has the advantage of depending only on the training data, without the need of handwritten rules.

Keywords: Backchannel · Neural networks · Data-driven prediction

1 Introduction

During a conversation, listeners usually provide feedback to the speaker. They indicate that they are still listening. These cues are often issued using different modalities. Examples are shaking the head or uttering short phrases like "OK". The intention of this is to make the speaker feel more comfortable while talking as they provide some form (positive or negative) of feedback. Those cues, so-called backchannels (BCs) are usually provided and perceived unconsciously. In contrast to this, a lack of BCs is very well noticed. It leads to the speaker feeling uncomfortable or explicitly asking for some form of feedback. Providing BCs during Human Computer Interaction (HCI) is one method of making the interaction with a Spoken Dialog System (SDS) more natural. The speaker has the feeling of being listened to. This might also help during the interaction via an automated telephone system.

Our approach tackles this problem with neural networks, a machine learning technique inspired by biological neural networks. They are a versatile tool

© Springer International Publishing Switzerland 2015
M. Kurosu (Ed.): Human-Computer Interaction, Part II, HCII 2015, LNCS 9170, pp. 329–340, 2015.
DOI: 10.1007/978-3-319-20916-6_31

which can be used for different tasks like function approximation, prediction of sequences, encoding or classification. The key feature of neural networks is their ability to learn without the need of handwritten rules. We therefore selected them in order to build a predictor for BCs with few handwritten rules as possible.

This paper is structured as follows: In Sect. 2, we look at other work in this area. Following that, we explain our approach in Sect. 3. We continue with the description of the experiments we conducted (Sect. 4) and an analysis of the results (Sect. 5). We finish with a conclusion in Sect. 6.

2   Related Work

Concerning the prediction of BCs, there have been many publications in the past years. On approach is to use a system that is rule based. Another approach is to use a classifier to predict BCs from a set of input features. With recent advancements in the field of neural networks, we trained a neural network to predict BCs.

2.1   Backchannel Prediction

There exist several approaches towards the prediction of BCs. They utilize different modalities in order to predict the occurrence of a BC, such as visual and auditory information. Examples are the tracking of head movement or prosodic features like pitch and power. All these information sources are based directly on signals originating from the speaker. Besides this information, derived sources like language models or part of speech tagged word sequences are also available. They rely on specially annotated data and provide information in addition to directly observable signals.

After their acquisition the input features need to be processed in order to determine the occurrence of a BC in a word sequence. Many approaches are rule based like the one described in Troung et al. (2010). These rule based approaches often make use of prosodic features to predict BCs and rely on handcrafted rules. Troung et al. (2010) claim that the most important indicators for the placement of a BC are phonetic phenomena occurring right before it. They emphasize pause and pitch, where the latter can either be falling or rising. One of the most important features in their approach is the duration of the pause as well as the duration of the pitch slope at the end of an utterance.

Creating rules for such systems is a time consuming process and includes manual work – which may be error-prone. With the availability of more computing power in recent years, the consequent paradigm shift towards data-driven methods also is reflected in the research of predicting BCs. In Morency et al. (2008), sequential probabilistic models (e.g., Hidden Markov Models, Conditional Random Fields) are trained on human-to-human conversations to predict multimodal listener BCs (e.g., eye gaze and spoken words). Another recent approach towards the generation of BCs is done by Kawahara et al. (2015) by means of a simple prediction model. They predict prosodic features of BCs based on the preceding utterance in order to overcome the BC monotony of most other systems.

In many research areas neural networks have seen a renaissance. Therefore, we used a neural network based approach to predict BCs in this work described in the upcoming sections.

Concerning the evaluation of BC systems, De Kok and Heylen (2012b) give an overview over many published papers. Most of the systems are only evaluated with objective metrics, either with Precision/Recall or with F1. A smaller number of systems is either only evaluated by subjective means (usually a user study) or by both, subjective and objective methods (e.g., De Kok and Heylen (2012a)). We also chose to perform both in our system because we liked to not only know the formal system performance, but also the usability for a potential SDS user. Furthermore, the BC systems named in De Kok and Heylen (2012a) used different margins of error: -500/500ms, -200/200ms, -100/500ms, 0/1000ms. We decided to use the error margin -200/200ms.

2.2 Neural Networks

Neural networks have been used for a variety of tasks like encoding, prediction or classification. In the area of dialogue modelling, Ries (1999) used them in a setup with HMMs to detect different speech acts. Something similar did Stolcke et al. (1998) and Stolcke et al. (2000) where they used a neural network to model dialogue acts. They did not focus on predicting BCs alone, instead they tried to model the different acts of a dialogue. We wanted to use deep belief neural networks (DNNs) Hinton (2006) to predict BCs. The hidden layers are pre-trained using denoising auto-encoders, similar to training of networks for extracting bottleneck features for speech recognition Gehring et al. (2013). After that, we use stochastic gradient descent combined with mini-batches for back-propagation training. We call this *fine-tuning* in this paper.

3 Backchannel Prediction with Neural Networks

We chose to use a neural network as part of our BC predictor because it is not only able to learn by itself how to perform a given classification task, but that it is also capable of generalizing to a great extend. By doing so, we can build a predictor for BCs without the need for writing extensive rules by hand. Since we have not built a BC predictor before, out goal is to build a system that archives a reasonable baseline, ideally matching the baseline from other works in the field.

We start by selecting an appropriate set of features to be fed into the network. The next step is the decide on a neural network design, as well as the training technique. The output of the neural network is then post-processed in order to produce the final set of predicted BCs.

Our experiments were conducted using the Janus Recognition Toolkit (JRTk) Woszczyna (1993). Although this toolkit is mainly developed for speech recognition, it is versatile and can be used in many applications. We used it to extract the features from the audio files and to process the data using neural networks.

3.1   Input Features

Looking at work that has been done in this field, many publications make use of
the pitch, the intonation and pause in terms of auditory features. We therefore
selected pitch and power for our experiments as well. We used a pitch tracker
Kjell (1999) and computed the signal power using methods provided by the
JRTk. We did not explicitly use pause information, but we let the neural network extract this information implicitly from the provided energy envelope. To
compute features from the input signal, we applied a window of 32ms length and
shifted that window with a step size of 10ms over the data. Power and pitch are
computed for each window, representing a frame. For each frame, this resulted
in two coefficients, one for power and one for pitch. The entire setup of feature
extraction and prediction is shown in Fig. 1

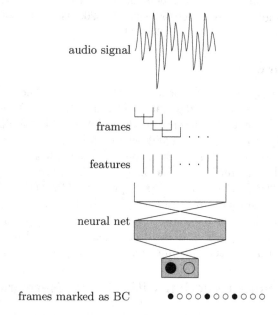

Fig. 1. Setup for extracting BCs

3.2   Neural Network Design

The input features are fed into a neural network for further classification. As
the occurrence of a BC is not provoked by a single point in time, we fed a
certain context around the current central frame into our network. By doing so,
we provide information about rising or falling pitch, as well as variances in the
signal power to the network.

The network itself consists of an input layer, one or more hidden layers and an
output layer. An example network featuring two hidden layers is shown in Fig. 2.
The input layer has as many neurons to match the dimensionality of the input
data. We did not present a single frame to the network, but instead a context

of several adjacent frames around a central frame. The output layer consists of only two nodes: One for predicting BCs and one for predicting non BCs.

For the training of the network, we use an approach similar to training a network to extract bottleneck features for a speech recognition system. First, we pre-train each hidden layer in an unsupervised fashion using denoising auto-encoders to guide the network weights into an appropriate range. The hidden layers feature a sigmoid as activation function. The network is then fine-tuned via back-propagation using gradient descent. For the error function we use cross-entropy and soft-max as activation function. The training samples are presented to the network in a random order.

After each round of training (epoch), the validation error of the network is computed using a validation data set that the network has not seen during training. This serves as an indication whether the classification performance of the network improves after one iteration of training. We also use this measure as a first indicator of the performance of the final system.

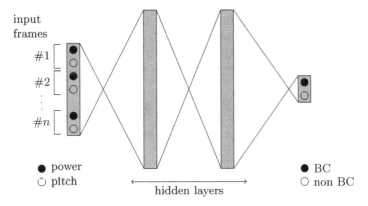

Fig. 2. Example of neural network featuring two hidden layers.

3.3 Post Processing

Our network features two output neurons, for predicting BCs and non-BCs. The output of the network is post-processed in order to obtain the label the current frame. We take the label from that neuron which has the highest output value. As final step, we apply a filter to suppress any BCs that are predicted within a window of 1 s after the last BC was output.

4   Experimental Setup

We first looked into the design and training of the neural network for the classification task. Afterwards, we then applied post processing to the output of the network to determine the final set of BCs. As pointed out in the related work section, the objective evaluation of the results is problematic. We therefore conducted a small user study to assess the subjective performance by humans.

As data we used dialogues from the Switchboard corpus, as the handling of the data is easier compared to data from meetings with a multitude of persons speaking and producing BCs at the same time.

4.1   Switchboard Corpus

The Switchboard Corpus (LDC97S62) consists of English telephone conversations that were collected within the United States. Each conversation features two channels, one for each speaker. The audio is sampled with 8kHz and quantized using the μ-law codec. We used in total 517 hours of speech, originating from 2400 dialogues. As BC, we marked the occurrence of the following utterances: "Um-hum", "Uh-huh", "Yeah right", "Oh", "Um", "Yes", "Huh", "Okay", "Hm", "Hum" and "Uh". Table 1 shows an overview of the used data sets. We assigned single conversations randomly to different data sets. We did not partition the data by individual speakers. Backchanneling is a mutual phenomenon between speaker and listener. Dividing speakers into different groups would therefore have required putting both participants of one conversation into one group. This was not feasible because two speakers had no more than one conversation.

Table 1. Overview of datasets

Data set	Length	# Dialogs	# BCs
Total	517 hours	2,438	53,270
Train	424 hours	2,000	43,900
Dev	42 hours	200	4,200
Eval	51 hours	238	5,170

4.2   Neural Network Design

As input for the network, we tested contexts of different sizes, covering 40,60 and 80 frames of context to the left and right. This results in a feature vector covering 0.81 s up to 1.61 s. We also varied the amount of nodes per hidden layer evaluating sizes of 64, 128, 256, 512 and 1024. In addition to that, we changed the amount of hidden layers and tested the performance on a network featuring just a single layer as well as up to 10 layers.

4.3   Training Data Selection

Initially, we estimated the appropriate mix of data for the training of the network. When training with data, the ratio between the different classes is important, as the network will implicitly learn an a-priori probability according to the distribution of the data. Hence, finding the right mixture is key.

When extracting the data for training the network, we extracted those parts of the audio, that caused the other speaker of the dialogue to utter a BC. Since other works use temporal features like the movement of the pitch over time, we extracted audio from the area around the occurrence of a BC. Our intention is to capture the data that lead to the utterance of that BC.

After having an initial network design, we also experimented with different history sizes before the appearance of a BC. We extracted data ranging from 1.5 s up to 3.5 s before a BC in order to train our network upon them.

4.4   User Study

We set up a user study as subjective evaluation means in order to be able to tell how well our BC production system works for users of a potential SDS. We designed an on-line questionnaire and embedded two audio files. We randomly chose two different conversations, extracted a middle piece with a length of ca. 60 seconds, and inserted BCs at the places which were predicted by the NN. The predictions of the first audio file were made by an NN trained on the audio data preceding the BCs by 2s, whereas the second audio file BC were predicted by an NN trained on 3 s of audio before the BCs.

Similar to Huang et al. (2010), we asked the participants to rate the amount and the placement of BCs, i.e. whether there were too few or too many and whether they were placed well or whether even possible placement opportunities were missed. Furthermore, we posed the question how naturally or artificially the system sounded to the user. The just named questions have been rated either on a 5-point Likert scale or as yes/no questions. Finally, the upcoming follow-up questions were presented to the participants: Which of the two backchannel audio files did you like the most? (possible answers: 1st, 2nd), Which type of backchanneler are you: Do you produce few, medium or many spoken backchannels? (possible answers: few, medium, many). To account for potential demographic effects, we asked for the gender and age of the participants.

5   Results

We first present the results from various objective evaluations and conclude this section by presenting the results from a small user study that we conducted.

For the objective evaluation, we used two different kinds of measures. First, we used the validation error of the neural network training as an indicator of the performance of a predictor based on a certain neural network. In a second step, we applied the post-processing to the output of the neural network in order to obtain the final BC positions. Based on those occurrences, we computed precision, recall and F-score to assess the performance of our system. We counted a BC as correctly predicted if our system predicted it in a window of 200ms before and after the actual BC. This is one of the measures that has been used in previous publications.

5.1 Neural Network Design

With this set of experiments, we assessed the performance of different architectures of neural networks. We extracted data using a window size of 1 s before and after the BC itself for training. Table 2 shows the validation error from different network configurations. The validation error decreases with adding additional layers. Configurations with 128 and 256 nodes show best results. The F-score of the systems using these different networks is shown in table 3. A similar improvement can be observed: Additional layers lead to a higher score. The best result is obtained with a configuration of 128 nodes per layer.

Table 2. Validation error of different network architectures.

# Layers	1	3	5	7
128 Nodes	0.202	0.196	**0.195**	0.196
256 Nodes	0.201	0.196	**0.195**	**0.195**
512 Nodes	0.202	0.196	0.196	n/a
1024 Nodes	0.203	0.196	0.196	n/a

Table 3. F-score of system based on multiple network architectures.

# Layers	1	3	5	7
128 Nodes	0.045	0.053	0.051	**0.060**
256 Nodes	0.044	0.053	0.056	0.058
512 Nodes	0.049	0.054	0.058	n/a
1024 Nodes	0.050	0.043	0.057	n/a

5.2 Context Size

We also considered different context sizes to be fed into the network. Using a context of 40 and 60 frames, we tested different configurations: In one experiment, we fixed the amount of nodes per layer to 256 and evaluated the performance of networks with a different amount of hidden layers. The validation error is shown in table 4, F-score in table 5. Both validation error and F-score again show better results when adding more layers. While the validation error benefits from a larger context, the best F-score result is archived by using a context of 60. In another experiment, we kept the amount of hidden layers fixed to 5 and varied the amount of nodes per layer. Table 6 shows the validation error of the network and table 7 the F-score. Here, the results differ. The best configuration in terms of validation error has a context of 60 and 128 nodes layer. Whereas the best F-score value originates from a system featuring 512 nodes per layer and a context of 40.

Table 4. Validation error of two context sizes, tested against several layer configurations.

# Layers	1	5	7
Context 40	0.201	0.195	0.195
Context 60	0.190	0.174	**0.173**

Table 5. F-score of two context sizes, tested against multiple layer configurations.

# Layers	1	5	7
Context 40	0.044	0.056	**0.058**
Context 60	0.022	0.022	0.023

Table 6. Validation error of various context sizes, amount of nodes per layer is changed.

# Nodes	128	256	512
Context 40	0.195	0.195	0.196
Context 60	**0.173**	0.174	0.175

Table 7. F-score of different context sizes, amount of nodes per layer is varied.

# Nodes	128	256	512
Context 40	0.051	0.056	**0.058**
Context 60	0.023	0.022	0.023

5.3 Training Data Selection

We also evaluated the use of different window sizes for the extraction of training data. We thereby varied the amount of non-BCs speech that is being extracted around the instance of one BC. For these experiments, we chose a network featuring 256 nodes, 5 hidden layers and a context of 40. Table 8 shows the validation error and the F-score of these experiments. The numbers indicate that a larger window size leads to both a better validation score and F-score. Although the validation error constantly decreases, the F-score peaks at a window size of 3s.

Table 8. Validation error of extraction lengths.

Metric	1.5s	2s	2.5s	3s	3.5s	4s
Validation error	0.206	0.195	0.162	0.136	0.117	**0.102**
F-score		0.020	0.056	0.082	**0.093**	0.078	n/a

5.4 Training Data Selection and Context Sizes

Since we saw improvements by increasing the amount of audio that is being extracted around one BC, we investigated the joint effect of increased context sizes with extraction lengths. The results are shown in table 9. Increasing both sizes has a positive effect on the validation error of the network as well as on the F-score of the entire system. By extracting data with a window size of 4 s and feeding a context of 60 into the network, we could archive the best F-score with 0.109.

Table 9. Combination of Context and Windowsize.

Context	Windowsize	Val. Error	F-score
40	3.5s	0.117	0.078
60	4.0s	0.101	**0.109**
80	5.0s	0.081	0.100

5.5 Subjective Evaluation

In total, 7 people participated in our user study. Most of them are doctoral students at the same institute, but do not work on the topic of backchanneling

Table 10. Results of the user study with a backchannel system with an NN trained on a 2 s and 3s span

Questions	1(3s)	2 (2s)
Amount of BCs appropriate (yes/no)?	5/2	0/7
Too few (1) / many (5) BCs?	3.25	5.00
Generally BCs placed well. (1=disagree,5=agree)	3.00	1.29
Many potential BCs missed. (1=disagree,5=agree)	2.86	1.29
Dialog with BCs sounds artificial (1) / natural (5)	3.00	1.43
Which audio file did you like the most?	7	0

themselves. Concerning the demographic characteristics, the participants' age ranges from 24 to 39 with an average of 29.3 years, 5 participants were male, 2 female.

As listed in Table 10, in total the first audio file is rated far better than the second one. Five of seven participants say judge the first audio file to contain an appropriate amount of BCs, while the all seven subjects say the second audio file does not contain an appropriate amount of BCs. The same tendency becomes visible in the second question whether there were too few or too many BCs in the audio: the average rating of 3.25 points on the 5-point Likert scale for the first audio also tells us that the participants are just fine with the amount of BCs inserted. On the contrary, audio file no. 2 gets the worst rating with 5.00 as all participants say the amount of BCs in the file is far too high.

Question #3 asked the participants about the placement of the BCs. They rate the placement in the first audio file with 3.00, so the placement is generally speaking "okay", but there is still space for improvement. At the same time, the second audio file is rated with only 1.29 meaning the placement is done badly. Question #4 mirrors whether many potential BCs were missed. Concerning this question, subjects reject this statement for the first (2.86) and the second audio file (1.29). Of course, the second file has missed fewer potential BCs as there are far too many in the audio right from the start, as the subjects state in the second question. This rating of the first audio file (2.86) is coherent with the rating of question no. 2 (3.25): on average there are slightly too many BCs in the audio, and the participants slightly disagree with the statement that many potential BCs would be missed. Question #5 about the perceived naturalness of the conversation with artificially inserted BCs was rated similarly to the general placement of the BCs: the naturalness of audio file no. 1 has an average rating of 3.00 and audio file no. 2 one of 1.43. This can be interpreted so that audio file no. 1 is quite natural, but there is still much potential for improvement, while audio file no. 2 is rated as far too artificial – as its placement of BCs is also rated badly. Concerning the follow-up questions, Table 10 clearly displays that all seven participants like the first audio file better as the analysis of all previous questions indicated. The results of the question, which type of backchanneler the subjects are themselves, whether they produce few, medium, or many BCs, are

Table 11. Which type of backchanneler are you: Do you produce few, medium or many spoken backchannels?.

Backchannels	few (A1)	medium (A2)	many (A3)
# of people	5	2	0

shown in table 11: 5 participants say they are using few BCs, while 2 say they are using a medium amount of BCs. This question is of course quite vage, but the results have the same tendency as the what we saw in the questions beforehand: our participants rather like fewer BCs.

We can conclude that the first audio file is clearly rated better, which is based on the BC prediction of a 3s-trained NN. This fact is in accord with the results of our objective evaluation: Table 8 shows that the validation error of the 3s NN is smaller as the one of the 2s NN. At the same time, the harmonic mean F1 is higher for the 3s NN than for the 2s NN.

6   Conclusion

We have presented a novel approach towards the prediction of backchannels using a neural network based system. We have performed experiments to evaluate different neural network architectures and training methods. Our approach is data-driven as it does not require a complex rule set. We only use one rule to prevent a new BC appearing within a 1 s window after another.

We examined various NN architectures as well as methods for training them. Our experiments show that using a network with more layers increases the performance of our system. Using a larger window size for data extraction increases the performance as well. Combining a larger window size during data extraction with a larger context size of the network improves the performance even more.

We confirmed the objective choice of system features by means of a final user study. It proves that we created an acceptable baseline system which can be improved by further development. Generally speaking, we plan to increase the perceived naturalness of the system by adding more features. This will be achieved by integrating different BCs opposed to the current approach, in which we only use "mhm"/"uh-huh". These could either be randomly inserted or determined by a more intelligent language model in a next step. Another aim of our future work is go beyond dialogs and apply BC prediction to multi-party conversations.

References

Woszczyna, M., Aoki-Waibel, N., Bu, F.D., Coccaro, N., Horiguchi, K., Kemp, T., Lavie, A., McNair, A., Polzin, T., Rogina, I., Rose, C., Schultz, T., Suhm, B., Tomita, M., Waibel, A.: JANUS 93: Towards Spontaneous Speech Translation International Conference on Acoustics, Speech, and Signal Processing (1994)

Stolcke, Andreas, et al.: Dialog act modeling for conversational speech. In: AAAI Spring Symposium on Applying Machine Learning to Discourse Processing (1998)

Kjell, S.: Pitch tracking and his application on speech recognition Diploma Thesis, University of Karlsruhe (TH)

Ries, K.: HMM and neural network based speech act detection. In: 1999 Proceedings of the IEEE International Conference on Acoustics, Speech, and Signal Processing, vol. 1. IEEE (1999)

Stolcke, A., et al.: Dialogue act modeling for automatic tagging and recognition of conversational speech. Comput. Linguist. **26**(3), 339–373 (2000)

Ward, N., Tsukahara, W.: Prosodic features which cue back-channel responses in English and Japanese. J. pragmatics **32**, 1177–1207 (2000)

Hinton, G., Osindero, S., Teh, Y.-W.: A fast learning algorithm for deep belief nets. Neural Comput. **18.7**, 1527–1554 (2006)

Morency, L.-P., de Kok, I., Gratch, J.: Predicting listener backchannels: a probabilistic multimodal approach. In: Prendinger, H., Lester, J.C., Ishizuka, M. (eds.) IVA 2008. LNCS (LNAI), vol. 5208, pp. 176–190. Springer, Heidelberg (2008)

Huang, L., Morency, L.-P., Gratch, J.: Parasocial consensus sampling: combining multiple perspectives to learn virtual human behavior. In: Autonomous Agents and Multiagent Systems (AAMAS), PP. 176–190 (2010)

Truong, K.P., Poppe, R., Heylen, D.: A rule-based backchannel prediction model using pitch and pause information. In: Interspeech, PP. 3058–3061 (2010)

de Kok, I., Poppe, R., Heylen, D.: Iterative Perceptual Learning for Social Behavior Synthesis, Centre for Telematics and Information Technology University of Twente. Technical report (2012)

de Kok, I., Heylen, D.: A survey on evaluation metrics for backchannel prediction models. In: The Interdisciplinary Workshop on Feedback Behaviors in Dialog, pp. 15–18 (2012)

Gehring, Jonas, et al.: Extracting deep bottleneck features using stacked auto-encoders. In: 2013 IEEE International Conference on Acoustics, Speech and Signal Processing (ICASSP). IEEE (2013)

Kawahara, T., Uesato, M., Yoshino, K., Takanashi, K.: Toward adaptive generation of backchannels for attentive listening agents. In: International Workshop Serien on Spoken Dialogue Systems Technology, pp. 1–10 (2015)

Towards Creation of Implicit HCI
Model for Prediction and Prevention
of Operators' Error

Pavle Mijović[1(✉)], Miloš Milovanović[2], Miroslav Minović[2],
Ivan Mačužić[1], Vanja Kovic[3], and Ivan Gligorijević[1]

[1] Department for Production and Industrial Engineering, Faculty of Engineering,
University of Kragujevac, Kragujevac, Serbia
{p.mijovic,ivanm,ivan.gligorijevic}@kg.ac.rs
[2] IT Department, Faculty of Organizational Sciences, University of Belgrade,
Belgrade, Serbia
{milos.milovanovic,miroslav.minovic}@mmklab.org
[3] Department for Psychology, Faculty of Philosophy, University of Belgrade,
Belgrade, Serbia
vanja.kovic@f.bg.ac.rs

Abstract. This paper describes development of a new generation of the interactive industrial workplace, through introduction of a novel implicit Human Computer Interaction (HCI) model. Proposed framework aims at being a foundation of a computer-based system that enables an increase of workers safety and well-being in industrial environments. Further aim is to enable an increase in production levels, together with improvement of ergonomics of the workplace. Specifically targeted environments are industrial workplaces that include repetitive tasks, which are in most of the cases monotonic in nature. Implicit HCI model could enable development of a specific technical solution that is meant to be an integral and inseparable part of a future workplace and should serve to predict human errors and communicate a warning to a worker. As such, system is meant to increase situational awareness of the workers and prevent errors in operating that would otherwise lead to work-related injuries (including causalities).

Keywords: Implicit HCI · Multimodal HCI · Neuroergonomics · EEG · Kinect

1 Introduction

Current technological context in HCI casts a view on computers that are regarded as solid-state machines relying on explicit interaction through mouse, keyboard and monitor. Although users became familiar with the devices that are enabling explicit HCI, they undoubtedly limit the speed and naturalness of HCI [1]. On the other hand, specific challenge in the direction of improvement of existing Human Computer Interaction (HCI) studies is to bring it closer to the communication patterns of human beings, and hence to create more "natural" interaction. Schmidt [2] provided a

© Springer International Publishing Switzerland 2015
M. Kurosu (Ed.): Human-Computer Interaction, Part II, HCII 2015, LNCS 9170, pp. 341–352, 2015.
DOI: 10.1007/978-3-319-20916-6_32

definition of implicit HCI as "An action performed by the user that is not primarily aimed to interact with a computerized system but which such a system understands as an input". This definition was preceded by the notion that the most of the interaction between people, and situation in which they are interacting, is implicitly exploited in communication [2]. This notion clearly outlines that an important part of natural interaction actually depends on implicit interaction. In that direction, the development of small, reliable and affordable mobile sensors opens a whole set of opportunities for natural interaction with computing entity through sensitive environments.

Multimodal HCI (MMHCI) present multidisciplinary research area including, but not limited to, psychology and gesture recognition [3]. Traditionally, MMHCI is used with the main aim to investigate the possibility of bringing closer computer technologies to users [3]. However, MMHCI research was mainly concerned with an explicit, rather than implicit interaction. In order to fulfill this gap current study is mainly aiming in investigating possibility for employing implicit MMHCI, particularly in industrial environment.

Industry workers', especially those working in assembly positions that require performing monotonous repetitive tasks are susceptible to mental fatigue and loss of concentration as time progresses. Their activities often require execution of tasks dependent on use of tools and/or operating a machine. In such a context, explicit interaction with computer becomes increasingly impractical. A new approach to communication is needed, through an interaction model that will be more natural. Stable foundation in building such interaction model in production workplace should be on different communication modalities that can ensure implicit interaction between worker and workplace, such as movement, voice, psychophysiological signals, etc.

2 Problem Statement

Throughout the industrial history, industrial accidents were mainly attributed to the equipment failure and system malfunctioning [4]. However, as technology became sufficiently reliable the remaining accidents are mainly attributed to human error [5]. As it was pointed out, human is often characterized as the most fallible element in the production line, and the main causes for these failures are limited mental and physical endurance that sometimes cause behavior and reactions to be unpredictable [6]. In other words, the human has an inborn tendency to failures, but at the same time the human can realize his or her faults and their reasons [6].

Although reliable automated systems can somewhat suppress workers operating errors and their consequences, they are still unable to assure completely "error free" industrial processes. One of the main reasons for chronic occurrence of human errors is that these systems demand the shift in the role of workers, from active operators' to the system control operators [7]. This shift introduced lowered mental workload to the operators, which further leads to the hypovigilance state of the operator and consequently the human error is still likely to occur. Another important notion is that despite of all the technological advancements, resulting in process automation, there are still many work places requiring operators' manual repetitive and monotonous actions [6]. The repetitive and monotonous actions are also known to induce the hypovigilance to the operator, leading to the lowered attention state of the operators, which could further lead to work-related injuries and industrial accidents [8].

Current practice in human factors and ergonomics (HFE) for studying the operators' cognitive abilities mostly rely on subjective questionnaires and measurement of operators' overall performance [9]. However, these methods are unreliable, since they mostly rely on subjective assessment and are dependent on the expertise of an interpreter of the collected data [9]. Another drawback is that the data acquisition and analysis is carried offline. Physiological measurements, on the other hand, are able to provide real-time data acquisition and processing, as well as objective results on one's mental states. In this context, researchers are proposing the use of computer-assisted methods that are attempting to directly acquire information on worker cognitive state and behavior using different types of sensing equipment [10].

Researchers almost exclusively agree that obtaining the information about vigilance, attention and mental fatigue can be done based on electroencephalography (EEG) and other physiological signals, such as Galvanic Skin Response (GSR) and Heart Rate Variability (HRV), [11, 12]. Until very recently, the major drawback of all established technologies for the non-invasive study of human physiological signals and brain function, was that they were confined to the highly controlled laboratory environments and conditions [10, 13]. However, the recent technological advances have enabled miniaturization of recording amplifiers and integration of wireless transmission technologies into the physiological sensors, opening a whole set of opportunities for estimating the various physiological states of the human in applied environments.

Another important notion is that many aspects of industrial work are physical in nature. On the one side, there are many tasks requiring manual action of the operator, e.g. object manipulation, lifting, pushing, pulling, etc. that are one of the major sources of work-related musculoskeletal disorders (MSDs). From the other side, automation has reduced the need of the operators' to conduct these manual tasks, however, the need of the operator to handle the automated processes did not sufficiently reduced the improper postures of the workers, which represents another source of work-related MSDs. There are different methods and tools existing for the ergonomic assessment of manual tasks and postures of the workers, such as self-reports, observational measurements and direct methods [14]. However, all of these methods have a lot of drawbacks and the biggest of them is that the analyses need to be carried off-line. Therefore, postural evaluation that can be carried out in real-time could provide benefits in practice.

Researchers are continuously working on developing supportive tools for identification and evaluation of potentially hazardous human motor tasks and postures with the main goal to improve ergonomics in work processes. Currently there are numerous tools that are based on manual observation by experts, or self reporting, such as QEC, manTRA, RULA, REBA, HAL- TLV, OWAS, LUBA, OCRA, Strain Index, SNOOK tables and the NIOSH lifting equation [15]. Most approaches in analyzing human movement are based on pose estimation techniques, that refer to the process of estimating the configuration of the underlying kinematic skeletal articulation structure of a person [16]. This representation can be reached using various sensor settings, starting from typical video cameras, variety of range cameras (structured light, time-of-flight, stereo triangulation etc.) or some combination of wearable sensors. In industry setting, researchers are working on applying this approach in defining work processes, preventing improper worker positions [17] and proper training and monitoring of new workers [18].

Ambition of this work lies in advancing interaction between worker and workplace. In order to reach this goal, we started developing a truly unobtrusive sensing workplace environment. By having unobtrusive motion sensing technology and mobile physiological monitoring system, one is able to monitor work activities without interfering with standard activities of industry worker. This could enable the development of human error detection and prevention system in a production workplace. Existing approaches are mostly limited to application in early stages of product design and workplace planning, and are confined to laboratory spaces. Contrary to existing systems, that mostly observe specific features that are considered relevant, contribution of our proposed approach is to integrate a more complete physiological and motion parameter set. In essence, our approach should provide a continuous and real time monitoring of worker activities in realistic production environment. Continuous input stream will be interpreted as implicit commands in line with the suggested human computer interaction model. In comparison to existing systems that require workers adoption to designed workplace, our approach should enable continuous improvement of the work process according to specific profile of the worker. Introduction of such a system into workplace environment is aimed to reduce workplace injuries, reduce work related errors, increase productivity and improve overall job satisfaction. This approach is aimed towards providing an automated system for monitoring of workers with different set of goals, such as improving ergonomics, detecting errors or as a tool for worker training and adaptation of workplace. This is based on the notion that continuous monitoring of the operators' behavior through his body movement and gestures, as well as his mental state, e.g. vigilance state, mental fatigue, arousal, etc. in operational environment, could decrease potential for serious errors and provide valuable information concerning the ergonomics of the tasks being performed [19].

3   State-of-the-Art

An overall research of software and hardware available on the market for biomechanical analysis indicated a number of largely diverse solutions. Larger companies (especially automotive) have made considerable financial investments in Motion Capture (MoCap) devices in recent years, example being: Impuls X2, motion capture system (PhaseSpace, Inc.); The ART Motion Capture (Advanced Realtime Tracking, Inc.); MOTION-VIEWTM (AllSportSysrems, Inc.), etc. These devices are well known, i.e. from the entertainment industry, where it is possible to animate a virtual character as a result of capturing real actor movements. Thanks to the expensive MoCap devices, it is possible to acquire positions of points (called markers) on a character's body in real time. Once the data has been acquired, there is a need to import it to the 3D simulation software, e.g. JACK (Siemens, Inc.), 3DSSPP (developed at university of Michigan, http://www.umich.edu/~ioe/3DSSPP/index.html), OpenSimulator (http://www.opensimulator.org) etc., in order to perform subsequent ergonomics analysis.

Although MoCap systems could offer highly precise ergonomic analysis, there are still certain bottlenecks in performing the on-line measurements in real-life industrial environments. The first difficulty for the industry, especially for small to medium enterprises (SMEs), is that technology for on-the-fly recording by MoCap systems is financially very demanding and often, it is necessary to devote an entire room to perform recording [20]. Further, the majority of MoCap Systems uses external sensors (Led diodes, Depth Of Field targets, etc.) that have to be attached to the person being recorded, which could interfere with workers everyday regular operations in industry. Another drawback for majority of recording systems is that there is no possibility of on-line recording of person's movements, together with the on-line analysis with the possibility for providing feedback to the operator in case of a bad posture position. To our knowledge, there are only two systems that could possibly be used for the on-line recordings and analysis: Real-time Siemens JACK & PSH Ergonomics Driver (Sinterial, Inc., http://www.synertial.com) and Cognito system [21]. However, the first system can be used when company is addressing the ergonomic aspects of manual operations during early stages of product design and manufacturing planning and there is a need to use the Synertials motion captures suits. On the other hand, the Cognito system uses on-body sensor network. These sensors are composed of tri-axial accelerometer, a tri-axial gyroscope and a tri-axial magneto-inductive magnetic sensor [21]. Therefore, Cognito systems does not record the movements of the worker, but uses the sensor readings as an input data to computer based RULA ergonomic assessment method and provide feedback when certain thresholds are reached.

Concerning current technologies, regarding real-time tracking of operators' mental fatigue and its ability to maintain desired alertness level, research and industry market has mostly been oriented towards the transportation sector, mining industry, etc., while production industry is left aside. In 2008th the Caterpilar, Inc. has published "Operator Fatigue: Detection Technology Review", the most recent critical review that has been done on the technologies regarding operators' fatigue real-time detection. In summary from that review, only three out of 22 top rated technologies are reported immediately available: ASTiD (Pernix), HaulCheck (Accumine) and Optalert (Sleep Diagnostics). Of these technologies only ASTiD and Optalert can be considered as fatigue detection technologies and are recommended for the immediate use by the Caterpillar, Inc. However, none of the proposed methods rely on the physiological signals, rather on the vehicle dynamics (ASTiD) and measuring the delay between the reopening of an eye after eye closure (Optalert).

Recently, two novel commercial fatigue detection systems emerged on the market, namely Smart Cap (EdanSafe, Inc.) and Driver State Sensor (DSS, SeeingMachines, Inc.). The DSS In Vehicle System (DSS-IVS) uses a console-mounted camera to track the driver's head and eyes, resulting in a continuous assessment of drowsiness and distraction. Using proven eye-tracking algorithms and image processing techniques powerful enough to accommodate eyeglasses, safety glasses and sun glasses (http://www.dssmining.com).

Smart Cap represent only commercially available system for fatigue detection that is based on the reliable EEG systems. EdanSafe's SmartCap solution incorporates brainwave electroencephalographic (EEG) monitoring technologies that provide a direct, physiological measurement of driver/operator fatigue in real time by sensing and analysing brainwaves (http://www.smartcap.com.au). However, this system is presented as an EEG system that is based on dry EEG electrodes. However, the desired signal quality is not achieved yet and the dry electrodes are still unable to reduce the movement artifacts, which related to the relative movement of electrodes against the head surface [22]. Further, this system is created only to monitor the operators' fatigue, but not the vigilance correlates and it is not suitable for the on-line monitoring of operators' attention level.

4 Proposed Approach

This work aims in development of an automated system for human error detection and prevention in a production workplace. System will rely on novel human-computer interaction system founded on implicit input. Underlying idea is to use unobtrusive motion tracking sensors to record worker body movement (BodyMovement), identify gestures (GestureRecognizer) and develop a model of optimal worker movement on a workplace (GestureAnalyser), Fig. 1. Using structured light technology captivated in Kinect^{TM} and LeapMotion^{TM} devices, we are able to capture body movements represented with estimated stick figure of body and hand pose estimations retrieved in time. This is possible to achieve utilizing MMK recorder (for Kinect^{TM}) and Leap-Motion SDK, adopted and developed at IT department of Faculty of Organizational Sciences (University of Belgrade). Based on this input it is intended to develop a Gesture recognizer, able to recognize generic gesture patterns on a workplace. Output from this module will feed in to application Gesture analyzer that we plan to develop in order to specify models of worker behavior on a specific workplace.

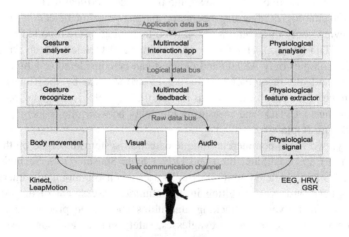

Fig. 1. Multimodal concept visualization

On the other track, we will also use physiological sensors such as EEG, GSR and HRV to record workers physiological signal (physiological signal), distinguish physiological features (physiological feature extractor) and attempt to detect worker attention state, mental fatigue, vigilance, engagement and emotional state (physiological analyzer), Fig. 1. For the second track, intention is to acquire physiological signals of worker, using concurrent physiological sensor technologies. For EEG recoding we will use state-of-the-art *SMARTING* device *(mBrainTrain, Serbia)*, an small in size and lightweight (80 × 50 × 12 mm, 55 gr) system for the purpose of recording the brain activity in the unrestricted environment. SMARTING amplifier can be tightly connected at the occipital sites to a 24-channel EEG recording cap (Easycap, Germany). For GSR recording we opt to use technology developed at University of Kragujevac, Department for production and industrial engineering. Further, commercial HRV sensor (Canyon) will be used, as it was previously validated as a good method for estimation of sleepiness and performance predictor. All physiological sensors are connected to recording computers via Bluetooth connection. Based on these recordings we will develop a physiological feature extractor, able to identify workers' relevant mental states. Output from this module will feed in to the application physiological analyzer that will be developed in order to specify a model of worker attention, vigilance, mental fatigue, engagement and emotional state for operational process. In order to improve the physiological analysis, and reach more stable conclusions, we will research the possibility of including the output from gesture analysis in to physiological analyzer decision-making process (Fig. 1). Since body movement represents a final result of cognitive effort, establishing correlation between noticed disturbance in worker gestures and mental state of the worker (acquired through his physiological signals) should enable us to early recognize and prevent possible mental or physical fatigue of worker.

In order to provide an adequate interoperability of defined components, a communication layer that carries some specific demands will be defined. It is important to note that interaction signal modalities need to be in almost perfect synchronization in order to obtain both fine time scale correlations between sensor observations and to reach necessary conditions for proper segmentation of event-related potentials (ERPs) observations from EEG recordings. Recently, Swarcwald Center for Computational Neuroscience (SCCN) developed the Lab Streaming Layer LSL, available at https://code.google.com/p/labstreaminglayer/), which is a real-time data collection and distribution system that allows multiple continuous data streams as well as discrete marker timestamps to be acquired simultaneously in an eXtensible Data Format (XDF, available at https://code.google.com/p/xdf/). This data collection method provides synchronous, precise recording of multi-channel, multi-stream data that is heterogeneous in both type and sampling rate, and is obtained via local area network (LAN). In order to use available features of the LSL recorder, the recording software of all devices used in this study were optimized with aim to allow real-time and synchronous data streaming.

Upon creation of optimal worker behavior (movement and physiological states) model, using the same set of sensors we can perform a real time worker supervision. A comparison can then be made between actual and expected models (Multimodal interaction app). System should be able to detect model deviation and suggest adequate feedback (Multimodal feedback). The existing workplace can therefore be extended to serve in a fail-safe capacity, by providing feedback information (Visual and Audio cues) about a possibly emerging problem (Fig. 1). For implementation of Multimodal feedback, initial idea is to use RGB (Red, Green, Blue) LED (light-emitting diode) strips for visual feedback and small-scale integrated speaker system for audio feedback. Special attention will be on finding user-friendly feedback system that does not increase stress levels and does not interfere with other workplaces. Further, proposed feedback systems would not interfere workers projected operations, on contrary it will be designed to increase workers' productivity, prevent lapses in attention, prevent bad postures and consequently decrease potential operating errors.

5   Current Progress

In order to conduct our initial study of worker behavior, upon which the model should be created, we created a full-scale replica of the existing workplace from our industrial partner (Fig. 2a) at Faculty of Engineering (University of Kragujevac), which is shown at Fig. 2. All major aspects of the existing workplace, including spatial ratios and microclimate conditions were completely replicated from industry. Further, a study for determination of placement of sensors used in this study was conducted and the position of the recording devices is presented on Fig. 2b. It is notable that sensors do not pose any movement restrictions for the participants in this study, and therefore, the simulation of a working process can be carried out without interfering with the process itself.

The workplace chosen for this study is replicated from automotive sub-component manufacturing industry and in laboratory settings, we simulate the assembly of the hoses used for the hydraulic brake systems in vehicles. The process itself is simple, comprising of six sub-actions which could be summarized as follows: (1) – Picking the rubber hose (blue box, on the right hand of participant in the study, Fig. 2); (2) – picking the metal extension, that should be crimped to the hose (yellow box, on the left hand side of the participant, Fig. 2); (3) – placing metal extension on the rubber hose; (4) – Placing unassembled part in the improvised machine (white box in front of participant, Fig. 2); (5) – upon placement of the unassembled part, the participant should press the pedal, with his right foot, in order to initiate the simulated crimping process; (6) – once the simulated crimping process is finalized, participant should remove the assembled part from the machine and place it inside the box with the assembled parts (grey box in front of participant, Fig. 2). Although the explained assembly process comprises of six sub-processes, it lasts roughly ten seconds and in industry settings one operator assembles approximately 2500–3000 parts in 8 h working shift. Therefore, this assembly operation presents typical repetitive and monotonous industrial task, which are known to induce vigilance decrement and mental fatigue. Moreover, the assembly process is carried out in sitting and static position, which require extended manual material handling, thus being suitable for our study, since it is well known that these kind of tasks impose also physical load for the operators if they are performed for the prolonged period of time.

(a)   (b)

Fig. 2. a – Authentic industrial workplace from our industrial partner; b - laboratory replica of the workplace with the set of sensors: 1 – Kinect™; 2 - Wireless EEG sensor (Smarting, mBrainTrain); 3 - Heart Rate Sensor (Cannoy); 4 – LeapMotion™; 5 - Galvanic Skin Response sensor (developed at our department) (Color figure online).

Participants in this study are supposed to be seated in the comfortable chair in front of an improvised machine (Fig. 2), while performing the simulated assembly task. In order to investigate the time-locked features of physiological signals, ERPs from EEG and skin-conductance level (SCL) from GSR signals, one functional modification was made in simulated work routine, in sense of information presentation to the participants. For example, evaluation of the ERP latency and magnitude can provide us important information about workers' cognitive state that can further be used as an input for the physiological feature extractor, i.e. P300 response can serve as an indicator for the amount of attention allocated to a task [23]. For that reason, instead of real information during the work process, including information on initiation of the assembly action, verified psychological sustained attention to response tast (SART) for estimating ones' cognitive ability were presented on the 24" screen from a distance of approximately 100 cm. The task specifications were programmed in Simulation and Neuroscience Application Platform (SNAP, available at https://github.com/sccn/SNAP), developed by the SCCN. The reason for utilizing SNAP software is its ability to send markers as strings to above-explained LSL and therefore, satisfying synchronization between physiological, as well as MoCap sensors can be achieved. We believe that this modification does not alter the working routine, while it provide access to the cognitive states of the participants simultaneously with the pose estimation of the participants, while performing simulated operation.

Data acquired during these recording sessions will be used for optimal worker behavior (movement and physiological states) model development for each of the constructed workplaces and specific worker. In the next steps we can develop an initial interaction model that will enable us to compare implicit inputs with defined models of optimal worker behavior and provide corresponding outputs. Further, development of interaction model will be data driven, input data that will be acquired in empirical studies will affect the parameters of the implicit input section of the system. Also, the output will be edited according to conclusions gathered in empirical studies in order to find the best possible feedback to worker. To summarize, final interaction model implementation will be reached through iterative-incremental development.

6   Discussion and Concluding Remarks

The main aim of presented work is to develop a new automatized, computer assisted observation method, by improving the interaction of worker with his work environment. The approach used relies on implicit multimodal human computer interaction. In the workplace setting, where worker is mainly focused on performing defined work activities, it is difficult to base communication between worker and is workplace on explicit interaction. In a world where people's movements and transactions can be tracked—where individuals trigger non-deliberate events just by being at a certain place, physical or virtual, at a certain time—the notion of interaction itself is being fundamentally altered [24].

Workers' activities in a workplace can be regarded as implicit interaction input towards system for error detection and prevention. Majority of the production workplaces are constructed in respect with guidelines given in ergonomic and other industrial standards, and work process is developed in such a manner to ensure optimal level of productivity. Compared to computers that are capable of executing given algorithm, humans are unable to perform projected repetitive activities, without variation in performance and deviation from projected work plan. With time, people become subject to physical and mental fatigue, which if not properly regarded may lead to drop in productivity or even induce work-related injuries. The purpose of the proposed system is to use novel HCI model involving implicit interaction input in detecting deviations from the projected work behavior and perform preventive actions by providing adequate feedback to worker. Interaction modalities as input in our approach are human gestures, body motion and physiological signals, and audio and visual signals will be delivered as an output feedback.

Currently this system reached a phase of initial laboratory installment and testing. System components for recording and monitoring of physiological signals and body movement are developed and initially tested. Communication and synchronization platform, that as a base uses open source technology called Lab Streaming Layer LSL, is developed and optimized. Acquisition modules are connected to communication platform via specifically designed and developed drivers.

A full-scale replica of workplace environment was built at Faculty of Engineering (University of Kragujevac). The workplace represents a work process of the assembly of the hoses used for the hydraulic brake systems in vehicles. Sensing equipment and computer components are integrated in to workplace environment based on iterative process of signal analysis and sensor placement.

Current activities of our research team are focused on developing and executing an initial round of experimental recordings in order to retrieve a first data set. This data set will be used in realization of the first version of implicit MMHCI model. Additionally, results will be used in iterative improvement of system components.

Upon these initial steps, our plan is to take the system to our industrial partner and perform a small-scale experimental study, using one of the replicated workplaces that were used in building a simulated, and laboratory environment. Output from these experiments will be used for system and models fine-tuning and preparation for a full-scale production environment, i.e. it is intended to create generalized model, which could be utilized on the majority of existing industrial workplaces. Finally, the system will be evaluated in a relevant, production environment, using workplaces not utilized in previous development. In order to achieve this, entire process starting from recording, specific workplace model development and enrolment of system in to existing production conditions will be conducted. This requires a larger scale empirical study.

Acknowledgments. This research is financed under EU - FP7 Marie Curie Actions Initial Training Networks - FP7-PEOPLE-2011-ITN. We would further like to acknowledge company "Gomma Line" (Serbia), for their assistance and advisory during the experimental set-up phase.

References

1. Pavlovic, V.I., Sharma, R., Huang, T.S.: Visual interpretation of hand gestures for human-computer interaction: a review. IEEE Trans. Pattern Anal. Mach. Intell. **19**(7), 677–695 (1997)
2. Schmidt, A.: Implicit human computer interaction through context. Pers. Technol. **4**(2–3), 191–199 (2000)
3. Jaimes, A., Sebe, N.: Multimodal human–computer interaction: a survey. Comput. Vis. Image Underst. **108**(1), 116–134 (2007)
4. Gordon, R.P.: The contribution of human factors to accidents in the offshore oil industry. Reliab. Eng. Syst. Saf. **61**(1), 95–108 (1998)
5. Hendy, K.C.: A tool for Human Factors Accident Investigation, Classification and Risk Management. DRDC Toronto TR 2002-057.   Defence R&D Canada (2003)
6. Hamrol, A., Kowalik, D., Kujawińsk, A.: Impact of selected work condition factors on quality of manual assembly process. Hum. Factors Ergon. Manuf. Serv. Ind. **21**(2), 156–163 (2011)
7. Young, M.S., Stanton, N.A.: Attention and automation: new perspectives on mental underload and performance. Theor. Issues Ergon. Sci. **3**(2), 178–194 (2002)
8. Spath, D., Braun, M., Meinken, K.: Human factors in manufacturing. In: Salvendy G. (ed.) Handbook of Human Factors and Ergonomics, 4th edn., pp. 1643–1666 (2012)
9. Parasuraman, R.: Neuroergonomics: research and practice. Theor. Issues Ergon. Sci. **4**(1–2), 5–20 (2003)
10. Parasaruman, R., Rizzo, M.: Neuroergonomics: The Brain at Work. Taylor & Francis, New York (2003)
11. Bonnefond, A., Doignon, C.N., Touzalin, C.P., Dufour, A.: Vigilance and intrinsic maintenance of alert state: an ERP study. Behav. Brain Res. **211**(2), 185–190 (2010)
12. Fowles, D.C.: The three arousal model: implications of Gray's two-factor learning theory for heart rate, electrodermal activity, and psychopathy. Psychophysiology **17**(2), 87–104 (1980)

13. Mijović, P., Giagloglou, E., Todorović, P., Mačužić, I., Jeremić, B., Gligorijević, I.: A tool for neuroergonomic study of repetitive operational tasks. In Proceedings of the European Conference on Cognitive Ergonomics, pp. 1–2. ACM (2014)

14. Diego-Mas, J.A., Alcaide-Marzal, J.: Using Kinect™ sensor in observational methods for assessing postures at work. Appl. Ergon. 45(4), 976–985 (2014)

15. Andreoni, G., Mazzola, M., Ciani, O., Zambetti, M., Romero, M., Costa, F., Preatoni, E.: Method for movement and gesture assessment (MMGA) in ergonomics. In: Duffy, V.G. (ed.) ICDHM 2009. LNCS, vol. 5620, pp. 591–598. Springer, Heidelberg (2009)

16. Moeslund, T.B., Hilton, A., Krüger, V.: A survey of advances in vision-based human motion capture and analysis. Comput. Vis. Image Underst. 104(2), 90–126 (2006)

17. Li, C., Lee, S.: Computer vision techniques for worker motion analysis to reduce musculoskeletal disorders in construction. Computing in Civil Engineering, pp. 380–387 (2011)

18. Ray, S.J., Teizer, J.: Real-time construction worker posture analysis for ergonomics training. Adv. Eng. Inform. 26(2), 439–455 (2012)

19. Gevins, A., Leong, H., Du, R., Smith, M.E., Le, J., DuRousseau, D., Zhang, J., Libove, J.: Towards measurement of brain function in operational environments. Biol. Psychol. 40(1), 169–186 (1995)

20. Horejsi, P., Gorner, T., Kurkin, O., Polasek, P., Januska, M.: Using Kinect technology equipment for ergonomics. Mod. Mach. (MM) Sci. J. 388–391 (2013)

21. Vignais, N., Miezal, M., Bleser, G., Mura, K., Gorecky, D., Marin, F.: Innovative system for real-time ergonomic feedback in industrial manufacturing. Appl. Ergon. 44(4), 566–574 (2013)

22. Chi, Y.M., Jung, T.P., Cauwenberghs, G.: Dry-contact and noncontact biopotential electrodes: methodological review. IEEE Rev. Biomed. Eng. 3, 106–119 (2010)

23. De Vos, M., Gandras, K., Debener, S.: Towards a truly mobile auditory brain–computer interface: exploring the P300 to take away. Int. J. Psychophysiol. 91(1), 46–53 (2014)

24. Sellen, A., Rogers, Y., Harper, R., Rodden, T.: Reflecting human values in the digital age. Commun. ACM 52(3), 58–66 (2009)

Development of Chat System Added with Visualized Unconscious Non-verbal Information

Masashi Okubo[✉] and Haruna Tsujii

Doshisha University, 1-3 Miyakodani, Tatara, Kyotanabe
Kyoto 610-0321, Japan
mokubo@mail.doshisha.ac.jp, suzy3250@gmail.com

Abstract. Face-to-face communications are performed by sending and receiving verbal and non-verbal information. And non-verbal information are sent and received consciously and unconsciously. In the face-to-face communication, this non-verbal information plays the important roles for smooth communication. In the case of text chat, we can send the some kind of non-verbal information, for example, the face marks, smiley and stamps to let the partner know our emotion and the true meaning of verbal information. However, it is difficult to treat the unconscious non-verbal information in text chat. Because of this, sometime we have a misunderstanding of text information. Therefore, we propose the text chat system which visualizes the unconscious non-verbal information of user. In the proposed system, the change of heart's pulse wave of user is reflected in the background color of text chat. In this paper, the detail of proposed system and the result of system evaluation by sensory evaluation are described.

Keywords: Unconscious non-verbal information · Text communication · Heart's pulse wave · Emotion

1 Introduction

The forms of real-time communication are broadly divided into face-to-face communication and non-face-to-face communication [1]. As shown in Fig. 1 on the left, in face-to-face communication users communicate effectively to understand each other by sending/receiving various kinds of non-verbal information including facial expressions, voice tones, gestures and nodding, and so on [2]. On contrary, in remote communication, the lacks of non-verbal information sometimes interfere with a communication. Especially in the text communication shown on the right in Fig. 1, many users attempt to express verbal information such as their feelings and intensions by adding non-verbal information including symbols, face marks and stamps consciously for smooth communication. However they hardly exchange unconscious non-verbal

© Springer International Publishing Switzerland 2015
M. Kurosu (Ed.): Human-Computer Interaction, Part II, HCII 2015, LNCS 9170, pp. 353–362, 2015.
DOI: 10.1007/978-3-319-20916-6_33

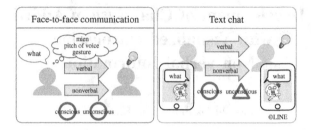

Fig. 1. Role of non-verbal information in face-to-face communication and text chat

information. However, it is said that the exchange of unconscious nonverbal information such as face colors and body motions plays an important role in face-to-face communication.

Therefore in this study, we propose a chat system enables to add unconscious non-verbal information and develop a prototype aiming to support smoother text communication in visualizing unconscious non-verbal information. A change of user's heart's pulse interval is used as the added non-verbal information. A heart's pulse interval is closely related to automatic nerve's activity and usually used as an index to estimate emotional stress. In general it is considered that giving a user moderate stress, the heart's pulse interval becomes short and the variability becomes little. Also it is considered that keeping a user in relaxed state, the heart's pulse interval becomes long and the variability becomes big. Additionally as a blood flow affects a change of face color...etc., we believe that visualization of the heart's pulse interval and visualizing such information to the text chat is reasonable.

In this study the influence of presenting the unconscious non-verbal information on users in text chat is investigated. We build the text chat system added unconscious non-verbal information obtained by visualizing heart's pulse interval variation and perform the experiment using the proposed system.

As related study in this field, Watanabe and his colleagues developed and evaluated the voice chat system in avatar communication, in which user's communication behaviors and breathing information was reflected to the avatar simultaneously. From the result of evaluation experiment, it was concluded that the system adding the breathing information improved a sense of presence and coexisting and that users found it preferable to the system without adding such information [3]. In our proposed system, the heart's pulse interval variation was used as the presented information. Recently a list-watch type sensor allowing measurement/visualization of pulse waves is available on the market, which is easier than using general physiological indexes including breathing information.

2   Chat System Added Unconscious Non-verbal Information

In this chapter, the method to reflect a change of heart's pulse interval as non-verbal information in text chat and the outline and configuration of the system are described.

2.1 Outline of Proposed System

The proposed text chat system was added non-verbal information sent out unconsciously. The user's heart's pulse interval was used as the non-verbal information to be added and the change was reflected into the color of balloon in the text chat. The heart's pulse wave was monitored by an ear-phone type sensor and the sensed information was sent to the server where the heart's pulse interval was measured. According to the temporal change of the heart's pulse interval, the background color of the user's text chat changed. Although the proposed system measured the heart pulse interval and controlled the text chat through the server, it seems that this system is able to be built as an application available on P2P for smart phone users.

2.2 System Configuration

Figure 2 shows the outline of the system. The user put on the earphone type sphygmograph made by Rohm Co., Ltd. The information of user's heart's pulse wave was sent to PC with Bluetooth and finally sent to the server with socket. In the server, the heart's pulse interval was detected from the pulse wave information received and the balloon color of the text chat was determined by comparing the length of the pulse interval received previously. When the user sent out the message, the color of the message and the balloon were sent to the client.

2.3 Detection Method of Heart Pulse Interval from Pulse Wave

In this study a user's heart's pulse interval is used as unconscious non-verbal information [1]. The method for detection of the heart's pulse interval is described as follows; the pulse wave information at rest was measured for 5 min and its average of the maximum and the minimum value was defined as threshold Th. Comparing the threshold Th and the pulse wave information, the time exceed the threshold Th (Time t_i)

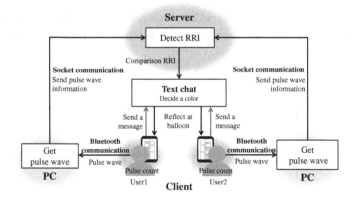

Fig. 2. System configuration.

was once stored, and the difference between ti and t_{i-1} is the heart's pulse interval. Moreover the average of the heart's pulse interval for 10 s was calculated. Comparing it to the previous average and the change was reflected to the balloon color in the chat system.

2.4 Representation Method of Change of Heart's Pulse Wave Interval in Chat System

The user's heart's pulse wave information for 10 s is sent to the server. After the heart's pulse interval is detected from that information, it is stored at the server. When the user sends a message, the proposed system executes comparison of the heart's pulse interval at that moment and the one of 10 previous second. The color of the balloon is verging to red when the heart's pulse interval becomes shorter and it is verging to blue when the heart's pulse interval becomes longer. If any change is not detected in the heart's pulse interval, the color of the balloon remained unchanged. The system has 9 colors stages changed by the interval length. The color determined is sent to the both users' terminals along with the user's message. The above process is conducted repeatedly every time the user sends a message and the color of the balloon is reflected (See Fig. 3).

3   Influence of Added Unconscious Non-verbal Information on User and Text Chat

In face-to-face communication, a face color, for example, is difficult to change con-sciously. However, sending/receiving this kind of unconscious non-verbal information plays an important role for smooth face-to-face communication. To investigate the influence of the added unconscious non-verbal information on a user's state of mind and text chat, the following experiment was performed using the proposed system.

3.1   Experimental Purpose and Method

To investigate the influence of the added unconscious non-verbal information on a user's state of mind and a text chat, the evaluation experiment with subjects was

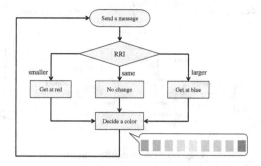

Fig. 3. Representation method of the change of the heart's pulse interval.

performed using the developed text chat system. 40 university students aged around 20 years were participated as the subjects. They worked in pairs during the experiment. The two types of experiments reflecting/without reflecting the change of the heart's pulse interval in the balloon color were performed. The number of statements and the result of questionnaire answered by the subjects after each experiment were compared. The pulse wave information at rest was measured for 5 min. previously, and then the experiment was carried out for 10 min. Additionally considering an order effect, the order of the two type's experiments was randomly shuffled per subjects.

3.2   Experimental Results

Figure 4 shows the average of the number of statement and the standard deviation. As the typing speed differs depending on the subjects, the number of statements under each experiment's condition is standardized by the average of the number of statements sent by each subject. No statistic difference is found between the chat system with or without reflecting the change of the subject's heart's pulse interval in the balloon color. There is high possibility that the change of the color has no impact on the number of the statement. Figure 5 shows the result of the questionnaire on the matching degree of the emotional change of the subject and the balloon color change. Many subjects have no idea whether their emotions are coincident with the balloon color or not. Moreover, Fig. 6 shows the result of the questionnaire on the degree of reading the partner's feeling by text chat under each experiment condition. In the case with reflecting the change of the heart's pulse interval in the balloon color, more subjects give positive

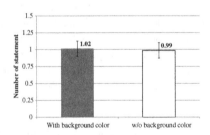

Fig. 4. Average and standard deviation of number of statement.

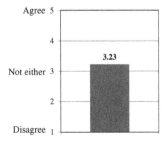

Fig. 5. Degree of coincidence between color of text balloon and feeling.

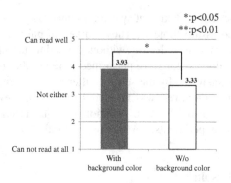

Fig. 6. Degree of reading partner's feeling by text chat.

answer to the question comparing to the case without reflecting. Thus the significant difference between two cases is found. In the case with reflecting the change of the heart's pulse interval in the balloon color, although the subjects are not aware of the coincidence between their feelings and the color reflected on their sides, they feel it possible to read the partner's feelings from the color reflected on the partners' sides using the same system. Further studies are needed to validate these results.

Figure 7 shows the result of the questionnaire on the degree of consciousness of the heart's pulse sensor. The either of the experiment conditions results in low consciousness. However the subjects' consciousness increases more in the condition reflecting the balloon color than in the condition without reflecting. There are significant differences between the two conditions.

Figure 8 shows the result of the questionnaire on the degree of reading the partner's feeling from the background color change. Figure 9 shows the result of the questionnaire on which system can read the partner's feeling change easily. Many subjects respond that they feel it easier to read the partners' feelings when using the system reflecting the change of heart's pulse interval in the balloon color. As the above result, it was found that many subjects have an intuitive feeling that they are able to read the change of the partners' feelings by the balloon color change.

As shown in Fig. 5 previously, the matching degree between the change of the subject's emotion and that of the balloon color is not high. Meanwhile, in Fig. 6, the

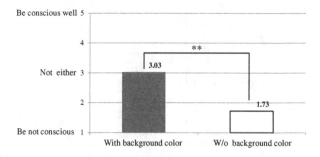

Fig. 7. Degree of consciousness of the heart's pulse sensor

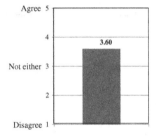

Fig. 8. Degree of reading the partner's feeling by background color's change.

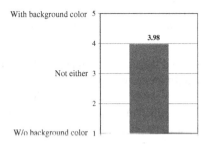

Fig. 9. System of reading the partner's feeling easily.

result of the degree of reading the partner's feeling is explored in details. Figure 10 presents the answers of the questionnaire shown in Fig. 5 which is filled out by each subject.

The subjects are divided into α and β groups. 14 subjects, who answer that the change of their emotions highly matches with the change of the balloon color, belongs to α group, and 7 subjects, who answer the matching degree is low, belongs to β group. The results of each group in each questionnaire are shown in as following.

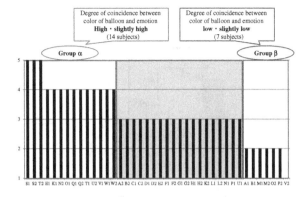

Fig. 10. Dividing participants into 3 groups by degree of coincidence between color of balloon and emotion.

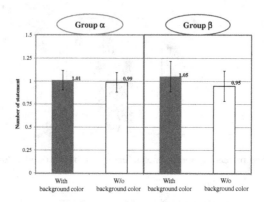

Fig. 11. Average and standard deviation of number of statement.

Figure 11 shows the average and the standard deviation of the number of the statement. Each group has no statistical difference between the cases with or without reflecting the change of the heart's pulse interval in the balloon color. Therefore, along with the result of Fig. 4, the difference in the matching degree between the balloon colors has no influence on the number of the statement.

Figure 12 shows the questionnaire result in each group, on the degree of reading the partner's feeling by text chat under each experimental condition. In α group, many subjects respond that they are able to read the partners' feelings easier in the case with reflecting the change of heart's pulse interval in the balloon color than in the case without reflecting the change and the significant difference is found. In contrast, many subjects in β group have no idea whether they are able to read the partners' feelings or not and no statistic difference is found. In short, it was found that the subjects in α group who respond their own feelings matches with the color change intuitively feel the partners' feeling change from the balloon color change.

The questionnaire result in each group on the degree of consciousness of the heart's pulse sensor under each experimental condition is shown as Fig. 13. It is found that either group is not aware of the heart's pulse sensor in the case without reflecting the

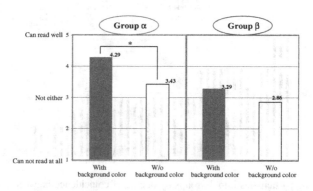

Fig. 12. Degree of reading the partner's feeling by text chat.

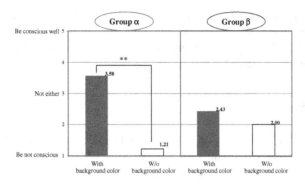

Fig. 13. Degree of consciousness of the sensor.

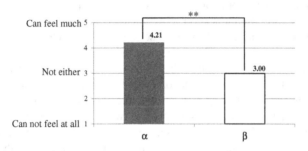

Fig. 14. Degree of reading the partner's feeling by balloon color changes.

change of the heart's pulse interval in the balloon color change. In addition, α group tends to be aware of detecting the heart's pulse wave in the case with reflecting the change of the heart's pulse interval in the balloon color change and the significant difference is found from the condition without reflecting the change.

Figure 14 shows the questionnaire result in each group on the degree of reading partner's feeling by the balloon color change. The group obtains higher evaluation than β group and has the significant difference between the both groups.

Moreover, Fig. 15 shows the questionnaire result on the system enables to read the partner's feeling change in each group. Comparing to the β group, the α group has more subjects who answer that they can read the partner's feeling easier when using the system reflecting the change of the heart's pulse interval in the balloon color and the - significant difference between each group is indicated.

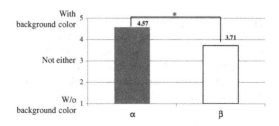

Fig. 15. Reading the partner's feeling easily.

Figures 14 and 15 indicates that the group recognizing the coincidence between the change in their feelings and in the balloon color change perceives the change in the partners' state of feelings by the balloon color change. Accordingly, it is shown that the proposed system is effective for this group.

4   Conclusions

This study aims to support a smooth text communication and develops a system visualizing the unconscious non-verbal information on a text chat. In particular, a user's heart's pulse interval was detected from a user's pulse wave. When the interval length changes, that information was reflected in the color of the balloon on the text chat. Additionally, the experiment to investigate the influence of visualized the unconscious non-verbal information on the subjects was performed in this study.

The result of the communication experiment using the proposed system shows whether the change of subject's heart's pulse interval is reflected in the balloon color has no influence on the number of the statement by the subjects. According to the result of the questionnaire, all in all, many subjects have no idea whether their own emotion match with the balloon color or not. In contrast, many subjects respond that the change of the state of the partner's feeling matches with the balloon color. Therefore the further study was conducted by sorting the subjects into two groups according to the matching degree of the change of their own feelings and the balloon color. As a consequence, it is shown that the group recognizing high matching degree perceives that they are able to read the partner's feeling as the balloon color changes. Also it is shown that the consciousness of detecting the heart's pulse wave increases as the balloon color changes. From these results, visualizing the unconscious non-verbal information on the text chat is very effective for the user who considers it as reasonable and it suggests that there might be high possibility to support the smooth communication.

A method for the control of the balloon color change will be necessary to be examined as future challenge. In addition, we are scheduled to examine the variability of the heart's pulse interval, the body temperature change and the other unconscious non-verbal information.

Acknowledgment. This work was supported by JSPS KAKENHI Grant Number 26560016.

References

1. Tamura, H., et al.: Human Interface. Ohmsha, Tokyo (1998). (in Japanese)
2. Kurokawa, T.: Non-verbal Interface. Ohmsha, Tokyo (1994). (in Japanese)
3. Watanabe, T., et al.: Visualization of respiration in the embodied virtual communication system and its evaluation. Int. J. Hum. Comput. Interact. **17**(1), 89–102 (2010)
4. Masaki, M.: Relationship between infraslow wave of ear plrethtysmogram and psychic tension –in comparison with skin potential refex and heart rate. Jpn. J. Psychol. **46**(4), 199–206 (1975). (in Japanese)

Implications for Design of Personal Mobility Devices with Balance-Based Natural User Interfaces

Aleksander Rem[✉] and Suhas Govind Joshi

Department of Informatics, University of Oslo, Oslo, Norway
{aleksre, joshi}@ifi.uio.no

Abstract. In this paper, we present a set of guidelines for designing personal mobility devices (PMDs) with body balance exclusively as input modality. Using an online survey, focus group and design workshop, we designed several PMD prototypes that used a natural user interface (NUI) and balance as its only form of user input. Based on these designs we constructed a physical and functional PMD prototype, which was tested using a usability test to explore how the balance interface should be designed. In conclusion, we discuss whether the guidelines from the literature could apply when designing PMDs and present a set of implications for the design of PMDs with balance-based NUIs based on both the guidelines and our own findings.

Keywords: Personal mobility · Embodied interaction · Natural user interface

1 Introduction

In July 2014, personal mobility devices (PMDs), such as self-balancing vehicles, were legalized on public roads by the Norwegian government. With the introduction of PMDs, a new market of cheap, environmentally friendly, and personal transportation vehicles would be available to the public. However, more than two months after the legalization the adoption rate was still very low [1], which suggested that the current vehicles had failed to meet the requirements of the public. This potential need for a redesign was the main motivation for our study on improving PMDs using a Natural User Interface (NUI) interaction approach. As such, we gathered user requirements through an online survey and designed several PMD prototypes using a focus group and design workshop. This was followed by a usability test on one of the designs to identify possible implications for the design of balance-based PMD interfaces.

This paper is structured as follows: We start by presenting related work on balance as input and user experience (UX) of movement-based interfaces, and use this literature to propose a list of design implications for the prototype and its interface. Next, we present the methods used to collect requirements, design and test the prototype using these implications. We then present the results from each of the methods, and finally discuss the proposed implications based on our findings.

© Springer International Publishing Switzerland 2015
M. Kurosu (Ed.): Human-Computer Interaction, Part II, HCII 2015, LNCS 9170, pp. 363–375, 2015.
DOI: 10.1007/978-3-319-20916-6_34

2 Related Work

Within Human-Computer Interaction (HCI), much of the research on balance-based interfaces so far revolves around balance as input in a virtual environment. In a study by Fikkert et al. [2], the authors compared the use of lower-body input to traditional hand held controllers using a Wii Balance Board and Wii Remote. They found that while using the remote to navigate was significantly faster, the balance board was both easier to learn and use and felt more intuitive to the users, and the users strongly indicated that they enjoyed using the balance board more. These results indicated that while a balance-based interface may not be as precise as a traditional button-based interface, it could still be easier to learn and provide a more fun and intuitive user experience.

Wang & Lindeman [3] conducted a study comparing two modes of balance control; isometric and elastic (tilt), with a leaning-based surfboard interface in a 3D virtual environment. The authors found that participants preferred the elastic board because it was more intuitive, realistic, fun and provided a higher level of presence. However, they found no significant difference in user performance, indicating that people prefer elastic balance interfaces over non-elastic, but that this preference has no impact on performance.

Haan et al. [4] demonstrated different scenarios where balance could assist traditional hand-operated input in a virtual reality (VR) setting. They tested the use of a balance interface as an interaction supplement in three different interaction modes (3D rotation, navigation and abstract control), both while sitting and standing. They found that all three modes worked well, but noted that side-to-side motion was slower and required more effort on the user's part in all modes. The authors concluded that the balance board was effective and easy to use, suggesting that the balance could easily be used in a wide variety of applications, even outside of VR.

Research on user experience is often concerned mostly with graphical interfaces and screens, but the rapid development of small integrated processors in the last decade has opened the door for UX research on embedded computers without any graphical or screen-based interface. In a study by Moen [5] the authors present the design process and user explorations of a wearable movement-based interaction concept called the BodyBug. This was created to explore full-body movement, as the interaction modality. Through their observations of users interacting with the BodyBug, they identified that the success of embodied user experience relies on having movement-triggers as well as a social excuse or reason to move, i.e. that these movement patterns are socially and culturally accepted in their context. Additionally, the authors observed large individual differences regarding which movements felt comfortable to the participants, suggesting that enforcing a set of pre-defined gestures or strict rules for a successful interaction may limit the user experience for users that feel uncomfortable with these kinds of body movements.

In a study by Larssen et al. [6] exploring movement-based input using a Sony Playstation2® and Eyetoy™, the authors used two existing frameworks for conceptualizing the interaction: *Sensible, Sensable, Desirable: a Framework for Designing Physical Interfaces* [7] and *Making Sense of Sensing Systems: Five Questions for*

Designers and Researchers [8]. The frameworks were used to categorize the movements of the participants during play, and look at how movement as input would hold as communication in the interaction. The authors found that both frameworks were valuable tools to aid researchers and designers in understanding the specific challenges that new interaction and input options present. They conclude that when movement is the primary means of interaction, the forms of movement, enabled or constrained by the human body together with the affordances of the technology, need to be a primary focus of design. Additionally, an intuitive and natural interaction through movement relies on appropriate mapping between movement and function.

Table 1. Our design guidelines for a PMD with a balance interface based on related work

Guidelines	Related work
1. Elastic interfaces increase user experience over isometric	[3]
2. Leaning from side-to-side requires more effort	[4]
3. A movement based interface relies on movement-triggers and a social excuse to move	[5]
4. There are large individual differences in which movements feel natural	[5]
5. The device must be designed around the forms of movement as allowed by the human body	[6]
6. Intuitive and natural interactions relies on appropriate mapping between movement and function	[6]

2.1 Design Guidelines from Related Work

Based on this literature we have assembled a set of guidelines for the design that we have attempted to incorporate in the design process of the prototype (see Table 1). We will return to these guidelines following our results to evaluate and discuss whether they can be used as design implications for future PMD interfaces.

3 Method

The aim of the study was to identify opportunities for improving PMDs using a NUI and lower-body input approach. We used Blake's definition of NUI *"A natural user interface is a user interface designed to reuse existing skills for interacting appropriately with content."* [9], and focused on designing an interface that: Would reuse existing skills to ease the learning curve, was "invisible" in the sense that it allowed input through direct manipulations of the device without any use of buttons, dials or switches etc. as metaphors, and finally that took advantage of the users' own intuition through tacit knowledge within a given context – in our case, motor skills and balance. In this paper, we present three of the methods used during the study; a survey to gather requirements, a focus group to generate design concepts and a formative usability test conducted before the implementation of the balance interface.

3.1 Survey

We conducted a quantitative online survey (N = 248) with the purpose of identifying user requirements and needs in the prototype. We used the following three PMD product categories as a way of framing the questions around familiar designs: Self-balancing/Segway, e-bike and electric kick-scooter. The users were asked to assess various attributes such as size, weight, safety and speed in order to identify what people like and dislike about each device category. This resulted in a list of good and bad attributes for each category that would lay the foundation for the requirement specification and become the basis for the design of the prototype.

The target group was adult Norwegians with a daily transportation need, and particularly people living in urban areas. The timeframe was set to two months. Participants were mainly recruited using online forums, had a fairly even age distribution (Mean = 37.83, SD = 3.19), but a gender distribution skewed towards males (81 %).

3.2 Focus Group and Design Workshop

To create a set of initial design ideas from the survey results and requirement specification, a focus group was chosen. This is a common method to use in combination with surveys and the pairing of these two methods are one of the leading ways of combining qualitative and quantitative research methods [10]. Additionally, because of the easy access to students with previous HCI experience at our department, it allowed for the collection of multiple perspectives in a group of people who are ordinary users in relation to PMDs, but have years of experience in conducting user-centered design and research. As a result, the focus group was coupled with a design workshop, allowing the participants to create simple paper prototypes from the generated ideas.

The focus group was conducted over approximately 2 h and included 7 participants. All participants were master students associated with the Department of Informatics at the University, and 5 of them were students of the Design, Use, Interaction program with years of experience in fields such as HCI, UCD and UX. The focus group did not have a structured set of questions, but instead used the survey results to fuel the discussion and encourage the participants to discuss if and why they agreed or disagreed with the results, adding a qualitative layer to the survey findings. Following this discussion was a brainstorming stage, where the participants generated ideas based on existing man-powered means of transport. These ideas were then discussed in relation to the survey results, the opinions of the participants, and the balance user interface. The participants formed groups of two or three and created prototypes from the two ideas that were found to be the best match with post-it notes of different colors to represent the added components for motorization; motor, battery, and electronics. Each group then presented their design to the others and explained their thoughts on how the prototype would be controlled. In the weeks following the focus group, the participants were contacted via e-mail to evaluate additional prototype iterations.

3.3   Usability Testing

Drawing on the results from the two previous activities, we continued with the design of a skateboard prototype. The paper prototypes from the workshop were unified and improved though multiple iterations with the help of the participants from the workshop. The resulting prototype was then built as a functional and testable electric skateboard design.

Initial user testing of the design included simulating the balance control with an app on a mobile phone as a formative usability test. The test (N = 14) was conducted inside a long hallway at the department over the course of three days with the purpose of learning how the balance interface should be designed and implemented, as well as getting early feedback on the design. The participants were recruited from the students that were studying in close proximity to the hallway. The prototype gained much attention from bystanders, but many were too afraid to try it themselves and only wanted to watch. The participants were observed while executing a set of basic tasks such as acceleration, maintaining a constant speed, turning and breaking. After the test, they completed a short, one-page form about their thoughts on the design and balance interface. Each test took only about a minute to complete, but many participants wanted to try it for longer. All participants were students at the department (both bachelor and master students), aged between 20 and 31. The simulation of balance was carried out by asking participants to lean forwards to put weight on the front of the board to accelerate. The actual acceleration was accomplished using a slider control on a Bluetooth connected mobile phone controlled by the user.

4   Results

4.1   Results from the Online Survey

Of the 248 respondents, only 15 (6.0 %) reported that they currently own a PMD. The same number of people reported having good prior experience with PMDs, followed by 24.6 % having tried PMDs once or twice, 36.3 % had only seen them in use and 33.1 % had no prior experience. This show that even with few PMD owners, there is a fair share of people who have tried riding a PMD at least once (30.6 %).

There was a significantly higher acceptance for the use of e-bikes than for Segways or electric scooters. Table 2 shows the willingness to use the three vehicles as a daily means of transportation.

Table 2. Distribution of people who could see themselves use a Segway, e-bike or electric scooter daily

PMD	Would use	Would not use	Don't know	Already owns
Segway	13.7 %	78.6 %	7.3 %	0.4 %
E-bike	51.6 %	32.7 %	13.7 %	2.0 %
Electric scooter	19.0 %	69.4 %	10.9 %	0.8 %

Based on the respondents answer in the previous question, they were divided into groups of positive (for answers "would use" and "already owns") or non-positive (for answers "would not use" and "don't know") and asked about which attributes they found the most positive or the most negative for each device type. These questions were not mandatory, so respondents could continue without checking any attributes.

When it comes to the Segway results (Table 3), the participants were particularly unsatisfied with the price, how they are perceived by others, size and weight, and safety. They were most satisfied with ease of use, range and the environmental aspects. Additionally, people who are positive to Segway use, mostly checked the opposite reasons, compared to those asked to list negative attributes. The exception is the ambiguous "Replaces alternative transport" vs. "Prefer alternative transport", which is frequently cited by both groups (see Table 3). The positive reasons given in "Other" were related to the enjoyment and fun of riding the Segway, while negative reasons were mostly related to health and elaborations on how people are perceived.

Table 3. Positive (left) and negative (right) citied attributes of the Segway

Most positive Segway attributes		Most negative Segway attributes	
Ease of use	60.0 %	Price	68.1 %
Replaces alternative transport	57.1 %	How I'm perceived	44.6 %
Range	28.6 %	Prefer alternative transport	38.5 %
Environmental	22.9 %	Size and weight	28.2 %
Speed	20.0 %	Safety	23.9 %
Size and weight	17.1 %	Other	22.5 %
How I'm perceived	14.3 %	Speed	10.3 %
Other	11.4 %	Range	8.0 %
Safety	2.9 %	Ease of use	4.2 %
Price	0.0 %	Environmental	2.8 %

Interestingly, all positive attributes were cited more frequently with the e-bike compared to the Segway, and almost all the negative attributes were cited less frequently. Beyond this, the most notable differences were that "how I'm perceived" was

Table 4. Positive (left) and negative (right) citied attributes of the e-bike

Most positive e-bike attributes		Most negative e-bike attributes	
Replaces alternative transport	70.7 %	Prefer alternative transport	40.9 %
Ease of use	69.9 %	Price	34.8 %
Range	56.4 %	Other	33.0 %
Speed	47.4 %	How I'm perceived	16.5 %
Environmental	41.4 %	Size and weight	15.7 %
Price	28.6 %	Speed	5.2 %
Size and weight	21.1 %	Safety	4.3 %
How I'm perceived	17.3 %	Range	3.5 %
Safety	13.5 %	Environmental	2.6 %
Other	12.0 %	Ease of use	1.7 %

much more rarely cited as a negative attribute, and that "range", "speed", "environmental", and "price" were cited much more frequently as positive e-bike attributes. The full list of e-bike results can be found in Table 4.

When it comes to electric scooters (Table 5), the results show that "size and weight", "ease of use" and "price" were rated the most positively while, "prefer alternative transport", "how I'm perceived" and "safety" were the most negative.

Table 5. Positive (left) and negative (right) citied attributes of the electric scooter

Most positive electric scooter attributes		Most negative electric scooter attributes	
Size and weight	63.3 %	Prefer alternative transport	41.2 %
Ease of use	53.1 %	How I'm perceived	36.2 %
Price	46.9 %	Safety	28.6 %
Replaces alternative transport	38.8 %	Other	19.6 %
Speed	28.6 %	Price	17.6 %
How I'm perceived	20.4 %	Range	13.6 %
Environmental	20.4 %	Size and weight	9.5 %
Other	16.3 %	Ease of use	8.0 %
Range	6.1 %	Speed	5.5 %
Safety	4.1 %	Environmental	0.0 %

4.2 Focus Group and Design Workshop Results

Only one of the participants had personal experience riding a PMD (during a Segway sightseeing tour), but all others were familiar with the concept. In general, all participants were in agreement with the main findings of the survey, stating that the e-bike was the most useful of the three because it operates and looks like a normal bike, and because it doesn't stand out as much as devices with an unique look. One participant said: "The only one I'd use personally would be the e-bike. The Segway looks like it's for obese or lazy people." They also found the e-bike to be the safest option of the three and liked that it can be used even with a depleted battery. "If the battery runs out on a Segway, I'm basically stuck, but if it runs out on an e-bike, it turns into a normal bike". The participants found the Segway category to be clumsy and impractical mostly because of its large size and weight, making it difficult to transport or use in combination with public transit systems, as well as difficulties related to parking. One participant asked, "What am I going to do with it when I go to buy groceries? It's too big to go inside the store, right?" The participants all found the Segway to be better suited in specialized tasks and used for in-doors transport of large buildings like airports, shopping malls, hospitals and schools, and agreed that it "looks way too silly" for normal urban transportation. Regarding electric kick-scooters, the participants were less vocal, but expressed concerns regarding the safety and stability of the vehicle at high speeds. "Is it really stable at high speeds? I don't think I would feel comfortable going 20 km/h on a kick-scooter." Otherwise, they agreed with the results, that the smaller size and weight was a plus, but that an e-bike or normal bike is still a better choice in most situations. They also noted that PMDs in general would probably benefit substantially from better facilitation in the cities, like more dedicated bike roads.

The brainstorming stage resulted in a long list of ideas such as electric skateboards or longboards, rollerblades, roller skis, snow racers, snake boards and more. Out of this list, the participants found the skateboard/longboard and rollerblades concepts to be the best fit for the requirements and chose to continue with these in the paper prototyping stage. The participants formed groups and discussed the optimal location of the various components, represented using post-it notes, as they created the paper prototypes (see Fig. 1). The participants discussed various design concerns as they made decisions, such as initiatives to hide the components as much as possible, keeping the device lightweight and distributing the weight equally on the front and back of the vehicle. Some of the groups also made minor alterations to their designs when they saw what the others had created (Fig. 2).

Fig. 1. Pictures from the focus group (left) and design workshop (right)

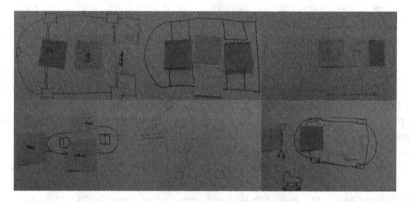

Fig. 2. Paper prototypes of the skateboard (top row) and roller blades (bottom row). Post-it note colors: Orange = motor, yellow = battery, pink = electronics (Color figure online).

4.3   Results from the Usability Test

In spite of several technical difficulties with the prototype during testing, virtually everyone who tried expressed how much fun it was to ride. The participants had mixed previous experience with skateboards and longboards (see Table 6), and those with little experience in particular had difficulties with keeping their balance and turning during their first few seconds on the board. However, they learned quickly and after only a minute you could see a noticeable difference, which was visible as they kept a straighter and more confident posture, showed improved turning ability and willingly increased the driving speed. Several of the participants wanted, on their own initiative, to ride the board back to the starting point after completing the test. Many of the participants also kept riding for longer than necessary, and some actually came back for more after a few minutes because they wanted to try again.

Table 6. Ratings of various attributes from the user test

Rating from 1 (very low) to 7 (very high)	Mean	Median	SD
Previous skateboard/longboard experience	3.29	3	1.94
Overall prototype satisfaction	6.14	6	0.84
Observed amount of leaning forwards and backwards	1.71	2	0.73
Observed ability to turn left and right	4.57	4.5	1.87

During the simulation, the participants were asked to lean forwards on the board to accelerate as if it was their body weight distribution that controlled the speed of the board. The amount of visible lean did not vary substantially between the participants (see Table 6). Some participants hardly showed any visible lean at all, and others leaned only a little bit. Thus, we did not witness large individual differences. The amount of lean on toes and heels (to turn the board) varied slightly more, but could have been related to the participants' previous board experience. Those with more experience leaned from side to side more visibly than those with less experience (Fig. 3).

Fig. 3. Participants standing on the prototype board

Next, the participants were asked how they would prefer the device to tilt elastically as they shifted their balance, between the choices: side-to-side (turning), front-to-back (accelerating/breaking), both or neither. 78.6 % of the participants said they wanted side-to-side tilt only, i.e. elastic when turning and isometric when accelerating and breaking, similar to a traditional longboard. Further, we asked how much weight should be applied on the front of the board before the vehicle starts accelerating. All participants gave values in a range between 60 % and 80 % of body weight (mean = 67.59, SD = 7.76). Finally we asked for suggestions on design improvements, and with the exception of two participants that called for balance as input rather than a simulation, all suggestions were related to various technical issues, mostly motor stuttering at slow speeds due to the use of an underpowered motor in the prototype (Fig. 4).

Fig. 4. Participants riding the prototype board during usability test

4.4 Design Implications

Revising our list of guidelines based on the results from the study, we present a list of design implications for PMDs using balance as input. We summarize these implications in Table 7. Most of the guidelines showed to be useful when designing a balance-based PMD interface. However, implication #1 was found only to be partially true while for implication #2 and #4, our results were inconclusive and further research is required.

Table 7. Design implications for balance-based PMD interfaces

Implications	PMD applicable
1. Elastic interfaces increase user experience over isometric	Partially
2. Leaning from side-to-side requires more effort	Unconfirmed
3. A movement based interface relies on movement-triggers and a social excuse to move	Yes
4. There are large individual differences in which movements feel natural	Unconfirmed
5. The device must be designed around the forms of movement as allowed by the human body	Yes
6. Intuitive and natural interactions relies on appropriate mapping between movement and function	Yes
7. Familiarity increases design acceptance	New
8. The interface should encourage visible body-movements	New

5   Discussion

As we have only simulated balance control, it is too early to draw any conclusions on the usability of the interface itself. Instead, we will evaluate the guidelines according to how well we found them to apply for the design of balance-based PMDs based on our results. When it comes to elastic vs. isometric interfaces (Table 7, implication #1), we found that for this form factor, maintaining the traditional skateboard design with elastic sides for turning and isometric front and back for accelerating and breaking was preferred by the vast majority of the participants. This could indicate that designing for familiarity in an interface is valued more than the added feedback gained from elasticity, and that a traditional skateboard design is preferred over a board with an elastic front and back, such as a self-balancing skateboard. However, this is not necessarily the case with other form factors. Similarly, we observed a lower amount of leaning on each foot (on the front and back of the board) compared to leaning on toes and heels to turn, which could indicate that side-to-side movement requires more effort (implication #2). On the other hand, it is certainly possible that this is simply a result of the participants knowing that any leaning on the front and back foot did not actually produce an effect during simulation. Furthermore, visible leaning is not required for changing ones distribution of balance between the feet, so this should be tested more thoroughly with a fully implemented balance interface.

As our design used an existing vehicle as a base and was kept as close to its original design as possible, users are given the same socio-cultural excuse to move while interacting with it as people riding traditional longboards (implication #3). Longboard riders certainly move while traveling, so these movement-triggers will transfer over to riders of electric boards. We witnessed only small individual differences in movements during the test, so we were unable to verify this implication (implication #4). There could be multiple reasons for this. First, operation of the board did not necessarily encourage large movements, thus it is expected to only see small movements being made by the participants. Had the design encouraged larger movements, the differences between participants may have been more noticeable when some of them were uncomfortable with performing large movements. Additionally, it is probable that people will be performing larger movements as they become more comfortable with the device. The participants only tested the vehicle for a few minutes, and most of them did not have extensive experience with a skateboard or longboard.

The proposed interface is designed to accelerate when the user leans on the front foot. We argue that this interaction is both appropriate and natural (implication #5 and #6) because it is what humans do instinctively to keep their balance when standing on an accelerating platform, thus the movement of the vehicle and user are working together to keep the user balanced and on the board. The opposite (leaning back to accelerate) would likely make the user lose their balance as the accelerating platform and the users balance would both contribute towards pushing the user off the board. Because of this, we consider both implications relevant for designing PMD interfaces.

Adding to the guidelines, we found it necessary to introduce a few additional design implications not covered in the literature. Both in the survey and focus group we found that the acceptance of a PMD would greatly increase if the design and interface was familiar (implication #7). Most people seem to be quite self-conscious when riding a PMD and they prefer to use vehicles that "blend in" in the urban landscape. We also found that devices where the rider has a static posture were perceived very negatively (implication #8). We would therefore encourage designers of future PMDs to take this into consideration and design interfaces that encourage some form of body movement. Whether this stems from a need for improved health or mere esthetics remains a question.

6 Conclusion

In this paper, we have presented a set of guidelines based on related work for the design of balance-based PMD interfaces. Using a survey, focus group, design workshop and usability test, we designed and tested a PMD prototype to evaluate our guidelines. Based on our results, we have verified and extended the guidelines to a list of design implications for PMDs with balance-based user interfaces. We found that most of the guidelines were applicable in our context. Additionally, we found that design and interface familiarity is essential for the acceptance and willingness to use a PMD, and that the interface should encourage visible body-movements in the interaction. As we have only simulated the interface in our tests, future work should further investigate these implications with a fully implemented balance interface.

References

1. Ståhjuling-salget gikk i stå: http://www.vg.no/forbruker/bil-baat-og-motor/bil-og-trafikk/staahjuling-salget-gikk-i-staa/a/23294798/. Accessed: 17 October 2014
2. Fikkert, W., Hoeijmakers, N., van der Vet, P., Nijholt, A.: Navigating a maze with balance board and wiimote. In: Nijholt, A., Reidsma, D., Hondorp, H. (eds.) INTETAIN 2009. LNICST, vol. 9, pp. 187–192. Springer, Heidelberg (2009)
3. Wang, J., Lindeman, R.W.: Comparing isometric and elastic surfboard interfaces for leaning-based travel in 3D virtual environments. In: 2012 IEEE Symposium on 3D User Interfaces (3DUI), pp. 31–38 (2012)
4. de Haan, G., Griffith, E.J., Post, F.H.: Using the Wii balance board as a low-cost VR interaction device. In: Proceedings of the ACM Symposium on Virtual Reality Software and Technology – VRST 2008, p. 289 (2008)
5. Moen, J.: From hand-held to body-worn: embodied experiences of the design and use of a wearable movement-based interaction concept. In: Proceedings of the 1st International Conference on Tangible and Embedded Interaction, pp. 251–258 (2007)
6. Larssen, A.T., Loke, L., Robertson, T., Edwards, J.: Understanding movement as input for interaction–A study of two Eyetoy™ games. In: Proceedings of OzCHI, vol. 4 (2004)
7. Benford, S., Schnadelbach, H., Koleva, B., Gaver, B., Schmidt, A., Boucher, A., Steed, A., Anastasi, R., Greenhalgh, C., Rodden, T., Gellersen, H.: Sensible, sensable and desirable: a framework for designing physical interfaces (2003)

8. Bellotti, V., Back, M., Edwards, W.K., Grinter, R.E., Henderson, A., Lopes, C.: Making sense of sensing systems: five questions for designers and researchers. In: Proceedings of the SIGCHI Conference on Human Factors in Computing Systems Changing our world, Changing Ourselves CHI 2002, vol. 1, pp. 415–422 (2002)

9. Blake, J.: The natural user interface revolution. In: Natural User Interfaces in .NET, 15th edn., pp. 2–43. Manning Publications (2010)

10. Morgan, D.L.: Focus groups. Annu. Rev. Sociol. **22**, 129–152 (1996)

Stage of Subconscious Interaction for Forming Communication Relationship

Takafumi Sakamoto$^{(\boxtimes)}$ and Yugo Takeuchi

Graduate School of Science and Technology, Shizuoka University, Shizuoka, Japan
dgs14010@s.inf.shizuoka.ac.jp, takeuchi@inf.shizuoka.ac.jp

Abstract. We assume that subconscious interaction is carried out to make possible the forming of a communication relationship with the object. To model this stage of interaction, two experiments were carried out. We created an experimental environment to observe the interaction between a human and a robot whose behavior was actually mapped by another human. In experiment 1, interaction with an unknown robot and a known robot were compared. As a result, the interaction property for each condition was confirmed. This result suggests that a stage of subconscious interaction does exist for recognition of artifacts as interaction partners. In experiment 2, we explore the relation between physical interaction and cognitive states by the think-aloud method. Behavioral data was analyzed by a Bayesian network (BN). As a result, it is obvious that BN structure relates to speaking data. This indicates that it is likely to model the process of subconscious interaction.

1 Introduction

It is expected that artifacts, such as robots, will increasingly be developed to cooperate with us and assume social roles in human society. While we can communicate with strangers because we know that other people possess the intellectual ability to form a relationship with us, it is difficult to communicate with an unknown artifact because it is unknown whether it can communicate with us or how it will behave. As humans, we recognize an agency depending on actual interaction. For example, we do not regard others who we pass in a crowd as communication partners, yet we often treat computers as agents [1]. It is necessary to clarify how people attribute agency status to an object through interaction. Humans can perceive the properties of an object or agent, such as its animacy and intention, by observing a moving geometric Figs. [2–4]. It has been previously shown that humans can recognize animacy and intention through interaction with an abstract shape robot [5]. These researches indicate that only actual behavior during the interaction can encourage the development of communication relationships between humans and artifacts. However, the experiments for almost all previous studies involved interaction between participants and objects beforehand through the experimental task. In real situations, people must first realize that the artifacts are capable of interacting with them and react to their actions in the early stages of the interaction. We hypothesize that this process is

© Springer International Publishing Switzerland 2015
M. Kurosu (Ed.): Human-Computer Interaction, Part II, HCII 2015, LNCS 9170, pp. 376–384, 2015.
DOI: 10.1007/978-3-319-20916-6_35

carried out subconsciously and that, after this process, the interaction shifts to the stage of conscious interaction in order to create a relationship. We define this subconscious process as the "stage of subconscious interaction". Assuming that this process exists, we conducted an experiment in which participants interact with an unknown entity.

2 Stage of Subconscious Interaction

In human communication, we can immediately recognize a partner as human. The human brain possesses an area that is specifically designed to detect the human body [6,7]. In addition, as can be seen from the phenomenon called "biological motion" [8], we have a specific perception for recognizing human body movement. On the basis of these abilities, other people are regarded as agents with which we can communicate. On the other hand, artifacts must have a physical appearance that can be recognized as an agency or, through interaction, encourage humans to perceive them as such. We focus on interaction, rather than physical appearance, because it can be used to design the form of an artifact. In previous research on interaction with artifacts, participant behavior based on the premise that the participants and artifacts can interact has been observed. However, in real situations, people must first realize that the artifacts are capable of interacting with them and react to their actions in the early stages of the interaction (Fig. 1). We hypothesize that this process is carried out subconsciously and that, after this process, the interaction shifts to the stage of conscious interaction in order to create a relationship. We define this subconscious process as the "stage of subconscious interaction" and attempt to clarify it. Until recently, many studies on interaction have used upper limb motion. Entire body movements, such as gait, differ from upper limb action [9]. While walking, humans unconsciously adjust direction and automatically avoid obstacles underfoot. Therefore, unconscious motions occur at a higher frequency than interaction using only the upper limbs. By using an abstractly shaped robot whose function is only moving a flower, we can observe lower-limb-driven interaction.

3 Experiment 1

3.1 Method

As shown in Fig. 2, we used two rooms as the experimental environment. Both rooms were constructed with similar appliances. The positions of the participants were mirrored by the robots. That is, the position of the robot located in one room mirrored the position of the participant in the other room. In this way, each participant was able to interact with the other participant without recognition of each other (Fig. 3). We used a Roomba vacuum robot controlled via Bluetooth. An encoder of the tires measured the robot's position. The participant's position was measured with a laser rangefinder. We assigned 10 pairs

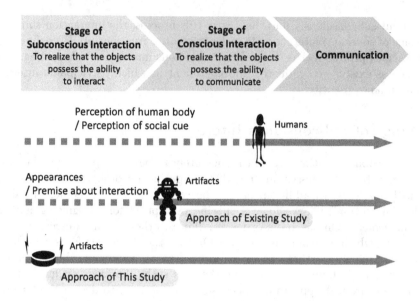

Fig. 1. Stage of subconscious interaction

(20 university students) to the unknown condition and the known condition. All participants were instructed to move freely within a three-meter square field. In the unknown condition, the participants were not told about the robot's behavior. The pair participant assigned to the known condition group was instructed, "The robot moves as an entity that you want to relate to." Their partner was told, "The robot moves as an entity that you want not to relate to." Every participant was left alone in the room, and the interaction between the participants and the robot was observed for three minutes. The participants then responded to questionnaires.

3.2   Results and Considerations

Figure 4 shows the result of the time rate of interaction in which both participants and robot ambulate at the same time. Under the known condition, the participants interact with the robot through the entire experiment time. On the other hand, interaction under the unknown condition is difficult to continue. In the case where an interaction was carried out continuously, the distance under the known condition changed more frequently than the distance under the unknown condition. These results show that the interaction pattern with an interaction partner that is a known entity differs from the interaction pattern with an unknown entity. It is easy for an interaction with unknown entities to become deadlocked. This points to the importance of the primary stage of the interaction between humans and artifacts. In this experiment, it is difficult to identify the point when the unknown condition participants realize that the robot can interact with them. To find that point, we carried out an experiment using a think-aloud method and try to clarify the relation between behavior and cognitive states.

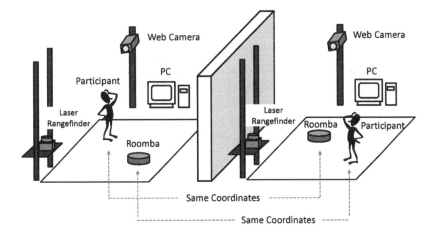

Fig. 2. Experimental setup

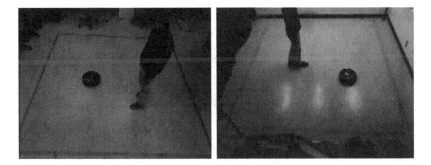

Fig. 3. An interaction scene

4 Experiment 2

4.1 Method

Apparatus. As shown in Fig. 5, we used two rooms as the experimental environment. Both rooms were constructed with similar appliances. The participants' movement was restricted within a circle three meters in diameter. The positions of the participants were mirrored by the robots. The position of the robot located in one room mirrored the position of the participant in the other room. In this way, each participant was able to interact with the other participant without recognition of each other. We used a Roomba controlled via Bluetooth. An encoder of the tires measured the robot's position. In addition, the robot's position was adjusted using a video camera. The participant's position was measured with a laser rangefinder. The participants put on a headset and audio recorder for recording their thinking aloud during interaction. In this way, we tried to specify how participants regarded robot behavior (action or reaction), and why participants moved.

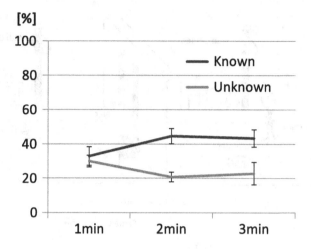

Fig. 4. Interaction rate

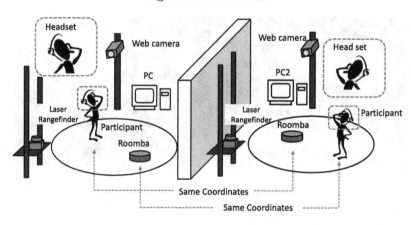

Fig. 5. Experimental setup

Participants and Experimental Task. Nine pairs (18 university students) participated in this experiment. The participant pairs were guided into the rooms separately without knowledge of their partners. The participants were required to say whatever they were thinking or feeling. To practice thinking aloud, participants performed the tangram for five minutes before an interaction. After the practice, the participants were instructed to move freely within the interaction field while thinking aloud. The contents of speech were recorded by voice recorder through a headset participants wore. The participants were not provided information about the robot's behavior. The participants were left alone in the room, and interaction between the participants and robot was observed for three minutes. The participants then responded to questionnaires.

4.2   Observed Data

We observed and analyzed the following data:

- Behavioral data
  - Log data of participant position (every 125 ms)
  - Log data of robot position (every 125 ms)
  - Interaction video
- Speaking data
- Questionnaires
  - Free descriptions about behavior of participant and robot.

4.3   Results and Considerations

We assume that humans often realize that a partner has the ability of forming a relationship with them through unconscious interaction. Thus, physical interaction seems to cause recognition of others who have the possibility of carrying out interpersonal interaction. By analyzing behavioral and speaking data, we try to model the relation between awareness of agency and physical interaction. With the think-aloud method, we can investigate participants' recognition of the behavior of the robot. We took dictation of the participants, and labeled these data. By focusing on speaking about robot behavior such as, "It's moving.", "It stopped." or "The robot is coming here.", and about themselves such as "I will stay here.", "I keep my distance." or "I will approach it.", the relation between speaking and behavioral data was explored. On labeling speaking about robot behavior, robot action and robot movement are distinguished. Speaking about robot behavior for participants, such as approaching or departing, is labeled as robot action, and speaking about robot behavior, such as moving or stopping, is labeled as robot movement. The physical interaction is analyzed using a Bayesian network (BN) because it can express the causal relationship between some parameters.

The participants' main actions were to approach the robot or to stand away from it. The participants' actions seem to be decided based on distance from the robot, previous participants' actions and previous robot actions. Therefore, the following values are used as parameters of the physical interaction.

$Dist$: distance between participant and robot
$\Delta Dist$: $Dist$ change from previous frame
V_P: perpendicular ingredient to robot position of participant's velocity
V_R: perpendicular ingredient to participant's position of robot's velocity
V_P^+: V_P of next frame
V_R^+: V_R of next frame.

However, the following limits were given beforehand:

- V_P^+ and V_R^+ do not become parents
- $Dist$ does not become parent of $\Delta Dist$.
- V_P and V_R do not have any parents.

Table 1. Relationship between arcs from $Dist$ and Speaking

From $Dist$	To V_P^+		To V_R^+	
	Connected	Unconnected	Connected	Unconnected
Robot Action	15(12.2)	50(52.8)	14(8.10)	51(56.9)
Robot Motion	12(14.8)	67(64.2)	8(9.84)	71(69.2)
Self Action	10(9.55)	41(41.5)	4(6.35)	47(44.6)
Other	145(139)	600(606)	87(92.8)	658(652)
(No Speaking)	374(380)	1656(1650)	257(253)	1773(1777)
$\chi^2(4, N = 2970)$	1.87 (n.s.)		6.80 (n.s.)	

observed frequency(expected frequency),*:$p < .05$, **:$p < .01$

Table 2. Relationship between arcs from $\Delta Dist$ and Speaking

From $\Delta Dist$	To $Dist$		To V_P^+		To V_R^+	
	C	UC	C	UC	C	UC
Robot Action	2(2.52)	63(62.5)	32(17.2)**	33(47.8)**	18(6.65)**	47(58.3)**
Robot Motion	5(3.06)	74(75.9)	25(21.0)	54(58.0)	1(8.09)**	78(70.9)**
Self Action	3(1.97)	48(49.0)	24(13.5)**	27(37.5)**	8(5.22)	43(45.8)
Other	21(28.8)	724(716)	194(198)	551(547)	55(76.3)**	690(669)**
(No Speaking)	84(78.6)	1946(1951)	513(539)*	1517(1491)*	222(208)	1808(1822)
$\chi^2(4, N = 2970)$	4.55 (insufficient)		31.0**		37.8**	

observed frequency(expected frequency),*:$p < .05$, **:$p < .01$

Table 3. Relationship between arcs from V_P and Speaking

	To $Dist$		To $\Delta Dist$		To V_R^+	
Robot Action	13(6.72)**	52(58.3)**	64(57.7)*	1(7.29)*	11(2.49)	54(62.5)
Robot Motion	10(8.17)	69(70.8)	65(70.1)	14(8.86)	0(3.033)	79(76.0)
Self Action	5(5.27)	46(45.7)	47(45.3)	4(5.72)	3(1.96)	48(49.0)
Other	64(77.0)	681(668)	707(661)**	38(83.5)**	19(28.6)	726(716)
(No Speaking)	215(210)	1815(1820)	1754(1802)**	276(228)**	81(77.9)	1949(1952)
$\chi^2(4, N = 2970)$	9.62*		49.6**		37.4(insufficient)	

observed frequency(expected frequency),*:$p < .05$, **:$p < .01$

BN structure was learned every second from behavioral data. Each data consists of 120 frames (15 sec of data). These data were treated as a continuous value. Each arc of learned BN and speaking labels every second were accumulated, and a chi-square test was carried out.

Tables 1–4 show the result of the chi-square test between arcs and speaking label frequency. Significant relationships were found to exist between arcs from $\Delta Dist$ and speaking label. By residual analysis, when the arc from $\Delta Dist$ to V_P^+ exists, speaking about robot action and self action is increased. Also, when the arc from $\Delta Dist$ to V_R^+ exists, labeling of robot action increases. A significant

Table 4. Relationship between arcs from V_R and Speaking

From V_R	To *Dist*		To *ΔDist*		To V_P^+	
	C	UC	C	UC	C	UC
Robot Motion	9(11.0)	70(68.0)	67(70.8)	12(8.25)	4(8.86)	75(70.1)
Self Action	5(7.13)	46(43.9)	38(45.7)**	13(5.32)**	4(5.72)	47(45.3)
Other	102(104)	643(641)	663(667)	82(77.8)	77(83.4)	668(661)
(No Speaking)	281(284)	1749(1746)	1829(1818)	201(212)	227(228)	1803(1802)
$\chi^2(4, N = 2970)$	11.4*		18.9**		33.2**	

observed frequency(expected frequency),*:$p < .05$, **:$p < .01$

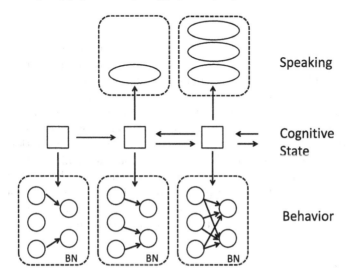

Fig. 6. Conception of modeling subconscious interaction

relationship was found to exist between the arc from V_R and speaking label. By the residual analysis, when the arcs from V_R direct to *Dist*, *ΔDist* or V_P^+, speaking labeled as robot action increases. The relationship between arcs from V_P to *Dist*Dist indicate the same result as V_R, but the relationship to *ΔDist* and V_R^+ is not obvious because some expected frequencies are less than 5. At this stage, the analysis is a restricted relation of single arc existence because of insufficient data.

5 Discussions

In this study, we aim to model the primary stage of interaction that a person undergoes in realizing that a robot has the ability to form a communicative relationship. As a first step, it is important to clarify the relationship between physical interaction and cognitive state. In this experiment, we try to model the physical interaction by Bayesian network and to explore the cognitive state by the think-aloud method. As a result, some arcs' existence relates to the speaking data. Because of the relation between arcs from V_R and speaking data, the existence of arcs from robot proximity to distance or participants seems to reflect robot action or reaction. This learning BN structure seems to be able to express the process of awareness that the partner has the ability to interact. Figure 6 shows the conception of modeling subconscious interaction. However, the effects of arcs' combination were not investigated because of insufficient data. Also, labeling of speaking data should be classified in a more detailed manner to model the process. A further experiment will be necessary to solve these problems.

6   Conclusion

To extract the subconscious interaction, we observed interactions with known and unknown robots whose positions were mapped by other participants. The participants under the unknown condition interacted more infrequently, and the interaction was more easily inhibited than for the known condition group. These results suggest that a stage of subconscious interaction exists for regarding objects as interaction partners. To model this interaction, another experiment was carried out. In this experiment, we tried to clarify the relation between behavioral and cognitive state by the think-aloud method. As a result, the learned Bayesian network structure based on behavioral data relates to the speaking data. By modeling the process, artifacts that are able to form relationships with humans will be designed, thus contributing to the promotion of communication and interaction between humans and robots.

References

1. Reeves, B., Nass, C.: The Media Equation. Cambridge University Press (1996)
2. Heider, F., Simmel, M.: An experimental study of apparent behavior. Am. J. Psychol. **57**, 67–70 (1944)
3. Tremoulet, P.D., Feldman, J.: Perception of animacy from the motion of a single object. Percept. **29**, 943–951 (2000)
4. Stosic, M., Brass, M., Hoeck, V.N., Ma, N., Overwalle, V.F.: Brain activation related to the perception of minimal agency cues: the role of the mirror system. NeuroImage **86**, 364–369 (2014)
5. Fukuda, H., Ueda, K.: Interaction with a moving object affects onefs perception of its animacy. Int. J. Soc. Robot. **2**, 187–193 (2010)
6. Downing, P.E., Jiang, Y., Shuman, M., Kanwisher, N.: A cortical area selective for visual processing of the human body. Sci. **293**, 2470–2473 (2001)
7. Kanwisher, N., McDermott, J., Chun, M.M.: The fusiform face area: a module in human extrastriate cortex specialized for face perception. J. Neurosci. **17**, 4302–4311 (1997)
8. Johansson, G.: Visual perception of biological motion and a model for its analysis. Percept. Psychophysics **14**, 201–221 (1973)
9. Kannape, O., Blanke, O.: Agency, gait and self-consciousness. Int. J. Psychophysiol. **83**, 191–199 (2012)

Interactive Sonification Markup Language (ISML) for Efficient Motion-Sound Mappings

James Walker, Michael T. Smith, and Myounghoon Jeon$^{(\boxtimes)}$

Mind Music Machine Lab, Michigan Technological University,
Houghton, MI, USA
{jwwalker,mtsmith,mjeon}@mtu.edu

Abstract. Despite rapid growth of research on auditory display and sonification mapping per se, there has been little effort on efficiency or accessibility of the mapping process. In order to expedite variations on sonification research configurations, we have developed the Interactive Sonification Markup Language (ISML). ISML is designed within the context of the Immersive Interactive Sonification Platform (iISoP) at Michigan Technological University. We present an overview of the system, the motivation for developing ISML, and the time savings realized through its development. We then discuss the features of ISML and its accompanying graphical editor, and conclude by summarizing the system's feature development and future plans for its further enhancement. ISML is expected to decrease repetitive development tasks for multiple research studies and to increase accessibility to diverse sonification researchers who do not have programming experience.

Keywords: Design research · Interactive sonification · Sonification markup language

1 Introduction

The primary aim of this paper is to describe the implementation and applications of a scripting language, Interactive Sonification Markup Language (ISML), designed for expediting the creation of different parameters and specifications for interactive sonification [1] research. Sonification [2] and specifically interactive sonification is multidisciplinary by nature, including computer science, psychology, HCI, acoustics, music, and sound design, etc. We hope to promote greater efficiency in implementing experimental parameters by demonstrating a method for allowing sonification researchers, even those with no programming experience, to efficiently alter the software specifications of an interactive sonification research platform.

To this end, ISML needs to be flexible enough to support a wide variety of experimental setups, yet simple enough to be easily produced and parsed. Thus, once the initial language specification was complete, our work focused on creating a graphical user interface (GUI) that could facilitate the creation of ISML scripts by non-programmers. Given that auditory display and sonification community has grown, this type of effort [e.g., Auditory Menu Library for auditory menu research, [3]] is expected to increase efficiency and accessibility to sonification research.

© Springer International Publishing Switzerland 2015
M. Kurosu (Ed.): Human-Computer Interaction, Part II, HCII 2015, LNCS 9170, pp. 385–394, 2015.
DOI: 10.1007/978-3-319-20916-6_36

The present paper briefly describes our sonification research platform that gave rise to ISML, the motivation for the development of ISML, the effectiveness of ISML in actual research, and the language features and GUI. Finally, limitations of the current system and potential expansions and improvements are discussed. A description of the ISML specification is then given in the appendix.

2   Background and Motivation

Interactive sonification research has various applications, such as enhancing learning effects and overall user experience. For example, research [4–6] suggests that a combination of physical interaction with sonified feedback improves users' learning. Other studies [7–9] have shown that interactive sonification can also provide users with a more enjoyable experience and improve accessibility to more diverse audiences.

To conduct active interactive sonification research on those multiple applications, we have developed the Immersive Interactive Sonification Platform (iISoP) [10], which generates sounds based on users' motion – location, movements, and gestures – tracking. We have built the iISoP system using the JFugue Library (i.e., Java API for Music Programming, www.jfugue.org). iISoP leverages the university's Immersive Visualization Studio (IVS), which consists of 24 42″ monitors connected to a computing cluster of 8 machines with high-end graphics cards for display, along with a Vicon tracking system composed of 12 infrared cameras for tracking objects inside the lab. In constructing iISoP, we have developed phased projects – interactive map, virtual instrument, and dance-based sonification as a testbed [see [10], more details].

The third phase of iISoP uses parameter mapping [11] to map data features—in this case, users' physical location, movements, and gestures—into sound. This is accomplished through the following process. Users (dancers, performing artists, kids, and robots) wear special reflective markers and thus, their movements can be tracked by the Vicon system, which relays the users' positional data to the head node on the IVS cluster. There, this information is parsed to generate an abstract visualization of the users' movements on the wall of monitors. The data is simultaneously forwarded to another computer running a program which parses the positional data to dynamically generate sounds or improvise real-time music in response to the users' movements.

However, if the method the audio parser uses for generating sound were fixed, this would limit the usefulness of the platform. Therefore, the motion-to-sound mapping should be configurable, so as to facilitate various kinds of research and experiments. Because many of the researchers (psychologists, sound designers, performing artists, etc.) using iISoP may lack programming experience, expecting them to configure the system by altering the source code by hand would be an unreasonable expectation.

ISML was developed to bridge this gap between the non-technical researchers and the research platform. ISML is a simple scripting language for configuring iISoP's motion-to-sound mapping. To make generating these scripts even easier, ISML includes a web-based GUI so that researchers can create a script simply by responding to prompts, rather than needing to learn ISML's syntax and semantics. This method of configuring the mappings is far more efficient and accessible to non-technical

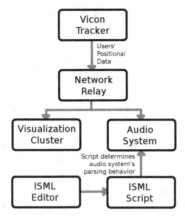

Fig. 1. ISML's role in the iISoP system

researchers than attempting to reprogram the system for every new experiment. Figure 1 illustrates ISML's role in the iISoP system.

The format of ISML's syntax is loosely inspired by markup languages, a system for annotating documents so that the annotations are distinguishable from the actual content [12]. Two major markup language standards are Standard Generalized Markup Language (SGML) and Extensible Markup Language (XML), the latter of which is a simplified version of the former designed to maintain its most useful aspects [13, 14]. While markup files are typically "documents" of various kinds, they can also represent arbitrary data structures [15]. ISML files, which can be thought of as an activity flowchart or state machine defining application behavior in response to external inputs, are more similar to the latter. Note that ISML is only inspired by these standards and does not make any attempt to conform to them.

ISML also bears similarity to scripting languages, since it is designed to automate the behavior of iISoP's sound generation application. Specifically, it is an example of an audio synthesis scripting language. Other languages of this type exist. A non-exhaustive list of examples includes the ChucK audio programming language [16], the C-based audio programming language Csound [17], the commercial Reaktor software, and the MPEG-4 Structured Audio standard [18]. Some of these systems use graphical interfaces for their scripting languages, while others are textual. Additionally, some of them support live coding, the ability to change the program's behavior while it is running.

By comparison, ISML scripts can be created in a graphical or textural manner. The present version of ISML does not support live coding. To the authors' knowledge, ISML is the only scripting language specifically designed to translate physical movements into dynamically generated sound, which makes it very different from other audio scripting languages.

3   Cost Efficiency: Programmer Time and Effort

Based on our own experience developing the system (two CS/ECE Ph.D. graduates and one CS undergraduate), creating a complete iISoP specification by programming it from scratch takes about 50 h for an experienced programmer. Reusing a preexisting specification in the creation of a new one would likely cut that time to about 20–40 %, or 10–20 h. Conversely, creating an equivalent specification for a research study using ISML takes about 5 h from scratch, or 1–2 h if reusing an existing specification, and has the added advantage of not requiring extensive training in programming. Getting ISML fully operational requires an initial time investment of approximately 70 h. Taking all of this into account, Table 1 compares the total specification development times of each approach, demonstrating that the time savings of using ISML as opposed to creating new specifications for different research studies with hard coding from scratch rapidly accumulate. It seems that the development cost of ISML "pays for itself" after approximately 3–4 specifications.

4   System Description

4.1   Overview

The iISoP system dynamically changes sound output via the following procedure. First, the system checks to see whether a set of conditions has been met; for example, "The user is currently moving at a speed equal to or greater than 1 meter per second". If these conditions are met, the system executes one or more actions; for example, "Change the key signature to C-major and the time signature to 4/4". Conditions are optional: It is allowed to specify a set of actions that is executed all the time, without any conditions being met.

Each set of conditions and actions is organized into an activity. Activities serve as a mechanism for grouping conditions and actions together. By having multiple activities, it is possible to have different sets of conditions and actions which can be checked and executed. Within an activity, all of the conditions must be satisfied in order for the actions to be executed; outside of that activity, its conditions do not matter.

Thus, considered collectively, activities and their conditions form a disjunction of conjunctions.

Table 1. Comparison of spec development times with and without ISML

Specifications	Hours (code)	Hours (ISML)	Total (code)	Total (ISML)
1	50	75	50	75
2	10–20	1–2	60–70	76–77
3	10–20	1–2	70–90	77–79
4	10–20	1–2	80–110	78–81
5	10–20	1–2	90–130	79–83

Lastly, activities are organized into *items*. Items provide a scoping mechanism for variables. ISML has 26 variables (a–z) available for use. However, each variable exists independently within the item in which it is used; that is, each variable has item scope. Within each item, all of that item's activities are executed in sequential order from top to bottom. Each item, and all of its activities, are executed (all conditions are checked and the corresponding actions are executed) every cycle of the system. There is no limit on the number of items an ISML script may contain.

The current version of ISML allows for two basic types of conditions: *object* and *comparison*. An *object* condition applies only to an object in the Vicon tracking system that possesses the user-specified name; for example, "left_foot". A *comparison* condition compares whether two values are equal to, greater than, or less than each other. Values that can be compared include constants, variables, current beats per minute, current velocity (in any of the X, Y, or Z axes, or the composite velocity on all three axes), average velocity, acceleration, proximity (the average distance between all tracked objects), current position, and elapsed time (which may be repeatable for conditions that are checked at regular intervals).

Additionally, the current version of ISML allows for the following types of actions:

- Assignment. Sets one value equal to an expression. An expression may be another value, or two other values with some arithmetic operation applied on them (e.g., a = b*c).
- Set the key signature.
- Set the time signature.
- Set the instruments being used.
- Play a specific sequence of notes.

4.2   Graphical Editor

Since ISML is designed to be usable by non-programmers, it includes a GUI for the creation of scripts via prompts. The GUI is written entirely in Javascript, so it can be run in a Web browser; and because it does not use any server-side code, it can be run from any computer.

The GUI's appearance is shown in Fig. 2. Upon startup, the user is presented with a blank script and can either access a comprehensive help guide, load an existing script, or begin creating a new script by clicking the "Add Item" button. From here, the GUI dynamically generates additional buttons for adding and deleting the various components of the script under development. To prevent mishaps, selecting a checkbox is required before deleting script components.

To aid user comprehension, each component of the GUI is indented and color-coded so that distinguishing different activities, condition sets, and so on, is more intuitive. Additionally, a "mapping summary" is generated on the side of the screen which summarizes the motion-to-sound mapping that has been created so far. These features help lighten the cognitive burden on the user by keeping the visual representation of the script organized.

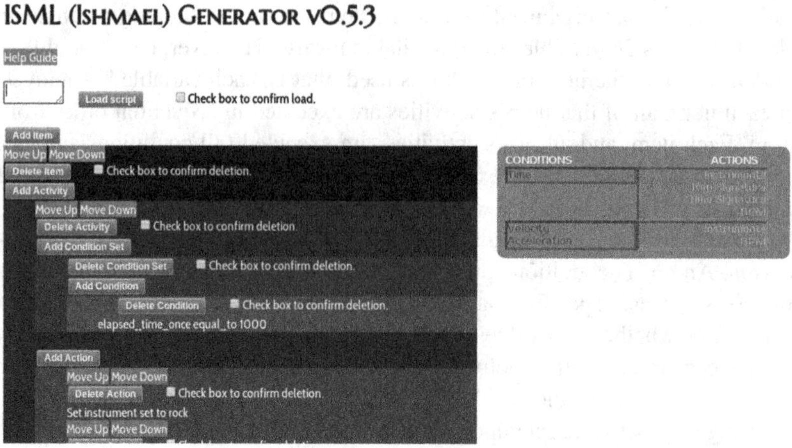

ISML (Ishmael) Generator vO.5.3

Fig. 2. Screen capture of the ISML graphical editor (Color figure online)

Once editing is complete, the user can download the valid ISML-formatted file by clicking the "Download ISML File" button. This file can be further tweaked by hand if desired, or loaded back into the GUI editor at any time for later revision.

4.3   Feature Development

The ISML specification and accompanying editor have gone through several small revisions. After initial development, the specification was changed from infix to prefix notation for easier parsing, and semantic error prevention was added to the GUI editor. Various other tweaks were applied to the specification to simplify parsing, and then the "mapping summary window" (Fig. 2, right side) feature was added. Finally, the color scheme was changed to be more visually pleasing. Both the ISML specification and the editor are in a fluid state and will undergo iterative development cycles with end users.

5   Discussion and Future Work

Faste and Faste [19] proposed four categories of design research. With ISML, we have seized on two of those categories: "research on design" by investigating our research process for possible enhancements; and "design of research" by planning and preparing for future research on the system. From our experience, the ability to rapidly generate new sonification configurations has already shown benefits, and the time savings will continue to accumulate as more research is conducted with the system. This approach will decrease repetitive development tasks for various experiments and increase accessibility to researchers from various disciplines, who do not necessarily have programming experience.

In the future, we intend to strengthen our claims of ISML's effectiveness with an empirical study and to continue developing ISML to improve its efficacy; for example, by adding features for volume control, panning, and audio filters. Additionally, the current version of ISML only supports the configuration of audio. In the future, we plan to add the ability to configure the visualization parameters and emotional parameters through ISML as well.

Appendix: ISML Language Format

ISML uses a format that encloses sections between tags, with the closing tag indicated by a slash (e.g., <tag> and </tag>). ISML supports the following tags:

```
<item></item>
<activity></activity>
<if><or><then></if>
```

Everything within a single item should be contained between <item> and </item> tags. The execution order of items is not defined; thus, items should be written to be independent of one another. Everything within an activity is contained between corresponding <activity> and </activity> tags. All activities within an item are checked and executed in sequential order. The content of each activity is in the following form:

```
<if>
condition_a1
condition_a2
...
<or>
condition_b1
condition_b2
<or>
...
<then>
action_1
action_2
...
</if>
```

Or alternatively, simply:

```
action_1
action_2
...
```

A condition set is defined as all the conditions contained between two tags. Any of the following forms are possible:

```
<if>
conditions
<or>

<or>
conditions
<or>

<if>
conditions
<then>

<or>
conditions
<then>
```

Conditions may have either of the following 2 forms:

```
object name_of_object
comparator value_1 value_2
```

Note that, for ease of parsing, ISML uses prefix rather than infix notation. Valid comparator tokens include:

```
equal_to not_equal_to greater_than less_than
```

Values may be any valid number, a variable name (a-z), or any token from the following list:

```
cur_velocity_x cur_velocity_y cur_velocity_z cur_velocity_composite
avg_velocity_x avg_velocity_y avg_velocity_z avg_velocity_composite
acceleration_x acceleration_y acceleration_z acceleration_composite
avg_proximity x_position y_position z_position elapsed_time_once
elapsed_time_repeatable bpm
```

Actions may have any of the following forms:
```
assignment
set key signature
set time signature
set instruments
play notes
```

Set key signature is denoted by any token from the following list:

```
c_major g_major d_major a_major e_major b_major fsharp_major csharp_major
a_minor e_minor b_minor fsharp_minor csharp_minor gsharp_minor dsharp_minor
asharp_minor
```

Set time signature is denoted by any token from the following list:

```
1/2 2/2 3/2 4/2 2/4 3/4 4/4 2/8 3/8 4/8 6/8 8/8
```

Set instruments is denoted by any token from the following list, which is slated for future expansion:

```
electronica rock orchestral
```

Assignments take the following form:

```
= value_1 operator value_2 value_3
```

The third value is optional. In the case of simply transferring one value to another, assign is used as the operator; e.g.,

```
= a assign cur_velocity_x
```

Values 2 and 3 may be any valid number, a variable name (a-z), or any token from the token list for conditions (cur_velocity_x and so on). Value 1 may only be a variable or bpm because it does not make sense to assign to other kinds of properties, such as velocity, which are read-only.

Valid operators include:

```
+ - * / % ^ abs
```

"Play notes" has the following form:
```
play_notes:note_list
```

References

1. Hermann, T., Hunt, A.: The discipline of interactive sonification. In: Proceedings of the International Workshop on Interactive Sonification (ISon), Bielefeld, Germany (2004)
2. Kramer, G., et al.: The sonification report: status of the field and research agenda. Report prepared for the National Science Foundation by Members of the International Community for Auditory Display (ICAD), Santa Fe, NM, USA (1999)
3. Raman, P., Davison, B.K., Jeon, M., Walker, B.N.: Reducing repetitive development tasks in auditory menu displays with the auditory menu library. In: Proceedings of the International Conference on Auditory Display (ICAD), pp. 229–237, Washington, D.C., USA (2010)
4. Antle, A.N., Droumeva, M., Corness, G.: Playing with the sound maker: do embodied metaphors help children learn? In: Proceedings of the International Conference on Interaction Design and Children, pp. 178–185, Chicago, IL, USA (2008)
5. Ferguson, S.: Learning musical instrument skills through interactive sonification. In: Proceedings of the International Conference on New Interfaces for Musical Expression (NIME2015), pp. 384–389 (2006)
6. Howison, M., Trninic, D., Reinholz, D., Abrahamson, D.: The mathematical imagery trainer: from embodied interaction to conceptual learning. In Proceedings of the SIGCHI Conference on Human Factors in Computing Systems (CHI2011), pp. 1989–1998, Vancouver, BC, Canada (2011)
7. Walker, B.N., Godfrey, M.T., Orlosky, J.E., Bruce, C.M., Sanford, J.: Aquarium sonification: Soundscapes for accessible dynamic informal learning environments. In: Proceedings of the International Conference on Auditory Display (ICAD 2006), pp. 238–241, London, UK (2006)
8. Jeon, M., Winton, R.J., Henry, A.G., Oh, S., Bruce, C.M., Walker, B.N.: Designing interactive sonification for live aquarium exhibits. In: Stephanidis, C. (ed.) HCII 2013, Part I. CCIS, vol. 373, pp. 332–336. Springer, Heidelberg (2013)
9. Jeon, M., Winton, R.J., Yim, J.B., Bruce, C.M., Walker, B.N.: Aquarium fugue: interactive sonification for children and visually impaired audience in informal learning environments. In: Proceedings of the 18th International Conference on Auditory Display (ICAD 2012), Atlanta, GA, USA (2012)
10. Jeon, M., Smith, M.T., Walker, J.W., Kuhl, S.A.: Constructing the immersive interactive sonification platform (iISoP). In: Streitz, N., Markopoulos, P. (eds.) DAPI 2014. LNCS, vol. 8530, pp. 337–348. Springer, Heidelberg (2014)
11. Hermann, T.: Taxonomy and definitions for sonification and auditory display. In: Proceedings of the 14th International Conference on Auditory Display (ICAD 2008), Paris, France (2008)
12. Coombs, J.H., Renear, A.H., DeRose, S.J.: Markup systems and the future of scholarly text processing. Commun. ACM 30(11), 933–947 (1987)

13. World Wide Web Consortium: Extensible Markup Language (XML) 1.0 (5th edn.) 2008. Web. 4 Oct 2014
14. Clark, J.: Comparison of SGML and XML. World Wide Web Consortium, 1997. Web. 4 Oct 2014
15. Philip, F.: Extremes of XML. XML London, 15–16 June 2013
16. Wang, G.: The ChucK Audio Programming Language. Dissertation, Princeton University, Princeton (2008)
17. Boulanger, R.: The Csound Book. MIT Press, Cambridge (2000)
18. Scheirer, E.D.: The MPEG-4 structured audio standard. In: Proceedings of the 1998 IEEE International Conference on Acoustics, Speech and Signal processing 1998, vol. 6. IEEE (1998)
19. Faste, T., Faste, H.: Demystifying 'design research': design is not research, research is design. IDSA (2012)

Adaptive and Personalized Interfaces

Defining and Optimizing User Interfaces Information Complexity for AI Methods Application in HCI

Maxim Bakaev[(✉)] and Tatiana Avdeenko

Novosibirsk State Technical University, Novosibirsk, Russia
bakaev@corp.nstu.ru, avdeenko@fb.nstu.ru

Abstract. The HCI has understandably become user-centric, but if we are to consider human operator and computer device as even components of a human-computer system and seek to maximize its overall efficacy with AI methods, we would need to optimize information flows between the two. In the paper, we would like to call to the discussion on defining and measuring the information complexity of modern two-dimensional graphic user interfaces. By analogy with Kolmogorov complexity (algorithmic entropy) for computability resources, the interface information complexity could allow estimating the amount of human processor resources required for dealing with interaction task. The analysis of the current results allows concluding that interface "processing" time by humans is indeed affected by the interface message "length" parameter, and, presumably, by vocabulary size. We hope the results could aid in laying ground for broader AI methods application for HCI in the coming era of ubiquitous Big Interaction.

Keywords: Model human processor · Interface design automation · Information complexity · Hick-Hyman's law

1 Introduction

Just as the recent emergence of Big Data field became the result of ongoing exponential growth of available and generated data, soon we may face the phenomenon of Big Interaction. The multiplicity and extensiveness of data sources, the diversity of user needs and tasks, as well as of interface devices and contexts of use, may leave us in a situation when hand-making of all the necessary human-computer interfaces by dedicated designers becomes impossible or economically unfeasible. A possible solution is employment of Artificial Intelligence (AI) methods, which may be able to ensure "good enough" interaction.

Indeed, there were already approaches and even products proposed that are able to automatically generate user interfaces for relatively simple tasks or for special contexts of use. For example, the usage of PUC system dedicated to the creation of standardized interfaces for various home appliances was reported to improve the interaction quality rates 2–4 times [1, p. 185]. In it, the language specially developed for describing interface models was simplified based on peculiarities of the task at hand – as such, it didn't allow specification of users tasks, because home appliances by and large don't

© Springer International Publishing Switzerland 2015
M. Kurosu (Ed.): Human-Computer Interaction, Part II, HCII 2015, LNCS 9170, pp. 397–405, 2015.
DOI: 10.1007/978-3-319-20916-6_37

imply complex multi-operational interaction. The interface code generation was based, in particular, on heuristic rules providing standardization of the interfaces' visual appearances and on ontological system for describing semantic equivalence of concepts used in various appliances descriptions.

Another example is SUPPLE system, used for creating alternative interfaces for users whose needs weren't considered in mainstream interface of a product or device, and for which the average increase in effectiveness of 62 % was reported [2, p. 45]. The authors noted that the system was most suitable for creating standard interfaces based on dialogue windows, because there is well-established taxonomy for them, which describes the possible interaction elements. The interface generation was considered as a discrete optimization problem, while input data were functional description of interface, the model of the platform's capabilities and limitations, the interface usage model, and criterion function incorporating parameterized quality indexes. This function would mostly cover "physical" parameters in interaction, such as movement time between interface elements, or their size. It should be noted that it was also able to consider the usage of interface by a specific user category, e.g. people with motor disabilities.

The above products could be said to belong with the so-called model-oriented approach, when abstract user interface is specified (PUC or SUPPLE), or somehow derived – from existing programming code (such as in Mickey or HUMANOID), from database model (GENIUS) or from high-level user tasks. The actual interface code generation is then based on knowledge-base rules or on optimization of certain interface parameters or expected quality indexes [2, pp. 3, 4]. Yet another representative here is RAS IACP's system that allows to denote design resolutions and to perform automated interface quality validation [3]. The system was also based on ontological approach that implies specification of concepts related to user interfaces, such as user tasks, use cases, information presentation, etc. When the interface model was automatically transformed into code, the interaction quality was insured via usability metrics also existing in the ontology, together with specialized language for specification their calculation algorithms.

All in all, the review of AI methods applicability in the HCI field could be summarized as the following directions, listed in the order of increasing intellectuality:

- Recommendation of design resolutions or providing relevant guidelines/patterns for user interface being created by human designer. Indeed, the so-called tools for working with guidelines are quite widespread, although the relevance issue remains problematic, which hinders their practical use (see reviews and reflections in [4, 5]).
- Validation of available user interface code and identification of errors or disadvantages [3]. Currently, automated validation tools mostly cover syntactical aspect only, and can hardly understand semantics. Some approaches for deeper analysis are proposed, in particular ones based on domain ontologies, but the involved prior effort generally outweighs the automation benefits, similarly to interface code generation mentioned below.
- Interpretation of available user interface code and the adjustment of ensuing interaction to match user needs, characteristics of interface devices, etc. E.g. modern web-browsers in a relatively non-intelligent way can vary webpage presentation due to many factors, mitigate code errors, etc.

- Designing user interface and generating its code based on provided specification [1, 2]. However, detailed specification of user interface using a formal language or as an interaction model becomes too extensive as the complexity of interaction increases, and the effort required to spell it out quite soon exceeds the one needed for making an actual user interface.
- Creating specification for the user interface based on "understanding" of full interaction context and the functions of the involved software, predicting user needs, etc. [6]. It seems a promising and possibly feasible approach for the Big Interaction era, although the results are likely going to remain somehow close to interface wireframes and be aesthetically inferior compared to "hand-made" solutions.

It should be noted, however, that the widespread optimization-based automated interface code generation has a fundamental problem in the Big Interaction era. Most often neither a designer nor a supporting system would have confidence in how exactly the interface is going to show. Obviously, optimizing distances between interface elements and their sizes (like in SUPPLE) has little sense for a web interface code processed and shaped by a web browser, not even considering varying screen sizes. Thus, we believe, the optimization could be founded on different principles, such as the measurements of information volumes transferred between human and computer. In our paper we call to the discussion on defining and measuring the information complexity of modern two-dimensional graphic user interfaces (GUI), which may be loosely based on Kolmogorov complexity (algorithmic entropy) and Halstead's software metrics. Possibly, information complexity can dictate optimal user interface structure and content, and lay ground for broader AI methods application in HCI.

2 Methods

There is no lack of study of "interface devices" present in a human body – for example, human's visual system throughput is estimated at 50–70 bit/s for passive perception of images (e.g. watching television), while for reading that implies comprehension the value drops to at least 30–40 bit/s. For the output tasks, speech allows up to about 50 bit/s, writing with a pen – 10 bit/s, while computer mouse and keyboard are at 3–5 bit/s and up to 25 bit/s respectively [7]. Currently, the applications of these data are quite limited, because there seems to be no accepted way to measure the amounts of information transferred between human and computer via user interfaces, except for simplest cases. The most straightforward way to quantify information contained in a user interface would be application of Hick-Hyman's Law, known to HCI researchers for already quite a long time.

2.1 Hick-Hyman's Law in HCI

As selection tasks that are prevalent in many modern interfaces may be represented as combination of choice and movement stages, the application of the infamous Fitts' and Hick's laws for modeling would seem a natural approach. We'd like to remind that W.E. Hick, applying Shannon's Information theory to psychological problems, observed that reaction time (RT) when choosing from N equiprobable alternatives is proportional to the logarithm of their number:

$$RT \sim k * \log_2(N + 1), \tag{1}$$

where k is the rate of gain of information. Later, R. Hyman reasonably noted that RT is in fact linearly related to information quantity, i.e. the entropy of the set of stimulus (H_T):

$$RT = a_H + b_H * H_T, \tag{2}$$

where a_H and b_H are empirically defined constants. The slope in thus formulated Hick-Hyman law (2), b_H, in simplest cases is believed to be equal to 150 ms, then the corresponding Hick's rate of gain of information (b_H^{-1}) is equal to 6.7 bits/s [8].

Unlike the Fitts' law that adequately models movement sub-stages, Hick's law generally falls short to describe cognitive performance, as the amount of information that needs to be processed (HT) is far more complex than log2(N+1) for any real tasks [9, p. 341]. With the experimental investigation described below we sought to improve the information measure and propose alternatives to the Hick-Hyman's law [10], so far by incorporating in the model visual search time, as a measure of information complexity.

2.2   The Experimental Investigation

Subjects. Twenty eight subjects took part in the experiment. Fifteen participants (4 male, 11 female) were elder people and their age ranged from 56 to 74 (M = 63.4, SD = 5.26), recent graduates of 36-h computer literacy courses held by People's Faculty of Novosibirsk State Technical University (NSTU). Thirteen subjects (5 male, 8 female) were recruited among NSTU students and general staff. They ranged in age from 17 to 30 (M = 23.9, SD = 4.38). All subjects had normal or corrected to normal vision. Eight (53.3 %) elder subjects reported having no experience in using computers or mouse before the computer literacy courses.

Experiment Design and Procedure. The experiment consisted of two parts: in the first (control) one the subjects were assigned typical movement tasks modeled with Fitts' law, while in the second one the participants were asked to perform selection tasks. The general experiment design was carried out in accordance with recommendations for Fitts' law experiments, provided in [11]. It was within-subjects, with two groups of participants – elder people and younger computer users. Before the experiment, data regarding the participants' age and gender were gathered. All subjects participated in the experiment voluntarily, and prior to the experimentation informed consents were obtained. Each subject then did a test run of trials with random combinations of A (distance to target), W (targets size), and N (number of targets in the second experiment), until fully understanding the assignment, to negate the effect of practice.

In the first experiment, the two main independent variables were size of a square target (W: 8, 16, 32, 64, 128) and distance to it (A: 64, 128, 256, 512, 1024). There were 7 different ID values (not all combinations were used), ranging from 1.58 to 7.01. The number of outcomes for each combination of A and W was lower than generally recommended (15 for each of ID values), because of the exploratory nature of the study and the intent not to tire the seniors.

The subjects were presented with two squares, a starting position and a target, dissimilar in shape and color. They were positioned randomly in relation to each other on a computer screen to negate the effect of movement direction. The subjects were asked to click the starting position with a mouse pointer and then, "as fast and as accurately as possible", move the pointer to the target and click it. Coordinates of both clicks were recorded; also if the second click was outside the target, error was recorded, and participant was taken to a next trial. The dependent variables were performance time (MT, between the two clicks) and error (E_1).

In the second experiment, the target would become visible on the screen only after participant's click on the starting position. False alternatives (of dissimilar shape and color, all of them identical, so overall vocabulary size n = 2) would appear together with the target. The number of alternatives was additional independent variable with 3 levels (N: 2, 4, 8), which were so far deliberately chosen not to exceed Miller's number of 7 ± 2. Also, there were A and W resulting in 6 different values of ID, ranging from 1.58 to 6.02, with 17 outcomes for each level of N. Again, the dependent variables were performance time (ST, between the two clicks) and error (E_2, clicks outside the target).

To measure and record the values of independent and dependent variables, an online application was developed with PHP and MySQL and used in IE web browser, with performance time measured with JavaScript to eliminate any server-side delay. The sessions with the two groups of participants, elder and younger, took place with 21-days interval in a same room on same computer equipment, with monitor screen resolution of 1024*768 pixels (thus constant S_0 of 1000*600 pixels).

Hypotheses. To confirm our reasoning, we identified several hypotheses to be checked in the subsequent experimental investigation:

H1. There is performance difference (time, accuracy) between movement and selection tasks.
H2. Hick's law is not adequate to model selection time.
H3. Visual search time is appropriate addition to movement time in modelling selection tasks.
H4. The proposed model is robust enough to plausibly model performance for different user groups.
H5. Movement and selection throughputs correlate per subjects and are affected by identical factors.

3 Results

First Part (Movement Tasks). The 15 outcomes for each of 7 ID values in the first part of the experiment resulted in 105 data for each participant, producing a total of 2940 data, of which 2888 (98.2 %) were considered valid. Invalid were the outcomes

Table 1. Mean MT and E_1 per Fitts' ID

ID	1.58	2.32	3.17	4.09	5.04	6.02	7.01	Mean (SD)
MT, ms	468	617	777	890	1039	1247	1425	922
	(251)	(303)	(379)	(374)	(395)	(483)	(507)	(503)
E_1, %	3.4	5.6	4.6	4.8	5.6	6.8	11.0	6.0

when subjects made an obviously erroneous click far from target or when the registered time was higher than 3000 ms. Table 1 shows mean values for movement time (MT) and error level (E_1) per Fitts' ID as well as overall ones.

MANOVA was used to test the effect of subjects' characteristics such as subject group (elder or younger), gender and experience (for this factor, the analysis was done for elder participants only) on MT and E_1. The effect of the experimental conditions in the first experiment was analyzed independently for the two subject groups. Predictably, distance (A) had significant effect on MT for both elder and younger participants. At the same time, the effect of distance was not significant for the number of errors committed by neither seniors ($F_{6,1502} = .9$; $p > .5$), nor their younger counterparts ($F_{6,1336} = 1.2$; $p = .29$). Size of target (W), besides significantly affecting MT for both subject groups, also had significant effect on error level for both elder ($F_{4,1502} = 5.5$; $p < .001$) and younger participants ($F_{4,1336} = 2.7$; $p = .03$). Post-hoc analysis indicated that only W = 8 px was significantly different in terms of committed errors, for both groups, and led to 10.2 % and 12.3 % errors for elder and younger subjects respectively. The interaction between distance to target and its size was not significant for either of the subject groups.

Second Part (Selection Tasks). The number of outcomes for each participant in the second part of the experiment was 51, producing a total of 1428 data, of which 1408 (98.6 %) were considered valid. Table 2 shows means for selection time (ST) and error level (E_2) per ID and number of targets (N) as well as overall ones.

Table 2. Mean ST (ms) and E_2 (%) per N and Fitts' ID

ID N	1.58	2.32	3.17	4.09	5.04	6.02	Mean (SD)
2	842	965	1016	1064	1238	1467	1034
	(318)	(423)	(409)	(283)	(405)	(530)	(414)
	3.6 %	7.2 %	6.4 %	8.4 %	7.3 %	7.1 %	6.6 %
4	814	953	1016	1121	1259	1660	1051
	(338)	(432)	(426)	(379)	(399)	(558)	(459)
	4.8 %	2.8 %	3.7 %	9.5 %	7.1 %	14.3 %	5.7 %
8	797	977	1020	1170	1328	1526	1061
	(315)	(480)	(392)	(424)	(478)	(439)	(461)
	4.8 %	6.4 %	9.1 %	8.4 %	7.1 %	24.0 %	8.1 %
Mean (SD)	818	965	1018	1118	1275	1552	1049
	(323)	(444)	(408)	(368)	(428)	(514)	(444)
	4.4 %	5.5 %	6.4 %	8.8 %	7.2 %	14.8 %	6.8 %

As in the first part of the experiment, a multivariate analysis of variance was used to test the effect of subject group and gender on ST and E_2. The results suggest highly significant effect of subject group on time ($F_{1,1404} = 365.8$; $p < .001$), with estimated marginal means of 1238 ms for elder subjects vs. 814 ms for younger ones. The effect of subject group on error was not significant ($F_{1,1404} = 1.8$; $p = .18$), in contrast to the first part of the experiment. The gender factor remained significant for both ST ($F_{1,1404} = 5.3$; $p = .022$) and number of committed errors ($F_{1,1404} = 5.0$; $p = .026$). As before, male participants on average were somehow faster, with 1001 ms vs. 1051 ms for female ones. The mean number of errors was 4.6 % and 7.8 % respectively. No significant interaction between the independent variables was observed.

Visual Search Time. To further examine the effect of N on ST (which did not clearly manifest in Table 2), we ran MANOVA test with ST and E_2 as dependent variables and N, W and A as factors. We found no significant effect for N on neither ST ($F_{2,1357} = .27$; $p = .76$), nor E_2 ($F_{2,1357} = 1.03$; $p = .36$). The effect of W was highly significant for both ST ($F_{3,1357} = 131.36$; $p < .001$) and E_2 ($F_{3,1357} = 6.05$; $p < .001$). Movement amplitude A significantly affected ST ($F_{3,1357} = 23.51$; $p < .001$), but not E_2 ($F_{4,1357} = 2.04$; $p = .09$).

We attempted preliminary regression models for ST with $\log_2(N)$ and Fitts' effective index of difficulty as factors, and N was not significant in the regression ($p = .308$), so we decided to exclude the number of objects from the visual search time model. Thus, we proposed the index of visual search difficulty (ID_{VS}) in the following form:

$$ID_{VS} = \log_2(S_0/S) = \log_2(S_0/W^2), \tag{3}$$

where S is equal to W^2 in case of our square targets. The justification is twofold:

1. The S_0/S represents the "length" of graphic interface as a message, i.e. the maximum number of elements of square S that it can contain. It seems reasonable to assume that users "process" not just the displayed objects, but the whole interface, including whitespace. Then S_0/S should take the place of N in Hick's law (1).
2. Parallels may be also drawn with motor behaviour described by Fitts' ID: then "search amplitude" S_0 corresponds to A and "search termination area" S – to W.

Hypotheses Check Results. Based on the analysis described in more detail in [10], we can make the following conclusions regarding the previously stated hypotheses.

H1.   Confirmed. Selection tasks took more time to complete and the accuracy was lower than for movement tasks. We'd like to note that the increase in performance time was nearly constant for the two subject groups, 187 ms for elder vs. 236 ms for younger participants, but the growth in error level for senior subjects was far more dramatic, at +75.0 %, which may be explained by poorer multi-tasking abilities of people in older age.

H2.   Confirmed. The number of alternatives (N) didn't have significant effect on ST, and $\log_2(N+1)$ was not significant in the regression.

H3.   Partially confirmed. ID_{VS} (3) was significant in regression for ST, but the resulting R^2 were lower than for movement tasks (see in [10]).

H4.   Confirmed. ST regressions with ID_{VS} factor were significant for both elder and younger subjects, and regression coefficients suggest that visual search task is relatively harder for seniors than movement task. This corresponds well to sharp increase (+75 %) in error level for elder participants in selection tasks.

H5.   Confirmed. Movement and selection throughputs are relatively highly correlated per subjects, and the effects of age and experience Fitts' throughput (TP) and TPS (see its formulation in [10]) are similar.

4   Conclusions

In our paper we raised the problem of quantifying information flows in human-computer systems, via introducing information complexity measure for user interfaces. The straightforward information entropy approach (2) has proved to be problematic in real circumstances, so we proposed to use visual search difficulty (3) to reflect the graphic user interface complexity. Search area size (S_0), sought element size (S) and the number of alternatives (N) were elected as primary factors for VST, while also employing vocabulary size parameter is the goal of our next experimentation. In the result of experimentation with 28 subjects of different age groups (described in more detail in [10]), visual search difficulty was suggested as the logarithm of the ratio between S_0 and S, with N not being significant.

Thus obtained mean value for proposed selection task throughput (TPS), 12.6 bit/s, seems to be consistent with established human visual processing capacity that ranges from 5 to 70 bit/s. It is known that tasks requiring deeper processing have lower capacity: perception of TV picture is at 50–70 bit/s, simple text reading – 40–50 bits/s, while text proof-reading – 18 bit/s [7, p. 62], so TPS was to be expected in the lower part of the range. However, the model is subject for further development, and we expect that the information complexity measure should be ID_{VS} multiplied by the vocabulary size – how many kinds of different objects, i.e. interface elements, are employed on the screen. Further development of our research implies closer analysis of the classic Kolmogorov's algorithmic entropy and Halstead's software "difficulty" measures.

We believe that ID_{VS} or the enhanced information complexity measure could be used in optimization when auto-generating user interfaces, as they are independent of absolute size measurement, which is of particular importance in adaptable web interfaces or multitudinous mobile interfaces. As we noted before, greater degree of AI methods utilization for creating user interfaces may be deemed necessary to cope with the Big Interaction, caused by ever-increasing diversity of users, their tasks, interface devices and contexts of use.

References

1. Nichols, J., Myers, B.A.: Automatically generating high-quality user interfaces for appliances. Doctoral dissertation, Carnegie Mellon University, Pittsburgh (2006)
2. Gajos, K.Z., Weld, D.S., Wobbrock, J.O.: Automatically generating personalized user interfaces with Supple. J. Artif. Intell. **174**(12–13), 910–950 (2010)
3. Gribova, V.V.: Automation of design, implementation and maintenance of user interface based on ontological approach. Doctoral dissertation, Institute of Automation and Control Processes, Far Eastern Branch of the Russian Academy of Science (2007) (in Russian)
4. Dearden, A., Finlay, J.: Pattern languages in HCI: a critical review. Hum. Comput. Interact. **21**(1), 49–102 (2006)
5. Chevalier, A., Fouquereau, N., Vanderdonckt, J.: The influence of a knowledge-based system on designers' cognitive activities: a study involving professional web designers. Behav. Inf. Technol. **28**(1), 45–62 (2009)
6. Bakaev, M., Avdeenko, T.: Indexing and comparison of multi-dimensional entities in a recommender system based on ontological approach. Computación y Sistemas **17**(1), 5–13 (2013)
7. Gasov, V.M., Solomonov, L.A.: Engineering psychology design of human interaction with technical instruments vol. 1. Visshaya shkola, Moscow (1990) (in Russian)
8. Longstreth, L.E., et al.: Exceptions to Hick's law: explorations with a response duration measure. J. Exp. Psychol. Gen. **114**, 417–434 (1985)
9. Seow, S.: Information theoretic models of HCI: a comparison of the Hick-Hyman law and Fitts' law. J. Hum. Comput. Inter. **20**(3), 315–352 (2005)
10. Bakaev, M., Avdeenko, T., Cheng, H.I.: Modelling selection tasks and assessing performance in web interaction. IADIS Int. J. Comput. Sci. Inf. Syst. **V VII**(1), 94–105 (2012). Isaías, P., Paprzycki, M. (eds.)
11. Soukoreff, R.W., MacKenzie, I.S.: Towards a standard for pointing device evaluation, perspectives on 27 years of Fitts' law research. Int. J. Hum. Comput. Stud. **61**(6), 751–789 (2004)

A Systematic Review of Dementia Focused Assistive Technology

Joanna Evans[1], Michael Brown[2(✉)], Tim Coughlan[2], Glyn Lawson[3],
and Michael P. Craven[4]

[1] Thales, Surrey, UK
joanna@evans6.me.uk
[2] Horizon Digital Economy Research, University of Nottingham,
Nottingham, UK
{michael.brown,tim.coughlan}@nottingham.ac.uk
[3] Human Factors Research Group, University of Nottingham, Nottingham, UK
glyn.lawson@nottingham.ac.uk
[4] NIHR MindTech Healthcare Technology Co-operative and Institute of Mental
Health, University of Nottingham, Nottingham, UK
michael.craven@nottingham.ac.uk

Abstract. This paper presents a systematic review which explores the nature of assistive technologies currently being designed, developed and evaluated for dementia sufferers and their carers. A search through four large databases, followed by filtering by relevance, led to the identification and subsequent review of papers. Our review revealed that the majority of research in this area focuses on the support of day-to-day living activities, safety monitoring, memory aids and preventing social isolation. We conclude that the majority of AT currently available support day-to-day living activities, safety monitoring and assisting healthcare. However these devices merely address the 'ease of living' rather than focusing on 'quality of life'. Although there are some devices which address social symptoms of Dementia, few address behavioural issues such as aggression and virtually none are available to support recreational activities. After discussing the implications of these findings, we finally reflect on general design issues for assistive technologies in this domain that became apparent during the review.

Keywords: Design: human centered design and user centered design · Technology: adaptive and personalized interfaces · Technology: interaction design · Technology: new technology and its usefulness · Dementia · Alzheimer's · Assistive technology

1 Introduction

This systematic review explores the types of assistive technologies which are currently being researched in relation to dementia care. By analysing trends in research to date, our aim was is to understand and reflect upon the state of the art in this area, and to highlight domains which appear underexplored, in order to guide future research in this area.

Demographic projections of an aging population in many countries pose a concern for elderly care services [21]. In particular, the increasing number of elderly people

© Springer International Publishing Switzerland 2015
M. Kurosu (Ed.): Human-Computer Interaction, Part II, HCII 2015, LNCS 9170, pp. 406–417, 2015.
DOI: 10.1007/978-3-319-20916-6_38

with dementia poses serious problems in terms of providing effective infrastructure to support sufferers, such as care homes, nursing and others. In the UK, 5 % of over 65 year olds have been diagnosed with dementia and 30 % of over 95 year olds suffer with the condition [11]. This causes problems in expenditure of healthcare, quality of care and increases pressure on caregivers due to a lack of resources [8].

Many elderly individuals prefer to stay in their home environment (Davies et al. 2008) and others do not have the option to move into residential care due to the cost of being admitted or lack of services. This situation places increasing pressure on family members and informal caregivers. However, there are systems which help to support independence for elder generations to enable them to remain at home [8], known as assisted living. Supporting individuals in their own home can prolong the admittance into care homes which merely transfers the stress and pressure onto the healthcare system and care staff directly [21].

Direct costs to the UK National Health Service and social care are currently estimated as at least £3.3 billion a year [17] and in the World's Alzheimer's report it was stated that by 2050 there will be 115 million people with dementia, emphasising the need for assistive technologies to be developed to ascertain whether they can reduce the prevalence of dementia and reduce the burden on caregivers [11].

The next section of this paper gives an overview of dementia in terms of its definition, typical symptoms and their implications for not only the individual but also their informal caregiver. Assistive technologies are then defined in terms of dementia, highlighting their importance and impact in society. Following this we describe the methods used to perform a systematic review of research papers focusing on the assistive technologies designed for those with dementia. Then we report the findings of this review, identifying which areas are currently under developed. Finally, concerns in the current technologies and critical factors for technology design are discussed.

2   Background

Alzheimer's is the most common form of dementia and accounts for 50–80 % of dementia cases [2]. It is a chronic progressive disorder that develops and leads to deterioration in the individual over time. It is a disease of the brain that damages and eventually destroys brain cells. This causes a range of symptoms resulting in difficulties throughout everyday life as a result of the loss of brain function [11].

Dementia is a complex condition, so diagnosis can take several months and many hours of medical testing. This is because the main symptoms of Dementia such as memory loss and cognitive impairments are similar to other pathologies and the 'normal' signs of aging. This often results in the symptoms being overlooked, which can lead to misdiagnosis. In addition to this, the early symptoms such as forgetfulness are often so subtle that it is difficult for friends and family to notice them. Finally, individuals showing related symptoms of mild cognitive impairment may or may not go onto to develop Dementia, which also makes early detection unreliable [7].

There is currently no cure for dementia, but some medication and therapies have been shown to reduce the behavioural and psychological symptoms, alleviating pressures and improving quality of life for individuals as well as their caregivers. Living with Dementia can make everyday tasks frustrating for individuals and cause burden and stress for their caregivers, often leading to anxiety [25]. Caregivers and family members often worry about leaving individuals with dementia alone due to their forgetfulness, risk of injury, memory to take medication and also their general safety. This inability to carry out daily tasks causes a reduced quality of life, poor self-esteem, and social isolation. This is a result of impaired executive function, leading to problems in planning, sequencing and attention control. Dementia sufferers also experience difficulties in communication, for example in using telephones to communicate with distant partners. These difficulties can be a further cause of negative social and emotional effects and creates greater isolation [20].

Caregivers reported that one of the main reasons they resorted to nursing homes is due to the sleep disruption to both the individual with dementia and themselves. This is supported by Rowe et al. [23] who found that sleep disturbance occurred in 58 % of a large sample of individuals who suffered with dementia and that this was one of the most stressful symptoms to caregivers. Their study on injuries in an emergency department found that 40 % of injuries occurred as a result of night time falls and that this resulted in 62 % of individuals not being able to return their own home, due to factures or dislocations, resulting in institutionalisation. This is a major concern for an individual's spouse, who is typically elderly as well and so vulnerable due to the physical effects of being a carer. The chronic stressors of caring for a spouse with Dementia can increase health problems due to a decreased immune system in not just elderly individuals but also younger people. This combined with a perceived workload and feelings of isolation reduces the carer's ability to look after their loved one, often leading to an earlier admission into a care home [24].

2.1   Assistive Technologies for Dementia Sufferers and Carers

The symptoms and effects of dementia presented above can be used to suggest that there is both high potential for assistive technologies to have a positive impact in this area, but also a need for these technologies to be designed with an in-depth understanding of constraints on interaction caused by the disease. Various types of assistive technologies have been developed to help to manage some of the symptoms of Dementia. The term 'assistive technologies (AT)' refers to a device that helps someone do a task that they otherwise would not be able to do, or enables a task to be carried out more easily and in a safer manner [3].

Assisted living can help maintain a healthy and safe environment to enable individuals to live independently and thus reduce stress and burden on informal caregivers [8]. Technological advances can help to slow the onset by keeping individuals cognitively active, improve quality of life and extend independence for longer and therefore prolong institutionalisation [7]. The range of AT are used to not only enhance individual quality of life, but also have the potential to reduce costs for society and public health systems. It is estimated that by prolonging admission into care homes it could save health care $12 billion annually in America alone [5].

3   Methods

In order to gain a deep understanding of the current state of assistive technology research and development in this domain, and to guide future research, a systematic review was carried out. This focussed on the types of technology reported to have been designed, developed and evaluated across a broad sample of research literature.

3.1   Data Sources and Search Strategy

In December 2014 we searched for English language articles indexed in the Pubmed, PsycINFO, Web of Knowledge and Scopus online repositories. We searched title, abstract and body text for the terms: ("assistive technology" OR "assistive device" OR "adaptive technology" OR "adaptive device") AND (Alzheimer's OR Alzheimers OR Dementia), with query logic modified to reflect the language used by each system. A total of 379 papers were initially identified.

3.2   Study Selection

Two stages of filtering were performed prior to full paper reviews, as illustrated in Fig. 1. Firstly the paper titles were assessed and 218 papers were rejected as duplicates or obviously irrelevant to the topic at hand. The abstracts of the 264 remaining articles were reviewed and a further 88 rejected as they were found to be irrelevant to this topic. Both stages of filtering were performed independently by two reviewers, and only the papers rejected by both reviewers were removed from the working corpus. This left 176 papers for the full review.

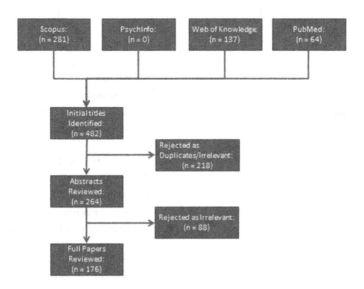

Fig. 1. Study selection process

3.3   Data Extraction and Synthesis

Two researchers independently reviewed the articles in order to identify the general and specific purpose of the technologies described in each case. Articles covering a wide range of technologies and those that did not mention a specific technology were coded as 'Miscellaneous: No Specific Technology'. Where a full paper was not found online, articles were requested directly from authors. If no response was received, they were coded as 'Miscellaneous: Article Not Found'. Where an article discussed multiple discrete technologies, each was considered separately. In the remaining 105 articles, a total of 233 technologies were described. From these technologies 22 specific purposes were identified, falling into 6 general themes, as illustrated in Table 1. Finally, in order to explore the significance of the number of technologies identified in each category a Chi Square test was performed on the six general themes.

Table 1. Systematic review of technologies for Dementia suffers

General theme	Number of technologies	Specific purposes
Safety devices	70	Fall prevention (n = 20)
		Cooking safety (n = 12)
		General sensors (n = 2)
		Tracking/wayfinding (n = 34)
		Leak detection (n = 2)
Memory aids	58	Time orientation calendars (n = 8)
		Item locater (n = 6)
		General reminders (n = 28)
		Reminiscing aid (n = 8)
		Medication reminders (n = 8)
Preventing social isolation	37	Communication aids (n = 32)
		Artificial companions (n = 5)
Supporting everyday tasks	33	Hand/body washing aids (n = 8)
		Incontinence/toilet assistance (n = 4)
		Simple task completion (n = 19)
		Dressing undressing (n = 2)
Clinical devices	28	Music therapy (n = 14)
		Symptom monitoring (n = 11)
		Rehabilitation (n = 1)
		Doll therapy (n = 2)
Leisure activities	7	Gaming (n = 4)
		Creativity/arts (n = 3)
Miscellaneous	71 papers	Full paper not found (n = 23)
		No specific technology (n = 48)

4 Results

A CHI Squared analysis revealed that the distribution of research across these themes was highly significantly different from an expected even split ($CHI^2 = 62.14$, $p = 4.39 * 10^{-12}$). Post hoc testing was then performed examining the adjusted residuals from each general theme and showed significant differences (at $p < 0.05$) for over representation of Memory Aids and Safety Devices and under representation of Leisure Activities and Clinical Devices, as show in Table 2.

Table 2. Chi squared adjusted residuals for differences in distribution to expected even split

Theme	Chi^2 adjusted residual
Memory aids	*2.71**
Safety devices	*4.60**
Preventing social isolation	−0.57
Supporting everyday tasks	−1.20
Leisure activities	*−5.279**
Clinical devices	*−1.986**

*significant at $p < 0.05$

4.1 Memory Aids

The review found that memory aids were one of the most common areas of reported AT research and development. For example, TV-based prompting systems can be used to remind people to have their lunch, take medication, or remind them that a family member is visiting. These reminders not only benefit the individual with Dementia, but also reduce the burden to caregivers as they no longer have to constantly remind individuals to carry out certain tasks [7]. This type of technology needs to strike a balance between flexibility and simplicity. It needs to have an appropriate range of prompts that suits the individual such as picture or verbal cues, but these cues needs to be simple to set up and generally usable.

4.2 Safety Devices

The most common theme across the developed technologies was safety devices. These ranged from fall prevention to the tracking of people with Dementia. There are a range of monitoring technologies such as wireless systems and sensors. These can be used to detect any unusual behaviour and provide continual feedback in individuals with dementia to their caregivers [9]. These technologies can be characterised into wandering, fall and navigation devices. Night time wandering is a major issue, but technologies can be used to assist caregivers [23]. However, 'assist' is the key term in this, as such forms of AT merely alert caregivers to the problem, and do not resolve the issue. Therefore while the caregiver's role is still essential, they are being provided with greater potential for awareness and for monitoring from a distance.

4.3 Preventing Social Isolation

Two types of device aimed at reducing/preventing social isolation were identified, aids to communication and artificial companions:

Communication Aids. The inability to recognise people and communicate easily has negative impacts on social interaction for people with dementia [26]. An example of this kind of tool is Social Memory Aid [16], which allows people with dementia to practise name and face recognition. The system allows the user to select photos where questions and clues are given about the friend or family member in order to prompt recall of their name. This helps with social interaction and is a tool which can be applied to aid communication such as the principles used in COGKNOW [13]. This system is a cognitive device combined with current smart home technology to provide a range of services. It was adapted to help combine verbal, written and visual information to aid recall in individuals with dementia to make phone calls independently. Its goal was to achieve patient empowerment and greater autonomy, and to enhance quality of life for mild dementia patients. In additional it aims to provide benefits to caregivers, by relieving them from some daily care tasks. The use of photos and verbal identification helped individuals to recognize partners more easily and confidently, and this improved their communication abilities by enabling them to decide who they wanted to call.

Artificial Companions. Robots are a new and emerging technology, which brings the potential to improve the quality of life for dementia sufferers through social care [4]. Due to the impaired cognitive abilities of people with dementia, they often find new technologies difficult to use. Therefore, robots need to be simple and easy to use whilst being complex enough to cause cognitive and social stimulation in order to reduce psychological distress or social withdrawal. However they still need to be complex enough to cause cognitive and social stimulation in order to reduce any psychological distress or social withdrawal in people with dementia [21].

The potential for robots to be applied in the home environment is supported by their ability to monitor health, remind patients to take their medicine and guide individuals around their home [21]. Companion robots such as Paro, have been developed based on these principles of animal therapy and have been found to help enhance moods, make social interactions possible and generally lead to a higher quality of life in studies conducted in Japan [2]. However cultural differences may impact on the wider uptake of these technologies: A study in a residential facility in New Zealand investigated the suitability of an elderly care robot: Guided, compared with Paro. Whilst Paro had been developed for people with dementia, Guided had only been tested on elderly users and had low acceptance. This highlights the importance of participatory design and gaining insight into sensitive cultural differences.

4.4 Supporting Everyday Tasks

A number of papers explored the use and value of technologies aimed at helping people with Dementia completing everyday tasks that are essential for independent living. The majority of these focus on personal hygiene or food preparation tasks.

Food and Kitchen Tasks. Preparing food, cooking and cleaning is a complex sequence of actions for an individual with cognitive impairments. Many difficulties in kitchen tasks result from sequencing problems, as the reduction in episodic memory causes forgetfulness in steps already taken. This results in repetitiveness and problems in locating items [26]. Computer vision algorithms can be used to detect a person's location and the stage of a task they are currently undertaking. This, combined with RFID tags which label and locate utensils, enables sensors to gather data and infer stages in an activity. This enables a technology to potentially recognise if an individual is not progressing through a task correctly. Dishman [10] looked at RFID tags attached to the utensils needed to make a hot drink and developed a technology which uses audio prompts to give an indication of steps to carry this out [24]. However these verbal commands can be too complex to understand, and so in contrast to this, the Cooks Collage used to visually display the previous six steps completed whilst cooking to help reorient the user to the rest of the process [5].

Personal Hygiene. People with dementia often find it difficult to complete daily tasks such as washing, brushing teeth and using the toilet. As in the kitchen technologies discussed above, video monitoring can be used to track these activities, and a technology COACH has been developed to help individuals carry out these activities [14]. COACH uses a video camera, hand tracking bracelets and machine learning algorithms to guide people through hand washing. It monitors the users' context and has the ability to give verbal aids, detect problems, and prompt the user to complete missing steps. Similarly the 'Friendly Rest Room' project [19] was established with the aimed to design a toilet that allowed greater autonomy and privacy, whilst maintaining dignity.

4.5   Leisure Activities

The clearest finding of this systematic review is a lack of research exploring technologies to support leisure activities. Only seven technologies were identified in this area, four relating to games, and another three that focus on arts and crafts. As the majority of people with Dementia are retired, much of their time could be spend on recreational activities, which could have a range of cognitive and wellbeing benefits. However, the results of the review suggest that technologies to support these activities and subsequently improve quality of life simply do not exist.

4.6   Clinical Devices

A small number of papers explored the use of technology for clinical purposes, be it early detection or therapy to relieve symptoms.

Symptom Monitoring. Diagnosis is usually accomplished via pen and paper tests however computer tests can be used for visio-spatial tests where a subject must match a shape in different orientations to an original shape shown. With a computer test, the images can be shown in 3D which helps to bring out subtleties that are not found in pen and paper tests as patients must mentally rotate the images in their head [12].

Therapy and Rehabilitation. Caregivers and family members often forget what individuals were like before their cognitive decline. Therefore multimedia biographies can be made which help individuals remember their past and can help reduce their tendency for disruptive behaviour. Interactive video systems are used to monitor the user whilst exercising in the home and give encouraging feedback to carry on completing the task. These systems are shown to help with social development and physical activity has been shown to reduce cognitive decline [1]. However, some systems need further development as they are sensitive to clothing, backlight and home objects.

5 Discussion

In addition to identifying the key technology areas in this domain and highlighting the amount of research currently published in each, a number of specific issues were identified over the course of the review.

5.1 Generalisability and Methodology Issues

Whilst there are lots of studies on the aging population in general, few studies worked with participants specifically with dementia. Therefore many studies have low ecological validity as they are not conducted on a representative sample. Although there are obvious ethical and practical difficulties, more research needs to be done in the specified target population in order to develop interventions which offer more appropriate care. Cross cultural studies are also important such as COGKNOW [13] which compared different cultures and this is important so as not to be culturally biased.

Many studies on dementia use interviews to assess individuals and caregivers, which is a valuable technique for gaining rich insights. However an overreliance on any single method can be detrimental to general understanding, and in this case, focusing solely on subjective reporting could result in a distorted view of this how assistive technologies are appropriated. It is also questionable whether their level of cognitive decline enables participants with dementia to know what help they need, in order to reliably help designers in developing technologies.

5.2 Acceptance and Stigma

The use of AT can result in feelings of frustration or embarrassment due to the stigmatism of relying on a device for support. Brooks [6], found that AT which needs users to wear any form of equipment can be perceived as a stigma. Although lots of technologies have the potential to reduce the burden for carers, most current systems are ineffective in real life situations due to their low acceptance rates [5]. Despite this, more empirical studies have found that AT are perceived as beneficial and necessary to individuals. Therefore it needs to be addressed how AT are marketed due to stigmatism which can impede acceptance and adoption. Acceptability is dependent on how a product makes the user feel, what they like about it, whether they think it is useful and its appearance. The use of AT is also influenced by confidence of the user, their fear of performance when using the technology and an awareness or acceptance for personal help and concerns that the technology may inconvenience others around them.

5.3 Awareness

Another issue to be addressed is that individuals may not know what is available or appropriate for their personal circumstances. In a survey analysing at the awareness of the existing supply of AT found that some devices were more well-known than others although living alone or with others made no difference to the awareness of technology available [22]. However those who live alone are more vulnerable and more should be done to increase awareness of the technology available to them. The survey identified gaps in the awareness of specific devices despite the AT usefulness and commercial availability. As well as this problem, it is difficult to access information of the range of AT as current technologies can only be found on charity websites however it is unclear where newer emerging technology can be purchased. This issue of awareness needs to be addressed to improve the accessibility of technologies so that they are more commercially available.

5.4 Importance of User Centered Design and Studies to Inform AT

For the future development of AT it is essential that user centred design and user testing is integrated further into the process. There is a range of literature used in order to inform the design of AT for people with dementia. Using interviews with individuals with dementia but also with their caregivers, enables designers to discover what the individuals with Dementia really want and need, as well as what their care givers want and would benefit from so as to increase acceptance [24]. It is not sufficient to simply understand the theoretical causes and implications of cognitive impairment, technologists need to understand what the user and their caregiver really wants from technology.

6 Conclusions

The majority of AT currently available support day-to-day living activities, safety monitoring and can assist in health care. However these devices merely address the 'ease of living' rather than focus on 'quality of life'. Although there are some devices which enhance social symptoms of Dementia, few address behavioural issues such as aggression and virtually none are available to support recreational activities. One potential area for development is recreational devices to encourage individuals with dementia to participate in hobbies which they once enjoyed. The range of technologies currently available illustrates a need for more context aware and intelligent software to be developed through extensive user testing and evaluation. This is essential as without design input from both individuals with Dementia and their caregivers, acceptance is often low. This can result in products not being used thus reducing opportunities for increasing independence as well as reducing burden to caregivers. To increase acceptance, AT should be low cost and non-obtrusive so as to reduce stigma. However development is restricted due to ethical considerations and difficulties in accessing appropriate participants.

References

1. Alm, N., et al.: A cognitive prosthesis and communication support for people with dementia. Neuropsychol. Rehabil. **14**(1–2), 117–134 (2004)
2. Alzheimer's Association: Aim: Establish a definition and over view of Alzheimer's. Source: No source given for the information provided. http://www.alz.org. Accessed 17 September 2011
3. Alzheimer's Society: Aim: Establish definition for assistive technologies with respect to Alzheimer's itself. Source: No source given for the information provided. http://www.alzheimers.org.uk. Accessed 17 September 2011
4. Bermelmans, R., et al.: Socially Assistive Robots in Elderly Care: A Systematic Review into Effects and Effectiveness. Elsevier (2012). doi:10.1016/j.jamda.2010.10.002. Accessed on 17 December 2012
5. Bharucha, A.J., et al.: Intelligent assistive technology applications to dementia care: current capabilities, limitations, and future challenges. Am. J. Geriatr. Psychiatry. **17**(2), 88–104 (2009). doi:10.1097/JGP.0b013e318187dde5. Accessed 29 October 2012
6. Brooks, N.A.: User's responses to assistive devices for physical disability. Soc. Sci. Med. **32** (12), 1417–1424 (1991)
7. Camilo, M.C., et al.: Everyday technologies for Alzheimer's disease care: research findings, directions, and challenges. Elsevier (2009). doi:10.1016/j.jalz.2009.09.003. Accessed 27 October 2012
8. Chembumroong, S., et al.: Elderly activities recognition and classification for applications in assisted living. Expert Syst. Appl. Elsevier (2012). doi:10.1016/j.eswa.2012.09.004. Accessed 17 December 2012
9. Demiris, G., et al.: Technologies for an aging society: a systematic review of "smart home" application. IMIA Yearbook Med. Inform. **3**, 33–40 (2008)
10. Dishman, E.: Inventing wellness systems for aging in place. Computer **37**(5), 34–41 (2004)
11. Hughes, J.C.: Alzheimer's and Other Dementias, 1st edn. Oxford University Press, Oxford (2011)
12. Lojkowska, W., et al.: SPECT as a diagnostic test in the investigation of dementia. J. Neurol. Sci. **203**, 215–219 (2002)
13. Meiland, F., et al.: COGKNOW: development of an ICT device to support people with dementia. J. Inf. Technol. Healthcare **5**(5), 324–334 (2007)
14. Mihailidis, A., et al.: The COACH prompting system to assist older adults with dementia through handwashing: an efficacy study. BMC Geriatr. **8**(1), 28 (2008)
15. Mittleman, M.S., et al.: Preserving Health of Alzheimer Caregivers: Impact of a Spouse Caregiver Intervention (2007). Accessed 27 October 2012
16. Morris, M., Lundell, J., Dishman, E.: Catalyzing social interaction with ubiquitous computing: a needs assessment of elders coping with cognitive decline. In: CHI 2004 Extended Abstracts on Human Factors in Computing Systems. ACM (2004)
17. National Audit Office: Improving services and support for people with dementia. Aim: Understand effects of dementia and ways in which to deal with the condition. Source: No source is given. The stationary office, London (2007) http://www.nao.org.uk/publications/0607/dementia_services_and_support.aspx

18. Orpwood, R., et al.: User involvement in dementia product development. Dementia **3**(3), 263–279 (2004)
19. Panek, P., Edelmayer, G., Magnusson, C., Mayer, P., Molenbroek, J.F.M., Neveryd, H., Schlathau, R., Zagler, W.L.: Investigations to develop a fully adjustable intelligent toilet for supporting old people and persons with disabilities – the friendly rest room (FRR) project. In: Miesenberger, K., Klaus, J., Zagler, W.L., Burger, D. (eds.) ICCHP 2004. LNCS, vol. 3118, pp. 392–399. Springer, Heidelberg (2004)
20. Perilli, V., et al.: Research in Developmental Disabilities. Persons with Alzheimer's disease make phone calls independently using a computer-aided telephone system. Elsevier (2012). doi:10.1016/j.ridd.2012.01.007. Accessed 18 October 2012
21. Robinson, H., et al.: Suitability of healthcare robots for a dementia unit and suggested improvements. Elsevier (2012). doi:10.1016/j.jamda.2012.09.006. Accessed 27 December 2012
22. Roelands, M., et al.: Awareness among community-dwelling elderly of assistive devices for mobility and self-care and attitudes towards their use. Elsevier (2002). Accessed 17 December 2002
23. Rowe, M.A., et al.: Reducing dangerous night time events in persons with dementia by using a night time monitoring system. Elsevier (2009). doi:10.1016/j.jalz.2008.08.005. Accessed 17 December 2012
24. Schoenmkers, B., et al.: Factors determining the impact of care-giving on caregivers of elderly patients with dementia: a systematic literature review. Elsevier (2010). doi:10.1016/j.maturitas.2010.02.009. Accessed 23 October 2012
25. Wherton, J.P., et al.: Problems people with dementia have with kitchen tasks: the challenge for pervasive computing. Interacting with Computers. Elsevier (2012). doi:10.1016/j.intcom.2010.03.004. Accessed 27 October 2012
26. Wherton, J.P., et al.: Technological opportunities for supporting people with dementia who are living at home. Int. J. Hum. Comput. Stud. Elsevier (2007). doi:10.1016/j.ijhcs.2008.03.001. Accessed 27 October 2012

Trust-Based Individualization for Persuasive Presentation Builder

Amirsam Khataei[(⊠)] and Ali Arya

School of Information Technology, Carleton University, 1125 Colonel by Drive,
Ottawa, ON K1S 5B6, Canada
akhataei@ca.ibm.com, arya@carleton.ca

Abstract. For most people, decision-making involves collecting opinion and
advice from others who can be trusted. Personalizing a presentation's content
with trustworthy opinions can be very effective towards persuasiveness of the
content. While the persuasiveness of presentation is an important factor in
face-to-face scenarios, it becomes even more important in an online course or
other educational material when the "presenter" cannot interact with audience
and attract and influence them. As the final layer of our personalization model,
the Pyramid of Individualization, in this paper we present a conceptual model
for collecting opinionative information as trustworthy support for the presentation content. We explore selecting a credible publisher (expert) for the supporting opinion as well as the right opinion that is aligned with the intended
personalized content.

Keywords: Presentation · Personalized · Trust · Opinion mining

1 Introduction

As discussed in our previous publication [1], presentations are effective way of communicating information, particularly in the field of education and e-learning. However,
the content of a presentation may not be completely beneficial and persuasive to all
users since it is not personalized for each recipient. Yale Attitude Change Approach [2]
specifies four kinds of processes that determine the extent to which a person will be
persuaded by a communication. These processes are:

1. Attention: The presenter must first address the intended audience.
2. Comprehension: The audience must understand the presented message.
3. Acceptance: The audience must accept the argument in the presentation.
4. Retention: The audience must remember the argument later.

It also elucidates the persuader main characteristic which is credibility. As defined
by Yale Attitude Change Approach credibility is summarized into expertise, trustworthiness, dynamism and sociability. Despite some of the differences, for the rest of
this document, we will use the terms credible, trustworthy, and expert interchange-
ably, as by expert we mean someone whom audience find credible and trustworthy. It
has been also frequently demonstrated that highly trustworthy and credible com-
municators prompt a greater positive attitude toward the position they advocate than

© Springer International Publishing Switzerland 2015
M. Kurosu (Ed.): Human-Computer Interaction, Part II, HCII 2015, LNCS 9170, pp. 418–428, 2015.
DOI: 10.1007/978-3-319-20916-6_39

do others with less level of credit [3]. As Sternthal and Dholakia said in [3], if a highly credible source inhibits counter arguing, whereas a less credible source does not, cognitive response predicts the superior persuasive power of a highly credible communicator.

In Personalized Presentation Builder for Persuasive Communication, we proposed a personalization model called, Pyramid of Individualization [4]. The intention of our model is to build a system in which with the help of aggregating user's social network information, the presenter is able to personalize the content of a given presentation. The proposed personalization consists of four layers:

1. Content assembler that collects appropriate content items through demographic segmentation.
2. Language modifier that increases text readability.
3. Personality trait modifier that revises the content by predicting user's personality.
4. Individual modifier that adds items related to each individual such as quotes, images, events, information shared by close relatives or trustable public figures/organization, etc.

Our main focus in this paper is the individual modifier (the fourth layer). The design for this modifier is based on the idea of enriching the personalized content with the flavor of personal data like family history or personal opinion. A simple example could be a restaurant's online flyer to promote people to reserve the restaurant for their future events. Incorporating the individual's personal photo from past festive events may enhance the sense of positive emotion towards persuasiveness of the advertisement in comparison to using a generic restaurant advertising image.

However using personal images in the intended personalized content is only a simple example of such individualization. An image of friends in a restaurant, or a quote from them describing their happy event there, can increase the likelihood of audience trusting that place even more. Various types of data such as user likes, postings, comments or events can be used in such "individualization". Our objective in this paper is to introduce the essential components involved in collecting supporting opinions from reader's trustworthy sources to support the personalized content.

Social networks are becoming the most common place for people to post information, express their opinion, and get reviews from other users. These activities result in the generation of a rich source of information on different aspects of life. Such user-generated information ranges from health and politics to product and service reviews. However, these "opinionative information" may be generated by different people with various relations to us. The opinion can be from an iconic public figure or organization who we strongly support or from our credible colleague who we personally know. On the other hand, they also may come from someone who is part of our social network but not trusted, or with different taste and standards.

The iconic public figure and our dear colleague share a common factor, which is trustworthiness. Dictionary definitions for trust include such terms as "confidence", "reliance", "expectation", and "hope". Kim Giffin studied theory of interpersonal trust within credibility context [5]. She shows that interpersonal trust is based upon a listener's perceptions of a speaker's expertness, reliability, intentions, activeness, personal attractiveness and the majority opinion of the listener's associates.

After discussing the technical issues of improving persuasiveness of personalized content by using opinion-oriented information, we focus on the central problems around designing the actual model. The next section of this paper, the related work and the motivation behind this research has been reviewed. Following that, we present some background information about the proposed model, a general overview of our procedure, and some implementation notes. Then we discuss some conceptual results and examples. Finally we describe how this system can be improved and what work remains to be done in the future phases of the research.

2 Related Work

In general, there are two main types of textual information: facts and opinions. Multiple solutions have been proposed and specialized in factual Information Retrieval (IR). These solutions have been discussed and used in the language modifier section of our personalization system. In this paper, the main focus is on identifying and using personal opinions. In the related literature, this is usually referred to as opinion mining or sentiment analysis [6].

With the rapid growth of the user-generated content published in social networks, a tool for mining the Web to capture sentiments and opinions at a large scale becomes essential. Due to importance of collecting products and services reviews by product vendors and policy makers, we have witnessed extensive interests in this line of research [7, 8]. Their focus has mainly been designing the system suitable for organizations to analyze and aggregate their customers' attitude towards a product or service and its features along different dimensions, such as time, geographical location, and experience. In our research, our focus is to retrieve the reviews for personalizing content to persuade readers'.

Bo Pang and Lillian Lee [6] published an inclusive survey that covers methods and approaches in the field of Opinion Mining (a.k.a. Sentiment Analysis). Their focus is on techniques to address new challenges raised by sentiment-aware applications, as compared to those that are already present in more traditional fact-based analysis. They have discussed a variety of topics from material on summarization of evaluative text and on broader issues regarding privacy and economic impacts that the development of applications based on opinionative information gives rise to. Enhancing percussive personalized content can become an addition to the above topics.

There have been also many studies within the field of trust-based social recommender systems. Some preliminary literature demonstrate the advantages of applying factor of trust in recommendation marking [9, 10]. These works focus on recommender systems that consider trustworthiness factor before recommending content to the user. One of the challenges in these systems is their trust rating mechanism. Predicting trust rating between content publisher and receiver is a critical task. For instance,

Golbeck and Hendler in their work on inferring binary trust relationships in web-based social networks considered those social networking sites where users explicitly provide trust ratings to other members [11]. However, for large social networks it is infeasible to assign trust ratings to each and every member so they propose an inferring mechanism, which would assign trustworthy/non-trustworthy rating to those who have not been assigned one. The missing element in their research is demonstrating the logic within an application context.

Although mining personal opinion and experience consists of a series of challenging procedures, evaluating the credibility of collected data has its own complexity. Microblogs can be sources of truthful news and also a tool to spread misinformation and false rumors. Castillo and Mendoza analyzed the information credibility of news propagated through Twitter using a classifier [12]. Their model uses features from users' tweets and re-tweeting behavior, from the text of the posts, and from citations to external sources. Based on their results, with precision and recall in the range of 70% to 80%, it is possible to classify messages as credible or not credible. On the other hand, Soo Cho [13] proposed to apply user profiling and LIWC (a text analysis software program) [14] to predict publisher's expertise. By collecting background knowledge about the publisher, the system assigns a certain level of reliability based on the subject of the content. Predicting the credibility of the content is an essential part of our individualization model and these approaches would be applicable in our proposed model.

3 Proposed Individualization Model

Nowadays, it is becoming evident that the views expressed on the web by a certain user can be influential to readers in forming their opinions on some topic [15]. In order to benefit from such a delicate concept, we need to be tactful enough with selecting an aligned opinion with our personalized contents from the right person for a particular reader. To understand the complexity of the process, consider the following scenario. We are looking to personalize an advertisement to highlight the benefits of a new tax policy. We have found a review from a democratic congressman regarding the new policy. The congressman is considered as an expert with a decent public credibility approval but the twist is the actual content reader is a republican. Due to differentiation between the expert and the reader political point of view, the expert may miss the credibility factor in the reader's eyes.

Our proposed model is a collaboration between multiple actors and assigned roles. The actors in this model are Individualization System, Reader, Expert and Author. While Individualization System acts as an automated content recommender, the reader and author are users who are interacting with the system. The expert is a user who will be known to the system through the reader. Table 1 defines some the term used in our model.

The challenge of collecting the proper supporting opinion consists of multiple sub processes. It begins with identifying the objective of the personalized content. After that we select the right expert and then collect the supporting opinion. The general overview of the process illustrated in Fig. 1.

Table 1. Summary of individualization model terminology

Actor	Role
Individualization system: the automated recommender or the personalization system	1. The personalized content can fall into personal (e.g. birthday event) and public (e.g. new tax policy) categories
	2. The system starts with authors opinion and then finds and uses supportive opinions to improve percussiveness of recommended personalized content
Reader: the intended personalized content receiver.	Authenticated to the system through his/her social network account
Expert: the expert might be the reader's close friend/family member or a public figure/organization which is trusted by the reader	Published the supporting opinion
Author: the presentation designer	Creating the presentation template and rule files

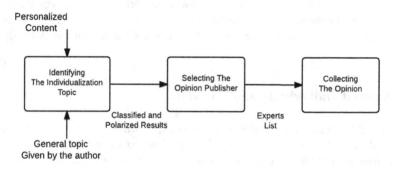

Fig. 1. General overview of individualizations model

3.1 Identifying Individualization Topic

Categorizing the personalized content is the first step towards mining supporting argument. The content main topic needs to be identified before an expert or a supporting opinion can be assigned to the personalized content. As discussed in our previous paper [4], a content assembler collects the contents by user profiling and applying author driven content rules. The content rules act like the logic to guide the recommender system with collecting, analyzing, and personalizing the content. The rules are essentially consisting of facts and goals. Facts are users' data (e.g. age, sex and income) and goals (e.g. increasing savings and higher education) are topics that author likes the personalization system to collect content for based on users' data. Once the rule is activated, the system begins with searching for information within the rule's goal context and recommends the most relevant content based on the criteria. Thus, rule goals can also be used as a way to categorize the content.

To avoid contradiction between supporting opinion and the content, the system first need to conduct polarity analysis on the content. For instance, following sentence implies a negative opinion:

"Returns are not guaranteed – While stocks have historically performed well over the long term, there's no guarantee you'll make money on a stock at any given point in time and you may lose all your principle".

However such an opinion is not a suitable candidate for the content as supporting opinion:

"Just made a $3,000 investment in stock last year and it turned into a $250,000 fortune within couple of years".

The polarity of a sentiment is the point on the evaluation scale that corresponds to our positive or negative evaluation of the meaning of this sentiment. A good practice is to verify whether the supporting opinion has the matching sentiment information as the intended personalized content. This achievable through existing third party public APIs like o2MC and Stanford NLP - Sentiment Analysis.

3.2   Searching for the Expert

Acquiring expertise in any domain is defined as going beyond ordinary learning from rule-based and fact-based "know-that" towards experience-based "know-how" [16]. Unfortunately, the data generated in social network accounts does not have the semantic structure which we see for product's review on a typical electronic commerce (EC) website. Such a data structure, allows publishers to build up reputation/expertness level in the community. In social networks, our tools are limited to number of likes and re-posts (re-tweets) plus polarity analysis on the comment. As illustrated in Fig. 2, our task in this part of proposed model is to generate a list of experts for a given topic.

There are two groups of experts: personal relatives and public figures/organizations. Personal relatives includes close friends and family members. Unlike well-known famous people/organizations (the second group), the system first needs to determine the quality of the relationship with the people in the first group. To achieve our goal, we rely on an unsupervised model to estimate relationship strength from interaction (e.g., communication, tagging) and common interests. By using the above idea, Xiang and Neville formulated a link-based latent variable model, along with a coordinate ascent optimization procedure for the inference [17].

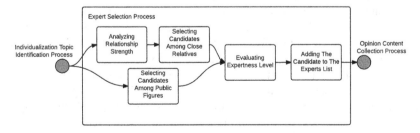

Fig. 2. General overview of expert selection process

Once the system filtered out reader's casual acquaintances with weaker relationship strength, it initiates a semantic approach to organize each of our candidates with the area of expertness within the given topic. Based on Dreyfus and Dreyfus terminology [16], this task has two phases.

1. Confirming the "know-that" factor:
   This task is summarized into processing/classifying candidate activities, and finding the total number of activities associated to the individualization topic. The activity is defined as candidate's posts and re-posts from other users. The post may also contain a link to a website which is also reflected in the classification. The goal is to define how well the candidate knows the topic.
2. Estimating the "know-how" factor:
   Well known readability indexes like flesch-kincaid [18], gunning FOG [19] or Coleman-Liau [20] are formulated to evaluate and indicate comprehension difficulty of a text or a passage. The calculated readability score for the candidate's published or the recommended content is the first source to determine the level of expertness. Although, there is no ranking mechanism in social network to build up reputation, number of followers, likes and re-posts can be applied towards estimating the reputation level.

To increase the likelihood of choosing the best possible supporting argument, the system generates a list of top experts for the given individualization topic instead of only selecting a single expert.

3.3   Collecting the Opinion

Sentiment analysis (opinion mining) [6] involves various methods and techniques that originate from Information Retrieval (IR), Artificial Intelligence (AI) and Natural Language Processing (NLP). This confluence of different approaches is explained by the nature of the data being processed (free-form texts) and application requirements (scalability, online operation) [21]. For the purpose of our research, we picked a typical opinion mining process that involves identifying, classifying and analyzing sentiment polarity. Besides, collecting the content, it conducts binary sentiment classification for instance, at emotional states such positive or negative. An overview of this section of the model is illustrated in Fig. 3.

Similar to the identifying individualization topic, in the first step, we need to identify the topics mentioned in the input data, and also associate with each topic the corresponding opinionative sentences. The available third party tools for opinion mining also allow us to distinguish between opinionative and non-opinionative phrases by performing subjectivity identification. This additional task is useful, since not all phrases that contain sentiment words are, in fact, opinionative.

The second step is to collect the supporting opinion. We need to assure that the opinion and personalized content sentiments are aligned. The same polarity analysis which we have applied for the personalized content can be reused during opinion mining. By comparing the result with the personalized content sentiment, the model can avoid creating contradiction between supporting opinion and the main content.

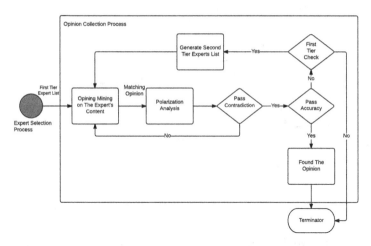

Fig. 3. General overview of opinion collection process

To simplify the comparison process, we are considering only binary polarity analysis by classifying contents into positive and negative groups. However, it is possible that the content has neutral or irrelevant sentiment category. In that case, we are not collecting opinions for the content.

Once the above steps are conducted, it is possible to select the closest matches to the target content as the supporting opinions. However, it is likely that the personalization system fails to find supporting opinions from the legitimate experts list or the accuracy level for the closest match is too low. To address the lack of supporting opinions, the model considers opinion mining through a second tier of experts recommended by the reader's preliminary experts (first tier of experts). This process is very similar to finding the first tier of expert's module. In social networks, transitivity means "the friends of my friends are my friends". The transposition of this property in our context implies "the reader trusts people who are assigned as credible sources by the reader's experts". Due to performance concerns and mitigating the risk of trustworthiness factor, we decided to not proceed with third or fourth tier sources.

4 Discussions

For a better demonstration of the methodology, we consider the following example of an educational piece on financial advice:

"Saving at least 10 to 15 % for retirement at an early age is a wise strategy. You will have to save less if you start early, and your savings will have longer to grow. Not all savings are guaranteed such as 401 K and stocks, so choose a savings option that is comfortable for you. One of the investment opportunities is in real-estate. Just four years ago, there were less than 25 annual starts in your neighborhood, and today it has grown to nearly 200 annual starts. It looks like the recovery is starting to occur even in the most exurban parts of Atlanta."

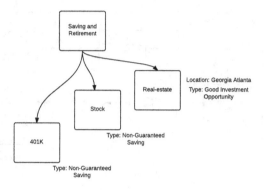

Fig. 4. Objective analysis example

The highlighted words in the above phrase are considered as objects. An object can be a product, person, event, organization or topic. Each object can be represented as hierarchy of components and sub-component. Each component in this hierarchy can have its own associated attributes. Figure 4 illustrates the relations between the objects and their attributes in the above example.

An opinion can be expressed on any component or attribute in the hierarchy. Using the mentioned tools for opinion mining in the proposed model, we are able to identify the objects as well as opinions that are likely to be relevant to the content. For instance, after searching through reader's social network, the system might generate results shown in Fig. 5. In this example, based on the generated experts list, the system decides to collect a tweet from the reader's close friends as well as a tweet from his trustable bank.

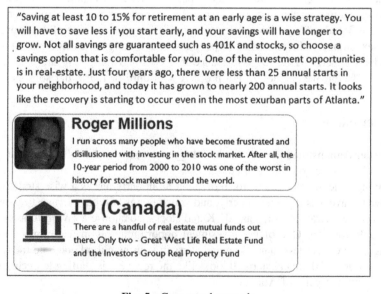

Fig. 5. Conceptual example

Our initial findings from previous publication [4] suggest that personalizing text can improve content persuasiveness. The accuracy of the result has a direct relation with the precision of the user social network contents. Based on the peer reviews on opinion mining, we identified polarity and modality at the local context with an estimated performance over 90 % precision and 50 % recall [22]. Comment threads can become another source of data for sentiment analysis and information retrieval. However, due to its unstructured nature, it requires entailment process and complex filtering methods, which is out of the scope of our work at this time.

5 Conclusion

In this paper, we have discussed our individualization model to enrich a personalization system with extracting opinion-oriented information. This model uses a corresponding 3-stage pipeline where the given content and user data will be used to collect opinionative information as supporting content to improve the overall persuasiveness of the content. The initial results demonstrate the ability of our model to increase the persuasiveness of content by enhancing it with supporting opinions from trustable sources. While further research is required to fine-tune all major parts of the model, the current design and findings are promising and show the potential use in many educational and otherwise informative applications, such as customer briefing, etc.

In addition to further research on technical aspect of the proposed system, more theoretical work is required to investigate the value of social network-based trust and who we can trust, the ethical issues associated with such persuasions (abuse of trust, privacy, etc.), the effectiveness of conflict resolution methods for opinions, and finding appropriate multimedia content from experts and the users themselves.

References

1. Khataei, A., Arya, A.: Personalized Presentation Builder. In: CHI, Toronto (2014)
2. Hovland, C.I., Janis, I.L., Kelley, H.H.: Communication and Persuasion: Psychological Studies of Opinion Change. Yale UP, New Haven (1953)
3. Sternthal, B., Dholakia, R., Leavit, C.: The persuasive effect of source credibility: tests of cognitive response. J. Consum. Res. **4**(4), 252–260 (1978)
4. Khataei, A., Arya, A.: Personalized presentation builder for persuasive communication. ACM SIGDOC's Communication Design Quarterly (2015)
5. Giffin, K.: The contribution of studies of source credibility to a theory of interpersonal trust in the communication process. Psychol. Bull. **68**(2), 104–120 (1967)
6. Pang, B., Lee, L.: Opinion mining and sentiment analysis. Found. Trends Inf. Retrieval **2**(1–2), 1–135 (2008)
7. Liu, J., Cao, Y., Lin, C.Y., Huang, Y., Zhou, M.: Low-quality product review detection in opinion summarization. In: Empirical Methods in Natural Language Processing and Computational Natural Language Learning, Prague (2007)

8. Ghose, A., Ipeirotis, P.G.: Estimating the helpfulness and economic impact of product reviews: mining text and reviewer characteristics. IEEE Trans. Knowl. Data Eng. **23**(10), 1498–1512 (2011)

9. Massa, P., Avesani, P.: Trust-aware recommender systems. In: RecSys, New York, NY, USA (2007)

10. Ma, H., King, I., Lyu, M.R.: Learning to recommend with social trust ensemble. In: SIGIR 2009 Proceedings of the 32nd International ACM SIGIR Conference on Research and Development in Information Retrieval, New York, NY, USA (2009)

11. Golbeck, J., Hendler, J.: Inferring binary trust relationships in Web-based social networks. ACM Trans. Internet Technol. **6**(4), 497–529 (2006)

12. Castillo, C., Mendoza, M., Poblete, B.: Information credibility on twitter. In: 20th International Conference on World Wide Web, Hyderabad, India (2011)

13. Cho, K.S., Ryu, J.-S., Jeong, J.-H., Kim, Y.-H., Kim, U.-M.: Credibility evaluation and results with leader- weight in opinion mining. In: Cyber-Enabled Distributed Computing and Knowledge Discovery, Huangshan (2010)

14. Pennebaker, J.W., Francis, M.E., Booth, R.J.: Linguistic Inquiry and Word Count. LIWC. net, Austin (2007)

15. Horrigan, J.: Online shopping. Pew Internet & American Life Project, Washington, D.C. (2008)

16. Dreyfus, H.L., Dreyfus, S.E.: Mind Over Machine: The Power of Human Intuition and Expertise in the Age of the Computer. Blackwell, Basil (1986)

17. Xiang, R., Neville, J., Rogati, M.: Modeling relationship strength in online social networks. In: The 19th International Conference on World Wide Web, New York (2010)

18. Kincaid, J.P., Fishburne, R.P., Rogers, R.L., Chissom, B.S.: Derivation of new readability formulas (Automated Readability Index, Fog Count, and Flesch Reading Ease formula) for Navy Enlisted personnel. Chief of Naval Technical Training: Naval Air Station Memphis

19. Gunning, R.: The Technique of Clear Writing, pp. 36–37. MCGraw-Hill, New York (1952)

20. Coleman, M., Liau, T.L.: A computer readability formula designed for machine scoring. J. Appl. Psychol. **60**, 283–284 (1975)

21. Tsytsarau, M., Palpanas, T.: Survey on mining subjective data on the web. Data Min. Knowl. Disc. **24**(3), 478–514 (2012)

22. Sauri, R., Verhagen, M., Pustejovsky, J.: Annotating and recognizing event modality in text. In: FLAIRS, pp. 33–339 (2006)

Context Elicitation for User-Centered Context-Aware Systems in Public Transport

Heidi Krömker and Tobias Wienken[✉]

Ilmenau University of Technology, Ilmenau, Germany
{heidi.kroemker, tobias.wienken}@tu-ilmenau.de

Abstract. In the area of public transport context-aware systems have great relevance regarding the barriers. The service of these systems can be adapted to the individual situation in order to support the user in carrying out his tasks during the journey. The adaption is based on the context of user which is mainly influenced by the user goals and the associated tasks. In the context-aware system development for public transport the early stages of requirements engineering require more detailed investigations. The research of this paper is focused on the initial context elicitation which is a precondition for the analysis and modelling of the context. The first part discusses the knowledge lack of the developer team about the context in the beginning of a development and presents a task-oriented context taxonomy of public transport to overcome this problem. Furthermore, the second part sets out to address the concerns of designing a concept of user data acquisition and provides a framework for the selection and combination of elicitation methods.

Keywords: Adaptive system · Context awareness · Requirements engineering · Context elicitation · Public transport

1 Introduction

By using public transport the passenger passes different stages during his journey, from planning the trip up to his arrival at the destination. During these situations the passenger is confronted with a large number of barriers regarding his journey, e.g. missing automation of passenger information as well as insufficient seating capacity. Therefore the passenger needs situational adapted support to master these barriers. This support can be realized by context-aware systems. Context-aware applications respond to changes of actual existing situation and optimize the service or the information automatically in accordance with the user goals. Because of that there is a rising potential of context-aware systems within the public transport.

The context is the initial point for all development activities in context-adaptive systems. Consequently the creation of context models is one of the first steps of development. However, the precondition for modeling is the initial capture of context data. Regarding this the developer teams are primarily faced with two challenges. During the early stages of requirements engineering the developers must have solid knowledge of context and the structure for planning and implementing the data research. Furthermore, the developers have to select appropriate methods for collecting data of

© Springer International Publishing Switzerland 2015
M. Kurosu (Ed.): Human-Computer Interaction, Part II, HCII 2015, LNCS 9170, pp. 429–439, 2015.
DOI: 10.1007/978-3-319-20916-6_40

potential users. This paper presents an approach for context elicitation of user-centered context-aware systems in public transport to solve the mentioned problems.

2   Background

Before discussing the challenges of context elicitation, a brief introduction is outlining what lies behind requirements engineering of context-aware systems and context of public transport.

2.1   Requirements Engineering of Context-Aware Systems

In general, context can be interpreted as the reification of a real situation [1]. However, from the user-centered point of view the user and his tasks form an inherent part of context [2]. This aspect considers Dey in his general definition by integrating the user in the definition and describing the task in the form of the interaction. "Context is any information that can be used to characterize the situation of an entity. An entity is a person, place, or object that is considered relevant to the interaction between a user and an application, including the user and applications themselves [3]." Furthermore, context-awareness describes the potential of a system to adapt to the circumstances of a certain users' situation. Therefore, context-aware systems can provide different functionalities, such as presentation of information and services to a user, performing of services automatically and tagging of context to use information for future retrieval [3]. In contrast to the division of the requirements engineering process into requirements elicitation as well as requirements analysis and modeling [4], this development phase of context-aware systems is enhanced by the requirements monitoring [5]. Here, the possible change of requirements during runtime is taken into account.

However, in this paper, the initial context elicitation is focused. To classify the context elicitation in the requirements engineering, the process by Sitou is presented (Fig. 1).

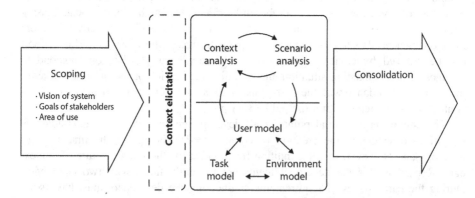

Fig. 1. Modified representation of the requirements engineering process for context-aware systems by Sitou [19].

The results of the phase scoping deliver the starting point and the limits for the context elicitation in the area of use. Afterwards the context elicitation can be executed by this specification. All information about person, place and any objects which are relevant for the task are collected. As stated by Adelstein et al., elements can be considered relevant if the information is needed for the adaptation of the task as well as the information improves the user's understanding of the task [6]. The collected data form subsequently the basis for the iterative analysis and the modelling, to generate the user model, the task model and the environmental model.

2.2   Context of Public Transport – A Task-Oriented Perspective

The motivation of a public transport passenger is based on the task in his or her personal agenda. The user needs the public transport to master ways between appointments and tasks of the daily routine. For that reason, the public transport can be considered as a link between single agenda elements [7]. Based on this perspective, the superior goal of "managing a journey" can be derived [8]. When analysing the structure of a journey, it can be divided into a sequence of phases – the so called journey chain. In the view of the Association of German Transport Companies, the journey is broken down into stages and it lists places where the passenger passes during a trip [9]. Hörold et al. divided this journey chain into eight stages, from planning the journey to arriving the desired destination [8] (Fig. 2).

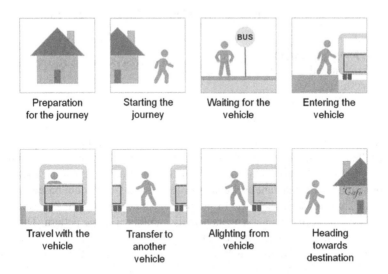

Fig. 2. Journey chain in public transport [16]

3 Challenges for Context Elicitation

The initial points for the presented approach are two essential challenges for the development team during the context elicitation phase: The needed basic understanding of user context as well as the specific requirements for context data elicitation.

3.1 Basic Understanding of User Context

According to Bauer and Spiekermann, the knowledge of the given situation is an essential precondition for identifying relevant context elements [10]. However, the necessary context understanding of the development team and the early execution time of context elicitation are mostly in contrary relation. This problem occurs especially in complex areas of use of the public transport. To specify the needed knowledge of the context for the development team, during the phase of scoping it the supported task of journey chain should already be determined. Thereon the data collection can be executed and subsequently the user, his goal and the resulting tasks as well as the relevant elements of the environment can be characterized.

Because of this, the development team should have a basic understanding and categorization of the public transport context at the beginning of context elicitation.

3.2 The Specific Requirements for Context Data Elicitation

The following enumeration gives an overview of the challenges for context data elicitation:

- Implicit knowledge of the user
- Formalization and communication of information
- Future systems
- Scope and detail degree of context to be collected
- Dependencies of context elements

Besides the context understanding, the design of a concept for data acquisition is a central challenge. When developing user-friendly systems, the potential user himself is the centre of data collection. On this account the question arises which methods are suited for acquiring the relevant user data. Context-aware systems are based on explicit and implicit knowledge of the user. In public transport, the implicit knowledge fragments occur e.g. in form of a passengers heavily habituated usage pattern. This kind of information cannot be easily formalized and communicated, because the determinant of an action is done on a subconscious level. Another challenge for the developer as well as the user are visionary systems like innovative assistance systems for mobility impaired passengers. In this case, the future context of an application has to be captured, though the user has only limited experiences of this scenario. On the system side, the developer must not only solve the problem of identifying relevant context elements but also the question of when the context elicitation should be stopped. Schmidt describes this question as non-trivial [11], because the complexity of this decision rises with the required detail degree as well as the number and the heterogeneity of entities, e.g. transport vehicle, driver, stop point, points of interest etc. Besides the scope, the developer has to face several content-related challenges regarding context. For example, in cooperation with potential users he has to define the necessary context elements for the adaption of a task (active) as well as the context element which enhance the users' understanding of a current task [6]. This poses a particular challenge, because numerous heterogeneous user types with different preferences and information needs exist in public transport [12]. Furthermore, the development team has to find dependencies between identified objects. So objects can have inherent relations [11] or specific values of objects only provide an added value for the application in combination with other objects [6]. In this respect, it is important to remember that users' context is not only influenced by public transport, but also by the users' daily routine.

The discussion of the challenge shows, that the characteristic of context aware systems and public transport context may be considered in the concept of context elicitation. Moreover, the consulted users have to be integrated in this decision making.

4 Approach for Context Elicitation in Public Transport

Taking the challenges in consideration the need of an approach occurs in order to overcome difficulties in this domain. Therefore an approach for context elicitation for user-centered context-aware systems in public transport is developed. The first part provides general context taxonomy of the public transport. Furthermore the second part presents a framework for the selection and combination of context elicitation methods.

4.1 Taxonomy of Public Transport Context

The proposed taxonomy can be defined as a categorization of the context information regarding the public transport. The taxonomy is of twofold importance for the interdisciplinary development teams. At first developer teams should enlarge the understanding of the public transport context in order to ensure the precondition of a context elicitation. The second purpose of categorization is the assistance in identifying relevant context elements.

Method of Taxonomy Creation. The taxonomy is developed within three steps: working model, abstraction and generalization and verification and refinement. In the first step the basic structure of the working model is defined by a combination of top-down-approach and bottom-up-approach. Afterwards the working model is elaborated by a workshop. [cf. 10] During the top-down-process existing context- taxonomies must be checked for suitability regarding public transport by a literature research. On the basis of the selected taxonomy an expert workshop identifies the involved user, the activities and the further relevant context elements with regard to the phase of the journey chain. An analysis of Kolos-Marzuryk identifies these parts as the core of a context model [13]. The extraction of the situational information is done by brainstorming and cord-sorting. To understand the user needs concrete scenarios and persons

of the public transport are provided for the participants of the workshop. The participating experts consist of transport company employees and usability engineers with
experience in public transport (n = 5). Part of the second step is to abstract and generalize
the created working model. Therefore, parts of the public transport taxonomy are
derived form the situational information of the scenarios and assigned to the selected
taxonomy from the beginning. Afterwards the created taxonomy of public transport is
verified and refined iteratively in cooperation with the experts.

Taxonomy of Public Transport Context. Based on Deys' definition of context, the
primary context types (location, identity, time and activity) [3] are used as the initial
point of the taxonomy. However, this classification is not considered to be sufficiently
specific in order to describe the situations of public transport in a differentiated manner.
Furthermore, the taxonomy should be more focused on the aspect of mobility.
Therefore the existing categories are expanded by the categories information, social
and environment [14].

Overall, the proposed approach to the description of public transport context
includes seven different categories: user, goal and the associated tasks, spatial context,
temporal context, environmental context, social context and informational context.
Besides these basic categories the taxonomy contains different degrees of abstraction,
macro level, micro level and situational level [cf. 10]. The level with the highest degree
of abstraction (macro level) is valid for all context-aware application in public transport. On this level the overall context of public transport is subdivided into the relevant
categories. The second level (micro level) substantiates each category and provides
support for the identification of relevant context elements in specific application
environments. Finally, the last (situational level) describes the relevant context elements of a given situation.

The taxonomy of the public transport should be introduced by an example of the
journey chain, the phase of the transfer to another vehicle (Table 1).

4.2   Framework for Selection and Combination of Context Elicitation Methods

As the second part of the approach a framework for selecting and combining of data
acquisition methods is provided. The goal is to support the developer team by selecting
the methods for an effective and efficient context elicitation regarding the prevailing
conditions.

Structure of the Framework. Based on the discussion of challenges above, four main
sections can be identified influencing the concept of a context elicitation in public
transport. These sections are the basic structure of our framework in combination with
the methods proposed. The first section, user, consists of aspects relating to the user as
a knowledge source. In that we distinguish between the organizational factors and the
characteristics of the user which could influence the quality of the collected insights.
The second section lists the factor related to the investigated tasks. Moreover, the third
section includes the pertinent factors regarding the context. The last section takes
account of the investigator and project conditions (Table 2).

Table 1. Taxonomy of the public transport

Marco level		Micro level	Situational level
General context categories of public transport		Refined context categories for passenger information systems	Relevant context elements for a given situation
Goal	Associated tasks	Preparation for the journey	Identifying the required time to transfer
		Starting the journey	Identifying the available time to transfer
		Waiting for the vehicle	Finding the departure point
		Entering the vehicle	- Finding the way to the departure point
		Travel with the vehicle	- Identifying the stop
		Transfer to another vehicle	- Identifying the stop point
		Alighting from vehicle	
		Heading towards destination	
User		Physical properties and conditions	Walking speed
		Mental properties and conditions	Current capacity
		Purpose of journey	Importance of purpose
		User preferences	Spontaneous need (e.g. shopping), safety
		Experience and knowledge	Knowledge of location and place
		Sociodemographic properties	
		Existing ticket and discount	
		External mobility impairments	Luggage
Context environment			
Spatial context		Information about user	Current position
		Information about departure	
		Information about destination / intermediate destination	Position of the stop/stop point
		Information about route	Distance to stop/stop point
Temporal context		Date and time	Current time
		Journey information	Planned end of journey
		Timetable information	Departure time
		Footpath information	Duration to stop/stop point
		Time information about destination	
Environmental context		Physical condition	Light, temperature, moisture, noise
		Social condition	Density of passengers
		Planning location – properties and equipment	
		Origin – properties and equipment	
		Destination / intermediate destination – properties and equipment	
		Vehicle – properties and equipment	
		Stop – properties and equipment	Barrier-free, shopping facilities
		Route – properties and equipment	
Social context		Other passengers	Fellow passenger
		Other passer-by	
		Service staff	Service staff at the platform
		Driver	
Informational context		Transport network information	Stop name
		Line information	
		Connection information	
		Disturbance information	Predicted departure time
		Navigation information	Direction for route
		Tariff information	

Table 2. Framework for selection and combination of context elicitation methods (based on [15, 17, 18]).

	Creative techniques			Observation		Inquiries		
	Brainstorming	6-3-5 Method	Six thinking hats	Field observation	Apprenticing	Questionnaire	Interview	Self-reporting
Factor user								
A large number of passengers	-	-	-	-	-	+	-	-
Short availability of passengers	-	-	-	+	-	+	-	-
Low motivation of passengers	-	-	-	+	-	+	+	-
Low abstraction capability of the passengers	-	-	-	+	+	+	+	-
High heterogeneity of the passenger preferences and restrictions	-	+	-	-	-	+	0	-
Troublesome group dynamics	-	+	0	-	+	0	0	+
Factor task								
High amount of implicit knowledge	+	+	+	+	+	-	0	-
A large number of visionary tasks	+	+	+	-	-	-	+	-
A large number of tasks which are difficult to formalize and communicate	-	-	-	-	+	0	-	-
Factor context								
Large scale of context	0	0	0	-	0	-	+	-
High detail level	+	+	+	+	+	-	+	+
High dependency	+	+	+	+	+	-	+	-
New elicitation of context	+	+	+	0	0	+	+	+
Enlargement of context	0	0	+	+	+	+	+	+
Other factors								
Missing experience in the application area	0	0	0	+	+	-	+	+
Missing experience of the method	0	0	-	0	-	-	-	-
Low cost budget	+	+	+	+	-	-	+	+

The involved methods are an extract from the spectrum of knowledge elicitation and can be grouped into three categories: creative techniques, observation, and inquiries. The selection is focused on the wide distribution and the manageable complexity in order to ensure the applicability.

The framework is intended to find a method for context elicitation in public transport. Because of this a description of the methods is not listed. A detailed description of the methods is, inter alia, discussed in [15, 17, 18].

The suitability evaluation of each method is carried out through a three-step scale: un-recommended, no influence and recommend. Each assessment shows, whether the method is recommended (+) or unrecommended (−) by the respective factor. A neutral factor which has no impact on the method is characterized by no influence (0).

Application of the Framework. Finally a three-staged procedure for selecting the suitable elicitation method should be introduced:

1. Preselection of methods based on the kind of examined knowledge
2. Analyzing the factors
3. Creation of a method mix

According to Rupp a distinction can be drawn between subconsciously, consciously and unconsciously knowledge. Based on this point of view a tendency regarding the suitability of the method can be concluded. Observing techniques are especially qualified for subconsciously knowledge. In contrast to that the best way to figure out consciously knowledge are questioning techniques. Unconsciously knowledge, e.g. in case of visionary tasks, appears mainly by using creative techniques [15]. During the second step the methods are compared among themselves according to the factors and potential methods are selected. Finally it is possible to compensate appearing weaknesses of the selected methods by combining them with further methods.

5 Conclusion

In this paper a task-oriented procedure is presented for the context elicitation in public transport. Based on the user's tasks, general context taxonomy of the public transport is developed in the first part. This context categorization pursues the aim to enhance the understanding from the developers of the context, since this knowledge of the user's context is the prerequisite for the early phase of the requirements engineering. Furthermore, the taxonomy facilitates the identifying of the relevant elements in the context of the public transport. This can be achieved because the tasks of the user limit the relevant scope of the situation. Beyond that the written composition shows the challenges of context elicitation for context-aware systems in the area of public transports. Based on these requirements, there will be developed a framework for the selection of an effective and efficient elicitation method. Finally, the usage limits of the framework should be discussed. In our understanding the taxonomy is only a tool for eliciting and structuring of the context. On this account the given taxonomy should be verified for validity in all developments and if necessary, depending on the aim, be adapted to the application. Regarding the method selection, there is an agreement with Rupp, who points out that the ideal method cannot be defined generally [15]. Therefore, the selection of factors have to be enhanced or adapted according to the prevalent project terms even for this introduced framework. Besides the factor the methods can also vary. The present selection is oriented on the broad distribution and the simple use. Depending on the project the usage of expansive methods could bring a clear added value.

Acknowledgements. Part of this work was funded by the German Federal Ministry for Economic Affairs and Energy (BMWi) grant number 19P12013B within the DynAPSys project. The DynAPSys project develops an agenda planning system for individual task and mobility planning from "door to door".

References

1. Finkelstein, A., Savigni, A.: A framework for requirements engineering for context-aware services. In: First International Workshop from Software Requirements to Architectures (STRAW 01) 23rd International Conference on Software Engineering. IEEE Computer Society Press (2001)
2. ISO 9241-210. Ergonomics of human-system interaction – Part 210: Human-centred design for interactive systems (2010)
3. Dey, A.K., Abowd, G.D.: Towards a better understanding of context and context-awareness. In: Proceedings of the CHI 2000 Workshop on the What, Who, Where, When, and How of Context-Awareness. Georgia Institute of Technology, Atlanta (2000)
4. Brügge, B., Dutoit, A.H.: Objektorientierte Softwaretechnik: mit UML, Entwurfsmustern und Java. Pearson Studium, Hallbergmoos (2004)
5. Siadat, S.H., Song, M.: Understanding requirement engineering for context-aware service-based applications. J. Softw. Eng. Appl. 5(8), 536–544 (2012)
6. Adelstein, F., Gupta, S.K.S., Richard, G.G., Schwiebert, L.: Fundamentals of Mobile and Pervasive Computing. MCGraw-Hill, New York (2005)
7. Wienken, T., Mayas, C., Hörold, S., Krömker, H.: Model of mobility oriented agenda planning. In: Kurosu, M. (ed.) HCI 2014, Part III. LNCS, vol. 8512, pp. 537–544. Springer, Heidelberg (2014)
8. Hörold, S., Mayas, C., Krömker, H.: Passenger needs on mobile information systems – field evaluation in public transport. In: Stanton, N.A., et al. (eds.) Advances in Human Aspects of Transportation Part III, pp. 115–124 (2014)
9. Verband Deutscher Verkehrsunternehmen (VDV): Telematics in Public Transport in Germany. Alba Fachverlag, Düsseldorf (2001)
10. Bauer, C., Spiekermann, S.: Conceptualizing context for pervasive advertising. In: Müller, J., Alt, F., Michelis, D. (eds.) Pervasive Advertising, pp. 159–184. Springer, London (2011)
11. Schmidt, A.: Ubiquitous computing-computing in context. Ph.D. thesis, Lancaster University (2003)
12. Mayas, C., Hörold, S., Krömker, H.: Meeting the challenges of individual passenger information with personas. In: Stanton, N.A. (ed.) Advances in Human Aspect of Road and Rail Transportation, pp. 822–831. CRC Press, Boca Raton (2013)
13. Kolos-Mazuryk, L., Eck, P., Wieringa, R.: A Survey of Requirements Engineering Methods for Pervasive Services. Report, University of Twente (2006)
14. Krogstie, J.: Requirement engineering for mobile information systems. In: Salinesi, C.B.A., Opdahl, A.L., Pohl, K., Rossi, M. (eds.) Proceedings of the 7th International Workshop on Requirements Engineering: Foundation for Software Quality (REFSQ 2001), Volume 6 of Essener Informatik Beiträge, Universität Duisburg-Essen, Essen (2001)
15. Rupp, C.: Requirements-Engineering und –Management. Carl Hanser Verlag, München (2014)

16. Hörold, S., Mayas, C., Krömker, H.: Analyzing varying environmental contexts in public transport. In: Kurosu, M. (ed.) HCII/HCI 2013, Part I. LNCS, vol. 8004, pp. 85–94. Springer, Heidelberg (2013)
17. Laplante, P.A.: Requirements Engineering for Software and Systems. Taylor & Francis Group, Boca Raton (2009)
18. Kotonya, G., Sommerville, I.: Requirements Engineering – Processes and Techniques. Wiley, Chichester (1998)
19. Sitou, W.O.: Requirements engineering kontextsensitiver anwendungen. Diss. Technischen Universität München, München (2009)

Personalization Through Personification
Factors that Influence Personification
of Handheld Devices

Jung Min Lee and Da Young Ju[(✉)]

School of Integrated Technology, Yonsei Institute of Convergence Technology,
Yonsei University, Incheon, Republic of Korea
{jmlee_0104,dyju}@yonsei.ac.kr

Abstract. In the close future, flexible bending display will emerge, bringing greater degree of freedom for users to personalize their devices. According to theoretical researches, the newly introduced technologies will be personified since people tend to be attracted to things that are similar to them, and treat them as if they were real people. Thus, this paper investigates what variables influence upon the personification of the flexible devices. To find these variables, interview was conducted on 10 individuals, asking how they would personify the device based on Paul Ekman's six basic emotions, and what kinds of variable influence their emotional change on the devices. As a result, the degree of angle, the speed and continuity of the movement and positioning of the device are the major factors that influence personification of flexible handheld devices.

Keywords: Flexible display · Personification · Personalization · Interaction design · User experience · Handheld devices

1 Introduction

In the early 2000s, revolution of the handheld devices occurred, changing from feature phone to the smart phone. This significant change in the user environment allowed users to experience greater degree of freedom on their interface. Along with this greater degree of freedom on usage of handheld devices, demand for personalization among the users has increased. Personalization of hand-held devices is significant since it fulfills individual's preference and increases productivity, satisfying the users' needs in general.

Indeed, software experienced significant development on personalization. However, hardware of the devices did not experience as significant change as the software development. Hardware of the devices is still limited, maintaining rigid and rectangular-shaped feature. Thus, hardware of the future handheld devices will be personalized in a way that the users can use them in more intuitive way alongside with the technology development. We perceive that personifying the deformable handheld device will fulfill the users' needs on personalization of their handheld devices. Herein, throughout this paper, we argue that the degree of angle, speed and continuity of the movement and positioning of the devices are the key variants that play decisive role to personify future handheld devices.

© Springer International Publishing Switzerland 2015
M. Kurosu (Ed.): Human-Computer Interaction, Part II, HCII 2015, LNCS 9170, pp. 440–447, 2015.
DOI: 10.1007/978-3-319-20916-6_41

2 Background

2.1 Personification Design

Relational researches and aestheticians perceive that people tend to be attracted to things that are familiar or similar to them. They argue that people perceive human-like of animal-like characteristics to be more beautiful because they unconsciously feel pleasured from them [2]. Related to this relational research, Uncertainty Reduction theory argues that this familiarity is crucial on developing any kinds or relationship, between human to human or between human to devices [2].

As Reeves and Nass also [13] advocates on their book, "The Media Equation", people tend to unconsciously treat computers, television and new media as if they were real people or real place [13]. In the other words, due to psychological and social factors, people tend to equate the media (x) equals to real people (y); x = y. Thus, as they argue it is necessary to "give computers some personality" for successful design of the interactive technical products [13].

This Uncertainty Reduction theory and Media Equation theory suggests that personification, giving human characteristics to non-human entities, will be one of the major promising design for the future technical products. For instance, designers tend to use human or animal's biological characteristics in order to attract and implement meanings on the object. Most well-known examples of personified technologies include humanoid robots, and other various robotic researches design their robots also use animal creatures to increase social interaction and support emotional bonding with humans [10, 16]. Thus, for successful commercialization of future technology, flexible handheld devices, it should maintain personified characteristics when it is first introduced into the public.

2.2 Flexible Display

There are various studies which investigated how the users may interact with the flexible devices [6–9, 11, 12, 14, 15]. There are various kinds of ways to change the shape of flexible displays, such as corner bending, swinging, rolling flipping, folding, twisting, crumpling, curving and zero-crossing. These kinds of shape changes can be implemented in different levels according to different factors. For instance, as Warren et al. [15] investigated how angle of the bending display can result different user experience, and Pederson et al. [11] also recognizes the role of speed on flexible display. However, how these variables influence emotional integration with the users is not widely explored.

There also had been researches which link the display with the emotions of the users [1, 3, 11]. Pederson et al. acknowledge that there is emotional response on the flexible display using Circumplex Model of Emotion, although they argue that it is not provide volatile feeling [11]. Bailenson et al. also recognizes how emotion factor is closely related to the user experience of haptic display using Paul Ekman's six basic emotions [1]. Paul Ekman's six basic emotions is the emotion model that propose that the happy, sadness, anger, fear, disgust and surprise are the universal basic emotions as it was identified by the analysis of facial expression of the people from different background [4, 5]. Likewise, we use six basic emotions for the analysis in this study because we believe that among various models of emotion, six basic emotions are the basic emotions that should be first introduced for the emotionally interactive flexible device in the future.

3 Methods

In order to find how people would personalize their personified flexible devices in the future, we conducted interview on 10 South Korean volunteers. The average age of the participants are 35.4, years old (SD = 13.92), where were male and 5 were female. On average, they commonly use 3 devices (SD = 0.94) on daily basis, and change their handheld devices every 25.2 months on average (SD = 6.81). Based on the seven point scale, participants rated average 4.7 on expected satisfaction on flexible devices that express emotion.

The interview lasted between 9–12 min for each participant. In the interview, clear plastic film that was cut and drawn into the size of iPhone 6 was given to the participants and was asked to freely personify the device based on 6 basic emotions of Paul Ekman. As they freely shape the plastic film to express the emotion, they were also asked how differently do they feel when they were bent, rolled, twisted the device in different angle and speed.

4 Result

4.1 Personification of Personified Devices

Through twisting, rolling, bending, curving and corner bending, participants personified the plastic film based on 6 basic emotion of Paul Ekman (see Table 1). Overall, participants preferred to express their emotion by bending> corner bending> rolling> twisting. Some emotion, such as 'disgust' and 'surprise', was personified similarly among most participants, created from the body image of a person vomiting when they are disgusted, and the a person bending their body backwards when they are surprised. However, for the other emotions, participants created different feature for the personification of devices.

For the most cases, the participants personified the device by perceiving the device-like plastic film as a human body. They imagined how their body moves when they feel such emotion, such as wave dancing when they are happy. They also personified their emotion by implementing facial expression, such as the movement of eyebrows and the shape of the lips. Apart from the body and facial movement, they tried to express the emotion abstractly, how their mind feels like when they are experiencing such feeling. For instance, P2 expressed 'anger' by rolling the device because his said his mind feel extremely small and self-protected when he feels angry.

Table 1. Personification of flexible device based on six basic emotions

Partici-pant	6 Basic Emotion					
	Happy	Sadness	Anger	Fear	Disgust	Surprise
P1						
P2						
P3						
P4						
P5						
P6						
P7						
P8						
P9						
P10						

4.2   Factors Influencing Emotion of Flexible Devices

For the in-depth analysis, affinity diagram was used to organize meaningful comments and ideas of the participants (see Fig. 1). The factors that influenced personification of flexible devices include the degree of angle and the speed of the movement as it was studied among other previous researches, and meaningfully, positioning of the device and consistency of the movement also provide different emotion to the participants.

Fig. 1. Affinity diagram of the interview

Degree of Angle. Most of the participants argued that different degree of angle provide different emotion. Six of the participants commented that the degree of angle plays crucial role on intensity of the emotion. For instance, P7 said that when the device with top corners bended is bent at smaller degree, it provides sad emotion, and when it is bended at larger degree, it provides the image of a person who is deeply depressed.

On the other hand, three participants viewed that implementing different degree of angle provide completely different emotion. For example, P9 said when the device is bent forward at 90°, it seems like a person vomiting, and when it is completely bent at 180, it gives the image of a person who is experiencing sadness. When it is slightly bent, at 20° for instance, it comes up with the image of a person who is bowing, a kind of way to greet the others in Asian culture.

Only one participant commented that different degree of angle does not provide any emotional change.

Speed of the Movement. All of the participants agreed that implementing different speed on the same movement and position of the handheld device can present different feeling to the users. For instance, as P1 argues, when the device rolls quickly, it seems like the device is trying escape or protect itself from the fearful situation. However, if the device rolls slowly, it looks like it is hiding itself from the others because it feels diffident or shy.

Consistency of the Movement. Through the interview, two main issues came up in relation to consistency of the movement of the flexible devices. Firstly, the device that moves single time provides different emotion from the device that moves repetitively. P4 commented that when the device quickly bends backwards single time, it seems like it is very surprised. However, when it repetitively bends backwards, it comes up with the image of children who are pestering for something to their parents.

Secondly, the device that consistently moves regularly gives different emotion form the device that moves irregularly. For instance, P5 commented that the movement of a device which create wave-like feature gives different body images. If the device moves at regular rhythmic speed, it seems like it is dancing. However, when the device moves irregularly, changing its speed from slow to fast and fast to slow, P5 recognize the device that is impatient and nervous.

Positioning. Although the device is bent at the same angle, positioning the device can provide different emotion to the individuals. For example, flexible device that is bending forwards slightly when it is standing present bowing gesture in Asian culture or nodding in Western culture. Although the device bent at the same angle, when the device bends forwards slightly when it is lying down drew the image of a person waking up.

5 Discussion

Taking Uncertainty Reduction theory and Media Equation theory to be valid, users will be more attracted to personified handheld devices in the future. Handheld devices can be personified through bending, twisting, rolling and corner bending the flexible display.

There may be contending perspectives on how to personify the handheld devices because each individual can perceive differently on what emotion does the personified device is trying to express. Here, instead of standardizing the movement of personified flexible display, we believe that future flexible display is more likely to be personalized among the users because apart from the social trend among users to characterize themselves from the others, personalization of the devices also plays crucial role on productivity. Indeed, this study finds that the users tend to personify the device in each personal ways, taking images of facial expression or body movement, or how their mind feel like abstractly.

For the personalization of personified flexible devices in the future, degree of angle, speed and consistency of the movement and positioning of the device should be considered as a key variant for the technological development of flexible display. The users would be able to freely personalize the movement of the flexible display that expresses emotion by controlling these variables.

6 Conclusion

Throughout this paper, we find two observations through the interview on 10 participants. First, people tend to personify the device by using how they express the emotion through their face or body movement, or how their mind abstractly feels like. Secondly, variants that influence personified bending display include: the degree of angle, speed and consistency of the movement and the position of the device. This study is significant as it outlines what factors should be considered to personalize the future flexible handheld devices.

Limitation and Future Work. The limitation of this paper is that the interview was held among South Koreans only. Thus, cross-cultural study on how the users from different backgrounds personify the flexible display can be researched for the future study. This study also does not suggest specified digit on what angle, which position and how fast the device provides the specific emotion. For the further research, these specific digits can be investigated. Matching the personified movement with the function that the device can provide can also be an interesting research for the future work. Although this paper focuses on the personification of handheld devices, it would also be interesting to see how people personify other kinds of devices, such as tablet PC or wearable devices.

Acknowledgements. This research was supported by the MSIP (Ministry of Science, ICT and Future Planning), Korea, under the "IT Consilience Creative Program" (NIPA-2014-H0201-14-1002) supervised by the NIPA (National IT Industry Promotion Agency).

References

1. Bailenson, J.N., Yee, N., Brave, S., Mergetm, D., Koslow, D.: Virtual interpersonal touch: expressing and recognizing emotions though haptic devices. Hum. Comput. Interact. **22**, 325–353 (2007)
2. Berger, C.R., Bradac J.J.: Language and Social Knowledge: Uncertainty in Interpersonal Relations. Edward Arnold, London (1982)
3. Dawson, J.Q., Schineider, O.S., Ferstay, D., Dereck, T., Link, J., Haddad, S., MacLean, K.: It's alive! Exploring the design space of a gesturing phone. In: Graphics Interface Conference 2013, pp. 205–212. ACM Press, Toronto (2013)
4. Ekman, P., Frisen, W.V.: Unmasking the Face: A Guide to Recognizing Emotions from Facial Clues. Prentice-Hall, New Jersey (1975)
5. Ekman, P., Sorenson, E.R., Friesen, W.V.: Pan-cultural elements in facial displays of emotions. Science **164**, 86–88 (1969)

6. Gomes, A., Nesbitt, A., Vertegaal, R.: MorePhone: a study of actuated shape deformations for flexible thin-film smartphone notifications, In: Proceedings of CHI 2013, pp. 583–592. ACM Press, Paris (2013)

7. Hemmert, F., Lowe, M., Wohlauf, A., Joost, G.: Animate mobiles: proximacally reactive posture actuation as a means of relational interaction with mobile phones. In: Seventh International Conference on Tangible, Embedded and Embodied Interaction, pp. 267–270. ACM Press, Barcelona (2013)

8. Lahey, B., Girouard, A., Burleson, W., Vertegaal, R.: PaperPhone: understanding the use of bend gestures in mobile devices with flexible electronic paper displays. In: Proceedings of CHI 2011, pp. 1303–1312. ACM Press, Vancouver (2011)

9. Lee, S., Kim, S., Jin, B., Choi, E., Kim, B., Jia, X., Kim, D., Lee, K.: How users manipulate deformable display as input device. In: Proceedings of CHI 2010, pp. 1647–1656. ACM Press, Atlanta (2010)

10. Li, J., Chignell, M.: Communication of emotion in social robots through simple head and arm movements. Int. J. Soc. Robot. 3, 125–142 (2011)

11. Pederson, E.W., Subramanian, S., Hornbaek, K.: Is my phone alive? A large-scale study of shape change in handheld devices using videos. In: Proceedings of CHI 2014, pp. 2579–2588. ACM Press, Toronto (2014)

12. Rasmussen, M.K., Pedersen, E.W., Petersen, M.G., Hornbaek, K.: Shape-changing interfaces: a review of the design space and open research questions. In: Proceedings of CHI 2012, pp. 735–744. ACM Press, Austin (2012)

13. Reeves, B., Nass, C.: The Media Equation: How People Treat Computers, Television and New Media Like Real People and Places. Cambridge University Press, Cambridge (1996)

14. Roudaut, A., Karnik, A., Lochtefeld, M., Subramanian, S.: Morephees: toward high "shape resolution" in self-actuated flexible mobile devices. In: Proceedings of CHI 2013, pp. 593–602. ACM Press, Paris (2013)

15. Warren, K., Lo, J., Vadgama, V., Girouard, A.: Bending the rules: bend gesture classification for flexible displays. In: Proceedings of CHI 2013, pp. 607–610. ACM Press, Paris (2013)

16. Yohanan, S., MacLean, K.E.: The role of affective touch in human-robot interaction: human intent and expectations in touching the haptic creature. Int. J. Soc. Robot. 4, 164–180 (2012)

Enterprise Systems for Florida Schools

Mandy Lichtenstein[(⊠)] and Kathleen Clark

College of Business, Florida Gulf Coast University, Fort Myers, USA
mdlichte@eagle.fgcu.edu

Abstract. The purpose of this paper is to show the impact of decision making about technology in school districts. During our research we found a lot of important information about decision making and forecasting. Furthermore, we also found information on EBusiness, along with Business Strategy, Structure, and Impact. All these important factors come together to help us understand where the Charlotte County's district went wrong in their decisions with their upgraded system. We explore our findings and present the results of how better planning can help other districts.

Keywords: Enterprise systems · Florida schools · FOCUS system · Hardware · IT department · Legacy system · Schools · Software system · System maintenance · System benefits · System implementation · System upgrades · Vendor

1 Introduction

Decision Making is becoming more important as technology expands, especially in public School districts. Decision making is defined as the steps taken while coming to a decision. We decided to do our case study on one of the local school districts in Florida to see if they have had any issues with their technology practices. We researched and choose to go with Charlotte County Public Schools.

1.1 Background Information

During our research, we found that Charlotte County Public Schools have a history of over 120 years. Originally, Charlotte County was part of Desoto County and the school sessions were held in the community hall during 1880s but quickly outgrew it at the time. They went ahead and built the first actual school building for the student community in 1888. Meanwhile, the modern district as we know today did not start until much later. The State of Florida and the County of Charlotte officially recognized the public school district during the 1920s when Charlotte became independent from DeSoto County ("Our history" 2014).

We found that the first is the Department of Innovation Through Technology (DoITT) which handles the hardware and software throughout the district. They handle the hardware in the individual schools and the administrative buildings. The second department is Information and Communication Services (ICS) which handles the data load of the county. Along with that they also handle the Student information system (SIS) throughout the county.

M. Kurosu (Ed.): Human-Computer Interaction, Part II, HCII 2015, LNCS 9170, pp. 448–458, 2015.
DOI: 10.1007/978-3-319-20916-6_42

We decided to concentrate our case study on the ICS department in Charlotte County Public School District. They manage the FOCUS School Software, which is their student information system platform. Their FOCUS School Software is the upgrade they did from their legacy system they originally were using. We found that in the beginning of 2009, the district started their research into different systems that could support all the functions they needed for the time, including IEP tools. According to The anonymous, Director of the ICS department, FOCUS is responsible for many of their tasks such as; "taking attendance, disciplining, grades, and student information for parent to see. There is also course history updates, along with transcript transmission to DOE, and State survey processes". The FOCUS software system was implemented throughout the district during the summer of 2010, while the schools were at a low operational capacity. They had about 150 people that were involved in implementing the software. Part of the implementation process was that they went live only after using testing servers and getting them to 99.98 % accuracy. They were able to get this done quicker than they were anticipating and were able to go live ahead of schedule ("Charlotte County" 2010).

We found that during our research in the four years since they implemented the system there has been a few issues that have come up. The most recent issue was that they were having difficulties "timing out" on the FOCUS/SIS because of the volume of data that is passing through it daily. According to The anonymous, they had to invest in and add two more front end servers to the FOCUS/SIS systems to correct this and they are still watching these for effectiveness today. They School district has 15,744 students currently throughout its 18 schools that the FOCUS system is accountable for.

1.2 Research Statement and Questions

Since we found they were having timing out problems with their FOCUS system that has become the main purpose of our case study. This means, helping other school districts avoid this issue when making upgrades to their system or upgrade form their original legacy system. We want to provide information about what we feel went wrong with Charlotte County's process. We believe the answer is quite simple and that is they needed to have a clearer understanding of the decision making processes to avoid the issues.

This can be done by understanding the ways other corporations do their decision making and trying to improve theirs. They could even going as far as making a case to the state to improve the decision making process in school districts because according to John, "School Districts are required to compare. They have to set specifications and requirements, along with comparing cost and other factors from as many vendors that will submit a bid". The decision making process brings in our research questions that we asked ourselves for this case study.

2 Literature Review

For the literature review section we are going to focus on what an ICS department is and why it is useful. The decision making process and why it benefits a decision. Along with the forecasting process and how it helps with correct predictions. Next it moves into Business Strategy, Structure, and Impact and how these factors impact school districts. Lastly, it moves into E-Business module and how Charlotte County School Districts website can be compared to and E-Business module because of the different departments linked on the webpage.

2.1   ICS Vs ICT Departments

During the research for the literature review, there were several sources that were found for the understanding of Information and Communication Departments (ICT). This department is just another name for the Information and Communications Services (ICS) department in the Charlotte County Public School District. According to research that was done in Nigeria companies have had positive significant relationships with their ICT adoption (Ladokun, p. 81). Here in the states, Charlotte County Public Schools has had the same type of adoption of their version of an ICT department. This department handles all of the reporting that the county school district does to the state. Along with all the reporting they do, they also manage the day to day operations within the FOCUS student information system such as daily backup of information and monitoring system performance.

According to another study, done by Sulaiman Alateyah, administrative processes within businesses need to have a separate department for the information and communication. To build a company for the future the different processes throughout Saudi Arabia are going electronic; therefore, making it important for an ICT adoption in the county. Moreover, this process is a growing trend worldwide making it easier for governments to get services to their citizens (Alateyah, p. 280). This process is very similar to the growing trend of ICS departments in the school districts around the United States. Furthermore, in Florida, all districts have an ICS department that takes care of the services for the students, parents, and, teachers, and other staff of the local schools. Not all of the departments are named the same but they all do the same thing by giving information. Meaning, they help out the local public school community with their data needs such as, getting transcripts to the graduating seniors or helping the alumni out getting theirs.

Along with the positives of the ICT departments there are also some challenges that come with having one. In Africa, Nigeria is having some trouble with theirs because of how sparse the internet connection is. The study that was done has predicted that the slow adoption levels throughout Africa for more ICT departments is caused by the lack of electricity supply and their poor communication infrastructure (Ladokun, p. 81). Even though, the Charlotte County Public School's ICS department has been around for many years there have been some issues that are from the department. The major one is the way the way school districts in Florida are required to make their decisions, which mostly are based on only comparing. The county had to forecast for the number of servers they would need both for the present and the future for their SIS system. They were not able to correctly forecast for this system, which was mainly due to the decision making processes that are required within the school district. These issues are different from the ones in Africa's ICT departments, but they show that even with having a good electricity and communication infrastructure there are still challenges that affect the United States ICS departments. These issues bring in the next subsection of how decisions making is done for small and large businesses and how incorporating some of that into school district policies can help out with planning better for future upgrades.

2.2 Decision Making

According to University of Massachusetts, there are seven steps to the decision making model. These seven steps are: identify the decision to be made, gather relevant information, identify alternatives, weighing evidence, choosing among alternatives, taking action, and review the decision and consequences ("Decision-making" 2014). These seven steps could help any company in their decision making process including public school districts.

Based on the decision making model, school districts need to review their decision making practices and implement improved policies. Since, schools districts base their decisions on comparing prices over any other factor it would be beneficial to them to look at other factors. According to research, we found for this case study, showed factors that decision making factors that helped most in small businesses are education, previous work experience, and technology experience (Spencer, p. 1203). These three factors are very important for the decision makers in school districts to have, maintain, and go by.

School districts need a decision maker who is educated in computers and has gone to school for either information systems or the computer science. Having an education is important because the decision maker will know more than someone that went to school for something else entirely. Having previous work experience along with technology experience should be one of the number one factors in the person who is responsible for the decisions in the school district. They need to understand what the systems can do that the district is interested in looking at. An even better decision maker would be one that has worked on the system in the past because they have that first-hand experience. These should always be factors while making decisions.

For Example, let's say a public school district hires a CIO or director that came from another state or district they would bring with them that knowledge they learned during their time working with that other district. They could make better decisions like is the current system in their new district better than the one they used in the previous district. What functions worked better in that other system that they could look to implement in their new district.

Since, we found out that public school districts are required to compare and most likely pick the lowest cost one to save the budget. It would make more sense for a district to have a CIO or directory with past experience in different systems so they can compare the ones they know or research new ones and avoid the random bids they get. There are many companies out there that have Student information systems available through their enterprises. Public school districts need to have better research done into each one of the student information system to get better information about them. It is not just the software they need to research but also the hardware that will support the software they need to make decisions on.

According to The anonymous, Charlotte County Public School District decided to make their adoption of the FOCUS School Software based on the "availability, cost and bit specs requirements". While they researched the FOCUS system, they should have seen what the other school districts thought about the system, because they only compare the size of the system to other school districts numbers. This experience relates to the research that found "decision making is driven though experience" (Spencer, p. 1197). The way school districts make their decisions seems to be on savings more than on experience because of all the comparing they are required to do.

According to Ardjouman, they did a study that found that barriers that affected smooth adoption of technology are "cost of technological tools, lack of technological skills, and uncertainty over business benefits from adoption and use of technology, technical problems, inadequate infrastructure and poor maintenance, limited access to internet, limited and unreliable sources of power" (Ardjouman, p. 188). Charlotte County Public School District did not have all these problems but the one that seems most like their problem is inadequate infrastructure of the servers. Considering that the problems they faced were fixed by adding more servers it shows that they did not have a good enough infrastructure to handle the amount of students, parents, and staff they have throughout the district.

Other research that we found shows that decision making in school districts is based on all the key stakeholder data to represent the aspects of the schools (Lai, p. 63). This would be a great method if school districts across the United States could give out questionnaires to their students, parents, along with the staff. They would generate data about what the community likes in the system the way it is and what they would like to see it do. This can then be interpreted by the school districts while they do research on the best possible student information systems.

In the end, school districts should update their decision making policies to include the seven steps so that they have decision makers with a great understanding of information systems through experience and education. They need to spend less time on the price of the system and more time on the functionality of that SIS. Lastly, they should ask questions to the local student community about what they like and do not like in the current system. This brings in the next subsection of the literature review the forecasting methods in school districts for long periods of time.

2.3   Decision Forecasting

Forecasting methods go hand and hand with the Decision making processes, because companies cannot make correct decisions if the forecasting models have errors in them. This is very true for school districts because along with their decision making processes the districts need to make sure they forecast their future systems correctly. According to The anonymous, Charlotte Countly Public schools forecasted for the FOCUS system "by comparing the size of their district with the size of other districts that were already using FOCUS system". This information should only be part of the forecasting not the only data they use. Normally forecasting should be set up as a five – year plan ("Five year" 2013). This plan should include at least three years historical costs to the information department. They should also look at the growth rate of the county over the last several years too. They could have predicted the amount of student data going in the SIS by this. This decision to just base on other districts was probably brought on by keeping their costs with in the budget they were allowed. Going with only this method does not hold up in the end because districts are always growing with their student population and need systems that can grow without trouble.

Along with traditional (original) forecasting tolls there are several new methods that have come up in the last 40 years to improve predictions. Two of these are Delphi method and Scenario method. Delphi method is about taking surveys and letting people answer number of questions in a setting where a strong dominate personality will not over shine the less dominate. So having surveys that are anonymous helps this greatly (Karlo, pp. 313–314). The more formal definition for Delphi method is that it is an organized communication procedure. This method really would not work out well in a school district for forecasting reasons, because most everyone that uses the systems are students and staff that do not know much knowledge about the system structure. On the other hand, this method would help more with decision making because it would give the IT staff ideas of how the general population of the school districts are liking the system.

The scenario method is used to avoid problems that might occur in the predictions by running different scenarios outcomes (Wright, p. 814). Since this method is for developing flexible long term plans it might be a good method for school districts to use. This could help them when planning because it can give different possibilities of growth rates for counties. For the case with Charlotte County's School District, it could have helped by predicting growth rates along with possibilities of the number of servers they would need for a long period span. They could then have taken a number in that range, then compared it to several other districts using FOCUS, and invested in the correct amount of servers to handle the school district data load.

Even with all the great reasons for having the scenario method involved with forecasting, there are some problems that come with it too. Studies have found that there are reasons why the predictions will come out so low. One such reason is that the planning team has a "narrow frame of references" (Wright, p. 814). This could be true with the case involving Charlotte County Public School's because they only used the comparisons of different school districts when making the decisions on the FOCUS system. This is a narrow way to do the forecasting because of the many other factors that is involved in a prediction such as growth rates.

2.4   Business Strategy, Structure, and Impact

Strategy, structure, and organizational impact is a huge element of performance and impact. In order for businesses to be successful, they will need to do a significant amount of research on the industry they are entering and how to come up with a reliable success strategy, the structure of the business and how it compares to competitors, and also the organizational impact on your business by the way it is set up. Companies, especially in the modern business era, should have some knowledge on how technology is shaping businesses and competition. Businesses should be able to make there IS systems friendly for smart phones, modern computers, and user interaction (such as social media). There are many different factors of this topic that businesses should consider when trying to keep up with competition and make a profit off of their operations.

According to a case study we read called "Five Types of Organizational Strategy," successful business strategies depend highly on cooperation between the different departments of the business. There are three recommended factors for a business to consider that will lead business down the right path to coming up with a proper success strategy for every department and one that will be a superior influence on competitors. Communication is the first factor and it is recommended that a business strategy should gear toward excellent communication skill between organizational members and external stakeholders of the company. For Charlotte county schools, they have implemented several different information systems in order to perform the different business functions such as for financial data entry, employee data, students and teachers for entering and viewing grades, teachers for student discipline, the main school system for sending out report cards and other county-wide notices, etc. (Steensen).

Intentions is another factor that is a sign of a good business strategy. When a company is planning out their objectives and goals, it is important that they know their intentions and plan their strategy based on their capabilities. Charlotte County Public Schools wanted to implement the FOCUS system to be friendly toward the growth of the technology industry. They were convinced that they were capable of providing a new system that is not just helpful for teachers and parents to access academic information about children, this system would also be more helpful for the students. For example, most of the middle and high school students in Charlotte County have direct access to an online account where they can view their grades and submit homework online. This is kind of like our Canvas system here at FGCU.

The third factor of a successful business strategy is realization. This means that a company needs to keep good track of the decisions that they make and the consequences (good or bad) of those decisions. The company needs to realize what strategies work best so that they can continue down that path, and also what isn't working out for them so that they can conduct more research on how they are going to improve and what actions need to be taken to make those improvements. For this school system, they do keep very good track of what works out for their system. For example, they identified that their database management system was unreliable. Having an unreliable database can cause problems for both the internal and external stakeholder's for the company. In order to fix this, they plan to spend the next year or so switching their DBMS system over to Microsoft SQL Server 2014 hoping that this will provide better efficiency for entering and retrieving data.

The five types of business strategies shared in this study include: Shared, Hidden, false, learning and realized strategy. Shared strategy consists of all the company's employees using reliable communication about decision making and how to go about reaching an objective. The school system that we are talking about demonstrates a little bit of a shared strategy between the two separate information systems departments. We interviewed the Information Communication services department which communicates with their main information technology department in order to plan for system maintenance, system installations, upgrades, etc. Communication is always a plus for a company because the two departments can give each other feedback on how to successfully come up with a strategy to improve the information system for Charlotte County Public Schools.

Integration is the part of a business structure that is strongly encouraged and mostly refers to digital integration such as an enterprise system. According to an article about business structure, integration is one of the top ways to save money and is strongly encouraged for companies to be able to communicate better throughout the departments (Aversano, Grasso and Tortorella). This is where we think that Charlotte County Schools sort of lacks in a successful business strategy. In the interview, the director mentions several different Information Systems for the different departments. One for the main software systems, one for educational purposes, and more for other departments such as financial, maintenance, etc.

When we are referring to the business structure for Information Systems, we want to think about how Information Technology actions are aligned with the objectives for top management. Part of this means the company using a cost-benefit analysis to compare the IS actions to departmental expectations and looking for signs of successful patterns (Aversano et al. 2012). An information systems needs to be properly designed so that management can easily make decisions about what needs to be done with the different applications for the system. For example, the school system will make decisions regarding how to set up the web interface for teachers and parents to access student information. The department for the employee payroll system will have different requirements that are essential for a payroll system. The way an Information System is set up will affect the performance of business activities and if systems do not function correctly, it could cost the company not only money damages but also reputational damages. An example of a negative outcome for the FOCUS system that we discussed is that there are times where the system times out and its users cannot access important educational data.

2.5   E-Business

E-business is a very interesting topic because it is growing all around the world and has a large influence on economic growth for most companies. E-business allows companies to reach out to its stakeholders through the internet to figure out what people are looking for and how to satisfy customer demand. E-business has enabled companies to make better management decisions by enabling all the departments of the company and business partners to collaborate through a virtual system about different ideas. Competitive advantage is a huge factor of E-business. Companies are now using the internet to compare their business models with similar companies that market to the same customers. We know that the school system is constantly comparing their business processes to that of other districts in the state. Unlike twenty years ago, it is almost impossible to complete business activities without some form of digital technology for the company.

According to the article we read about virtual information systems, a successful business environment will be mostly virtual with the ability to transfer data to internal and external users, to provide background information and history about the organization, and also to interact with customers (could mean marketing goods and services for some companies). The Charlotte county school system does have a good virtual business structure. Even though there are some improvements that need to be made such as integrating the IS activities into one department instead of two, they do have a reliable online communication system where the different business departments of the school system can come together and make the decisions. (Kuettner and Schubert). There are of course several risks associated with ebusiness strategies, one of them being the revealing of unwanted information to competitors. Maybe Charlotte County Schools doesn't want Lee County to know what they are doing with all their systems because they want to be known for this strategy.

Customer Web interface is probably what most people think of when the hearing term E-business. This type of interface is most commonly known today and is probably one of the best ways to enable interaction for your business. A company's web interface should be designed efficiently so that the user can easily get hold of the information they need to. The Charlotte County School System has a main web site that people can access to find out information on the schools as well as links to the different departments and contact information. Though this is not an actual software system that integrates the different functions of the company, the different departments are integrated into this website. There are a set of links on the home page that are appropriate for students and teachers, information on the different schools, academic calendar information, a page for employees, department information, and even a link for candidates to apply for a career. This is very important for any company because if customers don not find what they are looking for on a business site, chances are that they will go somewhere else. Companies also need to think about the visual aids of their web interface. If a web site has inappropriate coloring or fonts that are too hard to read, it could cost the company because users will be scared away from the interface. For each department of the school system, there is an employee who is responsible for updating and maintaining the web page for that particular department. It is the responsibility of the communication information systems department to make sure that all required updates are made on the interface and that any technical issues with the system are addressed to the IT software department.

Data management is another important component of E-business. Because most company transactions happen online, data should be set up to automatically be stored in a database. For Charlotte County Schools, they are required to keep all students and alumni students on record for a specific period of time. That means whenever a new student gets enrolled into a Charlotte County Public School for the first time, their name will be stored in a big database for all the students in the district. This needs to be set up so that will be easier for a database administration employee to retrieve records and edit them if necessary. We already discussed that they are changing over to a new DBMS system next year.

3   Methodology Used

While we were gathering information about Charlotte County Public school district for our case study, we used two methods: research and interviewing. During our research, we found a lot of information about the school district through their website about the different systems they are currently using district wide. We found their newest released technology plan that was just published for the next five years for the county. Through this research, we also learned about the school district having the two information technology departments. Meanwhile, we originally decided to concentrate on the FOCUS school software, because we found a lot of information about the software on the distributer's website. During the research process and interviewing process we ended up finalizing on the idea of decision making instead of what system would be better than FOCUS. It was after this that we started researching about decision making processes. We also went ahead and researched all of the software that The anonymous said they had such as: "Sungard Bitech, FOCUS School Software, and Follett Destiny". A lot of hours went into all this research for the case study.

Furthermore, we decided to spend our time concentrating on the ICS department over the DoITT one. We used the Interviewing method to get more information about the school district and their information technology department. We decided it would be best to talk to one of the members who works in the ICS department. We noticed that The anonymous is the director of that particular department and decided to contact him for help. He is about the number two person in the technology department of the district, right under the CIO. The CIO takes care of the DoITT side of the district though, which is why we decided to go with the ICS side. The anonymous has a team for all their software they support throughout the district; for example, FOCUS school software. We initially contacted him to ask for his help in answering questions and within a week he got back to us. He had no problem answering interview questions for us. He asked that we do all our interviews through emails because of how busy he is during the school year. The first time, he got back to us within a day with the first half of interview questions. He got the rest of those questions answered by the end of the following day. Furthermore, about two weeks later we sent him our last few questions for the second interview on their decision making processes. He got those answered and back to us within 24 h. He really worked with us because if he did not know answers to the questions then he went into the district records to find out for us what the answer was. Now that the Methodology is talk about, the data analysis can be determined.

4 Conclusion

After conducting this case study research, we have learned a lot about the IT departments for school districts and how most of them handle day-to-day operations. The reason why we chose a school district instead of a retail company was to learn something different about management strategies and decision making. For the most part, we are not dealing with customers buying merchandise and the company making a profit off of that. We are dealing with an Information Systems department that is in high need of improvement and also needs to be functioning correctly at all times in order to not inconvenience a large number of people. To work for this department is not easy and requires a lot of communication, success strategy development, and decision making skills. The director of the CIS department seemed to be pretty happy with the FOCUS system and does not plan on implementing another system any time soon.

However, for some of the other systems they probably could have done a little more research on finding reliable vendors to avoid frequent maintenance issues. As far as where The Charlotte County School District is concerned with updating the IT systems, we don't see that happening any time soon. Based on the results from the interview, they seem pretty happy with the FOCUS system and do not plan on switching in the near future. The will probably need to eventually because the process of IT systems will more than likely change dramatically over the years and the FOCUS system may eventually become obsolete. Also, they may eventually find that other school districts are doing better productively and financially, which they may then realize they need to discuss the possibility of implementing a new system. All this is possible but there is not really any way of knowing how soon or far off this would happen (could be five or ten years from now). We enjoyed learning about the Charlotte County School Information Technology System and how they help the district succeed in its operations.

References

Alateyah, S.A., Crowder, R.M., Wills, G.B.: Identified factors affecting the intention of Saudi Arabian citizens to adopt e-government services. Int. J. Innov. Manag. Technol. 5(4), 280–286 (2014). doi:10.7763/IJIMT.2014.V5.527

Aversano, L., Grasso, C., Tortorella, M.: A Literature Review of Business/IT Alignment Strategies. Case Study Research. Department of Engineering, University of Sannio, Italy (2012)

Charlotte County Schools, Florida (2010). http://focusschoolsoftware.com/success/charlotte-county/

Decision-Making Process (2014). http://www.umassd.edu/fycm/decisionmaking/process/

District Mission (2010). http://www.yourcharlotteschools.net/district/aboutus.cfm

Five Year Forecast News (2013). http://www.swanton.k12.oh.us/5_Year_Forecast

Karlo, K., Palmroos, P. The Delphi method in forecasting financial markets—an experimental study. Int. J. Forecast. 30(2), 313–327, (2014). http://dx.doi.org/10.1016/j.ijforecast.2013.09.007

Kuettner, T., Schubert, P.: IT-based competitive advantage: a cross-case comparison of business software usage. Case Study Research. Koblenz, University of Koblenz-Landau, Universitaetsstr, Germany (2012)

Ladokun, I.O., Osunwole, O.O., Olaoye, B.O.: Information and communication technology in small and medium enterprises: factors affecting the adoption and use of ICT in Nigeria. Int. J. Acad. Res. Econ. Manag. Sci. 2(6), 74–84, (2013). http://ezproxy.fgcu.edu/login?url=http://search.proquest.com/docview/1500940251?accountid=10919

Our history (2014). http://www.yourcharlotteschools.net/district/history.cfm

Spencer, A.J., Buhalis, D., Moital, M. A hierarchical model of technology adoption for small owner-managed travel firms: an organizational decision-making and leadership perspective. Tourism Manag. 33(5), 1195–1208, (2012). http://dx.doi.org/10.1016/j.tourman.2011.11.011

Steensen, E.F.: Five Steps of Organizational Strategy. Case Study Research (2013)

Wright, G., Goodwin, P.: Decision making and planning under low levels of predictability: enhancing the scenario method. Int. J. Forecast. 25(4), 813–825, (2009). http://dx.doi.org/10.1016/j.ijforecast.2009.05.019

Toward Usable Intelligent User Interface

Nesrine Mezhoudi[(✉)], Iyad Khaddam, and Jean Vanderdonckt

Louvain Interaction Laboratory, Louvain School of Management (LSM) - Place
des Doyens, 1, Université catholique de Louvain (UCL),
1348 Louvain-la-Neuve, Belgium
{nesrine.mezhoudi,jean.vanderdonckt}@uclouvain.be

Abstract. Context-awareness of interaction with intelligent user interface has
been considered as a potentially important factor of their usability. A fair
amount of research has been conducted to identify and help developing
advanced adaptations in order to streamline interaction with systems. However,
it has to be noted that adaptations could have an adverse impact when it does not
meet users expectations. Thereby 'Context-awareness' as well as 'user-
centeredness' become more crucial to improve the quality of interaction as
well as UIs. Inter-twinned with intelligent techniques, HCI proved an ability to
be more intuitive, nevertheless a significant lack of transparency and controllability and predictability were detected. This work is aimed to improve the
quality of interaction to fit intelligent user interface performance. We focus on
interaction as a key factor for improving the user satisfaction and the interface
usability during use. This paper considers major issues and challenges of
improving interaction with user interfaces during their use by considering the
ISO2941. It presents a methodological proposal for guiding UI developers to
designs predict and evaluates interaction quality with regards to well-defined
dialog principles.

Keywords: Adaptation · Intelligent user interfaces · Controllability · Predictability · Transparency · ISO2941-110

1 Introduction

The complexity of interactive intelligent systems relies mainly upon three factors:
system, human and interaction [4, 5, 8]. Recent works focus on context-awareness and
user-centeredness for improving the User Interface (UI) quality and reducing interaction complexity. Adapting UI during use to the user, the platform and the environment
is a promising means towards accessible technologies. The literature shows that
adaptation manifests in different modalities regarding the human intervention degree.
Adaptations range from user-controlled adaptable mode to fully-automatized (intelligent) adaptive mode. Existing adaptation approaches present their pros and cons.
Adaptable systems promote controllability and maintain a high understandability and
satisfaction level. This advantage is the main pros of such approach, because customization (personalization) dialogues overload users and present a significant barrier
for end-users with different profiles and abilities. On the other side, despite their
advanced mechanism to automatically adapt to user preferences and the insignificant

M. Kurosu (Ed.): Human-Computer Interaction, Part II, HCII 2015, LNCS 9170, pp. 459–471, 2015.
DOI: 10.1007/978-3-319-20916-6_43

required workload, adaptive systems are still showing a high unpredictability and are considered confusing. Adaptive UIs (fully-automated) demonstrate their capacity to improve tasks achievement in terms of time and finality [2], to increase accurateness [11], users performance [10, 32].

However in most of the cases, adaptive behavior is at the root of inconsistencies that lead to decrease UI usability levels. Such adaptations are often seen as not transparent and lack controllability and reduce the predictability level [2]. This illustrate an increased yield spread may also be explained in terms of a more general customizability/human-cost tradeoff, which relies on user cognitive skills that acquire, process, decide and act at runtime. This was a critical issue discussing the advantages and disadvantages of intelligent UI and direct manipulated interfaces [29]. However with the growing complexity of UI direct manipulation is no more sufficient to handle interaction. Maes [30] claims for augmenting interface with intelligent behavior to improve usability and act on behalf user.

We believe that adaptivity and UI intelligence are not less relevant than direct manipulation for usability. Intelligent User Interface (IUI) challenges for usability are widely discussed, related development methods, adaptations technique, and maintainability [19]. The research in [20] identifies main proprieties for evaluating interactive system from different scopes and provides extensive definitions of concepts. However the issue is still intensified. Three main criteria were defined in the literature to assesse and criticize interfaces: (1) *Controllability*: it represents the capacity and tolerance of system to support user-initiated customization of the interface [31]. (2) *Predictability* which focuses on the extent to which past and present interface allows user to determine the outcome of future interactions, it is about actions and effects [16, 27], and (3) *Transparency* that concerns the honesty [27] of system. It presents the capacity of the user to understand adaptation and interpret perceived information.

In this work, we aim at promoting those criteria within a methodological structure to guide UI development and improve reliability and usability of intelligent UIs. The structure of this paper is as follows: Sect. 2 presents an overview of previous works. Section 3 presents a background of intelligent system usability and challenges that they are facing. Section 4 introduces the well-balanced model for intelligent usable adaptation and focuses on issues of predictability, transparency and controllability of adaptation. Section 5 concludes the paper and discusses future directions.

2 Related Work

Quite few studies in the literature paid attention to different IUI adaptations approaches shortcomings and called to consider an intermediate adaptivity level [5, 15]. Proposed solutions were mainly devoted to overcome the transparency and controllability deficiencies while keeping advantages of automatic adaptivity [5]. IUI shortcoming involve allowing the personalization by giving the user control over the UI design, making the system predictable so that it gives consistent reaction given the same user's feedback within the same context, and making the system transparent so that the user can understand approximately internal system inferences.

One way to achieve this performance consisted on allowing the user a partial control on adaptation. This solution defines a mixed-initiative adaptation method that combines adaptable and adaptive behaviors. Researchers in [9, 13] argues for mixing both behaviors to balance out the controllability and the predictability levels. Bunt presents a literature review discussing the relevance of the Mixed-initiative UI topic and stresses the necessity of the current adaptive systems to provide end-users with an adaptive mechanism assisting the personalization process [3]. Along the same lines, A Mixed-initiative solution MICA was proposed by [21], it consists on an adaptable system allowing users to personalize the UI, while assisting them by recommending customization. The system reinforces the comprehensibility. Evers [13] addressed controllability in adaptive UI by integrating the users in the system's self-adaptation loop. Both implicit and explicit controls were supported, implicit control defines the user's influence and the explicit control allows the user to change the adaptive behavior of the application [13].

Transparency was addressed from different perspectives, Dessart et al. [10] targets the transparency via animated transitions displaying the adaptation process explicitly to the end user. The transparency was addressed in a different way by self-Explanatory UI, which have the capacity to provide the end-user with information about its purpose, structure and design. Predictability was stressed as a crucial evaluation criterion for adaptive UI [15, 16], however the majority of works don't address transparency in an explicit way with focused solutions.

Table 1 establishes the coverage of analyzed works for each criterion. The analysis of existing works leads to identifying one significant issue: None of existing methods takes into accounts all of these criteria with an integral prospect. While these considerations need to be taken into account simultaneously to ensure that the approach is in compliance with the extents outlined in technical criteria.

Further we believe that the interaction quality and the UI usability concerns exceed these criteria. On the other hand, despite the authoritative nature of international standards for usability, many of them are not broadly considered. Commonly, standards

Table 1. Visual analysis and comparison of existing works coverage

Legend ●□Completely fulfills ◖□Partially fulfills ○□Does not fulfill * Not specified	Controllability	Predictability	Transparency
Bunt 04	●	◖	○
Bunt 09	●	◖	*
Garcia 10	*	○	●
Dessart 11	*	○	●
Ever 12	●	○	*
Gajos 04	●	◖	*
Demeur 08	○	○	●
Eisenstein00	*	◖	*

are established to provide valuable tools for promoting HCI best practices. Their completeness, their relevance to practices as well as their cost/benefits are widely discussed [4, 17]. To overcome such a weakness we believe that establishing standards to support interaction quality and system usability is of great importance. We argue for complete covering and support of standard principles within a well-established structure. To that end we refer to the ISO9241-110 to define a methodological guidance structure for supporting interaction with intelligent user interface.

3 Requirements and Challenges

3.1 Requirement for IUI Usability

The above-defined criteria were of paramount importance to the assessment of the literature and expected to contribute the improvement of their usability are: Controllability, Predictability and Transparency [6, 7, 14, 15, 27]. By the analysis of the related works and tools, as presented previously, the main IUI shortcoming is still the lack of systems that reinforce and support all criteria from early development stages (in a powerful, robust, and complete manner). We present here identified requirement:

R.1 The support of **controllability** represents the capacity and tolerance of system to support user-initiated customization of the interface [27]. Many works (e.g. [21, 29]) argues for providing user full control over automatic adaptations as a major requirement of acceptable adaptive systems. An intelligent UI require an improved support of user, in which user, depending on their preferences and need must be able to adjust their UIs and then being able to accept or decline system decisions [22].

R.2 The support of predictability focuses on the extent to which past and present interface allows user to determine the outcome of future interactions, it is about actions and effects [15, 16, 27, 31]. Gajos [15] considers that an adaptive system is predictable if it follows a strategy users can easily model in their heads, and evaluated predictability effects on user satisfaction. We assume that the accuracy and the predictability of the UI increased user satisfaction. Tsandilas [31] draw attention to the negative effect of inadequate adaptation accuracy on user performance in adaptive menus. Intelligent UI should maintain a height satisfaction level among their users. Accordingly providing accurate adaptation for the user context enhances such satisfaction and increases the subjective predictability of the system's behavior.

R.3 The **support of transparency** concerns the honesty [27] of system. It presents the capacity of user to understand adaptation and interpret perceived information. [19] argues for transparency as one on main usability principal for intelligent user interfaces. Only few approaches were aimed to increase the transparency of automatic adaptations have been published [10, 14]. Dessart et al. [10] suggest animated transitions for viewing the adaptation process to the user and develop a catalogue of "adaptation operations" to support continuity in the UI perception at runtime. Other approaches aim at a deeper user understanding of the system's adaptations by providing detailed justifications [19, 27]. However, it seems questionable if and how these approaches can match perceptual, cognitive and motor impairments in users.

All above-mentioned shortcomings agreed on the fact that successful adaptations must not result a confusing situations and should avoid the trouble of losing control over the user interface for end-users who must be at the heart of adaptation. Their involvement could be achieved by providing non-technical designers and typical users with user-friendly techniques for managing adaptations depending on their aptitudes at different levels: perceptual, cognitive and motor. Existing works promote above selected criteria in different ways and by different policy, however they still suffers from shortcomings and most of existing methods covers partially such concepts [19].

3.2 Challenges

Context-aware interaction requirements were investigated within different perspectives. Nowadays, the adequacy of interaction scenario to the user and the context is an essential requirement. Interaction depends on the context of use and situation complexity but above all on user preferences and abilities. The main interaction issues could be summed within three points: incomplete user model, lack of user involvement and complex adaptation model [27].

Improve Users Support: Establishing an effective personalization requires recognition of user's preferences. However it is difficult to obtain accurate and sufficient user representation from user profile and abstract user models. A new trend of user centered adaptation focuses on accruing information on users based on their interaction and feedbacks. Back to the year 1983, [18] defines feedbacks as "information about the gap between the actual level and the reference level of a system parameter which is used to alter the gap in some way". This seems promising to improve their involvement in system decisions and consequently their satisfaction. The consideration of user feedbacks and preferences during interaction for adaptations is intended to increase the user satisfaction degrees by time and reduce the system complexity [27].

Improve Decision-Making Process: The system involves several complex models that require more inferences to support too high functionality such as acquiring, considering up-to-date contextual facts and adapting the UI at runtime. Although there were successful adaptive systems, they did not often make use of particular users' preferences and context's circumstances at runtime. A context-aware adaptation should have a crosscutting impact on the software design and appearance depending on the interaction's context with an insignificant cost [33]. Designing a responsive adaptation at runtime is still a challenge in HCI since there is no agreed technique for learning and executing appropriate adaptations during interaction neither an approach to manage unanticipated situations. UIs adaptivity over time considering acquired data during use is still a major UI requirement. However, system adaptation and decision-making is a double-edged sword. On one hand, it enhances UIs pervasiveness and proactivity. On the other hand it could increase the user's workload leading to frustration. Accordingly, systems that adapt and change their behavior to better-fit users' requirements could disturb user and interrupt predictability, further perceptual transparency is not enough to maintain understandability. Context-aware interaction involves three main basis: (1) giving the user control over the system, (2) making system decisions predictable so that it always agree with users' expectations, and (3) ensuring system transparency so that the user can understand internal inferences. These requirements are widely revealed in the literature [19, 32].

We aim at improving interaction by considering effectively usability principles. This improvement can enhance the user experience and maintain UI usability within the growing complexities of interfaces functionality and their changing contexts. To overcome this complexity we put forward user as the heart of interaction and adaptation process. Reliability to human behavior is a requirement. We consider Rasmussen's model, which has been extensively used over the last two decades for human behavior modeling. The model rationalizes the Human (user) behavior controlling a complex dynamic system [28]. This model sum up human performance within three levels of behavior: skill, rule, and knowledge. The purpose is not only to advance adaptation; it is to address the challenge of usable adaptation, taking into account different user needs with an integral prospect.

This work suggests a well-balanced guidance model to counterbalance the cost of adaptation principles with cognitive user behavior. It also suggests that system adaptation have to be examined and matched in terms of the level of focus (knowledge, skill, rule) and usability principle that they provide.

4   A Methodological Structure

To address previous provoked requirements, a set of key points were analyzed and lead to the definitions of consistent design decisions for usable intelligent UI (Table 2). The solution focused on two main points: the support of human behaviors for improving the

Table 2. Requirements and associated design decisions for context-aware intelligent interaction

Shortcoming	Requirements	Design decisions
S1: Limited controllability	R1: Provide users an interaction model regarding their ability and experience: Improve the support of user intervention	DD.1 Support of user behavioral model: Processing layer. Provide users an adequate interaction, and a compliant controllability depending on their skill and ability etc.
S2: lack of predictability	R2: Improve the support of user preferences and reduce the gap between system decision and user expectation: Enhance the support of user expertise and competence	DD.2 Support of user affective model: Executive layer: Regarding the rule engines, to provide inference and reasoning, user preferences and expectations should be considered
S3: Partial transparency	R3: Support of user expertise level. Improve the transparency of adaptation changes (display): Advance the transparency of system decision-making mechanism	DD.3 Support of user cognitive model: Perception layer: Varied complexity levels must be supported for users with different expertise levels and various knowledge

reliability of interfaces and the consideration of dialogue principles ISO9241-110 to streamline the interaction. Table 2 illustrates a categorization of dialogue principle within three layer regarding human performance and interface quality.

4.1 Support of Human Behavior

The human performance consequences of particular types of interaction constitute primary evaluative criteria for adaptation and interaction design. Accordingly, user reliability is a key factor for performing usability evaluation [1]. Several works focused on reliability for guiding and structuring the assessment of usability. This need results from the need for context-awareness [1]. Usability support tools aim at a better understanding of the emergent dynamics of interaction. Reliability is concerned with identifying, modelling, and quantifying the probability of human errors during interaction with systems.

Existing reliability methods are based on a cognitive model more appropriate to clarify human behavior. It is evident that any attempt at understanding human performance needs to include the role of human cognition. Such understanding includes many relevant findings from cognitive psychology, behavioral science, neuroscience, human factors and human reliability analysis. Several models were developed to support human models. Most of existing works refers to Rasmussen proposal (1984), for instance [11, 12, 26]. Rassmussen models is based on classification of human behavior divided into skill-based, rule-based, and knowledge-based, compared to the cognitive level used. The terms skill, rule and knowledge refer to the degree of conscious control exercised by the individual over his or her activities. Supporting skill- and rule-based behaviors in familiar tasks, more cognitive resources may be devoted to knowledge-based behaviors, which are important for managing unanticipated events accordingly improve system transparency and predictability [12]. This support enhance system' problem-solving and decision-making, and action execution.

4.2 Support of Dialogue Principles: ISO9241-110

Dialogue principles are a valuable reference to confirm design quality. The aim is to offer an effective user experience during interaction. The international standard ISO9241-110 [20] addresses the ergonomic design of interactive systems and defines seven values supporting interaction. These values of dialogue design are recommended to be applied during analysis, design and evaluation of interactive systems. We assume that such guidelines involving current best practices can assist stakeholders and enable controlled analyses and unified evaluation tool.

ISO9241-110 design principals are defined "without reference to situations of use, application, environment or technology (Table 3)". Existing works applied design principles within different user-centered design process, (e.g. [23–25]).

Consistent with the aim of considering well established abstracted design principles to avoid major design weaknesses, We argues for their use at any stage of a user-centered development process. Interaction quality contributes in the improvement

Table 3. Association between requirements and respective Design Decisions taken

Interaction principals (Rasmussen Model)	ISO 9241-110	Definition
Transparency (*Knowledge*)	Self-descriptiveness	Each dialog step is immediately comprehensible through feedback from the system or is explained to the user on his or her requesting the relevant information.
	Suitability for learning	The dialog guides the user through the learning stages minimizing the learning time.
Predictability (*Rule*)	Suitability for the task	The dialog supports the user in the effective and efficient completion of the task.
	Conformity with user expectations	The dialog corresponds to the users task knowledge, education, experience, and to commonly held conventions.
Controllability (*Skill*)	Controllability	The user is able to maintain direction and speed over the whole course of the interaction until the point at which the goal has been met.
	Error tolerance	Despite evident errors in input, the intended result my be achieved with either no or minimal corrective action having to be taken.
	Suitability for individualization	The dialog is constructed to allow for modification to the user's individual needs and skills for a given task.

of system usability. It depend on the context of use, the effectiveness of interaction differs with regard to user profile. Considering information about user behavior model and cognitive process can increase system usability and provide stakeholders guidance for designing and maybe evaluating interaction.

Further user characteristic (such as the age, preferences, gender), users cognitive models provide a significant improvement for UI. It will be useful to recognize user, knowledge, rules and skills in order to cover their preferences and enhance their interaction experience. The ISO9241-110 standard includes interaction-guiding principals that could assist the design of user interface dialog. In order to enhance the user centeredness of such principles, Table 3 presents ISO9241-110 classified with regards to the user cognitive model of Rasmussen. The KRS model provides a practical framework that link user's judgments, decisions, actions and experience. It provides a model of human performances for supporting the design and evaluation of UIs integrating quantitative and qualitative models.

4.3   Structure Supporting Intelligent Interaction

We assume that meeting users requirements and preferences effectively and efficiently during interaction should consider a conjunction of above detailed principal and concerns. Interaction is intended to maintain usability while keeping full visibility of user performance and behavioral model. The main purpose of this work is to make a step toward usable intelligent UI. It is aimed to provide system designers with a tool (structure) to help the development of intelligent interfaces that invoke a good representation among users. This tool consists on a guidance that allows bridging the gap between user expectation and system decisions during interaction in order to support usability improve reliability and enhance user satisfaction.

We assume that usability improvement relies to harmoniously integrating controllability, predictability and transparency above described. Human reliability during interaction could be achieved via a two different ways:

- In the anticipatory stage, as a post analysis of the potential situation of interaction and as assessment of the interaction quality.
- In post-interaction, to comprehend and recognize involved features that influence human performance during interaction in order to improve user satisfaction.

Satisfaction is then an obvious consequence. In particular, there was a need for further development regarding the integration of quality and human aspects for one exposure scenario. To that end, the proposed structure reflects Rasmussen user performance model within interaction principals. Further, such principal are endorsed by relating to ISO9241-110 dialogue principals for designing interaction. The advantage of this integration is the particular importance accorded to the end-user significance and/or involvement when determining and agreeing context-aware interaction with intelligent system. The human support during adaptation allows guiding, verifying and improving their accuracy rather than the improvement of system intelligibility to meet user expectation. System should learn through interacting with the user and its environment otherwise, it would only repeat its mistakes. Different technique support system intelligence (e.g. learning by observation or knowledge's).

We refer to cognitive aspects of user's performance and we consider three levels to model user behavior: skills, rule and knowledge (SKR) defined by Rasmussen. Considered layers (SKR) [28] enhance the user-centeredness and human reliability of the method. We define the adaptation process with a full coverage of three levels:

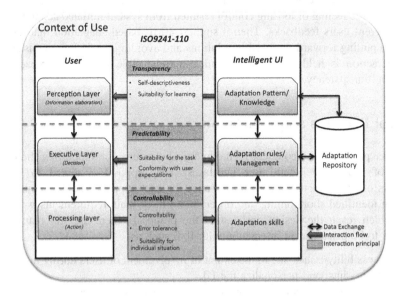

Fig. 1. Context-aware intelligent interaction architecture

The first layer hold **Skill** feature *(control* theory), it regards the concrete interaction flows allowing user to act and access to information. From the system side it denotes the capacity of system to support users intervention. As well, it presents the ability to take such intervention into consideration for the improvement of adaptation performance via the advanced algorithms allowing knowledge learning. Several solutions targeting controllability were convoyed and reviewed in the related works; most of them focus on the user feedback. This level has to do with controllability, errors tolerance and suitability for situation (context-awareness) principals.

The **Rules layer** regards the Executive layer of users. This layer concerns *predictability* and human situation assessment and decision making process. On the system side the implementation of decision-making algorithm and optimization strategies is responsible for the management of contextualization. The aim is to ensure greater convergence between human reasoning and the decision-making algorithms in order to prevent distortions of users and fraud. Accordingly predictability could not be seen only as a consequence of controllability, but require to be investigated in term of deduction, reasoning and problem solving algorithms. At this layer mainly two-dialog principals are to be considered: the suitability for the task and the conformity with user expectations.

The **knowledge layer** is aimed to ensure a common understanding of adaptations and interfaces changes. From the user side, the Perception layer is responsible for this feature. It concerns information processing bloc and refers to the acquisition of incoming information for instance comprehending, relating, grouping etc. The UI support this feature within different perspective. The main intent is to insure that users correctly interpret perceived information. We argue that a transparent adaptation improves accessibility among systems.

Within this prospect, we established the methodological structure view supporting a user-centered adaptation with regard to usability criteria. An approach supporting the aimed synergetic adaptation will be convoyed. First it solves the controllability issues and reduces the feeling of loosing control resulted from system-initiated adaptations by using different users feedbacks. Then it support a ML based adaptation management algorithm putting forward predictable solutions and avoiding confusing inconsistency. This interaction is held by a simple and comprehensible graphical representation supporting transparency.

5   Final Remarks and Conclusion

This paper presented a theoretical methodological structure for supporting the development of usable intelligent user interfaces. The proposal is aimed to support de-signers of an interactive system to enhance the user support when designing UIs. Based on identified shortcoming and observation, three main requirements were provoked which result the design decision of the proposal. There are still many open questions to be discussed in interaction with IUI, such as,

- The accessibility issues due to the extent of involvement of users during interaction to control, adjust and personalize the UI,
- The consideration of context-awareness and all its consequences,

- transparency of adaptation decision and adaptation display to end users.
- the reliability of end user, preferences, profile, expectation, needs etc.
- compatibility of interaction with usability principals.

The proposal focused mainly on interaction with an intelligent user interface. Interaction contributes the user's experience when using systems. Accordingly a well-designed interaction imparts a sense of trust to the system accordingly it enhances usability. The main structure benefits at this level are the consideration of the ISO standard for dialog in principle and forwarding human behavioral model throughout integrating Rasmussen models. This work will be extended by; (i) a methodological guidance for designing IUIs' interaction with regards to usability and UX requirements. (ii) a cost benefits analysis awarding the trade-off between providing greater implementation of context-awareness and avoiding frustrating automatized changes. (iii) an instantiation case studies.

References

1. Andre, T.S., Hartson, H.R., Belz, S.M., McCreary, F.A.: The user action framework: a reliable foundation for usability engineering support tools. Int. J. Hum. Comput. Stud. **54**(1), 107–136 (2001)
2. Augusto, J.C., Zhang, T.: Boulevard: affective adaptive user interface. In: Proceedings of the 10th International Conference on Intelligent Environments. IOS Press, Amsterdam, July 2014
3. Bertini, E., Calì, A., C, T., Gabrielli, S., Kimani, S.: Interaction-based adaptation for small screen devices. In: Ardissono, L., Brna, P., Mitrović, A. (eds.) UM 2005. LNCS (LNAI), vol. 3538, pp. 277–281. Springer, Heidelberg (2005)
4. Bevan, N.: International standards for usability should be more widely used. J. Usability Stud. **4**(3), 106–113 (2009)
5. Brusilovsky, P., Karagiannidis, C., Sampson, D.: Layered evaluation of adaptive learning systems. J. Continuing Eng. Educ. Life Long Learn. **14**(4), 402–421 (2004)
6. Bunt, A., Conati, C., McGrenere, J.: Mixed-initiative interface personalization as a case study in usable AI. AI Mag. **30**(4), 58 (2010)
7. Bunt, A., Conati, C., Mcgrenere, J.: What role can adaptive support play in an adaptable system. In: Proceedings of 9th International Conference on Intelligent User Interfaces. ACM (2004)
8. Boy, G.A. (ed.): The Handbook of Human-Machine Interaction: a Human-Centered Design Approach. Ashgate Publishing Ltd., Farnham (2012)
9. Chang, Y.H.J., Mosleh, A.: Cognitive modeling and dynamic probabilistic simulation of operating crew response to complex system accidents—part 1 overview of the IDAC model. Reliab. Eng. Syst. Saf.(2006, in press). http://www.sciencedirect.com/science/article/pii/S0951832006001232
10. Dessart, C.-E., Genaro motti, V., Vanderdonckt, J.: Showing user interface adaptivity by animated transitions. In: Proceedings of the 3rd ACM SIGCHI Symposium on Engineering Interactive Computing Systems, pp. 95–104. ACM (2011)
11. Di Pasquale, V., Iannone, R., Miranda, S., Riemma, S. An Overview of Human Reliability Analysis Techniques in Manufacturing Operations. INTECH (2013)

12. Embrey, D.: Understanding human behaviour and error. Hum. Reliab. Associates **1**, 1–10 (2005)

13. Evers, C., Kniewel, R., Geihs, K., Schmidt, L.: Achieving user participation for adaptive applications. In: Bravo, J., López-de-Ipiña, D., Moya, F. (eds.) UCAmI 2012. LNCS, vol. 7656, pp. 200–207. Springer, Heidelberg (2012)

14. García Frey, A., Calvary, G., Dupuy-Chessa, S.: Xplain: an editor for building self-explanatory user interfaces by model-driven engineering. In: Proceedings of the 2nd ACM SIGCHI Symposium on Engineering Interactive Computing Systems. ACM (2010)

15. Gajos, K.Z., Czerwinski, M., Tan, D.S., et al.: Exploring the design space for adaptive graphical user interfaces. In: Proceedings of the Working Conference on Advanced Visual Interfaces. ACM (2006)

16. Gajos, K.Z., Everitt, K., Tan, D.S., Czerwinski, M., Weld, D.S. Predictability and accuracy in adaptive user interfaces. In: Proceedings of the SIGCHI Conference on Human Factors in Computing Systems (2008)

17. Gram, C., Cockton, G. (eds.): Design Principles for Interactive Software. Springer, Berlin (1996)

18. Herczeg, M.: Software-Ergonomie: Theorien, Modelle und Kriterien für gebrauchstaugliche interaktive Computersysteme, Oldenbourg Verlag, München (2009)

19. Höök, K.: Steps to take before intelligent user interfaces become real. Interact. Comput. **12** (4), 409–426 (2000)

20. ISO 9241-110: Ergonomics of human-system interaction – Part 110: dialogue principles. International Organi- sation for Standardization, Geneve (2006)

21. Kaber, D.B., Endsley, M.R.: The effects of level of automation and adaptive automation on human performance, situation awareness and workload in a dynamic control task. Theor. Issues Ergon. Sci. **5**(2), 113–153 (2004)

22. Kniewel, R., Evers, C., Schmidt, L., Geihs, K.: Designing usable adaptations. In: David, K., Geihs, K., Leimeister, J.M., Roßnagel, A., Schmidt, L., Stumme, G., Wacker, A. (eds.) Socio-Technical Design of Ubiquitous Computing Systems. Springer, Berlin (2014)

23. Maguire, M.: Methods to support human-centred design. Int. J. Hum. Comput. Stud. **55**(4), 587–634 (2001)

24. Maguire, M.: Using Human Factors Standards to Support User Experience and Agile Design. Loughborought Design School, Loughborought University (2013)

25. Mentler, T., Herczeg, M.: Applying ISO 9241-110 dialogue principles to tablet applications in emergency medical services. In: Proceedings of 10th International ISCRAM Conference (2013)

26. Mosleh, A., Chang, Y.H.: Model-based human reliability analysis: prospects and requirements. Reliab. Eng. Syst. Saf. **83**(2), 241–253 (2004)

27. Peissner, M., Edlin-White, R.: User control in adaptive user interfaces for accessibility. In: Winckler, M. (ed.) INTERACT 2013, Part I. LNCS, vol. 8117, pp. 623–640. Springer, Heidelberg (2013)

28. Rasmussen, J.: Skills, rules, knowledge: signals, signs, and symbols and other distinctions in human performance models. IEEE Trans. Syst. Man Cybern. **13**(3), 257–266 (1983)

29. Shneiderman, B.: Direct manipulation for comprehensible, predictable and controllable user interfaces. In: Proceedings of 2nd International Conference on Intelligent User Interfaces (1997)

30. Shneiderman, B., Maes, P.: Direct manipulation vs. interface agents. Interactions **4**(6), 42–61 (1997)

31. Tsandilas, T., Schraefel, M.C.: Usable adaptive hypermedia systems. New Rev. Hypermedia Multimedia **10**(1), 5–29 (2004)
32. Tsandilas, T., Schraefel, M. C.: An empirical assessment of adaptation techniques. In: CHI 2005 Extended Abstracts, pp. 2009–2012. ACM, New York (2005)
33. Wickens, C.D., Hollands, J.G.: Engineering Psychology and Human Performance, 3rd edn. Prentice Hall, Upper Saddle River (2000). ISBN 0-321-04711-7

Suturing Space: Tabletop Portals
for Collaboration

Evan Montpellier[1], Garrett Laroy Johnson[2], Omar Al Faleh[1],
Joshua Gigantino[2], Assegid Kidane[2], Nikolaos Chandolias[1],
Connor Rawls[2], Todd Ingalls[2], and Xin Wei Sha[1,2(✉)]

[1] Topological Media Lab, Concordia University, Montréal, Canada
xinwei@mindspring.com
[2] Synthesis Center, School of Arts, Media and Engineering, Arizona State
University, Tempe, USA

Abstract. Most video-conferencing technologies focus on 1-1, person-to-person links, typically showing the heads and shoulders of the conversants seated facing their cameras. This limits their movement and expects foveal attention. Adding people to the conversation multiplies the complexity and competes for visual real estate and video bandwidth. Most coronal meaning-making activity is excised by this frontal framing of the participants. This method does not scale well as the number of participants rises. This research presents a different approach to augmenting collaboration and learning. Instead of projecting people to remote spaces, furniture is digitally augmented to effectively exist in two (or more) locations at once. An autoethnographic analysis of social protocols of this technology is presented. We ask, how can such shared objects provide a common site for ad hoc activity in concurrent conversations among people who are not co-located but co-present via audio?

Keywords: Collaboration technology · Lifelong learning · Collaboration technology · Problem-based learning · Inquiry-based learning · Project-based learning · Blended learning · Collaborative knowledge construction · Interdisciplinary studies · Social media · Social networking · Social processes · Teams · Communities · Surface computing · Technology-enhanced learning · Technology-rich interactive learning environments · Suturing spaces · Tabletop displays · Augmented reality · Mixed reality · Collaborative work · Interior design · Furniture design · Responsive architecture · Interactive architecture · Smart architecture · Smart objects · Realtime media · Real-time interactive media · Responsive media · Live video · Live audio · Gestural interfaces · User interfaces · Computational matter

1 Introduction

Since the early 2000s, video chatting has become a mainstay in everyday communication. Theses person-to-person links are well equipped for mimicking the conditions of co-located interactions. Facing their cameras, the illusion of locked gaze is created by the tightly coupled camera and screen of a laptop or desktop computer

© Springer International Publishing Switzerland 2015
M. Kurosu (Ed.): Human-Computer Interaction, Part II, HCII 2015, LNCS 9170, pp. 472–484, 2015.
DOI: 10.1007/978-3-319-20916-6_44

configuration. This has somatic and social implications; foveal attention – eye contact – is expected for the duration of the conversation (arguably much longer than in co-located interactions). Adding people to the conversation multiplies the complexity and competes for visual real estate and video bandwidth. Most coronal meaning-making activity is excised by this frontal framing of the participants — an approach which has been adapted by some to address the scaling up of co-discussants.

Instead of spotlighting single entities as talking heads, our approach to augmenting collaboration and learning focuses on making furniture and objects that effectively exist simultaneously in multiple locations. By focusing attention on a common table instead of faces, we avoid the problems of representing people: the complexities of gaze tracking, focusing cameras or microphones. We ask, how can such shared objects provide a common site for ad hoc activity in concurrent conversations among people who are not co-located but co-present via audio?

Our Table of Content (TOC) uses tables mated with two way, continuous live-video. Each table has a projector and a camera beaming down onto the surface of the table. Video capture from one side to transmitted to the remote projector and vice versa. As a result, objects placed on one table appear projected on the other. This focuses attention on what is being discussed and on a common tabletop on which props, diagrams and simple gestures can be used with ad hoc freedom. Should the collaborators wish to see their remote counterpart's faces, they can add a standard technology like Skype. We provide an omni-directional microphone and good speakers so that people can speak at any time in the flow of conversation without having the overhead of human gaze tracking. This conveys everyone's presence and enables ad hoc concurrent engagement.

We rethink the process and methodology of designing for shared spaces. Rather than fixing on tele-projecting people or transporting things and data objects from location to location, we think of a single place that exists in two locations. We call this technique "suturing", borrowing consciously from topology. There is no need for mated objects be the same size or shape so long as symbolic and social activity coordinate those objects. Just as in topology one can suture two manifolds together by a "gluing map" that identifies dissimilar shapes, designers can identify objects that are quite different.

We emphasize the design metaphor that the TOC is furniture existing in two or more places at once. It is not a "communication channel" that requires dial-up protocols for initiating or terminating a device; the TOC is engineered to run continuously so that people can gather around it and start using it at any time. We leverage all the existing social and technical protocols people use to get together around, and for sharing a table. Rather than treat collaboration as a telecommunication problem, we build furniture as sites of common activity.

The video [1] shows how this technology works. We implemented our common table in our labs in Montreal and Phoenix to serve several series of seminars. The seminars vary in format between round-the-table verbal discussions and single-speaker presentations.

In this paper, we focus on the social protocols which emerged from these sessions. To begin, we discuss precedent work in many-to-many conferencing or furniture-based telematic networking. Following, we briefly outline the TOC's technical specifications. Turning to the element our observations of how we as humans interacted with each other through the table, we discuss our negotiations with etiquette; how should we coordinate and interleave our interventions using tokens, gesture, vocal signals, etc.? In this vein, we share how our mediated communication affected perceptions of politeness and rudeness related to focus and attention. Here, we deal with the mixture of different streams of communication, such as augmenting the table with "foveal" media such as the talking-heads videos of remote interlocutors or text messaging. Secondly, we discuss the interaction of sharing space, which allows for people and objects to "overlap" in unique ways. Privacy and trust are important issues dealt with in the TOC's design, which we investigate here as well. Finally, we propose future work to be done which respond to these first experiments.

2   Methods

2.1   Problem Statement

Aside from the engineering problems, some of the questions we address with this platform include:

- Coordinating Conversation. How should people coordinate and interleave their interventions using tokens, gesture, vocal signals, etc.?
- Time Zone. How can we handle time zone differences? Three hours between Montreal and Phoenix, 8 or 9 h between Phoenix and London or Athens?
- Live vs Recorded. How do people mix live events with recorded audio, video or documents?
- Foveal vs Ambient Attention. How do people mix the table with foveal media such as the talking-heads videos of remote interlocutors?

2.2   Literature Review

Using tabletop surfaces as communication and collaboration platforms has been a research interest for many institutions in academic and technological circles. Dating back to experiments at Xerox Parc, Video Walls described in [2] where California and Oregon research offices were connected to promote spontaneous interactions between people in the two different locations, which ranged from social to work-related interactions. This focus on collaborative and networked solutions that extend beyond the computer screen and into everyday spaces are among the interests of many researchers and groups, and are used for many different applications that aim to enhance collaborative work across remote locations. Other examples include [3–5].

Reference Fish et al. [4] provides an affordable and easy to use setup to create a tabletop collaboration platform by using an overhead projector, top-mounted tracking cameras, and a standard table surface for the projection. This project focuses on gesture recognition and computer vision tracking to enable collaborative manipulation of shapes, figures, and interface elements. While the set of this project is similar to that in the Table of Content, we avoid designing the interaction to a specific set of tasks, and instead leave the platform open for a multitude of use cases that rely on the augmented presence without the computational complexity. Our work on the Table of Content draws on this long history of research and experimentation, but with a conscious effort to avoid reproducing work that has already been done, and to approach the challenge from a different perspective.

Reference Costanza et al. [6] presents a survey of mixed reality applications, use cases, challenges (mostly technical), futures, and HCI considerations in mixed reality applications. In the survey, the tabletop interaction project, which was developed at the Innovation Center Virtual Reality (ICVR) at ETH Zurich, uses of overhead table projection and computer vision tracking to augment people's interaction with regular office supplies such as pens and rulers. The Holoport project allows for extending the regular meeting tables with a virtual one in a different location, thus allowing for a face-to-face meeting with remotely connected counterparts. We draw similarities from these projects since our Table of Content uses an augmented tabletop as a meeting and collaboration platform that allows participants to use everyday object and projected imagery as tools for this collaboration.

Reference Ehnes [8] addresses the issue of content presentation, retrieval, and sharing, through projecting meeting notes and relevant documents on the table top. It applies similar technique as [6] in allowing users to manipulate and move documents and figures through computer vision tracking, but relies on objects with special marking and shapes on and around the table to be the facilitator of that interaction. This project implements the possibility of scalability, where it could be deployed on multiple meeting tables that can share and exchange documents between themselves.

Concerns over privacy and spatial social behavior in networked remote locations, as well as distinguishing between place and space as two different concepts in networked mixed reality solutions has been addressed in [9] by drawing on social and linguistic definitions of regular spatial practices and definitions, and attempting to refining them in the context of networked solutions as design considerations. This is also approached in [8] where concepts of co-location and social conventions in shared and connected spaces are studies in different experiments from collaborative writing, to collective design changes, and to tabletop interactions.

2.3 Methods and Materials

Each terminal point in a Table of Content network consists of the following pieces of hardware:

Furniture:

- *Table:* An oval table painted matte white.

Video:

- *Projector:* a projector mounted vertically above the table, projecting downward onto it.

- *Camera:* a monochrome video camera mounted vertically above the table, pointing downward to capture video of the table.[1] The camera has an optical filter that passes infrared light and blocks visible light so as to prevent the camera from capturing the projected image, resulting in a feedback loop.

Audio:

- *Microphone(s):* one omnidirectional microphone suspended above the centre of the table, or multiple shotgun or cardioid microphones positioned to pick up audio from different sectors of the table.
- *Speaker(s):* a wide-spectrum audio transducer mounted to the underside of the table, or an array of two to four speakers attached to the ceiling above the table.
- *Amplifier:* an audio power amplifier capable of driving the speaker(s).

Lighting:

- *Controller:* a DMX lighting controller[2] that controls the ambient lighting array, allowing the lights to be animated by data extracted from the video and/or audio feeds.
- *Dimmer packs:* A set of DMX dimmer packs,[3] which vary the brightness of the ambient lighting array.
- *IR emitter:* an infrared light to illuminate the table without washing out the projected image.[4]
- *Ambient lighting array:* an array of lightbulbs suspended from the ceiling and attached to the DMX control system to provide animatable ambient lighting.

Computer:

- A computer running custom patches (available at https://github.com/Synthesis-ASU-TML/Synthesis) written in Max/MSP/Jitter (TML uses a 2011 Mac Pro).

The Software:

- masking and mapping
- fluids and particles
- weighted control between local and remote feeds
- Recording and playback: The Software allows for recording the video feed which is acquired from the overhead camera, and encoding the feed into video files that will be stored on the local computer's hard drive. Once the feed is recorded and stored, it can be used as a video source that could be streamed and mapped onto the other tabletop in case of inactivity or intentional change of the feed source. This feature is

---

[1] Currently a Point Grey Research Flea2 1394 camera; http://www.ptgrey.com/flea2-ieee-1394b-firewire-cameras.

[2] E.g. Enttec ODE: http://www.enttec.com/index.php?main_menu=Products&pn=70305.

[3] E.g. the Chauvet DMX-4: http://www.chauvetlighting.com/dmx-4.html.

[4] E.g. the Raytec Vario-8 LED IR emitter: http://www.rayteccctv.com/products/view/vario-low-voltage/vario-i8.

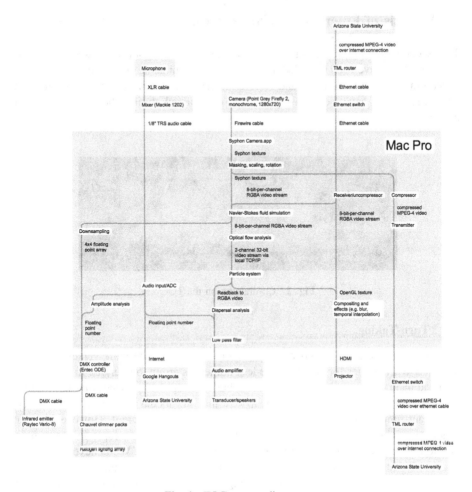

Fig. 1. TOC system diagram

implemented to account for important events or meetings that happened in one of the two locations, but was not streamed live due to time shift or schedule conflicts.

- key software: Max/MSP/Jitter, Syphon, syphon camera, syphon recorder (for documentation and looping)
- ffmpeg and the Jitter [vipr] external (Fig. 1).

2.4 Data Collection

In order to obtain relevant experimental results that are experiential in nature, we employed an autoethnographic method inside a qualitative methodology using a grounded theory approach. Data was archived as email, video collections and a series of shared online documents. Data was coded, excerpted and analyzed for relevant information regarding current behavioral practices and enhancements to the Table of Content system.

3   Analysis of Emergent Social Protocols

This section presents the design considerations resulting from the observations and analysis which have been recorded during our TOC seminar sessions. These are mainly concerning the social protocol and interaction patterns that have emerged during the seminars, which have been discussed and categorized during the iterative design process (Fig. 2).

Fig. 2. Co-drawing on the TOC

3.1   Turn-Taking

Imbalances between the number of people on one side of the table versus the other often led to difficulties for people in the less-numerous group to interject. In such cases, the local band overrode the video and audio bands. Corporeal presence during a formal discussion demanded attentiveness in a way that the media streams do not; if one discussant ignores a co-present interlocutor, it is readily apparent. However, in our conditions, it was much less apparent to the speaker whether people in the remote location were paying attention to his or her transmitted speech. We believe that this is also partly due to seminar convention, in which the desire to interject is signified through a silent but visible act, namely raising a hand. In our conditions, simply waving ones arms below the camera did not provide an adequate remote analog to this, because the projected video was less compelling of attention, and all the more so when it was rendered illegible by the plethora of notebooks, coffee cups, and snack bowls covering a well-attended seminar table.

To mediate turn-taking between our co-located seminar discussants, we employed an intuitive solution: electing one person to act as the liaison between the two groups, deliberately making space in the conversation for each side to speak and prompting responsive engagement between the two groups. Our events organized around/through the table benefited greatly from the designation of a facilitator on each side, whose roles were to monitor the conversational dynamics and actively bridge the conversation between the two groups. The delegation of speaking permissions imparted a strong feeling of administrative cohesiveness and experiential togetherness, not unlike in co-located seminars, which remedied perceived notions of social instability or unbalance.

3.2   Etiquette of Attentiveness or Politeness and Rudeness

Our experiences of rudeness or politeness of attentiveness whilst using the TOC differed from norms of face-to-face conversation (co-located or remotely located). In face-to-face conversations, visibly switching one's bodily orientation/attention away from an interlocutor (e.g. by checking messages on your phone, looking something up on the computer, going to get an object from elsewhere in the space) may be interpreted as rude. However, the many-to-many dynamic of conversations mediated by the TOC rendered the social dynamic pliant in this regard. If an interlocutor was speaking and noticed in the projected image that remote discussant was working on his or her computer, the speaker did not interpret this as distraction on the side of their remote counterpart. This derived in part from the fact that foveal attention/ Skype-talking-head-style visual presence was never established. Thus activity seen from a birds' eye view did not represent a deviation from signifiers of attentiveness (e.g. eye contact) that were never present in the first place. Attentiveness was mainly signified within the audio domain via practices such as turn-taking. Once a conversation was established, each speaker in the sequence assumed (though not necessarily with justification) that the other participants were listening. Thus, our device that supported "multi-band communication."

3.3   Multi-band Communication

We designed the TOC to scaffold four separate communication bands: visual, auditory, ancillary, and corporeal. Each of these bands has specific characteristics and "bandwidth."

In the audio band, bandwidth was relatively narrow, at least during intentional activities such as seminars when dialogue between remote locations was desirable. Typically, for reasons both of perceived attentiveness and intelligibility, turn-taking conventions precluded more than one person speaking/being heard at a time. When this one-at-a-time speaking protocol is observed, we suggest that the audio band is the main region where individual identity is established. In the absence of the habitual legibility of body language that comes from a head-on perspective, we contend that the audio region also acts as the main site of non-lexical signalling (e.g. tone of voice, rhythm of speech).

Video was the domain of (a) relatively impersonal presence and (b) symbolic information. In terms of presence, the sight of arms, cups, the tops of heads, etc. in the projected image gave a sense of the type and quantity of activity taking place at the table, but was relatively thin compared to face-based video chatting in terms of conveying personal information (e.g., body language). Our participants' attention sometimes drifted from the projected image without feeling like the quality or focus of the conversation was compromised. This changed when deliberate visual signifying activities (e.g. collaborative drawing) occurred, since these activities required collaboration from all parties (e.g. to clear space on the table so that the drawn images or text could be seen, and to participate in the co-creation of images). Video was high-bandwidth in the sense that multiple distinct activities could take place around the table without garbling the signal, although we found that intelligibility did decrease as the visual complexity/density of the set of objects on either table increased.

Fig. 3. Clocks superimposed on the Table of Content

The ancillary band is a catch-all term for all communication between people around remote tables that took place via media other than the tables themselves. SMS or instant messaging are two examples of this category. During seminars, those researchers charged with driving the technical set up often communicated with each other over established internet chat platforms to work out calibration issues (e.g. "what's your port"? or "lower the contrast please"). Arguably, communication in this region could take place in parallel to the intra-table video and audio streams without disrupting them (although prominently texting during a seminar was locally interpreted as rude) (Fig. 3).

Finally, the local/corporeal band simply designates activity which took place locally at either table, with the full "bandwidth" of a conventional meeting/conversation.

3.4   Overlapping in Shared Space

The overlaying of projected images of bodies onto corporeally-present bodies is a unique intersection which produced a range of effects, whose specificity is, we argue, determined by the context of the conversation at hand. In some cases, occupying the same space as someone's image produced feelings of intimacy (similar to the territory explored in [10]); this was more plausible when familiarity already exists, or when the event taking place was less formal. During a seminar, on the other hand, situating oneself in the same space occupied by the image of someone who is currently speaking appeared as a sign of impoliteness, inasmuch as one is not making (visual) space for the speaker. Then again, aligning one's body with the image of a remote speaker who is dominating the conversation produced or conveyed at times feelings of identity. In our seminars, both sides of our conversation aligned a clock on the TOC, to the purpose of keeping track of daylight time zone differences between Phoenix and Montreal. This further emphasizes the metaphorical singularity of our TOC, which exist simultaneously in distinct two time zones.

3.5   Privacy and Trust

Privacy. Insofar as the table streams video and audio data to remote locations, and also records video and audio for later viewing, we considered seriously the question of privacy. The transmit-receive function of the table was apparent even without explanation simply from its physical design (a visible microphone, a projector showing a remote location and a camera capturing the table). Often, when people encountered the table for the first time, one of the first questions they asked was, "Is that thing streaming?" or "Am I being recorded?" Arguably, the essence of surveillance technology is the non-consensual capture, remote viewing and storage of data. Surveillance practices involve a hierarchy, setting some people as informed viewing subjects over others as ignorant viewed objects. We considered it best to orient the table away from such an unethical structure at the level of engineering/design. Since the constant telematic connection of the remote tables was integral to establishing a sense of the tables existing as a single object shared between two spaces, we suggest that the media streams be regarded as providing two types of data, namely presence and representation. The video and audio components of the table provide a sense of remote presence without conveying representational content. In order to sense remote presence, we simply needed to see perturbations in the audio and video streams that have no apparent local cause.

Trust. The Table of Contents can be used as a playback medium for recorded materials that are managed by users from the respective sides at ASU and Concordia. These videos are designed to be played in a loop during times of inactivity, or at will by user interaction in case of specific events of mutual interest. Earlier discussions about computing the level of activity, or performing specific gesture analysis, as a trigger for the recording process has precipitated several privacy and trust concerns that needed to be dealt with on the design stages. For this reason, our implementation necessitated a clear, intentional, and embodied gesture to start and stop the recording by clicking on an unambiguous interface element. Making the content available for streaming was enabled by users on each side. This was an immediate solution to handle concerns about content storage and availability. New models for managing storage, content, and interaction paradigms to control these issues, are being discussed for future implementations.

4 Implications and Moving Forward

4.1 Turn Taking

In order to facilitate turn-taking, we suggest integrating a gesture recognition engine into the table, designing a gesture that causes a difficult-to-ignore visual signal on the remote table. This could be as simple as causing the table's brightness or colour to pulsate, an agreed-upon cue that the other side wishes to speak. Again, this gesture could be something as elegant as haptic or auditory feature detection evoked by scratching or tapping on the table, or as gross as a large red button in the middle of the table. The design of said gesture should not interfere with the "gesture-space" of actions that people normally perform at a table. For example, looking for hands placed on the table would not be a good strategy, as people often rest their hands on the table by default.

4.2   Privacy

In order to secure users of their privacy without losing the ability to visualize real-time presence, we suggest streaming a low-resolution version of the overhead camera feed from Phoenix and use it as a control matrix for a particle system in Montreal, and vice versa. In this case, only the particle system is being displayed on the table - the full-resolution video feed (which we are calling the "representational" feed) does not appear. When someone in Phoenix moves at the table, the particles in Montreal would be disbursed accordingly. The rhythm and intensity of the particles' movement conveys a nuanced sense of presence – even of the genre of activity taking place, without literally representing the image of the remote party.

Acoustically, we suggest running the microphone feed through a low-pass filter, so that the cadence of speech can be heard but the content is unintelligible. This solution will be run in parallel with s more poetic implementation where the mic audio will be run into a feature extraction object that sends the resulting data stream (but not the audio) to the other side, where the data would control musical or abstract sonic instruments creating a sonification of presence. In this case, we can imagine hearing a set of synthetic chimes playing with the cadence of a remote person's speech. Here again, we have a means of conveying presence without non-consensually broadcasting meaning.

The solutions which we describe here could be implemented as default behaviours for the table. Should a party wish to establish representational communication, a gesture (corporeal, spoken, GUI-based, etc.) could be used to "clarify" the visual and auditory streams, replacing the low-res information with full-frequency audio and full-resolution video. In sync with our concerns in the social protocol aspect of the design, "opening of the table" should be designed to require a two-way handshake (the same way in which invitations to voice or video calls work in Skype). Alternately, each side could autonomously decide to clarify or obscure their streams independent of the status of the other side's streams. The important point, we believe, is that in a perpetually-running communication system, the broadcasting or storage of data should require voluntary and intentional initialization.

4.3   Recording

Managing the storage and archiving of the recorded media presents multiple challenges on the technical and interaction levels, and on the level of administering the availability of the content. Recording long sessions and storing them on local hard drive has resulted with very large file sizes, and presented us with the danger of losing the entire content in case of a software crash during the recording process. We suggest an implementation that sets a maximum buffer length for recorded media, which splits long recording sessions across multiple files, thus preserving the content from any software-caused loss or damage, and allows for the implementation of a distributed archival system over multiple storage units. Future implementations will include a management console that allows users on each side to control the availability of their recorded content.

We suggest another poetic way for users to interact with the table's video feed over time; objects left on the table for a certain period of time could "burn in" to the video feed, with their images persisting for a duration that corresponded exponentially to the duration of their physical presence on the table, with the option to dismiss the burn effect with gestural or timed expiry system. This effect could run in parallel to our above-described recording format, with the former being suitable for giving a sense of temporally-distorted presence and the latter being more suited to representational purposes (e.g. the archiving of seminars).

4.4 Time Differences

The time difference between Phoenix and Montreal has so far not been of major consequence, as it is easy enough to follow standard protocol for planning geographically-remote meetings and make the time difference explicit in scheduling. Larger time differences move work days more significantly out of sync; which presents a design challenge for developing combined live/recorded effects to most effectively suture these spaces. We are interested in further investigating the social protocols which emerge from this configuration. These will include preparing for the scenarios where one party would leading the other one in the conversation (e.g. Athens would be recording events that Phoenix would later view), and the case where the two parties would treat the system as a way to leave audiovisual messages for each other. Although we consider these circumstances relating to the genre of intentional, planned activity that the table has mostly been used for to date - the question of how time differences might affect the perception of occasional/casual activity around the table while it is perpetually running feels is another question we are interested in pursuing.

5 Conclusion

In this paper, we presented the results of experiments with a table-based video conferencing system. We began by outlining the technical specifications of this system. Our focus was to share our observations regarding the emergent social protocols of this system, such as turn-taking, interleaving recorded and live video materials, interactions in physical space, etiquette, and multiple simultaneous streams of communication. Finally, we propose future areas of development in this project, including changes to interfacing, considerations of privacy, and the more organic integration of playback materials.

References

1. Montpellier, E.: The Table of Content (2014). https://vimeo.com/105478904. Accessed 10 Jan 2015
2. Goodman, G., Abel, M.: Communication and collaboration: Facilitating cooperative work through communication. Off. Technol. People 3(2), 129–146 (1987)

3. Sirkin, D., Venolia, G., Tang, J.C., Robertson, G.G., Kim, T., Inkpen, K., Sedlins, M., Lee, B., Sinclair, M.: Motion and attention in a kinetic videoconferencing proxy. In: Proceedings of the 13th IFIP TC 13 International Conference (2011)
4. Fish, R.S., Kraut, R.E., Chalfonte, B.L.: The videowindow system in informal communication. In: Proceedings of ACM Conference on Computer Supported Collaborative Work (1990)
5. Johanson, B., Fox, A., Winograd, T.: The stanford interactive workspaces project. VLSI J. 1–30 (2004)
6. Costanza, E., Kunz, A., Fjeld, M.: Mixed reality: a survey. In: Lalanne, D., Kohlas, J. (eds.) Human Machine Interaction. LNCS, vol. 5440, pp. 47–68. Springer, Heidelberg (2009)
7. Bekins, D., Yost, S., Garrett, M., Deutsch, J. Htay, W.M., Xu, D., Aliaga, D.: Mixed reality tabletop (MRT): a low-cost teleconferencing framework for mixed-reality applications. In: VR 2006 Proceedings of the IEEE Conference on Virtual Reality (2006)
8. Ehnes, J.: An automated meeting assistant: a tangible mixed reality interface for the AMIDA automatic content linking device. In: Filipe, J., Cordeiro, J. (eds.) Enterprise Information Systems. LNBIP, vol. 24, pp. 952–962. Springer, Heidelberg (2009)
9. Harrison, S., Dourish, P.: Re-placeing space: the roles of place and space in collaborative systems. In: Proceedings of ACM Conference on Computer Supported Collaborative Work (1996)
10. Sermon, P.: Telematic dreaming. http://www.medienkunstnetz.de/works/telematic-dreaming/. Accessed 21 Dec 2014

Violin Fingering Estimation According to the Performer's Skill Level Based on Conditional Random Field

Shinji Sako$^{(\boxtimes)}$, Wakana Nagata, and Tadashi Kitamura

Nagoya Institute of Technology, Gokiso-cho, Nagoya, Showa-ku 466-8555, Japan
{s.sako,kitamura}@nitech.ac.jp
nagata@mmsp.nitech.ac.jp

Abstract. In this paper, we propose a method that estimates appropriate violin fingering according to the performer's skill level based on a conditional random field (CRF). A violin is an instrument that can produce the same pitch for different fingering patterns, and these patterns depend on skill level. We previously proposed a statistical method for violin fingering estimation, but that method required a certain amount of training data in the form of fingering annotation corresponding to each note in the music score. This was a major issue of our previous method, because it takes time and effort to produce the annotations. To solve this problem, we proposed a method to automatically generate training data for a fingering model using existing violin textbooks. Our experimental results confirmed the effectiveness of the proposed method.

1 Introduction

With a violin, the same pitch can be produced by several fingering patterns, and players decide which fingering to use. In general, the optimum fingering differs according to a player's skill level. For low-skill players, fingering that is easily played is optimum, whereas for high-skill players, fingering that allows the best performance expression is optimum. From this point of view, it is important to consider the skill level of the player in the field of automatic fingering estimation techniques.

Some studies have focused on fingering estimation for a plucked or bowed string instrument [1–5] or for the piano [6–8]. The methods proposed in these studies estimate the easiest fingering and can not recommend suitable fingering for various skill levels; however, one promising approach is a method to describe the relationship between fingering and music score by using a stochastic model such as [5,7]. We have been working on the research of violin fingering estimation based on such a stochastic model approach. Our goal is to estimate the natural violin fingering according to the player's skill level for any musical compositions. It is considered to be a human-centered design in assistive technology for musical instrument training. In this paper, we propose the technique for violin fingering estimation according to the performer's skill level based on a conditional random field (CRF).

© Springer International Publishing Switzerland 2015
M. Kurosu (Ed.): Human-Computer Interaction, Part II, HCII 2015, LNCS 9170, pp. 485–494, 2015.
DOI: 10.1007/978-3-319-20916-6_45

Fig. 1. Examples of violin fingering for different skill level

2 Methodology

2.1 Violin Fingering and Our Previous Study

Figure 1 shows examples of violin fingering for beginners and intermediates players. The violin player decides whether playing needs to be easy or whether performance expression is appropriate. We also realize that this priority is influenced by the note length. If the note is short, ease of play becomes a higher priority because playing a succession of short notes is more difficult. When the note is long, expression has a higher priority because playing longer notes is easier. Expression also has a higher priority when the skill level is high.

From this point of view, we previously proposed a fingering estimation method based on a hidden Markov model (HMM) [9]. In our previous study, we regarded fingering as the hidden state and the notes in the musical composition as the observation. We defined the priority of performance expression based on note length and skill level, and this priority was used to determine the output probability. Because note length also influences ease of transition from one fingering pattern to another, we defined the degree of change between fingering patterns based on note length, and this degree of change was related to transition probability.

Model parameters were estimated from textbook fingering patterns; however, that method requires fully annotated fingering for training HMM, making it difficult to prepare the training data. In general, partial fingering patterns are described in violin textbooks. We had to create a large amount of complementary fingering data manually in order to train fingering estimation models, which required a lot of time and the skill and knowledge of violin playing.

2.2 Outline of Our Method

Figure 2 shows an overview of our complementary training method using partial fingering data. The initial model is trained by using the completed fingering

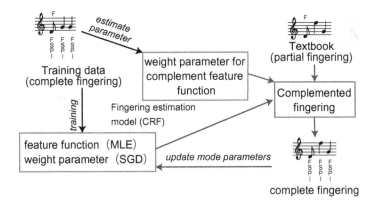

Fig. 2. Overview of our complementary training method using CRF

data that has been fully complemented manually in the same way as in our previous study. Parameters of complementary feature function are estimated from complete fingering data. Then, partial fingering data is complemented by using the CRF, and the model is updated using the complemented fingering data. In this study, we adopted well-known stochastic gradient descent (SGD) method to train CRF. This cycle is repeated under the convergence condition.

2.3 Basic Idea of Fingering Model Using CRF

In this paper, we propose a framework for training the fingering estimation model using a partial fingering data from violin textbooks. To accomplish that, we model violin fingering using the concept underlying the CRF as shown in Fig. 3. This model is an extended version of our HMM-based fingering model. State sequences s is the left-hand state sequence, and output o is the note and rest sequence in the score. We assume that the state changes for every note and that the state sequence is a Markovian process. To simplify the problem, the model has the following restrictions: the score is monophonic, and only the factors pitch, note length, and rest length are considered by this model.

Each note information of o can be represented as set of pitch information p, expressiveness e and changeableness c. Expressiveness e depends on the parameter w^l representing the skill level.

The four elements are represented by the following variables: finger number FN, string SP, hand position HP and finger interval FI.

$$s_n = \{x_n^{FN}, x_n^{SP}, x_n^{HP}, x_n^{FI}\} \tag{1}$$

The objective function for the fingering estimation is defined as Eq. (2) by using potential function $\Phi(o, s)$.

$$\hat{s} = \arg\max_s P(s|o) = \arg\max_s \frac{\exp(\Phi(o, s))}{z(o)} \tag{2}$$

Here, $z(o)$ is a normalization term.

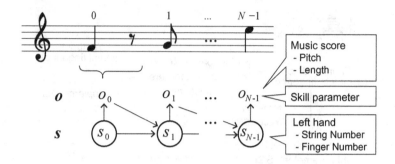

Fig. 3. Outline of our fingering model

2.4   Potential Representation

CRF potential function Φ is represented as a linear combination of feature functions as follows:

$$\Phi(o,s) = \sum_n \sum_{i,j} w_{i,j} f_{i,j}(o_{n-1}, o_n, s_{n-1}, s_n) \tag{3}$$

In this study, feature functions of CRF are represented by a probability density function because the degree of expressiveness e and changeableness c are continuous values. Both e and c have been introduced to accommodate skill levels in our previous study (please refer to [9] for more details). There are four features: state feature, transition feature, expression feature, and pitch feature. Due to the number of states being too large, each feature is defined individually for each element except for the pitch feature.

2.5   State Feature

This feature represents the appropriateness of the hands of the state. To simplify the model, we assumed that feature is independent of each element. The state feature function is defined as Eq. (4) as the logarithm of the probability of occurrence of each element.

$$f_{1,j}(s_n) = \log P(x_n^j) \tag{4}$$

It can be considered as $j \in \{\mathrm{FN}, \mathrm{HP}, \mathrm{FI}\}$, because this feature does not depend on the violin string.

2.6   Transition Feature

This feature represents the appropriateness of the transition of the state, and its feature function is defined as the logarithm of the Laplace distribution or the exponential distribution, where the variance of distribution depends on the degree of changeableness c. It is noted that this feature also depends on the finger numbers before the transition. The details of transition the probability are described in [9], and a simplified example is represented by Eq. (5).

$$f_{2,j}(o_{n-1}, s_{n-1}, s_n) = \log f_{\text{Lap}}(x_n^j; x_{n-1}^j, k_j c_n) \tag{5}$$

Here, $f_{\text{Lap}}(x; \mu, \sigma^2)$ is the Laplace distribution with mean μ and variance σ^2. It can be considered as $j \in \{\text{SP}, \text{HP}, \text{FI}\}$, because the transition of finger numbers does not depend on the appropriateness of fingering.

2.7 Expressiveness Feature

This feature represents the appropriateness of the expression. The frequency of expression can be approximated by log-normal distribution. The feature function is represented as Eq. (6). It can be considered as $j \in \{\text{FN}, \text{SP}\}$, because expressiveness depends on both finger number and string.

$$f_{3,j}(o_n, s_n) = \log f_{\text{LN}}(e_n; \mu_{j,x_n^j}, \sigma^2_{j,x_n^j}) \tag{6}$$

2.8 Pitch Feature

The relationship between state and pitch is represented as Eq. (7). The state corresponds to the pitch to set the probability to zero, otherwise set the probability to ∞.

$$f_4(s_n, o_n) = \begin{cases} 0 & \text{state } s_n \text{ correspond to pitch } p_n \\ -\infty & \text{state } s_n \text{ does not correspond to pitch } p_n \end{cases} \tag{7}$$

3 Automatic Fingering Completion

In general, fingering is not described for every note in commercial fingering textbooks. One reason is that an easily guessed part is often omitted. In addition, fingering information is represented by finger number only, with string information provided only as required. To use such partial fingering data as training data, it is necessary to create a full fingering data by completion.

3.1 Outline of Completion Method

In this study, we introduce a new method for a semi-automatic completion method by using a fingering estimation framework based on CRF. At first, we focus on the difference between described and non-described fingering in the textbook. As for non-described parts, only a small change in the state of the hand would be expected; on the other hand, a large change in the state of the hand is expected at locations where the fingering is described.

These relationships can be represented by changing the weights of the feature by the described or non-described fingering in the textbook. Finally, a potential function for the automatic complement is represented as Eq. (8).

$$\Phi_{cmp}(o, s) = \sum_n \sum_{i,j} \alpha_{i,j}(n) w_{i,j} f_{i,j}(o_{n-1}, o_n, s_{n-1}, s_n) \tag{8}$$

Here, $\alpha_{i,j}(n)$ is the function that changes the weight by the described or non-described fingering:

$$\alpha_{i,j}(n) = \begin{cases} \alpha_{i,j}^0 & \text{fingering is not described at } n^{th} \text{ note} \\ \alpha_{i,j}^1 & \text{fingering is described at } n^{th} \text{ note} \end{cases} \tag{9}$$

Here, $\alpha_{i,j}^0$ means fingering was not described at the nth note, while $\alpha_{i,j}^1$ means fingering was described at the nth note.

An optimal complemented fingering can be searched from the state sequence through the textbook fingering by using the potential function. Complement state sequence can be represented as Eq. (10) for the set of state sequences S_{text} that satisfy the textbook fingering.

$$\hat{s}_{cmp} = \arg\max_{s \in S_{text}} \frac{\exp(\Phi_{cmp}(o, s))}{z(o)} \tag{10}$$

4 Training Method Using Textbooks

Figure 4 shows an outline of our training method. Our goal is to train the fingering estimation model from textbooks. In order to obtain automatic complemented fingering data from textbooks, an initial fingering estimation model is required. In this study, we use an initial data set with a small amount of manually complemented fingering data. Estimation of auto-complemented fingering data and updating of model parameters is repeated. The termination condition for this process is the case where a concordance rate of $(t_1 - 1)^{th}$ and t_1^{th} complemented fingering is equal to or more than $\alpha\%$.

4.1 Parameter Estimation for θ

The parameter set of the feature function consists of an occurrence probability of each element of 57 dimensions in total. These parameters are estimated in the same manner as [9].

4.2 Parameter Estimation for ω

It is not necessary to consider the weight, since the pitch feature can not be defined only as zero or one. We have to estimate an 8-dimensional feature weight in total.

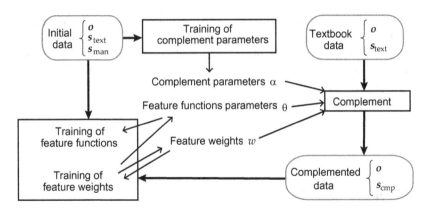

Fig. 4. Outline of the training method

In general, the weight parameter of the CRF is estimated by using the limited-memory Broyden-Fletcher-Goldfarb-Shanno (L-BFGS) method in cases of batch training. On the other hand, a stochastic gradient descent (SDG) method is used in cases of online training. In the batch training, parameters are updated by using all training data. An advantage of the batch method is the stability of convergence, but the computational time is a problem. In the online method, training is performed using the training data sequentially. An advantage of the online method is that the calculation time is small, but the problem is instability of convergence. In this study, one data set corresponds to the whole music score, which contains several hundreds notes.

The gradient vector of SGD is defined as Eq. (11), and the weight update equation is defined as Eq. (12).

$$g(o^{(d)}, s^{(d)}) = f(o^{(d)}, s^{(d)}) - \sum_s f(o^{(d)}, s) P(s|o^{(d)}) \tag{11}$$

$$w^{t_2+1} \leftarrow w^{t_2} + \eta_{t_2} g(o^{(d_{t_2})}, s^{(d_{t_2})}) \tag{12}$$

Here, t_2, d and η_{t_2} represent the number of updates of the weight, index of training data and training coefficients, respectively. In the online training, the update process is performed in units of one music score. d is defined as the remainder obtained by dividing the t_2 and D. $P(s|o^{(d)})$ can be calculated efficiently using a forward-backward algorithm.

In the SGD method, the training result is often strongly affected by the data that is used in the most recent update cycle. For this reason, training coefficient η_{t_2} is defined to be reduced by the weight parameter update cycle t_2. Determination condition of convergence L_2-norm, which is a change in ratio of weight, is used. A summary of these ideas can be written as Eq. (13).

$$\Delta_{t_2} = \sqrt{\sum_{i,j} \left(n\left(w_{i,j}^{t_2}\right) - n\left(w_{i,j}^{t_2-1}\right)\right)^2} \tag{13}$$

Here, $n(\cdot)$ is a function to normalize such that the sum of the weight is equal to one. Δ_{t2} is divided by the number of occurrences $N^{(d)}$ because it is strongly affected by the high frequency of occurrence data. Because it is considered to be dependent on the data (music), we use the average of the last D times. It is considered to have converged if the average is less than the threshold value b. The update performed at least D times.

$$\sum_{i=t_2-D+1}^{t_2} \frac{\Delta_i}{N^{(d_i)}} < b \tag{14}$$

4.3   Complement Parameter α

Dimensionality of the complementary parameters is twice the number of dimensions of feature weights. Our complementary parameters are represented by the ratio of the weight of fingering the described part and the non-described part.

Complementary parameters are defined as Eq. (15). Here, w_{all}, w_0, and w_1 are weight parameters corresponding to training from all notes, fingering described notes and fingering non-described notes, respectively.

$$\alpha_{i,j}^k = n\left(w_{i,j}^k\right) / n\left(w_{i,j}^{\text{all}}\right) \qquad k = 0, 1 \tag{15}$$

5   Experiment and Results

5.1   Settings

We performed a fingering estimation experiment to confirm the differences between our complementary training method using partial data and our previous training method using complete data. We used sixteen musical pieces (total 4,594 notes) from some textbooks for intermediate violin students. We also used one musical pieces (total 101 notes) for the initial model. Sixteen musical pieces were used to generate the complemented fingering data that was used for training the CRF model. The intermediate test data set comprised fourteen musical pieces (total 2,265 notes) that did not overlap with the training data.

By the preliminary experiments, some parameters of the training were set as follows: $a = 99.5\%$, $b = 3.0 \times 10^{-5}$, $\eta_{t_2} = 10^{-3} \times 0.7 e^{t_2/D}$, $w^l = 1.0$.

5.2   Results

Figure 5 shows the average concordance rate obtained from the experiment. The horizontal axis represents the amount of data used for training the initial model. The proposed method obtained equivalent performance to the previous method that was trained using the complete data set. In addition, the proposed method was superior to the previous method even when the training data of the initial model was small. The results show that it is possible to greatly reduce the manually complemented fingering data. In particular, cost of preparing training data has been reduced to about 1/45 by using proposed method.

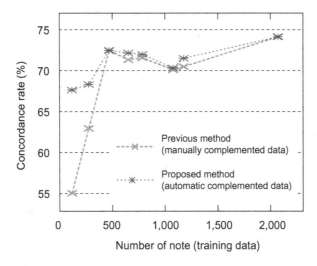

Fig. 5. Result of fingering estimation experiment using proposed training method and previous training method

6 Conclusion

In this paper, we proposed a CRF-based violin fingering estimation model and complementary training method by extending our HMM-based violin fingering estimation method according to skill level. Our complementary training method, using partial fingering data, showed the same performance as the previous training method using the complete fingering data. In other word, high-precision fingering estimation model can be obtained from small amount of manually complemented data. Our study also makes simplifies and reduce the time cost in the training data creation task.

There are still some issues, however, about the naturalness of the estimated fingering, especially in the performance expression, which depends on slur, volume, and other factors. In our future work, we will consider such another information obtained from the music score other than note information.

Acknowledgement. This research was supported in part by Japan Society for the Promotion of Science (JSPS) KAKENHI (Grant-in-Aid for Scientific Research) Grant Number 26730182, and The Telecommunications Advancement Foundation.

References

1. Radisavljevic, A., Driessen, P.: Path difference learning for guitar fingering problem. In: Proceedings of the International Computer Music Conference, pp. 456–461 (2004)
2. Miura, M., Hirota, I., Hama, N., Yanagida, M.: Constructing a system for finger-position determination and tablature generation for playing melodies on guitars. Syst. Comput. Jpn **35**(6), 10–19 (2004)

3. Tuohy, D.R., Potter, W.D.: A genetic algorithm for the automatic generation of playable guitar tablature. In: Proc. the International Computer Music Conference, pp. 499–502 (2005)
4. Radicioni, D., Scienza, C.D., Lombardo, V.: Guitar fingering for music performance. In: Proc. the International Computer Music Conference. (2005) 527–530
5. Hori, G., Kameoka, H., Sagayama, S.: Input-output hmm applied to automatic arrangement for guitars. Journal of information processing **21**(2), 264–271 (2013)
6. Hart, M., Bosch, R., Tsia, E.: Finding optimal piano fingerings. The UMAP Journal **21**(2), 167–177 (2000)
7. Yonebayashi, Y., Kameoka, H., Sagayama, S.: Automatic decision of piano fingering based on hidden markov models. In: Proc. the 20th International Joint Conference on Artificial Intelligence. (2007) 2915–2921
8. Kasimi, A.A., Nichols, E., Raphael, C.: A simple algorithm for automatic generation of polyphonic piano fingerings. In: Proc. the 8th International Conference on Music Information Retrieval. (2007) 355–356
9. Nagata, W., Sako, S., Kitamura, T.: Violin fingering estimation according to skill level based on hidden markov model. In: International Computer Music Conference (ICMC) and Sound and Music Computing conference (SMC) 2014. (2014) 1233–1238

Interactive Motor Learning
with the Autonomous Training Assistant:
A Case Study

Ramin Tadayon[✉], Troy McDaniel, Morris Goldberg,
Pamela M. Robles-Franco, Jonathan Zia, Miles Laff, Mengjiao Geng,
and Sethuraman Panchanathan

Center for Cognitive Ubiquitous Computing, Arizona State University, Tempe,
USA
{rtadayon, troy.mcdaniel, pamela.franco, jonathan.zia,
mlaff, mgengl, panch}@asu.edu, mgoldberg@ieee.org

Abstract. At-home exercise programs have met limited success in rehabilitation and training. A primary cause for this is the lack of a trainer's presence for feedback and guidance in the home. To create such an environment, we have developed a model for the representation of motor learning tasks and training protocols. We designed a toolkit based on this model, the Autonomous Training Assistant, which uses avatar interaction and real-time multi-modal feedback to guide at-home exercise. As an initial case study, we evaluate a component of our system on a child with Cerebral Palsy and his martial arts trainer through three simple motion activities, demonstrating the effectiveness of the model in representing the trainer's exercise program.

Keywords: Autonomous Training Assistant · Computer–based learning · Multimodal interface · User experience and usability · Human centered design and user centered design

1 Introduction

Under the guidance of therapists and trainers, many individuals have successfully acquired and reacquired motor skills in rehabilitation and training programs worldwide. A critical component in that success has been the introduction of at-home components to rehabilitation and training, the benefits of which have been well-noted [1, 2]. However, since trainers and therapists often cannot be present for the at-home self-practiced segment of an individual's training, individuals often fail to perform the recommended amount of at-home exercise in the long term [3]. Given that the intensiveness of therapy has been known to correspond with health outcomes [4], this is a critical issue for motor recovery in general.

To remedy this issue, telerehabilitation and outpatient rehabilitation programs and other at-home services are seeking an optimal mechanism for therapist-prescribed, self-managed exercise in the home environment. One of the key elements in this process which lacks evidence in research is the design of a feedback environment and

© Springer International Publishing Switzerland 2015
M. Kurosu (Ed.): Human-Computer Interaction, Part II, HCII 2015, LNCS 9170, pp. 495–506, 2015.
DOI: 10.1007/978-3-319-20916-6_46

interface to allow individuals to complete computer-based home therapy for upper limb motor acquisition and recovery [5].

To explore this issue, we are developing a model and toolkit for the delivery of customized exercise programs by therapists and trainers in the home. The toolkit, entitled "The Autonomous Training Assistant" (ATA), is a computer-based system which utilizes multi-modal concurrent feedback and the guidance of a virtual avatar to represent the trainer's presence in at-home training.

The system consists of three main components:

1. An interactive exercise interface in which a virtual avatar acts as an individual's trainer at home
2. Authoring software which allows to assign customized exercise routines
3. A rod-shaped training device, the "Intelligent Stick", through which individuals interact with the virtual trainer.

This system motivates and empowers individuals to take control of their home exercise using a model of action observation which provides fine-grained feedback and knowledge of performance in real-time. An overview of related work in Sect. 2 indicates the need for an effective feedback environment which we explore in the implementation and evaluation of the model and ATA toolkit. In Sect. 3, we describe the model for motor-learning which motivates our toolkit's design. In Sect. 4 we describe the details of our implementation and initial design of the avatar software, Intelligent Stick prototype, and authoring interface. In Sect. 5 we evaluate our initial prototype of the Intelligent Stick prototype for both usability and accessibility, as well as the effectiveness of our training model in representing a training program, in a case study involving a child with Cerebral Palsy and his martial arts trainer. We conclude in Sect. 6 with directions for future work including a longitudinal study of the effectiveness of the ATA in the home environment.

2   Related Work

2.1   Action Observation Model

A primary weakness in many solutions for at-home motor learning is the lack of a cognitive model for learning to inform the design and implementation of the system. An early attempt at outlining such a model for stroke rehabilitation emphasized the need for frequent repetition of the specific motor tasks pertaining to an individual's goals, as well as the importance of visual information in the environment in directing an individual's posture and form during motor training [6]. These foundational principles have resulted in a wide variety of strategies to induce motor learning in individuals undergoing rehabilitation [7]. While these interventions serve well within specific clinical contexts of motor learning, a more flexible model for motor skill acquisition is required for a minimally-invasive solution within the home environment, in the physical absence of a therapist.

Recently, the action observation model has been touted in research as a viable solution to this problem [8]. This model conveys motor learning as an interaction between the subject and a demonstrator, where the subject first observes as the demonstrator performs the required motion and degree for each exercise, then attempts to replicate the demonstrator's motion [9]. Neuroscience points to the activation of "mirror neurons" as the catalysts of learning through action observation and motor imagery for both the upper and lower extremities, in the presence or absence of a visible effector limb [10–13]. The application of the action observation model to the design of games and gaming environments for at-home motor learning has yet to be explored. We utilize the action observation model in the development of the Autonomous Training Assistant.

2.2   Feedback Environments

While the action observation model provides insights into the method by which individuals interact with therapists and trainers to acquire motor skills, it is an incomplete model of the motor learning process because it does not fully explain how these skills are reinforced through repetition, and does not fully grasp the role of the trainer or therapist in this process. The other component which completes this explanation is the feedback model. The elements of this model include the frequency and nature of the feedback, and the sensory channels through which this feedback is communicated to the subject. Earlier work by Hartveld and Hegarty describes the most critical aspects of feedback from therapists in a physiotherapy context [14]: it is frequent, flexible and qualitative, and can be conveyed both verbally and nonverbally. More intriguingly, this work also points out that the equipment used in therapy can also play a critical role in providing feedback that is quantitative, objective, immediate and accurate, which can complement a trainer's feedback and provide the information that trainer needs to assign new goals for the subject on a regular basis.

These findings are the basis for our inclusion of the Intelligent Stick device within the Autonomous Training Assistant not only as a game controller, but also as equipment which provides feedback to the user. More recent studies on feedback within rehabilitation and training have revealed further details on how it can be most effectively administered. One such study by Parker et al. suggests that the given feedback be customizable [15]. Several works emphasize the benefits of multi-modal feedback but caution that the effectiveness of multimodality vary by individual [16]. The virtual presence or representation of a therapist or trainer is described as an effective strategy for delivering this feedback in the absence of a real therapist [17]. We explore this feedback in the Autonomous Training Assistant through both the Intelligent Stick and the virtual trainer.

3   Proposed Model and Approach

Based on the above principles, we propose the following model for the acquisition of motor skills in rehabilitation and training, consisting of the subject (the observer) and the trainer (the demonstrator):

- **Action Observation:** The observer watches and listens as the demonstrator performs and explains an exercise using a piece of training equipment at the expected degree of motion.
- **Motor Imagery:** As the observer watches and listens, he or she imagines completing the motion with his or her body, creating a mental mapping of the motion.
- **Action Replication:** The observer then attempts to replicate the demonstrator's motion using the training equipment. During these attempts, the user receives feedback from both the demonstrator and the equipment which comprises knowledge of performance (pacing, posture, progression toward the targeted degree of motion) and knowledge of results (number of successful completions of the required motion, improvement since previous session). This feedback is frequent, accurate, verbal and non-verbal, multi-modal, and occurs in real-time.
- **Evaluation:** During each attempt, the observer uses the information provided through feedback to evaluate his or her performance, and attempts to improve performance on the next attempt.
- **Assessment:** The demonstrator assesses the observer's performance and, based on this information, forms a new set of goals (pacing, degree of motion, number of repetitions) to assign in the next session.

This version of the action observation model ensures that the principles for successful rehabilitation and training [6] are met while the components of observational learning [9] are preserved. We use this model to design a solution for at-home exercise by introducing a key middle-agent into the process: the **virtual trainer**. This trainer, embodied as a virtual avatar within the home environment, serves as the facilitator of indirect at-home interaction between the **real trainer** (we will use "virtual" and "real" to distinguish between these two entities in this paper) and **trainee**. The virtual trainer is programmed with a real trainer's exercise program and training protocol on a per-trainee basis (the interface, motions and goals are different for each individual using the software). The virtual trainer uses this information to conduct and oversee an individual's at-home training, including the following roles:

- **Demonstrate** visually and provide a description for each motion.
- **Measure and record** an individual's performance in real-time using the parameters given by the real trainer.
- **Provide feedback to an individual** in real-time on each attempt of an exercise using the protocol provided by the real trainer (knowledge of performance).
- **Provide overall data to an individual** on his or her performance after a completed session for each exercise, based on the parameters given by the real trainer (knowledge of results).
- **Provide data to a real trainer** on an individual's performance per exercise, per session, on all of the parameters listed by the real trainer. This information should be usable by the real trainer to assess the trainee, view progress over time, and provide new goals for each parameter to the virtual trainer.

This framework of interaction, based upon the action observation model given above, is summarized in Fig. 1.

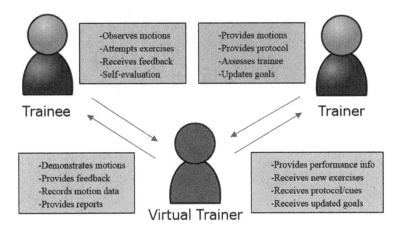

Fig. 1. Interactions between virtual trainer and trainer/trainee

4 Implementation

To implement the framework for interaction shown above, we designed the Autonomous Training Assistant as a proof-of-concept prototype to determine how well the framework can facilitate at-home training in a real-world scenario. We focus the scope of our implementation to upper extremity motor rehabilitation for individuals with mild to moderate hemiparesis (motor impairment in one arm with full function in the opposite arm). While this is a very limited scope due to its specificity, it serves as an initial testing point for our proof of concept. We reserve the generalization of this approach for future work in which we will explore lower extremity function and applications toward other populations.

4.1 Intelligent Stick Prototype

The Intelligent Stick is a rod-shaped training stick which is held and swung by the trainee to complete at-home motion training. Every exercise designed with the ATA system uses the Intelligent Stick as training equipment. We chose to include the Intelligent Stick prototype due to the critical role of training equipment in obtaining objective measures of performance and providing physical feedback to the user [14]. A design sketch of the prototype is shown in Fig. 2. The design consists of a hollow tube molded with plastic resin durable enough to protect the inner hardware in case of drops or collisions, and interior modules including a vibration motor, a power supply, an accelerometer with high-frequency sampling, a gyroscope, and Bluetooth interface for communication with the software.

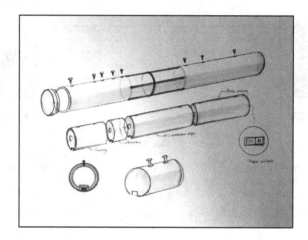

Fig. 2. Intelligent Stick prototype design sketch

4.2   Motion Authoring

We include Motion Authoring software in the ATA system to initialize and update the virtual trainer with the training tasks, feedback cues, and goals of the trainer. The same software provides data on performance to the trainer to allow them to assess and monitor and individual's performance and progression through the training, and to assign new goals for exercises as well as entirely new exercises.

The primary challenge in developing this software is to create a definition of a motion task that is flexible enough to cover as wide a range of different motions used by as many different trainers/therapists as possible. To help us achieve this task, we focus specifically on upper-extremity motion exercises with a single degree-of-freedom. This limits the software and the system to motion tasks in which the major joints of the arm (wrist, elbow, shoulder) are rotated along a single plane. While this presents a major limitation to our current implementation (limited domain of exercises captured in the software), it enables us to simply and accurately represent a motion within the software and simplifies the interface for trainers, allowing them to adjust goals with numeric entry.

Using these restrictions, we define a **motion task** via the following properties:

(a) Name of the motion
(b) Text description of the motion
(c) Primary limb (elbow, shoulder, wrist) involved in the motion
(d) Unimanual (left or right arm) or Bimanual
(e) Axis of rotation (x, y, or z)
(f) Starting position
(g) Degree of motion
(h) Expected average speed of motion (pace)
(i) Body posture
(j) Time limit to complete the exercise

We represent the trainer's feedback on these motions as a series of feedback cues. Each **feedback cue** is defined with the following attributes:

(a) Parameter of feedback (progression, pacing, posture.)
(b) Threshold of feedback (ex. "pace drops below ½ of expected speed".)
(c) Feedback modality (Visual, Audio, or Physical)
(d) Description of feedback

A **training protocol** then simply becomes a set of feedback cues with the attributes above.

4.3   Virtual Training Software

To administer the at-home training component of the ATA using the information obtained from the Motion Authoring system, we developed a software interface which communicates with the Intelligent Stick prototype above to allow a trainee to complete the exercises assigned by a trainer. This software is developed in the Unity platform and the current prototype has been deployed on PC. The software consists of a Heads-Up Display (HUD) which displays visual information on an individual's progress and a 3D embodiment of the virtual trainer which demonstrates the motion and mirrors (imitates) the trainee's motion as he or she attempts the exercise. The software may be automated (screens are timed and progress automatically) or controlled manually, depending on the individual's comfort with keyboard usage. Each exercise contains the following screens:

- **Exercise Title:** Name of the exercise is shown.
- **Demo:** Virtual trainer demonstrates the intended motion task with a text description on the screen.
- **Main Exercise Screen:** Virtual trainer mimics the user's motion with the Intelligent Stick while feedback is given as selected by the user's real trainer.
- **Report:** Shows individual's performance in terms of number of reps completed, previous number of reps completed, and highest number of reps completed by that individual for that exercise.

A screenshot showing an example of the software interface is shown on the left in Fig. 3. This interface can vary between individuals, as the actual information shown on screen to each individual is determined by that individual's real trainer via the Motion Authoring interface. This allows trainers to adapt not only the exercises and their complexity, but the complexity of the interface itself, based on each individual's progress.

Because the sensors on the Intelligent Stick are insufficient for detecting and recording information such as body posture, an additional sensing mechanism is needed. In our implementation, we include the Kinect motion sensor as a simple, non-intrusive method by which to collect information on body posture. This sensing is shown in the screenshot on the right of Fig. 3.

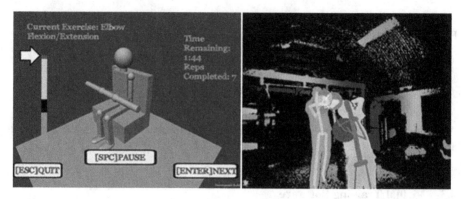

Fig. 3. Virtual Trainer software interface (left) and Kinect body motion capture (right)

5 Case Study

In a previous user study, we evaluated the usability of the Intelligent Stick prototype and motion authoring software with users who have no motor impairment [18]. Through this study we eliminated the most basic issues with the usability and accessibility of our device. In order to determine the usability and accessibility of the system in a rehabilitative setting, and to test the ability of our model to completely capture an interaction between trainer and trainee, we conducted a case study of the ATA system between a trainer and a trainee who meets the current user restrictions of our prototype (hemiparesis, upper extremity motor impairment, mild to moderate degree of impairment).

5.1 Procedure

The subject of the case study was a 12-year-old child with Cerebral Palsy who is hemiparetic as a result of the condition. The individual is undergoing martial arts defense training as a form of motor rehabilitation; consequently, the individual's martial arts instructor became the trainer in the study. The study was conducted in the trainer's martial arts training facility, and since the training already involved the use of stick equipment for martial arts defense techniques, we focused on basic stick training exercises as a testing platform for the Intelligent Stick device. The study was split into three sessions: regular training with the trainer's stick equipment, training using the Intelligent Stick without vibrotactile feedback, and training using the Intelligent Stick with vibrotactile feedback.

For each session, we observed the interactions between the trainer and trainee on a set of four basic exercises: elbow flexion/extension, wrist flexion/extension, bimanual steering, and wrist ulnar deviation in the paretic arm. The first three of these exercises involve bimanual motion while the last exercise is unimanual. The exercises themselves are single-degree-of-freedom exercises selected by the trainer as a part of his training program, and each meet the limitations and restrictions of our model. For each exercise, the trainer began by demonstrating a motion task to the trainee for one minute and then guided the trainee through five minutes of exercise with that motion task. We recorded each session, observing the subject's response to the trainer's feedback and to the prototype. In the third session (Intelligent Stick device with vibrotactile feedback) vibrational cues from the Intelligent Stick were used to replace the trainer's feedback in indicating when the trainee had reached the targeted degree-of-motion for each exercise. Observational data was used to compare the response of the trainee to this feedback relative to the trainee's response to the trainer's feedback. Furthermore we collected feedback from the trainer and trainee on the usability and accessibility of the device, including weight, strength of vibro-tactile cueing, and grip comfort.

5.2   Results

We began by capturing the four required motions using numeric values defined by the trainer under the definition of motion tasks within our model (speed shown in degrees/sec and time shown in minutes):

From the three sessions, we were able to observe the following categories of feedback from the trainer to the trainee during each exercise, all of which serve as quantifiable parameters within our model:

The feedback from the trainer was consistent across all three sessions, and was formatted to match the definition of a feedback cue within our framework. An important attribute of the audio modality was that, as most of the feedback was delivered verbally within this modality, it was given sequentially rather than in parallel. For example, if the subject's posture and pacing both required correction, the trainer would correct one before correcting the other, with priority given toward posture over pacing. This feature of the feedback (priority assigned to one category over another when overlaps occur) is currently not present in our model and will be incorporated in our next iteration of the design.

For the session using vibrotactile feedback from the Intelligent Stick prototype, the trainer selected progression as a parameter and chose the endpoints of the motion (the rest point and the targeted degree-of-motion point) as the critical points which would trigger half-second vibrations from the device. The Intelligent Stick behaved as follows for the third session: for each motion, the stick would vibrate at the starting position and ending position (the targeted angle of motion) of the motion. The instructor chose the range-of-motion for each exercise based on his current training program. These values are shown in Table 1. The stick sent a vibrational signal at the start and end points listed above for each exercise in the third session. The subject was informed of the purpose of these vibrations before beginning the session, and responded to the vibrations as though they represented the stick equipment touching the palm of the trainer to represent a fully-completed motion.

Feedback on usability was generally positive across all exercises. The trainer and trainee were both satisfied with the weight of the device and the responsiveness and amplitude of the vibrotactile feedback. However, there was a major concern with accessibility: as the subject had a weak grip strength in the paretic hand, it was difficult to secure a grasp on the device, which would hamper the subject's ability to use the

Table 1. Case study motion tasks

Name	Descrip.	Limb	Typ.	Axis	Strt.	End	Spd.	Posture	Time
Elbow flex/ex	Hold stick at rest on knees, curl elbows up and down	Elbow	Bi.	X	0	60	20	Seated, elbows tucked in	5
Wrist flex/ex	Hold stick at rest on knees, curl wrists up and down	Wrist	Bi.	X	0	30	30	Seated, elbows tucked in	5
Steer	Hold stick out in front, standing, tilt left and right	Should.	Bi.	Y	0	45	22.5	Standing, arms straight	5
Wrist uln. dev.	Hold stick upward in one hand, tilt fwd and back.	Wrist	Uni.	Z	0	25	25	Seated, elbow tucked in	5

equipment at home. To remedy this, we incorporated the same solution which the trainer used with his regular equipment: we added a strap mechanism to secure the subject's grip on the device which consists of a simple band that wraps around the wrist and is secured with a velcro strip. With the added grip mechanism in place, the subject was able to proceed through the training by using the Intelligent Stick prototype device as if it were regular training equipment.

6   Conclusion and Future Work

While the results of this initial study provided limited information regarding the efficacy of the virtual trainer as a solution deployed in the home setting, it has indicated that our model of action observation can be successfully incorporated within an existing training program by capturing the motion tasks and training protocol of the trainer. To address the effectiveness of the virtual avatar, we have begun a longitudinal case study wherein the same subject will use the device with regular monitoring and updates from the trainer in the home setting, using the training parameters shown in Tables 1 and 2, for a period of 6 months. The results of this deployed solution in long-term at-home training will provide further insights into how this model for motor learning can constitute an effective, optimal interface and training environment in the absence of a real trainer.

Upon demonstrating this to be a successful case for this subject, we will then take steps in future work toward generalization of the model and toolkit by addressing issues with respect to accessibility and usability across other populations, including the stroke population, and issues with respect to model accuracy and capacity for representation across multiple trainers and training programs. As the domain of training programs and assessment strategies by trainers captured within the toolkit continues to

Table 2. Case study training protocol

Parameter	Modality	Threshold	Description
Progression	Audio	Subject reaches one of the endpoints of the motion, or reaches the halfway or ¾ point in the motion	Verbal feedback: "Good job, you're halfway there." "You're almost there." "Good, now bring it back down to starting position"
	Physical	Subject stops before reaching the targetted degree-of-motion for the exercise	Trainer uses hand to nudge the stick up to the targetted degree-of-motion
	Visual	No threshold	Trainer positions his palm at the targetted degree-of-motion, encourages subject to touch the palm of his hand with the equipment
Pacing	Audio	Subject drops below half the expected speed or motion or moves at twice the expected speed, or subject's speed of motion is inconsistent across the motion	Verbal feedback: "You are moving too slowly. Pick up the pace" -"You are moving too quickly. Try to slow it down" -"Try to keep a consistent pace" -"Good, keep this pace"
Posture	Audio	Subject's elbows move out, no longer touch sides of body	Verbal feedback: "Tuck in your elbows"

grow, so should the definition of motion tasks and feedback cues to accommodate the variation in these protocols. We hope that this model for training will serve as a foundation for a new generation of exergaming interfaces which can directly attribute their design choices upon the training strategies of expert therapists and trainers.

References

1. Wijkstra, P.J., Vergert, E.M.T., van Altena, R., Otten, V., Kraan, J., Postma, D.S., Koëter, G.H.: Long term benefits of rehabilitation at home on quality of life and exercise tolerance in patients with chronic obstructive pulmonary disease. Thorax **50**, 824–828 (1995)
2. Legg, L., Langhorne, P.: Outpatient service trialists: rehabilitation therapy services for stroke patients living at home: systematic review of randomised trials. Lancet **363**, 352–356 (2004)
3. Shaughnessy, M., Resnick, B.M., Macko, R.F.: Testing a model of post-stroke exercise behavior. Rehabil. Nurs. **31**, 15–21 (2006)
4. Smith, D.S., Goldenberg, E., Ashburn, A., Kinsella, G., Sheikh, K., Brennan, P.J., Meade, T. W., Zutshi, D.W., Perry, J.D., Reeback, J.S.: Remedial therapy after stroke: a randomised controlled trial. BMJ **282**, 517–520 (1981)

5. Parker, J., Mountain, G., Hammerton, J.: A review of the evidence underpinning the use of visual and auditory feedback for computer technology in post-stroke upper-limb rehabilitation. Disabil. Rehabil. Assist. Technol. **6**, 465–472 (2011)

6. Carr, J.H., Shepherd, R.B.: A motor learning model for stroke rehabilitation. Physiotherapy **75**, 372–380 (1989)

7. Krakauer, J.W.: Motor learning: its relevance to stroke recovery and neurorehabilitation. Curr. Opin. Neurol. **19**, 84–90 (2006)

8. Ertelt, D., Small, S., Solodkin, A., Dettmers, C., McNamara, A., Binkofski, F., Buccino, G.: Action observation has a positive impact on rehabilitation of motor deficits after stroke. Neuroimage **36**, T164–T173 (2007)

9. Mulder, T.: Motor imagery and action observation: cognitive tools for rehabilitation. J Neural Transm. **114**, 1265–1278 (2007)

10. Garrison, K.A., Winstein, C.J., Aziz-Zadeh, L.: The mirror neuron system: a neural substrate for methods in stroke rehabilitation. Neurorehabilitation Neural Repair. **24**, 404–412 (2010)

11. Ezendam, D., Bongers, R.M., Jannink, M.J.A.: Systematic review of the effectiveness of mirror therapy in upper extremity function. Disabil. Rehabil. **31**, 2135–2149 (2009)

12. Sütbeyaz, S., Yavuzer, G., Sezer, N., Koseoglu, B.F.: Mirror therapy enhances lower-extremity motor recovery and motor functioning after stroke: a randomized controlled trial. Arch. Phys. Med. Rehabil. **88**, 555–559 (2007)

13. Modrono, C., Navarrete, G., Rodríguez-Hernández, A.F., González-Mora, J.L.: Activation of the human mirror neuron system during the observation of the manipulation of virtual tools in the absence of a visible effector limb. Neurosci. Lett. **555**, 220–224 (2013)

14. Hartveld, A., Hegarty, J.R.: Augmented feedback and physiotherapy practice. Physiotherapy **82**, 480–490 (1996)

15. Parker, J., Mawson, S., Mountain, G., Nasr, N., Davies, R., Zheng, H.: The provision of feedback through computer-based technology to promote self-managed post-stroke rehabilitation in the home. Disabil. Rehabil. Assist. Technol. **9**, 529–538 (2013)

16. Bongers, B., Smith, S.: Interactivating rehabilitation through active multimodal feedback and guidance. Smart Healthcare Applications and Services, pp. 236–260 (2010)

17. Jung, H.-T., Takahashi, T., Choe, Y.-K., Baird, J., Foster, T., Grupen, R.A.: Towards extended virtual presence of the therapist in stroke rehabilitation. In: 2013 IEEE International Conference on Rehabilitation Robotics (ICORR), pp. 1–6 (2013)

18. Tadayon, R., Panchanathan, S., McDaniel, T., Fakhri, B., Laff, M.: A toolkit for motion authoring and motor skill learning in serious games. In: 2014 IEEE International Symposium on Haptic Audio Visual Environments and Games (HAVE) (2014)

Distributed, Migratory and Multi-screen User Interfaces

Living Among Screens in the City

Bertrand David[(✉)] and René Chalon

CNRS, Ecole Centrale de Lyon, Université de Lyon, LIRIS,
UMR5205 Lyon, France
{bertrand.david, rene.chalon}@ec-lyon.fr

Abstract. Screens have become the apparatuses through which we encounter the world. However, this does not simply mean that our use of screens has increased, but rather that our relationship towards them has changed the way in which we see and live. Through screens we get knowledge and communicate with other people as well as with what is all around us, particularly the urban environment. Individuals and screens have become the inseparable elements of a single communicational and social system raising the fundamental questions of its comprehension and governance. The proliferation of screens and new information and communication technologies (ICT) is accomplishing a perceptive revolution. Our goal is to study the use of screens in the city and propose a new ecosystem contributing to their better use and mastery.

Keywords: Screens · Large screen · Public screen · Private screen · In mobility interaction · Informational ecosystem

1 Introduction

Nowadays, we use a number of screens: personal (smartphones, tablets, etc.), terminals (computers, ATMs, ticketing machines, etc.) and large information screens (airports, railway stations, etc.) or advertising screens. We use them more or less appropriately, and the gap between appropriate use and lack of knowledge is constantly growing. By analyzing this situation we can observe several facts or phenomena.

Firstly, we observe that our relationship towards screens has changed how we see and live. Through screens we get knowledge and communicate with other people as well as with what is all around us, particularly the urban environment. The proliferation of screens and new information and communication technologies (NICT) is accomplishing a perceptive revolution. However, we observe many problems relating to use of these screens.

One hypothesis is that the user is lost in a "world of screens". He does not see why he should have to use a terminal for a new service. Yet he uses such terminals as ATMs, ticket distribution machines, self-service kiosks, etc. It would appear that, faced with the terminal, customers does not perceive that the screen allows interactivity, thus providing the product or service they want. It is indisputable that the user now has smartphones or tablets and is flooded with digital images (e.g. screens in the subway, shops, etc.). There is a lack of benchmarks for distinguishing the services of small screens (mobile phones) versus those large screens (especially as television becomes

© Springer International Publishing Switzerland 2015
M. Kurosu (Ed.): Human-Computer Interaction, Part II, HCII 2015, LNCS 9170, pp. 509–518, 2015.
DOI: 10.1007/978-3-319-20916-6_47

interactive), personal screens versus public displays, passive displays with "push" information versus interactive screens. The first challenge of public screens is the heterogeneity of users faced with such screens: young "geeks", foreigners, people with no computer knowledge, the elderly, and the disabled. So how can we build a reliable interactive solution used by a heterogeneous population working in public places (stations, shops, government offices, schools, universities, etc.)?

To help discover appropriate use of these screens, we must first identify where they are today and how they have evolved from the point of view of human (uses) and technologies.

2   What Is a Screen Today? Mobility, Tactility, Interactivity, Connectivity, and Immersivity

Following the emergence of the cinema, our experience of screens was modified first by television and later on by laptops, smart and mobile phones, and today by large public street screens, which have inaugurated some radical novelties in our experience of screens [1]:

- Mobility. Mobilization of the screen surfaces (smart phones, tablets etc.) produces a peculiar mobilization of the gaze and a transformation of individual and collective habits especially within the urban environment.
- Tactility. Touch screen technology changes interaction and integration between the body and the screen and raises new perceptive constellations.
- Interactivity. Social user screen interaction destroys the traditional representative relationship with the world, producing an intertwining of activity and passivity, as well as allowing users to develop creative employments and practices of the devices themselves.
- Connectivity. Increasing diffusion of connected devices and media convergence develop a new relationship with space and time.
- Immersivity. Post-cinematographic media entail a peculiar sentiment of immersion into the screens, which can be compared to those experienced by the beholder in paintings, the cinema and in the print-on-paper reading experience.
- Ownership (public/private). Public and private screens when traveling: How to use them to decorate the city? How to indicate the way (on public display and/or private screen). How to inform citizens via public and/or private display screens. How to interact with public and/or private display screens.

In our work, we examine, identify, class and propose situations that can be characterized by opposite positions such as: small screen compared to large screen; public screen in relation to private display; fixed screen with respect to mobile screen; user and screen by static situation; mobile user and fixed screen; interaction experiencing user mobility; multiuser collaboration screen; inclusion of the display in proxemics; content aware screen of user presence (explicitly or automatically selected); contents of the screen after the user; contents of the screen projecting the user's location; different interaction techniques to be used, including a tangible user interface and the user interface for media content distribution screens.

Technologically speaking, we find the answers in 3 technologies that are booming: 1/Mobile and cooperative Internet: which can be used everywhere and to which everybody can contribute, 2/Internet of things: automated information exchange to prompt the user only when it is necessary or useful. 3/Location-based services: to increase usefulness of the information conveyed (by limiting its scope of service - utility). To be able to present each user with useful information, the system must know that the user exists: by his/her profile, location, and priority interests. By combining behavioral logic, ubiquitous computing and ambient intelligence the system is able to provide this appropriate information.

3 The Future of the Screens

The screen seems to be destined to integrate all of our actions, thus transforming our expectations and desires. By taking into account our present experience of screens, we plan to identify foreseeable future perspectives and social issues.

Indeed, the dominant position of screens in our society and culture engenders new perceptive, affective and cognitive behaviors, both individual and collective– the phenomenon of Augmented Reality is an example that still needs to be explored – and raises social issues such as the apprenticeship problem, the generational effect, and screen addiction.

4 Screens in the City

Our experience of screens has ultimately become plural and interactive, transforming our relationship with the world and with others, as well as the appearance of the devices all around us and that of urban public spaces [2]. Actually, on the one hand, screens allow us to know the urban environment and to move around in it (geo-localization software, Augmented Reality, etc.), while, on the other, they cover up the means of transportation surfaces, and of buildings (screen facades), like a new skin.

5 Proposal of a New Ecosystem

We propose to apply to information the metaphor of water states (solid, liquid and gaseous) (Fig. 1). We take into account the usual three states of water: solid, liquid and gaseous with the following assumptions: solid - materialized information on a physical medium, liquid - information scrolling (flowing) in front of us, gas - the invisible information circulating around us. Information in solid state is conveyed for example by free newspapers, or is fixed on information panels. Information in liquid state is that scrolling across large screens in the city and found on the facades of buildings, underground corridors and shopping centers, as well as on public transportation bus shelters. Information in gaseous state, invisible and impalpable, is that reaching our smartphones and tablets. Our concern is how to accommodate this liquid information, how to use it, how to make it useful, how to influence it, but also how to avoid being

| Solid, fixed infor-
mation, non-updatable | Liquid information, public
and updatable | Gaseous information, private
and updatable |

Fig. 1. Information in different states (solid, liquid and gaseous) in the city

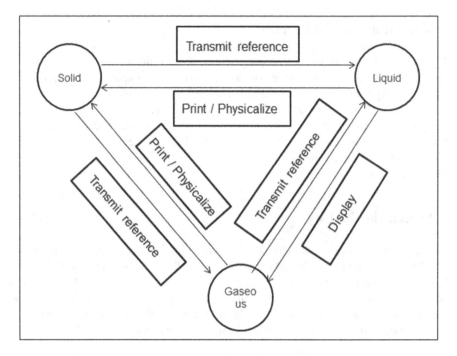

Fig. 2. State transformation operations

invaded, submerged, how to protect us from it, etc.? In this approach we also need to explore and define handling and transfers from one state to another: How to intervene in liquid mode information? How to customize liquid information? How to interact with liquid information?

5.1   State Transformation Operations

In this water metaphor based ecosystem we need to show how these different states can be changed. As indicated in Fig. 2, all state changes are possible.

The operation called "Transmit reference" is the operation which is able to send identification of solid information [3] to the system. At present the usual method

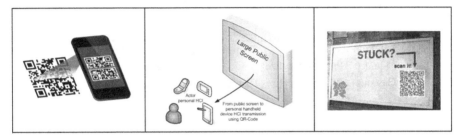

Fig. 3. Information flow between screens

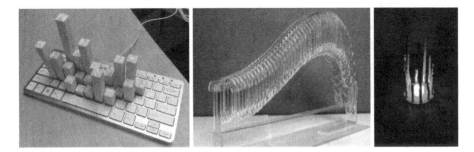

Fig. 4. Examples of physicalization [5–7]

employed is QR-Code transmission, or another appropriate identification code transmission [4] (Fig. 3).

The operation called "Print/Physicalize" proposes two approaches; the first is the classical print-of-paper based on a printer, or pdf generator transmitting a pdf file which could be printed later. The second is the emerging approach called "physical visualization" or "data sculpture", which is able to transform information into a physical form that can then be presented as a new and original expression of the information (Fig. 4).

The last operation called "Display" is a classical operation designed to present (display) gaseous information on the screen. Naturally, a large number of visualization techniques can be used for this purpose, depending on the size of the screen, transmission conditions (QoS- Quality of Service) and its expected use and by whom it is used (see Table 1).

5.2 Communication Between Screens

In multi-screen situations, mainly between personal and public screens, it is important to be able to transfer interesting information from one screen to another, mainly public to private, so as to be able to reuse this information later. The other direction (private to public) is also interesting and we shall discuss this later in this paper. The main method for moving information is by using a QR-code approach [4] (Fig. 3) or a solution proposed by H. Jin [5].

Table 1. State Transformation Operation

From /To	Solid	Liquid	Gaseous
Solid		Transmit reference	Transmit reference
Liquid	Print/Physicalize		Transmit reference
Gaseous	Print/Physicalize	Display	

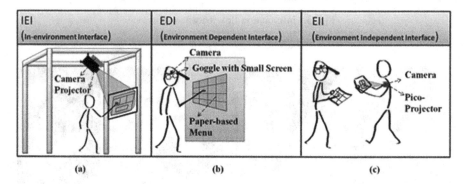

Fig. 5. Interaction techniques in mobility

5.3   Interaction Techniques in Mobility

We identified four main interaction techniques in mobility. The first is classical use of smartphone or tablet multi-touch based interaction. The three others are more original, as explained in Jin [8, 9] for the first one (Fig. 5a) and Zhou [10] for the last two (Fig. 5b & c)). They are called In-Environment Interaction, Environment Dependent Interaction and Environment Independent Interaction, respectively.

5.4   Use of Public Screens

Public screens are very frequent in the city. They can be small or large and are used for different raisons. While advertising is a main use, a more useful application is based on information provision with public transportation information, cultural and sport programs, weather and pollution situation, etc. Naturally, the location and size of these screens must be compatible with the information proposed [11]: short messages giving appropriate information to passing users (readers) in minimum time in busy areas, more detailed information in waiting areas, multi-user information for all passengers present such as airport schedules, etc. All these aspects must be taken into account when designing these public screens [12]. These screens are mainly non-interactive [13] i.e. the content does not depend on users observing it. We considered it interesting to study different solutions for content modification in relation with users observing such screens [14] and identified three situations that we propose to analyze:

1. Interaction with large distant screens is also an interesting challenge.
2. Interaction with large nearby screens is an interesting situation which could use the answer proxemics interaction approach [16].
3. Content dependence on present users: If the system is able to identify who is in the screen vicinity, it could decide to display information directly related to them.

Let us explain these three aspects in some more detail.

Interaction with Large Public Distant Screens. The three main characteristics of large public screens to be taken into account are in the title: large, public and distant:

- Large screens allow sharing of main information, mainly static, with more dynamic and contextual ones.
- Public screens mean that the nature of information must be controlled in order to validate message content with respect to public communication (to whom, language used, words and messages to avoid, communication style, etc.). Two approaches can be proposed, namely either initial agreement mainly with professionals respecting communication rules, or intermediary agreement on fly validation (moderation) of sent messages and information, mainly for non-identified participants.
- Distant screens mean that the corresponding interaction must use an appropriate manipulation (interaction) style. Several solutions were proposed, including indirect interaction which can be more or less sophisticated [15]. We consider that preparation on the tablet of information to be displayed concerning layout and inserted content is a potential approach. A more limited approach is insertion of information in a predefined zone, either able to receive only textual information, finalization of which i.e. color, font, etc. are predefined, or offering more extensive possibilities with image display and choice of finalization.

Proxemics Interaction with Large Nearby Screens. Another approach for large public screens relates to nearby screens. In this case, proxemics principles [16] can be used for it to share its surface between several users according to their distance (Fig. 6). For distant users, a small part of the screen is devoted to publishing small images or brief messages. For closer users, a larger surface is proposed for more informative and explicit messages. Users very close to the screen are able to interact and communicate normally with the screen [7].

Fig. 6. Proxemics interaction [16]

Fig. 7. Contextualization in the city

Contextualization in the City. Citizens can be provided with very attractive services if the information system is able to know their logical or geographical position and, more generally, their behavioral profile [17]. By tracking their current position, it can provide them with appropriate contextual information and display this information either on their personal screen or on public screens such as store windows. This is the case of targeted advertising (if it is possible to match the desired product and its location in the store). It is also possible to use city orientation screens to guide a user to a particular destination, i.e. a visiting itinerary for a tourist, or how to get to a particular destination (soccer stadium).

It is naturally important that the user can choose the level of identification which will be used during this contextualization. His /her name, first name, an alias or an avatar can be used on public screens to guide or solicit him /her. These choices are proposed to allow respect of his /her private life if so requested (Fig. 7).

5.5   Information Fountain

One interesting object in the city is the bus-stop [18]. It can both receive and broadcast information, thus playing a role of hotspot. We can identify its role as a concept of "information fountain" providing and receiving information. It can play an important role in the relationships between citizens as well as with public transportation officers.

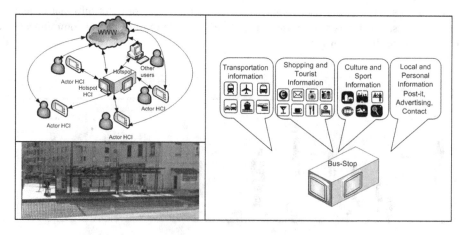

Fig. 8. Bus-stop as an information hotspot and/or fountain [18]

Bus-stops form the location of different screens which can be used for information on city activities (transportation, shopping, and tourist, cultural and sports information, etc.) as well as for exchanging information between citizens and support for local advertising. Messages can be sent via the bus-stop to the bus driver to inform him of a particular situation (stroller, bicycle or wheelchair transportation). All these services can be attached to the bus-stop and used by citizens (Fig. 8).

6 Conclusions

In this paper we discussed the use of different screens, public or private, large or small, mobile or static and we proposed a new ecosystem clarifying their use in relation with the water metaphor applied to the information. We explained the meaning of solid, liquid and gaseous information and the transformation operations. We also introduced the "Information fountain" concept. Contextualization and interactivity are the main goal for the new generation of public screens as well as smooth communication between all screens, small or large, public or private, with appropriate relationships with users. Respect of privacy is an important consideration, but in an appropriate way, i.e. strict respect for whoever so wishes, but allowing personal implication in exchanges if the user agrees and wants this. Interdisciplinary studies are needed to appreciate and identify different kinds of behavior [19, 20].

References

1. Carbone, M.: (2015). http://vivreparmilesecrans.wix.com/vivreparmilesecrans
2. David, B., Yin, C., Zhou, Y., Xu, T., Zhang, B., Jin, H., Chalon, R.: SMART-CITY: problematics, techniques and case studies. In: ICCM 2012 8th International Conference on Computing Technology and Information Management, Seoul, Korea, pp. 24–26 (2012)
3. Jin, H., Xu, T., David, B., Chalon, R.: Direct migrator: eliminating borders between personal mobile devices and pervasive displays. In: 2014 IEEE International Conference on 5th Pervasive Computing and Communications Workshops (PERCOM Workshops), pp. 557–562 (2014)
4. Rouillard, J.: Contextual QR codes. In: The Third International Multi-Conference on Computing in the Global Information Technology, ICCGI 2008, pp. 50–55 (2008)
5. (2011). http://www.cmybacon.com/2011/06/keyboard-frequency-sculpture/
6. Stusak, S., Tabard, A., Sauka, F., Khot, R.A., Butz, A.: Activity sculptures: exploring the impact of physical visualizations on running activity. IEEE Trans. Vis. Comput. Graph. **20** (12), 2201–2210 (2014)
7. Moere, A.V., Patel S.: The physical visualization of information: designing data sculptures in an educational context, Design Lab, Faculty of Architecture, Design and Planning, The University of Sydney, Australia (2009). http://infoscape.org/publications/vinci09
8. Jin, H., David, B., Chalon, R.: Exploring initiative interactions on a proxemic and ambient public screen. In: Kurosu, M. (ed.) HCI 2014, Part II. LNCS, vol. 8511, pp. 567–577. Springer, Heidelberg (2014)
9. Jin, H., David, B., Chalon, R.: Novel proxemic interactive platform for sociable public zone in smart city. In: Botía, J.A., Charitos, D. (eds.) 9th International Conference on Intelligent

Environments IE 2013 (Sociable Smart City 2013 workshop) Athens, Greece. Ambient Intelligence and Smart Environments 17. IOS Press, Amsterdam (2013)

10. Zhou, Y., Xu, T., David, B., Chalon, R.: Innovative wearable interfaces: an exploratory analysis of paper-based interfaces with camera-glasses device unit. Pers. Ubiquit. Comput. **18**(4), 835–849 (2014)

11. Bendinelli, A., Paternò, F.: Design criteria for public display user interfaces. In: Kurosu, M. (ed.) HCI 2014, Part I. LNCS, vol. 8510, pp. 623–630. Springer, Heidelberg (2014)

12. Nebeling, M., Matulic, F., Norrie, M.: Metrics for the evaluation of news site content layout in large-screen contexts. In: Proceedings CHI 2011. ACM Press, pp. 1511–1520 (2011)

13. Huang, E.M., Koster, A., Borchers, J.: Overcoming assumptions and uncovering practices: when does the public really look at public displays? In: Indulska, J., Patterson, D.J., Rodden, T., Ott, M. (eds.) PERVASIVE 2008. LNCS, vol. 5013, pp. 228–243. Springer, Heidelberg (2008)

14. Müller, J., Alt, F., Schmidt, A., Michelis, D.: Requirements and design space for interactive public displays. In: ACM Multimedia, pp. 1285–1294 (2010)

15. Gilliot, J., Casiez, G., Roussel, N.: Impact of form factors and input conditions on absolute indirect-touch pointing tasks. In: Proceedings of CHI 2014. ACM (2014)

16. Greenberg, S., Marquardt, N., Ballendat, T., Diaz-Marino, R., Wang, M.: Proxemic interactions: the new ubicomp? Interactions **18**(1), 42–50 (2011)

17. Dey, A.K., Abowd, G.D.: Towards a better understanding of context and context-awareness. In: Proceedings of the Workshop on the What, Who, Where, When and How of Context-Awareness. ACM Press, New York (2000)

18. David, B., Zhou, Y., Xu, T., Chalon, R.: Mobile user interfaces and their utilization in a smart city. In: ICOMP 2011 - The 2011 International Conference on Internet Computing as part of WorldComp 2011 Conference, Las Vegas, pp. 18–21, July 2011

19. Carbone, M.: Vivre par(mi) les écrans aujourd'hui (2014). http://vivreparmilesecrans.wix.com/vivreparmilesecrans#!colloque/c1q25

20. IMPEC: Interactions Multimodales par Ecran (2014). http://impec.ens-lyon.fr/archives-208361.kjsp?RH=1382969175190&RF=1382968657183

Delegation Theory in the Design of Cross-Platform User Interfaces

Dagmawi L. Gobena[1]([⊠]), Gonçalo N.P. Amador[2], Abel J.P. Gomes[3], and Dejene Ejigu[1]

[1] Addis Ababa University, Addis Ababa, Ethiopia
dagmawi.Lemma@gmail.com, ejigud@yahoo.com
[2] University of Beira Interior, Covilhã, Portugal
gamador@it.ubi.pt
[3] Instituto de Telecomunicações, Covilhã, Portugal
agomes@di.ubi.pt

Abstract. The amalgamation of various technologies to support the needs of new computing models has become prevalent in computing environments like ubiquitous computing. Amalgamation means here heterogeneity caused by not only the coexistence of various devices in the same computing environment, but also the diversity between software, users as well as interaction modalities. The platform heterogeneity together with additional needs of interaction modalities and the proliferation of new technologies pose unique challenges for user interface (UI) designers and developers. We consider the problem of heterogeneity as a demand of collaboration between platforms (device and system) that are owned or controlled by a human user. Hence, we drive the concept of delegation to be implemented in a peer-to-peer model, where one peer (known as *delegator*) delegates another peer (known as *delegatee*) to run a UI (or a single interaction-modality) on its behalf. Thus, the delegatee uses its own capabilities to present the required UI or interaction-modality.

Keywords: Cross-platform UI · UI migration · Distributed UI

1 Introduction

Delegation is the act of appointing others in order to discharge a certain responsibility on behalf of the appointer. The concept of delegation may appear in various forms and within diversified context. Nevertheless, in any form of delegation, there are two parties – the *delegator* and the *delegatee*. The former empower or appoint the later to discharge a task on its behalf.

Accordingly, we argue that, an interaction might be held across a platform if a device is appointed to run the user interface (UI) on behalf of another device while the service of the task runs at the delegator end. This approach is similar to some existing services such as remote desktop. But in remote desktop, identical interaction modality is considered between peers. We include the possibilities of assimilating diverse interaction modalities using peer-to-peer model. Each peer is autonomous to apply the interaction modalities as per their capabilities. For example, a visual modality might be converted

M. Kurosu (Ed.): Human-Computer Interaction, Part II, HCII 2015, LNCS 9170, pp. 519–530, 2015.
DOI: 10.1007/978-3-319-20916-6_48

into voice interaction at the peer delegated to run a certain UI. Thus, in this paper, we extend the concept of delegation to be applied in developing cross-platform UI within ubiquitous computing, which is characterized by heterogeneity of diverse elements.

The heterogeneity is caused by the coexistence of various devices in the same computing environment as well as due to the diversity between software, users, interaction modalities and environments.

It happens that two of the prominent approaches (i.e., UI distribution and UI migration), usually followed in the development of cross-platform UI, focus on a particular aspect of the heterogeneity – mostly the device [2]. But, while having heterogeneous environment, if the UI is generated based on a specific context (e.g., the device, user, task, interaction modalities, etc.), it is likely that the usability of the system would be reduced entailing several usability issues [1]. Furthermore, since both UI distribution and UI migrations are often based on client-server model, the entire cross-platform UI environment is subjected to single point of failure.

Rather, we consider the problem of heterogeneity as a demand of collaboration between platforms (device and system) that are part of the computing environment (e.g., wearable platform like a smart watch) or controlled by a human user.

We are motivated to develop the theory of *UI delegation* to sustain an alternative approach in the development of cross-platform UI within a peer-to-peer model where one peer (known as *delegator*) delegates another peer (known as *delegatee*) to run a UI/interaction-modality on its behalf. This means that the *delegatee* is autonomous and uses its own capabilities to present the required UI/interaction-modality. In other words, the UI (resp., interaction modality) generated (resp., used) by the delegatee does not need to be identical to delegator's one, but has to perform the function to achieve the same goal. Thus, we consider the concept of *UI delegation* as an opportunity to take advantage of heterogeneity, so that interaction can be extended and usability can be improved using the capabilities of the *delegatee*. For example, a list box widget can be used "on behalf of" radio button for implementing "choice" concept in the interaction. Similarly, instead of visually reading a text from the screen it can be converted to audio and played if the capability exists. Thus, audio listening can be used "on behalf of" of visual reading.

Summing up, the theory of *UI delegation* is presented in this paper to take advantage of heterogeneity inherent to different devices, systems, users, interaction modalities co-existing in a ubiquitous environment. In Sect. 2, we briefly review the literature related to concepts of cross-platform UI and types of user interfaces. The main constructs of theory of *UI delegation* are then discussed in Sect. 3. In Sect. 4, we discuss the *common interface language* (CIL) as a protocol for realizing *UI delegation* within the context of heterogeneous environment. Finally in Sect. 5 we made our conclusion.

2   Literature Review

Ubiquitous computing comprises various platforms to achieve its goal. These platforms are heterogeneous in type, technology, as well as function. For example, browsing the Internet is a common function that can be supported by various computing devices in the same environment, but such devices make usage of different browsers, display sizes, screen resolutions, operating systems, etc. – even by different users and in different contexts. Because of this, one of the characteristics of ubiquitous computing is *heterogeneity*. [1] In this setting, users interact with devices implicitly or explicitly using different interaction modalities [2].

The heterogeneity of the platforms can be felt at various levels and from different perspectives: users, UI designers, as well as the usability of the system. With respect to users, they are required to learn new UI and interaction modalities. Regarding the usability of the system, the learning curve of the user could take more time until the user becomes adequately proficient and efficient in dealing with the system. From designers' perspective, they may be required to develop unique UIs for each platform [3].

Vanderdonckt [4] classifies the UI design for heterogeneous platforms as per the situation that causes the diversity. Therefore, the UI design may focus on the presence of multiple users or, alternatively, on the usage of multiple monitors, devices, platforms, and displays [5].

Nevertheless, designing various versions of same UI for distinct platforms operating within the same environment entails several problems. Foremost, there would be duplication of effort in the UI development process and also.

- changing/adding/removing features consistently across each platform could be cumbersome [6], and this leads us to the problem of *maintainability* of each type of platform;
- introducing new platform may require rework, since it is important to have new design for supporting the newly added platform; and this would challenge the *scalability* of the environment.

Another approach in cross-platform UI development is adapting a UI for the context of a platform by automatically *generating* the UI or, alternatively, *migrating* UI [7–9]. In this regards, UI distribution and UI migration have become two of the prominent approaches. These approaches are followed as general UI development approaches [10–14]. In [14], distributed and migratory UIs are discussed as two independent concepts.

In UI distribution, UI elements are distributed across platforms, so that, in some cases, this may create duplication of UI elements [14]. For example, in [15], a multi-client (multi-platform) UI is presented using the model-view-controller (MVC) architecture that stores different versions of a webpage (UI) on the server for each predefined platform; and a controller is responsible for selecting one of the UI versions that most fits a particular platform from which the users operate. Also, UI distribution depends on predefined UI elements created at design time and available (or distributed across platforms) with a certain platform/user context in mind.

The action of transferring a UI from one device (source) to another device (sink) is called UI migration; the UI itself is known as migratory UI, which is "said to be *migratable* if it has the migration ability" [16]. Migratory ability is the ability of a UI element to be rendered at a remote peer. Hence, UI designers can decide on the part of the UI that shall be migrated across platform as the need arise. Thus a UI can be migrated partially or completely [10]. However, the interaction modality between the peers remains the same. Hence mono-modality is often followed [10].

Migrating UI can help a user to continue computing on the go. Thus, unlike distributed UIs, during migration not only the structure of the UI element but also their content is maintained and migrated [10, 14]. For example, if a user selects a checkbox on an interface before migration, then that checkbox shall appear as selected checkbox across a platform where the UI is migrated and rendered.

Migratory UIs can be seen as a particular type of distributed UI. Berti et al. [10] indicated that a UI migration process is mainly started on-demand. That is, if the user desires to continue the interaction on a different platform, but using exactly the same UI.

What distributed and migratory UI have in common is that they both run over the client-server computing architecture. Consequently, in addition to the unsolved problems of *scalability* and *maintainability*, these UIs suffer from lack of reliability because the UI server is a single point of failure.

In our opinion, the current cross-platform UI development methods need a different dimension, where a UI can be automatically generated from runtime UI related information about the device, the system and human user. It is here that delegation theory and delegated UIs come into play.

The notion of delegation is applied in some areas of computing. For example in [17], devices with less computing power benefits the computational power of delegated devices with higher computational power for assigning and revoking privileges to users in pervasive environment. Haddadi also developed a theory, in agent-based system, by taking "an internal perspective to model how individual agents may reason about their actions" [18]. This is further developed in [19], where it is stated that "in delegation an agent A needs or likes an action of another agent B and includes it in its own plan, thus, A is trying to achieve some of its goals through B's action". According to Castelfranchi et al., A is said to be the "client", while B is the "contractor" [19].

Since heterogeneous environment introduce several diversified platform capabilities at each distinct peer, this opportunity shall be consider in improving usability of the system by letting the user to interact through collaborated capabilities. Hence, we foresee a different dimension of cross-platform UIs that can be realized by delegating a peer to run a UI on behalf of another peer. For example, it is more convenient to compose a message on the standard keyboard than on virtual keyboard of small handheld device. Thus, thought the actual messaging service (e.g., SMS) can be delivered via a mobile phone, for instance, the user could be more satisfied if allowed to interact with its standard keyboard for the purpose of composing the message. Hence, the usability can be improved if the mobile phone delegates the desktop only for the HCI aspect of the messaging system.

According to the works and techniques we found in the literature, at the time of automatically generating a specific UI across platform within a certain computing environment, they focus only on one of the views (user, device or system). Though it is common practice to consider the user and platform capabilities in UI development at design time [20], this is not the case at runtime. For example, responsive web development approaches as well as solutions presented by Zhang et al., in their pattern based approach [7], the focus is on screen size adaptation. On the other hand, Jeffery et al. [6] focused on the functionality of the appliances while Sauter et al. focused [15] only consider the device type, just to mention a few works.

Therefore, we hypothesize that if each peer within the environment describe its UI capabilities and store it locally, advertising or making them available to other peers using the same protocol (i.e. CIL) whenever needed, and if there is at least another peer (*delegatee*) that matches its capabilities literally or by transmutability, then it is possible to run the UI or interaction modality on behalf of the *delegator*.

In this paper, delegating the build-ups of a UI on some device in the computing environment means that we are not using the client-server computing model anymore, but the peer-to-peer computing model. So,

1. since each peer is responsible to maintain and locally store its own capabilities, it is always possible to authorize new peers signing up and in the environment; i.e., the environment can be scaled up easily,
2. since the desired UI or interaction modality is generated during interaction, there is no need to create the UI element at design time (e.g., a menu to access a certain functionality), thus the environment would be easy to maintain.

Moreover, we assume a holistic approach of the UI by considering triplet views (the user, device and system) in cross-platform UI, but not in partiality of any of the views. This is especially useful when the peers communicate their capabilities during the delegation process. Thus, delegated UIs sustain themselves on *autonomy* of the delegatee, as well as on *transmutability* of capabilities between the delegator and the delegatee.

3 Theory of UI Delegation

There are two decision makers in delegation: the principal (*delegator*) and the agent (*delegatee*). The *delegator* decides whether to initiate the delegation or not while the *delegatee* may be willing to participate in the delegation process or not [21] Thus, both the *delegator* and *delegatee* are autonomous. Hence, *UI delegation* shall take place within a peer-to-peer model.

In *UI delegation,* the *delegatee* may initiate the delegation process on-demand or automatically. The delegation process can be initiated on-demand if the user wants to continue the interaction with the system but using another peer possibly owning more suitable capabilities. For example, a user who wants to compose an email that would be sent from its smartphone may wish to use a standard keyboard attached to his desktop computer. Hence the user shall initiate the delegation process manually so that the smartphone may delegate the desktop. Likewise, automatic delegation can be initiated by the *delegator* if a peer believes it is deemed important to do so. For example, in a situation where a user interacts within a context-aware system using the speech/audio modality at a desktop in his/her office, once the user changes the location and enters in to a noisy zone, a peer may decide to switch to the visual modality while delegating the UI on handheld device so that the user may continue the interaction using visual modality, providing that the *delegatee* peer is dressed up with the desired capabilities.

On the other hand, the *delegatee* peer might be willing or not to participate in the delegation process. Furthermore, considering a heterogeneous environment where peers are dressed up with various capabilities, and are able to support diversified functionalities, not all the peers shall participate in *an instance of a delegation process.* Accordingly, the peers can be classified as *delegatee, candidate* or neither. Thus, in the delegation process:

- A peer is said to be *delegatee* if it responds to a *delegation request* and necessarily selected by a *delegator* peer
- A peer is said to be *candidate peer* when it responds to a *delegation request*

Therefore, a reply to a *delegation request* indicates that the responding peer is willing to take part in the delegation process.

In order to participate in *UI delegation,* each peer shall describe its supported capabilities and store them locally. This can be done at design time and modified as required to incorporate new capabilities or removing undesired ones. However, selection of capabilities and rendering the UI accordingly can be done at runtime. The local description is then used when a peer creates and transmits a *delegation request,* and when a peer checks the degree of matching of its capabilities with other peer. The former is responsibility of the *delegator,* while the latter is responsibility of the *delegatee.*

3.1 Delegation Request

A peer willing to delegate another peer shall create a *delegation request* to peers within the same environment in order to be aware of existing capabilities available across such environment. Thus, a *delegation request* conveys a partial description of a UI or interaction modalities in terms of the desired capabilities required to build a usable interaction. Therefore, the *delegator* peer shall describe the required capabilities and then send them as a *delegation request* for each peer in the environment. At this stage, only basic information about the UI to be delegated is required.

For example, if there is a selection widget in the prospective UI to be delegated, then only its basic information is required, but not the details, such as the content (value) of the widget and the data structure (data type). As explained further ahead, delegation requests and communication between peers can take place using a XML-based protocol.

3.2 Degree of Matching

Having the *delegation request* in the form of XML description, each *candidate peer* shall compute the degree of matching M between capabilities, which is used to determine how much a peer's capability resembles to what is requested by the *delegator* peer. In this regards, three possible conditions can be considered:

1. There is identical capability
2. There is similar but not identical capability
3. The requested capability is not available.

In the case that the capability is identically supported by the *candidate peer*, the value of *M* is incremented by 2; if the homologous capabilities are similar, the value of *M* is incremented by 1; otherwise, the capability does not exist on the candidate delegatee side, even using transmutation, so the value of *M* shall be decremented to discourage the competing *candidate peer* so as to minimize the chance of appointment as *delegatee*. Thus, after computing the value of *M*, each *candidate peer* P_i returns M_i to delegator as its value of *M*. Therefore, for a given list of capabilities in the *delegation request* with size *N*, the maximum possible value that P_i can attain (i.e. if all the capabilities in the *delegation request* identically matches the corresponding local capabilities maintained by the *candidate peer*) is given by:

$$M = 2N \tag{1}$$

On the other hand, if all the capabilities in the *delegation request* can be supported by the *candidate peer*, using similar capabilities but not identical capability, then the value of *M* would be:

$$M = N \tag{2}$$

Therefore, suppose the number of candidate peers is *n*, then it is most appropriate to select a peer with the highest *degree of matching*, which is given by

$$\text{MAX } (M_1, M_2, \ldots, M_n) : 1 < i < n \text{ and } N \leq M_i \leq 2N \tag{3}$$

Thus, the *UI delegation* holds:

- if there exists an active peer that responds to *delegation request*, and
- if Eq. (3) is satisfied.

Nevertheless, Eq. (3) is subjected to design decision and the UI developers might decide letting the delegation to prevail if $N < M$, but if $N \approx M$ variation may occur with respect to Eq. (3).

3.3   Flow of *UI Delegation*

The following flow of steps intends to clarify the idea of *UI delegation* that is presented as within a heterogeneous environment.

1. user starts operation at platform p_i $(i = 1, 2, \ldots, n)$, *where n* is the number of platforms within the environment;
2. after a while, the user changes its location;

3. platform p_i is aware of the new user location (for example, the absence of UI can be traced/anticipated if the user is not responsive in a certain given time, and location service can be then used to learn about the new location of the user)
4. platform p_i broadcasts *delegation request* message M_{pi}, given by Eq. 4

$$M_{pi} = \{d_i, h_i, s_i\} \tag{4}$$

where d, h and s stand for the desired device, human and system capabilities respectively, that should be considered while applying the UI or interaction modality at the delegatee end;
5. platforms within the environment *advertise* their *degree of matching* with M_{pi};
6. platform p_i delegates device p_j since p_j better supports the desired capabilities;
7. platform p_j uses the description of M_{pi} to generate as per the locally maintained capability

$$M_{pj} = \{d_j, h_j, s_j\} \tag{5}$$

8. user operates at platform p_j using the delegated UI.

Therefore, since not all platforms in the environment are the most adequate for the delegation, the respondent peer that most fits the required capability will become the delegatee.

4   The CIL Protocol

In order to maintain the collaboration between peers, as well as to standardize how capabilities are represented and exchanged between peers, the peers shall use the CIL (Common Interface Language) as a protocol for describing: the *capabilities*, the *presentation*, and the *message to be exchanged between the peers*.

Furthermore, each description shall abide the syntax and semantics as defined in the *CIL-definition*.

We create *CIL-definition* using XML-schema for setting the constraints and structure of the descriptions that would be used between the peers. Hence, description for representing the UI, message, and capabilities shall be validated as per the *CIL-definition*.

The *CIL-definition* is created using three broad aspects deemed to be important in any HCI: the *human*, *device* and *system*. As indicated in the following fragment of the XML-schema, these three views are represented as the top-level elements of a taxonomy for cross-platform interfaces, so that any description shall be created under either of these elements.

```
<complexType name="CIL">
  <all>
    <element name="_HumanBeingView"
  type="xs:_HumanBeingView"
    maxOccurs="1" minOccurs="0">
</element>
<element name="_DeviceBeingView"
  type="xs:_DeviceBeingView"
    maxOccurs="1" minOccurs="0">
</element>
<element name="_SystemBeingView"
  type="xs:_SystemBeingView"
      maxOccurs="1" minOccurs="0">
</element>
  </all>
<attribute name="Version" type="string"/>
<attribute name="id" type="string"/>
</complexType>
```

The _HumanBeingView and _DeviceBeingView are used to define the required elements and respective constraints useful to describe human and device capabilities. For example, a human capability is the eye sight, so we need to specify whether or not a given individual is trichromat or colorblind.

```
<xs:_HumanBeingView>
  <xs:Sensory>
    <xs:Vision Supported="true" Preference="1">
      <xs:ColorBlind>true</xs:ColorBlind>
    </xs:Vision>
  </xs:Sensory>
  <xs:Effector Supported="true" Preference="2">
    <xs:Touching Supported="true" Preference="0">
        <xs:ArmCount>0</xs:ArmCount>
    </xs:Touching>
  </xs:Effector>
</xs:_HumanBeingView>
```

Thus, child elements are created under each of those top-level elements in the schema, which are useful to describe and represent:

- the human physical interaction capabilities;
- the device interaction modalities, with a focus on the input and output mechanisms possibly supported by the device

However, it is not important to create an exhaustive description of capabilities using all the elements defined within the schema. Rather, each peer shall locally describe and store its own capabilities using the same schema, so that such list of capabilities can be used.

- when determining the *degree of matching M* after receiving a *delegation request.*
- to describe UI that to be run at a certain *delegatee* end

For example, if a *delegator* desires to run a UI that is meant to support a colorblind user, then part of the *delegation request* description shall include this information under the _HumanBeingView.

The presentational description (or description of the running UI/interaction modalities) has to be created in accordance to the elements and the respective constraints set under _SystemBeingView. Nevertheless, the elements under this element can be used to describe platform capabilities related to services useful for HCI as well. For example, a text-to-speech conversion capability that may exist at one of the peer can be described under the _SystemBeingView within the presentation element.

The extent how CIL is used might vary at different level of the delegation process. For example, though we include all the possible generic information that can be required and useful to describe UIs or interaction modalities using XML-schema, it may not be important to use the entire structure; for instance for *delegation request.*

```
<complexType name="Widget">
  <sequence>
  <element name="WidgetClass" type="xs:WidgetClass"
      maxOccurs="1" minOccurs="1">
  </element>
    <element name="WidgetStructure"
type="xs:WidgetStructure"
      maxOccurs="1" minOccurs="1">
  </element>
  <element name="WidgetContent" type="xs:WidgetContent"
      maxOccurs="unbounded" minOccurs="0">
  </element>
  <element name="WidgetState" type="xs:WidgetState"
      maxOccurs="1" minOccurs="0">
  </element>
  <element name="WidgetSize" type="xs:WidgetSize"
      maxOccurs="1" minOccurs="0">
  </element>
  </sequence>
  <attribute name="WidgetID" type="string"></attribute>
  <attribute name="Identifier" type="string"></attribute>
  </complexType>
```

For example the above schema can be useful to describe the basic information about a particular widget that severs as a build-up of the UI. In this case, the Widget is an element that is defined under the WidgetSet, which is used to represent the form of explicit interaction. And the Widget element is further described by its class, using the WidgetClass element. Other parts of the schema shown in the above code are useful for defining the presentational description, but can be less relevant within the *delegation request.* Therefore, each peer within the environment, where *UI delegation* is applied, has to describe its capability using as per the *CIL-definition* and store it locally; and when required a peer can advertise its capability in the form of *delegation request* or for computing the *degree of matching* in response to *delegation request.*

It is important to note that the entire schema we created for CIL can be updated and improved by incorporating new elements to include new UI style or interaction modalities. But peers participating in the *UI delegation* process shall describe their capabilities and store is locally using the same version of the schema, known as *CIL-definition.* At this stage of our study, four classes of widget are identified: `selection`, `text`, `view` and `switch`. However, it has to be noted that this classes may appear in any form across various platforms. For example, choice can be presented in the form of radio, checkbox, list box, etc. Thus what is needed during *delegation request* is the basic information that shows whether the candidate peer supports the `selection` class or not.

5 Conclusion

In the *theory of UI delegation* we have identified four constructs. The concept of CIL is the main construct that is useful to realize the communication and collaboration between peers. Yet, the peers may appear as *delegator, delegatee* or *candidate* peer. Thus peer type is the second construct in the theory. However, the distinction between *delegatee* and *candidate* peer related to two other important constructs: *delegation request* and *degree of matching.* We argue that it is possible to generate at runtime a more usable UI across platforms as well as build scalable and maintainable heterogeneous environment by following the theory of *UI delegation.* Nevertheless, delegation is based on trust, thus more work has to be done regarding trust management between the *delegator* and *delegatee.* Also, though broadcasting the *delegation request* for all the peers is one option, it could be bandwidth intensive. Therefore, how to select most appropriate *candidate* peer remains as an issue in trust computing for future works.

References

1. Byeong-Ho, K.: Ubiquitous computing environment threats and defensive measures. Int. J. Multimedia Ubiquit. Eng. **2**(1), 47–60 (2007)
2. Albrecht, S.: Implicit human computer interaction through context. Pers. Technol. **4**(2–3), 191–199 (2000)
3. Meixner, G.: Past, present, and future of model-based user interface development. i-com **10** (3), 2–11 (2011)
4. Vanderdonckt, J.: Distributed user interfaces: how to distribute user interfaces elements across users, platform and environments. In: The 11th Congreso Internacional de Interacción Persona–Ordenador (Interacción 2010), Valencia, Spain, pp. 3–14 (2010)

5. Melchior, J., Grolaux, D., Vanderdonckt, J., Van Roy, P.: A toolkit for peer-to-peer distributed user interfaces: concepts, implementation and applications. In: EICS, USA, pp. 69–78 (2009)

6. Nichols, J., Myers, B.: Creating a lightweight user interface description language: an overview and analysis of the personal universal controller project. ACM Trans. Comput.-Hum. Interact. **16**(4), 17–37 (2009)

7. Radu, V.: Application. In: Radu, V. (ed.) Stochastic Modeling of Thermal Fatigue Crack Growth. ACM, vol. 1, pp. 63–70. Springer, Heidelberg (2015)

8. Nilsson, E., Floch, J., Hallsteinsen, S., Stav, E.: Model-based user interface adaptation. Comput. Graph. **30**(5), 692–701 (2006)

9. Ghiani, G., Paternò, F., Santoro, C.: On-demand cross-device interface components migration. In: Proceedings of the 12th international Conference on Human Computer Interaction with Mobile Devices and Services, MobileHCI 2010, Lisboa, Portugal, pp. 299–308 (2010)

10. Berti, S., Paternó, F., Santoro, C.: A taxonomy for migratory user interfaces. In: Gilroy, S. W., Harrison, M.D. (eds.) DSV-IS 2005. LNCS, vol. 3941, pp. 149–160. Springer, Heidelberg (2006)

11. Sørensen, H., Raptis, D., Kjeldskov, J., Skov, M.: The 4C framework: principles of interaction in digital ecosystems. In: ACM International Conference on Pervasive and Ubiquitous Computing (UbiComp 2014), USA (2014)

12. Elmqvist, N.: Distributed user interfaces: state of the art. In: Gallud, J.A., Tesoriero, R., Penichet, V.M.R. (eds.) Distributed User Interface. Human-Computer Interaction Series, pp. 7–12. Springer, London (2011)

13. Frosini, L., Paternò, F.: User interface distribution in multi-device and multi-user environments with dynamically migrating engines. In: EICS, USA, pp. 55–64 (2009)

14. Paternò, F., Santoro, C.: A logical framework for multi-device user interfaces. In: The 4th ACM SIGCHI Symposium on Engineering Interactive Computing Systems (EICS 2012), Denmark, pp. 45–50 (2012)

15. Sauter, P., Vogler, G., Specht, G., Flor, T.: A model–view–controller extension for pervasive multi-client user interfaces. Pers. Ubiquit. Comput. **9**(2), 100–107 (2005)

16. Grolaux, D., Van Roy, P., Vanderdonckt, J.: Migratable user interfaces: beyond migratory interfaces. In: The First Annual International Conference on Mobile and Ubiquitous Systems: Networking and Services, MOBIQUITOUS 2004, Cambridge, pp. 422–430 (2004)

17. Pham, A.: Privilege delegation and revocation for distributed pervasive computing environments. In Abraham, G., Rubinstein, B., (eds.) Proceedings of the Second Australian Undergraduate Students' Computing Conference, pp. 136–141 (2004)

18. Haddadi, A.: Communication and Cooperation In Agent Systems: A Pragmatic Theory. Springer-Verlag, New York (1996)

19. Castelfranchi, C.: Towards a theory of delegation for agent-based systems. Robot. Auton. Syst. **24**(3), 141–157 (1998)

20. Mayhew, D.: The Usability Engineering Lifecycle: A Practitioner's Handbook for User Interface Design. Morgan Kaufmann Publishers, San Francisco, USA (1999)

21. Bendor, J., Glazer, A., Hammond, T.: Theories of delegation. Annu. Rev. Polit. Sci. **4**, 235–269 (2001)

Current Challenges in Compositing Heterogeneous User Interfaces for Automotive Purposes

Tobias Holstein[1,2]([✉]), Markus Wallmyr[1], Joachim Wietzke[2],
and Rikard Land[1]

[1] School of Innovation, Design and Engineering,
Mälardalen University, Västerås, Sweden
Tobias.Holstein@tobidesign.de
[2] Department of Computer Science, University of Applied Sciences,
Darmstadt, Germany

Abstract. Composition (i.e. merging distinct parts to form a new whole) of user interfaces from different providers or devices is popular in many areas. Current trends in the automotive area show, that there is a high interest in compositing interfaces from mobile devices into automotive user interfaces. "Apple CarPlay" and "Android Auto" are concrete examples of such compositions. However composition is addressed with challenges, especially if the parts are originally designed for different purposes.

This paper presents the problem statement of compositing heterogeneous devices. Furthermore, it presents a layer model showing architectural levels, where compositions can take place and for each of these layers challenges have been identified.

Keywords: Design · Human factors · Ubiquitous interoperability · Heterogeneous · Platforms · User interface · Composition · Hypervisor · Virtualization

1 Introduction

Every device provides a certain user interface (UI), designed for the device's purpose, i.e. the use cases, stories and specifications that developers, designers and usability experts built the interaction around when creating the device. Even when using the same type of technology in two devices, the interaction might be quite diverse, for example due to different environments or user groups targeted. Some devices integrate a multitude of different types of functionality, such as a mobile phone with camera, phone functionality as well as applications (Apps). These devices have been designed from the beginning to fulfil those purposes. However there are also cases, where devices of different purposes (heterogenous devices) are subject of a composition.

© Springer International Publishing Switzerland 2015
M. Kurosu (Ed.): Human-Computer Interaction, Part II, HCII 2015, LNCS 9170, pp. 531–542, 2015.
DOI: 10.1007/978-3-319-20916-6_49

This can currently be observed in the automotive industry where car manufacturers and original equipment manufacturer (OEMs) seek alternative approaches to integrate new features. Driven, among others, to reduce development efforts and costs as well as providing new features in a short time. One approach is the integration of mobile devices into cars [3]. The basic idea is to take advantage of already established application platforms, instead of reimplementing applications for automotive platforms, gaining effort and time.

Mobile devices are increasingly important in our everyday life as the way mobile devices are used has changed drastically over the last decades. While the first mobile phones were solely used to make phone calls, they are now used e.g. to surf the World Wide Web (WWW), to post information on social platforms and listen to music. The amount of Apps available on mobile devices increases rapidly [16,23,29]. This trend is supported by open platforms, fast development cycles and a large constant contributing community.

Vehicle technology has become increasingly advanced over the last decades. While the primary functionality of a vehicle is still driving from A to B, many additional features towards infotainment, entertainment, comfort systems as well as increasingly advanced driver assistance have been introduced. These features have turned car user interfaces into increasingly complex systems. Making the effort for developing, testing and maintaining automotive systems extensive, also highly due to various automotive related requirements and safety regulations. Numbers indicate that up to 40 percent of the production cost of a car are due to electronics and software [10].

The idea to integrate mobile phones and vehicles is in itself not new, however the degree of integration have increased as technology has provided new opportunities. Today, graphical user interfaces (GUIs) of mobile phones are being completely integrated into in-vehicle-infotainment systems (IVISs) [4,12,18]. This kind of composition of heterogeneous devices (i.e. car and phone) is though fragmentary. There are often drawbacks when the composition takes place, which offers material for an investigation into the different challenges and layers of compositions. The results may indicate whether the approach of reducing development efforts and costs can actually be successful or not.

The contribution of this paper is threefold. First, we present the problem of integrating heterogenous devices into homogenous systems with focus on automotive and mobile devices. Second, we introduce a model containing different layers, in which composition can take place and third, we show examples of challenges providing limitations and resulting constraints.

The remainder of this paper is divided into the following sections. Section 2 gives a short introduction to different types of UIs. It is followed by a section that goes into related work and shows the inter-disciplinarity of this research area. Section 4 covers the problem statement. The last sections will introduce the layer model for composition and discuss the challenges applicable with each of the layers. The paper will finish with conclusions and future work.

2   Types of User Interfaces

Different classifications of UIs types have been made [31]. These classifications also extends and evolves over time as new technologies, inventions and compositions of different UIs appears in different types of interaction. To provide a foundation further chapters these subsections gives an overview of UI types discussed.

2.1   Hardware UI / Haptic UI

Hardware UIs (HUIs) are tangible, i.e. pieces of hardware that you can actually touch and feel. Standard elements found in HUIs are e.g. LEDs, flip-switches, wheels and levers.

In vehicles, buttons replaced flip switches decades ago. Advanced vehicle bus systems digitally connect everything and therefore many controls can have multiple purposes. Also combined controls like a push/turn control knob are used in modern UIs. Newer versions of this control include a touch pad at the top of the knob, which is used for gesture and script recognition [6].

In mobile devices the multi purpose use of HUIs has been there from the beginning. The number of HUIs on a mobile device has over time also been reduced, where a lot of interaction has been focused at certain places. Which brings us to display based UIs.

2.2   Display-Based UI

While the display itself is an element of HUIs, because of its physical form and appearance, it is also the basis for other UI types.

Graphical UI. The first graphical user interface (GUI) has been introduced in 1981 as part of the "Xerox Star workstation" [27], which used the WIMP (windows, icons, menus, and a pointing device) interaction style. This type of UI was later adapted by Apple and other companies.

GUIs in cars are used in IVIS and also in fully digital cluster instruments, which gain in popularity. These digital solutions provide flexible options for designs, i.e. displaying different content can easily be done and by a software update additional functionality can be added without affecting the HUI.

Touch-Screen. Touch-Screens allow an interaction directly on the screen without any intermediate device (e.g. a mouse or joystick). They are commonly used in e.g. portable navigation systems, mobile phones and also in IVIS. It has became a standard method to manage the complexity and to increase usability of device interaction. However touch-screens are reluctantly used in automotive UIs, because research shows, that the distraction of the driver while using a touch-screen is seen to be too high [26]. One reason for that is the missing haptic feedback (compared to buttons/wheels). Drivers cannot feel whether a button was pressed or not and need to check the visual feedback, which causes a measurable distraction. However the distraction is lower compared to using a mobile device while driving [20].

In addition multi-touch capable touch-screens made a new interaction style possible, which is referred to as Post-WIMP. It was first introduced by Van Dam in 1997 [13]. This interaction style is used in OSs like Android and iOS.

2.3   Car UI

A car UI is a combination of multiple different UI types. A typical and well-known part is a HUI for the primary task of driving the car, including e.g. the steering-wheel, pedals, gear shift and speed gauges. If a fully digital instrument cluster is used a GUI will be part of the overall UI as well.

UIs in newer vehicles offer access to about 700 different functions (e.g. BMW Series 7 [7]). However the difficulties of handling 700 buttons, or flip switches in a dashboard, in terms of dashboard design and usage, are significant. Therefore design decisions are required to cope with the trade-off between features that are quickly accessible and features that are not [21].

Modern IVIS use a combination of touch-screens or normal screens for the GUI and a HUI for controlling it. The approaches of car manufactures differ greatly and an extreme example can be seen in Tesla's Model S, where a large touch-screen has replaced all HUIs normally presented in a center console, which is used to access all in-vehicle functions [30].

2.4   Mobile Device UI

In addition to touch-screen, GUI and buttons, mobile devices provide a wide range of sensors, which can be seen as a part of the UI. Sensors are used to enrich the user experience and to support certain use cases. A magnetometer for example can be used to change the GUI from portrait to landscape mode and vice versa. Other sensors (e.g. gyroscope, proximity sensor and accelerometer) are used for navigation, games and even fitness/health applications. A list of typical sensors as well as input/output modalities can be found in [2] and [14, p.49].

3   Related Work

The topic of compositing, i.e. combining and/or integrating, heterogeneous devices has been covered in various research publications. Following is an overview on the current research and commercial solutions to show the different approaches in this area.

Software, which uses virtualization mechanisms to run multiple operating systems on the same hardware platform, is often referred to as "hypervisor". A hypervisor can be classified in two different types: Type one (or native, bare metal) hypervisors run directly on the host's hardware to assign the hardware components and to manage guest operating systems. Type two (or hosted) hypervisors run as a normal application within a conventional operating-system environment. A well- known type two hypervisor software is "VMWare".

In [22] compositing of GUIs from a partitioned IVIS is shown. Partitions, i.e. multiple OSs, are running concurrently on one hypervisor. Applications running on those OSs are presented in a homogeneous GUI, which is provided by a component called "compositor". Applications have to provide a GUI that fits into the overall GUI. In this approach the physical UI has not been considered.

Instead of using the cars UI as a base for the composition the authors of [15] uses a mobile device as compositor. Therefore all data from the car is redirected to the mobile device, where it is processed and visualized. The mobile device becomes a portable IVIS.

Another approach is a link between services of a mobile device and the cars UI. In [28] services and UIs are exchanged between car and mobile device. The GUI is built dynamically by exchanging HTML5 UI descriptions. Services are connected through exchange of interface descriptions for each available service.

Bose [8] introduces a concept called "Terminal Mode" for integration of a mobile phone UI into a car UI using an extended VNC protocol [25]. Extensions include categories and authorization for applications. This approach is very similar to MirrorLink [12] which relies partly on the VNC protocol to replicate the phones display content on the remote UI.

The newest developments in the automotive industry have been introduced by Google and Apple. In order to gain access to a new market both companies try to prepare their OSs "iOS" and "Android" for the automotive consumer market. Proprietary protocols denoted as "Apple CarPlay" [4] and "Android Auto" [18] are currently developed and introduced through OEMs to the consumer market. This allows users to connect and integrate their mobile phone to the cars UI. [1] describes some limitations based on a first evaluation.

For completeness it has to be mentioned that software solutions like VNC [25], TeamViewer and Windows Remote Desktop, can be used to achieve a similar integration of GUIs for Desktop OSs (i.e. Windows, Linux, MacOS). In general these are for the WIMP interaction styles.

4   Problem Statement

Designing user interaction that integrate UIs from different devices or applications into a combined homogeneous UI is fundamentally problematic as it introduces two opposing forces. One force is to have different UIs appear in a consistent experience in the combined interaction (i.e. look-and-feel). The opposing force is to keep consistency with the fixed original UIs of the application or device. E.g. the applications from different mobile devices or operating systems appear as one UI within the vehicle, while at the same time keeping the heritage to the original user interaction of the device.

Different devices are built for different purposes and these purposes result in different design choices being made when designing the device [11]. With

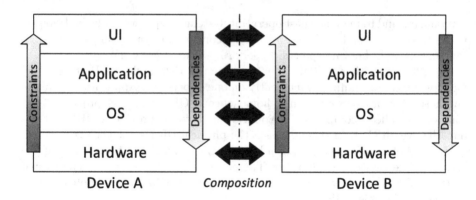

Fig. 1. Two devices with layers for compositions

heterogeneous devices being integrated, the set of interfaces will vary, e.g. a mobile phone has a different set of inputs and outputs than the interface of a car. Depending how and where the integration is performed, different constraints arise for the combined user interaction, which will be discussed in the following sections.

5   Layer Model

Compositing different devices or systems can be performed at different logical layers. In this section these layer are presented. The model is inspired by the OSI (Open Systems Interconnection) model and the layers are selected around the notion of separation of concern and the separation of different functionality in hardware and software. The layers are depicted in Fig. 1, which also shows constraints and dependencies. Definitions made in lower layers may appear as constraints in higher layers and higher layers strongly depend on lower layers. Higher layers may also force requirements towards lower layers, which have to be considered in a composition.

5.1   Hardware Layer

In the hardware layer composition is made at the physical hardware level by integrating different input and output components on mechanical or electrical level. Input components include for example buttons, knobs, microphones, joysticks and sensors. Output components include e.g. displays, speakers, vibration and LEDs.

An example of composition on this layer is using a video switch to share a display and its associated buttons between different devices. When changing channel on the display the image from the next device will be displayed and input signals will be sent to that device.

5.2 OS Layer

When a composition is performed at the OS layer, one set of hardware is used to run different OSs. This is typically done using virtualization techniques, i.e. using a hypervisor. OS integration using a hypervisor could be done in two ways. Either by having the OSs run in parallel with no knowledge of each other, a *type one hypervisor*. Alternatively, one OS is aware of the other OSs and manages the sharing of resources, a *type two hypervisor*.

An example of composition on this layer is having an OS handling critical tasks, which has control of the display and shared hardware resources. This designated OS can then show information from other OSs on the display and send input information back to them, ensuring that critical information is always shown when necessary.

5.3 Application Layer

In the application layer different applications or services are part of the composition, running on one OS. The implementation of applications usually requires libraries or services. Those provide an application programming interface (API) for developers, giving possibilities to share information and to let different kind of services collaborate. This layer is separated from the UI layer, because different applications may provide different UIs.

An example of composition in the application layer is a vehicle navigation application where a service is integrated presenting friends locations position and messages from a communication service.

5.4 UI Layer

In the UI layer the composed experience is considered. It is at this layer where the actual input and output modalities will meet the user as one UI. When fully embracing integration at the UI layer the different parts integrated is reshaped and composed to provide a rich user experience. While on the other hand if diverse parts is put together at lower layers the composed result may be a diverse UI.

An example of integration on the UI layer are technologies such as Apple CarPlay and Android auto where an app presents an adapted UI in the dashboard with respect to the phone UI.

6 Composition Challenges

In this section we present 13 identified challenges when compositing heterogeneous devices. The following list was created based on experiences and studies, but contains only significant challenges. However, those challenges show that no architectural layer is without challenges.

6.1   Hardware Layer

Challenge 1: Compositing the different hardware interfaces of two heterogeneous devices (e.g. different CPUs or GPUs, number of buttons, or screen-sizes).

One approach to address this challenge is to create a new device that fulfils all minimum requirements of each device in a composition. For example a composition of an Android device and an IVIS, would require the new target platform to fulfil the minimum requirements [17] for the Android device as well as for the IVIS. However, targeting the minimum requirements could also mean to sacrifice features, leading to incomplete user experience.

Another approach is to create a device with the maximum available configuration of both entities. For example a composition of two devices, one device with five buttons and another device with ten buttons. The composited interface would therefore have 15 buttons. However, if an upper layer is able to handle mapping or reassigning buttons, the number of buttons could be reduced.

Challenge 2: Compositing and sharing certain hardware that have a very specific use and context, potentially resulting in misinterpretation of information or delayed reaction. An example is sharing vibration as a mean to notify the user: A mobile phone may use vibrations to inform the user about incoming phone calls or messages, whereas a vehicle could use vibrations for lane assistance alertness [9]. The user would have to determine what the source of the notification is, if the same haptic feedback was used for both scenarios. In a driving situation this could result in loss of valuable reaction time.

6.2   OS Layer

Challenge 3: Compositing common hardware resources in virtualized OS environments. While one OS itself provides a level of abstraction from the hardware, the hypervisor will face challenges with singleton hardware resources when integrating two or more OSs. An example is how to decide which input signals should be routed to which of the OSs. A keyboard device might be assigned to one OS, therefore it cannot be used within another OS. The determination of which input belongs to which OS might also depend on higher layers, for example the current state of an application.

Challenge 4: Compositing different OS behaviours. When multiple OSs share the same screen, but aren't aware of it, challenges occur when it cannot be made sure that certain outputs are received by the user. This can result in some functionality not working as expected. An example from mobile systems is the notification system. In a single OS a message shown on top of all other applications, where the user has to take an action to proceed, will be visible as expected. One approach in a shared environment is to define a set of rules, e.g. priorities or other rule sets to make sure that OSs can force important messages to be shown on the screen. However defining these rules is yet another challenge and the way these notifications are presented is part of the UI layer.

Challenge 5: Compositing OSs without the full set of hardware. An OS might require a certain hardware component in order to provide full functionality, which may not be available in the given hardware layer. An approach is to provide virtual hardware via the hypervisor, which on one side offers the expected interface to the OS and on the other side works with the actual given hardware layer. For example buttons of a mobile device, which are not available in a center console of a car, can be replaced by virtual hardware and triggered through software. The challenge increases when interfaces are more complex, such as e.g. the routing of voice commands.

Challenge 6: Compositing different devices behaviour experience. As an extension of *challenge 5* the hypervisor may potentially provide a virtual device working as an adapter between the embedded platform and the OS, however the user experience might be significantly affected due to the challenges supporting all potential use cases. Such example is trying to virtualize the input of a touch screen when only buttons are available. Certain operations will be difficult to transform (e.g. multi touch operations). A more hypothetical example is the virtualization of a mobile device magnetometer. The usage of such sensors is fundamentally different in a car than a mobile device. A car might use it for crash detection and the mobile device to detect if the device is flipped into different directions. Using the sensor of the car would not cover all use cases of the mobile device, as the car cannot be flipped over. One approach could then be to use a button, which if pressed releases a signal in order to trigger a rotation by 90 degrees. The mapping of incompatible interfaces can however lead to limitations, e.g. allowing only rotations by 90 degrees, which will be a constraint to upper layers.

6.3   Application Layer

When compositing multiple services or APIs into a new application, the application will obviously depend on the services and APIs used. These dependencies are likewise *challenges*, and the following examples will elaborate on that.

Challenge 7: Composition with dependencies on the APIs provided by applications and services. If properly used the application will work as long as the APIs deliver the requested data and accept the given input. However, if an API is not used according to its specification or the expected use cases, the application might work in this version, but may break when the next API update occurs.

Challenge 8: Composition using external services causes a strong dependency. Integration into social- or information providing services can be attractive, but if a service is changed or stops to exist the application will fail. An example is using web services providing GUIs via HTML5. Even though the web service delivers HTML5 according to standard, it might contain HTML5 elements which are not supported by the renderer application in the car. This challenge and *challenge 7* become significant worse when development cycles and update rates of diverse systems is taken into consideration.

Challenge 9: Compositing two devices at application layer using remote connectivity protocols, e.g. VNC or MirrorLink. The OSs of each device run independently, but provide their services and GUIs via protocol to remote applications.

The remote application must then handle the challenge within interaction with the OS, i.e. sending the equivalent of the Mouse, Keyboard or touch command needed, while the same application receives an update of the GUI.

6.4   UI Layer

Challenge 10: Compositing different graphical design languages to form a homogeneous experience. The challenge is, that each type of device or service has different visualization and branding guidelines [5,19,24], which are more or less mandatory to follow when designing for that type of device. For example the look-and-feel of a car UI will differ from the look-and-feel of a mobile device UI.

Challenge 11: Compositing different sets of usage scenarios from the original user interfaces. A mobile device and its applications are designed for use on other distances from the user than a vehicle display. An example is screen utilization. With the mobile display the user can vary the distance depending on eyesight and content displayed. Whereas on the vehicle display text size etc. must be at a size that support users with varying eyesight.

6.5   General Challenges

Challenge 12: Compositing with dependencies and constraints of other layers. As already indicated by earlier presented challenges, a decision at one layer may lead to constraints and dependencies in other layers, i.e. new challenges. An example for this is the screen resolution in the hardware layer, affecting the design of the visual appearance of a GUI.

Challenge 13: Compositing devices with different life cycles causing diversity and constraints over *time*. This is a type of challenge that exists in a general level, applicable across all layers. For example a car may be bought every 10 years, while a mobile device may be replaced every two years. 10 years ago smartphones were fundamentally different than today and predicting what will come in the future is merely making a guess.

7   Conclusion

In this paper we have studied the composition of heterogeneous user interfaces. Furthermore we defined a model where composition approaches can be divided into different architectural layers. Last, but not least we discussed the challenges, limitations and constraints that relate to these layers. While the list of challenges is not complete for each layer, it shows that no architectural layer is without challenges. Based on identified approaches and challenges it seems that no approach can fully composite two heterogeneous interfaces without substantial adaptations at one or both sides.

It is possible to convert basic inputs from one element to another and it is also possible to pass basic outputs from one element to another. However, this is only a basic level of composition. In order to really composite a homogeneous experience the whole device composition must be considered, from the physical attributes to the combined UI, considering both output and input methods.

8   Future Work

There are several areas in composition of heterogeneous interfaces where we would like to extend our work. One area is to perform further evaluations on each layer to further investigate the constraints and limitations.

Another intent is to explore deeper into the usability, usefulness and user experience on the UI layer, in order to provide better user interaction of composited devices.

References

1. Airbiquity: Apple carplay: Ready for connected car prime time? (2014). http://www.airbiquity.com/news/blog/airbiquity-white-paper-apple-carplay-ready-connected-car-prime-time/. Accessed on 19 September 2014
2. Allan, A.: Basic Sensors in IOS: Programming the Accelerometer, Gyroscope, and More. O'Reilly Media Inc, Sebastopol (2011)
3. Alliance, O.A.: Open automotive alliance - a global alliance of technology and auto industry leaders (2014). http://www.openautoalliance.net/. Accessed on 01 November 2014
4. Apple: Apple carplay - the best iphone experience on four wheels (2014). https://www.apple.com/ios/carplay/. Accessed on 16 October 2014
5. Apple: Designing for IOS (2014). https://developer.apple.com/library/ios/documentation/userexperience/conceptual/mobilehig/. Accessed on 20 October 2014
6. Audi: Dialoge - das audi-technologiemagazin, January 2014. https://www.audi-mediaservices.com/publish/ms/content/de/public/broschueren/2014/01/14/Dialoge_-_Das_Technologiemagazin_01-14.standard.gid-oeffentlichkeit.html
7. BMW: Bmw technology guide: idrive (2014). http://www.bmw.com/com/en/insights/technology/technology_guide/articles/idrive.html. Accessed on 20 October 2014
8. Bose, R., Brakensiek, J., Park, K.Y.: Terminal mode: transforming mobile devices into automotive application platforms. In: Proceedings of the 2nd International Conference on Automotive User Interfaces and Interactive Vehicular Applications, pp. 148–155. ACM (2010)
9. Brandt, T., Sattel, T., Böhm, M.: Combining haptic human-machine interaction with predictive path planning for lane-keeping and collision avoidance systems. In: Proceedings of 2007 IEEE Intelligent Vehicle Symposium (2007)
10. Broy, M.: Challenges in automotive software engineering. In: Proceedings of the 28th International Conference on Software Engineering, pp. 33–42. ACM (2006)
11. Buxton, B.: Sketching User Experiences: Getting the Design Right and the Right Design. Morgan Kaufmann Publishers Inc., San Francisco, CA, USA (2007)
12. Consortium, C.C.: Mirrorlink (2014). http://www.mirrorlink.com/. Accessed on 22 October 2014
13. van Dam, A.: Post-WIMP user interfaces. Commun. ACM **40**(2), 63–67 (1997)
14. Dorau, R.: Emotionales Interaktionsdesign, vol. 1. Springer, Berlin (2011)
15. Geier, M., Becker, M., Yunge, D., Dietrich, B., Schneider, R., Goswami, D., Chakraborty, S.: Let's put the car in your phone! In: Proceedings of the 50th Annual Design Automation Conference, p. 143. ACM (2013)

16. GmbH, A.: Number of android applications (2014). http://www.appbrain.com/stats/number-of-android-apps. Accessed on 1 November 2014

17. Google: Android 4.4 - compatibility definition (2013). http://source.android.com/compatibility/android-cdd.pdf

18. Google: Android auto (2014). http://www.android.com/auto/. Accessed on 16 November 2014

19. Google: Android design (2014). https://developer.android.com/design/index.html. Accessed on 20 October 2014

20. Heikkinen, J., Mäkinen, E., Lylykangas, J., Pakkanen, T., Väänänen-Vainio-Mattila, K., Raisamo, R.: Mobile devices as infotainment user interfaces in the car: contextual study and design implications. In: Proceedings of the 15th International Conference on Human-Computer Interaction with Mobile Devices and Services, MobileHCI 2013, pp. 137–146. ACM, New York (2013)

21. Kern, D., Schmidt, A.: Design space for driver-based automotive user interfaces. In: Proceedings of the 1st International Conference on Automotive User Interfaces and Interactive Vehicular Applications, pp. 3–10. ACM (2009)

22. Knirsch, A., Theis, A., Wietzke, J., Moore, R.: Compositing user interfaces in partitioned in-vehicle infotainment. In: Boll, S., Maa, S., Malaka, R. (eds.) Mensch Computer 2013 - Workshopband, pp. 63–70. Oldenbourg Verlag, Mnchen (2013)

23. Microsoft: Microsoft by the numbers - the windows phone store features more than 300,000 apps and games (2014). http://news.microsoft.com/bythenumbers/index.html. Accessed on 1 November 2014

24. Microsoft: Windows design guidelines (2014). https://dev.windows.com/en-us/design. Accessed on 20 October 2014

25. Richardson, T., Stafford-Fraser, Q., Wood, K.R., Hopper, A.: Virtual network computing. IEEE Internet Comput. 2(1), 33–38 (1998)

26. Rümelin, S., Butz, A.: How to make large touch screens usable while driving. In: Proceedings of the 5th International Conference on Automotive User Interfaces and Interactive Vehicular Applications, pp. 48–55. ACM (2013)

27. Smith, D.C., Irby, C., Kimball, R., Verplank, B., Harslem, E.: Designing the star user interface: the star user interface adheres rigorously to a small set of principles designed to make the system seem friendly by simplifying the human-machine interface. Byte, pp. 242–282 April 1982

28. Sonnenberg, J.: Service and user interface transfer from nomadic devices to car infotainment systems. In: Proceedings of the 2nd International Conference on Automotive User Interfaces and Interactive Vehicular Applications, pp. 162–165. ACM (2010)

29. (TechCrunch), S.P.: itunes app store now has 1.2 million apps, has seen 75 billion downloads to date (2014). http://techcrunch.com/2014/06/02/itunes-app-store-now-has-1-2-million-apps-has-seen-75-billion-downloads-to-date/. Accessed on 1 November 2014

30. Tesla: Example ui (2014). http://www.teslamotors.com/sites/default/files/blog_images/model-s-photo-gallery-14.jpg. Accessed on 22 October 2014

31. Wikipedia: User interface – wikipedia, the free encyclopedia (2014). http://en.wikipedia.org/w/index.php?title=User_interface&oldid=630749818. Accessed on 3 November 2014

A Framework for Distributing and Migrating the User Interface in Web Apps

Antonio Peñalver[✉], David Nieves, and Federico Botella

Center of Operations Research University Institute,
Miguel Hernández University, Elche, Spain
a.penalver@umh.es

Abstract. Nowadays, the advent of mobile technologies with increasing functionality and computing power is changing the way people interact with their applications in more and more different contexts of use. This way, many traditional user interfaces are evolving towards "distributed" user ones, allowing that interaction elements can now be distributed among heterogeneous devices from different platforms. In this paper we present an HTTP-Based framework for generating and distributing UIs (User Interfaces) of custom applications, allowing device change with state preservation. We use a schema-based definition of DUIs (Distributed User Interfaces), allowing the specification of the elements to be distributed. The framework is based on open standards and supports any markup-based web language. We provide a graphic case of use implemented in HTML5.

1 Introduction and Related Work

In a short period of time, the way people interact with computers has changed. The wide variety of devices that people can use today has an important effect on the way users interact with them: computers, tablets, smartphones, and so on. Particularly, new mobile devices provide ubiquitous access to information and services as well as the possibility of fulfill more and more desktop-related tasks with them.

These advances open up new possibilities for interaction, including the distribution of the User Interface (UI) among different devices. The UI can be divided, moved, copied or cloned among heterogeneous devices running the same or different operating systems, maintaining its current state. These new ways of handling the UI are considered under the emerging topics of Distributed User Interfaces (DUIs) and Migratory Interfaces (MIs). DUIs are related to the distribution of one or many elements, from one or many user interfaces, in order to support one or many users, to carry out one or many tasks, on one or many domains, in one or many contexts of use [1]. Migratory user interfaces [2] are able to automatically move among diverse devices, allowing the users to continue in real-time their task after changing the device in use [3].

In this paper we propose a full client/server-based architecture to support DUIs that allows us to distribute the UI of any web-based application among different users in ubiquitous heterogeneous environments. The framework handles

© Springer International Publishing Switzerland 2015
M. Kurosu (Ed.): Human-Computer Interaction, Part II, HCII 2015, LNCS 9170, pp. 543–553, 2015.
DOI: 10.1007/978-3-319-20916-6_50

the registration process of applications and clients, as well as the distribution of the UIs and the communication between them. The state of an interactive session for each user is stored and saved between different devices. We use our formal description method for developing DUIs [4], our AUI model [5] and our schema-based approach to automatically construct a concrete DUI from an XML specification [6] as a basis for developing our framework.

Many research works have studied and proposed different implementations to the concepts of Distributed and Migratory User Interfaces. In [7] a software environment called Oz/Mozart supporting distribution is presented. It allows migrating windows and receiving events from the elements of an interface previously distributed. This is a non-HTTP-based approach and requires using non-standard web languages. In [8] an XML-based framework supporting collaborative web browsing is proposed. It uses a new XML language with specific tags in order to describe the UI, and XSL-T transformations to construct the HTML interface. A web page is split and then replicated to all the users. This approach needs a Java Applet at the client side. In [9] a framework for dynamically distribute UI's among several devices is developed. It is based on an HTTP Interface Distribution Daemon (IDD) and RelaxNG schema language is used to describe the XHTML interface, defining constraints for each element, attribute and text values. The proposal requires implementing a new HTTP command in order to avoid server timeouts. Recently, in [10] a framework that supports user interface distribution in web-based and android devices is presented.

In [11] a partial migration web system is proposed. It uses different abstraction levels to define the UI and allows migration between big displays and mobile devices. Different modules translate the original interface into a new one suitable for the new device and a proxy server captures interaction between the browser and the original web site. In [12] a system for dynamic generation of web interfaces supporting migration between different platforms is proposed. The approach uses a proxy server again to adapt the content to the target platform.

The rest of the paper is organized as follows: First the basic components of the framework architecture, including elements and communication schema are discussed. Then, an example of application is described. Last section provides conclusions and further work.

2   Architecture

This section is devoted to explain the architecture of the framework. The essential part of the framework is a Java Servlet that manages distributed interactive sessions for each connected client, passing messages from clients to applications and vice versa. The only requirement for a client to connect to the framework is a web browser supporting AJAX (Asynchronous JavAscript and Xml) in order to send and receive XML data without reloading the entire page each time an event arises.

2.1   Communication Model

Communication between applications and framework as well as communication between framework and clients is based on the REST (Representative State Transfer) model, where procedure calls are performed by conventional HTTP requests using standard URL nomenclature. The Servlet processes an HTTP request and replies with an HTTP response message using the HTTP 1.1 version specification, including only GET and POST standard commands. Some ad-hoc commands have been implemented in order to perform the different tasks the Servlet can perform. Table 1 shows a summary of all the Servlet commands and their descriptions.

Two different XML-based messages are used: "event" and "action". When the user performs an action during an interactive session (e.g. clicking on a button) an action message is sent to the framework. Then, the message is forwarded to the application that has to execute the action at the server side. After that, an event message may be triggered by the application and then returned to the framework that will forward it to all the clients interested in a specific type of event. Thus, as a result of a client action over a device, an event may be triggered and sent to multiple devices, and the UIs of these devices updated accordingly. It should be noted that each event message is stored in a repository within the server, so that clients connecting later can apply for and update the status of their interface. This allows us to migrate the interface between different devices maintaining the application state.

Figure 1 shows the action/event communication model with applications on the left side and clients on the right side. The information flows between client interface and framework and between framework and clients. We also need a middleware layer composed by two new APIs: one at server-side, which acts as an intermediary between framework and applications and other one at client-side, acting as an intermediary between framework and clients.

The former is required to parse and interpret XML-based action messages and translate them to native function calls of the application. The code depends on the particular application but we selected again the Java language because it supports both XML and HTTP over almost every operating system and platform. The latter is devoted to manage communication between framework and clients. We selected JavaScript language, as it can directly retrieve and submit XML data. Received XML documents can be processed through the Document Object Model (DOM) interface. This way, the communication with the server is performed in the background, so user interaction with the application is carried out asynchronously, and the updates of the UI are dynamically executed.

2.2   Client Pull

HTTP protocol is a stateless communication method but client devices may send action messages to the framework at any time. Each message is encapsulated as a POST HTTP command. When the framework accepts the POST command, it processes the message and replies by triggering an application event. This

Table 1. Servlet commands to allow bi-directional communication between clients and applications.

Command	Description
validate_user	The Servlet logs a client in the framework from a valid username and password. A unique client id is generated and then returned to the user in a cookie
validate_application	Allows registering a new application. An app name and an app key are required. The Servlet looks for the application in the *application.xml* file. If all is correct, a unique application id is generated and then returned in a cookie
user_logout	The Servlet unregister the specified client and then he/she is redirected to the login page
application_logout	The Servlet unregister the application with the specified Id
ui	Specifies the user sub-interface selected by the user. The body of the request includes all the required data. When the request is received, a new session starts and a new cookie id is sent to the user. Then, a new web page with the required sub-interface is generated, sent and rendered in the client device
session_end	When the user ends her/his session, the selected sub-interfaces are released, and then the user is redirected to the application selection page
action	Depending on each application, this command allows to specify different user interactions with the interface. The body of the request includes an XML document with the information needed for the Servlet to process the action. The actions are stored in the application message queue
event	If an application changes its state, a new event is generated and sent to the Servlet encapsulated in XML format. The event is stored in the message queue and sent to all the clients interested in such event in order to upgrade the state of their interface
pull	This command allows both clients and application to ask the Servlet for incoming messages (actions and events)

event may be sent to many clients, but as clients do not run a server to listen for incoming requests, the message cannot be delivered with a classic HTTP POST command. Bi-directional communication between clients and applications is required, because if the state of an application changes, all the clients must be informed. The same applies at server side, where an application must be notified when a client triggers an action. In order to overcome these drawbacks, we use Client-Pull technique for bi-directional communication. Server-Push method is an efficient technique, but it is difficult to implement using AJAX at the client side, so we use the Client-Pull. Client-Pull allows clients and applications poll for actions and events by sending requests to the framework at regular time

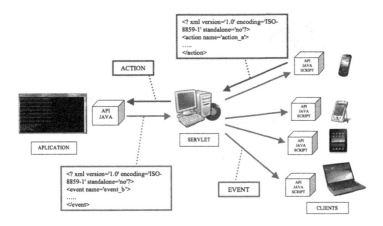

Fig. 1. Action/Event communication model and middleware layer at the server and client sides.

intervals. This way, the framework answers with an action or event message if there is anything to report. Thus, standard HTTP protocol and AJAX can be used. Pull messages are implemented as standard POST commands, and then data is encapsulated in XML format before being submitted.

2.3 Distribution

Prior to the use of the framework, both clients and applications must be registered in the framework. Application registration is performed by means of an XML configuration file with a pre-defined schema specification called *aplicalions.xml*, and then stored in one of the framework folders. The schema specifies the services that an application provides. The file includes tags to specify the application folder and the sub-interfaces that can be distributed. A "state" attribute allows us to specify whether the sub-interface can or cannot be distributed to more than one user at the same time.

Another important file is *globals.xml*, including important configuration information for the Servlet, such as connection port, applications paths, names for the cookies and so on. Client registration is performed in a slightly different way: first, the end user connects to the framework through an URL and a list of applications is showed with available services. Second, the user selects an application sub-interface.

Then the framework runs an XML instance generator algorithm producing a valid XML instance (concrete DUI in a markup language like XHTML or HTML5), taking into account the constraints specified in the schema. Finally, the UI is sent to the client and rendered in her/his device. Each service is marked as "exclusive" or "collaborative" in the configuration file. If "collaborative" option is specified, then the sub-interface can be duplicated and used in a collaborative session among different users. If "exclusive" option is specified, the service is available only for one user. At low-level, we use an identification cookie that is

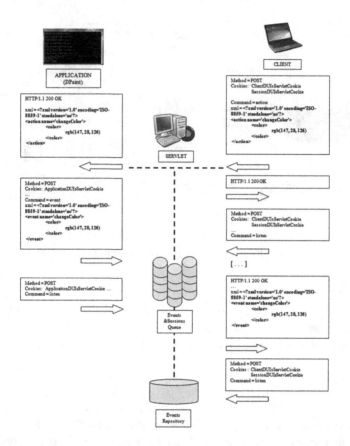

Fig. 2. Actions and Events interaction scheme.

used in subsequent requests in order to register a client. The client is validated by using a user name and a password. Then a session cookie is also generated and sent in order to link application and client. At the server side, each application is also provided with an identification cookie, which is sent to the framework in every new message.

Figure 2 shows the action/ event communication process for an ad-hoc drawing application we have developed to test the framework. The application is a standard drawing application with different sub-interfaces: canvas, color palette, etc. that can be distributed among different clients. The left column shows interaction between the application and the framework. On the right side we can see interaction between the framework and one client. Both, application and client send "pull" messages to check if there is any pending message from the framework. First, the client sends an action message with a "color change request". The message is sent to the framework, encapsulated in XML format, with the color selected by the user. Then the framework receives the command and redirect it to the application.

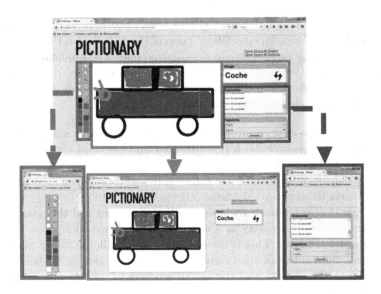

Fig. 3. DPictionary. Interface distribution options for the cartoonist role.

The Java API middleware at server-side processes the message and triggers the events that are also encapsulated in XML format, and then sent to the framework that forwards it to all the clients that selected the color palette sub-interface. The message is received by the Javascript middleware API at client side and then the UI is changed properly with the new current color in the palette. In this context, when a user selects a color in the color palette, all the clients will paint with that color in advance.

The framework stores events and actions in a FIFO queue. Although the figure model is a simplification (one client and one application), when multiple clients are collaborating, the framework has to forward event messages over multiple pull requests. Consequently, the framework needs a message queue to store and control the flow, letting applications and clients to retrieve messages at their own rate. When a new client logs into the system, all the application events stored in the queue are sent to the device, so that the initial state for the new client is just the same that the state of the rest of clients whose sessions began before. This way, our framework supports the concept of "Migratory" interface, as users do not need to restart their applications for each device change and they are migrated seamlessly across devices.

3   DPICTIONARY: A Graphic Distributed Interface

In order to test the performance and functionality of our proposal, some applications have been developed and their interfaces distributed using the framework described in the previous sections. Here we provide a distributed Pictionary, based on HTML5, using some of the advanced features of this new version of the standard, for managing graphical interfaces (the new <canvas> tag and Javascript). We have developed a DUI version of the well-known Pictionary game with very similar functionality than the original one. The application is multi-user, allows distribution and migration and provides two user roles: cartoonist and player. It consists of four different services with several sub-interfaces, three for the cartoonist and one for the players:

- *Canvas*: The cartoonist can draw on it, but it is also used as a viewer for the rest of users. It also includes a text box containing a word representing what the cartoonist has to draw.
- *Palette*: This is a toolbar with some drawing tools that are distributed together: pencils, erasers, thickness, objects, colors, etc.
- *Players panel (Cartoonist)*: Includes the list of players and the answers. The cartoonist can select a player as a winner and the game ends.
- *Players panel (Player)*: This is the only interface available to the player role. It includes the canvas (a read only version), the current score label, a text box to write the answer and the list of answers of all the players (like the cartoonist's one).

Figure 3 shows the interface for the cartoonist role with the canvas, the toolbar and the players panel. They can be displayed together of distributed between different devices. For instance, the tool palette could be displayed on a smart-phone, the canvas on a tablet and the players panel on a PC. Although the player interface could be distributed equally, we provide all the elements of the interface together.

DPictionary implements several actions that user can perform: "Draw", "Erase", "Erase All", "Change Object", "Change Thickness" , "Change Color", "New cartoon", "Winner", "Answer", "New player". Each action has its own XML schema grammar in order to specify all the required parameters so that the application can perform the action. All of them use the <action> tag with the "name" attribute. Although the current implementation already has several actions, it would be very easy to extend the application functionality extending the schema and adding new commands accordingly.

In Fig. 4 an action/event diagram for the "Winner" action is displayed. The cartoonist selects player two as winner of the current game and a new action named "scorePoints" is sent to the framework. The message includes the winner's name. The framework processes the message, adds 30 points to the "pointsPlayer" XML tag, and then a new event is sent back to the players. Each player receives the same message, but only the winner adds the new points to her/his score. As the framework stores in a queue all the actions and events raised since the beginning of an interactive session, if a user init a session in a different device, the state is automatically migrated to the new device and the user can keep playing as he did in the previous device. The user can continue the interaction from the same point where it was left, without having to restart from scratch.

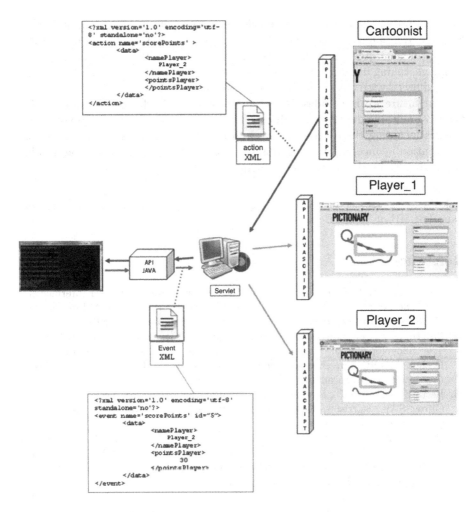

Fig. 4. DPictionary action/event diagram with three clients: the cartoonist and two players. The cartoonist select the winner and an action is sent to the framework. .

4   Conclusions and Further Work

In this paper we have proposed a framework that allows distributing user interfaces among heterogeneous client devices. Our proposal is based on a JAVA servlet that manages registration of clients and applications and bi-directional communication between them in a transparent way. The framework uses REST model over classic HTTP connections, so the only requirement for a client to establish an interactive session is an Internet browser supporting Javascript. The framework supports any XML-based user interface description language and we have provided an example based on an HTML5 graphical interface.

Constraints related to the distribution process itself are defined through W3C Schema grammars. After the DUI has been defined, an XML instance generator algorithm generates a new XML instance (concrete DUI) in any markup-based language, taking into account the constraints specified in the schema. The framework allows device change with state preservation.

Our future work includes the definition of a metric that allows us to decide the most suitable distribution scheme. This metric will require the use of device profiles including the device features and the formal definition of the "optimal distribution" concept. Thus, the distribution of the elements could be decided automatically by the framework, depending on the device's features.

Acknowledgments. This research is partially funded by the project 11859/2011 from Bancaja-UMH of Miguel Hernández University of Elche.

References

1. Vanderdonckt, J.: Distributed user interfaces: how to distribute user interface elements across users, platforms, and environments. Proceedings of X International Conference on Interaccion Persona-Ordenador (Interaccion 10) (2010)
2. Paterno, F.: User Interface design adaptation. In: Soegaard, M., Dam, R.F. (eds.) The Encyclopedia of Human-Computer Interaction, 2nd Ed. The Interaction Design Foundation, Aarhus. http://www.interaction-design.org/encyclopedia/ user_interface_design_adaptation.html
3. Berti, S., Paternó, F., Santoro, C.: A taxonomy for migratory user interfaces. In: Gilroy, S.W., Harrison, M.D. (eds.) DSV-IS 2005. LNCS, vol. 3941, pp. 149–160. Springer, Heidelberg (2006)
4. Peñalver, A., López-Espín, J., Gallud, J., Lazcorreta, E., Botella, F.: Distributed user interfaces: specification of essential properties. In: Gallud, J.A., Tesoriero, R., Penichet, V.M. (eds.) Distributed User Interfaces. Human-Computer Interaction Series, pp. 13–21. Springer, London (2011)
5. Gallud, J.A., Peñalver, A., López-Espín, J., Lazcorreta, E., Botella, F., Fardoun, H.M., Sebastián, G.: A proposal to validate the user's goal in distributed user interfaces'. Int. J. Hum. Comput. Interact. **28**, 700–708 (2012)
6. Peñalver, A., Botella, F., López-Espín, J., Gallud, J.: Defining distribution constraints in distributed user interfaces. J. Univers. Comput. Sci. **19**, 831–850 (2013)
7. Grolaux, D., Van Roy, P., Vanderdonckt, J.: Migratable user interfaces: beyond migratory interfaces. In: Mobiquitous, pp. 422–430. IEEE Computer Society (2004)
8. Han, R., Perret, V., Naghshineh, M.: WebSplitter: a unified XML framework for multi-device collaborative Web browsing. In: Proceedings of the 2000 ACM Conference on Computer Supported Cooperative Work, pp. 221–230 (2000)
9. Vandervelpen, C., Vanderhulst, G., Luyten, K., Coninx, K.: Light-weight distributed web interfaces: preparing the web for heterogeneous environments. In: Lowe, D.G., Gaedke, M. (eds.) ICWE 2005. LNCS, vol. 3579, pp. 197–202. Springer, Heidelberg (2005)
10. Frosini, L., Paterno, F.: User interface distribution in multi-device and multi-user environments with dynamically migrating engines. In: Proceedings of Engineering Interactive Computing Systems (EICS2014), Rome, Italy (2014)

11. Ghiani, G., Patern, F., Santoro, C.: Partial Web interface migration. In: Proceedings of the International Conference on Advanced Visual Interfaces, Rome, Italy (2010)
12. Bandelloni, R., Mori, G., Patern, F.: Dynamic generation of web migratory interfaces. In: Proceedings of the 7th International Conference on Human Computer Interaction with Mobile Devices and Services, New York, NY, USA (2005)

UniWatch - Some Approaches Derived from UniGlyph to Allow Text Input on Tiny Devices Such as Connected Watches

Franck Poirier[1(✉)] and Mohammed Belatar[2]

[1] Lab-STICC, University of Bretagne-Sud, Campus de Tohannic,
56000 Vannes, France
franck.poirier@univ-ubs.fr
[2] Technology and Telecom, Rue Dayat Aoua, 10090 Rabat, Morocco
mohammed.belatar@gmail.com

Abstract. Smartwatches are a fast-expanding type of interactive device that allow users to directly access to many applications on smartphone. At the moment, smartwatches lack a usable means of text entry. In this paper, we propose a new approach of text entry on smartwatches called UniWatch. At first, we give a state of the art concerning text entry on small devices. Then, we recall our past approaches of text entry and more particularly Uniglyph, a text input method for handheld devices that used a 4-button keyboard. Secondly, we describe and compare the different adaptations of Uniglyph for tiny connected devices such as smartwatches. All the proposed adaptations require only three buttons or three simple finger strokes on the screen. Thirdly, we examine the role of word completion and word prediction for such devices.

Keywords: Text input · Virtual keyboard · Word prediction · Connected watch · Smartwatch · Internet of things

1 Introduction

Smartwatches are on the wrist wearable computers that in addition to providing time give access to some functionalities of the smartphone. For example, the user can directly answer or make calls from his/her wrist, receive a notification of a message, take a snapshot or a short video... It is important to note that an essential functionality is absent from marketed smartwatches. Currently it is not possible to enter text directly on a virtual keyboard displayed on the watch screen.

The user must use the vocal assistant built-in application to communicate (S Voice on Android, Siri on IOS). The problem is that voice communication is not always possible or appropriate to the context of user interaction: voice is problematic in noisy environments and raise privacy issues in public spaces [19]. Voice communication is provided because there is currently no effective virtual keyboard on smartwatches.

From our point of view, text entry is a major functionality that should be present on all mobile or wearable devices [12]. The lack of usable text entry keyboard is probably a key reason for failure of wearable devices like smart glasses (i.e. Google Glass).

© Springer International Publishing Switzerland 2015
M. Kurosu (Ed.): Human-Computer Interaction, Part II, HCII 2015, LNCS 9170, pp. 554–562, 2015.
DOI: 10.1007/978-3-319-20916-6_51

In this paper, we propose some ways for text entry on smartwatches derived from UniGlyph. We call this approach UniWatch.

2   Related Works

For most of the smartphone applications, text entry is a key component. Smartwatches are usually presented as a new device that enables joint interaction with the smartphone. The paradox is that text entry is extremely limited on the smartwatch. We can therefore assume that the mass adoption of smartwatches is strongly conditioned by the possibility to enter short text with a smartwatch. That is why text entry on smartwatch is a major research challenge.

For the last two years, different text input methods for smartwatches have been proposed.

Few text entry methods are on the market for smartwatches, e.g. Fleksy [8], Minuum [13], Swype [21]. These three methods are based on a full QWERTY keyboard. Keys are so tiny that the finger touch does not hit the only desired key, the entry is disambiguated by lexical predictive algorithms. Predictive technologies are not perfect and are not suitable in typing abbreviations, acronyms, proper nouns... Due to the fat finger problem, it seems that a static QWERTY keyboard is not the right solution for smartwatches.

ZoomBoard [15] is one of the first methods based on a zooming user-interface (ZUI) paradigm. It provides a full QWERTY keyboard. The tiny keys around the finger press are iteratively enlarged, the user refines the finger position in order to point to the desired key, once this key is reached, zooming stops and the key is typed upon pressing.

Dunlop et al. [6] propose to divide the watch screen into seven zones, six big ambiguous keys, three at the top of the screen and three at the bottom and a center zone for the input entry field. OpenAdaptxt [14] is used for entry disambiguation and swipe gestures allow to change modes (alphabetical/numerical, lower/upper case, punctuation...), complete a word or enter a space.

DragKeys [4] is a circular keyboard composed of 8 ambigouous keys arranged around the text cursor. At most five letters are assigned to each key. To enter a letter, a first dragging gesture is made toward the key associated with the desired letter and a second dragging gesture in order to move the letter on the text cursor line.

Another approach is to use IR proximity sensors to capture gestures performed above the device, for example Gesture Watch [10] and HoverFlow [11]. This approach has the advantage to reduce screen occlusion but needs specific mechanisms, doesn't provide tactile feedback, and is not very discrete.

Xia et al. [23] use the watch face as a multi-degree-of-freedom mechanical interface. Their proof of concept supports continuous 2D panning on the watch screen, twist, tilt and click. They developed a series of example applications but don't envisage to input text with this kind of approach.

ABCDEFGHIJKLMNO
PQRSTUVWXYZ
0123456789

Fig. 1. The UniGlyph character set and the associated input keys: diagonal-shape key, loop-shape key, straight-shape key.

3 Uniglyph Text Input Method

UniGlyph [17] is a text entry method for handheld devices derived from Glyph [16, 18]. The methods of the Glyph family are based on the structure of Latin characters composed by a specific sequence of primitive shapes (curve, stroke, loop...).

For UniGlyph, the set of primitive shapes is reduced to only 3 symbols: (1) diagonal stroke, (2) curve and (3) horizontal or vertical line. Each primitive shape is dedicated to one key of the keypad called respectively diagonal-shape key, loop-shape key and straight-shape key.

Each letter of the English alphabet is represented by only one primitive shape according to the shape of the uppercase letter. In order to recall the coded key, the user needs to follow a very simple rule (Fig. 1):

- if the capital letter contains a diagonal stroke, then click on the diagonal-shape key (1);
- otherwise, if it contains a loop or a curving stroke, then click on the loop-shape key (2);
- otherwise, click on the straight-shape key (3).

As there are many more characters than primitives, each primitive corresponds to a set of letters. The expected word is deduced by a linguistic predictor like for all the ambiguous keyboards (T9®, SureType®, iTap®...).

The UniGlyph keypad contains three shape keys and one command key used to jump to the different input modes and to select the expected word.

4 Initial Design of UniWatch - An Adaptation of UniGlyph for Tiny Connected Devices

Form Factor Problem. The smartwatch screen is very small, from 1.2 (Pebble) to 1.6 inch. (Galaxy Gear). So, it is impossible to finger tap on a complete keyboard on such a so tiny screen in order to enter text. A smartwatch screen can just contain a small number of keys, buttons or icons. The solution proposed by Dunlop and al. [6] with seven keys on the screen occupies the whole screen, without referring to the magic number of Miller, it seems reasonable to have fewer keys on the watch screen. It is

a   b   c

Fig. 2. Three approaches for texting: a- one key per input primitive shape, b- directly drawing the stroke ('/', '(', '|'), c- one flick per input primitive shape. (Red text and arrows are only for explaining the figure. They are not displayed on the screen of the watch) (Colour figure online).

reasonable to enter text on a small keyboard only if the keyboard contains just very few buttons.

The UniGlyph approach is a good candidate for text entry on smartwatches because it minimizes the keypad to only 4 keys, even 3 if the commands are entered by a gesture directly applied on the watch. Gesture Watch [10], HoverFlow [11] or Xia and al. [23] have shown that sensor-based gestures (opposed to touch-based gestures) are suitable for controlling the text entry. More generally, with small devices or in mobility, it is better to combine the strengths of multi-touch gesture with motion- sensing gestures [9].

UniWatch, the adapted version of UniGlyph requires only three keys. It is especially well suited to input text on a smartwatch.

We propose different ways for entering text on the smartwatch screen with UniWatch.

Ambiguous Key Approach. The direct adaptation of UniGlyph is to use a 3-key keypad, each key corresponds to one input primitive. The original command-key can be replaced by sensor-based or touch-based gesture. The easiest solution is to directly touch the text field in order to validate one of the predicted words. These three keys can be placed on the lower side of the screen (Fig. 2-a) or in each corner. The interaction technique consists in button taping.

As with the method proposed by Dunlop [6] each key is ambiguous, a disambiguation engine gives word completion and word prediction. Another common feature is the number of keys across the width of the screen (3). Considering the finger size and the screen size, it seems difficult to put more than three or four keys at the bottom of the screen. A simple calculation shows that these keys occupy around 20 % to 25 % of the screen space.

With this approach, the user interaction is limited to single taps on the keys. Due to the size of the keys, even on the go, the risk of error is very low.

Single-Stroke Entry Approach. Another way is to use the touch screen capability by directly drawing the shape of the input primitives (diagonal stroke, curve or straight line) on the screen (Fig. 2-b). This approach is not new if we refer to the watch AT-550 made by Casio in 1984 [3]. With this watch, the user entered a calculation by drawing on the watch screen with a stylus, one after another, each operand. In 2014, this approach is re-used by Microsoft Research in the Analog Keyboard Project [2].

In our case, according to UniGlyph method, the primitive shapes are reduced to only 3 symbols ('/', '(', '|'), each one corresponds to a single stroke and each one is quite different from the others. Finger drawing on the screen watch is easy and comfortable on a so tiny screen. In this way, the risk of error is also very low.

The advantage compared to the previous approach is that screen is not occupied by buttons.

Flick Gesture Entry Approach. The third approach is based on flick gestures on the screen to enter the input primitives and to control all the process steps of text entry. Flick gestures are used for a long time [22]. A flick gesture is a particularly fast way for entering a command, the gesture direction is significant but not the amplitude.

The flick gestures can be executed from the center towards one side of the screen (top, bottom, left or right side).

Figure 2-c shows one of the possible mappings, a flick bottom down-left is for the diagonal stroke ('/'), a flick down is for the curve stroke ('(') and a flick down-right for the straight stroke ('|').

The difference with the previous approach is that the mapping between the flick and the primitive shape is arbitrary, the user must learn it. However, as there are only three primitive shapes, the mapping is very easy to learn and remember. With the *single-stroke entry* approach, the user directly writes the primitive shape on the screen. He/she just thinks which shape is associated to the desired letter. With the *flick gesture entry* approach, the user must think to the right key and, in addition, to the mapping between the key and the flick gesture.

5   Qualitative Comparison of Approaches

Each approach has some advantages and disadvantages. Text typing involves complex and numerous motor, perceptual and cognitive processes [5]. Because of this complexity, it is impossible to decide which is the best approach. Decision criteria must be established and the right approach must be chosen according to these criteria.

Table 1 presents a comparison of the three proposed approaches. Some drawbacks are associated with the user and other are related to the characteristics and limitations of the watch.

The decision taken is to go with the solution that favors the usability which means the ease of use, the familiarity, the comfort, the reliability and the entry speed.

The advantages and disadvantages are interpreted according to the concept of usability. Table 2 presents a subjective evaluation of the three methods in regard to the criteria of ease of use, familiarity, comfort, reliability and entry speed.

The *ambiguous key* approach gets the best score (12 points), the *flick gesture entry* approach follows (9 points) and the *single-stroke entry* approach seems to be the less usable (8 points).

Table 1. Comparison of the three approaches

Ambiguous keys	Single-stroke entry	Flick gesture entry
Advantages	Advantages	Advantages
Easy to use without learning (labeled keys).	Familiar mode of interaction (handwriting shapes).	Quickness of the flick gesture.
Classical button-based interaction.	Easy to draw primitive shapes.	Practically no risk of gesture recognition error.
Error-proof solution (button press).	Direct mapping between shape handwriting and desired letter.	
	Buttonless interaction.	
Disadvantages	Disadvantages	Disadvantages
Screen space occupation.	Lack of guidance on the screen.	Lack of mapping between flick orientation and desired letter.
Poor exploitation of tactile interaction possibilities (only taps on button).	Handwriting feedback superimposed on the information displayed.	Need to recall two informations: the right coding primitive shape and the associated flick gesture.
	Occlusion due to finger drawing.	
	Small risk of handwriting recognition error.	
	Slowness of handwriting process.	

Table 2. Evaluation according to the criteria of usability

Score range from 1 (low) to 3 (high)	Ambiguous keys	Single-stroke entry	Flick gesture entry
Ease of use	3	2	1
Familiarity	2	2	1
Comfort	2	1	2
Reliability	3	2	2
Entry speed	2	1	3
Total score	12	8	9

6 Quantitative Comparison of Approaches

It would also be interesting to base the comparison of the three approaches on a quantitative prediction model. The most suitable model is KLM (Keystroke Level Model). KLM is part of the wider GOMS-related work of Card, Moran, and Newell based on the Model Human Processor (MHP) proposed by the same authors. KLM is used to estimate the time taken to complete simple data input tasks by combining few input operators associated to timing constants. The main advantage of KLM is to describe tasks as a sequence of the operators and predict user interaction times without needing to create prototypes.

El Batran and Dunlop [7] have extended KLM for mobile touch interaction with three new operators for three new interaction techniques on mobile devices: tap, swipe and zoom. The extended KLM predicts user movement times for swiping (MT_S), taping (MT_T) and zooming (MT_Z),.

Based on this model, we can estimate the time for entering a n-length word (T_W) with our three approaches:

- $T_W = T_M + MT_T^n + T_M + MT_T$ for the *ambiguous key* approach
- $T_W = T_M + MT_D^n + T_M + MT_T$ for the *single − stroke entry* approach
- $T_W = T_M + MT_S^n + T_M + MT_T$ for the *flick gesture entry* approach

where T_M is the time for mental preparation, MT_T is the movement time for taping a button, MT_D is the movement time for drawing a primitive shape and MT_S is the movement time for flicking (flicking and swiping are considered equivalent).

In each expression, the first term (T_M) corresponds to the time spent for mentally preparing the touch operators, the second term (MT^n) is the time for entering a n-length word, the third time (T_M) is needed for scanning the word prediction list and the last term (MT) is the time for choosing the desired word.

According to Fitts' law, MT is expressed as:

$$MT = a + B \cdot ID \text{ and } ID = \log_2(D/W + 1)$$

where ID is the index of difficulty, W is the width of the target and D is the amplitude of the movement. The coefficients a and b are usually determined empirically for a given device (mouse pointing, finger pointing, stylus pointing…).

In our case, for *button entry* or *flick gesture entry*, W and D are between one third and one half of the screen size, the D/W ratio is in the order of 1. Consequently, the index of difficulty is approximately 1. For this value of ID, El Batran and Dunlop found a predicted time for flicking of 70 ms and a predicted time for button pointing of 80 ms.

For our part, we experimentally found that MT_D, the time for finger drawing a primitive shape on the watch screen is approximately 100 ms.

In conclusion, there is no significant difference between our approaches from the total interaction time perspective (T_W).

7 The Problem of Word Prediction

Whatever the chosen approach, the text input is ambiguous. The expected word must be deduced by a linguistic predictor then validated by the user. In the context of tiny devices used on the go, the lexical prediction is absolutely essential in order to facilitate text entry.

The simplest way is to use the default predictor of the smartphone linked to the watch (QuickType for IOS, Next Word Prediction for Android, Sense Input for HTC…).

Assuming that only very simple posts with abbreviations such as TTYL (*Talk To You Later*), IDTS (*I Don't Think So*), RYOK (*Are You OK*), SYT (*See You Later*), IDK (*I Don't Know*), B4 (*Before*), TY (*Thank You*)… will be entered on the tactile screen of a connected watch, it must be preferable to use a specific predictor [1].

Moreover as the typing sentences are very short and probably not syntactically correct, the default linguistic predictor is not suitable. The most useful and most effective is just to present the word completion and the current word prediction without taking account of the all context of the sentence.

In order to personalize and speed up text entry, a limited set of predefined sentences should be fixed by the watch user. For example, *"I can't answer you, I'm doing my jogging"* or *"at what time you will go back home"*.

It is important to note that processes that allow to speed up the entry, such as keyboard shortcuts, access keys, hot keys or word completion are especially appreciated by users. They allow to reduce the number of interaction and to increase the pace of interaction. They correspond to one of the 8 Golden Rules expressed by Shneiderman (*"Enable Frequent Users to Use Shortcuts"*) [20] and also one of the eight ISO-Standard 9241-110 Dialogue Principles (*"Suitability for Individualization"*).

The fact is that a simple sentence consists of around 8 to 12 words. With software keyboards for mobile devices or even smart watches, a trained user achieves an average of 8 to 12 words per minute (wpm). So, without shortcuts, writing a simple phrase takes more than one minute. In the specific context of interaction with a smart watch, one minute or more for texting is too long. As it is difficult to memorize a long list of abbreviations, a list of 25 to at most 40 common English abbreviations seems to be sufficient for covering lots of situations and speeding up the text entry.

8 Discussion and Future Directions

In this paper, we have analyzed different recent works on smartwatch text entry. We have designed a new approach called UniWatch derived from the UniGlyph method and have explored three input strategies based on touch buttons, finger drawing and flick gestures. We have performed a qualitative and quantitative comparison of these approaches. We have found that there is no significant difference between them from the quantitative point of view. On the other hand, from the qualitative point of view, the *ambiguous key* approach based on key taps has been judged more usable. Whatever the approaches, we have insisted on the necessity of a specific word predictor well fitted for short and not syntactically correct sentences and the importance of textual shortcuts.

In conclusion, taking into account the qualitative and quantitative analyzes, we think that the *ambiguous key* approach is preferable because it implies a better feedback (the primitive shape is recalled on the key), it is easiest to use (minimization of the working memory load compared to the *flick gesture entry* approach), it is quick and reliable.

In the next future, we will develop a proof of concept prototype of UniWatch based on ambiguous keys and textual shortcuts adapted to the context of use of a smartwatch.

References

1. Agarwal, S., Arora, S.: Context based word prediction for texting language. In: Proceedings of the 8th RIAO International Conference on Large-Scale Semantic Access to Content (2007)
2. The Analog Keyboard Project. Microsoft Research (2014). http://research.microsoft.com/en-us/um/redmond/projects/analogkeyboard

3. Buxton, B. The Mad Dash Toward Touch Technology. Business Week, 21 October 2009
4. Cho, H., Kim, M., Seo, K.: A text technique for wrist-worn watches with tiny touchscreens. In: Proceedings of ACM UIST 2014, pp. 79–80. ACM Press, Honolulu (2014)
5. Cooper, W.E.: Cognitive Aspects of Skilled Typewriting. Springer-Verlag, New York (1983)
6. Dunlop, M., Komninos, A., Durga, N.: Towards high quality text entry on smartwatches. In: Proceedings of ACM CHI 2014, pp. 2365–2370. ACM Press, Totonto (2014)
7. El Batran, K., Dunlop, M.: Enhancing KLM (keystroke-level model) to fit touch screen mobile devices. In: Proceedings of the 16th International Conference on Human-Computer Interaction with Mobile Devices and Services, pp. 283–286. ACM Press (2014)
8. Fleksy keyboard. www.fleksy.com
9. Hinckley, K, Song, H.: Sensor synaesthesia: touch in motion, and motion in touch. In: Proceedings of ACM CHI 2011, pp. 801–810. ACM Press, Vancouver (2011)
10. Kim, J., He, J., Lyons, K., Starner, T.: The gesture watch: a wireless contact-free gesture based wrist interface. In: Proceedings of 6th International Semantic Web Conference ISWC 2007, pp. 11–13, Busan (2007)
11. Kratz, S., Rohs, M.: Hoverflow: exploring around-device interaction with IR distance sensors. In: Proceedings of MobileHCI 2009, pp. 1–4. ACM Press, Bonn (2009)
12. MacKenzie, S., Tanaka-Ishii, K.: Text Entry Systems: Mobility, Accessibility, Universality. Morgan Kaufmann Publishers, San Francisco (2007)
13. Minuum keyboard. www.minuum.com
14. Montaparti, S., Dona, P., Durga, N. Meo, R. D.: OpenAdaptxt: an open source enabling technology for high quality text entry. In: Proceedings of CHI Workshop on Designing & Evaluating Text Entry. ACM Press (2012)
15. Oney, S., Harrison, C., Ogan, A., Wiese, J.: ZoomBoard: A Diminutive QWERTY Soft Keyboard Using Iterative Zooming for Ultra-Small Devices. In: Proceedings of ACM CHI 2013, pp. 2799–2802. ACM Press. Paris (2013)
16. Poirier, F.: Glyph: a new stroke-alphabet for stylus-based or key-based text entry. In: Baranauskas, C., Palanque, P., Abascal, J., Barbosa, S.D.J. (eds.) Proceedings of HCI International 2005. Springer, Heidelberg (2005)
17. Poirier, F., Belatar, M.: UniGlyph: only one keystroke per character on a 4-button minimal keypad for key-based text entry. In: Baranauskas, C., Palanque, P., Abascal, J., Barbosa, S. D.J. (eds.) Proceedings of HCI International 2007, vol. 2007, pp. 479–483. Springer, Heidelberg (2007)
18. Poirier, F.: Text entry methods for handheld devices or for AAC writing system. In: Proceedings of ACM CHI 2012. ACM Press, Austin(2012)
19. Sawhney, N., Schmandt, C.: Nomadicradio: speechand audio interaction for contextual messaging in nomadic environment. ACM Trans. Comput. Hum. Interact. 7(3), 353–383 (2000)
20. Shneiderman, B., Plaisant, C.: Designing the User Interface: Strategies for Effective Human-Computer Interaction. Addison Wesley, Boston (2004)
21. Swype keyboard. www.swype.com
22. Venolia, G, Neiberg, F.: T-cube: a fast, self-disclosing pen-based alphabet. In: Proceedings of the SIGCHI conference on Human factors in computing systems - CHI 1994, pp. 265–270. ACM Press, Boston (1994)
23. Xiao, R., Laput, G., Harrison, C.: Expanding the input expressivity of smartwatches with mechanical pan, twist, tilt and click. In: CHI 2014, pp. 193–196. ACM, Totonto (2014)

A Model-Based Framework for Multi-Adaptive Migratory User Interfaces

Enes Yigitbas[(✉)], Stefan Sauer, and Gregor Engels

s-Lab – Software Quality Lab, University of Paderborn,
Zukunftsmeile 1, 33102 Paderborn, Germany
{eyigitbas, sauer, engels}@s-lab.upb.de

Abstract. Nowadays users are surrounded by a broad range of networked interaction devices for carrying out their everyday activities. Flexible and natural interaction with such devices in a seamless manner remains a challenging problem, as many different contexts of use (platform, user, and environment) have to be supported. In this regard, enabling task continuity by preserving the user interface's state and adapting it to the changing context of use can help to improve user experience despite possible device changes. The development of such multi-adaptive migratory user interfaces (MAMUIs) involves several challenges for developers that are partially addressed by frameworks like CAMELEON-RT. However, supporting the development of user interfaces with adaptation and migration capabilities is still a challenging task. In this paper, we present an integrated model-based framework for supporting the development of MAMUIs.

Keywords: Model-Based user interface development · Adaptive user interface · User interface migration

1 Motivation

To day users are surrounded by a broad range of networked interaction devices (e.g. mobile phones, laptops, tablets, smartwatches, terminals etc.) for carrying out their everyday activities. Allowing for flexible and natural interaction with such devices in a seamless manner remains a challenging problem, as many different contexts of use (platform, user, and environment) have to be supported.

Figure 1 shows a usage scenario of such a distributed interactive system. Purchasing a train ticket is carried out by the use of different devices which provide different interaction interfaces. In this scenario, the ticket purchase is first prepared on a home PC entering the reservation dates (date and time for round-trip). In transit, the user is able to book additional services (luggage service, seat reservation, hotel reservation at destination) via smartphone. Finally, the printing of the ticket is done at the ticket machine. Focusing on this example scenario, one can see that different devices can be used to access and modify the information provided by the user interface. In this regard, a device change can cause a context change, which has to be considered for an intuitive and flexible task continuation. The major problems in developing cross-device user interfaces for such scenarios are: lack of efficient development methods for generating multiple user interfaces for different platforms, poor adaptation to the context of

© Springer International Publishing Switzerland 2015
M. Kurosu (Ed.): Human-Computer Interaction, Part II, HCII 2015, LNCS 9170, pp. 563–572, 2015.
DOI: 10.1007/978-3-319-20916-6_52

use, and inadequate support for seamless migration of user interfaces across different devices.

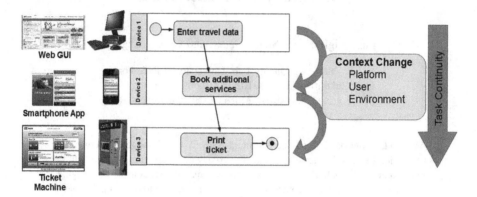

Fig. 1. Example scenario

Regarding the scenario mentioned above, enabling task continuity by preserving the user interface's state during migration and adapting it to the changing context of use can help to improve user experience despite possible device changes. The development of such multi-adaptive migratory user interfaces (MAMUIs) is partially addressed by frameworks like CAMELEON-RT [3]. However, the following factors remain challenging:

- Multi-platform capability: Increase efficiency of multi-platform user interface development across heterogeneous computing platforms (Windows, iOS, Android, Windows Phone etc.).
- Adaptation capability: Establish adaptation mechanisms that enable (semi-) automatic user interface adaptation as reaction to context changes.
- Migration capability: Share an application's user interface and client-side logic across multiple heterogeneous devices in order to support distributed transactions.

In this paper, we present an integrated model-based framework for supporting the efficient development of MAMUIs that enable task continuity and adaptivity to context changes. The paper is structured as following: First, we present related work in the area of model-based development and user interface migration as well as user interface adaptation. Then, we present architectural patterns as basic solution concepts for addressing the challenges of MAMUI development. Based on these architectural patterns, we describe our integrated model-based development framework for MAMUIs. Finally, we conclude with a summary and an outlook for future research work.

2 Background

Focusing on the topic of model-based development of multi-adaptive migratory user interfaces (MAMUIs), multiple aspects have to be taken into account: The model-based development approach for creating UIs and existing approaches for the migration and adaptation of UIs.

2.1   Model-Based Development

Model-based development methods have been discussed in the past for various individual aspects of a software system and for different application domains. This applies to the development of the data management layer, the application layer or the user interface layer [8]. The CAMELEON Reference Framework (CRF) [6] provides a unified framework for model-based and model-driven development of UIs. CAMELEON-RT [3] is an extended version of this framework which represents an abstract reference model for developing the run-time infrastructure for distributed and migratable user interfaces. There are already different approaches such as [4] or [11] which propose model-based development of UIs. These approaches mainly focus on model-based development and its technological implementation aspects. However, aspects like task continuity under device changes, which increase the flexibility of using different UIs, are not sufficiently integrated in the model-based development process.

2.2   UI Migration

UI migration is an important concept to transfer a UI or parts of it from a source device to a target device in order to carry a UI and its state across different devices and to enable mobile, distributed interaction. An example solution for partial Web migration to mobile devices is presented in [7]. Refinements of this concept and architecture proposals for UI migration are described in [15] and [16]. There are also model-based approaches for the dynamic distribution of UIs as described in [12] for example. However, an integrated UI migration process, supporting adaptivity to context changes is not fully covered yet.

2.3   UI Adaptation

Adaptive UIs have been promoted as a solution for context variability due to their ability to automatically adapt to the context-of-use at runtime. Norcio and Stanley consider that the idea of an *adaptive UI* is straightforward since it simply means [13]: "The interface should adapt to the user; rather than the user must adapt to the system." Based on [2] we can generally differentiate between the following types of adaptive UIs:

- **Adaptable User Interfaces** allow interested stakeholders to manually adapt the desired characteristics; example: a software application that supports the manual customization of its toolbars by adding and removing buttons.
- **Semi-Automated Adaptive User Interfaces** automatically react to a change in the context-of-use by changing one or more of their characteristics using a predefined set of adaptation rules. For example: an application can use a sensor to measure the distance between the end-user and a display device, and then trigger predefined adaptation rules to adjust the font-size.
- **Fully-Automated Adaptive User Interfaces** can automatically react to a change in the context-of-use. However, the adaptation has to employ a learning mechanism, which makes use of data that is logged over time. One simple example is a software application, which logs the number of times each end-user clicks on its toolbar

buttons and automatically reorders these buttons differently for each end-user according to the usage frequency.

A classification of different adaptation techniques was introduced by Oppermann [14] and refined by Brusilovsky [5]. UIs with adaptation capabilities have been proposed in the context of various domains and there are also proposals for integrating adaptive UI capabilities in enterprise applications (e.g. [1]). Still, the aspect of automated adaptation is not sufficiently covered during the migration process of a UI regarding to context changes.

3   Architectural Patterns for MAMUIs

In order to support the development of MAMUIs we have identified basic architectural patterns to address the identified challenges: Multi-platform, Adaptation and Migration capabilities.

3.1   Multi-Platform Capability

For increasing the efficiency of multi-platform user interface development it is important to overcome the process of implementing interfaces for M heterogeneous devices with N different contexts while maintaining N*M architectural models and code for all the variants of the same UI. The model-based development process proposes a stepwise approach. At the beginning, models of abstract user interfaces are specified that are then transformed to models of concrete user interfaces. Eventually, the final user interfaces are generated by model-to-code transformations. Such a modeling and generation process is described by the CAMELEON Reference Framework which is illustrated in Fig. 2. The top layer *Task & Concepts* includes a task model that is used for the hierarchical description of the activities and actions of individual users of the user interface. The abstract user interface (*AUI*) is described in the form of a dialogue model that specifies the user's interaction with the user interface independent of specific technology. The platform specific representation of the user interface is described by the concrete user interface (*CUI*), which is specified by a presentation model. The lowest layer of the framework is the final user interface (FUI) for the target platform. The vertical dimension describes the path from abstract to concrete models. Here, a top-down approach is followed, in which the abstract description of relevant information about the user interface (AUI) is enriched to more sophisticated models (CUI) through model-to-model transformations (M2 M). Subsequently, the refined models are transformed (model-to-code transformation, M2C) to produce the final user interface (*FUI*). Based on this architectural pattern, it is possible to enable multi-platform capability for the different UIs that are generated during the development process.

3.2   Adaptation Capability

While the architectural pattern above described, supports multi-platform UI generation, it is not sufficient to develop adaptive UIs, because there are no means to model

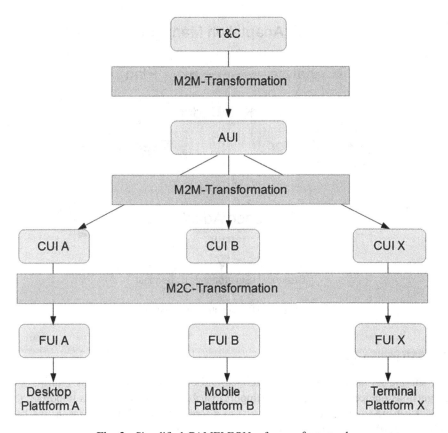

Fig. 2. Simplified CAMELEON reference framework

adaptivity. Nevertheless, the model-based development process offers flexibility to extend it for the development of adaptive components. In this context we have analyzed different architectural concepts for self-adaptive systems such as MAPE-K by Kephart and Chess [9] and the 3-layer reference architecture by Kramer and Magee [10]. As a result of this analysis, we have identified the need for an architectural pattern for representing the adaptation process (see Fig. 3). Such an architectural pattern for UI adaptation can be characterized by an *Adaptation Manager* that monitors the *Managed/Adaptive UI*. The *Managed/Adaptive UI* can run on different platforms (PC, smartphone and terminal). The *Adaptation Manager* consists of five main components that work in the following way: The *Monitor* component is responsible for observing the context information. Context information changes are then evaluated by the *Analyze* component to decide whether adaptation is needed. If so, the planning of an adaptation schedule is done by the *Plan* component. Finally, the adaptation operations are performed by the *Execute* component, so that an adapted UI can be presented. The *Knowledge* base is responsible for storing data that is logged over time and can be used for inferring future adaptation operations.

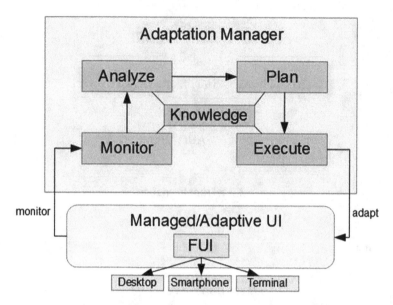

Fig. 3. UI adaptation manager

3.3 Migration Capability

For sharing an application's user interface and client-side logic across multiple heterogeneous devices and in order to support distributed transactions it is important that
the UI can be transferred from a source to a target device. For this reason, we have
defined a further architectural pattern called UI migration (see Fig. 4).

In order to support this in a seamless manner, we have to enable task continuity
during the migration process so that the state of the UI is carried over and the presentation is adapted to the target device and its context. For reaching this goal, the
source platform triggers a migration request to the *Migration Server*. This can be done
manually by request of the user or automatically based on context information events,
like for example, low battery status of a mobile device. The *Migration Server* accepts
the migration request to transfer the current *FUI A* to the selected target platform. For
supporting the migration process, the *Migration Server* consists of four main components. The *Task Mapping* component is responsible for determining which activities of
the task model are supported by the target platform. After establishing a mapping on
the task level, the *State Mapping* component captures the state of the migrating *FUI A*.
This state is the result of the history of user interactions with the application including
previous input data. The *CUI Redesign* component provides a mapping on the CUI
level by rearranging the CUI model of the migrating UI for the special needs of the
target platform. It considers platform information like display size or resolution for this
purpose. Finally, the *FUI Adaptation* component returns as a result of the *Migration
Server* a *Context-adapted FUI A'* that is activated on the target platform.

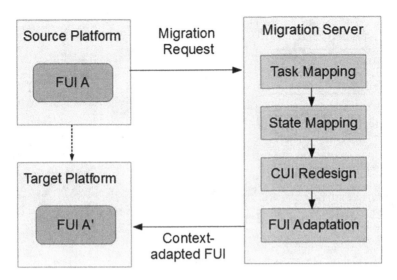

Fig. 4. UI migration

4 Model-based Framework for MAMUIs

In the previous section, we have presented different architectural patterns for developing MAMUIs. While these patterns address basic solution concepts for tackling the different challenges, it is important to design an integrated framework which combines the several aspects of multi-platform capability, adaptation capability and migration capability. For this reason, we propose our MAMUI Reference Framework which supports the development of migratory user interfaces that can extend across a variety of devices and are adaptive to context changes like platform, user and environment. The MAMUI Reference Framework which is depicted in Fig. 5 consists of four main parts: *UI Generator*, *Adaptation Manager*, *Migration Server* and *Context Manager*.

The *UI Generator* is responsible for generating the final user interfaces (FUIs) for the different platforms (Desktop, Mobile, Terminal, etc.). The generation process is based on the CAMELEON Reference Framework where a transformational approach is preceded. At the beginning of the transformation process, task models are created which describe the activities and actions of individual users of the user interface. The task models are then transformed to abstract UI models (AUI) which describe the user's interactions with the user interface independent of a specific technology. In a next transformation step, the concrete UI models (CUI) for the different platforms are created. Finally, by using model-to-code transformations the final user interfaces (FUIs) are generated.

The *Adaptation Manager* is responsible for monitoring the adaptive FUIs and adapting them to the different kinds of context changes. In order to support adaptation mechanisms at different levels of the CAMELEON Reference Framework, the *Adaptation Manager* consists of three adaptation layers. *Task Feature Adaptation* enables changes in the task models such as, for example, minimizing the task feature set based

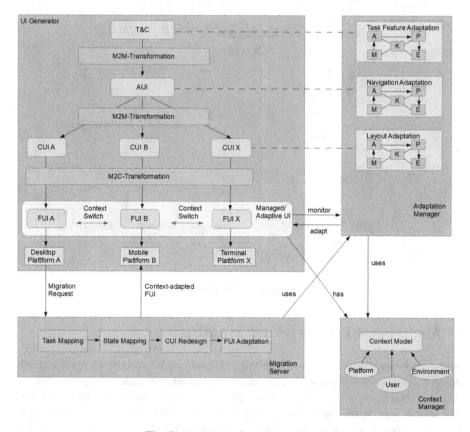

Fig. 5. MAMUI reference framework

on the context information. This means for instance that task activities which are not executable on particular platforms or for some predefined user roles are not represented in the FUI. Similarly, the adaptation layer *Navigation Adaptation* is responsible for changing the navigation flow of the FUI by manipulating the AUI model. Based on the context information, it is also possible to perform changes in the CUI models in order to reach *Layout Adaptation*. For specifying the different changes in the adaptation process, the *Adaptation Manager* makes use of an adaptation model. The adaptation model is encoded in the adaptation layers. In the adaptation model different adaptation rules based on the ECA (Event-Condition-Action) paradigm and the *Context Model* are defined, which are evaluated at runtime to react to the context changes.

While a final user interface (FUI) is running on a particular platform, a context switch may happen by changing the device. For this purpose, a *Migration Server* can accept a migration request from a source platform for migrating the current FUI to a target platform. In order to support the migration process, several steps are provided by the Migration Server as described in detail in Sect. 3.3. First, a task mapping between the source and target platform is done. This is necessary in order to adjust the different task activities so that executable tasks are selected for the target platform. After that, a state mapping of the user interfaces is established, so that preconfigured UI features and input data are carried over to the target platform. In the next step, the CUI model of the current platform is redesigned in order to adapt it for the target platform considering the context changes. For reaching this goal, the *Migration Server* makes use of the described layers of the *Adaptation Manager*. Finally, the context-adapted FUI is activated for the target platform.

The *Context Manager* operates on a *Context Model* that is divided into a *Platform*, *User* and *Environment* model. The *Context Manager* provides useful context information for the Managed/*Adaptive UI*, so that the *Adaptation Manager* is able to observe context changes that are addressed by related adaptation rules defined in the adaptation model.

With the interplay of its described main components, the proposed MAMUI Reference Framework provides a basic solution concept to support multi-platform, adaptive and migratory UI development. In our ongoing research work, we are currently developing an integrated development environment to address the main parts of the MAMUI Reference Framework. This will include the modelling and transformation of the core UI models at different levels and also the modelling of aspects like adaptation and migration. Future work will include the evaluation of our integrated development environment based on practical example scenarios.

5   Conclusion and Outlook

This paper presents an integrated model-based framework for supporting the development of multi-adaptive migratory user interfaces (MAMUIs). We have referred to a cross-device user interface usage scenario from practice, which served as a basis to show the different challenges in this context, e.g. multi-platform, adaptation and migration capability. In order to address these challenges, we have described different basic solution patterns for supporting the development of MAMUIs. Based on these architectural patterns, we have presented our integrated model-based MAMUI Reference Framework. Our future work will focus on the development and evaluation of a modelling and execution workbench based on the proposed MAMUI Reference Framework.

References

1. Akiki, P.A., et al.: Integrating adaptive user interface capabilities in enterprise applications. In: Proceedings of the 36th International Conference on Software Engineering (ICSE 2014), pp. 712–723. ACM (2014)
2. Akiki, P.A., et al.: Adaptive model-driven user interface development systems. ACM Comput. Surv. **47**(1), 1–33 (2014). Article 9
3. Balme, L., Demeure, A., Barralon, N., Calvary, G.: CAMELEON-RT: a software architecture reference model for distributed, migratable, and plastic user interfaces. In: Markopoulos, P., Eggen, B., Aarts, E., Crowley, J.L. (eds.) EUSAI 2004. LNCS, vol. 3295, pp. 291–302. Springer, Heidelberg (2004)

4. Botterweck, G.: A model-driven approach to the engineering of multiple user interfaces. In: Kühne, T. (ed.) MoDELS 2006. LNCS, vol. 4364, pp. 106–115. Springer, Heidelberg (2007)

5. Brusilovsky, P.: Adaptive Hypermedia. In: User Modeling and User-Adapted Interaction, vol. 11, pp. 87–110. Kluwer Academic Publishers, March 2001

6. Calvary, G., Coutaz, J., Thevenin, D., Limbourg, Q., Bouillon, L., Vanderdonckt, J.: A unifying reference framework for multi-target user interfaces. Interact. Comput. 15, 289–308 (2003)

7. Ghiani, G.; Paternò, F.; Santoro, C.: On-demand cross-device interface components migration. In: Proceedings of the 12th international conference on Human computer interaction with mobile devices and services (MobileHCI 2010), pp. 299–308. ACM (2010)

8. Hussmann, H., Meixner, G., Zuehlke, D. (eds.): Model-Driven Development of Advanced User Interfaces. Springer, Heidelberg (2011)

9. Kephart, J.O., Chess, D.M.: The vision of autonomic computing. Computer 36(1), 41–50 (2003)

10. Kramer, J., Magee, J.: Self-managed systems: an architectural challenge. In: Proceedings of 2007 Future of Software Engineering (FOSE 2007), IEEE Computer Society, Washington, DC, USA, pp. 259–268 (2007)

11. Link, S., Schuster, T., Hoyer, P., Abeck, S.: Modellgetriebene Entwicklung grafischer Benutzerschnittstellen (Model-Driven Development of Graphical User Interfaces). i-com 6, Nr. 3, Oldenbourg, München, pp. 37–43 (2008)

12. Martinie, C., Navarre, D., Palanque, P.: A multi-formalism approach for model-based dynamic distribution of user interfaces of critical interactive systems. Int. J. Hum.-Comput. Stud. 72, 77–99 (2014)

13. Norcio, A.F., Stanley, J.: Adaptive human-computer interfaces: a literature survey and perspective. IEEE Trans. Syst. Man Cybern. 19, 399–408 (1989)

14. Oppermann, R.: Individualisierte systemnutzung. In: Paul, M. (ed.) GI – 19. Jahrestagung, Computergestützter Arbeitsplatz, pp. 131–145. Springer, Heidelberg (1989)

15. Paternò, F., Santoro, C., Scorcia, A.: Ambient intelligence for supporting task continuity across multiple devices and implementation languages. Comput. J. 53(8), 1210–1228 (2010)

16. Yanagida, T., Nonaka, H.: Architecture for migratory adaptive user interfaces. In: Computer and Information Technology, CIT 2008, pp.450-455 (2008)

Games and Gamification

A Dome-Shaped Interface Embedded with Low-Cost Infrared Sensors for Car-Game Control by Gesture Recognition

Jasmine Bhanushali, Sai Parthasarathy Miduthuri,
and Kavita Vemuri[✉]

International Institute of Information Technology, Hyderabad, Hyderabad, India
{jasmine.bhanushali, saiparthasarathy.miduthuri}
@students.iiit.ac.in, kvemuri@iiit.ac.in

Abstract. This paper proposes a steering wheel like interface using infrared sensors suitable for in-car control, car-game control or any interface with spin or turn hand gesture. Most of the interfaces introduced to-date use touch, position/depth sensing using cameras or proximity sensors positioned in a 2-D configuration. The electronic screen used for touch interface requires the user to maintain contact with specific positions on the screen. In contactless interfaces the sensors or camera are placed in a planar configuration, and complex gestures like turns or twist is intensive signal analysis. In the proposed preliminary model we introduce a contactless gesture recognition design shaped as a dome to allow natural hand movement for turns and tested to control a virtual object mimicking the movement of a car-wheel. The system recognizes hand movements like forward (translated as acceleration), backward (deceleration/slow), steady-hold (cruise), lateral for braking, turns-clockwise (right turn of the wheel) and anti-clockwise (left-turn of the wheel)– using 9 low-cost IR sensors embedded in a dome-shaped structure. The convex shape reduces interferences from adjacent sensors to a significant extent and allows for capturing distinct gestures. The inclusion of the acceleration and braking action to be controlled by the hand movement is to test and reduce leg and hand reflexes difference in the human visuo-motor feedback response system. The Hidden Markov Model was used for 5 basic gestures deduced from the IR signal analysis. The first version of the system was tested on a 3D virtual wheel-like object simulating a car tire. Real-time user gesture data tested against this model gave an overall average accuracy of 88.01 % for the five gestures The user gestures were timed and were in the range of 140-300 ms depending on the gesture sequence. Some of the limitations of the first version of the design being addressed are noisy signals to reduce errors in gesture recognition. Secondly we need to test this on a comprehensive driving simulation to collect empirical data on the adaptation of the hand movement to control braking and acceleration.

1 Introduction

Hand gestures recognition techniques and interfaces [1] has been the focus of research for a long time as it provides natural way for users to interact with devices and virtual objects. Current gesture recognition concepts are generally touch, motion or vision-based or a

© Springer International Publishing Switzerland 2015
M. Kurosu (Ed.): Human-Computer Interaction, Part II, HCII 2015, LNCS 9170, pp. 575–583, 2015.
DOI: 10.1007/978-3-319-20916-6_53

combination of two or more to enable advanced interactions like detecting simultaneous multi-user play requiring depth and random motion. Touch based screens are restrictive to 2-d surfaces while motion and vision sensors are less restrictive but computationally intensive and also require considerable training for really natural gesture recognitions. Natural gesture recognizers are requisite for virtual or real 3-D object manipulation or for interaction with robots, from ergonomics and functional aspects.

Non-touch based gestural systems work with signals from ultrasonic sensors, infrared (IR) sensors, simple webcams or expensive depth cameras. Infrared,ultrasonic and camera sensors enable non-touch based gesturing, making them tenable for use in interactions with systems installed in public places. Wearable interfaces like wrist-watch [2] and gloves [3] embedded with IR or motion sensors are also being tested and found to be accurate but are either expensive or constrained in functionality. Wearable gloves [3, 4] embedded with infrared or ultrasonic sensors or pressure sensors are accurate in picking up finger bends and twists gestures usually not easy to detect using a full-body movement capturing camera sensor system. Finger bending and rotation was collected from a finger ring iRing [5] by measuring the reflectance from the skin. The problem with wearable gear is customization and personalization of the glove material which is expensive and unhygienic for public spaces as in a gaming club or a museum. Vision-based gesture recognition using cameras [6, 7] are considered to be the most accurate and flexible in terms of repository of actions that the user can commit. In games particularly, gesture and motion capturing has transferred the experience of the player and the device which has captured players imagination is the Kinect (TM: Microsoft Cooperation) which was similar to the Nintendo wii [8] fitted with accelerometers to detect 3-D gestures in open space. The depth-sensing cameras like Kinect and Xtion (http://www.asus.com/Multimedia/Xtion/) have enabled full body action and can extract hand gestures recognition from the depth data [9, 10] . In terms of analysis, depth sensing cameras rely on fairly extensive computing of the depth data from color [11] or 3D information extracted from the hand and finger posturing [10] and hence the set of gestures are large covering most natural hand movements like trajectories. A simpler device is the Leap Motion (https://www.leapmotion.com/) which is equipped with a depth sensing camera principally used for hand tracking and gesture recognition. Combining touch and air-gestures a taxonomy of interactions to be used on mobile devices was evolved [12] and is interesting method to capture expressivity. Gesture recognition systems set up in public places for particular applications like viewing pictures or in browsing through a library collection [13] using a simple camera is tenable for public places where hygiene and wear-tear are concerns. Using a simple webcam [14] demonstrated an interface for public spaces using an efficient vision algorithms. A multi-HMM model was applied on data collected from Kinect depth camera and a wearable inertia sensor resulting in improved recognition in real-time in realistic conditions [15, 16]. Wearable cameras for motion capture [17] allows for outdoor data capture of relative and global motion and used in animation movies. Capturing precise hand or finger movement is still a challenge because detection from image analysis in real-time is subject to lighting and filtering the visual clutter of the background.

Infrared sensors [18] have gained a special preference in human-system interaction due to the ease of signal analysis as it basically works as a proximity sensor.

Differential pyro-electric IR sensors and an ordinary camera [19] for gesture and hand detection respectively showed a sensitivity upto 1.2 m by a method of detection by collecting continuous signals of left to right and vice-verse in addition to clockwise and counter clockwise hand gestures. Hand-tracking and gesture recognition using only IR sensors was also tried in SideSight [20], where the IR sensors are fixed on to the side of a mobile device to track movement of the fingers. An application HoverFlow detects hand gestures over a mobile phone [21] using IR sensors, the same application was also tested on a wearable pendant. The dome shaped device with inexpensive IR sensors reported in this study is a unique physical configuration where the shape of the structure automatically supports the gestures like turn or twist.

The hardware configuration and architecture is mostly varies with the targeted application or usage, for example car-racing games controlled by external mechanical devices had IR sensors embedded [22, 23] on a car steering wheel with specific positions to sense, a click, tap or turn to where a support vector machine was used to analyze the data. In gaming, Kinect is the most versatile interface and popular among players equipped with a depth and RGB camera,IR sensor and tilting motor and microphones. Other niche applications where fixed set of predefined gestures like play, stop, next etc., is employed in music control [24, 25].

Compared to the touch-screen and vision-based gesture recognizers the IR based sensor arrays work optimally with simple gestures like hand-swipes and most importantly are inexpensive option. We propose an unique physical design embedded with off-the-shelf inexpensive IR sensors that enable recognition of free hand turns, a forward, backward move and left/right swipe using the Hidden Markov Model (HMM) [26] Viterbi algorithm for gesture recognition. The signals from the hand-gestures on the device was used to manipulate a virtual object mimicking the actions of a car-wheel. Two gestures translate to driving functions, acceleration and braking, by human-leg and an attempt was made to study differences if any in the visuo-motor response between the hand and leg.

2 Methods and Materials

The hardware used are off-the-shelf low cost components and include 9-pairs of Infrared (IR) LED transreceivers, an Arduino microcontroller which collects the analog signals from the sensors, and a 5 V power supply mainly. The testing was done for two conditions with or without a visual feedback of a representation of a virtual object indicating the direction of movement of a wheel. This testing analyses if the gestures require focused attention and also if mid-flight corrections is possible when looking at the object movement. The cost of the device can be further reduced by replacing the Arduino with a high-speed analog to digital convertor. The IR proximity sensors are noisy due to ambient IR radiation, power supply fluctuations and manufacturing defects as these are non-calibrated inexpensive LEDs. In the calibration stage, the minimum and maximum values of each sensor was stored in the microcontroller and used as reference to normalize each reading and also identify the active LED. The HMM toolbox in MATLAB was used to process the sequences. The flow chart is indicative of the processes applied is shown in Fig. 1c.

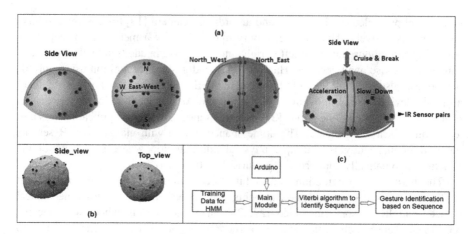

Fig. 1. (a) The virtual rendered device with the arrows showing the gestures and the top/side view. (b) The actual prototype made using paper-mache and (c) the process represented as a flow-chart.

The HMM was trained for 5 input gestures, as shown in Fig. 1a, which are Turn-left/right, forward (accleration) and back (deceleration) and the IR on the top used for cruise (constant speed) and also for pumping action in braking by up-down gesture.

2.1   Automatic Training

For every input sequence in the training the expected gesture is known. Hence for every gesture there exist sequences of states corresponding to it. A list was made of the sequence of states corresponding to each gesture according to the index number of the LED. Then the expected state sequence and the obtained observations were given as inputs to MATLAB programme. The code then finds the closest similarity in the values and accordingly fills in the state for every observation. If an observation occurs which corresponds to a state in the expected sequence, that time instant in the observation is set to have the same state in the state sequence. This state sequence was also confirmed manually in order to check for errors. All of the data was then stored in a loadable file for each use of the device. In the training phase the HMM generates a state transition matrix and emission matrix based on the state sequence and the observation sequence and the Viterbi algorithm uses this matrix to estimate the state sequence given a set of observations in the gesture recognition stage. The algorithm logic is provided below:

Algorithm:

For each input observation value received:

1. Convert current observation value to binary
2. Identify the indices of LEDs giving an output HIGH, and store in C_SEQ
3. For each member of expected sequence
   a. Check if member belongs to array C_SEQ
   b. If member found in C_SEQ, then
   c. State_Value[curr] = member_index

    d. If member not found in C_SEQ then

    e. State_Value[curr] = index with a HIGH in C_SEQ

    f. curr = curr + 1;

4. Store both observations and corresponding state sequences in Training Database.
5. Use to train Identification Model for HMM.

2.2   Identifying Gesture

After each person does the observation the values obtained are sent to the HMM Viterbi algorithm. This algorithm is trained from the dataset obtained from the states and observations given in the training period. The output of the Viterbi algorithm is a set of states corresponding to observations. This set of states is almost always very similar to one of the 5 gestures. We then found the probability of the sequence corresponding to each gesture and finalize on the one with the maximum likelihood. Next the algorithm weighs the starting states as higher and reduces the weight as the index in the state sequence array moves towards the end. Thus it makes sure that an incomplete correct sequence has more weight than a complete wrong one which has some non-matching or out of state numbers (that may confuse the identification process). Thus the sequences with lower probability are ignored, giving us a correct answer.

    Algorithm:

1. For each gesture, a set of possible state sequences was determined stored in a table – Ideal_Seq.
2. Create two weighting arrays:
    a. y = size(Ideal_Seq, columns) down to 1
    b. z = size(Viterbi_Output) down to 1 z = z . z
3. Initialize a histogram of size(Ideal_Seq, rows)
4. For all state sequences in Ideal_Seq
    a. For all members in a state sequence
      i. Check if member belongs to Viterbi_Output, and store indices in an array x
      ii. If member belongs, then vote for that sequence in the histogram with a number obtained by multiplying the weight of the member_index in z with the weight of member_index in y.
    b. Find percentage match
5. Return the state sequence index number with maximum percentage match as the output.

3   Results and Discussion

A set of five gestures and the envisoned actions: (1) North_South (over the top) – Deacceleration. (2) North_west turn-anti clockwise. (3) North_east turn – clockwise. (4) East_west and (5) South_north (over the top)- acceleration were tested. The directional reference are with respect to the top-most point of a steering-wheel being north and the anti and clockwise movement was selected in accordance which how one turns a steering wheel holding the top for taking a turn. Each gesture was briefly

Table 1. The accuracy estimates from the HMM for each testing state participant for the 5 gestures and the average. Gest 1: North_South (over the top). Gest 2: North_west turn. Gest 3: North_east turn. Gest 4: East_west and Gest 5: South_north (over the top).

Person No.	Percentage Accuracy					
	Gest.1	Gest.2	Gest.3	Gest.4	Gest.5	Average
1	66.67 %	58.33 %	75 %	100 %	83.33 %	76.67 %
2	66.67 %	75 %	83.33 %	91.67 %	75 %	78.33 %
3	75 %	83.33 %	83.33 %	100 %	91.67 %	86.67 %
4	100 %	83.33 %	91.67 %	83.33 %	91.67 %	90.00 %
5	66.67 %	75 %	100 %	100 %	91.67 %	86.67 %
6	91.67 %	100 %	83.33 %	91.67 %	91.67 %	91.67 %
7	91.67 %	91.67 %	100 %	91.67 %	91.67 %	93.34 %
8	91.67 %	75 %	83.33 %	100 %	100 %	90.00 %
9	91.67 %	91.67 %	75 %	91.67 %	100 %	90.00 %
10	100 %	100 %	100 %	91.67 %	91.67 %	96.67 %

described to the subject and each of these gestures was repeated 15 times by 16 different people. The binary value obtained from the sensors at each time instant was stored with a period of 30 ms between two instants. This data was then sent to the auto-training function, which generated a state sequence. For testing, each of the gestures were performed 12 times by 10 people different from the ones who contributed in the training phase (Table 1). The gestures were demonstrated to the testing subjects once and each gesture was repeated 6 times with and similar number of times without the visual feedback by all subjects. The gestures were first briefly described to each subject and then asked to perform the gesture. The presentation of the visual stimuli was counter-balanced to take care of learning from previous similar gesture movement. Visual feedback of the gesture had almost no impact on the accuracy.

From the accuracy estimates (Table 1) the gesture (Gest 4) which is the translatary motion from left to right is the highest while north_west (Gest 2) to turn left seems to be the most difficult to commit. Figure 2 presents the accuracy calculated for the 5 gestures for the two conditions with/out visual feedback of the change on the virtual object. The probability of accuracy increased as the subject did the gesture multiple times and got used to it. The probability also seemed to increase if users saw someone else performing the gestures before them. The total average accuracy for all gestures in both conditions was 88.01 % with nearly 85.67 % with visual feedback while it is 90.33 % without. Interestingly, the design's ease of use is exemplied by the 100 % accuracy by 6-7 trails by the users. The 'stop' or 'cruise' gesture's results is not presented as it was 100 % accuracy as the sensors collect the reflected signal either when the hand is held at a constant distance from the sensor or moved laterally. An additional gesture (Gesture 4) was included but does not have a literal action on the application used for tested but can translate to a 'flip' command if used as a music player controller. The visual stimuli seems to slightly distract the subject during gesturing.

As demonstrated by the results the device shows promising potential as an inexpensive alternative to camera or wearable gesture sensors. The device allows for

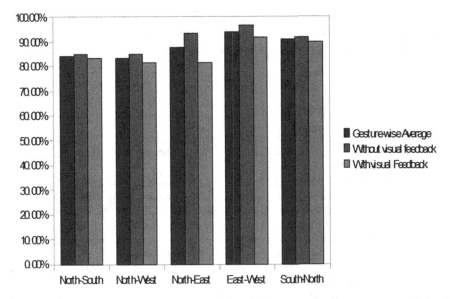

Fig. 2. The accuracy estimates from 10 testing phase participants. The data are averages for each gestures and the 2 conditions (with/out visual stimuli) and the overall average.

recognition of complex natural gestures like rotation or turning with high accuracy. The nicheness is the minimal training that is required to start using the device. Though, the first application tested was a steering-wheel like interface, the gestures can also be used to control music players with same set of gestures. The slightly lower accuracy with a visual interaction could be similar to the condition when learning to drive it takes a while to synchronize the motor action to the visual system. The testing on difference of hand and leg reflex for acceleration (South_North motion) and brake (steady position over the top) and role of visual-motor response was inconclusive.

4   Conclusion

The unique design with sensors at calculated separation to minimize noise from interference of signals shows promise as a gesture recognizer. Our basic aim was to come up with an ergonomic and integrated control device for in-car control, but the device can also be used in any application platform which requires non-contact control of virtual or real objects requiring rotation action specifically. One such usage in real-world is in assembly-line automation and control by factory-floor personnel, where touch-based systems have higher wear-tear compared to non-touch gesture interfaces. The design can also be tested in public places like museums where touch-based mechanical or electronic screens are expensive, unhygienic and requires regular maintenance. Extensive experiments are required to confirm if the transfer of controls like acceleration and braking to the hand as against the traditional leg will translate to faster reflex reactions and is important study for design of futuristic electronic vehicles.

Future work on the idea includes design and testing on a car-simulator. We have also not exploited the depth sensing, which would in principle increase the gestures set and hence the number of controls that can be manipulated.

References

1. Pavlovic, V.I., Sharma, R., Huang, T.S.: Visual interpretation of hand gestures for human-computer interaction A review. IEEE Trans. Pattern, Anal. Mach. Intell. **19**(7): 677–695 (1997)
2. Amstutz, R., Amft, O., French, B., Smailagic, A., Siewiorek, D., Troster, G.: Performance analysis of an HMM-based gesture recognition using a wristwatch device. In: International Conference on Computational Science and Engineering, CSE 2009, Pp. 303–309 (2009)
3. CyberGlove Systems. CyberGlove Systems website. http://www.cyberglovesystems.com/
4. Han, Y.: A low-cost visual motion data glove as an input device to interpret human hand gestures. IEEE Trans. Consum. Electron. **56**(2), 501–509 (2010)
5. Ogata M., Sugiura Y., Osawa1H., Imai M.: iRing: intelligent ring using infrared reflection. In: UIST 2012 (2012)
6. Lee, D., Park, Y.: Vision-based remote control system by motion detection and open finger counting. IEEE Trans. Consum. Electron. **55**(4), 2308–2313 (2009)
7. Wachs, J.P., Kölsch, M., Stern, H., Edan, Y.: Vision-based hand gesture applications. Commun. ACM **54**(2), 60–71 (2011)
8. Schlomer, T., Poppinga, B., Henze, N., Boll, S.: Gesture recognition with a wii controller. In: Proceedings of TEI (2008)
9. Zhang, Z.: Microsoft kinect sensor and its effect. Multimed. IEEE **19**(2), 4–10 (2012)
10. Dominio, F., Donadeo, M., Zanuttigh, P.: Combining multiple depth-based descriptors for hand gesture recognition. Pattern Recognit. Lett. **50**, 101–111 (2014)
11. Doliotis P., Stefan A., McMurrough, C., Eckhard, D., Athitsos, V.: Comparing gesture recognition accuracy using color and depth information. In: Proceedings of the 4th International Conference on Pervasive Technologies Related to Assistive Environments, PETRA 2011, pp. 20:1–20:7 (2011)
12. Chen, X.A., Schwarz, J., Harrison, C., Mankoff, J., Hudson, S.E.: Air+touch: interweaving touch & in-air gestures. In: UIST 2014 (2014)
13. Stenger, B., Woodley, T., Cipolla, R.: A vision-based remote control. Comput. Vis. **285**, 233–262 (2010)
14. Roccetti, M., Marfia, G., Semeraro, A.: Playing into the wild: a gesture-based interface for gaming in public spaces. J. Vis. Commun. Image R. **23**, 426–440 (2012)
15. Liu, K., Chen, C., Jafari, R., Kehtarnavaz, N.: Fusion of inertial and depth sensor data for robust hand gesture recognition. IEEE Sens. J. **14**(6), 1898–1903 (2014)
16. Liu K., Kehtarnavaz N.: Comparison of two real-time hand gesture recognition systems involving stereo cameras, depth camera, and inertial sensor. In: Proceedings of SPIE Conference on Real-Time Image and Video Processing, paper no. 91390C, April 2014
17. Numaguchi1, N., Nakazawa1, A., Shiratori, T., Hodgins, J.K.: A Puppet Interface for Retrieval of Motion Capture Data. In: SIGGRAPH 2011 Symposium on Computer Animation (2011)
18. LeBlance, D., Hamam, H., Bouslimani, Y.: Infrared based human machine interaction. information and communication technologies. In: ICTTA 2006. 2nd vol. 1 (2006)

19. Erden, F., Bingöl, A.S.,Çetin, A.E.: Hand gesture recognition using two differential PIR sensors and a camera. In: Proceedings of IEEE 22nd Signal Processing and Communications Applications Conference, pp. 349–352 (2014)
20. Butler, A., Izadi, S., Hodges, S.: SideSight: multi-"touch" interaction around small devices. In: Proceedings of UIST 2008, pp. 201–204 (2008)
21. Kratz, S., Rohs, M.: HoverFlow: expanding the design space of around-device interaction. In: Proceedings of MobileHCI 2009, pp. 1–8 (2009)
22. Koyama, S., Sugiura, Y., Ogata, M., Withana, A., Uema, Y., Honda, M., Yoshizu, A., Sannomiya, C., Nawa, K., Inami, M.: Multi-touch steering wheel for in-car tertiary applications using infrared sensors. In: Proceedings of AH 2014 (2014)
23. Doring, T., Kern, D., Marshall, P., Pfeiffer, M., Schoning, J., Gruhn, V., Schmidt, A.: Gestural interaction on the steering wheel: reducing the visual demand. In: Proceedings of the SIGCHI Conference on Human Factors in Computing Systems, pp. 483–492. ACM (2011)
24. Masui, T., Tsukada, K., Siio, I.: MouseField: a simple and versatile input device for ubiquitous computing. In: Mynatt, E.D., Siio, I. (eds.) UbiComp 2004. LNCS, vol. 3205, pp. 319–328. Springer, Heidelberg (2004)
25. Henze, N., Löcken, A., Boll, S., Hesselmann, T., Pielot, M.: Free-hand gestures for music playback:deriving gestures with a user-centred process. In: MUM 2010, 1–3 December (2010)
26. Rabiner, L.R., Juang, B.H.: An introduction to hidden markov models. IEEE ASSP Mag. 3 (1), 4–16 (1986)

Evaluating a Public Display Installation with Game and Video to Raise Awareness of Attention Deficit Hyperactivity Disorder

Michael P. Craven[1,2(✉)], Lucy Simons[1,3], Alinda Gillott[4],
Steve North[5], Holger Schnädelbach[5], and Zoe Young[1]

[1] NIHR MindTech Healthcare Technology Co-Operative, The Institute
of Mental Health, Jubilee Campus, Nottingham NG7 2TU, UK
{michael.craven, lucy.simons, zoe.young}
@nottingham.ac.uk
[2] The University of Nottingham, Faculty of Engineering Electrical Systems
and Optics Research Division, Nottingham, UK
[3] Faculty of Medicine and Health Sciences, Division of Psychiatry
and Applied Psychology, Nottingham, UK
[4] Nottinghamshire Healthcare NHS Trust, Intellectual and Developmental
Disabilities Service Specialist Services Directorate, Highbury Hospital,
Nottingham NG6 9DR, UK
alinda.gillott@nottshc.nhs.uk
[5] Mixed Reality Laboratory, School of Computer Science, The University
of Nottingham, Nottingham NG8 1BB, UK
{steve.north, holger.schnadelbach}@nottingham.ac.uk

Abstract. Networked Urban Screens offer new possibilities for public health education and awareness. An information video about Attention Deficit Hyperactivity Disorder (ADHD) was combined with a custom browser-based video game and successfully deployed on an existing research platform, Screens in the Wild (SitW). The SitW platform consists of 46-in. touchscreen or interactive displays, a camera, a microphone and a speaker, deployed at four urban locations in England. Details of the platform and software implementation of the multimedia content are presented. The game was based on a psychometric continuous performance test. In the gamified version of the test, players receive a score for correctly selected target stimuli, points being awarded in proportion to reaction time and penalties for missed or incorrect selections. High scores are shared between locations. Questions were embedded to probe self-awareness about 'attention span' in relation to playing the game, awareness of ADHD and Adult ADHD and increase in knowledge from the video. Results are presented on the level of public engagement with the game and video, deduced from play statistics, answers to the questions and scores obtained across the screen locations. Awareness of Adult ADHD specifically was similar to ADHD in general and knowledge increased overall for 93 % of video viewers. Furthermore, ratings of knowledge of Adult ADHD correlated positively with ADHD in general and positively with knowledge gain. Average scores varied amongst the sites but there was no significant correlation of question ratings with score. The challenge of interpreting user results from unsupervised platforms is discussed.

© Springer International Publishing Switzerland 2015
M. Kurosu (Ed.): Human-Computer Interaction, Part II, HCII 2015, LNCS 9170, pp. 584–595, 2015.
DOI: 10.1007/978-3-319-20916-6_54

Keywords: Cultural interface · Game design · Gamification · Gamification interface · Architectures for interaction · Interaction design · Multimedia design · Real life environments · Display networks · Healthcare technology · Public health · Mental health · Attention deficit hyperactivity disorder · Adult ADHD · ADD

1 Introduction

In recent years there has been a marked growth in the use of digital tools in healthcare. In particular there is increased interest in using digital technologies in the domain of mental health and one specific area of interest is public awareness campaigns aimed at improving health education and reducing stigma. The clinical area of interest for this project is Attention Deficit Hyperactivity Disorder (ADHD), a neurodevelopmental condition that is characterised by three core behaviours: inattention, hyperactivity and impulsivity. It is typically thought that around 3–5 % of school aged children have ADHD, with lifetime persistence for the majority. Research has found public uncertainty about the validity of ADHD as a diagnosis and scepticism towards ADHD treatment which could impact on access to, and engagement with, appropriate diagnosis and treatment.

Networked Urban Screens (interconnected multimedia displays) are a technology that offers new possibilities for social interactions in public spaces, with potential for use in public health campaigns. With the aim of realising an engaging experience, an information video about ADHD was combined with a custom, browser-based video game and deployed on an existing networked displays research platform, Screens in the Wild (SitW) [1, 2]. The platform consists of large 46-in. touchscreen or otherwise interactive displays running a web browser, a camera, a microphone and a speaker, currently deployed at four urban locations in England (Fig. 1a). The screens, two in Nottingham and two in London, England, are networked together via a central server. The networking allows users to see video streams of other users at remote locations and for local browser applications to share data.

The video content was a shortened (2 min) version of a film originally produced to accompany a resource pack 'Making Sense of Adult ADHD' that was produced in 2013 by Nottinghamshire Healthcare NHS Trust, aimed at educating patients and healthcare professionals about ADHD in adults (Fig. 1b). In the video, patients who had been treated by the Trust speak about their experiences of living with ADHD and the benefit of having a diagnosis. The game 'Attention Grabber' was developed from an initial proof-of-concept by the authors [3], then a commercial graphics design company and web designer were contracted to implement a polished version with attractive graphics and animations (Fig. 2). The game is based on a psychometric reaction time and impulse control test for ADHD with the addition of game elements. The adapted test presents stimuli on-screen for approximately 2 min, where players are instructed to watch a sequence of different fruit but to touch only one type, bananas, and ignore the rest. Scores are awarded as the game progresses dependant on reaction time and penalties are given for incorrect or missed selections. During the game, text feedback is provided to players across the top of the screen such as "Lightning!!

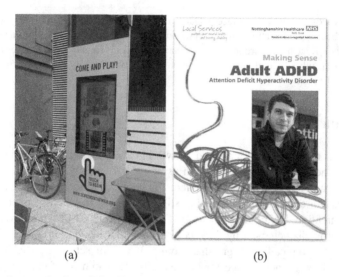

(a)   (b)

Fig. 1. (a) Screens in the wild (SitW) public display platform, photograph of one location (b) Resource pack 'making sense of adult ADHD', Nottinghamshire healthcare NHS trust.

(a)   (b)

Fig. 2. Design of attention grabber game (a) Final home page layout with high scores and webcam feeds at bottom (b) Example of game play on the touchscreen.

+1125", "Not bad +700", "Missed it! −200" or "Wrong fruit! −100". The player's score is compared to the location's high score at the end and the local high score is uploaded to the server to be shared amongst the four locations. Further work by the project team was carried out to fully integrate the game with the SitW platform.

Examples of awareness initiatives for mental health that use game elements are few [3], but where these have been implemented these have not been evaluated explicitly. In order to integrate evaluation into this application, four questions were embedded in the application: three questions (on a 4 point scale) before the video and one after. Data from game plays, video viewing and answers to the questions were captured on the SitW network server and subsequently analysed after the installation had run for 5 months. The technical design aspects of the installation will first be described in detail, including the testing process, followed by the results, analysis and discussion.

2 Technology and Data Capture Overview

2.1 The 'Screens in the Wild' Network

The 'Screens in the Wild' (SitW) Network is an output from research into Urban Screens and their potential applications for communities and culture [1, 2]. A novel feature of SitW is that it moves the state-of-the-art from standalone Urban Screens, as frequently seen in many city centre squares, into Networked Urban Screens where there is a shared interaction between screens and their content [4–6]. The SitW network consists of a set of urban screen nodes (currently numbering four), based in two cities in England, UK: Nottingham (Broadway cinema, BW, and New Art Exchange, contemporary visual arts space, NA) and London (Walthamstow 'The Mill' community space, WA, and Leytonstone public library, LE, later moved to Edgware Rd. 'Church Street neighbourhood centre', ER, due to refurbishment of LE during the period of the project). All the nodes featured a touchscreen attached to the glass of an outside window. NA was augmented by a touch-pad on the right of the screen due to the lack of transfer of touch through the glazing particular to that site.

The key functions of the SitW platform, Attention Grabber web-app and video application are now described. Table 1 details the components found at each screen node in the SitW Network (some available via GitHub [7]).

Figure 3 shows the system architecture for the SitW system. Conceptually, SitW consists of four layers: Screen Client Layer, Middleware Layer, Administration Layer and Data Store Layer. The SitW system architecture uses UNION, an off-the-shelf client/server infrastructure to provide real-time multi-user functionality for applications across the screen network, henceforth called the Interaction Server [8].

2.2 Attention Grabber Web App and Server Interactions

The game Attention Grabber [4] is a web app written in HTML5/JavaScript and designed to run in either the Chrome or Firefox browser (full-screen mode). Implemented on SitW, the app is based on a single URL, with all game play screens and their visual components and behaviours being programmatically hidden or revealed as required. From the user perspective, this generates a game play sequence of: the game, three initial questions (Q1, Q2 and Q3), an informational video about ADHD and a final question (Q4). Animated features to attract player to the home screen included flashing fruit and horizontally wiping text "Are you paying Attention?" etc.

Table 1. The components used in each in SitW screen node

A networked Windows PC (running Windows 7 Professional), which is remotely administered.
A 46" screen (mounted vertically in portrait mode) inside a partner venue, i.e. behind a glass window.
A mechanism to enable interaction with the screen, through the glass window (varies from node-to-node, according to the glass specification). Touch Foil or SitW component: Light-keypad (planned availability via GitHub [7]).
A camera and speaker (both available 'off-the-shelf') operate through the glass, making the installation interactive.
A secondary camera, recording interactions 24/7 to protect the system and to ensure ethical research principles.
Custom client software written to enable communication with a web-based schedule file, switching a program of applications, as required for one or more screens. This application also communicates with a server to share 'interaction events' between the screens in the network. Note: real-time manual override of the schedule is also possible (for demos, testing etc.), via a custom web interface (planned availability via GitHub [7]).
Software tools for securing the scheduled content from user-tampering and retaining browser 'kiosk-mode'.
A physical case to contain/protect the hardware elements.
Decals and visual branding around the screen - design varies between nodes.

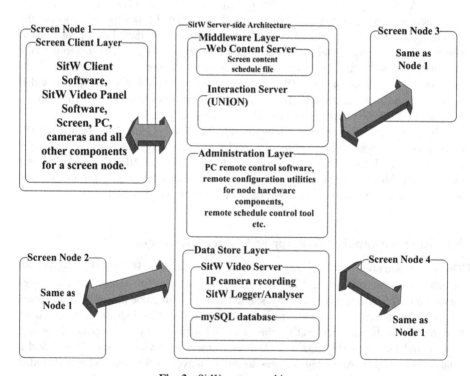

Fig. 3. SitW system architecture

SitW functionality was added to the original web app using the SitW Experience Template (planned availability via GitHub [7]). This is a single JavaScript file (sitw.js) that can be included in a JavaScript-based web app to provide UNION Interaction Server functionality [8]. Video playback in Attention Grabber was provided by the SitW component ScreenBase-Simple-Video (planned availability via GitHub), an embeddable version of the ScreenBase-Video-Player (available via GitHub). This provides a basic, customisable MP4 video player, with controls and layout suitable for use on a SitW screen node. This is implemented in JavaScript and is readily embeddable into other JavaScript-based web applications.

Location awareness of any instance of Attention Grabber, running on a specific SitW screen node, may be uniquely identified by a two-digit location code, passed as a parameter in the content URL. The SitW Screen Content Schedule File (hosted on the Web Content Server) provides the appropriate URL to each screen via the SitW Client Software. Therefore, each local instance of Attention Grabber knows where it is located when communicating with the Interaction Server.

Attention Grabber's awareness of screen location is also used to update the four game high scores, as displayed on the game interface. It can briefly be noted that Networked Urban Screens may have multiple modes within which content experiences are shared by the user. Two of the fundamental modes are: synchronous (the content is shared in real-time, similar to an online multi-player action game) or asynchronous (the content is shared 'as and when', similar to social networks). Attention Grabber is asynchronous in nature because it is possible to play the game (even competitively) on your own without players being simultaneously present at the other screens. The high score feature makes the experience shared, even though game play may occur in a chronologically staggered manner. The data sharing is made possible by the SitW Interaction Server. When each instance of Attention Grabber is loaded by the web browser, it connects to the Interaction Server and registers for relevant Interaction Events. It is provided with a 'snapshot' of the current high scores (for each of the four screens) and these are immediately displayed. If a user at any of the screens generates a score that exceeds the current local high score, this improved score is shared with all connected instances of Attention Grabber and they immediately update the appropriate high score. The high scores are saved by the Interaction Server as 'persistent attributes'. This means that they will survive not only a disconnection of all Attention Grabber clients from the Interaction Server, but also that they persist following a restart of the server. User responses to Attention Grabber's questions are stored in a database, using server-side PHP coding and MySQL. Table 2 show the fields captured to the database for each user session.

A session (or part session) is saved as a database record in one of the following situations: when any Attention Grabber 'Restart' button is pressed; any screen inactivity timeout is triggered (indicating that the user has abandoned at some stage); the 'Finish' button is pressed. Since abandonment timeouts can trigger the generation of a part-record, examples causes of part-records in the data might include: The game has been played, but the user has then abandoned before the questions and video; the user leaves at any point during the questions; the user leaves during video playback. Therefore, only a touch on Attention Grabber's 'Finish' button will generate a record that has all of the required data. Attention Grabber was also implemented with backend administration web page, password protected and available only to the research team.

Table 2. Data fields captured during each session

session_id	A unique identifier
dateAndTimeCreated	A timestamp for the session
sitw_screen_code	The two-digit location code for the SitW screen node
user_attention_score	The user's game score
question_1	
question_2	
question_3	
question_4	
video_interaction_from_user	A Boolean field, with a value of TRUE indicating that video playback was completed (as by a programmatic event) AND question 4 was answered

From this location, it was possible to review all collected questionnaire data and to download data as a CSV (Comma Separated Value) file.

2.3 Testing

Application usability and playability was tested in 3 phases. First, iterative usability and play testing on local PCs (involving the entire project team) was conducted from June 2014 when the graphics and web designer were contracted until handover back to the project team two months later. Most changes were made by the web design contractor and some additional refinements after handover. Changes included: modifying wording of questions, textual information on the game screen and names of graphical buttons; replacing all radio buttons with graphical buttons; addition of the "Restart" buttons and a 'Next' button on each question to allow confirmation of the selected answers to questions; adding a "Play Again" feature; reduced presentation period but increased visible/invisible ratio within period for each stimulus; adjustment of time-outs; adjustment of the score/penalty balance.

Second, field testing was conducted at the two Nottingham locations (BW and NA) using heuristic evaluation with two of the team at the same location separately (one playing, one noting errors) with a third member of the team monitoring the server, contactable by mobile phone to perform a remote reset in the case of errors. High score and question data upload to the server was also tested from each site.

Third, further field tests were conducted between the two Nottingham locations to test the transfer of high scores from one site to other after play (via the server). These tests involved the same three members of the project team through multiple plays at both locations and with the remote server monitor, all with mobile phones. It was also possible to check in an adhoc manner evidence of game plays by the public at the other sites by virtue of the high scores changing and to further check data collection on the server-side database of the question answers and score data.

Phase one iterative usability and play testing was completed over two months from June 2014. The second and third phases were conducted over one month with final testing one week before the official launch on 4th September 2014.

3 Results

Following the day of the launch, data collection continued for 5 months from 5th September 2014 to 4th Febuary 2015, with the application running and playable for 5 h a day in the morning (1½ h, 8:00–9:30), late afternoon (2½ h, 15:30–18:00) and evening (1 h, 20:00–21:00) except for location NA, which was accessible to users for 3 h a day (1 h on Sundays) due to shutters on the window at other times. Outside these times the platform was running other SitW applications. In addition one in London screen, LE, was moved to the ER location with a downtime of one month. At all locations there was a short break during the holiday period where the server was not being monitored and so applications were not deployed. This resulted in a maximum total playable period of 670 h over 134 days each for BW and WA, 369 h over 134 days for NA, 155 h over 31 days for LE and 310 h over 62 days for ER after the screen had been moved from LE.

Over the total playable time of 2174 h, a total of 781 plays were recorded after cleaning the data to remove duplicate database entries due to restarts/time-outs. On average a game was played every 2.78 h, or around two per day in the playable period. Of these 194 (25 %) plays included at least one question having been answered, the rest being game plays without any answers (and by implication no watching of the video). Also, from the total of 194, 142 players (73 %) answered question Q4 which implies that the video was also watched to the end. Table 3 shows the distribution of scores at the 5 locations showing there were few outliers (only in LE for 2.5SD and none for 3SD). Some variation in scores is apparent between sites. The highest mean and maximum scores were at BW. The lowest mean and max scores were at NA which is likely to have been a result of the different user interface (separate touch-pad).

Table 4 shows the results from the embedded questions after data cleaning. It can be seen from the answers to Q1 (N = 194) that 85 % players agreed playing the game had made them think about their attention span: 39 % rating 'a lot', 17 % 'some', 29 % 'a little' and 15 % 'not at all'. For Q2 (N = 174) 73 % of players knew something about ADHD: 32 % rating 'a lot', 24 % 'some', 17 % 'a little' and 27 % 'none at all'. For Q3 (N = 157) 71 % of players were aware of Adult ADHD: 41 % rating 'a lot', 17 % 'some', 13 % 'a little' and 29 % 'not at all'. For Q4 (N = 143) most (93 %) players agreed that their knowledge had increased from watching the video with 41 % rating 'a lot', 15 % 'some', 37 % 'a little' and 7 % 'not at all'.

Results were subsequently analysed using IBM SPSS software to investigate any statistical differences between locations and to test correlations with score. ANOVA tests on answers to Q1, Q2, Q3 and Q4 versus location showed significant differences (p < 0.05) for all locations. Post hoc tests showed these differences were mostly due to locations ER and NA however there were some other differences (e.g. at LE and the other locations) which are also suggested from looking the mean ratings in Table 4. Since location NA has a different (touch-pad) interface this may have been a factor but it is difficult to theorise much more since differences may have been due to a number of factors including other technical issues (especially since it was not possible to test the game at ER after the move), characteristics of the location (e.g. library versus cinema) or player population differences (e.g. age or other demographics).

Table 3. Score results from game plays, where embedded question(s) were also answered

Location	Mean	2.5SD	Mean + 2.5SD	Mean-2.5SD	Max	Min	N
All	3103	14784	17887	−11681	14395	−3600	194
BW(1)	7051	14441	21491	−7390	14395	−3100	75
LE(2)	−1107	8090	6983	−9196	8540	−3500	13
WA(3)	1530	12184	13714	−10654	13460	−3400	68
NA(4)	−1766	4030	2264	−5795	1760	−3600	26
ER(5)	2453	13263	15716	−10810	10125	−3200	12

Table 4. Results from the embedded questions

Question	Screen Location (Group number)	Rating scale, N(numerical rating)				Sub-total of N(1–4) responses	Mean rating
		A lot N (1)	Some N(2)	A little N(3)	Not/None at all N(4)		
Q1. Did playing the game make you think about your own attention span?	BW(1)	28	15	22	10	75	2.19
	LE(2)	6	2	0	5	13	2.31
	WA(3)	25	12	26	5	68	2.16
	NA(4)	15	4	4	3	26	1.81
	ER(5)	1	0	5	6	12	3.33
Q2. How much do you know about ADHD?	BW(1)	26	16	11	20	73	2.34
	LE(2)	8	2	3	0	13	1.62
	WA(3)	18	20	12	14	64	2.34
	NA(4)	4	3	3	12	22	3.05
	ER(5)	0	1	1	0	2	2.50
Q3. How aware are you that ADHD affects adults?	BW(1)	25	15	10	19	69	2.33
	LE(2)	8	0	0	3	11	1.82
	WA(3)	27	10	9	12	58	2.10
	NA(4)	4	1	0	12	17	3.18
	ER(5)	0	1	1	0	2	2.50
Q4. How much has the film increased your knowledge of ADHD?	BW(1)	26	13	23	2	64	2.02
	LE(2)	7	0	1	0	8	1.25
	WA(3)	25	8	14	8	55	2.09
	NA(4)	0	0	15	0	15	3.00
	ER(5)	0	1	0	0	1	2.00

Within-subject correlations between answers to questions were also investigated. This analysis proved more insightful since there was a strong positive correlation between answers to Q2 and Q3 (Pearson Correlation coefficient 0.811, $p < 0.001$) and between Q2 and Q4 (Pearson Correlation coefficient 0.516, $p < 0.001$) and moderate positive correlation between Q3 and Q4 ((Pearson Correlation coefficient 0.433, $p < 0.001$). These relationships were maintained for all location sub-groups (relevant for locations where there were enough answers to a question). Differences of ratings between Q2 and Q3 were investigated using paired samples t-tests but only one significant result was found with a mean difference Q2–Q3 of 0.24 at location WA ($p < 0.05$). Overall, knowledge of ADHD and awareness of Adult ADHD were similarly rated and positively correlated to increase in knowledge. Correlation of Q1 (and other Qs) with score was investigated but no relationship was found.

4   Discussion and Conclusions

The implementation of a mental health awareness vehicle using a browser based game and educational video was successfully realised within 3 months on an existing networked public displays platform, Screens in the Wild. The Attention Grabber game appeared to be stable and playable and the SitW platform performed well for the purpose of delivering the multimedia content and to facilitate a degree of connectedness between players, through the web-cam feeds and score sharing, although the impact of the latter on the study results was not investigated. We are not aware of any public health campaign that has attempted to gather data by the use of questions embedded in a urban screen multimedia application, at least in the domain of mental health. Nearly 800 plays were recorded in the 5-month period, indicating it is possible to engage the passing public with this approach.

Results indicate evidence of good public engagement with the application since 25 % of players who took the time to finish the game were prepared to answer the embedded questions afterwards, and most (73 %) of those who answered the first three questions immediately following the game also watched the video to the end and answered the final question to finish the experience. This shows it is possible to gather data even in an unsupervised setting once the audience is engaged, although it is not possible to say how much the game was responsible for this other that it provided an attractive means to initiate engagement. We cannot say much about the majority who played the game without answering the questions (e.g. was this due to multiple plays by the same player or did these players not wish to answer questions?) but it is also clear that the game was of interest on its own aside from the rest of the installation.

Responses to the embedded questions provide insights into prior knowledge of ADHD and the learning achieved through engagement with the application. The game was moderately successful in prompting people to think about their own attention span (with 39 % rating 'a lot'). We had not anticipated existing awareness of ADHD impacting into adulthood to be so high (with 41 % rating 'a lot'). Nevertheless, results indicate further increase in knowledge through this campaign since most (93 %) of the participants who progressed to the end of the video presentation, featuring adults who had been diagnosed with ADHD, agreed it had increased their knowledge. Therefore, when engaging with the entire content, Attention Grabber can be considered a successful approach to public health education and awareness. Differences across the locations in the answers to the embedded questions are not easy to explain and could be varied. Furthermore there was also no relationship found between the game scores and the question answers which was quite surprising, at least for Q1, although on the other hand being asked to 'think about' attention span is perhaps neutral with respect to performance and a different wording could have been used, in hindsight.

This limited ability to interpret results is one of the trade-offs from using technology in public where people are free to use it how they like and where information about individuals is not available to researchers (at least, without reviewing hours of webcam material to obtain visual clues e.g. multiple plays by the same person). Whilst further questions could have been added to gain information about individuals it would have increased the burden and time taken to complete the task, and public participants are free to walk away at any time if they become bored or just decide to carry on their day, going back to what they were doing before being attracted to the display. Other possible solutions could include spot surveys at the locations or inviting players to answer additional questions off-line (e.g. via a QR Code that players could follow to a web page via their mobile phone), but it is likely that either approach would only yield data for a small proportion of the sample.

Overall, our findings are promising in relation to the potential for utilising Networked Urban Screens for the purpose of public health awareness, specifically mental health awareness. This suggests merit in further research to develop both the methods for engagement and evaluation to add to this evidence.

Acknowledgments. For MC, LS and ZY the research reported in this paper was conducted though the NIHR MindTech Healthcare Technology Cooperative (www.mindtech.org.uk). The views expressed are those of the author(s) and not necessarily those of the NHS, the NIHR or the Department of Health. They wish to thank Caroline Falconer, also of MindTech, for advice on the statistical analysis. The SITW platform (www,screensinthewild.org), which was originally funded through EPSRC grant EP/I031413/1, is provided by HS, SN and Lei Ye at the Mixed Reality Lab. The authors acknowledge the graphic design work for Attention Grabber by Crocodile House, Nottingham, who also produced the condensed film, funding for which was raised from a prize awarded to AG and others for the Nottinghamshire Healthcare NHS Trust 'Making Sense' resource for Adult ADHD. Five Creative in Derby was contracted on the Attention Grabber web design.

References

1. Screens in the Wild, Accessed 16 February 2015. http://www.screensinthewild.org/
2. Schieck, A.F.G., Schndelbach, H., Motta, W., Behrens, M., North, S., Ye, L., Kostopoulou, E.: Screens in the wild: exploring the potential of networked urban screens for communities and culture. In: Proceedings of the International Symposium on Pervasive Displays (PerDis 2014), pp. 166–167. ACM, Copenhagen, Denmark (2014)

3. Craven, M.P., Young, Z. Simons, L., Schnädelbach, H., Gillott, A.: From snappyapp to screens in the wild: gamifying an attention hyperactivity deficit disorder continuous performance test for public engagement and awareness. In: 2014 International Conference on Interactive Technologies and Games (iTAG), pp. 36-42. IEEE Press, Nottingham, UK, 16-17 October 2014, ISBN 978-1-4799-6795-7/14. 10.1109/iTAG.2014.12

4. North, S., Schnädelbach, H., Fatah gen Schieck, A., Motta, W., Ye, L., Behrens, M., Kostopoulou, E.: Tension space analysis: exploring community requirements for networked urban screens. In: Kotzé, P., Marsden, G., Lindgaard, G., Wesson, J., Winckler, M. (eds.) Human-Computer Interaction – Interact 2013, 8118, pp. 81–98. Springer, Heidelberg, Germany (2013)

5. Davies, N., Langheinrich, M., José, R., Schmidt, A.: Open display networks a communications medium for the 21st century. IEEE Comput. **45**(5), 58–64 (2012). Open Display Networks a Communications Medium for the 21st Century

6. Memarovic, N., Langheinrich, M., Alt, F. The interacting places framework – conceptualizing public display applications that promote community interaction and place awareness. In: Proceedings of the International Symposium on Pervasive Displays (PerDis 2012), pp. 1–6. ACM, New York, USA (2012)

7. GitHub–SitW repository, Accessed 16 February 2015. https://github.com/screensinthewild

8. UNION Platform, Accessed 16 February 2015. http://www.unionplatform.com

An Investigation of Reward Systems in Human Computation Games

Dion Hoe-Lian Goh[(✉)], Ei Pa Pa Pe-Than, and Chei Sian Lee

Wee Kim Wee School of Communications and Information,
Nanyang Technological University, Singapore, Singapore
{ashlgoh, eil, leecs}@ntu.edu.sg

Abstract. Human Computation Games (HCGs) harness human intelligence to tackle computational problems. As in any game, a fundamental mechanism in a HCG is its reward system. In this paper, we investigate how virtual reward systems evoke perceptions of enjoyment in HCGs. Three mobile applications for location-based content sharing (named Track, Badge and Share) were developed for an experimental study. The Track version offered a points-based reward system for actions such as contribution of content. The Badge version offered different badges for collection while the Share version served as a control which did not have any virtual reward system. The experiment had a counterbalanced, within-subjects design. For each application, participants performed a series of tasks after which a questionnaire survey was administered. Results showed the Track and Badge applications were perceived to have more accurate and complete content than the control (Share) application. Further, participants reported being more engaged when using the former two applications.

Keywords: Human computation games · Reward systems · Points · Badges · Experiments · Output quality · Enjoyment

1 Introduction

Human Computation Games (HCGs) harness human intelligence to tackle computational problems. That is, while individuals engage in enjoyable HCG gameplay, they generate useful outputs as byproducts [8]. Put succinctly, HCGs are dual-purpose artifacts which generate computational outputs and offer entertainment at the same time. Hence they can be termed as games with a purpose (GWAPs) as defined by [22]. They could also represent a genre of computainment, a portmanteau of words computation and entertainment [8]. As such, enjoyment and computation are the most striking features of HCGs. This very characteristic indeed distinguishes HCGs from games for pure entertainment where enjoyment is considered to be the single most important goal [20].

HCGs leverage on the observation that people want to be entertained and games in general attract large numbers of players worldwide. Therefore, utilizing games is a promising way to motivate people to contribute their time and effort to a given computational endeavor. HCGs have been employed in a number of areas including image tagging, music annotation and ontology generation (e.g. [10, 22]). One well-known

© Springer International Publishing Switzerland 2015
M. Kurosu (Ed.): Human-Computer Interaction, Part II, HCII 2015, LNCS 9170, pp. 596–607, 2015.
DOI: 10.1007/978-3-319-20916-6_55

example is the ESP Game [22] in the context of image labeling, which is considered to be difficult for computers but easy for humans. Two randomly paired players on the Web are shown an image. The game requires a player to guess keywords which might be used by his/her partner to describe the given image. Players are rewarded points when their labels match. The ESP Game produces labels as byproducts of gameplay which can later be used to improve Web-based image search. Recently, HCGs have also been utilized in the mobile context, especially to garner location-based content. Indagator [13] incorporates gaming elements into content-sharing activities. Players can share and browse media rich location-based information, and earn points by rating and creating content. Using these points they can play mini-games, lay traps, and obtain treasure.

As in any game, a fundamental mechanism in a HCG is its virtual reward system [17]. Rewards translate a player's investments in terms of in time and effort spent in a game into a form that is quantifiable, comparable and communicable [9]. Rewards thus provide feedback to a player on his/her status within a game so that appropriate actions may be taken. As well, rewards allow a player to ascertain his/her performance against other players within a game. Put differently, rewards provide an enjoyable experience for individuals, motivating them to continue engaging in gameplay [23]. Two common types of virtual reward systems in games are points and badges [7]. Points represent a player's numeric score in a game and indicate achievement, progress, and/or wealth. Badges are awards that are non-numeric in nature. They indicate a player's status, and also mark the achievement of goals and in-game progress.

Despite the importance of virtual reward systems, there is little research in their use in HCGs. Due to the entertainment-output generation duality of HCGs [8], reward systems could signify gaming and/or output generation achievements, and hence could be perceived differently from entertainment-oriented games. In particular, since HCGs generate computational outputs, do players perceive reward systems differently when assessing output quality? This is important because if individuals do not perceive a HCG as generating useful outputs, its primary aim is rendered ineffective, leading to potential non-usage. More fundamentally, how do reward systems evoke perceptions of enjoyment in HCGs? Understanding enjoyment is important since this is a critical factor of sustained gameplay.

In the present study, we therefore aim to investigate the above two research questions. We first developed three applications: a mobile HCG that employs a point-based reward system, another mobile HCG that utilizes badges as rewards, and finally, a non-game-based mobile application to serve as a control. We then compare perceptions of the three applications in terms of enjoyment and output quality using frameworks derived from our prior work and extant literature.

2   Related Work

2.1   HCGs and Location-Based Content Sharing

HCGs are a genre of human computation system that is driven by entertainment experience cultivated from playing games [8]. In particular, HCGs are designed for people to perform computations that are typically trivial for humans, but challenging for computers such as knowledge creation tasks [22]. Recently, due to the mobility and accessibility afforded by mobile devices, HCGs have been implemented on the mobile platform. In particular, work has been done on creating HCGs for acquiring location-based content.

The Gopher Game [3] is an example HCG that facilitates geospatial content sharing through the performance of information creation tasks conducted by a game agent called a gopher. Players can either create a new gopher and assign tasks, or pick it up as they move around their physical world and help the gopher to complete its mission by supplying situated photographic and textual content, and earn game points for their good performance. Next, the Hidden View Game [15] gathers the latest information to keep maps and street views up-to-date. Players are shown a street view image and tasked to identify whether the given labels exist or not in the latest street view. Players earn game points based on the accuracy of their contributions and how quickly they accomplish the task.

In addition, HCG like PhotoCity [21] incentivizes players not only with points but also an ownership status that represents the player's accomplishment in the game. In particular, players of this game create images of real-world buildings at the positions anchored by flags on the map and earn game points for their relatively accurate contributions. Besides earning points, a player who contributes the most images of a building will eventually capture this building and his/her name appears under the castle icon.

2.2   HCGs and the Reward Systems

As the success and sustainability of HCGs is highly dependent on players' participation [22], it is critical that compelling rewards for human computation activities are provided. Prior research on entertainment-oriented games and information systems suggests that rewards are able to support ongoing users' engagement even if they do not enjoy the activity itself [23]. Accordingly, HCGs employ various forms of additional virtual rewards along with the intrinsic reward that players could experience from HCG play such as enjoyment [16].

One commonly used reward system is a point system that awards game points to various user behaviors [12]. In addition to being the most basic form of reward afforded by entertainment-oriented games [23], the point system has been shown to be effective in guiding users towards particular behaviors in various contexts such as enterprise social networking, peer-to-peer, and online learning communities [7]. As well, most location-based HCGs to date have been dominated by awarding points to players in exchange for their contributions of geospatial content.

An alternative approach to incentivize players which has received comparatively less attention in the HCG context is a badge system. Rather than signifying achievement as a single aggregate value (i.e., points), badges manifest a player's interest and experience because they are awarded for completing specific activities or clearly stated conditions and have associated visual representations [17]. Badges can therefore be seen as goals that players can strive for, and they also provide clear information about how far players have progressed towards the goal [2]. As people may escalate their behaviors when they get closer to the goal, badges may affect users' behaviors differently than points.

Although different virtual reward systems may have varying impacts on players' behaviors, no study to date, to the best of our knowledge, makes comparisons across these systems. Instead, prior studies in crowdsourcing environments have compared the relative effectiveness of virtual and financial rewards (e.g., [18]). Although influential, whether a particular virtual reward is more dominant than the other could not be observed in such studies. The present study therefore aims to examine the effectiveness of virtual reward systems for HCGs for location-based content sharing.

2.3 Perceived Enjoyment and Output Quality

Given that HCGs are built upon individuals' desire to be entertained while generating useful computations as byproducts of gameplay [22], enjoyment and output quality are two primary factors that determine the success of these games. As such, HCGs should be enjoyable for individuals to motivate them to generate more useful outputs. Enjoyment is also known to be the most important gratification obtained from playing games [20]. In media psychology literature, [19] contend that media enjoyment encompasses three dimensions, namely affect, cognition, and behavior. The affective dimension focuses on an individual's affective or emotional experiences, while the cognitive dimension centers on an individual's experiences gained through evaluative judgments in response to the media. The behavioral dimension focuses on individuals' behaviors when they are engrossed in the media.

In common with user-generated content applications, output is the noticeable aspect of HCGs, and hence perceived output quality is another important factor [11] that influences usage. Prior research on quality assessment of informational content suggests that output quality is a multi-faceted construct; hence, the use of multiple quality dimensions is necessary [16]. In particular, quality dimensions of accuracy, completeness, relevancy, and timeliness have been shown to be significant in affecting users' attitudes and perceptions of online information-oriented applications [1]. In order to examine the effectiveness of virtual reward systems for our mobile HCG, the present study analyzes whether players' perceived enjoyment and output quality differ between point and badge reward systems.

3 Methodology

3.1 Applications Developed for the Study

To address the research questions, we developed three mobile applications (named Track, Badge and Share) for an experimental study. The primary reason for developing our own applications for the study as opposed to using existing ones was that we would have better control over the look-and-feel of the interfaces.

All three applications had a similar purpose of supporting the contribution of location-based content. In particular, the three applications offered a map-based interface that indicated locations with content that could be accessed. In Fig. 1, such locations are indicated by a house icon. Figure 2 shows an example of content contributed by users. Other users are also able to review and/or rate these contributions.

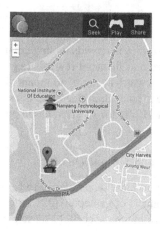

Fig. 1. Map-based interface for accessing location-based content

Fig. 2. Content contributed by users

Through the map-interface, new content can also be created, in which case, a form appears for users to complete.

Besides these common features, the Track version was a HCG that offered a points-based virtual reward system. Points were awarded based on actions such as contribution of content, reviews and ratings. The goal was to acquire as many points as possible, and this was encouraged via a leaderboard that ranked the top ten players (see Fig. 3). Through the points system and leaderboard, the Track HCG fostered the creation of location-based content.

Next, the Badge version was a HCG that encouraged users to contribute location-based content by offering different badges for collection. Each badge is associated with actions concerning creation, reviewing or rating of location-based content. Badges were displayed on users' publicly accessible profiles, encouraging them to collect as many as possible. Put differently, a user's collection of badges would

Fig. 3. The track HCG's leaderboard

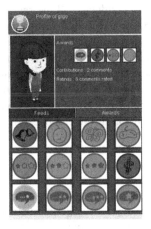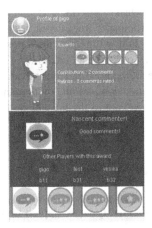

Fig. 4. The badge HCG's list of badges

reflect his/her reputation and status in the game. Figure 4 shows the badges available for collection, with the ones acquired by a user being highlighted. By selecting a particular badge, all users who have acquired it will be displayed.

Finally, the Share version was a non-game-based mobile application that served as a control. It did not have any reward system and offered the basic features for contributing and accessing location-based content described above. Users could access a page in Share that showed the number of contributions, comments and ratings performed. This information was made not available to other users.

3.2 Participants and Procedure

Sixty-seven participants (36 males and 31 females) with an average age of 25.84 were recruited from a local university for the present study. Most (74 %) had used social network applications and shared information using mobile devices. Among our participants, 47.8 % of them had a background in computer science, information technology or related disciplines, 38.8 % were from engineering disciplines, while the remainder were from disciplines such as arts, social sciences and business. Further, the majority of participants (61.2 %) were players of online games. Although a university-based sample does not reflect the entire population of potential HCG users, it may reasonably represent the population that is involved in online games. Prior studies have shown that university students can represent an important age demographic of overall online game players and mobile Internet users [24].

The study was an experiment which employed a within-subjects design where participants used all three applications (Track, Badge and Share). This experiment was also counterbalanced to reduce order effects. Here, participants were divided into subgroups with each performing a different combination of the applications. Additionally, participants performed a distractor task before using each application.

The experiment was held over a number of sessions, with each having a maximum of 10 participants. Consistency across sessions was ensured by using the same set of instructions and tasks. The same researchers also conducted all the sessions. For each application, participants were given a familiarization session in which they used it for practice tasks. Following this, they performed a series of tasks for about 15 min including view of content, creation of content, rating existing content and either viewing the leaderboard (for Track), badge list (for Badge) or their personal status (for Share). Upon task completion, participants completed a questionnaire that measured the constructs relevant to the present study, namely, perceived information quality and perceived enjoyment. These steps were repeated for all three applications.

3.3 Measures

All items in the questionnaire that were used to measure perceived enjoyment and perceived output quality were adapted from prior research (e.g., [6, 16]) Each item was measured along a 5-point Likert-type scale with 1 representing strong disagreement and 5 representing strong agreement. Prior to analyzing the data, principal component factor analysis with varimax rotation was used to test the validity of all the constructs in the study. Items that were highly loaded (0.5 and above) were retained in the analysis. Reliability analyses were then carried to ensure that items under each construct were interrelated.

Using the tripartite media enjoyment model proposed by [19], the present study assessed perceived enjoyment along three dimensions. Twelve items were utilized to measure perceived enjoyment, and were adapted from prior studies (e.g., [6]). As expected, three factors emerged from the factor analyses performed across participants' responses for the three applications. Good internal reliabilities were found for these three factors with Cronbach's alpha values of $.96_{Track}$, $.92_{Badge}$, and $.90_{Share}$ for affective, $.95_{Track}$, $.88_{Badge}$, and $.89_{Share}$ for cognitive, and $.92_{Track}$, $.91_{Badge}$, and $.91_{Share}$ for behavioral enjoyment. These factors are discussed as follows.

- **Affective:** Measures the extent to which the user perceives emotional experiences during gameplay.
- **Cognitive:** Measures the extent to which the user perceives favorable thoughts and beliefs about HCGs such as being worthy, effective, and interesting.
- **Behavioral:** Measures the extent to which the user perceives deep involvement in HCGs.

Output quality was operationalized as information quality since our applications generate location-based information outputs. This was assessed with twelve items adapted from [16]. Four factors were extracted from the factor analyses performed for the three applications. Again, all factors were found to have good internal reliabilities with a Cronbach's alpha values of $.84_{Track}$, $.88_{Badge}$, and $.89_{Share}$ for accuracy, $.88_{Track}$, $.86_{Badge}$, and $.89_{Share}$ for completeness, $.88_{Track}$, $.91_{Badge}$, and $.92_{Share}$ for relevancy, and $.84_{Track}$, $.82_{Badge}$, and $.84_{Share}$ for timeliness.

- **Accuracy:** Assesses the extent to which information generated is correct, reliable, and accurate.
- **Completeness:** Assesses the extent to which information generated contains sufficient details for one's needs.
- **Relevancy:** Assesses the extent to which information generated is appropriate, relevant, and useful.
- **Timeliness:** Assesses the extent to which information generated is current, timely, and up-to-date.

4 Results

Table 1 shows the means and standard deviations of participants' perceptions of the applications. One-way ANOVAs were performed to compare each variable across the three applications. Significant differences were found in two output quality variables (accuracy and completeness) and all enjoyment variables. Post hoc comparisons using Tukey's test were then conducted:

- **Accuracy:** Differences in perceptions of accuracy were found to be statistically significant [$F(2,198) = 5.47$, $p = .005$]. Post hoc tests indicated that participants perceived the Track and Badge applications as providing more accurate information than Share. Differences in perceptions between Track and Badge were non-significant.
- **Completeness:** A similar pattern of findings was found for perceptions of completeness [$F(2,198) = 5.42$, $p = .005$]. Specifically, Track and Badge were viewed similarly and both were rated higher than Share.
- **Affective enjoyment:** The differences between applications were again statistically significant in terms of perceptions of affective enjoyment [$F(2,198) = 11.96$, $p = .001$]. Post hoc tests showed that participants perceived the Track and Badge applications to provide higher levels of affective enjoyment than Share. There were no statistically significant differences in perceptions between Track and Badge.

Table 1. Means and standard deviations for perceptions of output quality and enjoyment (N = 67)

Variable	Application type mean (SD)		
	Track	Badge	Control
Accuracy*	3.40 (.64)	3.38 (.64)	3.10 (.75)
Completeness*	3.31 (.72)	3.25 (.71)	2.92 (.82)
Relevancy	3.44 (.72)	3.33 (.77)	3.23 (.72)
Timeliness	3.45 (.64)	3.36 (.63)	3.20 (.74)
Affective*	3.27 (.74)	3.48 (.66)	2.90 (.74)
Cognitive*	3.25 (.70)	3.61 (.72)	2.93 (.77)
Behavioral*	3.22 (.74)	3.21 (.81)	2.87 (.76)

*Statistically significant differences between the three applications at $p < 0.05$.

- **Cognitive enjoyment:** Participants perceived the applications as providing cognitive enjoyment differently [$F(2,198) = 14.47$, p = .001]. Here, both Track and Badge performed better than Share. Further, Badge was perceived to be more cognitively enjoyable than Track.
- **Behavioral enjoyment:** Perceptions of behavioral enjoyment displayed a similar pattern of findings as that of affective enjoyment [$F(2,198) = 4.49$, p = .012]. Both Track and Badge were viewed similarly and both were also rated higher than Share.

5   Discussion

This research advances the literature on virtual reward systems in HCGs by investigating their influence on perceptions of enjoyment and output quality. Our results suggest that reward systems enhance enjoyment emotionally, cognitively and behaviorally. HCGs also increase perceptions of the quality of outputs when compared to applications with no reward systems.

Unsurprisingly, our participants derived greater enjoyment from the applications that used either virtual reward system as opposed to the one without. This is in agreement with related research (e.g., [4, 7]) demonstrating that reward systems result in enjoyment during gameplay. Put differently, this augurs well for HCGs in that they have the potential to serve as motivators for harnessing human intelligence over non-game-based approaches for human computation.

From a more nuanced perspective, virtual reward systems enhance affective enjoyment as the actual and/or potential rewards and received evokes emotions [14] such as happiness, pleasure, excitement, frustration, to name a few. These emotions in turn translate into greater investment in terms of time and effort, and hence enjoyment. Reward systems also result in greater levels of cognitive enjoyment likely because players have to be more mentally involved when using a HCG. That is, a player not only has to perform computations, but also develop strategies to attain the various rewards offered by the HCG [2]. In the context of Track and Badge, this referred to performing computations to obtain points and badges respectively. Interestingly, our results show that between the two reward systems, participants using Badge derived more cognitive enjoyment than Track. Here, we surmise that acquiring badges required more strategizing because of the cognitive effort involved. In particular, players had to select the badge(s) they desired and then performed computations in a manner that could achieve their aims. Further, the collection of various types badges could have been more appealing than simply collecting points. Finally, reward systems enhance behavioral enjoyment when compared to non-game-based applications. This is expected since the incentives provided by the system would motivate players into deeper gameplay, resulting in greater immersion [5]. Specifically, players become motivated to engage in HCGs in the quest to acquire more points and badges.

In terms of output quality, virtual reward systems appear to positively influence our participants in terms of perceptions of accuracy and completeness. In particular, both Track and Badge performed similarly well, and outperformed Share (the non-game-based application). Put differently, the use of reward mechanisms conveyed the impression that the quality of outputs generated was better than applications that did not provide incentives. Here perhaps, participants felt that the effort put into earning points (Track) and badges (Badge) translated into higher quality outputs. In contrast, the Share application provided only statistics on the number of contributions made by a participant, and the lack of rewards could have perhaps translated into a perceived lack of indication of quality. Interestingly, relevance and timeliness was perceived similarly across all three applications. In the light of the significance of the other attributes of output quality, this may signify that relevancy and timeliness were viewed as comparatively less critical. First, relevancy is very much dependent on context of use [16], and the current study's context-free nature could have contributed to our results. Second, timeliness of information in the online context has been found to be under-emphasized by users [11] because of the assumption that online environments provide current information in the first place.

6 Conclusion

Our work was motivated by the fact that virtual reward systems are important in any game, including HCGs, and yet, there is little work in studying how users perceive them in terms of perceived enjoyment and output quality. We incorporated two common virtual reward systems (points and badges) into separate mobile HCGs and compared against a non-game-based mobile application for location-based content sharing. Our findings augur well for usage of HCGs, virtual reward systems, and their utility in generating computational outputs.

From a research standpoint, we investigated the enjoyment afforded by virtual reward systems through a nuanced perspective by investigating the phenomenon through three dimensions. Here, we found that virtual systems enhanced enjoyment of HCGs emotionally, cognitively and behaviorally. In addition, we treated perceived output quality as a multi-dimensional construct and found that virtual systems increased perceptions of accuracy and completeness.

From a practical perspective, our findings suggest the importance of virtual reward systems in motivating human computation, and more generally for crowdsourcing platforms that rely on the contributions of users. Developers of such applications should consider incorporating elements of virtual reward systems to attract users and sustain usage even if their intention is not to develop complete games. Thus for example, simply awarding points for contributions made, awarding badges or trophies for various tasks completed, and allowing these achievements to be shared within the community may be sufficient enough to engage users.

Although this research has yielded valuable insights, there are several limitations which give rise to possible new directions for future research. First, this research collected data from one human computation domain which is location-based content sharing. It is unclear whether our results will generalize to other computation contexts. Further, this study employed a very basic gameplay for content creation. It is possible that other game genres such as adventure and simulation, each of which presents specific gameplay styles comprising certain game elements, may influence perceptions of the virtual reward systems differently. For better generalizability, it would therefore be instructive to carry out investigations in different human computation domains using different HCG genres.

Acknowledgments. This work was partially supported by Nanyang Technological University Academic Research Fund (Tier 1), Grant No. RG64/14.

References

1. Alkhattabi, M., Neagu, D., Cullen, A.J.: Information quality framework for e-learning systems. Knowl. Manage. E-Learn: An Int. J. **2**, 340–362 (2010)
2. Antin, J., Churchill, E.F.: Badges in social media: a social psychological perspective. In: CHI 2011 Gamification Workshop. Vancouver, BC, Canada (2011)
3. Casey, S., Kirman, B., Rowland, D.: The gopher game: a social, mobile, locative game with user generated content and peer review. In: The International Conference on Advances in Computer Entertainment Technology, pp. 9–16. ACM Press, New York (2007)
4. Denny, P.: The effect of virtual achievements on student engagement. In: SIGCHI Conference on Human Factors in Computing Systems, pp. 763–772. ACM Press, New York (2013)
5. Ermi, L., Mäyrä, F.: Fundamental components of the gameplay experience: analysing immersion. In: DiGRA 2005 Conference: Changing Views: Worlds in Play, pp. 15–27 (2005)
6. Fang, X., Zhao, F.: Personality and enjoyment of computer game play. Comput. Ind. **6**, 342–349 (2010)
7. Farzan, R., DiMicco, J.M., Millen, D.R., Dugan, C., Geyer, W., Brownholtz, E.A.: Results from deploying a participation incentive mechanism within the enterprise. In: SIGCHI Conference on Human Factors in Computing Systems, pp. 563–572. ACM Press, New York (2008)
8. Goh, D.H., Ang, R.P., Lee, C.S., Chua, A.Y.K.: Fight or unite: investigating game genres for image tagging. J. Am. Soc. Inform. Sci. Technol. **62**, 1311–1324 (2011)
9. Jakobsson, M., Sotamaa, O.: Special issue - game reward systems. game studies. Int. J. Comput. Game Res. **11**(1) (2011). http://gamestudies.org/1101/articles/editorial_game_reward_systems

10. Krause, M., Takhtamysheva, A., Wittstock, M., Malaka, R.: Frontiers of a paradigm: exploring human computation with digital games. In: ACM SIGKDD Workshop on Human Computation, pp. 22–25. ACM Press, New York (2010)
11. Kim, B., Han, I.: The role of trust belief and its antecedents in a community-driven knowledge environment. J. Am. Soc. Inform. Sci. Technol. **60**, 1012–1026 (2009)
12. Konert, J., Gerwien, N., Göbel, S., Steinmetz, R.: Bringing game achievements and community achievements together. In: 7th European Conference on Game Based Learning (ECGBL), pp. 319–328 (2013)
13. Lee, C.S., Goh, D.H.-L., Chua, A.Y.K., Ang, R.P.: Indagator: investigating perceived gratifications of an application that blends mobile content sharing with gameplay. J. Am. Soc. Inform. Sci. Technol. **61**, 1244–1257 (2010)
14. Lee, H., Doh, Y.Y.: A study on the relationship between educational achievement and emotional engagement in a gameful interface for video lecture systems. In: Ubiquitous Virtual Reality (ISUVR), pp. 34–37. IEEE (2012)
15. Lee, J., Kim, J., Lee, K.: Hidden view game: designing human computation games to update maps and street views. In: 22nd International Conference on World Wide Web Companion, pp. 207–208 (2013)
16. Lee, Y.W., Strong, D.M., Kahn, B.K., Wang, R.Y.: AIMQ: a methodology for information quality assessment. Inf. Manage. **40**, 133–146 (2002)
17. Lewis, I., de Salas, K., Wells, L.: Features of achievement systems. In: 18th International Conference on Computer Games: AI, Animation, Mobile, Interactive Multimedia, Educational & Serious Games (CGAMES), pp. 66–73. IEEE (2013)
18. Massung, E., Coyle, D., Cater, K. F., Jay, M., Preist, C.: Using crowdsourcing to support pro-environmental community activism. In: SIGCHI Conference on Human Factors in Computing Systems, pp. 371–380. ACM Press, New York (2013)
19. Nabi, R.L., Krcmar, M.: Conceptualizing media enjoyment as attitude: implications for mass media effects research. Commun. Theor. **14**, 288–310 (2004)
20. Sweetser, P., Wyeth, P.: GameFlow: a model for evaluating player enjoyment in games. Comput. Entertain. **3**, 1–24 (2005)
21. Tuite, K., Snavely, N., Hsiao, D. Y., Tabing, N., Popovic, Z.: PhotoCity: training experts at large-scale image acquisition through a competitive game. In: SIGCHI Conference on Human Factors in Computing Systems, pp. 1383–1392. ACM Press, New York (2011)
22. von Ahn, L., Dabbish, L.: Designing games with a purpose. Commun. ACM **52**, 58–67 (2008)
23. Wang, H., Sun, C.T.: Game reward Systems: gaming experiences and social meanings. In: DiGRA 2011 Conference: Think Design Play, pp. 1–12 (2011)
24. Wu, J., Liu, D.: The effects of trust and enjoyment on intention to play online games. J. Electron. Commer. Res. **8**, 128–140 (2007)

Is Gamification Effective
in Motivating Exercise?

Dion Hoe-Lian Goh[1(✉)] and Khasfariyati Razikin[1,2]

[1] Wee Kim Wee School of Communications and Information, Nanyang
Technological University, Singapore, Singapore
{ashlgoh, khas0003}@ntu.edu.sg
[2] SAP Research and Innovation Singapore, SAP Asia Pte Ltd,
Singapore, Singapore

Abstract. Despite the benefits of exercise, many individuals lack the motivation to integrate it into their daily lives. Recently, there has been a growing interest in the use of game principles in non-game contexts to make an activity that is perceived to be challenging, tedious or boring more enjoyable. With increased enjoyment through the infusion of game elements, it is expected that individuals will be more motivated to partake in the activity. Given this backdrop, the present study seeks to ascertain the utility of gamification for promoting exercise among individuals. We used Fitocracy as the gamification platform. Our results suggest that gamification improves not only attitudes towards and enjoyment of exercise but also shapes behavior in terms of increase in exercise activity. These findings augur well for gamification platforms and their usefulness in motivating exercise among individuals. Finally, our work suggests design implications for applications that aim to gamify exercise.

Keywords: Gamification · Enjoyment · Social support · Exercise

1 Introduction

Exercise is one of the best ways to sustain an individual's physical and mental well-being. Multiple studies have shown that regular exercise can reduce many health risks and diseases such as cardiovascular disease [26], diabetes mellitus [16], hypertension [25], osteoporosis [7], and obesity [12]. Despite these benefits many individuals lack the motivation to integrate regular exercise into their lives as some may perceive that such activities are less enjoyable and tiring compared to sedentary activities [30]. As well, lack of time and lack of social support have been cited as reasons [33]. Because of the risks involved in physical inactivity, there is a need to devise innovative solutions to motivate individuals to exercise.

Research has shown that enjoyment plays an important role in promoting exercise, and may be manifested as positive feelings such as fun and pleasure [3]. Enjoyment of the exercise has been found to have a strong relationship to exercise participation [9, 35] as it is a commonly cited reason for engaging in exercise. Additionally, there is also a body of literature that suggests the relationship between social support and level of

© Springer International Publishing Switzerland 2015
M. Kurosu (Ed.): Human-Computer Interaction, Part II, HCII 2015, LNCS 9170, pp. 608–617, 2015.
DOI: 10.1007/978-3-319-20916-6_56

exercise. For example, the positive emotions derived from social interaction reinforce the positive experience of exercise, leading to further activity [10].

More recently, there has been a growing interest in the use of game principles in non-game contexts with the aim to increase user engagement and enjoyment [8]. Known as "gamification", this idea seeks to make an activity that is perceived to be challenging, tedious or boring more enjoyable through the infusing of game elements. With increased enjoyment, it is expected that individuals will be more motivated to partake in the activity.

The current research landscape has focused on the application of the integration of game principles to motivate individuals to start exercising. These studies have focused on design of applications through the inclusion of game principles and social support [e.g. 17, 22]. Another thread of research has focused on immersive exergames that involves the use of human kinetics to interact with the game elements as a way to increase the player's energy expenditure. Despite this promising approach, there is mixed evidence surrounding the resulting energy expenditure and intensity of the activities compared to traditional exercise [36]. Further, little is known about the effectiveness of the gamification applications in motivating individuals to exercise. Given this backdrop, the present study seeks to ascertain the utility of gamification for promoting exercise among individuals.

This paper will be organized as follows. The next section will focus on related work. The following section will highlight the method employed in this work. This will be followed by presentation of the results. This paper will close with a discussion of the results as well as concluding thoughts on this work.

2   Related Work

Exercise-related applications with gamification features adopting game principles as part of the players' exercise activities. In these applications, users have the flexibility of selecting any type of traditional exercise that they would like to do and log the exercise that they have done. Users are rewarded with incentives such as points and badges. In this process, activities with game principles are entwined [4]. The social network of users in these applications also plays an important role in motivating the users to engage in exercise. Other users provide encouragement and advice to the user [17]. By fusing game principles with the availability of social support from other players, users would supposedly be motivated to exercise.

Rewards as well as social support are common features that have been integrated in gamified applications. The main aim of including rewards is to incentivize users' effort that is embodied in points and badges [37]. Points provide a form of feedback to users of their performance in terms of effort and intensity put into the exercise [21]. For instance, more points are awarded to them for engaging in exercise longer, increasing the number of repetitions or putting more effort into the exercise. Badges are another form of reward that function as a status affirming, source of reputation, and achieving a goal [2]. In terms of social support, users are encouraged to post and share their activities as a form of accountability and motivation [23]. Others in the social network are able to "like" the posts and contribute to comments as way of encouraging the users and sharing information [34].

Enjoyment for motivating exercise in gamified applications is brought about and enhanced through the presence of the game principles. It has been identified in prior studies to have a strong correlation with exercise [9] and it is important leverage on it to motivate exercise [14]. This is because enjoyment is considered to be a more proximal and is seen to be a tangible outcome of exercising compared to other factors. It is an affective outcome of exercising during which endorphins are released to improve the individual's mood and is easily experienced by individuals as an after effect of exercising. As a consequence, enjoyment could alter an individual's perception of the actual effort put into exercise [e.g. 1]. Additionally, it could push the individual to exert more effort to the activity [28]. At the same time, it leads to the intention to undertake the activity in the future that may lead to sustain the engagement in exercise [35]. In the long run, exercise provides the psychological and sociological benefits in addition to the physiological benefits.

Social support is also a feature in gamified applications that could improve the effectiveness in motivating exercise. In general, social support refers to the way social relationships help to buffer stress on health and well-being [5]. Studies have highlighted that social support is related to the motivation to exercise. It has been suggested that social support provides the initial motivation in undertaking the exercise activity [11]. Further, it has been observed to have positive correlations with sustained exercise engagement [6]. Social support in motivating exercise could be examined in several aspects. Appraisal support is a type of social support gained from the social interactions in the network of users, and it provides a sense of encouragement for them. This is because the platform enables them to share their struggles with others who may be facing the same issues as them [27]. This support provides a sense of reinforcement to the individual in maintaining their health. Information provision is another type of social support where exercise-related information is provided by others in the social network. Users no longer rely solely on health-related professionals to seek health-related information as they can now also seek this from others who have similar issues online [23, 31]. Put differently, receiving information from others in the social network would improve users' knowledge and increase their motivation to exercise.

3   Methodology

Given the objective of this paper, we employed a pre-test/post-test experimental design to determine the effects of gamification on physical exercise. This approach takes into account users' perceptions before the intervention and after the intervention to enable us to examine the differences in their perception of physical exercise with respect to the influence of the gamification and social support features.

Prior to the study, participants were asked to complete a questionnaire survey eliciting their exercise habits in terms of the type of exercise and frequency they engaged in them, their attitudes and their level of enjoyment of the exercises they performed. They also completed questions related to their demographic information. Next, participants were introduced to Fitocracy where its gamification features were presented. They were then asked to use the platform as part of their exercise routine for a month. Thereafter, a similar questionnaire survey was administered to elicit participants' exercise habits, attitudes and level of enjoyment.

The measures for attitude were adopted from the Exercise Motivations Inventory [20]. This 44-items measure a diverse set of reasons for engaging in exercise activities. The reasons that could be elicited from the scale include stress management, weight management, recreation, social recognition, enjoyment, appearance, ill-health avoidance, competition, fitness and health pressures. The measures for habit were based on the types of exercise that the participants did as well as the frequency of engaging in the exercises. The measures for level of enjoyment were adopted from Physical Activity Enjoyment Scales (PACES) [18]. This 18-items measure the extent an individual enjoys engaging in any physical exercise, regardless if it was done for exercise or for sports.

As mentioned previously, we used Fitocracy (http://fitocracy.com) as the gamification platform for this study. Fitocracy may be characterized as an online social network that combines gamification elements to motivate people to improve their fitness. In Fitocracy, users log their exercise activity (Fig. 1) and points are awarded based on the benefits of each activity that users engage it. Users may level up once they reach certain point threshold levels (Fig. 2). To add an element of competition, users are also ranked in a leaderboard based on points earned (Fig. 3). Fitocracy also offers social networking features that allow users to follow others, view and comment on their exercise activities and join special interest groups. Launched in 2011, the site reached 1 million users in 2013 and has garnered awards and recognition for promoting health and fitness online. Given its popularity, Fitocracy is thus an appropriate platform for studying the influence of gamification on exercise activity.

In total, 100 participants comprising 48 males and 52 females with an average age of 28 years were recruited. Participants with Computer Science and IT training made up the bulk of the participants (47 %) in addition to those educated in life and health sciences as well as healthcare (19 %). The remainder of the participants had engineering, arts, humanities and social sciences, hospitality and tourism, business, advertising, design and media and education backgrounds. Web sites were the main

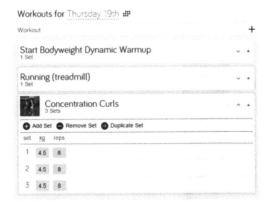

Fig. 1. Logging exercise activities in Fitocracy

source for the participants to find health and fitness information (79 %). Additionally, they used various social media platforms for information sharing on health and fitness. All of the participants were concerned with their health and fitness, but did not engage in the activity regularly. At the start of the study, most of the participants exercised at least once a week, performing activities such as walking, jogging and swimming.

4 Results

Participants' exercise attitudes, enjoyment and habits were measured before and after the study. The differences of their perceptions towards exercise were examined using paired sample t-tests. At the same time, the participants' comments corroborated with the statistical findings. Here, they shared their opinions on the game principles in motivating them to exercise after using Fitocracy for a month.

Fig. 2. Levelling up to a new level after reaching a milestone

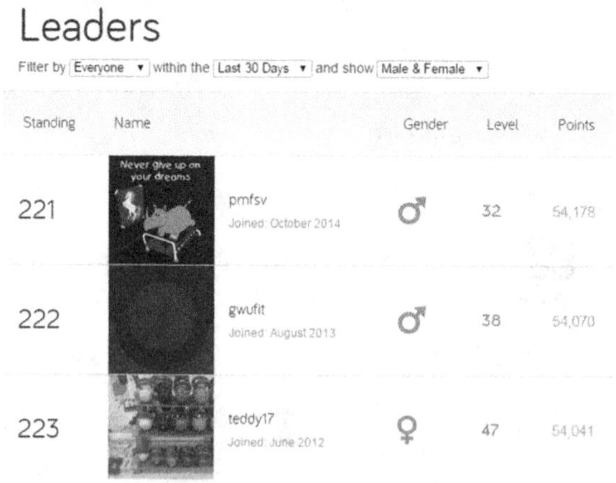

Leaders

Filter by Everyone ▼ within the Last 30 Days ▼ and show Male & Female ▼

Standing	Name		Gender	Level	Points
221		pmfsv Joined: October 2014	♂	32	54,178
222		gwufit Joined: August 2013	♂	38	54,070
223		teddy17 Joined: June 2012	♀	47	54,041

Fig. 3. Ranking users in leaderboard

Overall, participants' attitudes towards exercise changed during the study. A paired sample t-test was conducted to determine the differences in their attitude towards exercising. It yielded a significant difference for prior to the study ($M = 107.56$, $SD = 16.21$) and after the study ($M = 114.99$, $SD = 15.72$); $t (99) = -4.89$, $p < 0.001$. This highlighted that the participants significantly improved their attitude towards exercise after using Fitocracy.

As for enjoyment, the participants shared that they enjoyed exercising. After using Fitocracy for a month, their perception towards enjoying exercise improved as determined through another paired sample t-test. The test showed significant differences in exercise enjoyment prior to the study ($M = 60.93$, $SD = 9.37$) and after the study ($M = 64.37$, $SD = 10.20$); $t (99) = -3.12$, $p < 0.001$. This result thus shows that participants enjoyed exercising significantly after using Fitocracy than before.

Finally participants improved their exercise habits by increasing the length of time engaged in exercise. A paired sample t-test was conducted to determine the difference in the time engaged in exercise prior to the study ($M = 49.28$ min, $SD = 10.95$) and after the study ($M = 53.26$ min, $SD = 14.15$) and it showed significant difference with $t (99) = -3.81$, $p < 0.001$. Put differently, as a result of using Fitocracy, there was a significant increase in the time spent engaging in exercising as compared to before using the application.

Qualitative comments obtained from participants after the experimental study also corroborated with our statistical findings. In particular, participants reported liking the ability to follow other Fitocracy users to track their progress for either inspiration or competition. One sentiment shared by a participant was that "*the leveling system and social aspect motivates me and push me to do more exercise*". In other words, the gamification features enhanced participants' enjoyment and the social support from other users motivated them to engage in exercise frequently.

With respect to enjoyment, participants found the gamification features in Fitocracy made exercising fun and enjoyable for them. These features motivated them continue engaging in exercise on a regular basis. A participant highlighted that "*the leveling up system seems to be a good way to motivate and encourage regular exercise (like playing a game).*" The points system that works in tandem with the levels feature provided a sense of meaning for participants in terms of the effort put in during the exercise activity. As points in Fitocracy are awarded based on the effort and the intensity that they had put in during the exercise session, it serves as a form feedback of their performance. Similarly, users are awarded badges when they reach a new level and these are displayed on their feeds as a form of recognition for the effort that they had put into their exercise. In sum, providing feedback and recognition of the participants' effort motivated them to improve themselves further.

In addition, participants were able to appreciate the support from other users in the Fitocracy network of users. Particularly, they shared that were able to find information about various topics that could improve their understanding on health and fitness. This form of informational support could further improve their motivation to exercise. This was shared by a participant: "*Fitocracy is a motivating website and is a bridge between the health and fitness community and health and fitness information seekers. It is a useful website for health and fitness information seekers.*" Another type of social support, appraisal support, was also found to be motivating for participants. One of them commented that "*I can take a look around my buddies' activities and follow their progress.*" In other words, being able to follow their friends' progress is an appraisal of participants' own progress, and this could be motivating for them.

Despite the integration of gamification features as a way to increase the motivation to exercise, there was a group of participants who felt that the competition embodied in the gamification features were demotivating to them. One participant shared that low scores were demotivating, "*Sometimes, if you have a constantly low score, motivation will fade away.*" For these participants, they points that they had scored compared with the rest of the users could not propel them to engage in exercising more frequently. This may provide a hint that competition between users may not be universally appealing and alternative ways of providing them with the motivation for engaging in exercise may be needed.

In summary, using Fitocracy for a month yielded significant differences in participants' attitudes, enjoyment and habits towards exercising. These findings are further substantiated through the qualitative comments provided by the participants. We found that the participants felt that the gamification features enhanced their enjoyment and provided a supportive environment that motivated them to engage in exercise. However, there were also those who felt that they were gamification features overemphasized the competitive aspect. This caused them to feel demotivated by the scores they had achieved.

5 Discussion and Conclusion

This paper examined the its influence of gamification on users' perceptions of exercise and actual exercise behavior. We asked participants to use Fitocracy, an application with gamification features that aims to encourage exercise, for a month. Their attitudes and habits towards exercise as well as perception of enjoyment were elicited at the start and at the end of the study. Our results suggest that gamification improves not only attitudes towards, and enjoyment of exercise but also shapes behavior in terms of increase in exercise activity. These findings augur well for gamification platforms and their usefulness in motivating exercise among individuals.

Based on our findings, we propose three design implications for applications that aim to gamify exercise. First, the results indicate that gamification features are effective in motivating individuals to exercise. This corroborates with other studies that had been done on gamifying exercise [e.g. 3, 22]. In order to do so, the activities associated with exercise are entwined with the game principles [4], and these principles have to be relevant to the context of use [29]. As noted above, points provide a form of feedback of the users' performance of the exercise undertaken. The information provided has to be relevant to the context and understood by the users. Similarly, the badges that are awarded when a milestone is reached have to be relevant to the context as well. By doing so, users would be more likely to continue engaging in exercise at their own volition.

Second, the outcome of our study suggests that social support features are essential in motivating individuals to exercise. Hence, it is important to include such features in gamified applications. There are a number of features that could be considered. One type of social support feature would promote appraisals of users' efforts by others in the social network [23]. For example giving "props" and commenting on a user's workout or status in Fitocracy would provide encouragement to the user. Similarly, informational support facilities could be made available for players to share or seek exercise related information. Here, status updates and comments are two such examples where players could post their workout, share relevant information and solicit advice from other players [27]. Another form of support would be a repository of exercise-related articles that could add to the players' body of knowledge and further propel them to improve their exercise habits.

Finally, not all players may favor the competitive aspect that is often part of gamification features. This could be due to the different types of needs that such users would have. For instance, users with a high need for achievement might find the competitive aspect found in gamification features to be more appealing that those with a low need for achievement [13]. Furthermore, the competitive aspect may be taken too far by users and bring about negative feelings [31]. For such cases, collaborative gamification features could be included to reduce this tension. A collaborative feature would encourage players to work together and focus less on the competition between players. This would include group challenges where two to four players come together to complete a task [e.g. 19].

There are limitations to this work that warrant further investigation. One limitation is that there was no control group used in the experiment to establish the actual effects of gamification on the motivational behavior for exercising [15]. Future work may seek to compare between a gamified application and a non-gamified application between two groups of users [e.g. 37]. Another limitation is that not all of the participants found the competitive elements to be motivating. This perception of gamification as being competitive is attributed to users' individual differences. Future work may propose a personalized approach to determine features that are appealing to both competitive and non-competitive users [e.g. 24].

Acknowledgements. The authors wish to thank Maung Kyaw Zin Ohn Maung and Htet Htet Aung for their help in collecting the data for this study.

References

1. Acevedo, E.O., Rinehardt, K.F., Kraemer, R.R.: Perceived exertion and affect at varying intensities of running. Res. Q. Exer. Sport **65**, 372–376 (1994)
2. Antin, J., Churchill, E.F.: Badges in social media: a social psychological perspective. In: CHI 2011 Gamification Workshop Proceedings. ACM (2011)
3. Baranowski, T., Cullen, K.W., Nicklas, T., Thompson, D., Baranowski, J.: Are current health behavioral change models helpful in guiding prevention of weight gain efforts? Obes. Res. **11**, 23S–43S (2003)
4. Campbell, T., Ngo, B., Fogarty, J.: Design principles in everyday fitness applications. In: ACM Conference on Computer Supported Cooperative Work, pp. 249–252. ACM (2008)
5. Cohen, S., Hoberman, H.M.: Positive events and social supports as buffers of life change stress. J. Appl. Soc. Psychol. **13**, 99–125 (1983)

6. Courneya, K.S., McAuley, E.: Cognitive mediators of the social influence-exercise adherence relationship: a test of the theory of planned behavior. J. Behav. Med. **18**, 499–515 (1995)

7. Dalsky, G.P., Stocke, K.S., Ehsani, A.A., Slatopolsky, E., Lee, W.C., Birge, S.J.: Weight-bearing exercise training and lumbar bone mineral content in postmenopausal women. Ann. Int. Med. **108**, 824–828 (1988)

8. Deterding, S., Sicart, M., Nacke, L., O'Hara, K., Dixon, D.: Gamification. using game-design elements in non-gaming contexts. In: 2011 Annual Conference Extended Abstracts on Human Factors in Computing Systems, pp. 2425–2428. ACM (2011)

9. Dishman, R.K., Motl, R.W., Saunders, R., Felton, G., Ward, D.S., Dowda, M., Pate, R.R.: Enjoyment mediates effects of a school-based physical-activity intervention. Med. Sci. Sport Exer. **37**, 478–487 (2005)

10. Estabrooks, P.A., Bradshaw, M., Dzewaltowski, D.A., Smith-Ray, R.L.: Determining the impact of Walk Kansas: applying a team-building approach to community physical activity promotion. Ann. Behav. Med. **36**, 1–12 (2008)

11. Eyler, A.A., Brownson, R.C., Donatelle, R.J., King, A.C., Brown, D., Sallis, J.F.: Physical activity social support and middle-and older-aged minority women: results from a US survey. Soc. Sci. Med. **49**, 781–789 (1999)

12. Ford, E.S., Kohl, H.W., Mokdad, A.H., Ajani, U.A.: Sedentary behavior, physical activity, and the metabolic syndrome among US adults. Obes. Res. **13**, 608–614 (2005)

13. Goh, D.H., Lee, C.S.: Perceptions, quality and motivational needs in image tagging human computation games. J. Inf. Sci. **37**, 515–531 (2011)

14. Hagberg, L.A., Lindahl, B., Nyberg, L., Hellénius, M.-L.: Importance of enjoyment when promoting physical exercise. Scand. J. Med. Sci. Sport **19**, 740–747 (2009)

15. Hamari, J., Koivisto, J., Sarsa, H.: Does gamification work?–A literature review of empirical studies on gamification. In: 2014 47th Hawaii International Conference on System Sciences (HICSS), pp. 3025–3034. IEEE, California (2014)

16. Helmerich, S.P., Ragland, D.R., Leung, R.W.: Physical activity and reduced occurrence of non-insulin-dependent diabetes mellitus. New Engl. J. Med. **325**, 147–152 (1991)

17. Kamal, N., Fels, S., McGrenere, J., Nance, K.: Helping me helping you: designing to influence health behaviour through social connections. In: Kotzé, P., Marsden, G., Lindgaard, G., Wesson, J., Winckler, M. (eds.) INTERACT 2013, Part III. LNCS, vol. 8119, pp. 708–725. Springer, Heidelberg (2013)

18. Kendzierski, D., DeCarlo, K.J.: Physical activity enjoyment scale. J. Sport Exer. Psychol. **13**, 50–64 (1991)

19. Lin, J.J., Mamykina, L., Lindtner, S., Delajoux, G., Strub, H.B.: Fish'n'steps: encouraging physical activity with an interactive computer game. In: Ubicomp 2006, pp. 261–278. Springer-Verlag (2006)

20. Markland, D., Hardy, L.: The Exercise motivations inventory: preliminary development and validity of a measure of individuals' reasons for participation in regular physical exercise. Pers. Indiv. Differ. **15**, 289–296 (1993)

21. Mekler, E.D., Brühlmann, F., Opwis, K., Tuch, A.N.: Disassembling gamification: the effects of points and meaning on user motivation and performance. In: CHI 2013 Extended Abstracts on Human Factors in Computing Systems, pp. 1137–1142. ACM, New York (2013)

22. Munson, S.A., Consolvo, S.: Exploring goal-setting, rewards, self-monitoring, and sharing to motivate physical activity. In: 6th International Conference on Pervasive Computing Technologies for Healthcare (PervasiveHealth) 2012, pp. 25–32. IEEE (2012)

23. Newman, M.W., Lauterbach, D., Munson, S.A., Resnick, P., Morris, M.E.: It's not that i don't have problems, i'm just not putting them on facebook: challenges and opportunities in using online social networks for health. ACM 2011 Conference on Computer Supported Cooperative Work, pp. 341–350. ACM (2011)

24. Orji, R., Mandryk, R.L., Vassileva, J., Gerling, K.M.: Tailoring persuasive health games to gamer type. In: SIGCHI Conference on Human Factors in Computing Systems, pp. 2467–2476. ACM (2013)

25. Paffenbarger, R.S., Jung, D.L., Leung, R.W., Hyde, R.T.: Physical activity and hypertension: an epidemiological view. Ann. Med. 23, 319–327 (1991)

26. Paffenbarger, R.S., Wing, A.L., Hyde, T.R.: Physical activity as an index of heart attack risk in college alumni. Am. J. Epidemiol. 108, 161–175 (1978)

27. Preece, J.: Empathic communities: reaching out across the Web. Interactions 5, 32–43 (1998)

28. Raedeke, T.D.: The relationship between enjoyment and affective responses to exercise. J. Appl. Sport Psychol. 19, 105–115 (2007)

29. Richards, C., Thompson, C.W., Graham, N.: Beyond designing for motivation: the importance of context in gamification. In: First ACM SIGCHI Annual Symposium on Computer-Human Interaction in Play, pp. 217–226. ACM, New York

30. Salmon, J., Owen, N., Crawford, D., Bauman, A., Sallis, J.F.: Physical activity and sedentary behavior: a population-based study of barriers, enjoyment, and preference. Health Psychol. 22, 178 (2003)

31. Toscos, T., Consolvo, S., McDonald, D.W.: Barriers to physical activity: a study of self-revelation in an online community. J. Med. Syst. 35, 1225–1242 (2011)

32. Toscos, T., Faber, A., Connelly, K., Upoma, A.M.: Encouraging physical activity in teens: can technology help reduce barriers to physical activity in adolescent girls? In: 2008 2nd International Conference on Pervasive Computing Technologies for Healthcare, Pervasive Health 2008, pp. 218–221. IEEE (2008)

33. Uchino, B.N.: Social support and health: a review of physiological processes potentially underlying links to disease outcomes. J. Behav. Med. 29, 377–387 (2006)

34. Van Kleek, M., Smith, D.A., Hall, W., Shadbolt, N.R.: The crowd keeps me in shape: social psychology and the present and future of health social machines. In: 22nd International Conference on World Wide Web Companion, pp. 927–932. ACM (2013)

35. Wankel, L.M.: The importance of enjoyment to adherence and pyschological benefits from physical activity. Int. J. Sport Psychol. 24, 151–169 (1993)

36. Warburton, D.E.R., Bredin, S.S.D., Horita, L.T.L., Zbogar, D., Scott, J.M., Esch, B.T.A., Rhodes, R.E.: The health benefits of interactive video game exercise. Appl. Physiol. Nutr. Metab. 32, 655–663 (2007)

37. Zuckerman, O., Gal-Oz, A.: Deconstructing gamification: evaluating the effectiveness of continuous measurement, virtual rewards, and social comparison for promoting physical activity. Pers. Ubiquit. Comput. 18, 1705–1719 (2014)

'Blind Faith'. An Experiment with Narrative Agency in Game Design

Deb Polson[⊠] and Vidhi Shah

Queensland University of Technology, Musk Avenue, Kelvin Grove,
Queensland 4079, Australia
{d.polson,vidhi.lalitshah}@qut.edu.au

Abstract. This paper reports on the current field of narrative-based game design through case study analysis with a particular focus on balancing high narrative agency with low production resources.

Keywords: Game design · Narrative agency · Design-based research · Case study analysis · Context review · Aesthetics · Mechanics · Dynamics

1 Introduction

Traditional narrative devices such as cliff-hangers, plot twists, character redemption, flashbacks and forwards in entertainment media have for a long time been exclusively associated with television and cinema. More recently, game designers have adopted these devices, but with varying levels of success. In 2011 Grand Theft Auto 5 was pitched as the "most ambitious game Rockstar has yet created", carving out "a bold new direction in open-world freedom... (and) storytelling" [1]. Even more pertinently, Heavy Rain was promoted as an "evolving psychological thriller filled with innumerable twists and turns, where choices and actions can result in dramatic consequences on the story" [2].

Designers of such dynamic game narratives will typically focus on producing a cinematic story world where players can respond intelligently to various scenarios and explicitly recognise the impact of their decisions on character development and plot progression. Providing the player with a high level of narrative agency typically requires a number of different possible endings, or a very intelligent system that allows players to actually experience the narrative world from within. As a result, only large commercial game studios have been able to raise the capital required to support the production of narrative worlds comparable to common cinematic experiences. However, regardless of substantial investments in technology and asset production, fans and critics discussing the narrative aspects of these games remain unconvinced [3].

On the contrary, independent (Indie) games are increasingly gaining respect both critically and commercially for recently producing innovative and diverse narrative-based games. Indie games are "usually produced by a small group, if not a single individual, in charge of designing, developing, and releasing the game" [4]. Telltale Games is an indie company that has recently experienced great growth due to the successful release in 2012 of *The Waking Dead* game, which won over ninety

M. Kurosu (Ed.): Human-Computer Interaction, Part II, HCII 2015, LNCS 9170, pp. 618–627, 2015.
DOI: 10.1007/978-3-319-20916-6_57

'Game of The Year' awards with the New York Times reporting, "these moments have more sadness and subtlety in them than other games muster in 40 h" [5]. *The Walking Dead* uses the comic book and TV show franchise to situate the game within the same world. The game is released in episodes having cliff-hangers, flashbacks and open endings similar to that of the television show and comic books.

This new breed of indie game companies, including Telltale Games, The Fullbright Company and House on Fire, have become significant contributors to innovation in game design despite having fewer resources for production. This raises interesting questions about the relationship between production costs and narrative opportunities, suggesting that one does not necessarily depend on the other. This paper suggests a new model for the analysis of recent narrative games that specifically locates them in a scale between low to high narrative agency and high to low production efforts to identify design strategies that may support emerging and independent game designers.

2   Design-Based Research

This project team adopted a Design-based Research (DBR) methodology, which emerged from the Learning Sciences, but has key attributes that can be applied to the design of any interactive artifact. In the original context, it is critical for a DBR project to explicitly improve educational practices through collaboration among researchers and practitioners and subsequently, lead to contextually-sensitive design principles and theories [6]. By adapting a DBR approach, we adopt the main tenets of the DBR project in a game design context as being in situ, collaborative, iterative, player focused, and most importantly, results in design artifacts essential for peer and public participation, scrutiny and reflection.

The relationship between theory and design is pivotal in DBR, as design experiments allow theories to be problematised, explored, tested, adapted and advanced through analysis in their naturalistic contexts [7]. HUB Studio [8] is a new initiative offering small teams of graduate students who excel in disciplines cognate to game development. In the case of the Blind Faith project, a small team of a designer, artist, animator, sound designer and programmer was formed and over twelve weeks produced a polished prototype. To support the production, an initial case study analysis was undertaken to refine design specifications that would ensure the project brief was within the scope of the teams' abilities and resource availability.

This paper reports on the formation of a case study analysis model that best serves the tenants of a DBR practice within the context of a small game studio with limited resources. More specifically, a case study model that produces results that can explicitly contribute, support and sustain a shared vision for creative collaboration and rapid production by demonstrating key project intentions such as the aesthetic and mechanic style and production scope. Consequently, this model had three main phases; case study selection, analysis and presentation.

3 Model for Case Study Selection, Analysis, Presentation and Application

This project is guided by the principle that the effective direction of a new project is strengthened by an initial context review in the form of a customised case study analysis. The works analysed previous to the commencement of production were selected based on their impact in the field of narrative-based indie games and are discussed by combining, adapting and extending a number of existing theoretical models.

The results of the case study analysis informed the iterative design process, as the findings became a critical communication device to demonstrate and focus the small production team on the intended outcomes of the project.

3.1 Main Selection Criteria

The key characteristics for selection included release dates, production scope and both critical and commercial acclaim. All games selected can be located in a scale between high narrative agency for effective player immersion and low resource requirements for feasible production.

Recently Released: The games selected for this study were released within the last two years to show current trends in narrative-driven games. It is essential to this study and creative process to understand the current tools and techniques available and how peers in the field have adopted them to achieve the best possible outcomes for narrative presentation and agency within certain limitations typical of independent designers.

Independently Produced: Each of the works were produced by small indie development companies, often without the benefits of publisher support [9] with focus on innovation in game design rather than technology as they have limited resources and are commonly known to be using standard equipment, free-to-use software, and digital distribution [10]. Unlike major commercial developers that typically have large capital investment, over 200 employees, and access to state of the art equipment such as motion capture and virtual reality (VR) technologies that allow a capacity for technical innovation such as inventive game engines.

Critical and Commercially Acclaimed: In addition to the production value, the critical acclaim each game received for their emotive narrative components, was also considered as criteria for selection. Awards, nominations, official online reviews and ratings have been used to measure the critical acclaim of the game. Popularity has been determined by user reviews, comments on social media sites, user ratings and sales.

Agency and Resource Scale: Each game considered for analysis was first placed on a graph with two intersecting axes; the horizontal axis starts at low and ends in high player agency and the vertical axis begins with low and ends in high production value. The games most relevant to this study can be found in the second quadrant of this graph representing a range of projects perceived to have low resource requirements with high narrative agency. This exercise resulted in a group of works that became a focus for analysis and demonstration of the scope and style of game.

At the commencement of this study, there were a growing number of games that best suited this set criteria such as Papers Please by Lucus Pope, released in 2013, Silent Age by Fireproof Games, in 2012 and the Walking Dead, by Telltale Games, in 2012. For example, The Silent Age is the debut release of indie developers, Fireproof Games and has achieved both critical and public acclaim with a 4.5 /5 star rating on the iTunes store with an estimated app worth of $1,015,740 [11]. Produced by a team of only six developers, The Silent Age uses a simple side-scrolling, point and click mechanic that employs a unique minimalistic 2D art style and is released episodically as income is generated by funds procured from the initial chapters. These qualities contribute to maintaining a low demand on production resources while resulting in high public participation and impressive revenue.

3.2 Combining, Adapting and Extending Analysis Models

A significant effort to examine certain aspects of narrative games had been applied during the selection phase. Subsequently, a broader contextual understanding of the defined field was achieved well before games were short-listed for deeper consideration. The analysis of the final selected works was framed by a combination, adaptation and extension of existing models and concepts adopted by this study.

Game World, Play and Rules: A slight adjustment to Aarseth's [12] original description of the 'three dimensions that characterize every game' being game play, game structure and game world. Game world refers to the fictional content of the game, including the narrative and/or events, the setting, characters and all of the sensorial qualities, such as visuals and audio. Gameplay refers to participants' actions, strategies and motives, determining specific situations and events in an effort to maintain the momentum of the game. Gameplay can also refer to the resulting social relations, players' knowledge, in-character and out-of-character communications. Game rules refers to the structural limitations set by the programmatic game conventions designed to assist and limit player progress.

This model is particularly helpful when identifying the primary features of a game and preparing a general game description, incorporating all of the main characteristics of an interactive narrative experience such as where a player is, what they do while they are there, and how they progress and ultimately win.

The MDA Model: Attention is given to understanding the relationship between the mechanics, aesthetics and dynamics of a game and how certain aspects of each are elaborated or compromised depending on the possible resources limitations influencing design decisions and player enjoyment. According to Hunkie [13] 'Mechanics' describes the particular components of the game, at the level of data representation and algorithms; 'Dynamics' describes the run-time behavior of the mechanics acting on player inputs and each other's outputs over time; and 'Aesthetics' describes the desirable emotional responses evoked in the player, when he/she interacts with the game system.

Papers, Please is a puzzle-thriller game focusing on the emotional struggle of an immigration officer on the border of fictional countries that had recently been at war with one another. Papers, Please is the work of one man over nine months. Using the lens of the MDA model, it is clear that disproportionate effort has gone into creating a complicated interaction mechanic to mimic the complex issues and difficult decisions involved in processing immigration. There are two modes available to the player, 'Story' and 'Endless'. The Story mode is mostly scripted with twenty different possible endings. On completing the story mode, players can switch to endless mode, where they then select one of three game-types namely, Timed, Perfection, or Endurance. Each game-type has a different scoring system where the player can also choose from four different rule sets for any game-type. A rule set determines which border checkpoint laws are in effect and which documents are required for travellers. This is an innovative way to extend narrative agency by allowing the player to exercise different decisions with a variety of consequences in the same game world. However, with limited resources, Pope made cuts in the aesthetic components such as the visual and sound assets of the game [14]. The low-resolution art style is evocative of first generation games of the 1980s and 1990s and conveniently takes advantage of the current nostalgia for games of this era [15]. The other consequential effect of exploiting a nostalgic aesthetic style is that it automatically sets a lower expectation of narrative agency than initially anticipated based on previous experience of games of this aesthetic quality.

Narrative Agency: Narrative agency in games can be rendered in multiple ways and supported by structures ranging from simple linear to complex emergent ones. Linear narratives always feature a plot where their authors have complete control [16]. However, when a player is able to influence a world that responds to player action – or seems to do so – they can experience a more rewarding feeling of agency [17]. These outcomes can be either local (immediate), where the player receives an instant impact of his or her choices in game, or global, where the player's choices impact the overarching plot of the game. This allows user interactions that can influence storylines while still delivering a meaningful experience. This team focused on how player agency can be presented and facilitated through the exploitation of both aesthetic and structural narrative devices that are feasible for small teams to produce.

The Walking Dead takes place over five episodes, each one using narrative elements such as cliff-hangers to keep players interested in returning to complete each season. The Walking Dead is a traditional 'point and click' adventure game where the player moves around each scene interacting with characters and objects, solving puzzles and participating in dialogue with other characters.

In contrast to Papers, Please, The Walking Dead episodes are primarily linear stories with limited narrative agency over how the story resolves. However, there is a high sense of narrative agency over how the story unfolds, as the player is forced to make decisions based on limited options in limited time that can dramatically impact the way a player encounters and interacts with characters immediately or much later in another episode. This focuses the players' narrative engagement on the local rather than the global impact by concentrating on dramatic interactions with the characters rather than ultimately controlling the story ending. This has two major benefits. The first being that this mechanic allows the game designers to maintain the integrity of the original and very popular comic book series and television show, while still offering the player a dynamic and emotional experience within the narrative world. Secondly, by limiting the availability of multiple endings, the production demands would have been considerably lower.

3.3   Case Study Presentation

In the context of a studio environment it is imperative to articulate a projects key objectives in terms that aid production and collaboration in small and larger teams. An effective team building technique is to present relevant case studies early in the project design process to demonstrate and discuss influential aspects of each significant work. This assists the team to understand and contribute to a shared vision of the aesthetic qualities and to appreciate the intended project scope. Subsequently, an initial session was arranged to summarise and present the key findings of a case study analysis to the small team of a designer, programmer, artist, animator and sound designer:

It is imperative that the presentation and discussion of selected games is part of an iterative process. For the first presentation, the games are introduced and the various models for analysis are demonstrated. The game world, play and rules can be best illustrated through screen grabs or recorded play-throughs. The researchers then demonstrate how game aesthetics, mechanics and dynamics are employed and manipulated. The critical and commercial impact can be partly calculated by refer-encing reviews and statistics of a games success.

As available production resources determine how all components of a game are considered and resolved, the initial presentation and discussion focuses on the resources used and development process undertaken by the creative teams of the selected games. This information is more available now than in the past as many of the indie developers report on their tools, process and progress in the form of blog posts, Facebook updates and twitter mentions. For this project, it was also helpful to contact independent game designers directly via email and various other online profiles.

The second discussion with the entire team occurred a week after the first pre-sentation everyone time to play the selected games and undertake individual research that relates more closely to their various roles in the team. For example the programmer concentrated on identifying the tools and techniques used to develop each game and evaluate the influence this may have on the approach taken to develop Blind Faith.

A significant result of the case study process was that the team was well versed in the way that they articulated their game design intentions and were able to consult with the industry mentors effectively and with deliberate aims for advancing their project. The mentor sessions were scheduled at key milestones of production and were hosted at both the mentors studio or at our HUB Studio as demonstrated in Figs. 1 and 2. It was found during the feedback sessions with industry mentors, that the style and techniques used to create Blind Faith, were recognized and the mentors often referred to the games that were analysed by the team and other games that were similar in terms of aesthetics, mechanics, dynamics and scope. This indicated that the shared case study analysis had been effectively utilized by the team.

Fig. 1. The team met with industry mentor John Passfield, the Director of Right Pedal Studios

Fig. 2. Dan Vogt, the co-founder of Halfbrick Studios, speaking in detail to the team offering valued advice about the effectiveness of the game mechanics in a late prototype of Blind Faith.

4   Blind Faith. a Synthesis of Contextual Design

As illustrated in Figs. 3 and 4, The Silent Age was had the greatest influence on the aesthetic and mechanic qualities of our Blind Faith game. Both games are comparable examples of the quality of work that can be produced with a team of 6 people and minimal access to production resources. Since both games follows a linear narrative, the story and art production can be tweaked and scoped in unison without the complication of also considering the impact of every decision on the ultimate outcome of the game. The Silent Age uses a unique minimalistic art style in a 2D environment, having low production demands. To assist on controlling the scope of production, a number of familiar literary and cinematic tropes such as time travel mechanics, flashbacks and cliffhanger endings are adopted.

In the tradition of The Silent Age, Blind Faith is a 2D side scrolling, point and click adventure game where the player assumes the role of Nina Renner, a young systems analyst. The game is set in the year 2029, during an era in which the afterlife has undergone privatisation. At the game's introduction, Nina finds herself waking up in what appears to be her afterlife, and which is, unbeknownst to her, a simulated version of consciousness set up by The Company. Due to a glitch in the system, Nina has awoken into this consciousness before all of her memories had the chance to be uploaded. It is up to Nina (the player) to move backwards in time to restore the missing memories, unlocking the firewall of her mind.

Fig. 3. A screen grab of the Blind Faith game

Fig. 4. A screen grab of The Silent Age Game

In this world, The Company offers services where people can upload their memories before they die and create a consciousness in which they may continue to exist for eternity. The player protagonist Nina Renner is introduced as she wakes up at the scene of a major car crash, whereupon she finds she is suffering from memory loss. By inspecting the environment and collecting objects, Nina, and by proxy the player, begins to learn more about the desolate world in which the game is set.

At the end of this first chapter, the protagonist meets Henry, a scientist who used to work for The Company and is living his afterlife in this augmented reality. He acts as a friend, partner and guide through the game, where they develop a unique bond which leads to his helping her to escape this world as the player progresses. Certain objects trigger flashbacks; these memories include areas accessible to Nina, which she may investigate in aid of reobtaining her memory. They hold clues about her life, provide an insight into her past, and also contain artifacts that may be required to move forward in the present timeline. The challenge for the player lies in aligning these clues in a way that unfolds the narrative and allows Nina to progress through the world towards the player objective. This objective is to unlock Nina's memories, escape the augmented world and unfold The Company's secrets before people affiliated with The Company become aware of her consciousness and kill her physical body in the "real" world in order to trap her inside their constructed afterlife.

The game interaction is limited to three actions: tap, tap and hold, and swipe. The player can move across the screen by tapping once for walking, or use multiple taps to run faster. An inventory (Nina's satchel) is provided in which re-useable objects and clues are held. The player can interact with multiple objects by dragging them on top of each other. Nina can move in and out of memories by clicking on certain objects that act as portals between the world. A minimal interaction pallet is provided for the players to allow them to have more time to immerse themselves in the narrative, allowing it to remain the focal point of the game. This interaction can be replicated on a computer, laptop, tablet and mobile device, making the game accessible on multiple platforms, however the game has been designed for optimum experience on a tablet.

References

1. Rockstar. http://www.rockstargames.com/newswire/article/19471/grand-theft-auto-v-official-announcement.html
2. Quantic Dream. http://www.quanticdream.com/en/#!/en/category/heavy-rain
3. Short, E.: Heavy Rain's Storytelling Gaps (2010). http://www.gamasutra.com/view/news/27972/Analysis_Heavy_Rains_Storytelling_Gaps.php. Accesssed on 24 January 2014
4. Ruffino, P.: Narratives of independent production in video game culture. J. Can. Game Stud. Assoc. 7(11), 106–121 (2012)
5. Sullentrop, C.: Putting the Guilt Back in Killing: Game Features Zombies With a Little Soul (2012). http://www.nytimes.com/2012/05/09/arts/video-games/walking-dead-game-departs-from-zombie-cliches.html?_r=0. Accessed on 24 January 2014
6. Wang, F., Hannafin, M.J.: Design-based research and technology-enhanced learning environments. Educ. Technol. Res. Dev. 53(4), 5–23 (2005)
7. Barab, S., Squire, K.: Design-based research: putting a stake in the ground. J. Learn. Sci. 13(1), 1–14 (2004)
8. HUB Studio. https://www.facebook.com/hubgames
9. Bates, B.: Game Design, 2nd edn, pp. 252–253. Premier Press, Boston (2004). Thompson Course Technology
10. Gril, J.: The State of Indie Gaming (2008). http://www.gamasutra.com/view/feature/3640/the_state_of_indie_gaming.php. Accessed on 20th June 2014
11. Metacritic: The Walking Dead Season 1 User Reviews. http://www.metacritic.com/tv/the-walking-dead. Accessed on 20th March 2014
12. Aarseth, E.: Playing research: methodological approaches to game analysis. In: Proceedings of Melbourne DAC. University of Bergen (2003)

13. Hunicke, R., LeBlanc, M., Zubek, R.: MDA: a formal approach to game design and game research. In: Proceedings of the AAAI Workshop on Challenges in Game AI, p. 04 (2004)
14. Pope, L.: Road to the IDF: Lucas Pope's Papers, Please (2014). http://www.gamasutra.com/view/news/209905/Road_to_the_IGF_Lucas_Popes_Papers_Please.php. Accessed on 1st March 2014
15. Sloan, R.J.S.: Videogames as remediated memories: commodified nostalgia and hyperreality in far cry 3: blood dragon and gone home. Games and Culture (2014)
16. Linssen, J.: A discussion of interactive storytelling techniques for use in a serious game. Technical report TR-CTIT-12–09, Centre for Telematics and Information Technology. University of Twente, Enschede (2012)
17. Mataes, M., Stern, A.: Façade: An experiment in building a fully-realized interactive drama. In Game Developers Conference – Game Design track, vol. 2 (2003)

Play to Remember: The Rhetoric of Time in Memorial Video Games

Răzvan Rughiniş[1] and Ştefania Matei[2(✉)]

[1] University POLITEHNICA of Bucharest, Spl. Independenţei 313,
Bucharest, Romania
razvan.rughinis@cs.pub.ro
[2] University of Bucharest, Schitu Măgureanu 9, Bucharest, Romania
stefania.matei@sas.unibuc.ro

Abstract. This paper examines video games that commemorate historical events, identifying 'family resemblance' features and specific rhetorical resources. We argue that the commemorative character of a game derives, typically, from four interrelated qualities: invoking a specific historical event, claiming a truthful representation, inviting empathic understanding, and offering players opportunities for reflection. Starting from the observation that time has an important role in achieving commemorative gameplay, we discuss several games in terms of narrative and procedural rhetoric, with focus on time-related mechanics. We propose a repertoire of design resources to assist the creation of meaningful games for remembrance.

Keywords: Serious games · Art games · Memorial game · Procedural rhetoric · Rhetoric of time

1 Introduction

Video games are becoming an increasingly versatile medium, used for entertainment and for serious purposes as well. They are employed in many contexts, inviting different forms of player engagement within the gameworld. Video games are used, among others, as learning spaces, simulations of reality, practice to enhance cognitive skills, and media for existential reflection or social critique. Still, their use as memorials is infrequent.

When games attempt to kindle remembrance, they may be contested as inappropriate (e.g. 'Imagination is the only escape' [1], 'Inside a dead skyscraper' [2]). The main argument takes into consideration the potentially entertaining character of games, which may affect the earnest character of commemoration. Critiques suggest that, by making major historical events subject to play, it runs the risk of transforming a solemn occasion into a trivial manifestation. Also, games may be considered inappropriate as spaces of commemoration, due their potential to reduce historical events to means for gaining profit. The commodification of historical events through gameplay is thought to contradict the ceremonial character of commemoration.

© Springer International Publishing Switzerland 2015
M. Kurosu (Ed.): Human-Computer Interaction, Part II, HCII 2015, LNCS 9170, pp. 628–639, 2015.
DOI: 10.1007/978-3-319-20916-6_58

In this paper we examine several games which refer to specific historical events, studying how they achieve their memorial character (or fail to do so). We look into their proposed narrative and also into their procedural rhetoric [3], particularly into how they handle time. We thus aim to develop an analytic framework for memorial games, useful for designers, players, scholars, reviewers – generally speaking, people who reflect about and through gameplay.

2   What Are Memorial Games?

We focus on video games that encourage players to remember meaningful historical events and to consider their significance. Specifically, we consider several games that address 9/11 terrorist attacks ("Inside a dead skyscraper" [2], "Undo 9/11" [4]), and the World War I ("Valiant Hearts. The Great War" [5], and "Great War Adventure" [6]).

There is no strict definition for what counts as a game, and this is even truer for what counts as a memorial game. Nonetheless, we shall attempt to sketch several elements that contribute to the 'family resemblance' [7] shared by this sub-genre:

1. *Invoking specific historical events*: In order to afford remembrance, a game must point to a specific historical event - either before, during or after gameplay. The game may refer to it explicitly, through its title or narrative [5, 6]; it may refer to it implicitly, through various design elements [2] – or it may reveal its reference in the end [8].
2. *Claiming truthful representation*: Games may enhance the relationship between players and the commemorated event by claiming truthfulness as regards facts, authenticity as regards experiences, or both. Multiple elements may contribute to this realism, such as including historical characters, accurate descriptions of events and places, or accurate models of technology and weapons.
3. *Inviting empathic understanding*: Digital media [9] and, specifically, games [10] may encourage empathy through technologically mediated knowledge. Memorial games can foster empathy with people who have lived through the respective event, even from multiple perspectives. Games thus become portals for travel in time and space: they re-create significant events for players to observe and contemplate.
4. *Offering players opportunities for reflection*: Games may encourage players to reflect on the significance of the event, either by telling its story, or by formulating a 'morale' on its broader meaning [11].

3   Video Games and the Rhetoric of Time

Starting from Huizinga and Caillois [12], play has been theorized and studied as a time outside time, a form of escape from the drills of daily life. In reply, other researchers have stressed the ordinariness of gameplay, how it is part and parcel of daily life, blurring the divide between play and work or other daily tasks [13]. A second thread of research inquiries into gamers' time management and time organization, answering concerns that games are addictive and detrimental to other pursuits [14]. In reply, researchers who study games as learning experiences [15] focus on how time spent in gameplay is meaningful and transformative, challenging the rhetoric of addiction [16]. Yet a third strand of research examines the use of time in game mechanics [17–21], in order to inspire game design.

In previous research we have discussed time as a heuristic in the design of educational games [21], highlighting the risks and opportunities for learning of various approaches to time. We now examine a different type of serious games, the so-called 'memorial games', and we aim to highlight how rhetorical uses of time can contribute to gameplay for remembrance.

3.1   Narrative and Procedural Rhetoric

Ian Bogost highlights the use of game mechanics as rhetorical tools specific to the game medium [3]. He argues that games have the power to persuade and express ideas through procedures that enable players to act in the gameworld. Accordingly, games "use procedurality to make claims about cultural, social, or material aspects of human experience" [3]. Games open new perspectives by creating possibility spaces for exploring different topics and life circumstances.

If we understand rhetoric as the art to persuade an audience, to covey a meaningful message, then both static and dynamic content contribute to the creation of meaning. Games gain significance through rules of play in the context of the entire gameworld they create – that is, procedural rhetoric gains momentum by being interlocked with a narrative rhetoric. This includes the description and evolution of characters and storyline(s), which develop in co-authorship with the player.

Video games become persuasive through 'playworld', mechanics and 'playformance' [22]. According to Gonzalo Frasca, playworld refers to the space, time, and physical objects involved in the game, all of which gain rhetorical qualities through audiovisual works (images, sounds, texts). Game mechanics refer to the rules that afford and limit action, define the meaning of specific combinations of players' gestures, and allocate success and failure. The same author defines 'playformance' as a physical manipulation of games in which cognitive strategies are involved to create meaning. Therefore, it is important to take into account the interplay between all rhetorical resources – graphics, music, text and voice, as well as game mechanics and modes of engagement.

3.2   The Rhetoric of Time

Time plays an important role in the procedural rhetoric of video games. Game designers and players rely on experiences of time to derive meaning from gameplay. At the same time, game mechanics may support or disrupt intended messages [23], and it is therefore interesting to look into instances of convergence and divergence between the use of time for gameplay and for commemoration. Games may also invite an explicit reflection on time in our lives, when gameplay time experiences resonate with real world concerns of time waste, rush, alienation, or finitude.

Also, games support a materialization of memory by making it possible to manipulate time, to develop unusual temporalities, and to create innovative experiences concerning the passage of time. In studying the commemorative character of the selected games, we propose a framework for studying time (Table 1), alongside three dimensions:

5. (1) *The timescape* [24] of the game, created through its playworld: In what temporal landscape is gameplay situated? In centuries, days, hours, minutes, split seconds? What is the temporal breadth and which is the temporal focus of gameplay, as regards the fictive world it opens for players?

6. (2) The *anatomy of time*, encouraged by game mechanics and players' actions: what sort of representations of time and actions in time are afforded in the game? Is it possible to replay scenes, to explore multiple time frames, to go back in time, to consider alternative or multiple timelines? Is it necessary to be fast or patient? What forms of synchronizations are invited in the game?

7. (3) The *temporal attitude*: How does the game encourages us to think about past, present and future? Is there a "Memento Mori" message, or a "live in the moment" inclination, or is there openness towards distant futures – among others?

We consider that time mechanics have an important role in accomplishing the remembrance function, following Treanor and Mateas' analysis [23] of the 'Madrid' game [25], addressing the terrorist attack of the 2004 Madrid train bombings. They conclude that the commemorative function is inconsistent with the rapidity with which players are supposed to light candles. It thus appears that a certain configuration of gameplay parameters such as speed, duration, cyclicity may be useful or, on the contrary, damaging to remembrance.

4 Remembering 9/11

Following this line of inquiry, we examine the rhetoric of games that address historical events, with focus on understanding how (and whether) the commemorative function is accomplished through time mechanics. We also examine how other elements of gameplay contribute to the formulation of a memorial message.

'Inside a dead skyscraper' (IDS) [2] is a brief game developed by La Molleindustria to serve as a 'music video game' for the song 'The building', by Jesse Stiles. In the game players own a device which allows them to read other thoughts. Armed with this equipment, the player flies, in a hazmat suit, around a tower in which an airplane has crushed, and, on the background of the song, can wander around and listen to what other people are thinking. Still, the game does not have a visible commemorative character, because its reference to 9/11 is implicit.

When examining player comments for IDS on Bart Bonte's blog [26], it is interesting to observe that some players see it as inappropriate, given the emotional burden of the event. Also, the game is not explicitly focused on the terrorist attack. Rather, it uses a setting that connotes the 9/11 events to reflect broadly on human nature and life, rather than to encourage remembrance of this momentous tragedy.

Table 1. Overview of time mechanics

Game	Timescape	Anatomy of time	Temporal attitude
'Inside a dead skyscraper'	Breadth: a couple of minutesFocus: thoughts, dialogue, flying with music	- "Take your time" orientation: players may spend time at leisure in the game, flying with music- Speed does not make a difference- There is a premium for exploration- There are three alternative endings- One may 'seize the moment' and become agentic in an alien, hostile world - or just remain an observer	Distant observation of daily present-time
'Undo 9/11'	Breadth: a couple of minutesFocus: shooting down planes	- It proposes a change of history- Players may play at will, as there is no ending win state/check	Intense engagement with shooting down menacing planes
'Valiant Hearts: The Great War'	Breadth: several yearsFocus: interacting with the surrounding world	- The story is narrated from multiple perspectives (there are four characters that populate the gameworld). Some events are played twice based on each character mode of experiencing the moment.- There is no situated passing of time. Players may spend whatever amount of time they want in completing a task.-Players may periodically receive clues that guide them in their	Intense engagement with surviving the war

(*Continued*)

Table 1. (*Continued*)

Game	Timescape	Anatomy of time	Temporal attitude
		adventure, thus speeding up the exploration.	
'Great War Adventure'	Breadth: several yearsFocus: interacting with the surrounding world	- There is no situated passing of time. Players may spend whatever amount of time they want in completing a task. The surrounding environment will not change unless a task is completed.- Players act in a static world where situated time is irrelevant.	Intense engagement with surviving the war

Even though the game invites reflection on the significance of a recognizable historical event, it does not provide players with clear ways of retrospective engagement. Players are cast into an incongruous timespace that generates disorientation and confusion in relation with the world they encounter. At the same time, the song as well as the game give players ample opportunities to immerse themselves in the playworld, *to reflect and to co-author an ambiguous, open-ended story.*

Lacking an accurate positioning in time or space, the procedural rhetorical of the game depicts the 9/11 event as *eternal*, unbound from specific circumstances. The player examines, through gameplay, *the tension between the great forces of history and human agency* – including a contemplation of people's self-centeredness in daily life.

The stark contrast between the scale of the tragedy momentary lack of awareness of New Yorkers minding their own lives has been used before in relation with 9/11, for example in Thomas Hoepker's photo [27]. Indeed, the photograph has become highly controversial – following similar lines of argumentation as we see in players' comments for IDS. It could also be that the *subtle irony of the nonplaying game character discussing human concerns discourages players from remembrance.* At the same time, such distancing from daily affairs *may actually derive from the very shift in perspective introduced by a commemorative attitude* – in line with W. H. Auden's comments on The Fall of Icarus [28] (also discussed by [27]).

We can thus see in IDS both resources for a commemorative orientation and rhetorical elements that distract attention from it, at least for some players. Therefore, the game does not have completely coherent mechanics to support commemoration. Still, it could be that coherence is not required for a commemorative game – which could thrive on ambivalence, fostering reflection. The game establishes a space in which *fiction and truthful representations coexist, inviting empathy with a diversity of participants to this mixed situation and leaving players an ample space for interpreting the situation, be it in a commemorative direction or not.*

'Undo 9/11' [3] is a casual shooting game, in which the player have to 'undo 9/11' by shooting down planes that aim to crush into the Twin Towers. While the game does point explicitly towards 9/11, its narrative and procedural rhetoric both undermine commemoration. The storyline lacks truthfulness: the players are not encouraged to recreate a plausible story or elements of the event in any meaningful sense. On the contrary, they are invited to 'prevent' terrorist attacks by smashing airplanes with the use of a laser cannon. There is no concern for human life (such as giving a thought to the passengers of the airplanes, or to any other humans possibly involved in the gameplay scene), thus there is no empathetic identification. The game aims exclusively for entertainment. The time mechanics put a prize on skilled synchronization and speedy reaction, *with no time for reflection – and also no reason for reflection.*

This analysis illustrates the fact that the commemorative character of a game is dependent on time mechanics and on the emergent temporal attitude. In order to achieve memorial functions, it is not enough for games to invoke historical events: they have to claim truthfulness and offer the chance of an empathic understanding of the event, while also encouraging players to reflect on the event.

5   Remembering the World War I

In what follows, we are going to present other two examples (Ubisoft's 'Valiant Hearts: The Great War' [5] and 'Great War Adventure' by Chemins de Phil et Lou [6]) to illustrate how the commemorative function is accomplished in historical games. The games are comparable in terms of storyline and thematic content. Both of them assign players with the role of participants in the World War I, while asking for engagement with the playworld in order to survive. Both games invite players to actively explore the historical events of World War I, thus gaining mediated access to a past realm, through technical artifacts and graphics. The action is placed during 1914-1918, focusing on battles on the Western front.

5.1   Reference to Historical Events

The players are chronologically guided in their tour by a narrative voice that contextualizes events and offers clues of interpretation. The narrative voice reports events, introduces characters, offers guidance for successfully playing the game, reveals emotions, and communicates soldiers' thoughts. Based on this strategy, the *games are translated into a story* under the control of an omniscient narrator who teaches players how to position themselves towards the gameworld situation. The narrative voice not only provides perspectives from which events might be observed, but it also instructs players to understand the game as a memorial. By taking the function of a companion all over the game, the narrative voice continuously reminds players that the game is about a significant time in history, namely the First World War.

5.2 Claims of Truthfulness

The games offer limited possibilities of acting in the gameworld. Both of the games are based on a script which has to be followed strictly, in order to successively complete tasks and navigate towards a particular end. Players are characters who have to recreate the universe made available to them by interacting with the medium in specific ways. *The procedural rhetoric puts players in situations to enact events with no space for change or reconfiguration* - thus conveying the message that history is as it was, with no attention to alternative, counterfactual histories. In performing these acts, duration becomes almost irrelevant, and all that players have to do is to discover the right way to accomplish a task. Even the death of a character through lack of skill is not interpreted as 'real' in the gameworld: the character is reanimated, and players are encouraged to repeat the action until they succeed. Therefore, the games' affordances recreate history as factual and objective, as a structure to be known (but not changed), based on events as they happened.

A polarity between history and biography emerges, as a consequence of limitation of players' actions imposed by game procedures. The game mechanics consolidate a view of the world in which the individual autonomy is constrained by social conditions. In this sense, both games present individual life as a product of contextual features. The characters embodied by players become human types, and their individuality is designed to be reliable and accurate in relation with the social circumstances presented in the story. This polarity between history and biography supports a rhetoric of engagement into a war which is not wanted by anyone, but which cannot be resisted and escaped. Players, similar to people from the past, must conform to its imperatives.

Claims of truthfulness are also to be found in developers' statement about the game, which presents the games as a product inspired by the events of the World War I. Considering that commemoration is a mode of assuming a view of the past shaped in the interaction between game, developers and public, then both 'Valiant Hearts: The Great War' and 'Great War Adventure' also achieve their memorial character though discourse. By means of reviews or other interactions that provide legitimacy to the events, the communities of gamers are encouraged to understand them as remembrance devices, and to play them as such. Therefore the *commemorative character is not necessarily intrinsic to the game: it can also be achieved through accompanying discourses*.

The memorial character is also achieved by making the games comparable to *virtual museums*. Each stage of play is accompanied by informative boxes that contain descriptions of objects, pictures, letters, articles, and proclamations whose existence is historically documented. By clicking on them, players interrupt the usual order of tasks and enter into a specific temporality which is a historical temporality of war different from a situated temporality of play (Fig. 1). These informative boxes contain trustworthy content and suggest that the games have to be taken seriously.

5.3 Empathic Understanding

These two games might be understood as part of the mnemonic socialization of an individual, offering the necessary resources to build collective identities though symbolic displays (ex. flags, clothes, badges). The games portray players as members of a nation with collective interest, strategies, expectations, and a common past. The rhetoric of commemoration implies a certain perspective from which the events are narrated. In this sense, the games propose forms through which the World War I might be known. "Valiant Hearts", through direct portrayal of negative characters (ex. Von Dorf), represent a critique of different actions or modes of organization (genocide, betrayal, revenge). Still, both games offer possibilities of direct engagement in the story which other memorial environments make difficult to accomplish, thus favoring immersion into the war world and empathy with soldiers or other participants.

The time developed in the two games is not a linear one. There is no constant flow or rhythm of events. Some actions are more intensively presented than others, facilitating the emergence of particular sensibilities necessary for players to assume the role of the commemorator. The games are accompanied by a certain emotionality which makes them similar to other memorial environments (such as cemeteries or monuments).

Valiant Heart: The Great War

Situated temporality of play   Historical temporality of war

Great War Adventure

Situated temporality of play   Historical temporality of war

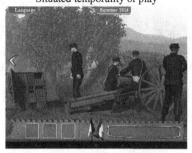 

Fig. 1. Temporalities of gameplay

5.4 Ways to Invite Reflection

Games also achieve their commemorative character by supporting a specific temporal attitude in which it is important to know and interrogate the past. Both'Valiant Hearts'and'Great War Adventure' cultivate reflection on the significance of historical events, thus enhancing their memorial function. The past appears as a plain object that might be assessed either based on its consequences in the actual world, or in relation with social values and norms. Consequently, it becomes a referential space to reflect about themes such as heroism, victimization, sacrifice, war crime, death and other related issues. The past is presented as an experience or arrangement that players are invited to be aware of by entering the game world and assuming to act in the environment made available to them. Implicitly, in both games the past appears as a realm that might be recreated through technological means and for remembering purposes.

6 Conclusions

We examine four games in order to highlight rhetorical resources that contribute to commemorative gameplay. These games are quite different as regards mechanics and emerging storylines, opening a space to discuss what constitutes memorial games, and how remembrance can be encouraged through gameplay.

We propose *four 'family-resemblance' features of memorial games*: reference to a historical event, concerns for truthful representation, invitation for empathic understanding of participants in that event, and opportunities for reflection (Table 2). While none of them is strictly necessary, various combinations may encourage a memorial function .

Table 2. Rhetorical resources for commemoration in the selected games

Game	Historical event	Concern for truthfulness	Empathy	Reflection
'Inside a dead skyscraper'	Implicit: 9/11	Present, but not central Fantastic elements are included into the game	Yes	Yes
'Undoing 9/11'	Explicit: 9/11	No	No	No
'Valiant Hearts'	Explicit: WWI	Yes, central	Yes	Yes
'Great War Adventure'	Explicit: WWI	Yes, central	Yes	Yes

We also discuss the *use of time as a rhetorical resource* to invite commemoration. We distinguish three dimensions on which we can analyze the temporality of a game: the game timescape, its anatomy of time, and its temporal attitude. Time mechanics may support or may hinder commemorative gameplay, for example by imposing to fast a rhythm to allow reflection, or by focusing on certain moments, highlighting them in the continuum of time. Commemoration may be achieved through different time mechanics, as well: both 'Valiant Hearts' and the' Great War Adventure' rely on a view of time as unidirectional and an understanding of history as immutable – but other games allow players to create alternative histories centered on the historical event, and to contemplate their significance.

Digital games offer a rich, yet underused and understudied medium for commemoration. The time has come to wield it more in order to bring young audiences, as well as the diversity of people who enjoy gameplay, in contact with the significant people and events that we want to remember.

Acknowledgement. This article has been supported by the research project "Sociological imagination and disciplinary orientation in applied social research", with the financial support of ANCS/UEFISCDI with grant no. PN-II-RU-TE-2011-3-0143, contract 14/28.10.2011.

This paper was co-financed from the European Social Fund, through the Sectorial Operational Programme Human Resources Development 2007−2013, project number POSDRU/159/1.5/S/138907 "Excellence in scientific interdisciplinary research, doctoral and postdoctoral, in the economic, social and medical fields –EXCELIS", coordinator The Bucharest University of Economic Studies.

References

1. Yaron, O.: Is there room for a Holocaust computer game?. Haaretz (2013)
2. La Molleindustria, Inside a dead skyscraper (2010)
3. Bogost, I.: The rhetoric of video games. In: Salen, K. (ed.) The Ecology of Games: Connecting Youth, Games, and Learning, pp. 117–140. MIT Press, Cambridge (2008)
4. Red Key Blue Key, Undo 9/11 (2014)
5. Ubisoft, Valiant Hearts. The Great War (2014)
6. Chemins de Phil et Lou, Great War Adventure (2014)
7. Arjoranta, J.: Game Definitions: A Wittgensteinian Approach. Game Studies **14**(1) (2014). http://gamestudies.org/1401/articles/arjoranta
8. Romero, B. Train (2009)
9. Rughiniş, C., Humă, B.: Massive multiplayer online advice: using forums to teach empathy in social professions. In: The 10th International Scientific Conference eLearning and software for Education - eLSE, pp. 1–7 (2014)
10. Belman, J., Flanagan, M.: Designing games to foster empathy. Cogn. Technol. **14**(2), 5–15 (2010)
11. Marinescu-Nenciu, A.P., Rughiniş, C.: Every day the same dream? social critique through serious gameplay. In: The 11th International Scientific Conference eLearning and Software for Education - eLSE, pp. 1–8 (2015)
12. Caillois, R.: The definition of play and the classification of games. In: Katie, S., Eric, Z. (eds.) The Game Design Reader A Rules of Play Anthology. The MIT Press, Cambridge (2006)
13. Warmelink, H.J.K., Harteveld, C., Mayer, I.S.: Press enter or escape to play deconstructing escapism in multiplayer gaming. In: Proceedings of DiGRA Breaking New Ground: Innovation in Games, Play, Practice and Theory, pp. 1–9 (2009)
14. Anand, V.: A study of time management: the correlation between video game usage and academic performance markers. Cyberpsychol. Behav. **10**(4), 552–559 (2007)

15. Gee, J.P.: What Video Games have to Teach Us about Learning and Literacy. Palgrave Macmillan, New York (2003)
16. Cover, R.: Gaming (Ad)diction: discourse, identity, time and play in the production of the gamer addiction myth. Game Stud. **6**(1), 15 (2006)
17. Zagal, J.P., Mateas, M.: Time in video games: a survey and analysis. Simul. Gaming **41**(6), 844–868 (2010)
18. Juul, J.: Introduction to Game Time. MIT Press, Cambridge (2004)
19. Tychsen, A., Hitchens, M.: Game time: modeling and analyzing time in multiplayer and massively multiplayer games. Games Culture **4**(2), 170–201 (2008)
20. Van Meurs, R.: And then you wait: the issue of dead time in social network games. In: DiGRA Conference Think Design Play, vol. 227(2004), pp. 1–12 (2011)
21. Rughiniş, R.: Time as a heuristic in serious games for engineering education. In: The 5th International Conference on Computer Supported Education CSEDU, pp. 580–585 (2013)
22. Frasca, G.: Play the Message. Play, Game and Videogame Rhetoric. Ph.D. dissertation. IT University of Copenhagen (2007)
23. Treanor, M. and Mateas, M.: Newsgames: procedural rhetoric meets political cartoons. In: Proceedings of the 2009 DiGRA International Conference: Breaking New Ground: Innovation in Games, Play, Practice and Theory (2009)
24. Adam, B.: Timescapes of Modernity: The Environment and Invisible Hazards. Routledge, London (1998)
25. Frasca, G.: Madrid (2004)
26. Bonte, B.: Bontegames - Inside a dead skyscraper (2010)
27. Jones, B.: The meaning of 9/11's most controversial photo. The Guardian (2011)
28. Auden, W.H.: Musee des Beaux Arts

'Sketchy Wives' and 'Funny Heroines'
Doing and Undoing Gender in Art Games

Cosima Rughiniş[(⊠)] and Elisabeta Toma

University of Bucharest, Schitu Măgureanu 9, Bucharest, Romania
{cosima.rughinis,elisabeta.toma}@sas.unibuc.ro

Abstract. Gender analysis of video games has increased its public visibility through the Gamergate controversy. We examine several casual art games in order to explore the diversity of both conventional and counter-stereotypical gender representations. We find significant reliance on stereotypical presentations, especially in 'sketchy wife' characters. Such tropes may offer rhetorical resources to communicate, in brief lapses of gameplay, messages about life, death and the human condition. We also find creative ways of tackling gender displays through character description and game mechanics. Art games may thus serve as a laboratory for experimenting with doing and possibly un-doing gender.

Keywords: Serious games · Art games · Procedural rhetoric · Gender

1 Introduction

The #Gamergate controversy [17] has brought to forefront of public debate the issue of gender in the video game culture, as a culminating point of a gradually increasing awareness of women's absence, stereotypical representation, and objectification in games and gaming communities. The rise of systematic critique regarding gender in videogames, exemplified by Sarkeesian's analysis of 'Tropes vs. Women' [22] has been paralleled by the growth of the indie 'art' games, which were too a topic of heated debates, mainly discussing whether they are proper games, or not. The so-called 'art games' claim to make a point about human condition and society, and occasionally to comment on the game genre itself, combining social critique and aesthetic statements, usually at the expense of conventional playability and fun. We take a closer look at gender in art games – an intersection that has received little explicit attention to date.

Given the attempt of art games to question received wisdom, to stimulate reflection and controversy, to 'modulate' reality [19] rather than escape it, we ask: How do they deal with femininity and masculinity? In her analysis of 'Tropes vs. Women', Sarkeesian praises three well-known art games for their take on death as a meaningful human (and women's) experience [23]: 'Dear Esther' [26], 'To the Moon' [7], and 'Passage' [18]. She also recommends 'Where is My Heart' [6], and 'Superbrothers: Sword & Sworcery' [25], as instances of games that subvert the 'Damsel in Distress' trope [24]. We start from these art games, and we examine them and several more in order to find out how they formulate femininity and masculinity. How is gender used as part of their rhetoric?

© Springer International Publishing Switzerland 2015
M. Kurosu (Ed.): Human-Computer Interaction, Part II, HCII 2015, LNCS 9170, pp. 640–648, 2015.
DOI: 10.1007/978-3-319-20916-6_59

2 Gender as a Rhetorical Resource: Gender Displays in Games

Players need to make sense of the game fictive world – characters, situations, scripts – while playing. Games include, therefore, clues on which players rely to interpret the situation and the available actions. Some of these signs amount to what Goffman terms 'gender displays' [9] – symbolic actions or features through which characters manifest their femininity or masculinity.

Gender is a rich and easily available cultural resource. Once a character is defined as masculine or feminine, a wide repertoire of stereotypes and scripts become available to players to make sense of what is expected from her or him and what is to be done. Occasionally, this affords the possibility to be surprised if expectations are contradicted by gameplay events. Gender is thus used as a rhetorical resource, enabling the delivery of a meaningful, persuasive message by alignment or misalignment with players gender-based expectations.

Therefore, it often happens that characters in games are explicitly gendered – either independently from players' choice, or through their options for a masculine or feminine character. This initial gendering is achieved mainly through appearance – using smaller or bigger bodies with gendered shapes, colors (such as pink/blue), clothing, and voice.

Characters display their gender not only through bodily appearance but also through their stories: what is their mission and role in the game? What are their actions? What are their personality traits? Invoking available stereotypical gender representations, some traits and roles are expected from characters by virtue of their gender: activity/passivity, authority/submission, emotionality/rationality, kindness/violence – and, of course, being a playable character versus a support, non-playable character.

There is an interplay between players expectations based on characters' gender, and the actual roles, actions and personalities that characters acquire or unveil through gameplay. This interplay may reproduce gender stereotypes or may challenge them, creating novel forms of femininity and masculinity, or just obscuring the distinction. As a consequence, gender is done - or undone [5] - through gameplay [28].

Games are not stories, of course [3, 14] – but they may generate stories through gameplay, with players as co-authors for the emerging narrative. Games are 'talkative' – but it is still players who must experience them, interpret and formulate their message [20]. Therefore, players also have a role in creating the kinds of femininities and masculinities that develop in the gameworld.

In the present paper we shall focus on the so-called casual 'art games'. These are typically indie games that claim to have something to say about the human condition – taking it upon themselves to kindle reflection, emotions, and deeper experiences in addition to, or instead of conventional entertainment. Casual art games are typically single player, and afford players a limited liberty in shaping the game story. Therefore, much of the gender displays in casual art games are constrained by game design.

In this paper we examine several games in order to identify various ways of using and thus re-creating femininity and masculinity through gameplay. Our guiding question is: what strategies for doing, re-doing and undoing gender can we find in casual art games?

3   Doing Gender: From 'Damsels in Distress' to 'Distressing Damsels'

In the typical 'damsel in distress' scenario frequent in video games [22], feminine characters wait to be rescued by masculine characters. This trope is not so frequent in the art games that we have selected. Still, there remains an unbalance in agency, as male characters are, as a rule, the playable characters ('ALZ' [4], 'Home' [13], 'Every day the same dream' [16], 'One chance' [2]). There are also a few games with two characters playable at once, including a man and a woman ('To the Moon' [7], 'One and One Story [15]').

Feminine characters are sometimes used to restrict the masculine character's actions, being depicted as 'distressing damsels' (such as in 'Passage' [18]), needing protection or attention ('One and One Story' [15]), and generally lacking agency ('Every day the same dream' [16], 'Passage' [18], 'ALZ' [4], 'Home' [13]). In several of the abovementioned games they appear only as 'sketchy wives' – cursory presences that serve to enhance the context for the masculine character's action ('Every day the same dream', 'Passage', 'ALZ', 'One chance').

In 'Passage' [18], an already classical art game by Jason Rohrer, the feminine character is portrayed as a companion. When she dies, the masculine character is slowed down, as a sign of his grief. As a companion, the feminine character does not get to be active. She only takes part in the mechanics of the game by slowing down the masculine character and making his accumulation of points more difficult, as they require more space to travel together and thus, occasionally, they do not fit through the labyrinthine paths.

In some games, actions are permitted regardless of the gender of the character, but the results differ by gender. For instance, the blue square in Rod Humble's 'The Marriage' [12], another art game which has received significant public and scholarly attention, enlarges when interacting with others, while the pink square enlarges when it gets close to the blue square. A message about a stereotypical view of men and women's needs in marriage is thus conveyed through the use of procedural rhetoric. The woman is portrayed as needing to feel loved by her husband, while the man is portrayed as needing contact with people outside his family.

When they are playable and even rescuers themselves, women characters' deeds may be constructed as witty or funny ('Superbrothers: Sword & Sworcery' [25]), somehow lacking the solemnity conventionally associated with men's heroism. While the heroine of Sword and Sworcery is not created through comical role-reversal [23], and she is carrying the quest through her own powers, her comments are whimsical, creating a humorous and often self-ironical atmosphere. We also found two 'serious heroines'. Interestingly, their quests are terminated by death - either through her own death ('Love's Cadence' [1]) or through the lover's death ('A love story' [11]).

In 'One and One Story' [15] both characters (the feminine and the masculine one) are playable at the same time, but the masculine one is more active and, also, he seems to be the narrator of the story. The feminine character also appears a few times as impossible to control and having to be saved by the masculine character. While the narrator tells the story "When she saw me she ran to me..." the feminine character becomes impossible to control and runs whenever she sees the masculine character, putting herself in danger. One of the players (TornPaperBird, 2014) ironically commented on the Kongregate website: "When she saw me, she ran to me.""Apparently not noticing the large pit of spikes that she could easily jump over."

Dylan Carter's 'ALZ' [4] is a game about a man with Alzheimer's disease, with difficulties in making sense of the world around him. His condition is expressed through glitches in the graphics, time and space jumps, and the reaction of his wife (or daughter?), whom he cannot recognize anymore. The 'sketchy wife' has a non-playable apparition in the game, in order to express concern and to illuminate the male's character condition.

Stephen Lavelle's 'Home' [13] is a game in which the playable character is an old person who arrives in a retirement home. The game play is built around the needs of the old man, with a rhetoric of failure [27]. Whatever the player does to fulfill Charles' needs, due to time shortage it is impossible to achieve balance and the physiological and psychological state of the character deteriorates very quickly. He inevitably becomes depressed, artificially fed, and confined to bed. When he finally gets to see his daughter, you understand from their talk that he has also lost his memory, not remembering that she comes to see him every Monday. Yet, he presents himself as happy, accepting his degradation – inviting players to question the typical family and social organization of elderly people's lives.

The main story in Home is about the physical deterioration associated with old age. Although the caretakers (all feminine characters) seem nice and supportive, the player is forced to fail at taking care of Charles' most basic needs, and nobody seems to be able to help him, not even his daughter. The feminine characters, although apparently invested with agency, cannot influence Charles' life.

'One Chance' [2] is a game focused on deciding how and with whom to spend your time, when the end of the world is near because of your own fault. The player is a scientist who accidentally invented a pathogen which will destroy the world in six days, and can now chose whether to go to work or spend time with his family. The wife has a cursory non-playable appearance and she is unavoidably killed at some point or another (either through suicide or murder), in all gameplay scenarios.

4   Un-Doing Gender?

We have identified two possibilities for un-doing stereotypical gender classifications and scripts, in the selected art games:

1. Feminine characters may be portrayed with *counter-stereotypical or androgynous roles, features and relationships*, thus disrupting established gender tropes; the 'funny heroine' is such an example – with humor deriving from masculine-feminine role reversal, or from characters' wit.

2. Gender may be designed as *ambiguous*, and sometimes as *irrelevant*, involving the player in the attribution and design of femininity and masculinity and making gender ideology a player's option.

4.1   Counter-Stereotypical Characters in 'a Love Story'

'A love story' [11] is a simple puzzle RPG. In 'A love story', it is the feminine character who has to overcome obstacles in order to meet the masculine character. Minimal color clues are used in character design to indicate gender: the feminine (playable) character is pink, and the masculine one is blue, while all other aspects are identical.

From a procedural point of view, the game makes a point about gender conventions, by using the feminine character as the rescuer and the masculine one as the rescued one. However, the narrative of the game does not render the heroine successful. At the end of the game, after being rescued several times, the masculine character dies.

Gamers may react to an unconventional approach to gender. One comment on the Kongregate website [11] is: "A real gentleman would walk all that way, climb those hills and would swim through those deadly lakes of water. Poor lady." (deadmonday 2012) Ironic or not, this comment is proof that breaking gender conventions is a noticeable activity.

4.2   Gender Irrelevance and Twists in 'to the Moon'

Freebird Games' 'To the Moon' [7] is an adventure RPG. John, a primary character - yet not the playable one - is old and dying. After his wife passes away, he hires a team of scientists to change all his memories of his life, so that he could die happy, with the knowledge that he accomplished his dream: to go to the Moon. The player does not know why John whishes to go to the Moon, but they find out that the Moon has a special significance for both John and his wife, River.

The team of scientists (Dr. Eva Rosalene and Dr. Neil Watts) is the playable character. The player gets to control each scientist in turn, one at a time, as the game requires it.

Gender becomes an aspect of the romantic connection between John and River. This portrayal of romantic love invokes traditionally gendered scripts, but only on a superficial layer. Both River and John are complex characters and their gender is not relevant for their passivity or activity in the game, or for their romance story. There are other characteristics rendering them passive or active, and they do not rely on sex differences, but on their background stories as they are revealed to the player during their search for clues. River has Asperger syndrome, which is important because it affects her capability of communicating important memories to John, while he also bears a grave problem. He had suffered a trauma in his childhood and was given strong pills to erase his painful memories, therefore making him unable to remember an important part of his and River's romance story together – a source of tension in their relationship.

Gender is used in order to build a romantic climate. There are resources that the player has to obtain in order to make sense of the game and solve the puzzle; however, gender is not relevant for these clues. The clues refer to John and River's memories together, but there are no stereotypes made available for giving meaning to the game.

Gender also appears in the professional relationship between the two scientists, though they are portrayed as complex personalities, with versatile and unpredictable reactions. For example, Dr. Rosalene is at first rather compassionate, while Dr. Watts more pragmatic - but Dr. Rosalene surprises the player when she eliminates River out of John's memory. When Dr. Rosalene tries to take River out of John's memory, Dr. Watts becomes the playable character and tries to stop Dr. Rosalene. She sends zombies for Dr. Watts and puts traps in his way. After this intermezzo, it appears that she had actually devised a hidden plan, turning out that her intentions were good and perfectly compatible with the romantic ideal of finding love. In the end, she appears as a mastermind. Moreover, the zombie scene is disruptive and humorous, enhancing Dr. Rosalene's sense of humor. The very end of the game also displays a strong emotional side to the until-then cynical Dr. Watts, inviting the player to re-interpret the masculine character altogether.

4.3 Minimalist Gender Clues in 'Superbrothers: Sword and Sworcery'

'Superbrothers: Sword & Sworcery' [25] is a witty and highly self-referential adventure RPG in which the playable character ('the Scythian') goes on a magical quest to find an artifact and vanquish the ghost that is guarding it. In her quest, she is aided by Logfella, Dogfella, and Girl.

The gender clues in this game are rare and either minimalist or ambiguous, as Dan Griliopoulos [10] argues. For example, when the playable character meets Girl and Logfella, it is one of the few instances with explicit descriptions for them, through which Girl is portrayed as "nice" and Logfella as "cool":

> "Far from the war-ravaged steppes of Scythia we met a dark haired girl in a sunlit Meadow. To the Mountain Folk of the Caucasus she was known as 'Girl' and she seemed nice."/"To the Mountain Folk of the Caucasus he was known as 'Logfella'& he seemed cool."

We notice here a stereotypical difference in the characters' descriptions: while the woman is presented as "Girl", her identity being solely based on her gender, the man is named "Logfella", his occupation being used as a gender display. Still, gender does not play a significant role in gameplay and in the emerging story (Fig. 1).

At first the gender of the playable character is unclear, since it appears as a pixelated figure with a sword. However, after encountering the two characters for which we obtain gender clues, we can also figure out the gender of the playable character, as it is visually rather similar with Girl, and with a smaller body size than Logfella (Fig. 2).

As for the procedural dimension of gender display, Logfella is not very helpful and the protagonist (a feminine character) is rendered as more heroic than him. The masculine character does not take on any of the responsibilities assigned during the quest, although he offers his help.

Fig. 1. Body differences between Logfella (left) and the Scythian (right)

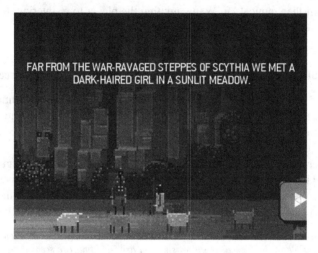

Fig. 2. Body similarities between the Scythian (left) and girl (right)

The Scythian is funny in a spiritual and witty way, while at the same time being a serious heroine. The humor of the game is not based on ridiculing her character or on role-reversal. However, through her slightly self-ironical voice ("We got the Megatome & we are the smartest!"), her success is rhetorically constructed as playful and lacks the dramatic effect that usually accompanies a masculine character's victory. She is not completely invested in her mission, approaching it with a certain ambivalence or 'half-belief' [21]. The dramatic element is only accomplished in the end, when she sacrifices herself. Although far from the stereotypical and unimaginative representations of women in popular video games, 'S: S & S' does not offer the counterpart to conventional male heroes – that is a serious, powerful heroine without the need to sacrifice herself, and who is able to finish the quest victoriously through her strengths and insights.

5   Conclusions

When examining a set of casual art games, we find that stereotypical gender representations are quite often used. For example, we identify 'the sketchy wife' as a frequent trope: a cursory 'wife' character that summarily communicates her care, more or less convincingly. We may explain the recourse to such benevolent sexism [8], at least partially, through the rhetorical constraint of making a point through short, ambiguous and ambivalent gameplay. Gender displays serve as a precious rhetorical resource in sketching characters which are instantly recognizable.

There are also games that feature innovative representations of masculinity and femininity, such as 'To the Moon' [7], 'Where is My Heart' [6], and 'Superbrothers: Sword & Sworcery' [25].

While art games make considerable less use of the gender tropes identified by Sarkeesian in mainstream games, such as 'Women as Background Decoration', 'The Damsel in Distress', or 'Ms Male Character' [22], we find that there is a frequent reliance on the 'sketchy wife' as a rhetorical resource for minimalist games to reflect on grave themes, such as mortality or alienation. At the same time, there is considerable depth in the portrayals of femininity in several art games – including the 'funny heroine' of 'S: S & S' [25], and the scientist team from 'To the Moon' [7]. In between these two design poles, the evolution of gender displays in art games remains an open question.

Acknowledgment. This article has been supported by the research project "Sociological imagination and disciplinary orientation in applied social research", with the financial support of ANCS/UEFISCDI with grant no. PN-II-RU-TE-2011-3-0143, contract 14/28.10.2011.

References

1. Love's Cadence. Kongregate.com (2012). http://www.kongregate.com/games/4urentertainment/loves-cadence
2. AkwardSilenceGames.One Chance (2010). http://www.newgrounds.com/portal/view/555181
3. Bogost, I.: The Rhetoric of Video Games. In: Salen, K. (ed.) The Ecology of Games: Connecting Youth, Games, and Learning, pp. 117–140. MIT Press, Cambridge (2008)
4. Carter, D.: ALZ (2014). http://www.newgrounds.com/portal/view/634905
5. Deutsch, F.M.: Undoing Gender. Gend. Soc. 21(1), 106–127 (2007)
6. Fabrik, D.G.: Where is My Heart. http://whereismyheartgame.com/
7. Freebird Games. To The Moon. http://freebirdgames.com/to_the_moon/
8. Glick, P., Fiske, S.T.: An ambivalent alliance. Hostile and benevolent sexism as complementary justifications for gender inequality. Am. psychol. 56(2), 109–118 (2001)
9. Goffman, E.: Gender Advertisements. Harper & Row, New York (1979)
10. Griliopoulos, D.: State of Play: Female Protagonists SMTG. State of Play (2014). http://www.showmethegames.com/2014/09/30/state-of-play-female-protagonists/
11. Hansa, W.: A Love Story. Kongregate.com (2011). http://www.kongregate.com/games/hansaW/a-love-story

12. Humble, R.: The Marriage. http://www.rodvik.com/rodgames/marriage.html
13. Increpare Games. Home. http://www.increpare.com/2009/10/home/
14. Juul, J.: Games telling stories? a brief note on games and narratives. Game Stud. **1**, 1 (2001)
15. MaTX222. One and One Story. Kongregate.com (2011). http://www.kongregate.com/games/MaTX222/one-and-one-story
16. La Molleindustria. Every Day the Same Dream (2009). http://www.molleindustria.org/everydaythesamedream/everydaythesamedream.html
17. Parkin, S.: Gamergate: A Scandal Erupts in the Videogame Community. The New Yorker (2014). http://www.newyorker.com/tech/elements/gamergate-scandal-erupts-video-game-community
18. Rohrer, J.: Passage. http://hcsoftware.sourceforge.net/passage/
19. Rughiniş, R.: Serious games as input versus modulation: different evaluations of utility. In: 26th Conference on People and Computers BCS-HCI 2012, pp. 175–184. ACM (2012)
20. Rughiniş, R.: Talkative objects in need of interpretation. re-thinking digital badges in education. In: CHI 2013 Extended Abstracts on Human Factors in Computing Systems, pp. 2099–2108. ACM (2013)
21. Rughiniş, R.: Work and gameplay in the transparent `magic circle' of gamification. In: Marcus, A. (ed.) DUXU 2013, Part II. LNCS, vol. 8013, pp. 577–586. Springer, Heidelberg (2013)
22. Sarkeesian, A.: Tropes vs. Women (2014). http://www.feministfrequency.com/
23. Sarkeesian, A.: Damsel in Distress (Part 2): Tropes vs. Women (2014). http://www.feministfrequency.com/2013/05/damsel-in-distress-part-2-tropes-vs-women/
24. Sarkeesian, A.: Damsel in Distress (Part 3): Tropes vs. Women (2014). http://www.feministfrequency.com/2013/08/damsel-in-distress-part-3-tropes-vs-women/
25. Guthrie, J.: Superbrothers: Capy.Sword & Sworcery. http://www.swordandsworcery.com/
26. The Chinese Room. Dear Esther. http://dear-esther.com/
27. Treanor, M., Mateas, M.: Newsgames: procedural rhetoric meets political cartoons. In: DiGRA 2009, (2009)
28. West, C., Zimmerman, D.H.: Doing gender. Gend. Soc. **1**(2), 125–151 (1987)

Gamification Effect of Collection System for Digital Photographs with Geographic Information which Utilizes Land Acquisition Game

Rie Yamamoto[1]([⊠]), Takashi Yoshino[1]([⊠]), and Noboru Sonehara[2]

[1] Faculty of Systems Engineering, Wakayama University, Wakayama, Japan
s165059@center.wakayama-u.ac.jp, yoshino@sys.wakayama-u.ac.jp
[2] Information and Society Research Division,
National Institute of Informatics, Tokyo, Japan
sonehara@nii.ac.jp

Abstract. As digital photos with geographic information are helpful as a new tourism resource, in this study we developed the "Photopolie" digital photo collecting system that includes geographic information. Through GWAP, which utilizes a land acquisition game, Photopolie defines photography targets that are useful as tourism resources, and promotes digital photo submission with accurate position information. Evaluation experiment results showed the following three points: (1) Through clarifying photography targets that are useful as tourism resources, and considering compatible gamification elements, there is the possibility of being able to collect more data. (2) User interaction has the possibility of motivating work. (3) It may be possible to maintain motivation for data submission for dynamic users who enjoy land acquisition games.

Keywords: Digital archive · Digital photograph · Location information · Motivation · GWAP (Games With A Purpose)

1 Introduction

Digital photos and videos of landscapes and reconstruction are thought to be valuable regional and tourist resources for stimulating a region. In order to preserve this scenery, digital photos and videos of every region that captures their cities is essential. However, most digital photos show bias towards where they are shot, since they are typically either tourist or private photos. In short, it is necessary to promote the digital photography of every area. Therefore, we considered that through encouraging the collection of digital photography that may serve as tourist resources for every region, and further reorganization of the collected data, the possibility would open up of being able to provide tourism information in a variety of forms, allowing the possibility to stimulate areas and help support tourism. In this study, we are constructing a digital archive for the

© Springer International Publishing Switzerland 2015
M. Kurosu (Ed.): Human-Computer Interaction, Part II, HCII 2015, LNCS 9170, pp. 649–659, 2015.
DOI: 10.1007/978-3-319-20916-6_60

purpose of supporting tourism by developing a digital photo collecting system called "Photopolie", which utilizes a land acquisition game. Hakodate Digital Museum for digital archive influenced tourism [1,2]. This system encourages the collection of digital photos that can be used as tourism resources for all regions through the use of GWAP, which utilizes a land acquisition game. A digital photo map is also provided to users by finding the association between digital photos and geographical information and mapping the data out into the map. Here, we suggest concentrating on collecting digital photos relating to parking lots. For example, if you could find out about tourist sites in unfamiliar areas or know about parking lots at commercial facilities prior to taking a trip by car, you could look up parking information at your destination, or cut down on time loss spent looking for parking lots. Knowing where there are handicap parking spaces is also useful information both for the handicapped individual and their family. In order to correlate more digital photos regarding parking lots with geographical information, we considered the appropriate gamification elements. In this paper, we will outline "Photopolie" and describe utilization experiments for the purpose of collecting digital photos of parking lots.

2   Related Work

GWAP (Games with A Purpose) is a game that produces profitable resources as a secondary effect that also has an accompanied purpose whenever a person plays it. In order to produce profitable resources, it is necessary to consider corresponding gamification elements. The ESP game [3] is the most popular example for research of GWAP. The ESP game is an online game wherein two randomly selected players are shown the same image and, without any mutual communication, the players input any words that come to mind from the image and score points if their words match. In this game, you are tagged by the picture as a secondary effect. As a study into GWAP, which aims for the large-scale collecting of digital photos, Tuite et al. have developed an online game for the purpose of large-scale data collecting in order to construct a 3D city model that hypothetically could be used for urban planning [4]. As a result of two competitions held between universities, a large amount of digital photos that captured city buildings from all angles was compiled. Among the students who participated in the game, various competitions for the highest score were used as motivation for data submission. The compiled digital photos that came from comparisons with 3D models constructed from digital photos shared on Flickr were useful for constructing even more detailed 3D models. Another relevant GWAP is the mobile game EyeSpy which Bell et al. have developed [5]. In this game, this game can collect photos and tags that would be useful for navigation. In this study, digital photos with correlated geographical information of various regions which are not tourist spots are collected by utilizing a land acquisition game. Gaining points and land through mutual player interaction is used to motivate the player.

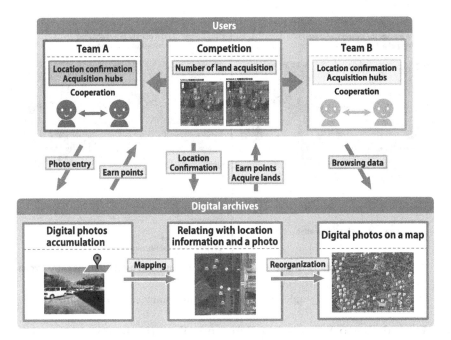

Fig. 1. System configuration.

3   Photopolie

3.1   Outline of Photopolie

Figure 1 shows the configuration of this system. It is composed of a digital archive that stores and reorganizes users who submit digital photos with location information and submitted digital photos. Location confirmation between users is performed in order to more make more accurate geographical information correlating with digital photos, enabling point and land acquisition. Users are motivated to submit data through mutual interaction by verifying each other's location. Users are separated between two teams, the allying team working among itself to acquire land and verify location information for digital photos. The opposing team competes for the most land acquisitions and photos with confirmed location. Thus, collecting digital photos of parking lots in every region is encouraged, and any stagnation of addition or updating of the digital archive is prevented. Digital photos that were collected for parking lots are mapped onto a map and reorganized as a digital photo map that gives parking lot information.

3.2   Functions of Photopolie

This subsection shows the functions of Photopolie.

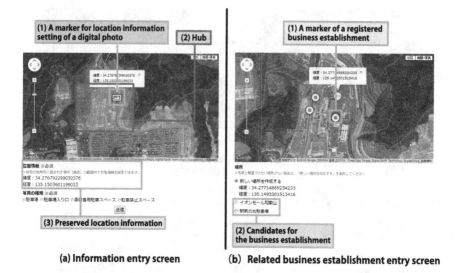

Fig. 2. An screen example of the digital photography submission function.

(1) Digital Photo Submission Function. With this function, is it possible to submit digital photos and geographical information regarding the place the photo was shot to the built digital archive. Users can upload digital photos, input information, obtain GPS information from Exif information, obtain their current location from their device, and transfer marks to Google Maps in Fig. 2-(a)-(1). This system is setup to separate a mesh on a map of Japan of the range possible to submit a digital photo of your position. The separation on the map uses a 1/4 regional mesh of the regional mesh code. The width of the mesh is 250 m. For the position that is the green square in Fig. 2-(a)-(2), it is necessary to set the digital photo location information only within the area surrounded by the green square We call the green square "hub". The submitted location information is displayed in Fig. 2-(a)-(3). Four types of digital photos, namely parking lots, parking lot entrances, handicap spaces, and no parking zones are laid out. Users can select a business establishment related a digital photo in Fig. 2-(b). Marks on Google Maps show location of registered business establishments in Fig. 2-(b)-(1). Registered business establishments nearby location information of a digital photo are displayed as candidates of the business establishment related a digital photo in Fig. 2-(b)-(2).

(2) Location Confirmation Function. With this function, geographical information from digital photos that were submitted by users is verified. It is possible to visit and confirm the place submitted as a digital photo's geographical information by pressing the "Confirm" button located in the list beneath Google Maps' digital photo's geographical information above the 125 m blue radius circle that centers on your current position. The rules for visiting the position of a digital photo and confirming its veracity is to make sure that it is a mark

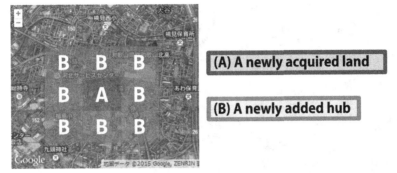

(1) Hub addition by acquired land

(2) Map of the acquired land situation

Fig. 3. A screen example of the land acquisition function.

that can be easily located. If the geographical information does not match with the digital photo, you can report it to the system by pressing the "Mismatch" button.

(3) Land Acquisition System. This system utilizes a land acquisition game. Each user confirms the digital photo's geographical information that members of the same team have submitted within the position, and any land in that position can be acquired when the whole team has a total of three digital photos that have had their position confirmed in the same location. It is possible to add the surrounding of the acquired land (Fig. 3-(1)-(A)) as a new hub (Fig. 3-(1)-(B)). You can view the acquired land situation in map for each team in Fig. 3-(2).

(4) Point Earning System. You can earn points with this function by submitting and confirming position of digital photos, and by submitting and adding

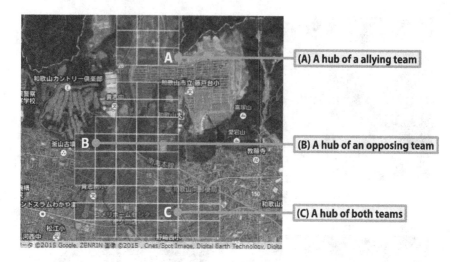

Fig. 4. Hubs on a location confirmation screen.

information. Once you have used 100 points, you can add a position. As you add positions, this adds merit to both your team members and yourself as it makes it easier to submit photos. While you cannot compare points between users with this system, it does add incentive to submitting data. This system was made to grant bonus points since it collects many digital photos for parking lots and correlates accurate geographical information with them. You can get points if you confirm a digital photo's geographical information in a hub of a allying team (Fig. 4-(A)) or a hub of an opposing team (Fig. 4-(B)). However you may get bonus points if you confirm a digital photo's geographical information in a hub of both teams (Fig. 4-(C)). Also, You can get bonus points if you submit various types of digital photos of business establishments.

4   Evaluation Experiment

4.1   Summary of Evaluation Experiment

This experiment was carried out from February 7, to February 14, 2015. There was also a midway survey on February 9 and a final survey at the end of the experiment. Participators were information science students (7 men, 5 women) residing in Wakayama. We asked users to use Photopolie on the web. Below are the experiment tasks.

(1) Submit three photos of parking lots for business establishments every day.
(2) Confirm geographical information for more than one photo submitted to Photopolie

Table 1. The number of submitted digital photos and the number of location confirmation.

UME team			MIKAN team		
	Number of submitted digital photos	Number of location confirmation		Number of submitted digital photos	Number of location confirmation
User A	42	38	User G	15	10
User B	55	12	User H	6	0
User C	13	17	User I	33	39
User D	21	8	User J	5	0
User E	13	0	User K	15	5
User F	4	0	User L	9	0
Total	148	75	Total	83	54

In this experiment, users were automatically assigned to two teams, UME (plum) and MIKAN (tangerine orange)[1]. Six people were assigned to the UME team (five men, one woman), and six people were assigned to the MIKAN team (two men, four women). The goal of this experiment was to promote the use of the digital archive and evaluate where data that could be used as tourism resources could be accumulated by having users use the system. Through the experiment, the following hypotheses were formed.

(1) Through utilization of the land acquisition game, collecting of digital photos for parking lots could be encouraged
(2) Through utilization of the land acquisition game, association with accurate position information for digital photos could be encouraged
(3) Through utilization of the land acquisition game, motivation to submit data could be preserved

Furthermore, manuals that explained how to use Photopolie were distributed before the experiment began. After the experiment, four information science university students were asked to evaluate photos that were collected. Evaluation contents are shown below.

(1) Determine where the digital photo is for a parking lot
(2) Match the type of digital photo

5   Experiment Results and Consideration

A total of 231 digital photos were submitted by users. Table 1 shows the amount of digital photos submitted by each user. The total of digital photos submitted

---

[1] UME (Plum) and MIKAN (tangerine orange) are a Japanese name of a fruit of a specialty in this area.

Table 2. Questionnaire survey about the experiment.

Question items	Team	Evaluation					Median	Mode
		1	2	3	4	5		
(1) I actively conducted the submission of digital photos for parking lots	U	0	1	0	2	3	4.5	5
	M	0	0	2	2	0	3.5	3,4
(2) The point earning system encouraged me to submit digital photos	U	1	0	2	3	0	3.5	4
	M	0	1	0	3	0	4	4
(3) It was difficult confirming geographical information of digital photos for parking lots	Both	0	1	4	3	2	3.5	3
(4) I checked the position information of a digital photography about a parking lot aggressively for a supporter team	Both	4	1	2	2	1	2.5	1
(5) It was difficult for me to understand a rule of "hub"	Both	0	1	4	4	1	3.5	3,4

- Evaluation: 1: Strongly disagree, 2: Disagree, 3: Neutral, 4: Agree, 5: Strongly agree
- "Evaluation" is the number of people.
- U: UME team, M: MIKAN team, Both: Both teams

by the UME team was 148, while the total for the MIKAN team was 83. After evaluating 231 of the collected photos, 165 of the total were determined to be for parking lots. Also, when users were asked to list photo types, digital photos that matched with the type that submitters gave was 126 out of 231 total. As a result of the midway survey, seven people responded, while ten responded to the final survey. The survey used the 5-point Likert scale (represented below as the "5 point evaluation"). The items of the 5 point evaluation were: "1: Strongly disagree", "2: Disagree", "3: Neutral", "4: Agree", and "5: Strongly agree".

5.1 Evaluations of Digital Photo Submission for Parking Lots

Perception Change of Data Submission for Land Acquisition Game.
For the survey item "I actively conducted the submission of digital photos for parking lots" listed in Table 2-(1), the UME team had a median of 4.5 and a mode of 5. Meanwhile, the MIKAN team had a median of 3.5 and a mode of 3 and 4. The following opinions in Table 1 for why that is were taken from User A and User I, who both submitted over 21 photos.

– The game got fun as my ally's land expanded.
– Since my team had not collected many photos, I took the initiative since I didn't want to lose to the opposing team.

For the survey item "The point earning system encouraged me to submit digital photos" in Table 2-(2), the UME team had a median of 3.5 and a mode of 4.

Meanwhile, the MIKAN team had both a median and mode of 4. From this, we assume users had a sense of rivalry with their opposing team and actively submitted data in order to earn points. From the above, it was learned that it was possible to encourage collecting of digital photos for parking lots from users who enjoyed the game.

Data Accumulation Effect Through Clarification of Photography Target. For the survey item "I submitted various types of digital photos of business establishments in order to earn bonus points", the below opinions were given as free-description answers.

- I took pictures at establishments where I could take numerous types of photos while being conscious of bonus points.
- Since I wanted to increase positions and needed to get more points, I thought to submit as many types of photos as possible for bonus points.

While it has been understood in experiments thus far that it is possible to encourage submission of digital photos through the point earning system, the bonus point earning system for when users submit various types of digital photos in business establishments encourages the taking of more digital photos for parking lots. Also, from evaluation results for digital photos, it can be assumed that over 50 % of digital photos collected can be accumulated as digital photos for parking lots categorized appropriately by type.

Evaluations for Association with Accurate Geographic Information. Results showed a total of 11 land acquisitions for the UME team and a total o 4 for the MIKAN team. From Table 2-(3), the survey item "It was difficult confirming geographical information of digital photos for parking lots" had a median of 3.5 and a mode of 3. From the free-description answers, we also got the following opinions: "It took time to properly photograph things at establishments with wide parking lots". "It was difficult getting present geographical information through the browser".

In the free-description answer portion of the survey in Table 2-(4), User A and User B, who both gave high evaluations, said that it was fun being able to acquire land, and that they actively confirmed locations and expanded their location in order to increase the total area that other members could submit photos for. User H said that "I could not actively back my team since I didn't know who was a member".

From the above, mutual user interaction has a possibility of giving incentive for actively confirming locations, as the acquiring of land and confirming positions with one another increases positions, making it easier to submit photos. However, confirming position information can be a burden for users, which splits evaluations. Also, since there was no system for communicating within teams, there is a necessity for a support system so users can collaborate.

5.2 Evaluations for Data Submission Motivation

Figure 5 shows the separately dated data submission of each user. The users who submitted data for more than four days and submitted over 21 digital photos were User A, B, D and I. In the free-description answer portion of the survey, User A and User I gave favorable views, stating that "it was fun being able to acquire land" and "I had fun. It was exciting being able to go to areas I normally do not go to". From this, we can assume the possibility of being able to preserve motivation for data submission for users that enjoy being able to acquire land and have initiative. From Table 2-(5), we see the possibility of the difficult game rules hindering the maintenance of motivation for data submission. It will be necessary to propose continued gamification elements, and will be our task here on out to make the rules easier for users to understand.

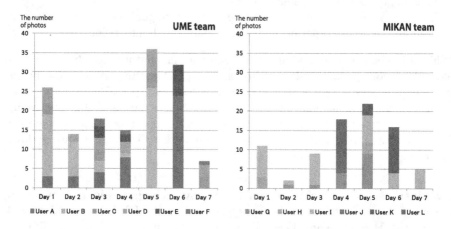

Fig. 5. The number of photos uploaded per a day.

6 Conclusion

This paper discussed the "Photopolie" image collecting system which utilizes a land acquisition game. Through utilization of the land acquisition game, we ran an experiment that encouraged use of a digital archive and evaluated whether data could be collected that could be used for tourism resources. The results of the experiment proved the following three points:

1. Through clarifying photography targets that are useful as tourism resources, and considering compatible gamification elements, there is a possibility of being able to collect more data.
2. User interaction has the possibility of motivating work.
3. It may be possible to maintain motivation for data submission for dynamic users who enjoy land acquisition games.

Hereafter, we will improve usability on smartphones and carry out privacy measures.

References

1. Toshio, K.: Tourism Informatics10. Tourism Information Services based on Digital Archives IPvol. 53(11), pp. 1192–1197 (2012) (in Japanese)
2. Masaki, T., Taku, O., Toshio, K.: Compilation of Photo Archives Using Historical Records of Hakodate IPSJDigital Document 2013-DD-88(9), pp.1-6 (2013) (in Japanese)
3. vonAhn, L., Dabbish, L.: Labeling images with a computer game. In: CHI 2004 Proceedings of the SIGCHI Conference on Human Factors in Computing Systemspp. pp. 319–326 (2004)
4. Tuite, K., Snavely, N., Hsiao, D., Tabing, N., Popovic, Z.: PhotoCity: training experts at large-scale image acquisition through a competitive game. In: CHI 2011 Proceedings of the SIGCHI Conference on Human Factors in Computing Systemspp. pp. 1383–1392 (2011)
5. Bell, M., Reeves, S., Brown, B., Sherwood, S., MacMillan, D., Ferguson, J., Chalmers, M.: EyeSpy, M.: supporting navigation through play. In: CHI 2009 Proceedings of the SIGCHI Conference on Human Factors in Computing Systemspp. pp. 123–132 (2009)

A Conceptual Model of Online Game Continuance Playing

Fan Zhao[1](⊠) and Qingju Huang[2]

[1] Lutgert College of Business, Florida Gulf Coast University, Fort Myers, USA
fzhao@fgcu.edul
[2] Experiment and Training Center, Hubei University of Technology,
Wuhan 430068, China
549941621@qq.com

Abstract. Today's online gaming customers are very demanding, hence there is a need for the game vendors and developers to understand and keep pace with customers' demands. The purpose of this paper is to survey the current literatures and summarize the reasons why users tend to play a certain online games longer. In this paper, we propose a research model to predict online games continuance play. We believe this framework will help both researchers and practitioners in game research, design and development.

Keywords: Online games · IS continuance · Intention

1 Introduction

In the past two decades, online games have gained popularity around the world. An online game adopted client server technology to let game players play the same game from different locations all over the world. Users can use computers, mobile devices or video game consoles to play the online games. There are variety online games available in the market. According to the new Online Game Market Forecasts report by Statista Incorporation [1], online game market will reach $41.4 billion at the end of 2015. In another report by Holodny [2], online gaming in the US is expected to be a 5.2 billion business by 2020. Online games are computer controlled games, including both PC games and video games, played by consumers over network technology, especially through the Internet. Online games can be categorized into multiplayer and single-player games. At present, multiplayer games, especially massively multiplayer online games (MMOG) are most successful among all online games. World of Warcraft, one of the famous MMOG, surpasses 100 million subscribers in 2014 [3].

The rapid growth of online games has caught the attention of the gaming industry. Investigation of consumers' online behavior becomes critical. According to Lo and Chen [4], the profitable life cycle of an online game goes down to 8 months to a year from 18 months to 3 years in average in the past. This means majority online game players switch their games every 8–18 months. Game developers try to make more profit from each game. However, they are facing two serious issues: market competitiveness and high demanding quality from customers. Every year, there are more than a hundred new online games available in the market from different game developers.

M. Kurosu (Ed.): Human-Computer Interaction, Part II, HCII 2015, LNCS 9170, pp. 660–669, 2015.
DOI: 10.1007/978-3-319-20916-6_61

Typical customers only focus on one or two online games at a certain time and customers are demanding on all aspects of the online games, including game stories, game graphics, game services, and so on [5]. Therefore, it is increasingly important to study the key factors for retaining customers in the game. As suggested by Semeijin et al. [6], maintaining customer loyalty not only lowers the cost of acquiring new customer, but also brings in substantial revenues. A typical revenue model of an online game is to charge subscribing fee every month. However, to attract more players, who are not willing to pay fees, most of the current online game developers start to offer the online games for free to the consumers. In the free games, their revenue model changed from collecting subscribing fee to allure customers buying virtual goods in the games. Therefore, the longer time players play the online games, the more money they possibly will spend on the game, and this will bring more revenue to the game vendors or developers. Few empirical research has been conducted on how to extend current customers' playing time and what are the variables impacting the online game continuance play. The purpose of this study is to review the current literature and establish a research model to explain what factors affect online game adoption and how to extend online game playing time.

2   Theoretical Background

There are many studies focus on how to persuade users to use IS or IT devices, such as research on IS acceptance models [7]. Recently, more and more researchers start to switch to post-adoption studies, such as how to attract consumers to continually use IS or IT devices, because IS/IT vendors and developer realize that retain their customers to keep using the IS or IT devices is getting more and more important to help them expand their revenue.

2.1   Post-Acceptance Model of IS Continuance

The initial IS continuance research model, explaining customer behaviors of their intentions to continually use IS or IT devices, was developed by Bhattacherjee based on expectation-confirmation theory (ECT) [8]. Bhattacherjee [8] argues that

- Users' extent of Confirmation, which represents the level of a customer's evaluative response regarding his/her expectations of the IS [9], is positively associated with their satisfaction of using the IS and is positively related to perceived usefulness;
- Users' perceived usefulness of IS, which is one of the key variables in technology acceptance model (TAM) [7], is positively associated with their satisfaction with IS use and associated with there is continuance intention;
- Users' level of satisfaction with initial IS use is positively associated with there is continuance intention.

The author summarizes that IS continuance more depend on users' first-hand experience with the IS. IS vendors and developer should adopt two different strategies to maximize their return on investments in customers' training: emphasize potential benefits to the new customers while educating continued users on how to use the IS efficiently [8].

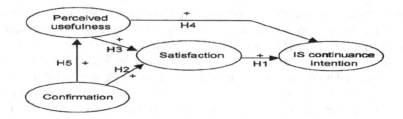

Fig. 1. A post-acceptance model of IS continuance

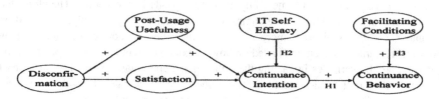

Fig. 2. An extended model of IT continuance

2.2   An Extended Model of IT Continuance

Based on the Post-Acceptance Model, Bhattacherjee, et al. [10] extend the model by adding three more variables: IT self-efficacy, facilitating conditions, and continuance behavior. Self-efficacy refers to one's conviction or belief in his/her ability to independently complete a certain task successfully [11]. According to previous research [12, 13], IT self-efficacy is a positive indicator to predict users' utilizations of computers and IS. Bhattacherjee, et al. [10] demonstrate that IT self-efficacy tends to cause users' belief in their ability to successfully utilize the IS right after their initial usage. However, they argue that and self-efficacy will not impact users' decisions/behaviors to continually use IT/IS. Facilitating conditions refer to the availability level of external resources required by IT usage, such as the speed of the Internet when users are playing online games. In the extended model of IT continuance, Bhattacherjee, et al. [10] conclude the following additional relationships:

- Users' IT self-efficacy is positively associated with their IT continuance intention;
- Users' perception of facilitating conditions is positively associated with their IT continuance behavior;
- Users' IT continuance intention is positively associated with their IT continuance behavior Fig. 2.

2.3   IS Use Continuance Intention Prediction Using Perceived Needs Fulfilment

Based on theory of human needs [14] and existence, relatedness and growth needs (ERG) theory [15], Yeh and Teng [16] develop a research model to predict users' IS continuance usage from perceived needs fulfillment. They claim that existence need from ERG theory, which refers to users' needs to perform the assigned job duty successfully, can be transferred to extended usefulness with perceived efficiency and perceived effectiveness. Additionally, the authors believe that relatedness need, which refers the individual intentions to communicate with other human beings, can be reflected to perceived relatedness to increase the users' interactions with others while using the IS. Similarly, growth need, which relates to "the urge of an individual to fully develop his/her potential", is transferred as perceived self-development fulfilment to obtain the opportunities to encourage users' learning, growth and self-development. In this research model, Yeh and Teng [16] suggest three new relations:

- Users' perceived needs fulfilment of IS use is positively related to their IS use continuance intention;
- Users' perceived needs fulfilment of IS use is positively related to their satisfaction with IS use;
- Users' extent of confirmation is positively related to their perceived needs fulfilment of IS use Fig. 3.

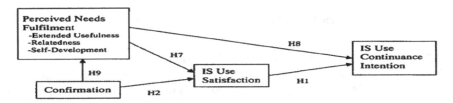

Fig. 3. Research model: predicting continuance intention using perceived needs fulfilment

2.4   Applications of Information Systems Continuance Models

2.4.1   Research Model Adopted to Mobile Applications

Hong et al. [17] compared three research models, TAM, expectation-Confirmation Model (ECM) by Bhattacherjee [8], and the proposed Extended ECM by the authors, in mobile Internet. Since this is an early study, authors are kind of misunderstand the three models. They include TAM as one of the continuance research model. According to Bhattacherjee [8], TAM is just an IS acceptance model which focus on the initial usage of IS while as the other two models in Hong et al.'s study are related to continuance usage of IS. One variable that this study added is perceived ease of use, which is adopted from TAM. In the context of mobile Internet, it is a reasonable factor that impacts the satisfaction and IS continuance Fig. 4.

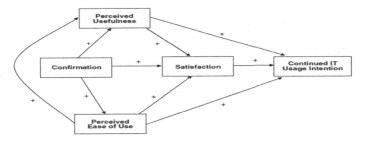

Fig. 4. Extended ECM

Chen et al. [18] expand the ECM with four more variables: Information Quality, System Quality, Process Quality, and Hedonic Value. Information quality, which refers to the quality of information output by the IS, and system quality, which focuses on the quality of functions/features in the IS, are generated from DeLone & MeLean research [19], whereas hedonic value, which refers to users' enjoyment of using IS, is adopted from Karaiskos et al. study [20] Fig. 5.

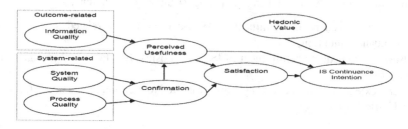

Fig. 5. Extended model of IS continuance for mobile applications

2.4.2 Research Model Adopted to Social Network

With the development of web 2.0, social network becomes to a popular study area. Extended from ECM, subjective norm and enjoyment were added to the research model in context of social network [21]. Different from most of the IS, social network focus on communications among users, therefore, subjective norm, which refers to a person's behavioral intentions influenced by people who are important to him/her, is positively related to social network use. Enjoyment is another special factor associated with social network because one of the purposes people use social network is to have fun. Therefore, authors demonstrate that enjoyment is positively related to satisfaction, continuance intention, and continuance usage of social network Fig. 6.

By comparing users in US and Taiwan, Ku et al. [22] propose another research model for social network continuance usage. Besides privacy concerns, region, and gender, which are three special factors in this study, perceived critical mass is a new variable in this model. Critical mass refers to the intention to use the social network when sufficient number of users are using the same system. Gratifications in this research model is the same factor as the previous one named enjoyment Fig. 7.

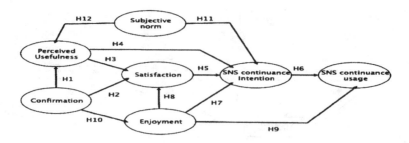

Fig. 6. Research model 1 for social network services

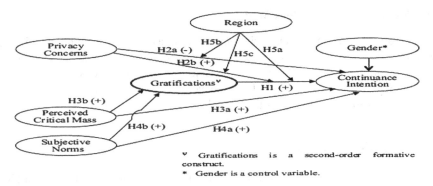

Fig. 7. Research model 2 for social network services

2.4.3   Research Model Adopted to Online Learning Technology

In the proposed research model, Limayem and Cheung [23] argue that habit of using a technology could cause the continuance use because habit strengthens the continuance activities or decisions without thinking about it or performing further decision making process [24, 25]. Habit is added as a moderator variable impacting on the relationship between continuance intention and continuance usage.

3   Proposed Research Model

Based on the previous research models and previous online game studies, we propose a conceptual online game continuance model as depicted in Fig. 1. This model integrates the motivational perspective into the original TAM and ECM. Discussions of this model are presented in the following sections.

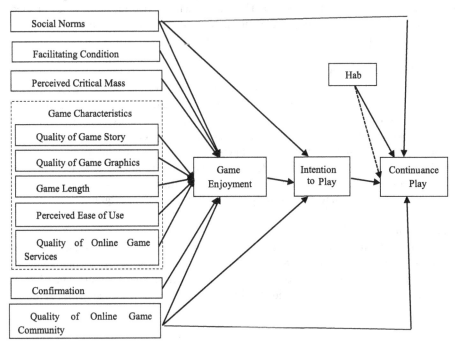

3.1   Variables from Previous Model

In the propose research model, social norms, same as subjective norms, facilitating condition, perceived critical mass, perceived ease of use, confirmation, enjoyment, intention, and continuance play are the variable explained in previous studies in the literature review section. Because of the specialty of online gaming, there are several more special variables adopted in this model.

3.2   Game Characteristics

Product quality is one of the crucial factors influencing customers' consumption [26]. For online products, since most purchasing and service activities are completed over the Internet, both product quality and service quality are important determinants of customers' behavioral intentions [27]. As online products, online games' quality is important. It includes but not limited to game story, game graphics, game length, and game operations.

3.2.1   Game Story

Most online games create virtual environments in the game. Game stories are often used to immerse game players in the virtual world. A good story attracts players' attention and increases players' curiosity to explore the virtual world. The story makes the game more enjoyable and fulfilling. These attractive tasks, like projects in real life, keep players continuously returning to the game whenever they have time to play [28]. A good story offers a wonderful growing space for the actors created in the game. From the beginning of the story, game players "watch" and "feel" the growth of their actors along the story phases. The good story environment let the players create the history using their actors in the virtual world. The players will cherish the stories they created in the game and this will bring them enormous enjoyment in the game and let them forget all the unpleasant things in their real lives [5].

3.2.2   Game Graphics

3D graphics has been receiving great attention recently due to its use in various applications such as movie making, 3D games, virtual reality modeling and 3D Graphical User Interface (GUI) development. Graphic attractiveness is a key element in creating an enjoyable user experience in online games [5]. Graphic designs for online games consist of static graphics, movement graphics and special graphics. Static graphics refer to the non-movement items in the game environment. A better design of static graphics makes players feel more real in the virtual world. Movement graphics includes all the movement design in the game, such as running, fighting, etc.

3.2.3   Game Length

The game length refers to the average time game players complete the online games by reaching the highest level of the actors, winning the final game items, or completing all the core game tasks. There is no best number to target regarding online game length because each online game is unique with special story and special game settings.

However, there could be an ideal length uniquely for each game [29]. For a certain game, players will not have enough time to enjoy the story and all the graphic designs in the game if the game is too short. On the other hand, if the length of the online game is extended too long, players may be exhausted and eventually quit if they can hardly see the end of the road. An appropriate game length will lead to an enjoyable experience.

3.2.4   Quality of Online Game Services

Service quality is one of the key factors in e-commerce success [30]. The quality of online game services are evaluated directly by game players according to the response promptness, problem solving ability, problem solving time, information richness of the game, attention to particular player needs, promise-keeping, game master (instant helper in the game) service behavior, and so on. Online players will perceive the services and make their judgments to determine the service quality. Their judgments significantly impact on their enjoyment of the game playing [31].

3.3   Online Game Community

An online community is defined as social groups of people who communicate with each other via network technology, such as Internet. Typically, each online community has a community theme, such as purposes or reasons why people are here, to attract more members. The theme of online game community is focus on the game to share information about game news, game experiences for different tasks and different types of actors, stories related to the certain game, social network communications, and so on. Through the online game community, players share their game information, seek helps from the community for game activities, and even build their social network beyond the game. The better quality of online game community motivates more players to gather and share information in the community, and in return stimulates even higher quality of the community. Players will feel comfortable and enjoyable if they have a social network in the game, which they build through the online game community. This community network also encourages their intentions to play the game and eventually increase their loyalty to the game [32].

4   Conclusions

The purpose of this study is to develop a theoretical research model regarding the key factors affecting customers' online game continuance usage based on a literature review. There are studies developed IS continuance research model and models for applications in mobile technology usage, social network adoption, and e-learning technology. However, there is no study focusing on the online game continuance playing area. This paper summarizes the previous IS continuance studies and proposes a complete research model to explain our research question: why there are online games that last over than 10 years while most of the online games only had short life less than 2 years.

References

1. Statista Inc., Market volume of online gaming worldwide 2012 (2012). http://www.statista.com/statistics/270728/market-volume-of-online-gaming-worldwide/
2. Holodny, E.: Online Gaming in The US Could Be A $5.2 Billion Business By 2020 (2014). http://www.businessinsider.com/morgan-stanleys-online-gaming-market-forecast-2014-9
3. "Blizzard reaches 100 M lifetime World of Warcraft accounts", 28 January 2014. Polygon.com
4. Lo, N., Chen, S.: A study of anti-robot agent mechanisms and process on online games. In: IEEE International Conference on Intelligence and Security Informatics, pp. 203 – 205 (2008)
5. Wu, J., Li, P., Rao, S.: Why they enjoy virtual game words? An empirical investigation. J. Electron. Commer. Res. **9**(3), 219–230 (2008)
6. Semeijn, J., Riel, A., Birgelen, M., Steukens, S.: E-services and offline fulfillment: how e-loyalty is crated. Managing Serv. Qual. **15**(2), 182–194 (2005)
7. Davis, F.D.: Perceived usefulness, perceived ease of use, and user acceptance of information technology. MIS Q. **13**(3), 319–339 (1989)
8. Bhattacherjee, A.: Understanding information systems continuance: an expectation-confirmation model. MIS Q. **25**(3), 351–370 (2001)
9. Anderson, E., Sullivan, M.: The antecedents and consequences of customer satisfaction for firms. Mark. Sci. **12**(2), 125–143 (1993)
10. Bhattacherjee, A., Perols, J., Sanford, C.: Information technology continuance: a theoretic extension and empirical test. J. Comput. Inf. Syst. **49**(1), 17–26 (2008)
11. Ajzen, I.: Perceived behavioral control, self-efficacy, locus of control, and the theory of planned behavior. J. Appl. Soc. Psychol. **32**(4), 665–683 (2002)
12. Compeau, D., Higgins, C., Huff, S.: Social cognitive theory and individual reactions to computing technology: a longitudinal study. MIS Q. **23**(2), 145–158 (1999)
13. Venkatesh, V., Morris, M., Davis, G., Davis, F.: User acceptance of information technology: toward a unifying view. MIS Q. **27**(3), 425–478 (2003)
14. Maslow, A.: A theory of human motivation. Psychol. Rev. **50**, 370–396 (1943)
15. Alderfer, C.P.: An empirical test of a new theory of human needs. Organ. Behav. Hum. Perform. **4**(2), 142–175 (1969)
16. Yeh, R., Teng, T.: Extended conceptualization of perceived usefulness: empirical test in the context of information system use continuance. Behav. Inf. Technol. **31**(5), 525–540 (2012)
17. Hong, S., Thong, J., Tam, K.: Understanding continued information technology usage behavior: a comparison of three models in the context of mobile internet. Decis. Support Syst. **42**, 1819–1834 (2006)
18. Chen, L., Meservy, T., Gillenson, M.: Understanding information systems continuance for information-oriented mobile applications. Commun. Assoc. Inf. Syst. **30**, 127–146 (2012)
19. DeLone, W., McLean, E.: Information Systems Success: the quest for the dependent variable. Inf. Syst. Res. **3**(1), 60–95 (1992)
20. Karahanna, E., Straub, D.: The psychological origins of perceived usefulness and ease-of-use. Inf. Manag. **35**(4), 237–250 (1999)
21. Yoon, C., Rolland, E.: Understanding continuance use in social networking services. J. CIS **55**(2), 1–8 (2015)
22. Ku, Y., Chen, R., Zhang, H.: Why do users continue using social networking sites? An exploratory study of members in the United States and Taiwan. Inf. Manag. **50**, 571–581 (2013)

23. Limayem, M., Cheung, C.: Understanding information systems continuance: the case of Internet-based learning technologies. Inf. Manag. **45**, 227–232 (2008)
24. Aarts, H., Verplanken, B., Van Knippenberg, A.: Predicting behavior from actions in the past: repeated decision making or a matter of habit? J. Appl. Soc. Psychol. **28**(15), 1355–1374 (1998)
25. Mittal, B.: Achieving higher seat-belt usage: the role of habit in bridging the attitude-behavior gap. J. Appl. Soc. Psychol. **18**(12), 993–1016 (1998)
26. Chinen, K., Jun, M., Hampton, G.: Product quality, market presence, and buying behavior: aggregate impages of foreign products in the US. Multinational Bus. Rev. **8**(1), 29–38 (2000)
27. Boyer, K., Hult, G.: Customer behavioral intentions for online purchases: an examination of fulfillment method and customer experience level. J. Oper. Manag. **24**, 124–147 (2006)
28. Sweetser, P., Wyeth, P.: GameFlow: a model for evaluating player enjoyment in games. ACM Comput. Entertainment **3**(3), 3–24 (2005)
29. Zeschuk, G., Muzyka, R.: Why don't people finish games? (2004). http://www.gamestar.com/12_04/features/fea_finish_jadeempire.shtml. Accessed on October 2008
30. Wang, Y.: Assessing e-commerce systems success: a respecification and validation of the DeLone and McLean model of IS success. Inf. Syst. J. **18**(5), 529 (2008)
31. Holsapple, C., Wu, J.: Building effective online game websites with knowledge-based trust. Inf. Syst. Front **10**, 47–60 (2008)
32. Hsu, C., Lu, H.: Consumer behavior in online game communities: a motivational factor perspective. Comput. Hum. Behav. **23**, 1642–1659 (2004)

A Lexical Analysis of Nouns and Adjectives from Online Game Reviews

Miaoqi Zhu and Xiaowen Fang[✉]

School of Computing, College of Computing and Digital Media,
DePaul University, 243 S. Wabash Avenue, Chicago, IL 60604, USA
miaoqi.zhu@gmail.com, xfang@cdm.depaul.edu

Abstract. The objective of this study is to develop playability heuristics by a lexical analysis of nouns and adjectives used in online game reviews. A revised lexical approach is adopted to analyze nouns and adjectives from 821,122 online reviews. Ninety seven (97) factors are extracted from the analysis. Based on the nouns and adjectives highly loaded on these factors, a new heuristic development process is introduced and 116 playability heuristics are developed. This study significantly expands the pool of playability heuristics that can be used by game developers for computer game design. The lexical method in this study demonstrates its effectiveness in developing interface design guidelines when a large number of online reviews are available on a system or product. It can be extended to other fields as well.

Keywords: Computer game · Lexical analysis · Online reviews · Factor analysis · Playability · Heuristics

1 Introduction

With the rapid economic growth of the computer game industry, the rising popularity of games and complexity of game-play call for systematic examination on play experience (PX) and playability.

According to the discussions that computer game systems are different from utility software [2, 13, 19] in many aspects including the user experience (UX), we can reasonably argue that a different set of playability heuristics should be introduced for computer games. Moreover, the resulting set should cover an array of common game design elements besides user interface.

As of now, only a handful playability heuristics [3, 6, 13, 17] have been identified by previous research. There are three major flaws in these heuristics: (1) the number of heuristics is small compared to traditional usability guidelines; (2) these heuristics are usually derived from a small dataset. They may not cover the most critical problems from players' perspective; and (3) these heuristics tend to focus on few types of games and may not be applicable to a wider spectrum of computer games.

Provided the success in exploring computer game traits by our revised lexical approach [24], the objective of this study is to initialize a set of playability heuristics through a similar process. Specifically, we argue that by incorporating nouns

© Springer International Publishing Switzerland 2015
M. Kurosu (Ed.): Human-Computer Interaction, Part II, HCII 2015, LNCS 9170, pp. 670–680, 2015.
DOI: 10.1007/978-3-319-20916-6_62

and gaming jargon terms, more context and subject information will become available for deciphering observed patterns. If a pattern proves to be prominent from interpreting the original reviews, it should be translated into a potential heuristics.

This study attempts to fill in the gap in game playability research and it aims at developing comprehensive playability heuristics through a lexical analysis of frequently-used nouns and adjectives by users. The paper is structured as follows: (1) playability and playability heuristics, (2) the lexical approach and prior lexical analysis, (3) lexical analysis of nouns and adjectives, and (4) results and discussions.

2   Playability and Playability Heuristics

There is no standard definition of playability presently. Usability-First [20] defines playability as "the degree to which a game is fun to play and is usable, with an emphasis on the interaction style and plot-quality of the game; the quality of gameplay". Sánchez et al. [18] view playability as the UX in videogames and define it as "a set of properties that describe the Player Experience using a specific game system whose main objective is to provide enjoyment and entertainment, by being credible and satisfying, when the player plays alone or in company." Paavilainen et al. [16] suggest that playability is the combination of gameplay and user interface, which can be further connected to concepts of intuitiveness, unobtrusiveness, fun, and challenge. Since the cores of these definitions lies on either game-play or usability, confusions exist between playability and usability. Above all, there are few playability heuristics that game professionals can easily apply with consideration of different aspects of gameplay.

To introduce some existing heuristics, Malone [13] pinpoints three motivational factors of designing enjoyable interfaces for educational games: (1) challenge, (2) fantasy, and (3) curiosity. The subsequent analysis generates a design framework, which has a far-reaching significance for ensuing playability research. Federoff [6] publishes the first playability heuristics set for the games of entertainment purposes. The set is developed in the light of traditional usability heuristics and game design principles. Desurvire et al. [3] create a heuristics set consisting of 43 items that fall into three categories. Korhonen and Koivisto [10, 11] become the first to develop playability heuristics for games running on mobile devices.

More recently, Pinelle et al. [17] develop a set of heuristics through analyzing 108 game reviews from GameSpot.com. Important issues are identified and classified from the reviews of certain PC games. They then translate initial findings into the principles at high level; however, the resulting set is more toward user interface problems thus less applicable when it comes to other design factors. With the trend of social networking games, Paavilainen [15] introduces an initial set of social game heuristics according to two design frameworks [9, 21]. The heading-level heuristics contain 10 items such as spontaneity and narrativity.

Each of aforementioned heuristics has its own strengths. However, they fail to cover views and opinions from the majority of players who have different tastes for games. This study strives to address this issue by examining a massive amount of online game reviews. Because these online reviews are tantamount to user-generated content from which players' experience is directly reflected, they will likely provide rich information and serve as a fertile ground for developing playability heuristics and/or design guidelines.

3   The Lexical Approach and Prior Lexical Analysis

The concept of lexical approach stems from the lexical hypothesis to study personality taxonomy in personality research. The lexical hypothesis states that when salient individual differences become socially relevant to human life, these distinctive attributes are likely to be encoded into nature languages. If many people recognize a difference, the difference may be expressed by similar words. Therefore, personality traits can be identified by exploring personality descriptive adjectives in natural languages. Through three basic steps summarized by Ashton [1], the original lexical approach helps discover five factors that later become the well-received Big Five personality factors: openness, conscientiousness, extraversion, agreeableness, and neuroticism [8].

Motivated by the lexical approach to understand human personalities, a revised lexical analysis is adopted in this study to analyze adjectives in online game reviews [22, 23]. This revised method has extracted six significant factors in game play experience: playability, creativity, usability, competition, sensation, and strategy. Based on the adjectives, a simple game design framework can be drawn, specifically, competition, sensation, and strategy can be regarded as the stimuli factors stimulating game enjoyment; on the other hand, playability, creativity and usability can be used to measure to what extent a computer game is successful.

However, the analysis of adjectives alone does not fully disclose the subjects and contexts when players write the reviews. Therefore, playability heuristics (i.e. design guidelines for computer games) are still some distance away. In this study, we plan to incorporate nouns in the lexical analysis because nouns may indicate the subjects described by the adjectives and therefore suggest more context-specific information. It is argued that a lexical analysis of the combination of nouns and adjectives will likely achieve two objectives: (1) Discovery of general patterns among online game reviews and (2) Context-specific information concerning different aspects of player experience. These two findings will likely lead to a prolific set of playability heuristics that would be a great help to game developers.

4   Lexical Analysis of Nouns and Adjectives

Two phases were involved in developing playability heuristics based on nouns and adjectives.

4.1   Phase I: The Lexical Analysis

There are mainly four stages in the revised lexical approach adopted in our early work [22, 23]: (1) Collecting online reviews, (2) Building a list of game descriptive adjectives, (3) Extracting ratings of adjectives from game players, and (4) Exploring patterns through factor analyses.

In our previous work [22, 23], we have downloaded 821,122 reviews from three major game websites (e.g., gamespot.com, gamestop.com, ign.com). The nature of those reviews varies self-reflection on game-play to objective introduction of game design and/or technical facts. Since nouns (including game jargons) are added in this study, we took some additional steps based on the work we've done in Stages 2 and 3 before [22, 23]:

- Step 1: Identifying nouns/noun phrases and jargon terms from original game reviews;
- Step 2: Extracting player ratings of nouns and jargon;
- Step 3: Refining the list and conducting factor analysis.

Step 1: Identifying Nouns/Noun Phrases and Game Jargon Terms. Four tasks were involved in this stage: (1) Parsing individual lexicons from raw texts and checking the part of speech (PoS); (2) Detecting nouns and phrases as non-adjectives in the sentences; (3) Dropping stop-words; (4) Registering overall frequency and the number of game reviews containing a word. Natural Language Processing (NLP) applications were developed using Perl to complete these tasks.

Since user-generated reviews are often poorly written with informal languages, this study adopts a simple parsing strategy. The NLP program examines a word's sense semantically instead of analyzing the entire sentence syntactically. WordNet [7, 14] is referred to as the main reference because it offers a wealthy lexical library that documents words of four PoS. Meanwhile, it provides a comprehensive set of senses for each word.

Based on 821,122 reviews, 21,535 distinctive nouns/noun phrases are found. The numbers of documents containing a noun range from 1 to 100,532. On the other hand, there are approximately 4,327 jargon terms carrying an absolute frequency ranging from 8,033 to 10.

Step 2: Extracting Player Ratings of Nouns. At this step, the online reviews were transformed to a matrix by a computer program as follows: (1) Each noun or jargon was regarded as an individual item. The terms were relabeled as the field names of the matrix table (2) All online reviews were retrieved one at a time. Each review about one game was processed as an individual document. If a term appeared in this review, the value for this noun or jargon (field) was set to 1. Otherwise, a zero value was registered. There were 821,122 records from which the ratings were obtained.   After variances of all terms were computed, those low variance terms causing computation errors were excluded. As a result, 4,342 items were retained in the final analysis. These terms were combined with the adjectives list produced in our prior lexical analysis [22] to form a new list. This new list was used as source dataset for the subsequent factor analysis.

Step 3: Refining the List and Conducting Factor Analysis. This step commenced from an exploratory factor analysis with Varimax rotation using SAS. Un-weighted least squares (ULS) method was employed, and communalities were estimated by square multiple correlations (SMC). 147 factors were obtained from the first round of analysis. Redundant information was noticed among the 147 factors. In other words, many factors seemed similar. To address this problem, we consolidated nouns with similar or identical meanings as what we dealt with adjectives. The process generated 3,044 groups of nouns. The items within each group are not only semantically relevant, but also statistically correlated.

After combining the 788 adjective groups from prior analysis, 1298 popular game jargons, and 3,044 noun groups, a new hybrid list of 5,130 terms was finally formed. It served as the base for an updated rating matrix by a slightly different conversion process. In particular, for each review, the number of distinct adjective or noun terms from the same group appearing in the same review was used as the value of this group in this review. A second factor analysis was then carried out.

The lexical analysis of nouns and adjectives led to 97 factors. Each factor was loaded with a group of nouns and adjectives relevant to each other for some reason. The next task was to interpret why and how these nouns and adjectives are related.

4.2   Phase II: Developing Playability Heuristics

In Phase II, each factor was analyzed in the following four steps in order to formulate playability heuristics: (1) Step 1: Sorting terms in a factor according to factor loadings, (2) Step 2: Identifying terms that may contribute to potential heuristics, (3) Step 3: Composing initial heuristics, (4) Step 4: Refining playability heuristics. Factor #31 is used as an example to illustrate these different steps.

Step 1: Sorting Terms in a Factor According to Factor Loadings. Ascript was written to rank the terms in a factor based on terms' loading values. The Part-of-Speech (PoS) tags were retained during sorting. It became immediately noticeable that highly-loaded terms in a factor may suggest a prominent game play context. Taking Factor 31 for example, the first three factor descriptors - "Japanese", "Anime" and "Turn-based" clearly represent the inherent characteristics of Japanese-RPGs. It is reasonable for them to stand out among other terms as players may have frequently used these three as generic descriptors. Other words such as "Anime-like" and "Japanese-style" with lower loadings also confirm this presumption. Those context-oriented terms introduce a primary context/background to understand the factor. Table 1 lists the words loaded on Factor #31.

Step 2: Identifying Terms that Contribute to Potential Heuristics. The list of each factor usually consists of nouns and adjectives with continuous factor loadings. This step is designed to short-list truly useful words for drafting playability heuristics. The entire list was studied in relation to the context. To ensure the validity of any playability heuristic to be developed, original player reviews were systematically examined.   Commonly-used words that hardly convey much useful information were first excluded. The following five types of words were considered irrelevant: (1) Terms reflecting a component in the game such as plot and character. In factor 31, some of the words are "daughter", "girl", "son", "dragon", "gust", and "incest". (2) Terms used in the title of a game or sequel. They can be a popular element in game storylines as well. With regard to Factor #31, some of these items are: "boy", "atelier", "sonata", "fencer", "saga", and "radiance"; (3) Terms entailing meta-data related to a game or sequel. "Composer" as a generic noun term is often mentioned in reviews of Final Fantasy. Reviewers keep mentioning its composer because of his excellent work on the soundtrack. Another term "Square-Enix"

Table 1. Nouns, adjectives and jargon terms loaded on Factor #31

Original terms and factor loadings	Selected terms for developing playability heuristics
japanese (a[1]): 0.2297	japanese (a)
anime (np[2]): 0.21537	anime(np)
turn-based(j[3]): 0.18741	turn-based(j)
boy daughter girl son (np): 0.15629	english (a)
english (a): 0.14535	side-quests(j)
dragon (np): 0.10936	cel-shaded(j)
atelier (np): 0.09365	anime-inspired(j)
side-quests(j): 0.08356	cel-shading(j)
cel-shaded(j): 0.08298	in-battle(j)
composer (np): 0.07932	level-grinding(j)
sonata (np): 0.07066	side-quest(j)
j-pop(j): 0.07043	non-playable(j)
scholar student (np): 0.06973	randomly-generated(j)
anime-inspired(j): 0.06962	fan-service(j)
saga (np): 0.06705	cell-shading(j)
cel-shading(j): 0.06435	translator (np)
aria (np): 0.06399	
in-battle(j): 0.06308	
gust (np): 0.06222	
....	
hearts (np): 0.01842	
oldie (np): 0.01819	
cleavage (np): 0.01709	
skit (np): 0.01645	
reincarnation (np): 0.01516	
censorship (np): 0.01486	
fandom (np): 0.01394	
highschool (np): 0.00937	
incest (np): 0.00413	

[1] Tag of "a" refers to adjective terms.

[2] Tag of "np" annotates nouns that do not play a role as adjectives in a sentence.

[3] Tag of "j" means gaming jargon and/or terminologies.

is the developer of Final Fantasy; (4) Terms emphasizing the theme or style of a game or sequel. In Factor #31, those items are: "spiky-haired", "anime-like", "over-world", "Japanese-style", "rpg-style", "adult-oriented", "j-pop", "zelda-like", and "anime-ish". (5) Terms describing generic features of gameplay. Those items loaded in Factor #31 are: "mid-battle", "action-rpgs", "friendship" and "auto-battle". As the result of this step, a shortened list of words was used to query the original reviews. Finally for Factor #31, 16 words were chosen for this purpose (see Table 1), and the first three context descriptors on this list are "Japanese", "anime", and "turn-based".

Step 3: Composing Initial Heuristics. Original reviews combined with nouns and adjectives belonging to a factor were systematically examined. The initial interpretations were then converted into playability heuristics in the light of general user-interface design principles. Playability heuristics were stated as specific as possible in order to preserve pertaining contextual information.   The process started with examining reviews that contain highly-ranked terms. In factor 31, the words "Japanese", "Anime", and "English" were used to query original reviews. This pattern in fact expresses players' support for keeping original voice-acting in certain themed games. Although language options are often available, most players prefer the original "Japanese" voice-acting, as it narrates stories better than "English". Since storytelling is an effective tool in user engagement, this finding is surely a unique discovery about game play. 146 online reviews with similar suggestions supported this heuristic.   "Side-quests" and "side-quest" encode the request for a fair playfulness in non-primary tasks. The reviews tell us that there should be plenty of fun side-quests so players will stay entertained. In addition, these secondary tasks may help players better explore the game world. 2,823 online reviews with similar suggestions supported this heuristic.   For factor #31, 12 out of 71 terms contributed to 10 raw playability heuristics. Table 2 presents two sample heuristics.

Table 2. Sample playability heuristics based on Factor #31

Terms	Playability heuristic (Draft)	Sample game review
English Japanese Anime	For English versions of Japanese-style games, users may prefer the original Japanese voice-acting with English subtitles	"I still prefer using Japanese voice w/English subs since there are some things that the Japanese could say better"
Side-quest Side-quests	Users expect fun side-quests in addition to the main tasks or missions	"A valiant attempt to add some spice to the over-populated SRPG Genre but boring side-quests and poor art hold it back"

Step 4: Refining Playability Heuristics. Two tasks were performed to refine the first draft of playability heuristics:

- Additional information was collected from original reviews to substantiate each drafted heuristic. The number and content of reviews related to each heuristic were analyzed. Sample reviews supporting a heuristic are presented along with it. Heuristics were re-worded to better reflect player comments. Heuristics without strong support in original reviews were removed.
- Similar heuristics were combined together and consolidated.

For Factor #31, 10 drafted items from previous phase were consolidated into 7 heuristics. In total, 116 playability heuristics were developed based on all 97 factors. They are grouped into three categories: playability, creativity, and usability. Table 3 shows some basic statistics about them. Through retrieving relevant reviews, it is noted that the number of online game reviews supporting a heuristic ranges from 51 to 7,611. Although some of these numbers might seem small in comparison to the total amount of reviews analyzed, they should be viewed in a very specific context rendered by a unique creative vision. The number of reviews per game ranged from 1 to 6,021 with an average of 56. Some playability heuristics may aim at certain type of games. Nevertheless, the factor analysis in the early lexical analysis has statistically substantiated the lexicon patterns that were used to derive the playability heuristics.

5 Results and Discussions

The lexical analysis of nouns and adjectives produced 116 playability heuristics. All of these heuristics have been verified and are supported by original player reviews. As shown in Table 3, 50 of these playability heuristics replicate the results from previous studies [4, 6, 10, 13, 17]. For instance, factors 17 and 26 are concerned about intruding or interrupting game-play. After reading original reviews, the corresponding heuristic in usability category was phrased as "a game should minimize the odds of pausing or interrupting user play during a mission." A similar rule, "the interface should be as non-intrusive as possible," has been discussed before under the scope of game interface [6]. Factor 51 helps us find a heuristic about character likability in game stories. As the result of examining original player reviews, the heuristic in the category of playability was formed as "a game can be humorous through its characters and stories". Although it sounds uncommon, a similar rule has been accepted as a final heuristic after large-scale survey studies [4]. The successful replication of 50 heuristics suggests that our findings are consistent with prior research and that the heuristics identified in this study are valid.

66 heuristics are newly discovered. This study substantially extends the pool of playability heuristics that game developers may apply. Since these heuristics were developed based on a fairly large amount of player reviews on a wide spectrum of computer games, they are able to cover many aspects of game-play that have never been possible in a-prior research. For instance, one heuristics advises designers to incorporate more connectivity features to support multiplayers mode. This becomes more demanding given the recent trend of mobile games, especially in a collocated setting. On the other hand, a couple of new heuristics may have been inexplicitly mentioned before, but they are much more elaborated this time. One example would be about replayability. Although Federoff [6] calls for designing re-playable games, there is a lack of details on how to achieve replayability. This study was able to produce 9 heuristics for re-playability, each of which proposes a specific strategy to improve replayability.

The playability heuristics have been developed to preserve specifics as much as possible. Although some researcher prefer a short list of heuristic rules, we argue that more specific heuristics are easier to use and are less likely misinterpreted by game developers. Because these playability heuristics were developed based on direct feedback from player, the specifics in the heuristics are accurate and will no doubt be a helpful source to game developers.

Overall, the discovery of the 116 playability heuristics indicates that the revised lexical approach is in fact effective and valid. By combining nouns and adjectives, the lexical analysis leads to discovery of lexicon patterns that contain specific contextual information. These patterns can then be used to develop valid playability heuristics. To summarize, the main advantages of the playability heuristics developed in this study include: (1) They are supported by a large number of online reviews and they truly represent player views on computer games. (2) They are based on the most critical issues in player experience since only the factors accounting for the most variances would be able to emerge from the factor analysis. (3) They provide much-needed specifics that cannot be easily derived from general design heuristics or theories. (4) They are comprehensive. These playability heuristics encompass a wide spectrum of computer games and different play scenarios. (5) The playability heuristics are expressed primarily by player language. They are easier to comprehend for game developers who often are also players themselves.

Table 3. Statistics about playability heuristics

Main category	Number of replicated heuristics	Number of new heuristics
Usability	19	22
Playability	28	38
Creativity	3	6
Subtotal	50	66

6 Conclusions

This study employed a revised lexical approach to analyze nouns and adjectives from over 800, 000 online game reviews. As a result, 116 playability heuristics were proposed. While these playability heuristics encapsulate an increasing amount of specifics, they also cover a wide range of topics about computer games. These playability heuristics can serve as useful design guidelines for different types of games. They clearly demonstrate the practical contributions of this study. From the theoretical perspective, this study provides strong evidence proving the effectiveness of the revised lexical approach. When mingling nouns and adjectives together, the revised lexical approach is able to discover the most important patterns in user experience with rich contextual information. These patterns can then be referenced to prepare design guidelines of a system or product. This new method can be easily extended to other fields for analyzing a large amount of online reviews on any user-oriented system or product.

To reiterate the rationale of this study, it is suggested that a lexical analysis of the combination of nouns and adjectives lead to two types of assets: (1) general patterns among players' reviews and (2) context-sensitive information associated with different aspects of players' experience. These two findings help introduce a prolific set of playability heuristics that would be of a great practical value to game researchers and professionals. Considering such a large dataset directly from game players, the resulting heuristics provide much-needed specifics to game professionals. Meantime, they cover a wide range of topics about computer games of various genres.

This new approach equips qualitative researchers with a rigorous, quantitative, and more controllable solution to analyze large amount of user-generated content. Its implications to the field of HCI and IS in general are profound.

Nevertheless, this study has its limitations as any other study would have. The present study used one coder to interpret the lexicon patterns and to develop playability heuristics. Although the playability heuristics proposed so far are all supported and verified by original player reviews, some potential heuristics might have been missed due the subjective reading of lexicon patterns. The language in the heuristics may also be refined to better serve game designers and/or developers. As the future research, we plan to hire additional game experts to continue the analysis of the lexicon patterns and develop new playability heuristics based on our revised lexical approach.

References

1. Ashton, M.C.: Individual Differences and Personality. Academic Press, San Diego (2007)
2. Barr, P., Noble, J., Biddle, R.: Video game values: human-computer interaction and games. Interact. Comput. **19**(2), 180–195 (2007)
3. Desurvire, H., Caplan, M., Toth, J.A.: Using heuristics to evaluate the playability of games. In: CHI 2004 Extended Abstracts on Human Factors in Computing Systems, pp. 1509–1512. ACM Press, New York (2004)
4. Desurvire, H., Wiberg, C.: Game usability heuristics (PLAY) for evaluating and designing better games: the next iteration. In: Ozok, A., Zaphiris, P. (eds.) OCSC 2009. LNCS, vol. 5621, pp. 557–566. Springer, Heidelberg (2009)
5. Entertainment Software Association. http://www.theesa.com/facts/index.asp
6. Federoff, M.: Heuristic and usability guidelines for the creation and evaluation of fun in video games. Unpublished Master Thesis, Department of Telecommunications, Indiana University (2002)
7. Fellbaum, C.: WordNet: An Electronic Lexical Database. MIT Press, Cambridge (1998)
8. Goldberg, L.R.: An alternative "description of personality": the big-five factor structure. J. Pers. Soc. Psychol. **59**(6), 1216–1229 (1990)
9. Järvinen, A.: Game design for social networks: interaction design for playful dispositions. In: Spencer, S.N. (ed.) Proceedings of the 2009 ACM SIGGRAPH Symposium on Video Games, pp. 95–102. ACM Press, New York (2009)
10. Korhonen, H., Koivisto, E.M.: Playability heuristics for mobile Games. In: Proceedings of the 8th Conference on Human-Computer Interaction with Mobile Devices and Services, MobileHCI 2006, pp. 9–16. ACM Press, New York (2006)
11. Korhonen, H., Koivisto, E.M.: Playability heuristics for mobile multi-player games. In: Proceedings of the 2nd International Conference on Digital Interactive Media in Entertainment and Arts, pp. 28–35. ACM Press, New York (2007)
12. Korhonen, H., Paavilainen, J., Saarenpää, H.: Expert review method in game evaluations: comparison of two playability heuristic sets. In: Proceedings of the 13th International MindTrek Conference: Everyday Life in the Ubiquitous Era, pp. 74–81. ACM Press, New York (2009)
13. Malone, T.W.: Heuristics for designing enjoyable user interfaces: lessons from computer games. In: Proceedings of the 1982 Conference on Human Factors in Computing Systems, pp. 63–68. ACM Press, New York (1982)

14. Miller, G.A.: WordNet: a lexical database for English. Commun. ACM **38**(11), 39–41 (1995)
15. Paavilainen, J.: Critical review on video game evaluation heuristics: social games perspective. In: Proceedings of the International Academic Conference on the Future of Game Design and Technology, pp. 56–65. ACM Press, New York (2010)
16. Paavilainen, J., Korhonen, H., Saarenpää, H.: Comparing two playability heuristic sets with expert review method: a case study of mobile game evaluation. In: Media in the Ubiquitous Era: Ambient, Social and Gaming Media, pp. 29–52. Information Science Reference, Hershey (2012)
17. Pinelle, D., Wong, N., Stach, T.: Heuristic evaluation for games: usability principles for video game design. In: Proceeding of the 26th Annual SIGCHI Conference on Human Factors in Computing Systems, pp. 1453–1462. ACM Press, New York (2008)
18. Sánchez, J.L.G., Simarro, F.M., Zea, N.P., Vela, F.L.G.: Playability as extension of quality in use in computer games. In: Proceedings of 2nd International Workshop on the Interplay Between Usability Evaluation and Software Development, I-USED, Uppsala (2009)
19. Sánchez, J.L.G., Vela, F.L.G., Simarro, F.M., Padilla-Zea, N.: Playability: analysing user experience in video games. Behav. Inform. Technol. **31**(10), 1033–1054 (2012)
20. Usability-First. http://www.usabilityfirst.com/glossary/playability/
21. Ventrice, T.: Building the foundation of a social future. http://www.gamasutra.com/view/feature/4210/building_the_foundation_of_a_.php
22. Zhu, M., Fang, X., Chan, S., Brzezinski, J.: Building a dictionary of game-descriptive words to study playability. In: CHI 2013 Extended Abstracts, Paris, France, 27 April–2 May. ACM, New York (2013). ACM 978-1-4503-1952-2/13/04
23. Zhu, M., Fang, X.: What nouns and adjectives in online game reviews can tell us about player experience? In: CHI 2014 Extended Abstracts, Toronto, Canada, 26 April–1 May. ACM, New York (2014)
24. Zhu, M., Fang, X.: Introducing a revised lexical approach to study user experience in game play by analyzing online reviews. In: Proceedings of the 10th Interactive Entertainment conference (IE 2014), 02–03 December 2014, Newcastle, NSW, Australia. ACM, New York (2014). ACM 978-1-4503-2790-9/14/12

HCI in Smart and Intelligent Environments

A Mashup-Based Application for the Smart City Problematic

Abdelghani Atrouche[1(✉)], Djilali Idoughi[1], and Bertrand David[2,3]

[1] Laboratoire de Mathématiques Appliquées-LMA,
Université A. Mira, Bejaia, Algerie
{atrouche.a,djilali.idoughi}@gmail.com
[2] Université de Lyon, CNRS, Lyon, France
[3] École Centrale de Lyon, LIRIS, UMR5205, Écully, France
bertrand.david@ec-lyon.fr

Abstract. A mashup is an application that combines data and functionalities from more than one source. It groups disparate data in ways that enable users to do new things or accomplish common tasks with newfound efficiency. The introduction of mashup applications and their increasing use by users in the field of e-Learning and e-commerce highlights new issues in a context called the "smart city". Indeed, transportation based on private cars, public transportation services and shared bicycles need appropriate user interfaces, which can be "mashuped" to allow an integrated approach to transportation related to weather conditions, real-time traffic situations and personal preferences. These new needs for composition and combination (orchestration) of existing web services and their underlying user interfaces are good examples of mashuping. First, we provide in this paper some valuable explanations on two kinds of orchestration: service orchestration and HCI (Human Computer Interface) orchestration. Secondly, we apply this global approach to the context of "smart cities".

Keywords: HCI · Mashup · Smart city · Orchestration · Service orchestration · User interface orchestration

1 Introduction

Today, the main challenge facing software developers is to cope with development complexity and adaptation to frequent changes. The practice of software engineering is particularly essential for developing applications which are human life oriented. The "software design component-based" approach [1] is a valid approach, even for non-interactive software. For interactive software, the HCI dimension (Human Computer Interface) is required, especially in order to be able to adapt the interface to user demand (services) when he/she is dealing with software using different interaction devices. The HCI should provide better utilization, more adapted to user context features. To reflect the behavior of the system and its ease of use and availability, we must design these user interfaces with the same rigor and concerns as the systems themselves. The user interface must allow usability of the features expected by the user in

© Springer International Publishing Switzerland 2015
M. Kurosu (Ed.): Human-Computer Interaction, Part II, HCII 2015, LNCS 9170, pp. 683–694, 2015.
DOI: 10.1007/978-3-319-20916-6_63

different conditions of use and different interaction devices, naturally also in mobility. Furthermore, the composition of services is related to elaboration of an appropriate HCI, allowing users to handle these new services by a well-organized orchestration. The introduction of ICT (Information and Communication Technology) in the daily life of citizens has led to the emergence of new appropriate economic, social and environmental needs. In this context, the goal of the smart city, a major application field, is to allow citizens to be smarter, i.e. to allow them instant and quick access to services proposed by the city such as energy, transportation, culture, sport, etc.

In this paper, we propose a global approach for designing and implementing interactive software, integrating non-interactive components within a logic of orchestration of services and human-computer interfaces in accordance with user tasks. This takes the form of providing their generation and composition (mashup) by orchestration of the HCI.

2   Mashup Applications

Mashups are defined as "the perspective of software engineering. A mashup is constructed by the assembly and the combination of several existing functions integrated into a new application" [2].

The term "mashup" was defined initially in the field of music, where it consists of remixing two (or more) sounds in order to obtain a new one. Mashup is primarily and usually performed for the so-called "drag&drop" applications from different sources. The mashup architecture is made up of three elements according to Merrill [3]: Data, Services and User Interface. Mashup aims at the composition of a three-tier application: (1) Data (data integration), (2) Application logic (process integration) and (3) User interface (presentation integration). Integration of heterogeneous data sources uses two main technologies: web services and Mashup. Integration implies that all relevant data for a particular bounded and closed set of business processes is processed in the same software application.

Moreover, updates in one application module or component are reflected throughout the business process logic, with no complex external interfacing. Data are stored once, and are instantaneously shared by different business processes enabled by the software application [3]. In the Mashup, every user can compose his/her own service with other services in order to create a new service. Mashup is a "Consumer Centric Application". The Mashup describes web 2.0 sites combining functions of one site with another site. Different pieces of UIs (User Interfaces) are integrated into a new web application. This approach requires composition and orchestration of web services.

The goal of service composition is to produce richer applications. In UI integrations, it is very important to have a component model that can support interactions and compositions. When the user has the privilege of editing the Mashup, he/she is able to construct multiple applications and multiple versions of Mashups.

3 State of the Art

The concept of mashups has been popularized in the web application domain as a result of a large number of well-known web-based systems, such as Google Maps (maps.google.com) and Flickr (www.flickr.com). Their main contribution was to release their APIs to the public, thus enabling developers to leverage existing web technologies and create new applications. By restricting the development process to feature composition, mashups enable developers to rapidly create custom applications aimed at niche audiences [4, 5]. Web mashups [6] have turned lessons learned from data and application integration into lightweight, simple composition approaches featuring a significant innovation: integration at UI level.

Besides web services and data feeds, mashups reuse pieces of UIs (e.g., content extracted from web pages or JavaScript UI widgets) and integrate them into a new web page. Mashups, therefore, show a need for reuse in UI development and suitable UI component technologies.

The web mashup [7] phenomenon produced a set of mashup tools, aiming at assisting mashup development by means of easy-to-use graphical user interfaces targeted also at non-professional programmers. It is convenient to separate the types of mashups into the following three categories: data, user interface (UI), and process. Data mashups combine two or more data sets to create a new data set. UI mashups combine familiar UI elements to create new applications. Process mashups combine two or more processes into a single execution. It is also worth noting that most mashups fall into more than one of these categories or can be implemented in different ways.

As the orchestration HCI has proved very useful in service composition, it is important to provide some more details on orchestration. Orchestration is seen as "a musical arrangement to involve several instruments and therefore their process" [8]. It is thus an agreement or an organization defined by process management. According to SOA, orchestration is a mechanism that defines the integration or composition operation of services. On the other hand, there is an approach, namely user oriented orchestration, where caution is required when using the HCI.

Web services and SOA (Service Oriented Architecture), viewed in a process-oriented perspective, need a particular language to define how services can be composed into business processes. Such definitions would allow abstract processes as well as executable processes to be described [9].

In most service orchestration approaches, such as BPEL [10], there is no support for UI design. Many variations of BPEL have been developed, e.g., aiming at invocation of REST services [11] or at exposing BPEL processes as REST services [12]. In terms of standard BPEL, orchestration is a process made up of a set of associated activities (e.g., sequence, flow, if, assign, validate, or similar), variables (to store intermediate processing results), message exchanges, correlation sets (to correlate messages in conversations), and fault handlers. As UI orchestration has proved very useful in service composition, it is important to provide some more details on these two orchestrations: Service orchestration and UI Orchestration.

It is generally accepted that the architecture of a mashup is divided into three layers:

- Presentation/user interaction: this is the mashup UI. The main technologies used are HTML/XHTML, CSS, Javascript, Asynchronous Javascript and Xml (Ajax).
- Web Services: the product functionality can be accessed using API services. The main technologies used are XMLHTTPRequest, XML-RPC, JSON-RPC, SOAP and REST.
- Data: handling data like sending, storing and receiving. The main technologies used are XML, JSON and KML.

Architecturally, there are two styles of mashups: Web-based and server-based. Whereas Web-based mashups typically use the user's web browser to combine and reformat data, server-based mashups analyze and reformat data on a remote server and transmit these data to the user's browser in its final form.

To contribute to orchestration studies, we decided to increase the number of layers to five to explicitly introduce the Service Orchestration Layer and the UI Orchestration Layer.

4 Smart City

Smart Cities refer to cities that aim to improve the living standards of citizens - not only by developing new physical infrastructures, but also by using information technology. These solutions bring services closer to the community and play a positive role in an environmental context, thus helping to build sustainable cities. A smart city is characterized by a set of ICT applications corresponding to a wide range of issues related to traffic, energy, urban mobility, security, etc. For all these applications, we can distinguish end-users i.e. citizens, visitors, and operators i.e. employees.

Citizens and visitors are able to use these ICT applications to make everyday decisions based on processed information which could not be used manually. These applications use various data sources to present a high-level view of current events and offer decision guidance to users. A combination of these applications in coherent and useful proposals seems understandable. This is the first situation requiring mashup of these applications. City employees or companies are in charge of operating these city infrastructures, such as a bus company or rental bikes, in order to allow end-users to use them. They also need to acquire some integrated and specialized applications in a wide range of fields such as town planning, optimization and organization of transportation, civil services, waste disposal and so on, which are, however, limited in the operational scope to their responsibilities. The Mashup approach is an answer to these requirements. To concretize our explanation, we describe in the next section a scenario issued from our smart city application field.

4.1 A Case Study or Scenario

To explain the mashup approach we describe a scenario in which citizens as end-users and employees as operators use five services. They are mainly oriented to transportation choices and related to observed situations made up of weather conditions, real-time traffic situations in public transportation and street circulation. These five services are as follows:

1. *Weather situation* is the service informing end-users in the short-term (less than 12 h) of weather conditions, allowing them to choose an appropriate means of travel.
2. *City atmospheric pollution service* provides users with the expected level of pollution for the same period.
3. *Bicycle rental fleet management service*, such as Vélo'V in Lyon, offers users the possibility to rent a bicycle with indication of availability in departure and arrival stations.
4. *Real-time vehicle traffic information service* provides overall city traffic information, as well as, more precisely, the local traffic situation (for a district).
5. *Real-time public transportation information service* is in charge of indicating bus, tram and metro traffic situations.

In our scenario, we have five web services: **weather application, traffic application, pollution application, management of rental bicycles** and **transportation management**. We use the UML Use case diagram to specify them (Fig. 1). Citizens use these services, and Operators (employees) are in charge of updating the status of these services.

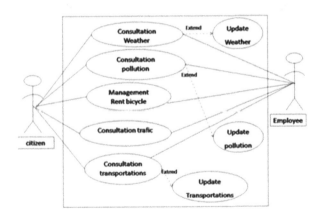

Fig. 1. Use case diagram of our Smart City scenario

These services are made up of several tasks which are either operator or end-user oriented. Operator-oriented tasks are working condition-oriented (such as indication of a new traffic jam area), while end-user tasks are use-oriented (to identify traffic jam areas). In both categories, more or less sophisticated tasks are provided such as simple observation of public transportation situation or appropriate trip structure between two points.

These services are, of course, Web services. They are available on various electronic devices located anywhere (personal apartment, public building, in street terminals and also and mainly personal devices i.e. tablets and smartphones). The main structure of these services is based on three parts: (1) specific application data, (2) SOA-based logical behaviors, and (3) user interface. However, the tasks proposed by each service are not available to everybody. Certain tasks are only operator-oriented, while others are end-user-oriented.

The first level of use is based on individual task (mono task) activation by the user interface and relates to a particular web service and corresponding User Interface. For example in Fig. 2, the end-user mono-task is weather consultation and the operator mono-task is weather update. In this relatively easy form of utilization, the application is not necessarily monolithic. It can use the mashup approach to indicate on the Google map the location of public transportation stations or traffic jam situations.

The second level of use is concerned with an integrated use of different tasks (called mashuped tasks) from different services in an integrated way; by interconnecting them with the mashup technology and orchestration of user interfaces. In Fig. 2, the end-user mashuped task aims at determining appropriate transportation in relation with weather and pollution conditions, street traffic and public transportation situations and bicycle availability. The Operator mashuped task allows him/her to modify public transportation in relation with increased pollution. At this higher level integration, the system is able to take into account weather conditions, atmospheric pollution, traffic conditions and user preferences (if they are available) in order to choose appropriate mono-mode or inter-mode transportation (same mode for all segments or different modes) (Fig. 2).

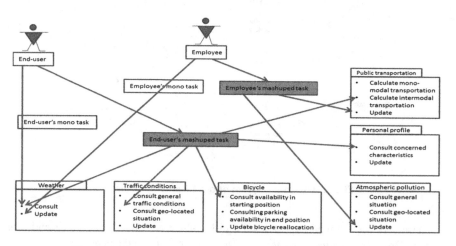

Fig. 2. End-User and Employee mono-tasks and mashuped tasks

5 Our Approach

5.1 Proposed Architecture

The architecture (Fig. 3) that we propose consists of five layers:

1. **User Interface:** the nearest layer to the user that presents to the user the final interface on his/her screen.
2. **UI Orchestration:** in this layer the UI orchestrator composes or integrates UI components allowing appropriate visualization and manipulation by users.
3. **Service Orchestration:** the layer where the Service orchestrator interconnects several services and their data in order to provide an appropriate functional answer as expected by the application. This interconnection is either a simple composition or a reasoning approach based on algorithm or knowledge manipulation.
4. **Services:** at this level all services are available and can access corresponding data sources located at the Data layer.
5. **Data:** this layer contains all sources of data needed by different services.

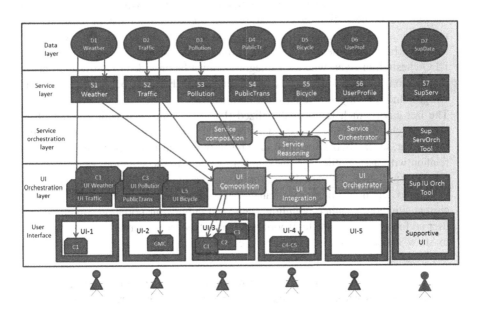

Fig. 3. The multi-layer mashup-based application architecture

On Fig. 3, we show an overall architecture model with 5 layers broadly explained hereafter with typical mashup situations related to our scenario:

- User interface 1 (UI-1) explains a classical situation where a UI component (widget) shows the current weather situation on the screen. The corresponding weather service task delivers current data.

- User interface 2 (UI-2) corresponds to the first mashuping situation, in which traffic situation data are not visualized as a list, but mashuped in a Google Map Component (GMC). In this case, application data are distributed geographically on the city Google Map.
- User interface 3 (UI-3) is in charge of delivering on the same screen information provided by different services. UI orchestration is easy, based only on composition of different UI components (widgets). Each widget is in relation with one task of the corresponding service, which is in charge of delivering appropriate data. In our case the user can observe at the same time weather, traffic and pollution situations.
- User Interface 4 (UI-4) presents a more sophisticated situation. The goal is to collect information concerning user profile, public transportation situation and bicycle availability in the departure station and space availability at the destination in order to offer the user an intermodal transportation based on several public transportation segments (bus, tram and metro) combined with bicycle segments (if the user profile is compatible with its use). For this application we have grouped all proposed aspects. We need to mashup different services in order to determine a composite transportation trajectory compatible with the user profile. Then we must find an appropriate presentation based on integration of different widgets. This means, at the service orchestration layer, that service orchestration must propose service reasoning able to find appropriate transportation segments with their transportation supports (bus, tram, metro or bicycle). It must then transmit this information to the UI Orchestration layer, where UI Integration must be provided to allow appropriate information presentation. At this layer, integration between public transportation widgets and the bicycle widget must be provided.
- The last case, which is not materialized (UI-5), is concerned with mashup of all services: choice of transportation in a composite intermodal way using, potentially, private car, several public transportation forms (bus, tram and/or metro) and bicycle in relation with user profile (age, bicycle ability, etc.), traffic situation, weather conditions and pollution. This service mashuping is reasoning- and/or algorithm-oriented in order to determine appropriate transportation segment scheduling according to the current situation (weather, pollution, traffic and public transportation conditions and user preferences. Once the transportation means has been determined, it is important to show chosen transportation schedule data appropriately. For this purpose, an integrated UI based on integrated widgets is needed.

In our architecture, two main layers are concerned with orchestration and mashuping: the **Service Orchestration layer** and the **User Interface orchestration layer**.

5.2   Service Orchestration Layer

At this layer, the **service orchestrator** is in charge of orchestrating services either by composition or by reasoning. Composition aims at unifying different services through seamless functional integration of aggregated sources. The resulting mashup is a new application, and participating sources are components of this new application.

Reasoning refers to integration of aggregated resources and services, which are connected by logical (reasoning rules) or algorithms in order to create new aggregated functionalities.

5.3   User Interface Orchestration Layer

At this layer, the **UI orchestrator** is in charge of orchestrating UI interfaces either by composition or by integration. The goal of UI composition is to present on the screen a collection of independent basic UI components (widgets). UI integration is concerned with integration of several UI components (widgets) into a single one.

5.4   Scenario-Based Explanations

Let us now show the role of these two orchestrators on our scenario situations:

1. UI-1 is a standalone application made up of Weather service (S1) and a UI-component showing and managing Weather visualization. The Service Orchestration layer and the UI orchestration layer are not concerned.
2. UI-2 is a Traffic management application made up of Traffic service (S2) and a UI component, Google Maps, allowing visualization of traffic data (situation) in a map perspective. This is what we call vertical mashup between a service and an open visualization application able to take into account the data to be projected on the map.
3. UI-3 is a mashuped application taking into account multiple data delivered by three services (Weather – S1, Traffic – S2 and Pollution – S3). At the service orchestration layer, no action is required: these services deliver independent data and propagate them to the UI Orchestration layer, where the UI Orchestrator uses UI composition to show on the screen three UI components, visualizing independently these data on a single surface.
4. UI-4 is a more sophisticated situation in which two orchestration layers are required. At service orchestration level, the service orchestrator asks Service Reasoning to group User Profile information, the Public Transportation situation and Bicycle management, treated by services S6, S4 and S5, respectively. Service reasoning is the service mashup which, in relation with user profile, indicates user ability to use a bicycle and elaborates a transportation schedule either mixing public transportation and bicycle segments or using public transportation only. The UI Orchestrator at the UI orchestration layer is in charge of integrating UI components C4 & C5 to show the trip structure.
5. UI-5 is, as described, a sophisticated mashuping at the service orchestration layer with weather, pollution and user profile conditions to determine the appropriate transportation solution based on an inter-modal aggregation. The optimized trip structure is presented in a mashuped single UI component showing the user the proposed trip.

It is important to observe that, at the Service Orchestration layer, mashuping is based on the study, connection and interrelation between different tasks available for each service. At the UI orchestration layer, the main goal is to deliver to each user in respect to his/her role, the appropriate user interface for both visualization and interaction. The buttons, menus and commands proposed are in relation with the user's accreditations, i.e. use for citizens, and management for city operators. The UI orchestration layer is in charge of managing task authorization and filtering.

Fig. 4. Large screen information scenarios concerning transportation proposals

5.5   Supportive User Interface

On the right side of Fig. 3 we show a new module added to the overall architecture model with 5 layers, as explained previously. This module, called the supportive User Interface [13], is in charge of creating new mashuped applications. Supervision data, supervision services, the Supervision Service Orchestration Tool and the Supervision UI Orchestration Tool are the main components of this module. The supportive User Interface offers users different possibilities for manipulation as well as facilitating manipulation of different services. Two working conditions are proposed: programming devoted to trained developers and a visual programming-oriented approach in which a light version of mashuping is provided to less trained developers and high-level users. Naturally, at the Service Orchestration layer, visual programming, i.e. graphical manipulation of concepts, is mainly used to compose tasks and data and to express relatively simple and easily expressed reasoning. At the UI Orchestration layer, composition of UI components (widgets) is supported as well as the low level of UI Integration. Naturally, the user-friendliness of this interface is the decisive factor for determining utilization: only by professional developers or also by experienced users (Figs. 4 and 5).

Fig. 5. Smartphone UI scenario

6   Conclusion

Application mashuping is a main and much appreciated approach for creating appropriate applications based on reuse of existing ones. In this paper, we tried to clarify this large and flourishing activity by means of multiple solutions and approaches. As our application field we took the smart city and its need to receive appropriate applications which can be elaborated by applying the mashuping approach. We proposed an architecture based on five layers, allowing both clear distinction of data, services and UI, as well as, with respect to mashuping, the Service orchestration layer and the UI orchestration layer. We consider this separation to be essential as Service orchestration and UI orchestration are very different. We explained the main mashuping techniques used at these two layers: composition and algorithmic or reasoning for service orchestration, and UI composition and UI integration for UI orchestration. We also proposed à supportive user interface, which is mashup application creation- or evolution-oriented, either with a programming interface for experienced developers or a visual programming-oriented approach for experienced users.

We are currently looking into the possibility of using this supportive visual programming- oriented interface while using mashuped applications in order to adjust their behaviors.

References

1. Yu, J., Benatallah, B., Casati, F., Daniel, F.: Understanding mashup development and its differences with traditional integration. IEEE Internet Comput. 12(5), 44–52 (2008)
2. Lizcano, D., Soriano, J., Reyes, M., Hierro, J.J.: EzWeb/FAST: reporting on a successful Mashup-based solution for developing and deploying composite applications in the upcoming ubiquitous SOA. In: Proceeding of the Second International Conference on Mobile Ubiquitous Computing, Systems, Services and Technologies, UBICOMM 2008, Valencia, Spain, pp. 488–495 (2008)
3. Merrill, D.: Mashups: the new breed of Web app: an introduction to mashups (2009). http://www.128.ibm.com/developerworks/xml/library/x-Mashups.html
4. Grammel, L., Storey, M.: An end user perspective on mashup making, University of Victoria Technical Report DCS-324-IR (2008)
5. Hartmann, B., Doorley, S., Klemmer, S.: Hacking, mashing, gluing: a study of opportunistic design and development. Pervasive Comput. 7(3), 46–54 (2006)
6. Caste, B.: Introduction to Web Services for Remote Portlets, IBM Developerworks (2005). http://www-128.ibm.com/developerworks/webservices/library/ws-wsrp/
7. Beinhauer, W., Schlegel, T.: User Interfaces for Service Oriented Architectures, July 2005. http://www.webservice-kompass.de/fileadmin/publikationen/User_Interfaces_for_Service_Oriented_Architectures.pdf
8. David, B., Chalon, R.: Orchestration modeling of interactive systems. In: Jacko, J.A. (ed.) HCI International 2009, Part I. LNCS, vol. 5610, pp. 796–805. Springer, Heidelberg (2009)
9. Erl, T.: Service Oriented Architecture, Concepts, Technology, and Design. Prentice Hall, Upper Saddle River (2006)
10. OASIS. Web Services Business Process Execution Language Version 2.0, April 2005. http://docs.oasis-open.org/wsbpel/2.0/OS/wsbpel-v2.0-OS.html
11. Pautasso, C.: BPEL for REST. In: Dumas, M., Reichert, M., Shan, M.-C. (eds.) BPM 2008. LNCS, vol. 5240, pp. 278–293. Springer, Heidelberg (2008)
12. Van Lessen T., Leymann F., Mietzner R., Nitzsche J., Schleicher D.: A management framework for WS-BPEL. In: ECoWS 2008, Dublin, pp. 187–196 (2008)
13. David, B., Chalon, R., Delomier, F.: Supportive user interfaces for MOCOCO (mobile, contextualized and collaborative) applications. In: Kurosu, M. (ed.) HCII/HCI 2013, Part V. LNCS, vol. 8008, pp. 29–38. Springer, Heidelberg (2013)

Design of a Bullying Detection/Alert System for School-Wide Intervention

Sheryl Brahnam[1(✉)], Jenifer J. Roberts[2], Loris Nanni[3],
Cathy L. Starr[2], and Sandra L. Bailey[2]

[1] Computer Information Systems, Missouri State University,
Springfield, MO, USA
sbrahnam@missouristate.edu
[2] Fashion and Interior Design, Missouri State University, Springfield, MO, USA
{jeniferroberts,cstarr,sbailey}@missouristate.edu
[3] DEI, University of Padua, Padua, Italy
loris.nanni@unipd.it

Abstract. In this paper we propose a bullying detection/alert system for school-wide intervention that combines wearables with heart rate (HR) monitors, surveillance cameras, multimodal machine learning, cloud computing, and mobile devices. The system alerts school personnel when potential bullying is detected and identifies potential bullying in three ways: (i) by tracking and assessing the proximity of known bullies to known students at risk for bullying; (ii) by monitoring stress levels of students via HR analysis; and (iii) by recognizing actions, emotions, and crowd formations associated with bullying. We describe each of these components and their integration, noting that it is possible for the system to use only a network of surveillance cameras. Alerts produced by the system can be logged. Reviews of these logs and tagged videos of detected bullying would allow school personnel to review incidents and their methods for handling bullying by providing more information about the locations, causes, and actors involved in bullying as well as teacher/staff response rates. In addition, false positives could be marked and fed back to the system for relearning and continuous improvement of the system.

Keywords: School bullying · Machine learning · Heart-rate monitoring · Face tracking · Emotion classification · Action classification · Computer technology

1 Introduction

A dominant stress factor for students today is being bullied at school. Bullying is defined as "any repeated negative activity or aggression intended to harm or bother someone who is perceived by peers as being less physically or psychologically powerful than the aggressor(s)" [22, p. 9]. Reports vary in the amount of bullying that takes place in the schools, in part because the rate of bullying varies by age and type of bullying, as well as by culture and subgroup. On an annual basis, it is estimated that somewhere between 20 % and 56 % of young people are involved in bullying [12], with involvement defined in terms of the roles of perpetrator, victim, or both (bully-victims). The most prevalent types of bullying, in descending order, are name calling, teasing,

© Springer International Publishing Switzerland 2015
M. Kurosu (Ed.): Human-Computer Interaction, Part II, HCII 2015, LNCS 9170, pp. 695–705, 2015.
DOI: 10.1007/978-3-319-20916-6_64

rumor-spreading, physical incidents, purposeful isolation, threats, stealing personal belongings, and sexual harassment [16]. Verbal bullying is more prevalent than physical aggression, and cyberbullying is the least prevalent [15]. Middle school children are more likely to be involved in bullying than are high school children [25], and certain subgroups are particularly at risk for bullying. For example, in one study 60 % of LGBT (Lesbian, Gay, Bisexual, and Transgender) youth reported victimization in a 30 day period compared with 28.8 % of heterosexual and cisgender youth [11].

The effects of bullying for all parties involved are devastating. Involvement in bullying is correlated with poor mental and physical health, including a higher incidence of psychosomatic illnesses [8]. Peer victimization is associated with high levels of stress and altered cortisol levels in stress tests [18]. Victims of bullying also have higher rates of absenteeism and receive lower grades than those who are not bullied [16]. Most troubling is the correlation between victims of bullying and depression, especially depression leading to suicidal ideation and behaviors, as well as other forms of self-harm [9, 12]. Suicidal ideation is reported for bullies as well, especially bully-victims [17]. Moreover, longitudinal research shows that bullies are at high risk for encounters with the law [23], and children who bully have trouble with relationships through adolescence into adulthood. Bullying can have lasting consequences not only for bullies and for victims [2, 16] but also for entire communities. Of those children who have perpetrated school shootings, 71 % were chronically bullied in their schools [29]. For all these reasons, bullying is considered a serious public health risk that must be addressed through interventions in schools [4].

Until fairly recently the prevention and intervention literature on bullying was relatively sparse [16]. In the last twenty years, a number of intervention studies have examined school programs, and the general consensus is that whole-school approaches are the best evidence-based methods for reducing school bullying [32]. Whole-school intervention programs generally include an anti-bullying policy, school-wide awareness raising, curriculum activities, a plan to deal with reported cases of bullying, and increased monitoring. Despite the international recognition of whole-school intervention programs, these programs reduce school bullying by only 20–30 %, according to a recent meta-analysis of cross-cultural studies on whole-school interventions [7]. Obviously, these programs leave much room for improvement.

One interesting finding in the aforementioned meta-analysis is that playground supervision is strongly related to program effectiveness. The need for schools to increase monitoring of students to prevent bullying has been widely recognized [32]. Most bullying takes place during unsupervised periods and in unsupervised areas at school [3]. According to a 2011 report from the U.S. Department of Justice on school crime [27], close to 50 % of bullying took place in the school hallway/stairwell, 22 % outside on the school ground, and 12 % in the bathroom/locker rooms. Observational studies have shown, however, that bullying is not always entirely covert. Peers are present in 85 % of bullying episodes, but peers rarely intervene to stop the bullying [26]. Some researchers have suggested that peers are pressured to be involved in the bullying for fear they will become victims themselves [26]. Moreover, Peers also rarely report the bullying after the episode [32].

Research also shows that increased monitoring is needed in the classroom. In the 2011 report cited above, approximately 33 % of bullying at school took place in the classroom, making it the second most frequent location for bullying [27]. As Atlas and Pepler have observed [3], when bullying occurs in the classroom it frequently goes undetected by teachers, and even when it is detected, teachers often fail to intervene.

Given this need for more effective monitoring, we propose a school-wide monitoring system that combines state-of-the-art machine learning systems with off-the-shelf technologies to detect bullying episodes. Some of the technologies utilized in our proposed system include smart ID badges, wearables with heartrate sensors for at-risk students, and surveillance cameras. A multimodal machine learning system located in the cloud processes the data produced by these technologies and alerts teachers and staff via mobile devices (or vibrating smart watches worn by teachers in the classroom) to potential bullying incidents.

Since each alert produced by the system would be logged and videos tagged, teachers and staff would be incentivized to implement interventions when bullying is detected. Moreover, reviews of the system logs and videos of detected bullying would allow school personnel to review their methods for handling bullying by providing more information about the locations, causes, and actors involved in bullying as well as teacher/staff response rates. In addition, false positives could be marked and fed back to the system for relearning and continuous detection improvement.

2 System Design

The basic idea of our bullying detection/alert system is illustrated in Fig. 1. This system combines smart school badges, wearables with heartrate (HR) monitors, surveillance cameras, multimodal machine learning, cloud computing, and mobile devices and is intended to tag videos and alert staff when bullying is detected.[1]

As illustrated in Fig. 2, the system identifies potential bullying in three ways: (1) by tracking and assessing the proximity of known bullies to known students at risk for bullying; (2) by monitoring stress levels of students via HR analysis; and (3) by recognizing actions, emotions, and crowd formations associated with bullying. The methods in system 1 focus on students who are known to have trouble with bullying. The methods in system 2 can specifically monitor at risk students or all students. The methods in system 3 are aimed at detecting any incident of bullying and involve the integration of several machine learning systems. Although some of these component systems could be employed alone for monitoring bullying (the tracking system, for instance), our vision is to combine all three systems into a larger bullying detection/ alert system.

---

[1] Another method for reducing bullying would be to give each student known to be at risk for bullying an alarm button that could be triggered whenever the student feared an imminent bullying situation. Most portable panic buttons, however, are expensive and conspicuous. If these buttons were noticed by other students, the at-risk students carrying them could be exposed to additional ridicule.

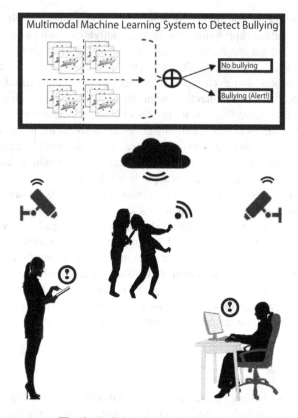

Fig. 1. Bullying detection/alert system

1. Tracking System	2. Stress Monitoring System	3. Bullying Detection System
Purpose: Track known bullies & students at risk	**Purpose:** Monitor stress levels of students	**Purpose:** Train classifier systems to recognize bullying
Methods: * Face tracking * Person re-identification * Smart IDs	**Methods:** * Wearable HR monitors * Person re-identification * Video pulse detection	**Methods:** * Emotion recognition * Crowd analysis * Action classification

Fig. 2. Three general systems that together will detect bullying

2.1 Tracking System

A tracking system is necessary for monitoring the locations of known bullies and students at risk for bullying. A known bully in a restroom, for example, with a known student at risk might be reason enough to issue an alert. As noted in Fig. 2, three methods could be employed (or combined) for tracking students. Two methods depend on surveillance cameras and one on smart chips in student IDs.

The two tracking methods that utilize video images make use of state-of-the-art face tracking and person re-identification algorithms. Face tracking combines face recognition/detection methods with a tracking mechanism and is a non-intrusive natural method for tracking people. Some recently proposed algorithms that might form the foundation of our face tracking system include [14, 31]. The basic idea of this system would be to track students through school buildings by recognizing their faces as they move from location to location. This technology would work best in close quarters where multiple cameras are available.

Person re-identification is defined as the task of recognizing a given person across any number of views (some non-overlapping) in a distributed network of cameras. Person re-identification is not dependent on face recognition/detection or other biometric markers, such as gait, but rather tracks the dominant colors in clothing and would be the technology of choice for tracking students across school grounds. Person re-identification would probably not work well, however, in schools requiring uniforms.

Person re-identification is challenging because the system must correctly identify the same person despite changes in illumination, pose, background, occlusions, and variability in camera resolutions and viewpoints. Because many surveillance cameras have low resolutions and cover large areas, an image of a student might be only a small number of pixels high by a small number of pixels wide. Despite these challenges, person re-identification is a fairly mature technology, with some of the most powerful algorithms having been developed in the last couple of years [19, 21, 28].

Another method for tracking students would be to utilize student IDs containing devices offering some means, such as radio frequency identification (RFID), for tracking people in real-time. Unlike person re-identification and face tracking, which requires surveillance cameras, smart IDs would be able to provide the location of students even in areas where cameras are socially prohibited, such as in restrooms, which, as noted in the introduction, are the second most common location for bullying in the schools [27]. Unfortunately, this technology is still in its infancy, and commercial systems that track items and persons are extremely expensive. Moreover, IDs are easily lost, misplaced, and left behind in bags and other belongings.

Despite the advantages smart IDs would offer, they are not a requirement. Depending on the saturation of surveillance cameras, face recognition and re-identification systems could also be employed to log students as they enter and leave school restrooms and other locations where cameras are prohibited, thereby reducing the need for this method of tracking.

2.2 Stress Monitoring System

Bullying produces stress in all parties involved: victims, bullies, and bystanders [3]. Since HR is correlated with stress and measures it reliably [8], it is important to detect it. There are two methods our system could use for detecting HR: surveillance cameras and HR sensors hidden in the clothing of students at risk for bullying.

The least obtrusive method for monitoring HR is through video magnification of skin pigmentation [24, 31], which is illustrated in Fig. 3. Video magnification reveals temporal variations that are impossible to detect with the naked eye. In [31] the authors

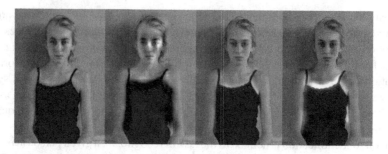

Fig. 3. Illustration of color amplification revealing blood flow as the heart beats

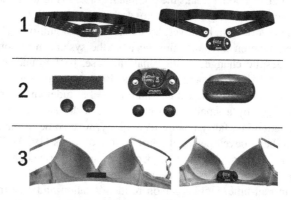

Fig. 4. Steps for concealing the DualTRNr monitor in teen's upper foundation clothing

propose an elegant realtime method for measuring pulse by magnifying the subtle variations in skin pigmentation as blood flows through the skin. Video magnification can also measure breathing rate by revealing low-amplitude motions [31], which might also be useful for detecting stress and anxiety. With video magnification it would be possible to detect the stress levels of any number of students.

One way to handle locations where surveillance camera are unable to detect pulse rates is to have students at risk for bullying wear clothing that place HR monitors in proximity to an area of the body where HR can best be detected yet remain discreet. HR is easily detected in the groin area, the temple area, and on the chest [5, 13]. As illustrated in Fig. 4, we are designing kits to hide off-the-shelf HR chest monitors in upper body foundation garments. Using any HR monitor with Bluetooth capability and an API, we could write software that would send HR information to our proposed system via the child's smart phone's internet connection.

Figure 4 demonstrates how the DualTRNr HR monitor (using a kit containing one Velcro fastener and two snappable soft pads) might be concealed in upper foundation clothing for females (ages 8–17). The same idea would apply to boys (ages 5–17) using t-shirts. Instructions for using this kit for girls appear in rows 1–3 of Fig. 4. In row 1 the DualTRNr HR sensor is unsnapped from the original strap. In row 2, one side of the Velcro strip is applied to the front of the HR monitor, and the snaps on the HR monitor are covered with the soft pads (since that side will be pressing into the skin). In row 3 the other side of the Velcro strip is attached to the underside of the garment. The DualTRNr HR sensor is then attached so that it fits next to the skin and registers the student's HR. Ideally, the HR monitor selected would come in three basic colors (white, black, and beige), which would help camouflage the HR sensors when worn with any upper body foundation garments.

2.3   Bullying Detection System

In this section we focus on three additional machine learning systems that could aid in the detection of bullying: (1) emotion classification, (2) action classification, and (3) crowd detection. Although none of these systems have been designed to detect the specific emotional displays, actions, and crowd formations indicative of bullying, we hypothesize that each of these technologies are capable of doing so.

Emotion recognition is an important area in HCI and has applications not only in affective computing but also in telecommunications, behavioral science, computer animations, etc. Because this technology plays an important role in so many domains, facial expression recognition is an active and mature area of research. For a recent review of some of the best approaches see [5]. For our purposes, an emotion classification system would work best with cameras that provide good views of faces, such as those located in hallways/stairwells and classrooms, two locations where approximately 83 % of reported bullying in the schools takes place [27].

Anger, contempt, and fear are some of the basic facial expressions that are most likely associated with bullying. Subtle differences in other emotional displays might also be associated with bullying. For example, bullies, victims, and onlookers might all smile, but each of these smiles would differ from each other and from smiles not associated with bullying. The bully might display a more sadistic smile, the victim a forced smile intended to appease the aggressor, and onlookers a smile suppressing fear or embarrassment, and each of these smiles would differ from smiles indicative of joy and delight. There is no reason to suppose that an emotion recognition system would be unable to discriminate subtle differences in emotional displays that are associated with bullying. In [13], for instance, a system is described that succeeds in distinguishing smiles indicative of delight from those that express normal social anxiety.

Crowd detection is a rather new area of research. In the last decade, research has focused on the automated analysis of higher level crowd characteristics, such as crowd configuration [1], abnormal crowd behavior detection [30], and real-time detection of violence [10], primarily by analyzing flow [10, 30] and recently through texture analysis [20]. Crowd detection applied to bullying would look at the way students group together to both witness and engage in bullying and would be very appropriate for video of the school grounds, where some 12 % of bullying occurs.

As noted in the introduction, physical incidents (i.e., behaviors such as hitting, kicking, throwing objects, or any form of overt violence toward another student) are the third most common form of bullying [16]. One way to detect actions associated with bullying would be to train classifiers to recognize actions associated with bullying. Such a system would be useful in all school-wide locations.

Action classification, like facial emotion classification, is an active area of research but far more complicated. Some challenges specific to action classification include large variations in action performance produced by variations in people's anatomy and spatial and temporal variations (including variations in the rate people perform actions) [6]. Distinguishing actions related to playfulness (such as wrestling and throwing objects at one another) from acts of bullying, will certainly prove an additional challenge. Solutions to this problem might include training the system to ignore actions involved in playing common children's games, adding social information to the system (e.g., a list of friends for each student), and integrating multiple systems (e.g., emotion classification with action classification).

Another possibility that should be mentioned is action classification using motion sensors, as proposed in [33], where researchers explored using the acceleration and gyro sensors found in some smart phones for detecting some actions associated with bullying. Distinguishing bullying from nonbullying activities using these sensors is difficult and probably only the at-risk students would comply in using the bullying detection app on their phones. As with smart IDs, phones can be misplaced or left behind. However, this is an option that could be useful if used in tandem with some of the other systems utilizing video images.

2.4 System Integration

In designing our Bullying Detection/Alert system we worked with the idea of integrating as many of the systems listed above as possible. As already mentioned, some systems, such as the tracking system, could function alone to at least alert personnel of potential problems with students at risk. HR monitoring, in contrast, would most likely function as an additional variable in other systems since HR increases for many reasons having nothing to do with bullying.

As illustrated at the top of Fig. 1, the Bullying Detection/Alert system would combine the decisions of all systems, including a simple rule-based system that might fire an alert and tag appropriate video when the tracking system detects a known bully approaching a known victim. In other situations, the combined decisions of all the systems would be summed to determine when to send out an alert to personnel. Based on the decisions of the systems, probabilities could be calculated that fire different levels of alert that could be sent to different locations and personnel depending on the type of alert and the location and severity of the bullying episode. Figure 1, for example, shows an alert being sent to a playground monitor's tablet as well as to a desktop located in some office. If bullying is detected in the classroom while the teacher is at the blackboard with her back to the class, the alert might trigger her smart watch to vibrate and even indicate, as displayed in Fig. 5, the general location in the classroom where the bullying activity is being detected. Interventions would depend upon school policy but could be as simple as a teacher turning her attention to the location indicated on her watch or for a monitor to approach the location in the playground where bullying is being detected.

Regardless of whether staff are able to intervene during a bullying episode or not, whenever bullying is detected, video from relevant cameras would be tagged and a list

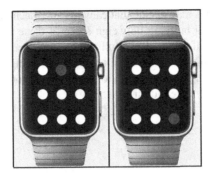

Fig. 5. A smart watch notifying a teacher of two separate bullying incidents and their approximate locations in the classroom (back middle and front right).

of bullying episodes and associated data (video and tracking information) archived. This information could be retrieved at a later time for review by school counselors and other personnel. Appropriate decisions could then be made regarding interventions (e.g., continuing to monitor the situation, changing seating arrangements in a classroom, speaking with those involved in a bullying episode, playing video back for a bully to watch and discuss, etc.).

3   Conclusion

In this paper we present a design for a bullying detection/alert system for school-wide intervention that combines wearables with HR sensors, surveillance cameras, machine learning systems, cloud computing, and mobile devices. The system alerts school personnel when potential bullying is detected, logs events, and tags video and other data for easy retrieval later by school personnel. The system identifies potential bullying by tracking and assessing the proximity of known players in bullying, by monitoring stress levels of students via HR analysis, and by recognizing actions, emotions, and crowd formations associated with bullying. Once bullying is detected, various levels of alerts produced by the system would be sent out to various devices, including smart watches, depending on both the level and the location of detected bullying events. Since all events would be logged and the videos and other data associated with the event would be tagged and archived, school personnel could review this material to implement appropriate interventions and assess the effectiveness of their whole-school strategies for reducing bullying.

Not addressed in this paper are security issues and some important ethical considerations in implementing a bullying detection system. Certainly the privacy of all associated with incidents of bullying would need to be safeguarded, and measures would need to be taken to ensure that students are allowed sufficient room for horseplay and appropriate expressions of anger and aggression. Some may fear that schools today are becoming more like prisons than institutions of learning with all the surveillance cameras and other security systems now being introduced throughout the educational system. Because the effects of violence and bullying are devastating for all parties involved, our communities may decide that cameras and machine learning systems that detect violence and school bullying outweigh some of these concerns. These systems need not be oppressive. If handled carefully, they could prevent physical and psychological harm to our children while simultaneously allowing for healthy expressions of negative affect. Reducing bullying and violence in the schools would certainly make our schools a better place for children to learn.

References

1. Arandjelovic, O.: Crowd detection from still images. In: British Machine Vision Conference (BMVC). University of Leeds (2008)
2. Arseneault, L., Walsh, E., Trzesniewski, K., Newcombe, R., Caspi, A., Moffitt, T.E.: Bullying victimization uniquely contributes to adjustment problems in young children: a nationally representative cohort study. Pediatrics **118**, 130–138 (2006)
3. Atlas, R.S., Pepler, D.: Observations of bullying in the classroom. J. Educ. Res. **92**(2), 86–99 (1998)
4. Barhight, L.R., Hubbard, J.A., Hyde, C.T.: Children's physiological and emotional reactions to witnessing bullying predict bystander intervention. Child Dev. **84**(1), 375–390 (2013)
5. Bettadapura, V.: Face Expression Recognition and Analysis: The State of the Art, Cornell University Library, arXiv.org (2012)
6. Brahnam, S.B., Nanni, L.: High performance set of features for human action classification. In: International Conference on Image Processing, Computer Vision, and Pattern Recognition (IPCV), Las Vegas, NV, pp. 980–984 (2009)
7. Farrington, D.P., Ttofi, M.M.: School-based programs to reduce bullying and victimization: a systematic review for the campbell collaboration crime and justice group. U.S. Department of Justice (2010). http://www.ncjrs.gov/pdffiles1/nij/grants/229377.pdf
8. Fekkes, M., Pijpers, F.I.M., Fredriks, A.M., Vogels, T., Verloove-Vanhorick, P.: Do bullied children get ill, or do ill children get bullied? A prospective cohort study on the relationship between bullying and health-related symptoms. Pediatrics **117**, 1568–1574 (2006)
9. Hanish, L.D., Guerra, N.G.: A longitudinal analysis of patterns of adjustment following peer victimization. Dev. Psychopathol. **14**, 69–89 (2002)
10. Hassner, T., Itcher, Y., Kliper-Gross, O.: Violent flows: real-time detection of violent crowd behavior. In: IEEE Conference on Computer Vision and Pattern Recognition Workshops (CVPRW), pp. 1–6 (2012)
11. Hatzenbuehler, M.L., Keyes, K.M.: Inclusive anti-bullying policies and reduced risk of suicide attempts in lesbian and gay youth. J. Adolesc. Health **53**(suppl. 1), S21–S26 (2013)
12. Hertz, M.F., Donato, I., Wright, J.: Bullying and suicide: a public health approach. J. Adolesc. Health **53**, S1–S3 (2013)
13. Hoque, M.E., Picard, R.: Acted vs. natural frustration and delight: many people smile in natural frustration. In: 9th IEEE International Conference on Automatic Face and Gesture Recognition (FG 2011), Santa Barbara, CA (2011)
14. Ishii, I., Ichida, T., Gu, Q., Takaki, T.: 500-Fps face tracking system. J. Real-Time Image Process. **8**(4), 379–388 (2013)
15. Juvonen, J., Graham, S.: Bullying in schools: the power of bullies and the plight of victims. Annu. Rev. Psychol. **65**, 159–185 (2014)
16. Juvonen, J., Wang, Y., Espinoza, G.: Bullying experiences and compromised academic performance across middle school grades. J. Early Adolesc. **31**, 152–173 (2011)

17. Kaltiala-Heino, R., Rimpela, M., Mamunen, M., Rimpela, A., Rantanen, P.: Bullying, depression, and suicidal ideation in finnish adolescents: school survey. Br. Med. J. **319**, 348–351 (1999)
18. Knack, J.M., Jensen-Campbell, L.A., Baum, A.: Worse than sticks and stones? bullying is associated with altered HPA axis functioning and poorer health. Brain Cogn. **77**, 183–190 (2011)
19. Munaro, M.B., Ghidoni, S., Tartaro, D.T., Menegatti, E.: A feature-based approach to people re-identification using skeleton keypoints. In: IEEE International Conference on Robotics and Automation, Hong Kong, China (2014)
20. Nanni, L., Brahnam, S., Ghidoni, S., Menegatti, E.: Automated crowd detection in stadium arenas. Northeast Decision Sciences Institute 2013. New York City, pp. 536–545 (2013)
21. Nanni, L., Munaro, M., Ghidoni, S., Menegatti, E., Brahnam, S.: Ensemble of different approaches for a reliable person re-identification system. Appl. Comput. Inform. (in press)
22. Olweus, D.: What We Know About Bullying. Blackwell Publishers Inc., Malden (1993)
23. Pepler, D., Jiang, D., Craig, W., Connolly, J.: Development trajectories of bullying and associated factors. Child Dev. **79**(2), 325–338 (2008)
24. Poh, M.-Z., Mcduff, D.J., Picard, R.: Non-contact, automated cardiac pulse measurements using video imaging and blind source separation. Opt. Express **18**(10), 10762–10774 (2010)
25. Robers, S., Zhang, J., Truman, J.: Indicators of School Crime and Safety: 2011, National Center for Education Statistics, U.S. Department of Education, and Bureau of Justice Statistics, Office of Justice Programs, U.S. Department of Justice, Washington, DC (2012)
26. Tattum, D.: Violence and Aggression in Schools, Trentham Books, Stoke-on-Trent, pp. 7–20 (1989)
27. U.S. Department of Justice Bureau of Justice Statistics. School Crime Supplement (Scs) to the National Crime Victimization Survey (2011)
28. Vezzani, R., Baltieri, D., Cucchiara, R.: People re-identification in surveillance and forensics: a survey. ACM Comput. Surv. **46**(2), 29:1–29:3 (2013)
29. Vossekuil, B., Fein, R.A., Reddy, M., Borum, R., Modzeleski, W.: The final report and findings of the safe school initiative: implications for the prevention of school attacks in the United States, Washington, DC (2002)
30. Wang, B., Ye, M., Li, X., Zhao, F., Ding, J.: Abnormal crowd behavior detection using high-frequency and spatio-temporal features. Mach. Vis. Appl. **23**(3), 501–511 (2012)
31. Wu, H.-Y., Rubinstein, M., Shih, E., Guttag, J., Durand, F., Freeman, W.: Eulerian video magnification for revealing subtle changes in the world. ACM Trans. Graph. (TOG) **31**(4) (2012)
32. Wurf, G.: High school anti-bullying interventions: an evaluation of curriculum approaches and the method of shared concern in four Hong Kong international schools. Aust. J. Guidance Counselling **22**(1), 139–149 (2012)
33. Ye, L., Ferdinando, H., Seppänen, T., Seppänen, E.: Physical violence detection for preventing school bullying. Adv. Artif. Intell. **2014**, ID 740358, 1–9 (2014)

Improving User Performance in a Smart Surveillance Scenario through Different Levels of Automation

Massimiliano Dibitonto[✉] and Carlo Maria Medaglia

DASIC, Link Campus University, Via Nomentana 335, 00162 Rome, Italy
m.dibitonto@unilink.it

Abstract. Artificial intelligence could be used to help users to better accomplish certain tasks, especially when critical or subjected to human errors. However, automating tasks could lead to other problems that could affect the final performance of the user. In this paper we investigate - from a Human Factors point of view - how different levels of automation (LOAs) may result in a change of user's behaviour and performances in smart surveillance systems. The objective is to find a correct balance between automating tasks and asking the user to intervene in the process. We performed tests (using qualitative-quantitative measures) to observe changes in performances, Situation Awareness and workload in relation to different LOAs.

Keywords: Levels of automation · Smart surveillance · Situation awareness · Usability · Mental workload · HCI

1 Introduction

Since the early history, humans tried to design and build tools to improve their life quality and their capabilities. Some of these tools are made to improve cognitive abilities. These could be defined as cognitive artifacts [16] that help us performing certain tasks, and give us the impression that our mental abilities are improved. One of the problems in designing a "smart" system is how tasks are divided between humans and machines, in order to achieve a certain goal, finding the correct balance between letting the system decide autonomously and giving the control to the user. However it is not always easy to decide when the user should take the control.

The balance between humans and automated systems could be better defined as Level of Automation (LOA). According to Kaber and Endsley [15]: "Level of automation refers to the level of task planning and performance interaction maintained between a human operator and computer in controlling a complex system". In the present work we will discuss how the right balance between the total automation and the manual control, with a right modality to deliver information to the user, could lead to a performance improvement in a video surveillance scenario.

M. Kurosu (Ed.): Human-Computer Interaction, Part II, HCII 2015, LNCS 9170, pp. 706–716, 2015.
DOI: 10.1007/978-3-319-20916-6_65

2   Smart Surveillance

There are many technologies and strategies involved to solve safety issues, however one of the most used is video surveillance. As Haering and colleagues [13] point out, monitoring is expensive and ineffective. Cameras alone produce a constant flow of data, but it is necessary the intervention of a human operator to understand the content of the video, recognize dangerous situations and react properly. In their study Haering and colleagues found that after 20 min of monitoring, the human attention lowers to an ineffective level.

To avoid this inefficiency the monitoring process could be automated using systems that are able understand and react to events. Tian and colleagues [18] define Smart Video Surveillance as: "the use of computer vision and pattern recognition technologies to analyze information from situated sensors".

Thanks to these techniques smart surveillance systems are able to work without human intervention, alerting the operative only when something happens (or according to different LOAs). However in real world conditions changes in illumination, occlusions and other phenomena could affect the effectiveness and robustness of a computer vision system, so the intervention of a human operator in some part of the loop is necessary.

However, during surveillance tasks, there could be long period of inactivity, resulting in an underload and boredom for the operator. On the other hand, attention levels of overloaded operators will drop in a short time.

As an example the user could be overwhelmed by information loosing the ability to perform their usual tasks effectively [14] or cold go outside of "the control loop" 10, loosing the awareness about the overall situation [1]. Indeed the main research focus in this area has been on the computer vision side and not on usability, reliability and efficiency of the interface.

3   Testing Different Levels of Automation

According to Parasuraman [17] automation does not merely supplant human activity but changes them and can impose new mental demands on the human operator. Automation can vary across a continuum, from a fully manual to a fully automated system and can be applied to different, replacing a function carried out by a human. To highlight where automation could meet humans activities, the author propose a simple four stage-view of human information processing, representing the way human achieve and process information to take a decision: (1) Sensory processing; (2) Perception/working memory; (3) Decision making; (4) Response selection.

Parasuraman uses these simple stages to draw a framework for automation design. To the four stages of (simplified) human information processing the author couples four classes of generic functions that could be automated in a system: (1) Information acquisition; (2) Information analysis; (3) Decision and action selection; (4) Action implementation. Each of these functions could be automated at different degrees, realizing a number of combinations that may require more or less the intervention of humans. Representing different levels of automation in a continuum, these categories could be an alternative way to look at the levels of automation proposed by Kaber and Endsley [15]. From these authors we can borrow some key points in the continuum that can be identified as: (1) Massive presence of the user and automation used as a tool; (2) Suggestion of the system to help the user; (3) Automatic action of the system vetoed by the user; (4) Autonomy of the automatic system.

In the present work we focus on Information Acquisition and Information Analysis classes. The acquisition could be automated intervening on sensing and registration of input data with filtering, highlighting or raw processing. The effect of the automation in this level could be seen in a change of the mental workload as, simply highlighting or filtering data avoid the user to search long lists of useless data. Moreover there is an effect on level 2 of Situation Awareness 9, related to the better quality of the signal provided, enabling a better understanding i.e. a clear video feed helps an operator more than one that is out of focus.

Automating analysis affects mainly perception and cognition of the user. The decision and the action selection imply the ability of the system to identify decision alternatives and eventually select one among them. The user tends to rely only on the automation. Parasuraman calls this over-trust phenomenon "complacency". This could be very dangerous when the automatic system fails. A user that is out-of-the-loop is not able to recognize errors of the system.

The experiment described below is designed to test how the user performance changes according to different levels of automation in a specific scenario. The results should help to find out how the user should be involved in the decision process without compromising the efficiency of the system.

3.1 Experimental Design

In the experiment we tested different levels of automation of a smart surveillance system, taking the one proposed by Dibitonto et al. [6] as a reference, to test the effect on an operator in terms of performance, situation awareness and workload. This context capture system is based on the combined use of computer vision and RFID UWD localization/identification system and is able to provide to the operator important information as the 3D position and the identity of people in the observed environment and some particular event (i.e. a fall, a person lying on the floor and a fire).

According to the model proposed by Parasuraman [17] we decided to vary level of automation only of Information Acquisition and Information Analysis classes, creating 3 different conditions: (1) Manual: no automation is applied; (2) Low system assistance: the system indicates areas with people inside (information acquisition). No information about identity is given. (3) High system assistance: the system provides real time identification and tracking of people in the scene. Moreover it detects some unusual events (i.e. fall detection) and operates some calculation on data achieved to help the user take a decision (information acquisition and analysis). We decided to not implement automatic decision levels due to the risks in terms of out-of-the-loop and over-confidence on the system.

3.2 The Simulators

To test different levels of automation three simulators have been implemented. The use of a simulator, using recorded video, presents some limitation as emotional responsibility, full communication, and real work practices cannot be fully addressed in a simulation 5. Despite these weaknesses, simulation is still a powerful technique. Moreover the use of recorded videos allows us to simulate precise conditions and the repeatability of the experiment, with a fixed ground truth. The three simulators have the same interface with a layout similar to the one used by Girgensohn and colleagues 11. The interface is constituted by: (1) a camera bank with 8 labelled video feeds (200 × 200 px); (2) a detail area to have an enlarged view (330 × 330 px) of a video feed; (3) a map of the observed area that is static in condition 1 while highlights room with people detected (condition 2) or draws placemarks with the real time position and identity of everyone in the scene (condition 3); (4) a control panel to send commands (i.e. raise an alarm or call rescuers) and receive system messages in conditions 3 (the number of people in the scene grouped by their role, alarms if some unusual event is detected).

All the alarms and important notifications were given in a textual way with blinking icons (2 Hz) drawing the attention of the user. Moreover we decide to show only essential information on the map (as position and role of persons in high system assistance condition) to avoid visual cluttering.The simulators were able to log on a csv file all the interactions of the user with the interface (Fig. 1).

3.3 Video Dataset

A video surveillance dataset has been recorded to perform the test. The dataset includes 21 min of a variable number of persons (3 to 7) acting inside an indoor environment recorded by a network of 8 synchronized cameras. Videos were recorded at the

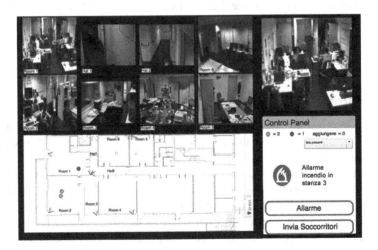

Fig. 1. The simulator in condition 3

resolution of 640×480 pixels at 30 fps. Video sequences were also manually annotated with ground truth. The dataset was recorded inside the laboratories of the University, the observed area is about 250 m^2, and the individuals involved are volunteer laboratory's members.

The activity of the users and the events have been scripted to create specific sequences that allows to test different aspects of a video-surveillance system and different task of the operator. Extra 5 min of video dataset, not annotated were made for training before preforming test.

3.4 Participants

Twenty-four participants (12 female) between the age of 25 and 35 (mean 29.5 SD = 3.36) volunteered the study. Participants had no prior experience of video surveillance tasks but they were confident in using computers. All the participants reported to be right-handed, with normal hearing and normal or correct to normal vision. To avoid learning effect each user tested only one condition.

3.5 Tasks

The participants have to monitor the video feeds of a laboratory where there are individuals belonging to two roles: workers (with a green jacket) and rescuers (with a red jacket). The participants were asked to look in particular for some conditions and to take proper actions according to certain rules: (1) check that the ratio between rescuers and workers is always at least 1:2 and, in case, call other rescuers, indicating the specific room where they have to go; (2) look for some events as: intruder (not worker/rescuer); fire; accident/injury for some worker; anything that may differ from the normal situation. In case of one of the latter the user has to call rescuers indicating the specific room where the emergency is. Regarding the last task there are multiple occurrences of such events: 4 times there is a wrong balance between the workers and the rescuers that has to be compensated by the user; 2 times there are alarms that have to be signalled by the users. Moreover a proper action has to be done in relation to different kinds of alarms.

3.6 Measures

A quali-quantitative approach has been used to measure various effects of different LOAs on users. Five different measures were taken during tests: (1) Performances; (2) Situation Awareness; (3) Eye Scanning Pattern; (4) Workload.

The performances were evaluated considering the success rate (effectiveness) and the time (efficiency) spent by the user to accomplish a certain task. We decided also to consider partially completed tasks. For example when a user recognizes a lack of balance between workers and rescuers but sends an incorrect number of rescuers.

The Situation Awareness was assessed through the combined use of a "freeze" 8 technique and of a self-evaluation questionnaire. The freeze technique was realized by obscuring the screen every 5 min (4 times in a test session) and asking to the user to draw, on a piece of paper representing the interface, the position of all the people detected in the videos. Users were asked to draw both on the map and on the camera bank, a symbol for workers and rescuers present on the scene.

The self-evaluation was made with a questionnaire the user had to fill for each freeze of the interface.

The way the user looks at the screen could be an important indicator about the strategies adopted and the mental workload. A Tobii® ET17 remote eye-tracking system was used for recording ocular activity of participants. This system allows the collection of ocular data calculating the gaze point on the visual interface (2D). From fixation data the scanning pattern (scanpath) was assessed. As reported by Camilli, Terenzi and Di Nocera [5] many works showed a relation between the scanpath and the mental workload of a user. Spatial statistic algorithms as Nearest Neighbour Index (NNI) [5], used to study special patterns, could be used to assess the spatial distribution produced by a pattern of fixation. Visual scanning randomness (or entropy) was found to be related to workload. Other studies [3] showed that when the temporal demand is the most relevant factor contributing to the total workload the randomness increases. In other words, transitions of fixations between different areas of interest (AOIs) were reduced when mental workload was high, indicating attentional narrowing. NNI index was calculated using the ASTEF tool [2].

3.7 Procedures

Before test session participants were trained on the interface performing sample actions (calling rescuers, firing alarms, zooming videos) and used it for 5 min (the same time interval used between each freeze). The participants were included in the sample only when they became able to perform all the operations needed for the tasks. Participants sat in front of the interface without other people in the room except for the facilitator and were asked to monitor the interface to accomplish the given tasks. The test lasted for 20 min and every 5 min the interface was masked and the user was asked to fill a SA questionnaire. The test was video recorded.

4 Data Analysis and Results

4.1 Performances

The sums of the proportions of tasks completed (6) were used as dependent variables in ANOVA statistic design using condition (Cond. 1 vs Cond. 2 vs Cond. 3) as fixed factor. There is statistical significance, $p < 0.05$, $F(2,21) = 5.2925$, among the different conditions.

Duncan post hoc testing showed statistical significance ($p < 0.05$) between condition 1 and 3 and between condition 2 and 3. These results may be related to the fact that the higher LOA implemented in Condition 3 could better support users during the tasks. If compared with the study of Girgensohn and colleagues [12] we can see that, in both cases, interactive spatial information helps the operator to perform better.

Moreover in condition 1 the user has to rely only on his/her perceptions and memory. In condition 3 there is an evident cue given by the control panel, that blinks and clearly indicates the number of workers, rescuers and the number of rescuers missing.

A qualitative evaluation made on the users' "thinking aloud" showed that users felt more confident about their choices in condition 3 as they could check their assumption with data reported in the control panel.

4.2   Situation Awareness

The means of the SA values were used as dependent variables in ANOVA statistical design with the conditions as a fixed factor. The results are only tending toward statistical significance $F(2, 21) = 2.6713$, $p = .09255$. Duncan post hoc test shown statistical significance between conditions 1 and 3 $p < .05$.

The main difference noticed was of qualitative nature. In condition 3 the users were able to give more details with less uncertainty. They were asked to "think aloud" during the test and during the filling of the questionnaire. While in condition 1 and 2 they often tried to make inferences to remember the number and the position of the people in the scene, in condition 3 they were more self confident and fast in compiling the questionnaire.

A remarkable condition concerns the second alarm. In this case a worker feels sick and slumps on floor, disappearing from the scene because occluded by a table. Without any other cue some participants supposed that the worker exited the scene in a moment of distraction. In condition 2 and, especially, in condition 3 indications on the map and on the control panel (number of workers and a fall detection system) helped to correctly interpret the sudden absence of the worker.

4.3   Eye Scanning Pattern

Fixations have been grouped into areas of interest (AOI) corresponding to the main elements of the interface: Camera bank (AOI 1); Map (AOI 2); Control panel (AOI 3); Video detail (AOI 4)

The means of fixation duration on each AOI for each minute have been calculated. This measure indicates the most used part of the interface and can highlight different strategies adopted by the users according to the tools and cues they could use. Of course this measure doesn't take into account the peripheral attention of the user that has shown to be attracted by sudden movements in video feeds or in the map or by alerts (blinking) in the control panel.

Proportions of ocular fixations per minute on the interface AOI were used as dependent variable in ANOVA statistical design by using the Condition (Cond 1 vs Cond 2 vs Cond 3) as fixed factor. It highlighted a main effect, $p < .05$ F $(6,63) = 2.7218$, of conditions on the user's scanpath. Duncan post hoc test showed statistical significance between condition 1 and 3 for fixations duration on AOI 2(map) $p < .01$ and on AOI 3(control panel) $p < .05$ as can be seen from the heatmap in Fig. 2. Another statistical significance has been found between condition 2 and condition 3 for fixations duration on AOI 2 $p < .05$ and on AOI 3 $p < .01$.

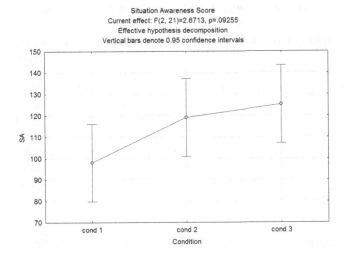

Fig. 2. Situation awareness assessment

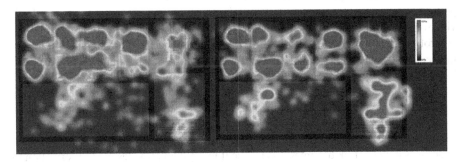

Fig. 3. The *number of fixations* in condition 1 (left) and condition 3 (right)

This could be related to the different use of these parts according to the different LOAs implemented. In conditions 2 and 3 map shows important information (presence and position of individuals) and in condition 3 the control panel shows the number of workers and rescuers and (eventually) the number of rescuers to call. As the results presented by Girgensohn and colleagues [12] the map help the operator to choose the video feed to look at, being the most used part of the interface (Fig. 3).

4.4 Workload

Users' fixations could give information about the path followed by the user across the interface to have another indicator about workload. The spatial distribution of eye fixations was assessed calculating the NNI using ASTEF [2].

In the work of Camilli et al. [3], is shown that when Temporal Demand [14] is the most loading component of the workload, the spatial distribution of eye fixation is more dispersed (i.e. more random, higher NNI values) respect to the fixations distribution recorded during easier task load conditions. Differently, when the most loading workload component is the Mental Demand, fixations spatial distribution is more grouped (i.e. less random, lower NNI values) respect to the fixations distribution associated with easier task load conditions.

The NNI mean values have been used as dependent variables in ANOVA statistical design using Conditions (Cond1 vs Cond2 vs Cond3) as fixed factor. The analysis showed a main effect, $p < .001$ $F(2, 21) = 21.699$, of condition on NNI. Duncan post hoc test showed that the effect is present also within the conditions. The decreasing of NNI could be interpreted as a decrease of the Temporal Demand. Indeed, supported by the map and the control panel the users doesn't have to look around to be prompt for the arrival of new information or to have a comprehensive view of the scene but can focus on specific areas.

5 Conclusion

Results showed that implementing different LOAs, without changing the interface layout, lead to the adoption of different strategies by the users, changing the action they perform to accomplish the given task. While the video feeds (camera bank and detail video) are the most used UI element in every condition, in condition 3 the map and the control panel, representing the visual output of the higher level of automation imple-mented, are used to have support to solve ambiguous cases, when information provided by video feeds were confused, due to many people moving though different rooms.

There is no significant effect on Mental Workload as, probably, the new tools provided change the sub-tasks that the users have to accomplish. Even if the user has a lower mental demand (less calculations and reasoning) he has to face a higher interface complexity with more elements to monitor. However, a decrease in Temporal Demand underlines how the task becomes less frantic if the system provides more information to the users. Indeed the user can get the information he/she needs from specific cues on UI (in condition 3) without having to search among all video feeds (as in condition 1).

During the test on condition 3 the users showed to don't rely totally on cues provided by the system but they used them as a confirmation. As the choice was not pre-compiled but the interface provided only a cue the user felt like was their own responsibility to check the correctness of the choice. However this alone doesn't avoid the risk to accept a wrong cue, due to an incorrect calculation of the system.

As a synthesis from these results it appears that the main effect of different LOAs on user is the change of strategy used to accomplish the given task. The multiplication of information sources (redundant and complimentary) had effect on the quantity and quality of information that the users are able to achieve and remember. The user is involved in the decision process and has enough elements to take a correct decision. This could be important to avoid underload and boredom with a positive effect on the users performances. Moreover results showed the importance of representing the information in an understandable le way to avoid the overload of the cognitive resources of users.

As a future evolution of the present work the research will be focused on the effect of natural interaction paradigms on human performance in a command, control and communication scenario.

References

1. Wiener, E., Renwick, L., E.C.: flight-deck automation: promises and problems. Ergonomics **23**(10), 995–1011 (1980)
2. Camilli, M., Nacchia, R., Terenzi, M., Di Nocera, F.: ASTEF: a simple tool for examining fixations. Behav. Res. Methods **40**(2), 373–382 (2008)
3. Camilli, M., Terenzi, M., Di Nocera, F.: Effects of temporal and spatial demands on the distribution of eye fixations. In: Proceedings of the Human Factors and Ergonomics Society Annual Meeting, p. 1248, SAGE Publications (2008)
4. Clark, P.J., Evans, F.C.: Distance to nearest neighbor as a measure of spatial relationships in populations. Ecology **35**(4), 445–453 (1954)
5. Di Nocera, F., Terenzi, M., Camilli, M.: Another look at scan path: distance to nearest neighbour as a measure of mental workload. In: de Waard, D., Brookhuis, K.A., Toffetti, A. (eds.) Developments in Human Factors in Transportation, Design, and Evaluation, pp. 295–303. Shaker Publishing, Maastricht (2006)
6. Dibitonto, M., Buonaiuto, A., Marcialis, G., Muntoni, D., Medaglia, C., Roli, F.: Fusion of radio and video localization for people tracking. In: Ambient Intelligence, pp. 258–263 (2011)
7. Dos Santos, I.J.A.L., Teixeira, D.V., Ferraz, F.T., Carvalho, P.V.R.: The use of a simulator to include human factors issues in the interface design of a nuclear power plant control room. J. Loss Prev. Process Ind. **21**(3), 227–238 (2008)
8. Endsley, M.R.: Measurement of situation awareness in dynamic systems. Hum. Factors J. Hum. Factors Ergon. Soc. **37**(1), 65–84 (1995)
9. Endsley, M.R.: Design and evaluation for situation awareness enhancement. Hum. Factors Ergon. Soc. Annu. Meet. Proc. Hum. Factors Ergon. Soc. **32**, 97–104 (1988)
10. Endsley, M.R., Kiris, E.O.: The out-of-the-loop performance problem and level of control in automation. Hum. Factors J. Hum. Factors Ergon. Soc. **37**(2), 381–394 (1995)
11. Girgensohn, A., Kimber, D., Vaughan, J., Yang, T., Shipman, F., Turner, T., Rieffel, E., Wilcox, L., Chen, F., Dunnigan, T.: DOTS: support for effective video surveillance. In: Proceedings of the 15th International Conference on Multimedia, p. 423. ACM (2007)
12. Girgensohn, A., Shipman, F., Turner, T., Wilcox, L.: Effects of presenting geographic context on tracking activity between cameras. In: Proceedings of the SIGCHI Conference on Human Factors in Computing Systems, p. 1167. ACM (2007)
13. Haering, N., Venetianer, P.L., Lipton, A.: The evolution of video surveillance: an overview. Mach. Vis. Appl. **19**(5), 279–290 (2008)
14. Hollands, J.G., Wickens, C.D.: Engineering Psychology and Human Performance. Prentice Hall, Upper Saddle River (1999)
15. Kaber, D.B., Endsley, M.R.: The effects of level of automation and adaptive automation on human performance, situation awareness and workload in a dynamic control task. Theor. Issues Ergon. Sci. **5**(2), 113–153 (2004)
16. Norman, D.A.: The'problem' with automation: inappropriate feedback and interaction, not 'over-automation'. Philos. Trans. R. Soc. B Biol. Sci. **327**(1241), 585–593 (1990)

17. Parasuraman, R., Sheridan, T.B., Wickens, C.D.: A model for types and levels of human interaction with automation. IEEE Trans. Syst. Man Cybern. Part A: Syst. Hum. **30**(3), 286–297 (2000)

18. Tian, Y., Brown, L., Hampapur, A., Lu, M., Senior, A., Shu, C.: IBM smart surveillance system (S3): event based video surveillance system with an open and extensible framework. Mach. Vis. Appl. **19**(5), 315–327 (2008)

Controlling the Home

A User Participatory Approach to Designing a Simple Interface for a Complex Home Automation System

Martin Eskerud, Anders Skaalsveen, Caroline Sofie Olsen,
and Harald Holone$^{(\boxtimes)}$

Østfold University College, Halden, Norway
{martin.b.eskerud,anders.skaalsveen,caroline.s.olsen,
harald.holone}@hiof.no

Abstract. This paper presents our experience with a Participatory Design approach designing an interface for controlling a home automation system. In a Future Workshop, users imagined that a home could be visualized as a graph, with nodes representing the devices in a household, and edges representing the interconnectivity between the devices. Participants later gave feedback on a refined mock-up of the interface, confirming that the idea of using a graph would be suitable for presenting the devices in a household. In the third iteration, users assessed a high-fidelity prototype. This evaluation focused on the graph interface's ability to control a home automation system, and its ability to create an overview of the devices. Based on the feedback from the participants, we concluded that the prototype was able to convey an overview of the devices, and that a graph based interface would be suitable for controlling a home automation system.

Keywords: Home automation · Participatory design · Future workshop · Graph based interface · Smart home

1 Introduction

Home automation is not a new idea [17], and can be traced all the way back to the 1850s, where Joel Houghton patented a device for automating the job of washing dishes [5]. Moreover, with the emergence of remote controllers, mobile devices, and the interconnectivity between different devices, home automation is becoming more accomplishable for the average Joe. However, if the development is only influenced by technology savvy individuals, we risk creating a system that may seem over complicated to the less tech savvy [2].

To avoid alienating the user, we sought out to create a user oriented design solution for a home automation interface. Using practices from Participatory Design (PD), we included users in all part of the design process [12]. Together we created a prototype for integrating and controlling household devices from a mobile device. The research questions were formulated as follows:

© Springer International Publishing Switzerland 2015
M. Kurosu (Ed.): Human-Computer Interaction, Part II, HCII 2015, LNCS 9170, pp. 717–728, 2015.
DOI: 10.1007/978-3-319-20916-6_66

RQ1: How can a potentially complex home automation system be controlled through a user interface focusing on simplicity? And how can the different household appliances be visualized to provide an overview of the different devices in the household?

RQ2: How can principles from Participatory Design be employed for designing an interface for such a home automation system?

2   Related Work

Home automation is the concept of creating automatic behavior with and between devices in the home. Controlling these devices remotely can be seen as a subgenre to home automation. This project will concern a suggested interface to this purpose. Many of the current interfaces for home automation are complex, "engineer style interfaces" where the user navigates by using a flora of menus and buttons. During prototype design, the idea of using a graph interface emerged, where the users suggested that a graph could be suited for our project's needs.

We reviewed several traditional interfaces for home automation: Mi Casa Verde[1], HomeOS[2], Homemaestro [9], as well as an internally developed home automation system at Østfold University College [10]. We also explored the current issues of the home automation domain as a whole for example as discussed by Brush et al. [2]. An example of the topics presented by Brush et al. were the issues which actual current users of home automation systems were experiencing.

2.1   Graph Interfaces and Visualizations

Graph interfaces are common in our everyday lives. Things such as the London Tube map and road maps stimulate people's ability to think in terms of graphs, and can be interpreted by users without a technical background [15].

The idea of using a graph for presenting information is not a new idea, in fact, it was estimated that 2.2 trillion graphs were published during 1994 [6], and it is very likely that this number is still growing. To the best of our knowledge however, the idea of combining a graph based interface with home automation is novel.

Although we did not find any relevant work regarding graph based interfaces for home automation systems, we did find other graph based interfaces and guidelines for graph interfaces which were of interest.

Freire and Rodriguez's article Preserving the Mental map [4] provided important guidelines when deciding how the user should be able to navigate the graph interface and which traits we should focus on when looking towards other graph based interfaces. The article emphasizes the importance of several aspects of graph interface design. One aspect is that the user should always be able to foresee the changes which they do to the interface. Furthermore, it is vital to

---

[1] http://getvera.com/.

[2] http://research.microsoft.com/en-us/projects/homeos/.

preserve the user's mental map of the interface, as losing a sense of direction means the abstract interface would fail.

This article influenced the light in which we discussed other graph based interfaces, such as Xenakis [1] and the Reactable [7]. Figure 1 shows the reactable application, where the user interacts with the direct manipulation interface by adding elements which become part of a beat.

Fig. 1. The Reactable app in use.

As previously mentioned, graphs are everywhere, but we could not find a graph interface used for home automation. We therefore based our prototype on existing applications within this field as well as existing graph interfaces intended for entertainment and other purposes.

3   Method

Our focus in this project has been to answer if a potentially complex home automation system can be controlled through an interface that would be easy for users to understand and use. As we aspired to develop the interface together with potential users, we employed Participatory Design (PD) to engage the participants. This section briefly presents the different methods used for developing and evaluating the prototype together with the participants.

3.1   Data Collection

As we wanted to involve the users in the whole process of developing the prototype, data were naturally collected throughout the project. These were collected through observation, interviews and questionnaires, using both quantitative and qualitative approaches. In the early phases of the project, users participated in a Future Workshop [14], a method from PD directed at enhancing the dialogue between designers and users. This session focused on concretizing issues with present day's solution regarding home automation, and a brainstorming where the participants developed ideas regarding how this situation could be improved [8].

In the subsequent phases of the development, the participants took part in two evaluations of the prototype. However, it is important to point out that the participants did not participate solely to test the interface. The feedback from the participants in the two evaluations were crucial for continuing the development of the design.

One of the techniques used for gathering data during the evaluations was the Think Aloud method [13]. When interacting with the prototype, the users were asked to think aloud explaining their actions and thoughts regarding the prototype. Further, to attain more information about the users' impressions of the prototype, we conducted individual semi-structured interviews after the participant had interacted with the prototype [3]. To gather quantitative data regarding the use of the prototype, the number of unique gestures was collected, making it possible to compare how the users interacted with the interface. Further, the data allowed for assessing different difficulties regarding the interface. Finally, to assess the prototypes usability, the users filled out a System Usability Scale[3].

3.2   Data Analysis

Using techniques from Grounded Theory, we extracted concepts from the interviews and observations [18]. To analyze the results from the System Usability Scale, the participants' scores for each question were converted as described by Jeff Sauro [11]. The scores end up on a 1-100 scale. A score above 68 is considered above average. Further, to make sense of the statistical data regarding the different user's unique gestures, descriptive statistics were used to visualize the results as graphs [16].

4   Design Iterations

The process of creating and developing a prototype together with participants consisted of three iterations. The first iteration was based on a method from Participatory Design (PD), where participants took part in a Future Workshop. The second iteration focused on further developing ideas from the first session into a low fidelity prototype. The prototype's viability was also evaluated in a preliminary usability testing. Based on feedback from usability testing in the second iteration, the third iteration focused on evolving the low-fidelity prototype into a high- fidelity prototype. Further, in the final iteration, the final prototype's functionality and usability were evaluated as participants again took part in a usability test.

---

[3] http://hell.meiert.org/core/pdf/sus.pdf.

4.1   First Iteration - Future Workshop

To create the prototype in the spirit of PD, the users were included in the design of the prototype already in the early stages of the project. The participants consisted of four students between the ages of 23 to 25, representing both sexes. To gather ideas, criticism of today's situation and possible solutions, users were invited to participate in a Future Workshop. In order to familiarize the user group with the project and the home automation domain, they first received a brief introduction to home automation. The participants were presented with already existing solutions and suggestions for possible interfaces. After the introduction, the users participated in a critique phase criticizing the current situation.

During the critique phase the participants expressed clearly that there had to be better ways of creating home automation user interfaces than the classic dashboard interfaces presented. After the critique phase, the participants described their vision of a home automation system. In a final phase, the users discussed how their previous ideas of a utopian home automation system could be implemented. During the Future Workshop, the participants proposed a design solution inspired by a graph. This idea was based on the belief that the inter-connectivity between the different appliances could resemble a graph, where the nodes represented the different devices, and the edges represented the connection between different devices. Further, the different rooms in a home could be viewed as a graph, where the different rooms represented nodes, and connections between the different devices in the rooms represented the edges. The users suggested that this would provide a good overview of the home and the devices within it. One participant mentioned:

> "There is a relation between these devices and they can communicate. Then, it can be considered a networks as well. A network with nodes, and relations between the nodes." (Man, 24)

The idea of controlling the household not only as a remote control, but also by creating different rules for how the devices should behave was also conceived by the participants. In the implementation phase of the Future Workshop, users suggested drawing a line between the devices in the graph, to create rules which would automate behavior between the devices. The idea of using a graph, and rules were ideas implemented in the second iteration of designing the interface.

4.2   Second Iteration - Low-Fidelity Prototype

The graph based interface from the first iteration was later created as a low-fidelity prototype, consisting of mock-ups created with Photoshop[4]. The programming languages PHP[5] and Javascript[6] were used to create a simple web-application containing a single frame for displaying the different mock-ups, see Fig. 2. These frames were enabled for user interaction through click, long click and drag.

---

[4] http://www.adobe.com/products/photoshop.html.

[5] http://php.net/.

[6] http://www.w3schools.com/js/.

Fig. 2. The low-fidelity prototype presenting rooms and appliances in a home.

To assess if the idea of using a graph would be a suitable way of presenting the different devices in a household, the prototype was evaluated in a usability test. Participating in the evaluation was six students between the ages 22 to 25, representing both sexes. Two participants had previously participated in the Future Workshop.

The test consisted of eight tasks, four of which focused on remote controlling home appliances, and four tasks that focused on creating rules between the different devices. After the tasks were finished, the participants were given a System Usability Scale form. After the users completed the form, a semi-structured interview was conducted for gathering qualitative feedback regarding the user's experience of the interface.

4.3   Third Iteration - High-Fidelity Prototype

As the usability test in the second iteration yielded good results, a final implementation of the prototype was developed as an Android application. Section 5 describes the prototype.

In the evaluation of the final prototype, we gathered feedback from the users on how well the graph interface worked in illustrating a home, and if they had control of the devices. Participating in the evaluation was five students between the ages of 23 and 34.

The users were asked to solve a set of tasks that were designed to resemble everyday scenarios. Afterwards, the users were asked to participate in a semi-structured interview [3], and then to fill out a questionnaire. The results from the evaluation is described in more detail in Sect. 6.

5   Prototype

This section describes the high-fidelity prototype for Android, resulting from the previous iterations described in Sect. 4. When starting the application for the first time, the user sees a white screen with circular room nodes in the middle of the screen as illustrated in Fig. 3. The movement of a node is animated to clearly show how it reacts to interaction. Having support for multi-touch, the application allows movement of multiple nodes simultaneously. In this prototype, the nodes are split into two categories, representing rooms and devices. Although they look rather similar, they have both different visual details, and behavior.

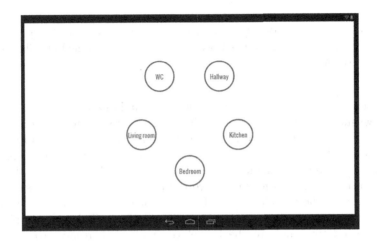

Fig. 3. The initial positioning of room nodes.

5.1 Rooms

Once the user taps or drags one or more nodes to the middle of the screen, the other ones drift to the edge of the screen to give space to the nodes in focus. The active nodes can either be dragged to the center of the screen, where two invisible slots take hold of them, or they can be put at the edge of the screen to be placed with the rest of the room nodes. The two invisible slots at the center of the screen "expands" the nodes, making the corresponding device nodes visible. The two slots reduce the space required in order to display all the devices, and make it possible to create connections between devices in different rooms.

5.2 Devices

When visible, the device nodes are drawn around their corresponding room nodes, connected by straight edges to illustrate their parent room node. In order to interact with the device nodes, three different gestures are used. The device nodes can be tapped to toggle its on/off state or to toggle the visibility of its child nodes. This depends on which type of device node the user taps.

The device nodes are split into three categories. The first category is for devices with binary states, which can either be turned on or off. When turned on, the outer ring of the node is colored green instead of grey to indicate the node's state. This, as well as the following category is depicted in Fig. 4.

Fig. 4. Device nodes from the high-fidelity prototype. The device node representing a coffee maker on the left can be toggled on and off. The device node for light on the right can be dimmed.

The second category handles floating values and enables the user to select a value within a given range. It is distinguished by its fragmented outer circle and its additional outer arc for indicating the selected value through its length. This node enables the user to perform tasks as for instance dimming lights and adjusting the volume of a music player. The gesture for adjusting the value of these nodes is a swipe-gesture where the user swipes from the inside of the device's circle to the outside. When the user's finger exits the circle, the node's text changes to display its value between 0 and 100 %. This value is given by the finger's relative angle to the top of the node with respect to its center. As the value displayed inside the device node is continuously updated, it allows the user to fine-tune it with more precision by moving the finger further away from the node. When the node is tapped and turned off, the current value is saved in order to be restored when the device is turned on again.

The third category allows devices to express multiple functions as child nodes of the corresponding device node. A stove for instance will often have multiple hot plates. These can then be illustrated as child nodes placed around the stove's device node. The child nodes of a device node are allowed to use icons instead of text to describe themselves. An example of this device node category is depicted in Fig. 5.

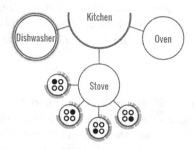

Fig. 5. The device nodes of the kitchen in one of our scenarios.

The interface enables users to create connections between nodes in order to apply rules for how the devices should affect each other. A user can for instance create a rule for instructing the light in the kitchen to turn on when the coffee maker starts brewing. These connections can be created by long pressing a node, which will cause it to detach from its fixed position around its room node, and dragging it on top of the node to be influenced. As the node is detached, the device which the interface runs on will vibrate and the connectable device nodes' border becomes dashed as a visual cue to the user that the dragged node can be dropped on top of them.

6   Results and Discussion

In this section we present and discuss findings emerging from the interviews, questionnaires and observations in the process of developing the prototype together with the users.

6.1   The Interface

During the future workshop, the users suggested a graph design for the prototype. The suggested solution showed potential for visualizing the devices in a household and providing control over a home automation system. Further, the solution seemed to be a promising improvement over the "engineer style" interfaces presented in Sect. 2.

When asked if the users felt in control, the participants expressed that the interface's features made it easy to feel in control over the different household appliances. In regard to the design, all but one of the users responded that the graph worked well as a way of visualizing the devices in a home. One participant explained that he found the node structure much more playful than traditional directory structure often found in other systems. As the participant explained:

> "This type of node structure is a lot more playful than a directory structure. If you look at Windows or Linux, you're always moving downwards into things, but being able to move across and outside of those things, and creating your own rules and connections - I like that a lot, I'm a fan of that train of thought." (Man, 24)

When looking at the time and number of clicks the participants used to solve the scenarios in the user test, we observed that the number of interactions were similar between the participants. However, they used different gestures when solving the tasks. Further, there was little variation between new users and users who had previously been involved in the development.

During the evaluation of the prototype, several participants commented on how smooth it felt to create rules to connect the devices together. Users agreed that the rule functionality added more value to the application, and that it would be less interesting if it worked only as a remote control. Further, the users responded positively to the haptic feedback provided by the different gestures. As one participant stated:

"I also like the idea of playing with the node and pulling it around....
It's the good feeling of pulling something around. Physically grabbing the
node." (Man, 34)

In addition, the scores from the SU scale[7] gave an indication that the overall usability of the interface was good. The average from the questionnaire was 84. A number above 68 is considered as above average usability.

6.2   The Use of Participatory Design

The participants' ideas, suggestions and experiences with the prototype was throughout the project an invaluable drive for developing the interface. By including the participants throughout the whole design process, we were able to gather valuable data that might not have been possible to obtain otherwise.

Due to limited time and resources, the group of participants consisted of students and PhD. candidates from the Faculty of Computer Sciences at Østfold University College. It is possible that the suggested graph based design is biased towards users with technological backgrounds. However, our findings suggest that less tech savvy users would be able to use the prototype satisfactory, as people interact with networks and graphs on a regular basis. Not having tested on users without a technical background in this project, it is difficult to foresee how a graph interface in this context would be perceived by the users in general. Nonetheless, the participants supported the use of a graph based interface when asked if they foresaw any problems with family members using the application. In unison, the users thought the concept of the prototype was sufficiently easy for anyone to learn.

Further, we purposefully involved two of the same users in several design iterations. This allowed us to compare gathered data from novice and seasoned participants to see if they behaved differently when using the prototype. In the evaluations of the prototype, we observed that new users suggested more drastic changes than the more seasoned participants. This may be attributed to the sense of ownership the experienced users might have had towards the prototype. However, little else was different between the two types of users.

7   Conclusion

In this paper we explore how a potentially complex home automation system can be controlled through a user interface designed with a focus on simplicity. Further, we wanted to create the solution in participation with the users.

Based on the results we gathered during the final user test, we can conclude that the interface did function well as an abstraction of the home and its devices. All users described that they felt in control of the devices, and that the graph interface worked well as a visualization of the home and its appliances.

---

[7] http://www.usabilitynet.org/trump/documents/Suschapt.doc.

Additionally, including the users throughout the process has undoubtedly been an invaluable element in the process of developing the interface. The participants did not only help evaluate the design's viability and usability, but their suggestions for design and improvement were a definitive driving force in the project.

8 Future Work

In this project we focused on designing a front end solution for controlling a home automation system. During the development of the prototype, suggestions for improvements emerged, and one of the paper's authors is presently developing the interface further.

For this project, we envisioned a future where the devices automatically connect and communicate by themselves. Another of the paper's authors is currently working on creating a prototype that allows smart devices to discover each other and intercommunicate using proven Web-technology.

Acknowledgements. First and foremost we would like to express our gratitude to the participants in this project. Their feedback has been invaluable. We would also like to thank the staff from the Faculty of Computer Sciences at Østfold University College for their support.

References

1. Bischof, M., Conradi, B., Lachenmaier, P., Linde, K., Meier, M., Potzl, P., Andre, E.: Xenakis - combining tangible interaction with probability-based musical composition (2008)
2. Brush, A.J., Lee, B., Mahajan, R., Agarwal, S., Saroiu, S., Dixon, C.: Home automation in the wild: challenges and opportunities. In: Proceedings of the SIGCHI Conference on Human Factors in Computing Systems, pp. 2115–2124. ACM (2011)
3. Clifford, N., French, S., Valentine, G.: Key Methods in Geography, 2nd edn. Sage Publications, UK (2010)
4. Freire, M., Rodriguez, P.: Preserving the Mental Map in Interactive Graph Interfaces. ACM, New York (2006)
5. Gref, L.G.: The Rise and Fall of American Technology. Algora Publishing, New York (2010)
6. Jones, R.W., Careras, I.E.: The empirical investigation of factors affecting graphical visualization. Behav. Res. Methods **28**(2), 265–269 (1996)
7. Jorda, S.: The reactable : tangible and tabletop music performance (2010)
8. Jungk, R., Müllert, N.R.: Future Workshops : How to Create Desirable Futures. Institute for Social Inventions, London (1996)
9. Karagiannis, T., Athanasopoulos, E., Gkantsidis, C., Key, P.: Homemaestro : Order from chaos in home networks. Technical report MSR-TR-2008-84, Microsoft Research, May 2008
10. Muntean, C., Johannesen, O.A.S.: User interface technologies for home appliances and networks (2013)

11. Sauro, J.: Measuring usability with the system usability scale (sus) (2011)
12. Sears, A., Jacko, J.A.: Human-computer Interaction : Development Process. CRC Press, Boca Raton (2009)
13. Shneiderman, B., Plaisaint, C.: Designing the User Interface : Strategies for Effective Human-Computer Interaction, 5th edn. Addison-Wesley Publ. Co, MA (2010)
14. Simonsen, J., Robertson, T.: Routledge International Handbook of Participatory Design. Routledge, New York (2012)
15. Steele, J.: Beautiful Visualization: Looking at Data Through the Eyes of Experts. O'Reilly, Sebastopol, CA (2010)
16. Trochim, W.: Descriptive statistics (2006)
17. Grinter, R.E., Edwards, W.K.: A home with ubiquitous computing: Seven challenges (2002)
18. Walliman, N.: Your Research Project (2005)

Enhancing Human Robot Interaction Through Social Network Interfaces: A Case Study

Laura Fiorini$^{(\boxtimes)}$, Raffaele Limosani, Raffaele Esposito,
Alessandro Manzi, Alessandra Moschetti, Manuele Bonaccorsi,
Filippo Cavallo, and Paolo Dario

The BioRobotics Institute, Scuola Superiore Sant'Anna, Pisa, Italy
{l.fiorini,r.limosani,f.cavallo}@sssup.it

Abstract. Recently we have assisted to the rise of different Social Networks, and to the growth of robots for home applications, which represent the second big market opportunity. The use and the integration of robotics services in our daily life is strictly correlated with their usability and their acceptability. Particularly, their ease of use, among other issues, is linked to the simplicity of the interface the user has to interact with. In this sense social networks could enrich and simplify the communication between the user and technology avoiding the multiplication of custom interfaces. In this work the authors propose a system to enHancE human RobOt Interaction through common Social networks (HeROIS). HeROIS system combines the use of cloud resources, service robot and smart environments proposing three different services to help citizens in daily life. In order to assess the acceptability and the usability levels, HeROIS system and services have been tested with 13 real users (24–37 years old) in the DomoCasa Lab (Italy). As regards the usability, the results show that the proposed system is usable for 4 participants (30.77 % M = 79.69 SD = 3.13) and excellent for 9 participants (69.23 % M = 90.05 SD = 3.72). Concerning the acceptability level, the results show that the proposed system is acceptable for 8 volunteers (61.54 % M = 77.02 SD = 4.23) and excellent for 5 participants (38.46 % M = 89.71 SD = 6.06).

Keywords: Service robots · Social network · Cloud robotics · Acceptability

1 Introduction

In recent years there has been a significant increase in the use of Social Networks [1]. The usage statistics indicate growing popularity for both Twitter and Facebook, with Twitter growing significantly faster than Facebook [2]. The rapid development and deployment of personal smart devices [3] helped to ensure that the social networks permeate anytime and anywhere in our life.

On the other side, ABI Research [4] highlights how robots for home applications represent the second major potential market opportunity for personal robotics. Several solutions show how robots could be integrated into smart homes and smart

---

L. Fiorini and R. Limosani are contributed equally.

© Springer International Publishing Switzerland 2015
M. Kurosu (Ed.): Human-Computer Interaction, Part II, HCII 2015, LNCS 9170, pp. 729–740, 2015.
DOI: 10.1007/978-3-319-20916-6_67

environments supporting the activities of daily life [5]. The use of robotic solutions in our daily life is consequent to the acceptability and usability of the proposed technology. Concerning the acceptability of the robot, three main issues are involved; that are the real willingness of the autonomous machine to be integrated, the positive attitude toward it in terms of appearance and services offered by the technology and a sufficient ease of use [6].

The ease of use of robotic solution as well as other smart devices is linked, above other issues, to the interface the user has to interact through and to the simplicity of this interface. Often different technologies have custom applications the user has to learn to use, making the usage of smart devices and robots more difficult. The use of several applications for each technologies decrease the ease of use of the smart environment itself.

In this context social networks could enrich and simplify the communication between the user and the smart technologies. In particular, in this work social networks are used to communicate with a smart home which integrated robot and smart environment.

Instead of using a new interface to manage smart home, the use of an already known one will help the user in using it.

2   Related Works

In literature there are examples on social networks integration with robotic agents. In [7] the authors compared the efficacy of Twitter to speech synthesis in communicating to waitress robot in a noisy environment. However the authors noted that the users involved in the experimentation don't like use Twitter to communicate to robot in the same room, but they preferred to use speech synthesis. Ma et al. [8] proposed a system composed by different social networks (Twitter, Google Calendar, MSN and SMS) to give instruction to the robot to accomplish surveillance and cleaning services. Nevertheless this system did not provide feedbacks to the user and not include external environmental network to extend robot sensing capabilities. Bell et al. [9] demonstrated the feasibility of producing "action" by a robot from social data. Particularly, in this work the user used Twitter to move the robot in the same room and to take a picture. They test their system with real end-user to analyze the feasibility of proposed service based on natural languages and social networks. However they underline the inefficacy to use tweet to command robot instead of voice recognition or other natural languages. Furthermore, another possible use of social networks in robotic applications was shown in [10]. In this work social networks were used as a resource of crowdsourcing allowing robot to access to the vast information available on Twitter.

Therefore, in this context, this paper aims to improve the state of the art by implementing a system which enHancE human-RObot Interaction by means of the inclusion of common Social Networks(HeROIS). HeROIS proposes a method to manage the remote interaction between the user and robotic agents creating a "link" between innovative services and already existing user interface in order to achieve the following advantages: (i) the user is able to exploit new services using social networks with which is already expert; this avoids the growth of new interfaces, each one specific

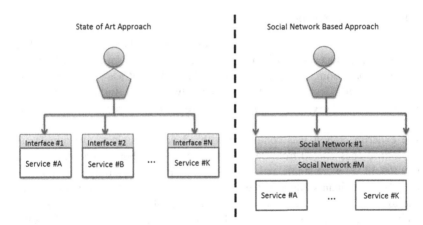

Fig. 1. Enhancing robotic services integrating common social networks in the system to avoid the multiplication of interfaces for the remote management of robotic services.

for a service (Fig. 1); (ii) the user is able to communicate with robotic agents both in the same environment and remotely, also overcoming problem of visibility under different networks. Moreover HeROIS system provides feedbacks to users.

HeROIS combines the use of cloud computing services (both commercial and custom), a domestic robot, called KuBo, a smart environments, to extend robot sensing capabilities, and two common Social Networks (Twitter and Google Services). The cloud resources include the indoor user localization algorithm, the social networks modules and a MySql database. KuBo exploits cloud robotics paradigm [11] because of several features rely on the cloud in order to increase the modularity of the overall system and to add other computational capabilities (see System Overview). Furthermore, this work aims also to qualitatively and quantitatively test the technological solution with real users in realistic scenarios to assess usability and acceptability levels. Particularly, the authors propose three robotic services to help citizens in reminder and surveillance tasks. The user by means of two interfaces (Google Calendar and Twitter) can access the HeROIS services and by means of Google Calendar on his smartphone can set important events anywhere and anytime; if the user is at home, at the proper time, the robot autonomously reaches the user acting as a physical reminder increasing the efficiency of the task. Furthermore, if the user is not at home he can receive information about the status of the house, and alarms on Twitter. Additionally, by means of Twitter message he can move the robot to remotely check the status of the house, through its autonomous navigation system.

3   Methodology

The evaluation of HeROIS performance was based on a specific experimental protocol, which envisaged the involvement of end-users, the use of a realistic living lab and the measure of appropriate metrics concerning the acceptability and usability of the entire service.

3.1   Experimental Settings

The proposed services were realistically tested in the DomoCasa Lab (Peccioli, Italy), which reproduces a fully furnished apartment of 200 sqm with a living room, a kitchen, a bathroom and two bedrooms [12]. DomoCasa is endowed with a service robot (KuBo robot) and two sensor networks (for further details see next paragraph). Furthermore, a gateway is used to gather sensor data to send to the cloud.

The experimentation was conducted with 13 young subjects (10 females and 3 males), whose ages ranged from 24 to 37 (29.62 ± 3.82). For which concerns marital status 9 (69.23 %) were single and 4 (30.77 %) married. Regarding educational level, 6 (46.15 %) participants attended the high school and 7 (53.85 %) graduated. About attitude towards the current technology, all participants were very familiar with PC, Smartphone and Tablet. Furthermore at least for hearsay, everybody had knowledge of most popular social networks such as Facebook, Twitter and Linkedin; however only 4 (30.77 %) and 5 (38.46 %) of them used respectively Twitter and Google Calendar.

3.2   Scenario Implemented During the Experimentation

In order to test the usability and the overall acceptance of the system, three different scenarios were implemented and tested with the users.

- **Environmental Alert:** user is not at home and the HeROIS system detects a critical unsafe situation, i.e. a window is open. It sends a tweet to the user and he can request a picture of the scene with a private message. For this particular scenario, the user was asked to be out of the DomoCasa holding a tablet.
- **Home Automation:** user is coming back to home. Through a *direct message* to the house Twitter account, or tweeting a new status adding the hashtag *"#kubo_service"* or tagging the Twitter DomoCasa account, the home is alerted to warm the environment. If the geolocalization is allowed, the smart home is also able to delay the operation based on the estimated time given through an interrogation to the Google Map service. In this scenario the user is out of the DomoCasa Lab, and send a tweet to the domocasa.
- **Robotic Reminder:** using Google Calendar tool, user can schedule appointments, drug therapies, etc. The system automatically addressed a robotic reminding service at the scheduled time, to remind through tweets the user about appointment or medication. In the experimentation phase, this scenario was divided into two part. In the first part the user was asked to call the robot to set an appointment in Google Calendar by means of the robot tablet. In the second part of the scenario, at the proper time, the robot act as a physical reminder for the user. In both case, the robot automatically reached the user. The scenario was concluded when the user gave to robot a voice feedback.

3.3   Metrics for Assessing the Acceptance of the Services

Acceptability has been defined as the "demonstrable willingness within a user group to employ information technology for the task it is designed to support" and the aim of acceptability is to understand the "factors influencing the adoption of technologies as planned by users who have some degree of choice" [13]. In order to understand the factors which determine the acceptability of ICT and robotics solutions, the issue should be addressed by borrowing social-psychology theories, a branch of the social sciences.

One of the first models developed to study the acceptance of the technology by an individual is the Technology Acceptance Model (TAM) [14] grown out of Theory of Reasoned Action (TRA) [15]. The TAM is based on the Perceived Usefulness and Perceived Ease of Use constructs which determine attitudes to adopt new technologies. This model was applied to the processes of adoption and use of many technology even if the social and normative variables are not taken into account. Progressively in order to provide a unified theoretical basis from which to facilitate research on technology adoption, the Unified Theory of Acceptance and Use of Technology (UTAUT) [16] was developed. The UTAUT is one of the most applied model and it is composed by four main constructs and four moderating variables. However UTAUT was developed for using technology at work so it doesn't always match with the purpose of studies about ICT and robotics solutions in everyday life. For these reasons in order to overcome this limit the UTAUT was adapted by Heerink et al. [17] to the specific technology of assistive and social robots. Starting from UTAUT and Heerink's study, we developed a specific and suitable questionnaire for the HeROIS system, based on a five point Likert scale, in order to investigate the usability and acceptability. In our study some constructs were omitted and others, such as Aesthetics and Perceived effectiveness were added.

The Table 1 shows the constructs of HeROIS questionnaire. Data from the survey were processed applying the following procedure. The construct reliability of the developed questionnaire was validated using the Cronbach's Alpha calculation [18], and a unique metric, ranged from 0 to 100, was defined for usability and acceptability score in order to identify three levels, i.e. not good (score < 65), good (65 ≤ score < 85) and excellent (score ≥ 85) [19]. A correlation analysis was performed in order to discover the relationship between data and, at this scope, the Mann-Whitney U and the Kruskal-Wallis tests were applied in order to compare different conditions and users.

4   System Overview

The architecture of the system, as depicted in Fig. 2, is based on three components: KuBo, the smart environments, and the cloud resources. The user by means of common social networks interfaces can access to proposed services. Particularly the system integrated two common social networks: Twitter (through the REST and Streaming APIs [20]) and Google Calendar (by Google API [21]).

Table 1. The HeROIS questionnaire constructs used in the experimentation

	Code	Construct	Definition
Acceptability	ATT	Attitude	Positive or negative feelings about the appliance of the technology
	ANX	Anxiety	Evoking anxious or emotional reactions when using the system
	PENJ	Perceived enjoyment	Feelings of joy or pleasure associated by the user with the use of the system
	AES	Aesthetics	Emotional reactions to the system appearance
	ITU	Intention to use	The outspoken intention to use the system over a longer period in time
Usability	PU	Perceived usefulness	The degree to which a person believes that using the system would enhance his or her daily activities
	PEOU	Perceived ease of use	The degree to which the user believes that using the system would be free of effort
	PE	Perceived effectiveness	The degree to which the user believes that the system would produce an intended or expected outcome

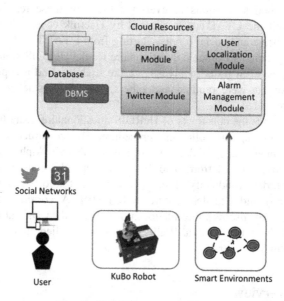

Fig. 2. HeROIS system architecture

4.1 KuBo Robot

During the design process of the platform two key points have been considered primarily: reduced dimensions to move easily in domestic environments, and high friendliness to enhance the robot acceptance. Hence, the robot is based on the youBot

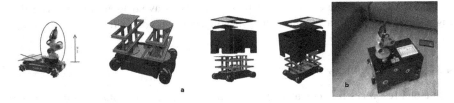

Fig. 3. (a) Design process of the KuBo robot. The overall height of the robot is elevated of about 30 cm and a new cover, made of black opal methacrylate, is mounted to an internal frame. In the last figure (b) is reported the final version of the KuBo robot with the KuKa arm.

[22], produced by KUKA, a small-sized holonomic mobile platform. In order to increase its acceptance, the original platform is modified with a design inspired by a typical "coffee table", a furniture commonly present in homes (see Fig. 3). The overall height of the robot is elevated of about 30 cm and a new cover, made of black opal methacrylate, is mounted to an internal frame. The final version of the robot, called KuBo (KUka roBOt) is shown in Fig. 3 and it can be with or without the KUKA arm. KuBo is equipped with an Hokuyo laser scanner, an Asus Xtion Pro Live RGB-D sensor, speakers, wireless microphone and a tablet. All the software modules are implemented in ROS [23]. KuBo is conceived as a platform with low computation capabilities that has to exploits cloud resources to carry out its task. The only on-board ability is the autonomous indoor navigation, which relies on the ROS navigation stack and uses the Dynamic Window Approach [24] for local planning and the Adaptive Monte Carlo [25] for indoor localization.

The other software functionalities rely on cloud resources, The text-to-speech module uses the Acapela service for the unknown sentences, otherwise they are stored locally to reduce the response time. The speech recognition module relies on the Google Recognition API. Using this tool, the robot has the potentiality to manage multi-languages without the need of specifics acoustic speech model.

4.2 Smart Environments

The smart environment is composed by two ZigBee Wireless Sensor Networks (WSNs). One WSN monitors the environment by means of several type of environmental sensors spread in the home. For instance Passive InfraRed (PIR) sensors, pressure sensor are placed under chairs or bed, switches on doors or drawers, GAS and water leak sensors are placed in strategic points of the house, while temperature, humidity and light sensors are distributed all over the house to monitor the status.

The second WSN is designed [12] to locate multiple users at the same time, using Received Signal Strength (RSS) [26]. It is composed of a ZigBee coordinator, a Data Logger, a wearable mobile node and a set of fixed ZigBee routers, also called anchors. Each anchor is located in a fixed place and computed the RSS as the ratio between the received and transmitted electromagnetic power on the received messages and transmitted this value to the data logger.

These two WSNs are set on different channels to avoid interferences. The data logger is connected to a PC through USB connection to collect data.

4.3   Cloud Resources

The cloud resources implemented are: the remind module, the twitter module, the user localization module and the alarm management module (Fig. 2). Furthermore a DataBase (DB) collects and stores data related to the environment, the alarms and user positions. A database management software (DBMS) manages the external queries to the database. This integration of physical agents with the cloud resources empowers the robot to outsource part of the software in the cloud [27].

4.3.1   Remind Module

The remind Module is based on Google Calendar API v3 with JSON data object for. NET. Using this API, it is possible to search and retrieve calendar events. Authenticated sessions can access private calendars, as well as create, edit, and delete both events and the calendars that contain them. Thus this module is able to link google calendar service with KuBo robot. The user set appointments through Google Calendar web page or the calendar of his mobile devices (if synchronized with google calendar); at a proper time this module sends a message to the robot activating the physical reminding services. In this experimental setting a provisional google account was created, thus the user can use it to set the appointments by means of KuBo tablet.

4.3.2   Twitter Module

The Twitter module is based on Twitter API for Python, which allows the use of both Twitter's Streaming and REST APIs. A provisional Twitter user was created in order to have an "entity" that could interact with users; during the description it is referred as KuBo_Tweet. The Streaming API could be used to create streams of the public data flowing through Twitter; for example, it was used to track any post on Twitter with hashtag #KuBo_Tweet or that had tagged @KuBo_Tweet. The REST API provided the programmatic access to read and write Twitter data; for example, it was used to reply to the users or to post Tweets with attached medias after a user's request. Using the Twitter Module a command line was created through an already known and spread interface, such as Twitter's web site or Twitter's app for mobile devices. In order to achieve a more natural communication, each users' request was interpreted in commands using a keyword approach through a regular expression search, to avoid problems as lower/upper case differences. Studies on use of semantic searches, for example using NLTK – Natural Language Toolkit [28] are planned, but a good trade-off has to be found in order to have a fast response for keyword research. About the privacy of sensitive information, such as photos of the home, settings on Twitter's account were used in order to limit the visibility of posts to a an ad hoc set of users.

4.3.3   User Localization Module

This module provides numeric (x, y) and semantic information (kitchen, bedroom …) on users position, to drive the KuBo robot and accomplish required services, by means of a sensor fusion algorithm and a Kalman Filter approach exploiting both range-free [29] and range-based [30] approach as suggested in [12]. User localization is performed by fusing heterogeneous information from the two WSNs. In case of sensor faults, the user position is estimated by fusing data from the remaining ones, improving the reliability and robustness of the service. The user position is stored into the DB and makes available for agents and users who need.

4.3.4   Alarm Management Module

The alarm management module analyses the data coming from the environmental WSN in order to identify potential danger situations or critical intrusions. In this system implementation several common alarm procedures are included such as door opening during night, water or gas leak and door/windows open when user is outside. When this module reveals a critical situations and the user is not at home, it activates the twitter module to alert the user. Instead if the user is at home, the KuBo robot is activated.

5   Results

The Cronbach's alpha is calculated to test the construct reliability and the cut-off value for being acceptable is 0.7 [31]. The Table 2 shows that reliability of the constructs is high, except for ANX and ITU. However values below even 0.7 can be expected because of the diversity of constructs being measured when dealing with psychological constructs [32].

The results of the questionnaire reveal interesting situations. As regards the usability (Fig. 4b), the results show that the proposed system is usable for 4 participants (30.77 % M = 79.69 SD = 3.13) and is excellent for 9 of them (69.23 % M = 90.05 SD = 3.72). In particular female participants perceive the HeROIS system more usable than male ones ($p < 0.05$) and also there is a statistically significant difference between married persons and singles in usability evaluation ($p < 0.05$). In effect, the high usability score is confirmed also by the score of each constructs, because the utility (PU M = 4.52 SD = 0.59), easiness (PEOU M = 4.63 SD = 0.56) and effectiveness (PE M = 4.18 SD = 0.56) are well evaluated by participants. Using a correlation analysis, there are no effects of gender, marital status and education level except for gender factor on PU results ($p < 0.05$) (Fig. 4a).

Table 2. Reliability of constructs

Code	Alpha Cronbach	Mean	DS
ATT	0,81	4,28	0,65
ANX	0,64	2,02	1,21
PENJ	1,00	4,85	0,37
AES	0,74	4,36	0,68
ITU	0,52	4,04	0,77
PU	0,86	4,52	0,59
PEOU	0,72	4,63	0,56
PE	0,78	4,18	0,56

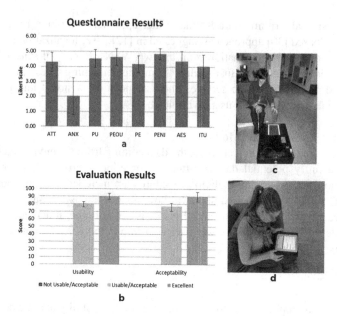

Fig. 4. (a) HeROIS questionnaire constructs results (b) The usability and acceptability results (c, d) Show the experimentation with real users in DomoCasa.

As regards the acceptability, the results show that the proposed system was acceptable for 8 volunteers (61.54 % M = 77.02 SD = 4.23) and excellent for 5 participants (38.46 % M = 89.71 SD = 6.06). In particular female participants evaluated the HeROIS system more acceptable than male ones ($p < 0.05$). About the intention to use (ITU M = 4.04 SD = 0.77), the sample would use this system every day and would pay an appropriate price for it, because the services provided by HeROIS are very useful and easy to use for them as confirmed by PU and PEOU results (Fig. 4a). Females were more likely than males to report using HeROIS system ($p < 0.05$). Furthermore this data was confirmed by the positive results about the appliance in everyday life of these service (ATT M = 4.28 SD = 0.65), especially for married persons ($p < 0.05$). Notably just low level of anxiety or negative emotional reactions were evoked (ANX M = 2.02 SD = 1.21) when volunteers used the system. On the contrary, feelings of pleasure were associated by the participants with the use of the system and the interaction of KuBo (PENJ M = 4.85 SD = 0.37) and in particular there was a statistically significant difference between man and woman ($p < 0.05$). In closing the aesthetics of KuBo was well judged (AES M = 4.36 SD = 0.68) because the KuBo was considered aesthetically appealing and suitable for a domestic use.

6   Conclusion

This paper presented HeROIS system which aims to enhance the human-robot inter-action with the integration of social networks. The system presented was based on KuBo robot, smart environments and cloud resources. In general, the proposed system was considered usable and acceptable by all participants, especially for women because females were more likely than males to spend time on Social Networks [33]. Furthermore in some cases there was a statistically significant difference between married persons and singles, maybe because married persons have a more busy life and the services provided by HeROIS system could be very useful for them. Nobody found the services "not usable" and "not acceptable". Furthermore the results highlighted how also persons which don't use social networks can use the system proposed without any problems. Future system development should include the analysis of privacy issues and the involvement of a large number of participants in the experimental settings.

Acknowledgment. This work was supported in part by the European Community's Seventh Framework Program (FP7/2007–2013) under grant agreement no. 288899 (Robot-Era Project). This work was also supported in part by Telecom Italia, Joint Open Lab WHITE, Pisa, Italy and OmniaRoboCare project - Programma Operativo Regionale CReO Fesr 2007–2013, Linea di intervento 1.5.a – 1.6, Bando unico R&S anno 2012.

References

1. Social Networking Fact Sheet (2014). http://www.pewinternet.org/fact-sheets/social-networking-fact-sheet/. Accessed 16 Oct 2014
2. BCS The chartered institute for IT (2013). http://www.bcs.org/content/conWebDoc/49824. Accessed 16 Oct 2014
3. Our Mobile Planet, Think with Google (2014). http://think.withgoogle.com/mobileplanet/en/ . Accessed 16 Oct 2014
4. Solis P., Carlaw, S.: Consumer and Personal Robotics. ABI Research (2013)
5. Moschetti, A., Fiorini, L., Aquilano, M., Cavallo, F., Dario, P.: Preliminary findings of the AALIANCE2 ambient assisted living roadmap. In: Longhi, S., Siciliano, P., Germani, M., Monteriù, A. (eds.) Ambient Assisted Living, pp. 335–342. Springer, Switzerland (2014)
6. Broadbent, Elizabeth, Stafford, Rebecca, MacDonald, Bruce: Acceptance of healthcare robots for the older population: review and future directions. Int. J. Soc. Robot. **1**(4), 319–330 (2009)
7. Emeli V., Christensen, H.: Enhancing the robot service experience through social media. RO-Man, 2011 IEEE. IEEE (2011)
8. Ma, X., Yang, X., Zhao, S., Fu, C., Lan, Z., Pu, Y.: Robots in my contact list: using a social media platforms for human-robot interaction in domestic environment. In: APCHI 2012, pp. 133–140. ACM, New York (2012)
9. Bell, D. et al:. Microblogging as a mechanism for human–robot interaction. Knowledge-Based Systems (2014)
10. Emeli, V.: Robot learning through social media crowdsourcing. In: IEEE/RSJ International Conference on Intelligent Robots and Systems (IROS), pp. 2332–2337, 7–12 October 2012
11. Kuffner J.J.: Cloud-enabled robots. IEEE-RAS International Conference on Humanoid Robotics, Nashville, TN (2010)
12. Cavallo, F., et al.: Development of a socially believable multi-robot solution from town to home. Cogn. Comput. **6**(4), 954–967 (2014)
13. Dillon, A.: User acceptance of information technology. In: Karwowski, W. (ed.) Encyclopaedia of human factors and ergonomics. Taylor & Francis, London (2001)

14. Davis, F.: Perceived usefulness, perceived ease of use, and user acceptance of information technology. MIS Q. **13**(3), 319–340 (1989)
15. Ajzen. I., Fishbein, M.: Understanding Attitudes and Predicting Social Behavior. Prentice-Hall, Englewood Cliffs (1980)
16. Venkatesh, V., Morris, M.G., Davis, G.B., Davis, F.D.: User acceptance of information technology: towards a unified view. MIS Q. **27**(3), 425–478 (2003)
17. Heerink, M., Kröse, B., Evers, V., Wielinga, B.: Measuring acceptance of an assistive social robot: a suggested toolkit. In: The 18th IEEE International Symposium on Robot and Human Interactive Communication Toyama, Japan, September 27–October 2 2009
18. Santos, J.R.A.: Cronbach's alpha: a tool for assessing the reliability of scales. J. Ext. **37**(2), 1–5 (1999)
19. McLellan, S., Muddimer, A., Peres, S.C.: The effect of experience on system usability scale ratings. J. Usability Stud. **7**(2), 56–67 (2012)
20. Twitter APIs. https://dev.twitter.com/overview/documentation. Accessed 17 oct 2014
21. Google Calendar API V3. https://developers.google.com/google-apps/calendar/. Accessed 18 Feb 2014
22. KuKa youBot official website. http://www.youbot-store.com/. Accessed 17 Oct 2014
23. Quigley, M. et al.: ROS: an open-source robot operating system. ICRA workshop on open source software, 3(3.2), pp. 803–821 (2009)
24. Fox, D., Burgard, W., Thrun, S.: The dynamic window approach to collision avoidance. Robotics Automation Magazine. IEEE (1997)
25. Thrun, S., Burgard, W., Fox, D.: Probabilistic Robotics. MIT Press, Cambridge (2005). ISBN 0-262-20162-3
26. Alhmiedat, T.A., Yang, S.H.: A ZigBee based mobile tracking system through wireless sensor network. Int. J. Adv. Mechatron. Syst. **1**(1), 63–70 (2008)
27. Kehoe, B., Patil, S., Abbeel, P., Goldberg, K.: A survey of research on cloud robotics and automation. IEEE Trans. Autom. Sci. Eng. (T-ASE) **12**(2), 1–12 (2015)
28. Natural Language Toolkit. http://www.nltk.org. Accessed 17 Oct 2014
29. Pivato, P., Palopoli, L., Petri, D.: Accuracy of RSS-based centroid localization algorithms in an indoor environment. IEEE Trans. Instrum. Meas. **60**(10), 3451–3460 (2011)
30. Yufeng, Q.J., Jianhua, M.: Integration of range-based and range-free localiza-tion algorithms in wireless sensor networks for mobile clouds. In: IEEE International Conference on and IEEE Cyber, Physical and Social Computing (2013)
31. Nunnally, J.C., et al.: Psychometric Theory, vol. 226. McGraw-Hill, New York (1967)
32. Kline, P.: Handbook of Psychological Testing. Routledge, New York (2013)
33. Lougheed, E.: Frazzled by Facebook? An exploratory study of gender differences in social network communication among undergraduate men and women. College Student J. **46**(1), 88–99 (2012)

aHead: Considering the Head Position in a Multi-sensory Setup of Wearables to Recognize Everyday Activities with Intelligent Sensor Fusions

Marian Haescher[1(✉)], John Trimpop[1], Denys J.C. Matthies[1],
Gerald Bieber[1], Bodo Urban[1], and Thomas Kirste[2]

[1] Fraunhofer IGD, Joachim-Jungius-Str. 11, 18059 Rostock, Germany
{marian.haescher,john.trimpop,denys.matthies,
gerald.bieber,bodo.urban}@igd-r.fraunhofer.de
[2] University of Rostock, Albert-Einstein-Str. 22, 18059, Rostock, Germany
thomas.kirste@uni-rostock.de

Abstract. In this paper we examine the feasibility of Human Activity Recognition (HAR) based on head mounted sensors, both as stand-alone sensors and as part of a wearable multi-sensory network. To prove the feasibility of such setting, an interactive online HAR-system has been implemented to enable for multi-sensory activity recognition while making use of a hierarchical sensor fusion. Our system incorporates 3 sensor positions distributed over the body, which are head (smart glasses), wrist (smartwatch), and hip (smartphone). We are able to reliably distinguish 7 daily activities, which are: resting, being active, walking, running, jumping, cycling and office work. The results of our field study with 14 participants clearly indicate that the head position is applicable for HAR. Moreover, we demonstrate an intelligent multi-sensory fusion concept that increases the recognition performance up to 86.13 % (recall). Furthermore, we found the head to possess very distinctive movement patterns regarding activities of daily living.

Keywords: Human activity recognition · HAR · Human computer interaction · Pattern recognition · Multi-Sensory · Wearable computing · Mobile assistance

1 Introduction

Smart glasses are the next generation of consumer wearables and will be increasingly used for Human Activity Recognition (HAR). While smart devices are equipped with various sensor modules, they became increasingly powerful and allow for an unobtrusive HAR [5, 6]. Still, today's activity recognition systems typically utilize data from a single sensor location, such as hip or wrist. However, with the proliferation of smart consumer devices, wearable sensor networks emerge and enable to provide data from multiple body locations [6]. This requires a different definition of a suitable sensor fusion strategy, which handles data from various locations and thus accommodates dynamic changes in network membership. With respect to pattern recognition tasks,

© Springer International Publishing Switzerland 2015
M. Kurosu (Ed.): Human-Computer Interaction, Part II, HCII 2015, LNCS 9170, pp. 741–752, 2015.
DOI: 10.1007/978-3-319-20916-6_68

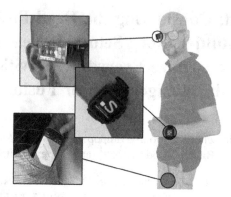

Fig. 1. The utilized wearable sensor system consisting of a smart glasses prototype, a smartwatch, and a smartphone.

it is interesting to understand which body location potentially contributes the most meaningful data for a discrimination between activities.

In this paper we investigate the possible contribution of a head mounted sensor for activity recognition tasks, both as a stand-alone sensor and as part of a wearable sensor network. To achieve this, a comprehensive wearable sensor system has been implemented, consisting of components for a multi-sensory activity recognition and sensor fusion, respectively. Therefore, we investigate 3 different sensor placements: a glasses frame (head), armband (wrist), and pocket (hip) as shown in Fig. 1.

2   Related Work

While activity recognition has become an attractive field of research over the past years [1, 5], different body positions and a variety of sensors have been evaluated to achieve different results in certain fields of applications. Lara et al. present further details on the categorization of sensors and sensor positions [11]. In the following, we will provide a brief overview on (1) HAR with smart devices in general (2) state of the art sensor fusion methods and (3) the few applications of head mounted sensors in relation to the HAR research.

2.1   Human Activity Recognition with Smart Devices

HAR provides widespread possibilities for applications [12]. Currently, activity recognition systems are emerging to a vast majority of different end-consumer products. While these products are primarily fitness applications for smartphones, which usually enable for a rudimentary distinction of very few activities or act as step counters, a recognition of sophisticated everyday activities cannot be achieved robustly and also not user independently yet [5, 6]. In contrast to conventional physical activity recognition, especially smartwatches allow for a broader range of different applications; such as sleep detection or applications in industrial environments [3].

When implementing a HAR-system, the concept of an *Activity Recognition Chain* (ARC) is a common concept, which follows a certain sequence of signal processing, pattern recognition, and machine learning techniques to allow a specific activity recognition system behavior as described by Bulling et al. [6].

2.2   Sensor-Fusion

While using multiple sensors and devices, an efficient sensor-fusion routine is essential, to still achieve an unambiguously classification result. A sensor fusion can be applied in different stages, either an early or later stage at the ARC. In general, using multiple sensors may increase recognition performance significantly [6, 18]. It has been shown, that a sensor fusion at later steps of the ARC (e.g. by combining feature vectors or applying a second classification), can be beneficial compared to an early fusion (such as directly after the preprocessing or segmentation) [18, 20].

Maurer et al. [14] present a sensor fusion concept that combines data from two accelerometers and an ambient light sensor directly after the feature extraction step. Results were collected on different body positions and the recognition accuracy ranged from 85.2 % to 92.8 % [14]. However, Zappi et al. [23] used a concept that implements a sensor-fusion to combine multiple classification results. This meta-classifier is based on a majority voting method and a Naïve Bayes implementation, which significantly increased the accuracy of the system. This top-level classification is a very popular approach and also used by many other researchers [16, 20].

Besides the great improvement of accuracy, the advantages of a sensor fusion are an increased robustness regarding faults or variability in sensor characteristics and a reduced classification problem complexity due to the possibilities of using different classifiers. Still, we face many challenges when fusing different types of sensors and data, such as high feature spaces when fusing at the feature extraction level or synchronization issues when using different sampling rates. Moreover, devices, sensors or single data streams may get lost at runtime [1, 6].

2.3   Application of Head Mounted Sensors

During the past years, it could be shown that the hip as a sensor position constantly provides best results regarding physical activity recognition with inertial sensors [5, 6]. The arm or wrist as a potential body position has also been analyzed in various early research approaches, e.g. in the works of Bao and Intille [2] or Maurer et al. [14], and found to be a desirable position for end-consumer products as well. With the emerging smartwatch technologies [3], these positions now become interesting again.

Another interesting position is the head, which provides very characteristic movement and orientation patterns [19, 21]. However, there is only very few work, which takes the head as a potential position for HAR into account. In 2000, Madabhushi et al. [13] presented a system to distinguish different human activities by analyzing the head in different monocular gray scale image sequences, and achieved decent results. Further research demonstrates a human fall detection and gear behavior with sensors attached to the head, such as described by Lindemann et al. [12] and Menz et al. [15]. A first real step towards inertial sensor based HAR was successfully performed by Hanheide et al. [9], who built a smart glasses prototype. The system was capable of distinguishing several motions and gestures via an integrated camera and accelerometer. Later, Windau and Itti [19] revealed a situation awareness system consisting of a pair of glasses and an IMU with an accelerometer and a gyroscope that was able to discriminate 20 different activities with an overall accuracy of 81.5 %. Lately, Ishimaru et al. [10] demonstrated an HAR implementation for Google Glass. By analyzing the blink frequency, using the integrated infrared proximity sensor, and head motion patterns, the team was able to recognize up to five different head activities (including *watching a movie*, *reading*, *mathematical problem solving*, *sawing* and *talking*) with an overall accuracy of 82 %.

Head mounted sensors, such as in glasses, headgear, or even hearing aids, yield the advantage of being fixed and always available while performing everyday activities. As a matter of fact, such devices are worn for longer periods of time in comparison to smartphones while also being relatively unobtrusive [10]. The former study outcomes of these very sparse research on head mounted inertial sensors already indicate the head as a sensor position to have great potential, which we try to address in this work.

3 Concept and Implementation

In this section we introduce our main concept of how to embed a head position into an efficient multi-sensory activity recognition system. First, we demonstrate our general sensor-fusion approach and afterwards we describe the setup and properties of our implementation, which comprises the positions: glasses frame (head), armband (wrist), and pocket (hip).

3.1 Sensor-Fusion Concept

Our sensor-fusion concept is a general approach that leverages the advantages of different sensor-fusion methods to support hierarchical sensor fusion. This way a flexible reconfiguration of sensor networks is enabled in response to possible changes in terms of network membership.

Our approach strictly follows the concept of the above mentioned Activity Recognition Chain (ARC) by fusing the data streams of every sensor at the last two stages while every sensor iteratively passes through the ARC. Meaning, every *sensor node* of the entire *sensor network* is passing the first four steps of the ARC. After the feature extraction, the concatenation of the particular feature vectors enables the fusion of a specific amount of nodes. These are used to form new *sensor groups,* which are taken into consideration for the following classification step. By applying a weighted majority voting, all classification results are finally being fused [19]:

$$\sum_{t=1}^{T} W_t d_{t,j} = max_{j=1} \sum_{t=1}^{T} W_t d_{t,j} \qquad (1)$$

The weight parameters for every sensor group are being specified a priori. We confirm that a simple majority voting, provides already promising results, even compared to more sophisticated methods, such as demonstrated by Zappi et al. [23].

For our system to perform an iterative, online sensor-fusion, the respective processing of the sensor nodes and groups needed to be synchronized. This is achieved on the one hand directly at the segmentation step by using sliding windows with varying lengths corresponding to the chosen sensor sampling rates, and on the other hand at the implementation level via the integration of *wait*-routines at every fusion step. Hereby, the time to fill all windows at the segmentation step for every sensor node will be the same and the recognition chain will temporarily stop just before a fusion step, to allow all other components to reach this step first. The sensor will not stop generating data for this short amount of waiting time; the data streams will just remain unused. After the final activity has been recognized, the ARCs of each sensor node will start all over again.

By applying this concept, most of the above mentioned issues are being automatically solved. Due to this statistic approach of synchronization, the sensor network itself deems to be very robust in terms of single data losses or delays. Furthermore, the fusion methods can be chosen arbitrarily, allowing an adjustment of the best setting to create a most effective tradeoff among the advantages of both fusion approaches.

3.2 System Configuration

We implemented a multi-sensory online system based on Java (Android) while relying on Bluetooth Low Energy devices, which we find to be highly efficient. This system incorporates our activity recognition and fusion concept in an object oriented manner, which enables for an utterly flexible configuration. Based on several preliminary studies, a literature research on state of the art methods and another conducted pilot study, we have determined a unique system configuration, which is being described in detail below.

Sensors. We have chosen three different sensor positions, which are the head, the wrist and the pocket of the user's pants. For all positions, an accelerometer has been applied (with a sampling rate of 32 Hz, since it is quite common for HAR [5, 6]), as well as a gyroscope (32 Hz) and temperature sensor (that is only sampled by 1 Hz, because the ambient temperature will not vary so fast) for the head position, lastly for the wrist the decibel level of a microphone (1 Hz). In past research it has been proven that accelerometers and gyroscopes are well suited for the recognition of activities and motion patterns. Moreover, the temperature and decibel values can be used to differentiate places and inside and outside locations, respectively [6].

Preprocessing. For all accelerometers low pass filters were applied to smoothen the raw signals. Additionally, the accelerometer in the pocket was treated with a special algorithm, which has already been used in preliminary studies [5] that allows an always-independent sensor orientation in relation to the world coordinate system. Therefore, the retrieved data will remain unaffected to any changes in the orientation of the smartphone in the pocket.

Segmentation. To segment the data, a static sliding window approach has been applied for each sensor [2, 6]. In respect to the sampling rates all windows contain data for duration of 8 s. Also the windows are overlapping by 50 % and thus create a segmentation delay of 4 s. Similar settings have proven to be reliable [2].

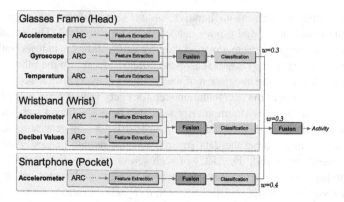

Fig. 2. Configuration of the fusion concept

Fusion. Our proposed fusion concept utilizes a position dependent fusion attempt, which firstly fuses all feature vectors of each single device position and later fuses again all classification results. The last fusion undergoes a majority voting. Because the hip is predestined to provide the best classification results, which literature [2, 5, 6] and own studies show, we weighted this position stronger (0.4) in comparison to the other positions; head (0.3) and arm (0.3). Therefore, the classification results of the pocket will be the final one, so to say (see Fig. 2).

Feature Selection. We selected features relying mainly on the research results of [1, 3, 11 and 22]. We picked several features and applied a feature selection calculation to get an appropriate amount of 8 different features distributed among all sensors. Besides default statistical measures, such as mean, variance or root mean square, those features were signal magnitude area, signal energy, mean crossing rate, dominant frequency and Activity Unit (AE), which basically describes the movement intensity in the three-dimensional space [3].

Classifiers. For all sensor groups, we applied the C4.5 decision tree, as it is being a very favorable classifier for HAR, because of its robust and simple implementation possibilities and low computational load [1, 4, 6, 7].

4   Evaluation

4.1   Apparatus

For the head position, we mounted a *SensorTag* from Texas Instruments at the right frame of a customary pair of glasses with the temperature sensor pointing outwardly. This setting was chosen due to the sensor arrangement in current smart glasses designs. The device recorded accelerometer data with a resolution of 6 Bit in a range of ± 2G, gyroscope data with a resolution of 7 Bit in a range of ± 256°/s and temperature values in °C.

For the position of the wrist we applied the smartwatch *Simvalley Mobile AW-420. RX,* which had to be worn at the wrist of the left arm in a usual manner. This device recorded accelerometer data with a resolution of 12 Bit with a ± 2G range and the decibel level additionally.

For the position of the waist, we utilized a smartphone, a *Google Nexus 4,* which had to be put into the left pocket of the subjects' pant, while the device orientation is irrelevant due to the applied preprocessing method of subtracting out the rotation of the sensor. The smartphone only recorded accelerometer data with a resolution of 13 Bit in a range of ± 4G. In addition, the smartphone also served as a hub device to process the data streams receiving from all other devices. Our system is enabled to run robustly for up to eight hours.

4.2   Study Design

In order to generate a ground truth configuration, we conducted a pilot study with one subject, which has an essential impact on our system configuration as described in Sect. 3.2. In our field study, we have chosen a set of different activities to allow the comparative assessment of the different positions and to enable the fusion options, respectively. Thus, we selected 7 target activities, which were classified with the data from all three devices, which can be viewed in detail in the following Table 1:

The subjects were asked to perform each activity for at least three minutes. The activities 3 to 6 have been executed outside at different locations, while all other activities were performed inside. The particular activity *Active* included the simulation of mobile phone usage and was performed while standing and holding the Nexus in one hand, accomplishing a text input.

4.3   Participants and Data Gathering

14 subjects (2 female and 12 male participants), who attended our field study, aged between 16 and 50 with an average age of 26.6 years and formed one test group. For every single subject and activity, the fused feature vector data has been collected *on the fly* with the hub device (Nexus) and dumped onto the internal storage as well as the ARFF-Files, to allow a convenient and efficient post-analysis in *WEKA.*

Table 1. List and description of all target activity classes

ID	Activity Name	Description
1	*Rest*	None or very little motion
2	*Active*	Slight, insignificant but noticeable motion
3	*Walk*	Slow to normal walking
4	*Run*	Fast walking to Running
5	*Jump*	Jumping up and down at on the spot
6	*Bicycle*	Riding a bike
7	*Office*	Office work in front of a Computer at a desk

4.4   Task and Procedure

To reach highly representative results and to enable differentiation between inside and outside activities, the data had been gathered in a non-laboratory environment. To receive a proper record of each activity, every subject had to wear the system for about 30 to 45 min. For each user, the system was required to record a trainings set first, which was merged with the ground truth data. The activities were trained successively in different sequences at varying locations and times. All subjects were supervised during the training procedure. Moreover, we figured out that weather conditions might have affected the recordings of the outside-activities.

5   Results

To make assertions about the classification performance of the devices and sensors, a leave-one-out cross-validation was performed and a cumulated confusion matrix was calculated with the results achieved for each case. This way the recall and precision[1] values could be easily calculated. To simulate the meta-classification, we created shell scripts, which calculated the prediction results of all cross-validations to generate confusion matrices as well. This section will first highlight the results of the single device performances, especially those, collected with the *SensorTag*. After that we will present the overall fusion results and list up some further implications, which can be drawn out of our investigations.

5.1   Single Devices Results

While only observing the results of the *SensorTag* (head position), the overall recall rate of the cumulated confusion matrix yields 76.01 % with a precision of 75.93 %. Taking a look at the other two measuring positions, the results of the smartwatch show substantially better performance with a recall rate of 79.20 % (Precision: 80.36 %). The smartphone only reached a slightly better recall of 77:56 % (Precision: 77.41 %). Especially the comparatively bad results in the pants pocket, were mostly due to the two most problematic classes *Rest* and *Office*, in which the most false negatives and false positives occurred. Nevertheless, the proportional good results of the glasses frame already indicate the head to be a suitable position for detecting daily activities.

5.2   Overall Fusion Results

To further improve the classification results, we applied a meta-classification above all classification results. This results in an increase of recall up to 86.13 % and in an increase of precision up to 86.20 % as well. The confusion matrix shows substantial

---

[1] The classification accuracy and recall rate are equivalent, when considering multi class classification problems. As we talk about recall, this can be seen analogous to accuracy or overall classification rate. For further information to the measures, please refer to [6] or [11].

Table 2. Confusion matrix of the meta-classification of all devices

		Classification							Recall	Precision
		Rest	Active	Walk	Run	Jump	Bicycle	Office		
Groundtruth	Rest	333	16	0	0	0	5	137	67.82%	77.44%
	Active	6	437	1	0	0	11	21	91.81%	91.04%
	Walk	0	1	458	2	2	28	0	93.28%	93.28%
	Run	0	0	5	432	53	1	0	87.98%	93.30%
	Jump	0	0	3	29	430	1	0	92.87%	88.66%
	Bicycle	1	8	24	0	0	443	5	92.10%	89.68%
	Office	90	18	0	0	0	5	380	77.08%	69.98%
								∅	86.13%	86.20%

similarities to those of the single devices (*see Table* 2). The most false classifications occurred with the activities *Rest* and *Office*, and a few error-classifications also appeared with the activities *Walk* and *Bicycle* as well as *Run* and *Jump*, respectively.

To allow further assumptions on top of the initial system configuration, we modified our two-step fusion concept by only fusing once. This means that we examined a fusion approach on the one hand by fusing the feature vectors of all sensors (*global feature-fusion*) and on the other hand by performing only one overall meta-classification (*global meta-classification*). To allow for a precise analysis of those modifications, we performed an independent samples, weighted One-Way ANOVA. First, we compared all wearing positions based on the *single device feature-fusion* (T1). Afterwards we compared the single device feature fusions of all 14 participants against the *global feature-fusion* modification and also against the *global meta-classification* modification (T2).

T1: Comparing the recall rates for all three positions; glasses frame ($M = 76.02$; $SD = 9.48$), armband ($M = 79.19$; $SD = 7.64$), and pocket ($M = 77.64$; $SD = 9.04$), did not yield any statistical significance as shown by a One-Way ANOVA ($F_{2,39} = 0.46$; $p = .64$). Therefore, no position enabled a significant better activity recognition of our tested activity set.

T2: At next we tested whether the *global feature-fusion* and the *global meta-classification* performed differently in comparison to each other and the *single device feature-fusions*. A One-Way ANOVA ($F_{4,65} = 5.01$; $p = .0014$) found a significant difference in terms of performance. Therefore, a Tukey HSD test suggests both, the *global feature-fusion* ($p < .01$; $M = 87.33$; $SD = 8.12$) and the *global meta-classification* ($p < .05$; $M = 86.23$; $SD = 8.68$) to perform significantly better than the *single device feature-fusion* of the head mounted glasses frame ($M = 76.02$; $SD = 9.48$). Comparing the *single device feature-fusion* for the armband ($M = 79.19$; $SD = 7.64$) to both global fusion concepts also shows a substantial performance increase in terms of recall rates, but which was not found to be statistically different by the Tukey HSD test. Furthermore, we obtained similar results for the *single device feature-fusion* of the pocket ($M = 77.64$; $SD = 9.04$), which was inferior to the *global feature-fusion* (Tukey HSD; $p < .05$). The *global meta-classification* showed no statistical difference in this case. Furthermore, a statistical significant difference between the two global fusion concepts could not be identified.

The results indicate that our two global fusion approaches (*global feature-fusion* and *global meta-classification*) performed better than the *single device feature-fusions* we introduced. The following Table 3 summarizes all recall and precision results of the above-mentioned settings.

Table 3. Overall classification results (R: Recall, P: Precision) of single sensors (red), single device feature-fusion (blue) and global fusion approaches (purple).

	Glasses Frame, Accelerometer	Glasses Frame, Gyroscope	Glasses Frame, Temperature	Armband, Accelerometer	Armband, Sound	Smartphone, Accelerometer	Glasses Frame, Feature-Fusion	Armband, Feature Fusion	Smartphone, Feature-Fusion	Global Meta-Classification	Global Feature-Fusion
R	77.26%	54.37%	24.50%	81.09%	34.87%	77.56%	76.01%	79.20%	77.56%	86.13%	87.34%
P	77.36%	54.26%	22.95%	81.87%	34.75%	77.41%	75.93%	80.36%	77.41%	86.42%	87.75%

5.3 Implications

By including the head position in our multi-sensory system, we were able to collect valuable data, which lead to the following findings:

1. While wearing all devices over several hours and performing everyday activities, we found uniqueness in the amplitudes of motion at position of the head. In respect to the other positions the head was surprisingly much more moved than the smartphone in the pants' pocket. Still, the wrist was moved more often, though.
2. The head shows unique motion data, which is characterized by the anatomical and physiological facts, that the head is connected to the entire body by the spine and the movement usually follows the users` eyes.
3. Comparing raw signals of various activities enables us to draw a generalizable statement in regard to the head movements: every-day activities such as *cooking, watching TV, driving a car,* or *playing a music instrument* can already be identified by typical head movement characteristics. This finding highlights the potential of the head position in a HAR application scenario.
4. In addition to the mentioned general outcomes, we were able to determine muscular microvibrations with customary inertial sensors. Those microvibrations could also be assessed at the head with the gyroscope of the *SensorTag* fixed at the glasses frame with a sampling rate of 100 Hz. We observed a microvibration frequency between 4 and 11 Hz. Similar observations could also be made at other positions of the human body [8].

6   Conclusion and Future Work

Our results show that human activity recognition can be substantially improved by integrating head-mounted sensors into a multi-sensory network. We found out that sensors positioned at the head provide characteristic motion data and enable for Human Activity Recognition. As a technical contribution, we demonstrated the integration and evaluation of head-mounted sensors into an existing activity recognition system. Hereby, we described possible features, classifiers, and further options for a sensor fusion and present a best-practice implementation as a proof-of-concept.

Future work will include the comparison of further sensor-types and different system configurations, while integrating more complex activity classes. This will also include different and more complex fusion approaches such as pre-classification routines, to allow for a rough and fine granulated classification, respectively. Nevertheless, regarding further development of smart devices, we believe the head to become an important position for practical HAR.

Acknowledgements. This research has been supported by the German Federal State of Mecklenburg-Western Pomerania and the European Social Fund; grant ESF/IV-BM-B35-0006/12.

References

1. Avci, A., Bosch, S., Marin-Perianu, M., Marin-Perianu, R., Havinga, P.: Activity recognition using inertial sensing for healthcare, wellbeing and sports applications: a survey. In: Proceedings of Architecture of Computing Systems (ARCS), pp.1–10. VDE (2010)
2. Bao, L., Intille, S.S.: Activity recognition from user-annotated acceleration data. Pervasive Computing, pp. 1–17. Springer, Berlin Heidelberg (2004)
3. Bieber, G., Haescher, M., Vahl, M.: Sensor requirements for activity recognition on smart watches. In: Proceedings of the 6th International Conference on PErvasive Technologies Related to Assistive Environments, 67. ACM (2013)
4. Bieber, G., Luthardt, A., Peter, C., Urban, B. The hearing trousers pocket: activity recognition by alternative sensors. In Proceedings of PETRA, 44. ACM (2011)
5. Bieber, G., Voskamp, J., Urban, B.: Activity recognition for everyday life on mobile phones. In: Stephanidis, C. (ed.) UAHCI 2009, Part II. LNCS, vol. 5615, pp. 289–296. Springer, Heidelberg (2009)
6. Bulling, A., Blanke, U., Schiele, B.: A tutorial on human activity recognition using body-worn inertial sensors. ACM Comput. Surv. (CSUR) **46**(3), 1–33 (2014)
7. Ermes, M., Parkka, J., Cluitmans, L.: Advancing from offline to online activity recognition with wearable sensors. In: Proceedings of EMBS, pp. 4451–4454. IEEE (2008)
8. Haescher, M., Bieber, G., Trimpop, J., Urban, B., Kirste, T., Salomon, R.: Recognition of Low Amplitude Body Vibrations via Inertial Sensors for Wearable Computing. In: Proceedings of Conference on IoT Technologies for HealthCare (HealthyIoT), Springer (2014)

9. Hanheide, M., Bauckhage, C., Sagerer, G.: Combining environmental cues and head gestures to interact with wearable devices. In: Proceedings of the 7th international conference on Multimodal interfaces, pp. 25–31. ACM (2005)

10. Ishimaru, S., Kunze, K., Kise, K., Weppner, J., Dengel, A., Lukowicz, P., Bulling, A.: In the blink of an eye: combining head motion and eye blink frequency for activity recognition with google glass. In: Augmented Human International Conference. 15. ACM (2014)

11. Lara, O.D., Labrador, M.A.: A survey on human activity recognition using wearable sensors. Commun. Surv. Tutorials IEEE **15**(3), 1192–1209 (2013)

12. Lindemann, U., Hock, A., Stuber, M., Keck, W., Becker, C.: Evaluation of a fall detector based on accelerometers: a pilot study. Med. Biol. Eng. Comput. **43**(5), 548–551 (2005)

13. Madabhushi, A., Aggarwal, J.K.: Using head movement to recognize activity. In: Proceedings of 15th International Conference on Pattern Recognition vol. 4, pp. 698–701. IEEE (2000)

14. Maurer, U., Smailagic, A., Siewiorek, D.P., Deisher, M.: Activity recognition and monitoring using multiple sensors on different body positions. In: International Workshop on Wearable and Implantable Body Sensor Networks. IEEE (2006)

15. Menz, H.B., Lord, S.R., Fitzpatrick, R.C.: Age-related differences in walking stability. Age Ageing **32**(2), 137–142 (2003)

16. Nam, Y., Rho, S., Lee, C.: Physical activity recognition using multiple sensors embedded in a wearable device. In Proceedings of TECS, 12(2), 26. ACM (2013)

17. Peter, C., Bieber, G., Urban, B.: Affect-and behaviour-related assistance for families in the home environment. In: Proceedings of PETRA, 47. ACM (2010)

18. Polikar, R.: Ensemble based systems in decision making. IEEE Circuits Syst. Mag. **6**(3), 21–45 (2006)

19. Windau, J., Itti, L.: Situation awareness via sensor-equipped eyeglasses. In: International Conference on Intelligent Robots and Systems (IROS), pp. 5674–5679. IEEE (2013)

20. Ward, J.A., Lukowicz, P., Troster, G., Starner, T.E.: Activity recognition of assembly tasks using body-worn microphones and accelerometers. IEEE Trans. Pattern Anal. Mach. Intell. **28**(10), 1553–1567 (2006)

21. Yang, C.C., Hsu, Y.L.: A review of accelerometry-based wearable motion detectors for physical activity monitoring. Sensors **10**(8), 7772–7788 (2010)

22. Zhang, M., Sawchuk, A.A.: A feature selection-based framework for human activity recognition using wearable multimodal sensors. In: Proceedings of the 6th International Conference on Body Area Networks, pp. 92–98 (2011)

23. Zappi, P., Stiefmeier, T., Farella, E., Roggen, D., Benini, L., Tröster, G.: Activity recognition from on-body sensors by classifier fusion: sensor scalability and robustness. In: Conference on Intelligent Sensors, Sensor Networks and Information, pp. 281–286. IEEE (2007)

Synchronization of Peripheral Vision and Wearable Sensors for Animal-to-Animal Interaction

Ko Makiyama[1]([✉]), Keijiro Nakagawa[2,3], Maki Katayama[4], Miho Nagasawa[4], Kaoru Sezaki[1,2], and Hiroki Kobayashi[2]

[1] Institute of Industrial Science, The University of Tokyo, Meguro, Tokyo 153-8505, Japan
{komakiyama,sezaki}@mcl.iis.u-tokyo.ac.jp
http://www.mcl.iis.u-tokyo.ac.jp/en_index.php
[2] Center of Spatial Information Science, The University of Tokyo, Kashiwa, Chiba 277-8568, Japan
{nakagawa,kobayashi}@csis.u-tokyo.ac.jp
[3] Cisco Systems G.K., Minato, Tokyo 107-6227, Japan
kenakaga@cisco.com
[4] Companion Animal Research, Azabu University, Sagamihara, Kanagawa 252-0206, Japan
m.katayama.07@carazabu.com, nagasawa@azabu-u.ac.jp
https://sites.google.com/a/carazabu.com/car_eng/

Abstract. It is considered that it can be one of the methods to use the animal-to-animal communication for getting over the difficulties of field survey. Carrier Pigeon-like Sensing System (CPSS) is one of the systems to realize effective inter-animal communication using wearable devices, but still the data-sharing section of this system is not evaluated comprehensively.

On this study, we evaluated data-sharing system by synchronizing the devices and peripheral vision using video data, and gave the guidance how should improve that.

Keywords: Human computer biosphere interaction · Wearable devices · Sustainable HCI · Field survey · Delay-tolerant network · Environmental monitoring

1 Introduction

Field surveys are meaningful for researchers for bringing much natural information in detail, but there are various obstacles during them. Most of them, especially in the area with limited or nonexistent information infrastructures such as forests, are highly depended on man power and have risks of accidents. Obviously, in the case of Japan, forested area is approximately 70 % of whole land and still much part of the land is the out of communication range [9],

© Springer International Publishing Switzerland 2015
M. Kurosu (Ed.): Human-Computer Interaction, Part II, HCII 2015, LNCS 9170, pp. 753–764, 2015.
DOI: 10.1007/978-3-319-20916-6_69

and unexpected typhoon occurs frequently (not only in Japan but also in lots of Asian-Pacific countries) and affects many people [7]. It cannot be easy to survey the area in severe climate like polar regions, deserts, or rain forests, neither. Also, in the case of the polluted area or battle zone, it becomes dangerous even only to enter the places. In addition, when conducting long-term investigations at such places or monitoring large scale, researchers have to go fields many times and sometimes maintain observation spots. As a result, that entails enormous costs with various aspects.

Remote sensing techniques can avoid such kind of situation and enable researchers to conduct efficient environmental research safely by using satellite images [3]. However, that depends on the sensor resolutions [28], and as we cannot acquire sound data through such images, the information we can get is limited. Thus, there are still several problems even in these methods.

Moreover, a threat of disaster to such inaccessible area like nuclear accidents or fires would harm wild animals, and the harms often follow several generations. For instance, bush warblers living in the forested area around the nuclear power plant in Japan, damaged in March 2011, are thought that they have some contamination on both the outside and inside of the body [14]. That means the pollution may carry over to later generations. Forest fire also affect on wild animals not only directly but indirectly, especially on the habitat environment. If forests are burned, that means animals lose their food a lot and it takes much time to be reproduced, so they have to find out little food which were left or even if they lay up food for winter, that becomes ruined [29]. For preserving and maintaining the ecosystems, long-term, extensive, and safe biological monitoring is required.

For these reasons, extensive and long-term field survey or biological research is needed for environmental monitoring, but has many problems for possibilities of human damages. Therefore, it is necessary to find the safe methods to get various environmental information, which is spatially and temporally satisfied, for researchers.

On this paper, firstly, we give an outline of the related work and show their problems in Sect. 2. Secondly, we suggest a method to solve them in Sect. 3. After that, we provide the result in Sect. 4, discussion in Sect. 5, and conclusions and future work in Sect. 6.

2   Related Work

2.1   Human Computer Biosphere Interaction

Recently, the concept of Human Computer Biosphere Interaction (HCBI), communication between humans and ecosystems using information technology beyond the physical distance, is put forward as extensions of Human Computer Interaction (HCI) and Human Computer Pet Interaction (HCPI) [18].

In the field of HCPI, there are a variety of studies such as Cat@Log [31]. Recently, responding to the increasing demand in pet industry, many researches related to active communication between humans and their pets using IT are conducted. In MyFitDog or FitBark, they are commercially developing their original collar-based devices for health care monitoring [8,20].

On the other hand, HCBI field conducts the communication between humans and biosphere like forests, wild insects, or wild animals. In the case of pets, as they contact with humans almost every day, they respond actively or the thoughts can be comparatively understood easily, while it is hard to comprehend the thoughts or actions of natural things. Therefore, in HCBI field, it can be one of the problems we should solve that how to catch or collect information or thoughts from nature.

Tele-Echo Tube is the equipment reflecting the concept of HCBI and creates the active communication with biosphere by hearing and calling out to natural sounds [16], while Cicada Fingerprinting System branches the HCBI concept to urban regions and estimates the places of users by using mobile devices to analyze the sounds of insects around them [1].

It is said that wild animals in the nature such as tropical forests communicate intricately each other [19]. Therefore, the combination of this inter-animal communication and ubiquitous computing would enable wild animals themselves to acquire and share the information around them [18]. However, the studies in the field of HCBI mostly just catch information around specific places, and in fact nature or wild animals neither acquires nor provides that extensively. Thus, the action or approach to humans by nature or animals is still weak in the aspect of interaction or mutual cooperation.

2.2 Carrier Pigeon-Like Sensing System

To realize the field survey cooperating with nature, based on HCBI concept, Carrier Pigeon-like Sensing System (CPSS), the data-collecting system through animals with wearable sensors as carrier pigeons do, was devised [17,22].

There are some studies applying wearable sensors to animals. Especially, for animals in industry, these are tested to realize precision farming such as the study gathering cattle autonomously by collar-based sensors [6]. CPSS is also one of the studies using wearable sensors.

Figure 1 shows the outline image of CPSS. Animals catch the environmental information such as temperature, luminosity, or records of encounters autonomously through the wearable devices on their backs ("Sensing"). With the sensors for the information, the devices also include acceleration sensors and communication modules. As to the communication step, the system consists of data-sharing system and "Animal Touch'n Go System". On the data-sharing system, they communicate with other animals they encountered to share the data they have collected. Animal Touch'n Go System is that wild animals can upload their own sensor data to the Internet by touching the base station in the area within communication range (data collection). Thus, through taking advantage of the interactions among wild animals, this system could realize safe and efficient field survey for humans. As the amount of electricity consumption of these modules for sharing data is about a hundred times as large as the sensors for collecting data, for long-term use, the system focused on animal behaviors for powering on the communication modules only at the time they share information. Therefore, even if the field is out of communication range, through this ad-hoc network that each animal becomes the node, it is expected to construct delay-tolerant network to collect the data in a long term and real time.

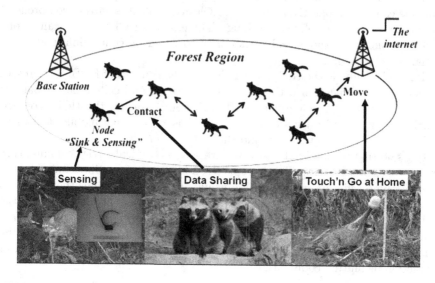

Fig. 1. The concept image of Carrier Pigeon-like Sensing System (CPSS) [21,22].

It is important for animal-to-animal data-sharing system to check whether animals communicate only when they encounter or contact, so such systems need to compare with other elements such as peripheral vision. As to data-sharing system, however, it has not been sufficiently (visually) evaluated yet. Actually, there is a problem that in the case of animal experiments using wearable sensors, unlike human experiments, it is difficult to confirm the reproducibility from a viewpoint of cruelty toward animals.

To check the reproducibility and get the visual information, using wearable cameras could be effective as we can detect what they do properly with them [15].

3   Proposed Method

On this study, we conducted the replication of the data-sharing system of CPSS in Azabu University and visualize the behaviors of dogs in order to evaluate the precision and recall of this system.

The data-sharing sensors in the bags (Fig. 2(c)) are placed on the dogs' backs (Fig. 3). Through the sensors, when encountering and contacting actively with the other, they exchange the information of their ID and accumulated at each time of encounter. In concrete, dog A send the letter "A" as the ID information to others and dog B send "B", everytime they communicate. At the time, as there is a real-time clock on the device, it can record when the ID data are transmitted or received. Also, we can understand how many times they receive the data through the record. In order not to cause data interruption immediately, transmitter continues to send the letter for about two seconds continuously every time dogs begin to transmit it to the other.

We adopted Arduino UNO R3 with Wireless SD Shield as the platform of the device. On the shield, we loaded XBee ZB (PCB Antenna type) as the communication module of ZigBee, Lilypad acceleration sensor (ADXL335), Real Time Clock module, and micro SD for recording (Fig. 2(a)). Sampling rate of the accelerometer is 20 Hz, and all the mechanism for powering on the communication module sets a parameter in the same way as CPSS. (When the displacement of the norm of the acceleration indicates more than 0.2 and pausing time continues from one to ten seconds, communication starts. If ten seconds elapse since the dog pauses, the sensor resets the count of pausing time [22].)

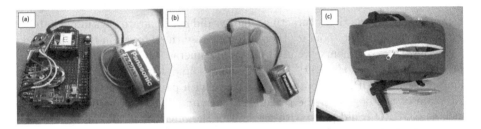

Fig. 2. The device (a) is covered by sponge for preventing them from shocks (b) and put in the bag (c). About 20 cm length and about 300 g weight in total.

For the experiment, we used two dogs. One (dog A) is Poodle (Standard), about 10 years old, whose weight is about 22 kg and the height is about 58 cm, and the other one (dog B) is Pembroke Welsh Corgi, about 3 years old, whose weight is about 11 kg and the height is about 32 cm. The dogs are kept by Azabu University. On the left side of Fig. 3 indicates the dogs. As the weight of the sensor is within the tolerable weight limit of wearable devise (5 % of the animal's body weight) [30], it is considered that the heaviness of the sensors does not largely affect on these dogs while this experiment.

At this time, focusing on the situation when animals encounter and contact each other, we attempted to reproduce that part. The right side of Fig. 3 indicates the field, a passage of Azabu University, and there is a garden plant and trees near the intersecting place. Each dog starts from the yellow star (the right figure) and encounters on the red-star place. The each road is about 10 m length. The experiment is conducted for 20 min from 9 o'clock (Dec. 22, 2014). To prevent dogs from running away, we had each dog on a lead and placed handlers for them. While the experiment, the dogs and the handlers go to and return from the intersecting place for 9 times. In the case of wilderness, animals contact the other actively for a while after their encounter, so considering they frequently

Fig. 3. The dogs with the devices on their backs (the upper-left figure: dog A; the lower-left figure: dog B) and the field (the right figure).

exchange the data on that contacting time, we did not separate dogs immediately, but made some time to contact them till they lose the interest in the other one.

While the experiments, we used GOPRO cameras (GOPRO HD HERO 3+) for acquiring video data [11]. Each handler bound a waist with the harness equipped with GOPRO like a belt, and move with paying attention to catching the state of the dog from the camera all the time. To use wearable interfaces such as GOPRO could place with no limit of the physical action, and enable us to move freer than handling minicams.

After acquiring the data, we counted the significant numbers of dogs' encounters or active contacts, communication attempt through these performances, and their communication success. As to the number of encounters or contacts, we checked the number of going to the other one's direction after pausing, and the significant number of the communication attempt of encounter or (active) contact, considering the error of the synchronization of communication devices and video data, we counted that when the error is within three seconds. Moreover, the attempt of every time from separated each other till starting again is excepted from the counts. In addition, we calculated the precision, recall, and communication success rate of the data-sharing system. On precision, we used the number of the attempt when they encounter or contact as the numerator and the number of communication attempt as the denominator, while on recall, the numerator is the same as precision and denominator is the number of encounters or contacts.

4   Results

Through the video data, we could precisely observe the dogs' behaviors, and four types of the performance, walking, pausing, shuddering, and sneezing were observed. Further, sometimes there were some gaps between the behaviors and devices' data. It can be thought that these errors have occurred at the time of the synchronization of the video and devices or the memory of these data.

Figure 4 indicates the one scene of the observation using GOPRO data. After encountering, the dogs contact each other some times. On 13:03 of the time of the experiment, dog B stared at dog A and was about to contact with it. On 13:07, dog B smelled dog A's hip. Before that, when dog B stepped up to dog A, dog B has just started attempting communication, but as dog A didn't notice dog B, it could not succeed. On 13:09, dog A noticed the dog B's presence and walked to it, and while walking, dog A started trying communicating with dog B. On this communication, dog A succeeded in exchanging the data, but it is thought that this data dog A has received was the data which dog B had transmitted once before it did on between 13:03 and 13:07. Then on 13:10, dog B set apart from dog A.

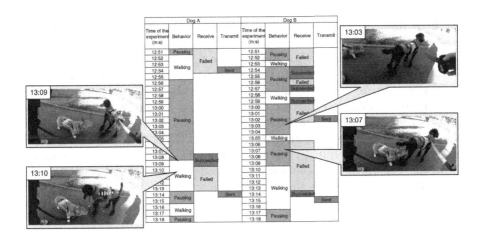

Fig. 4. Example of the observation

The results of the counts are described on Table 1. The difference between dog A and dog B has emerged according to this table. It can be thought that one of the reasons of the difference between the number of communication success of dog A and that of dog B is that each dog sometimes received the data the other transmitted once before they tried communicating at the same time. Based on these counts, precision, recall, and communication success rate were calculated, and using precision and recall, F-measures, the harmonic means of them, were also computed (the following equation) [13]. At this time, in order to evaluate precision and recall equally, we adopted $\beta = 1$.

$$F = \frac{(1 + \beta^2) \times precision \times recall}{(\beta^2 \times precision) + recall}$$

Table 1. Results of the significant numbers of counts

Element of the count	Dog A	Dog B
Encounters or (active) contacts	53	69
Communication attempt	42	35
Communication attempt while the encounters or contacts	23	27
Communication success while the encounters or contacts	15	20

In addition, we also calculated the ratio of the time when the communication module does not consume the power to the time length of the experiment (time saving rate of communication time).

The results are on Fig. 5. According to the result, precision, recall, F-measure, and communication success rate are 54.8 %, 43.4 %, 48.4 %, 65.2 % as dog A, and 77.1 %, 39.1 %, 51.9 %, and 74.1 % as dog B. Therefore, it can be confirmed that both dogs can communicate in an accuracy of about 60 to 70 percent based on about 50 % as F-measure. As to such precision (50 to 75 percent) and recall (about 40 percent), however, these figures are still low, so there are rooms for improvement in the data-sharing system like making some mechanisms considering animals' individual differences (as there are differences between dog A and B) to completely construct the system that animals communicate only when they encounter or contact. On the other hand, power-consuming time of communication has shortened more than 95 % in both dogs (96.9 % for dog A and 95.1 % for dog B). Accordingly, this system has great power saving performance.

On this experiment, we could construct some index scales of concrete individual difference of animals through the differences of precision and recall of communication attempt at encounters or contacts.

5 Discussion

At this time, it is thought that dogs move according to handlers' actions, and it would be necessary to adopt the experiment form that can keep dogs from moving along with the handlers, including the utilization of the dog run, in order to make it closer to the real and natural dog movements. Also, it is needed to prevent dogs from getting accustomed to encounter or contact with each other within the realms of possibility.

To evaluate communication efficiency more comprehensively, as a control experiment, we have to have the continuous communication-attempting experiment in the same condition. As to this time, we could check how long they shortened the communication-attempting time, but not completely confirm how much they lose the chance of mutual communication or how poor the communication efficiency becomes provided that the communication modules consume the power continuously. Therefore, as one of the future works, it is necessary to compare the actual power consumption before and after the installation of that power-saving system.

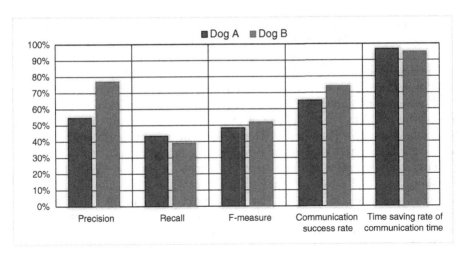

Fig. 5. The results of each dog's rates.

Referring to the number and the position of cameras, it is also important to set the experiment to get both qualitatively and quantitatively sufficient video data enough to understand each action of precisely without limiting the movements. In HUMANEVA-II, video data is taken from in the front and rear directions and the right and left directions of the objects with enough space for them [27]. Also, if GOPRO is equipped on an animal's back directly, the peripheral vision could be checked from its eye level, and understand every fine movement properly [15]. As this research, it is desirable to set cameras to observe from enough viewpoints from animals to precisely understand the motions, and there is still room for improvement.

The concept of CPSS enables wild animals to record extensive information on the long-term basis and share it with humans without any harm each other. Thus, finally, this mutual cooperation is expected to establish the sustainable ecosystem, and develop the study field of disaster prevention without any accident. In addition, with the technology like this, humans can monitor the ecology of wild animals distantly, so the study would contribute to further development of the research fields of animal life or action and epidemic, or protection of crops from harmful birds and beasts [10,14].

Especially in Japan, there are some area humans are still not able to enter under the influence of nuclear plant accidents on March, 2011. The dose rates of much ground surface are beyond 20 μSv/h even though the area is far from the plant, and many animals are still there while the residents are evacuated [18]. Thinking of these residents difficult to come back to their own hometown, outsiders shouldn't make enemies of them by intervening or fixing any equipment into there. On the other hand, the animals don't enforce any living or social constraint to them and trust each other [23]. Accordingly, the technology like CPSS is socially cooperative for both humans and animals, and meaningful to carry out for grasping the actual ecosystem condition. Referring to dose rates, Pocket Geiger Type 5 could be useful as it can be added into Arduino sensors [24].

Further, in the case fixing large equipment into fields or putting it close to wild animals for effective biological research, the animals, regarding differences with former memories as sense of discomfort and threats, would run away. As a result we cannot conduct the effective study in natural condition. In addition to solving this problem, the equipment of a wearable device such as this study would be advantageous for the animal. With this equipment, an animal would stand out comparing with others, and finally it could be beneficial for survival [4].

This study connects humans to wild animals in the place out of communication range and creates the mutual cooperation by ubiquitous computing. Thereby, this would strengthen the presence of HCBI in HCI field for such "socially extreme" cooperation, and in terms of the continuous contribution to environmental preservation by that, the study would also support the field of sustainable HCI [2].

Most of the parts of the study field of animal behavior recognition are still unexpected. For example, some animal anecdotes like "Animal suicide", people have deeply discussed for many years, or even usual actions of animals like shuddering are still partly understood by subjectivity of humans, and these are debatable [26]. Thus, it is obvious that lots of new facts can come to light in this research field. To speak such a knowledge, video data is necessary. Understanding animal behaviors through video data can support other various studies. In the case of veterinary medicine, there are still many unknown things why or when the diseases animals sometimes suffer from occurs (epilepsy etc.) [5,12], and it is needed that the signs of such illness are checked through video data. Also, in the future, to lower the cost of the medical technology for such diseases, it is important to construct the remote network system that we can know the habits, health status, or actions of animals in real time as well as humans [25].

6   Conclusion and Future Work

We have checked the accuracy of the data-sharing system of CPSS with peripheral vision using video data, and our research could confirm that it was important to consider the individual difference of animals and upgrade the accuracy of the extraction of their behaviors for animal-to-animal communication.

As the future work, based on the results, we are going to improve the animal-to-animal communication system, especially the part of power saving. In concrete, by using some methods of animal behavior recognition, we will make the system of the encounter detection in consideration of individual difference of animals. Also, we are precisely showing the improvement of the system performance of that communication efficiency. Our last goal is to construct the delay-tolerant inter-animal network for safe and effective field and biological survey.

Acknowledgements. This research is supported by MIC: Strategic Information and Communications R&D Promotion Programme (SCOPE) (No.142103015). We would like to thank all the students who helped with the experiment.

References

1. Aoki, S., Kobayashi, H., Sezaki, K.: Cicada fingerprinting system: from artificial to sustainable. In: Proceedings of the 12th International Conference on Mobile and Ubiquitous Multimedia, p. 36. ACM (2013)
2. Blevis, E.: Sustainable interaction design: invention & disposal, renewal & reuse. In: Proceedings of the SIGCHI Conference on Human Factors in Computing Systems, pp. 503–512. ACM (2007)
3. Butle, D.R., Walsh, S.J.: The application of remote sensing and geographic information systems in the study of geomorphology: an introduction. Geomorphology **21**(3), 179–181 (1998)
4. Darwin Charles, R.: On the origin of species by means of natural selection, or the preservation of favoured races in the struggle for life (1859)
5. Davis, K.A., Sturges, B.K., Vite, C.H., Ruedebusch, V., Worrell, G., Gardner, A.B., Leyde, K., Sheffield, W.D., Litt, B.: A novel implanted device to wirelessly record and analyze continuous intracranial canine eeg. Epilepsy Res. **96**(1), 116–122 (2011)
6. Doniec, M., Detweiler, C., Vasilescu, I., Anderson, D.M., Rus, D.: Autonomous gathering of livestock using a multi-functional sensor network platform. In: Proceedings of the 6th Workshop on Hot Topics in Embedded Networked Sensors, p. 5. ACM (2010)
7. Fan, K., Wang, H.: A new approach to forecasting typhoon frequency over the western north pacific. Weather Forecast. **24**(4), 974–986 (2009)
8. Fitbark. http://www.fitbark.com/. Accessed: 03 February 2015
9. Forest area (% of land area) in japan - trading economics. http://www.tradingeconomics.com/japan/forest-area-percent-of-land-area wb-data.html. Accessed: 13 January 2015
10. Giannachi, G., Kaye, N., Shanks, M.: Archaeologies of Presence: Art, Performance and the Persistence of Being. Routledge, London (2012)
11. Gopro hd hero 3+. http://www.gopro.com. Accessed: 26 January 2015
12. Howbert, J.J., Patterson, E.E., Stead, S.M., Brinkmann, B., Vasoli, V., Crepeau, D., Vite, C.H., Sturges, B., Ruedebusch, V., Mavoori, J., et al.: Forecasting seizures in dogs with naturally occurring epilepsy. PloS One **9**(1), e81920 (2014)
13. Hripcsak, G., Rothschild, A.S.: Agreement, the f-measure, and reliability in information retrieval. J. Am. Med. Inform. Assoc. **12**(3), 296–298 (2005)
14. Ishida, K.: Contamination of wild animals: effects on wildlife in high radioactivity areas of the agricultural and forest landscape. In: Nakanishi, T.M., Tanoi, K. (eds.) Agricultural Implications of the Fukushima Nuclear Accident, pp. 119–129. Springer, Heidelberg (2013)
15. Iwashita, Y., Takamine, A., Kurazume, R., Ryoo, M.: First-person animal activity recognition from egocentric videos. In: 2014 22nd International Conference on Pattern Recognition (ICPR), pp. 4310–4315. IEEE (2014)
16. Kobayashi, H., Hirose, M., Fujiwara, A., Nakamura, K., Sezaki, K., Saito, K.: Tele echo tube: beyond cultural and imaginable boundaries. In: Proceedings of the 21st ACM International Conference on Multimedia, pp. 173–182. ACM (2013)
17. Kobayashi, H., Kudo, H.: Carrier pigeon-like sensing system: beyond human-red forest interactions. In: Proceedings of Balance-Unbalance International Conference (2013)
18. Kobayashi, H., Ueoka, R., Hirose, M.: Human computer biosphere interaction: towards a sustainable society. In: CHI 2009 Extended Abstracts on Human Factors in Computing Systems, pp. 2509–2518. ACM (2009)

19. Leigh, E.G., Rand, A.S., Windsor, D.M., et al.: The ecology of a tropical forest. seasonal rhythms and long-term changes. The ecology of a tropical forest. Seasonal rhythms and long-term changes (1983)

20. Myfitdog. http://myfitdog.com/. Accessed: 03 February 2015

21. Nakagawa, K., Kobayashi, H., Okuno, J., Sezaki, K.: Suggestion of the sleep control technique using the habits of animal considering field survey (in Japanese). http://www.csis.u-tokyo.ac.jp/csisdays2013/csisdays2013-ra-pdf/C14.pdf. Accessed: 12 February 2015

22. Nakagawa, K., Kobayashi, H., Sezaki, K.: Carrier pigeon-like sensing system: animal-computer interface design for opportunistic data exchange interaction for a wildlife monitoring application. In: Proceedings of the 5th Augmented Human International Conference, p. 27. ACM (2014)

23. Philo, C., Wilbert, C.: Animal Spaces, Beastly Places: New Geographies of Human-Animal Relations, vol. 10. Psychology Press, Routledge (2000)

24. Pocket geiger type 5 (radiation watch). http://www.radiation-watch.org/p/english.html. Accessed: 26 January 2015

25. Pollard, J., Rohman, S., Fry, M.: A web-based mobile medical monitoring system. In: International Workshop on Intelligent Data Acquisition and Advanced Computing Systems: Technology and Applications, pp. 32–35. IEEE (2001)

26. Ramsden, E., Wilson, D.: The suicidal animal: science and the nature of self-destruction. Past Present **224**(1), 201–242 (2014)

27. Sigal, L., Balan, A.O., Black, M.J.: Humaneva: synchronized video and motion capture dataset and baseline algorithm for evaluation of articulated human motion. Int. J. Comput. Vis. **87**(1–2), 4–27 (2010)

28. Small, C.: Estimation of urban vegetation abundance by spectral mixture analysis. Int. J. Remote Sens. **22**(7), 1305–1334 (2001)

29. Smith, J.K., Lyon, L.J., Huff, M., Hooper, R., Telfer, E., Schreiner, D., et al.: Wildland fire in ecosystems. effects of fire on fauna. General Technical Report-Rocky Mountain Research Station, USDA Forest Service (RMRS-GTR-42) (2000)

30. White, G.C., Garrott, R.A.: Analysis of Wildlife Radio-Tracking Data. Elsevier, San Diego (2012)

31. Yonezawa, K., Miyaki, T., Rekimoto, J.: Cat@ log: sensing device attachable to pet cats for supporting human-pet interaction. In: Proceedings of the International Conference on Advances in Computer Enterntainment Technology, pp. 149–156. ACM (2009)

On the Usability of Smartphone Apps in Emergencies

An HCI Analysis of GDACSmobile and SmartRescue Apps

Parvaneh Sarshar[(✉)], Vimala Nunavath, and Jaziar Radianti

Department of ICT, University of Agder (UiA), Kristiansand, Norway
{parvaneh.sarshar,vimala.nunavath,
jaziar.radianti}@uia.no

Abstract. It is very critical that the disaster management smartphone app users be able to interact efficiently and effectively with the app during an emergen-cy. An overview of the challenges face for designing mobile HCI in emergency management tools is presented in this paper. Then, two recently developed emergency management tools, titled GDACSmobile and SmartRescue, are studied from usability and HCI challenges point of view. These two tools use mobile app and smartphone sensors as the main functionality respectively. Both have a smartphone app and a web-based app with different UIs for their different user groups. Furthermore, the functionality of these apps in the format of a designed scenario, fire onboard a passenger ship, will be discussed.

Keywords: Emergency management tools · Smartphone apps · Mobile HCI · Fire emergency · Mobile usability

1 Introduction

Unfortunately, disasters and emergencies happen all around the world every day or even every hour, and most of them are not even man-made but natural. They can be in a small scale such as a fire in a building or in a large one such as a tsunami hitting several coastal countries. When a disaster strikes, mapping the threat and getting the precise information and overview of the hazard become the most crucial and challenging tasks. There is a long list of ICT-based technologies (esp. software) that have been developed in recent years in order to successfully support these tasks, emergency management procedures, and actors involved in disasters (victims and emergency responders). For instance, crisis mapping tools such as [1–3] or disaster and crisis smartphone apps presented in [4–6].

By including ICT as a necessary component of emergency management, useful interfaces for emergency systems are required. The user interface (UI) and the usability of these systems are highly critical. We may hear from people around us complaining about the usability or interface of software or apps they use daily, but this cannot be the case for emergency management tools, such as smartphone apps that are developed to support emergency responders and victims. They need to be reliable and effective even when users are under stress. When facing disaster scenarios, momentous decisions rely on the effectiveness and efficiency of these technological tools to provide the

© Springer International Publishing Switzerland 2015
M. Kurosu (Ed.): Human-Computer Interaction, Part II, HCII 2015, LNCS 9170, pp. 765–774, 2015.
DOI: 10.1007/978-3-319-20916-6_70

information and communication processes. Users of the emergency management systems are under more pressure to [7]: absorb information rapidly, judge its sense,
meaning, relevance, and reliability, decide what the options for action are and make
effective decisions accordingly. Therefore, the accomplishment of a series of cognitively demanding steps rely on the effectiveness of the technology (e.g., apps) and the
design of the human-computer interaction (HCI) used in emergency scenarios.

There are several studies on the role of HCI and its challenges for mobile devices
(also known as Mobile HCI) (see e.g., [8–12]), in emergency management (see, e.g., [7,
13, 14]). In this paper, we study these challenges extracted from the literature and their
corresponding solutions. Then, we investigate whether these challenges have been
addressed in two crisis management tools that authors with a thorough understanding
about their features have used in their research, i.e. GDACSmobile [15] and SmartRescue application [16]. The former is an information system that acts as a real-time
multi-hazard platform using smartphones and Twitter. The latter is an application for
both monitoring hazard developments and tracking victims during a disaster applying
smartphone sensors and a publish-subscribe platform. This paper also studies the
usability of these two apps in a designed emergency scenario, a fire onboard a ship.

The rest of this paper is organized as follows. Section 2 describes the challenges in
designing HCI. Section 3 explains the two selected applications and their corresponding mobile HCI challenges in details. In Sect. 4, the usability of these apps in an
emergency scenario will be studied. Section 5 concludes the paper.

2   Challenges in Designing HCI

There are many challenges in designing HCI for emergency management smartphone
apps. There are some general challenges, such as: software challenges (e.g., menu,
navigation, browsing, image, and icon), hardware challenges (e.g., screen size, battery
life, keyboard, touch screen, and mobility), Internet connectivity, attempting to provide
users with powerful computing services and resources through small interfaces [9], the
fat finger problem [10] referring to the fact that finger touch is much more imprecise
than pointing with a mouse in terms of addressed pixels. In addition to these general
challenges, there exist some specific challenges from HCI point of view for smartphone
apps developed for supporting emergency issues that can be found in [7].

It is important to have a non-complex UI that helps victims in danger and stress or
rescuers to handle the emergency management apps as easily as possible. This can be
done by limiting the number of functionalities available on a single screen or within one
mobile app [12]. The mobile app developers should also consider that their user groups
might be elderly, disabled people, children, or even injured people. Flentge et al. [13] also
proposed that the design of HCI for those working in the disaster field should be different
from those in the command and control posts. They suggest audio and/or video interaction
for those working in the affected area and multi-user interfaces for crisis management
teams working in the command posts. In the same paper, they have listed the following
challenges of designing HCI for incident management: (1) Reduction of complexity,
which addresses the need for a compact form of presenting information in an emergency
situation, the ease of use, and the simplicity of user interfaces; (2) Priority of the primary

task, which states that interacting with emergency management tools should not distract responders from their main tasks and responsibilities; (3) Heterogeneity of the involved actors, which recommends that the UIs of the emergency management tools should support all kinds of users from victims to experienced, well-trained users; (4) Heterogeneity of ICT, which points out that the involved organizations have different technological systems. Therefore, flexible and adaptive user interfaces are needed; (5) Security and privacy, which concerns the information security and data privacy of the developed tools; and (6) Context-awareness, which deals with the adaption of interfaces to users, devices at hand, and environments. Context information can have a substantial impact on emergency response by contributing to an accurate view of the emergency situations.

In the next section, we present the two emergency management apps, GDACSmobile and SmartRescue and discuss if the six above-mentioned challenges have been addressed in designing HCI of these two apps by the developers.

3 Studied Applications

In this section, we give an introduction on GDACSmobile and SmartRescue apps. We study how the developers of these two apps have tackled the HCI design challenges mentioned in the previous section by [13]. The results are summarized in Table 1. The reason for selecting these two apps, as discussed in Sect. 1, is that the authors had the opportunity to employ them in their research and in a serious emergency game designed by the ISCRAM summer school.

3.1 GDACSmobile

The GDACSmobile project has been developed by the Information Systems Department of the University of Münster and the Joint Research Centre (JRC) of the European Commission aiming to expand GDACS by community involvement. The goals of GDACSmobile project are: to enhance the quality of circulated information using smartphone apps and Twitter; to reduce the level of uncertainty in the received information from Twitter by means of bounded-crowdsourcing; to be able to exchange information and coordinate emergencies in the first phase after a major disaster using smartphones.

The GDACSmobile system consists of a smartphone client app which is used for accessing content and sharing/updating information, and a web-based server application which is employed for data (e.g., reports on a disaster) retrieval, storage and analysis. GDACSmobile can be used by both disaster management professionals ("authorized/registered users") and the affected population ("public users" or "authorized users") to share their observations from the affected area as "situation reports", both via the GDACSmobile client app for mobile devices, and via Twitter. Via the client app, both users group can also receive updated reports providing them by valuable information to support their decision-making. Figure 1 shows some screenshots of the UIs of the client app for an authorized user[1].

---

[1] For detailed information on the functionality of GDACSmobile app, please refer to: http://portal.gdacs.org/Portals/0/SocialAndMobile/GDACSmobile%20User%20Guide.pdf.

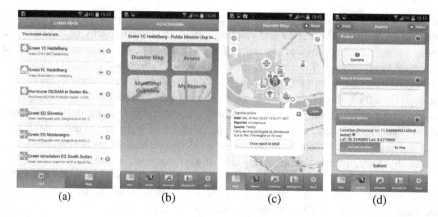

(a)   (b)   (c)   (d)

Fig. 1. (a) A map view of the alerts, (b) The main menu for each selected alert, (c) Map showing all reports related to the selected alert and its corresponding information window, (d) Reporting page.

3.2   SmartRescue

The SmartRescue project started in 2012 in the Centre for Integrated Emergency Management (CIEM) [17] at the Universitetet of Agder (UiA), Norway. The aim of this project is to apply latest technologies in smartphones to support victims in need and rescuers. The project also has several goals: detecting fire and predicting its future development; using advanced sensors embedded in smartphones in order to assist crisis managers to locate victims during the evacuation procedure; constructing risk-minimizing evacuation plans; avoiding congestion in escape routes.

(a)   (b)   (c)   (d)

Fig. 2. (a) The main menu, (b) The "Setting" page, (c) The "Subscriber" page, the user can choose what sort of sensor data to receive. The same option exists for the "Publisher". (d) The map a building that is showing the location of the user (blue marker), the location of the publishers (typically victims, red markers), and the location and condition of the fire in different areas of the building (red and green circles) (Color figure online).

To accomplish these goals, a smartphone-based app with the ability of processing sensor readings into useful information for the crisis responders was developed. It consists of a robust content-based publish-subscribe mechanism that allows flexible sharing and receiving of sensor data. A publisher is the user who wants to share the data that his/her SmartRescue app has sensed by the sensors in the smartphone. A subscriber is the user who wants to receive this sensed data. A user can be both publisher and/or subscriber. The system also employs a machine learning technique that predicts the fire status in the next couple of seconds. In addition to the smartphone app, there is a web-based server available for data collection and analysis, which also acts as a subscriber. Figure 2 presents some screenshots of the UIs of the SmartRescue app for both user groups (victims and rescuers).

3.3   HCI Analysis for GDACSmobile and SmartRescue Apps

The table below discusses if the developers of the apps, GDACSmobile and SmartRescue, have addressed the challenges of designing HCI when developing their apps for emergencies.

Table 1. HCI Analysis for GDACSmobile and SmartRescue apps

Challenges	GDACSmobile	SmartRescue
Reduction of complexity	The main goal of this app is to increase understanding and reduce visual complexity of the reports coming from the users. For example, by showing all reports in one map and using relevant icons.	The ease of use and simplicity have been a permanent goal of the SmartRescue app development. For example, victims can share their location, their condition and the condition of the area they are in only by switching on the "publisher" button. The same process is required for rescuers as "subscriber".
Priority of the primary task	The priority can be established by giving the client app only to the leaders of the rescuing teams at the site. At the command and control room, usually one or two people are in charge of the server side. Though, the app supports the primary tasks of both victims and the emergency responders.	This can be one of the most challenging issues when introducing smartphones as new supporting systems in emergencies. It can be resolved by managing the dynamic of the rescue teams and studying who is the most suitable person to use the app in those teams (leaders or firefighters). Though, the app supports the very primary task of both victims and the rescuers.

(Continued)

Table 1. (*Continued*)

Challenges	GDACSmobile	SmartRescue
Heterogeneity of the involved actors	The UI of this app is designed to support all user groups such as public users (e.g., victims), registered users, and administrator. In the web-based server, the user can be either an administrator or a registered user.	The UI is the same for different users (i.e., victim, firefighters, emergency manager) of SmartRescue app. All users can see all the data available on the app, if they want to. In a more mature development stage, there will be different UI for victims and responders.
Heterogeneity of ICT	It supports iOS and Android operating systems. The smartphone app needs the Internet connection to work, although it stores data in the phone when it is offline and transfers data to the server when it is online.	This app is only available for Android smartphone. The publisher loses the data when net-work connection is not available. Broker buffers data in the phone/server when it is offline and transfers data to the subscriber when it is online.
Security and privacy	Using bounded-crowdsourcing for data collection, authorizing users and other features in this app prove that information and users' privacy have been highly secured.	Users are connected to each other's sensor and location information through the publish-subscribe platform, without requiring them to know each other's phone numbers. The location markers only show the phone serial numbers, but not the name of the phone owners or their phone number as a part of the privacy protection.
Context-awareness	Emergency workers, as the first responders in the field can collect context information using their mobile devices. The client app is designed for different user groups as discussed above. In addition, it is compatible with different devices. The users can give information about their location using the map and the condition of them and their surroundings by sending text or image to the server from the affected area.	Sensors embedded in the smartphones can sense and send the context information regarding the surrounding of the smartphone owner. It senses the user's environment (e.g., humidity, pressure, temperature) and movement. Based on these sensor readings, it automatically locates the origin of fire, tracks its development and predicts the future development of the fire. The app can also track people by indoor positioning system which is very useful for emergency responders in the fire disasters.

4   SmartRescue and GDACSmobile in Practice

In this section, an emergency scenario, a fire on a cruise (i.e., a passenger ship) with about 5 floors and more than 1000 passengers and crews onboard is defined. The aim of having this scenario is to investigate the usability of the two chosen apps in practice.

4.1   Defining the Scenario: Fire Onboard a Passenger Ship

When fire is noticed by any of the passengers or crew, first the crew and then the captain of the ship will be informed. After informing the captain, the corresponding crew will go directly to the location to assess the situation. When the fire is approved, then the captain asks for more information to get an overview of the situation. Depending on the size and location of the fire, the captain should decide if it is an emergency or not. If the fire is steadily spreading over the other parts of the ship and is difficult to extinguish, then the captain considers it as an emergency and asks other emergency organizations to join in extinguishing the fire and evacuating the passengers. The captain then sounds the general alarm to initiate the mustering of the passengers, and then if necessary gives the order to abandon the ship. The ship crew alerts the passengers and tries to evacuate the entire ship or a part of it, while other crew members have to extinguish the fire. The crew acts as emergency responders. The crew of the ship is trained to act as firefighters and first aid team. They follow the orders given by the captain of the ship.

When fire spreads from one compartment to another, crew tries to close the compartment to prevent fire from spreading. The captain will give all the necessary information to the ship company, if they require while managing emergency. On the ship, there will be an on-scene commander (OSC) who reports the situation to the captain (operational commander (OPC)). The OSC will distribute all the fire teams for different tasks like cooling down areas above, on the sides and below, and search of the areas affected by the smoke. Based on the reports from the OSC, the captain will make the decisions. The ship has hospital and trained first aid team that take care of the injured passengers. The chief officer is the medical person onboard, and reports to the OPC. If the injured passengers need medical attention urgently, then they will be taken by helicopter.

Utilizing GDACSmobile Onboard. By getting onboard the ships and as part of the safety instruction, passengers are asked to install the client app on their smartphones. They are also informed about the hashtag they need to use for reporting or getting reports through Twitter. In order to use the GDACSmobile app, several crew members have been selected as authorized users in case of emergency. When the passengers of the ship notice a fire, they can use either the GDACSmobile client app or Twitter to report about the emergency situation by sending messages with text and/or with image. For instance, passengers can send their locations in the ship with directions in form of text or pictures. The information which is sent by passengers will be received by the emergency responders onboard in order to help the victims. When passengers use client app, they can send message as public users to get help from or to report about the situation. But passengers have to use a hashtag for sharing the information via Twitter. Victims of the emergency can view the other submitted reports as a list or on map view when the administrator accepts the report and makes them available. With the available reports, users (either authorized or public) can get the overview of the situation by viewing the map. Reports from authorized users are considered accepted by default. These reports are used for evacuating and helping the victims of the ship.

Utilizing GDACSmobile at the On-Scene Coordination Centre. When the reports are submitted by both passengers and the crew of the ship through the client app or via Twitter, administrator (chosen by the captain) on the web-based server will view the reports and edit the received reports, he can either public accept, accept, reject, or just save the reports to be later used for helping the victims and the emergency management. Administrator is able to add extra information such as description and comment to the available reports. By using GDACSmobile app, emergency responders can receive the emergency related data to get an overview of the situation as well as to help the victims by alerting the public via Twitter. OSC can use these reports to assign the tasks to the other crew of the ship and also to inform to the OPC i.e., the captain. OPC uses these reports to assess the situation and take the decisions on evacuating, providing first aid, and managing the emergency.

Utilizing SmartRescue Onboard. For the security and the safety procedure, before the journey starts, the passengers of the ship are asked to install this app in their smartphones in order to send the information to the emergency responders during an emergency. When fire is noticed and reported, crew of the ship will inform the captain and then a group will go to the location of the fire. They can locate the fire using the SmartRescue app. They can act either as a publisher (to send information) or a subscriber (to receive information). The passengers, who chose to be publishers, send sensed data from their smartphones. Some of the crew members, as subscribers, receive the published data such as the location of the passengers, their condition (if they are moving or not), the location and condition of the fire. They can also receive data about the temperature, pressure, and the humidity of the area the publisher is in. This generates a global picture of the fire. The app can also predict how the fire is going to develop in the near future using Bayesian networks (BN). The crew members who are acting as firefighters inform the OSC and he informs the OPC about the emergency procedure. Thus, the captain can make decisions about the evacuation procedures, extinguishing plan, and so on.

Utilizing SmartRescue at the On-scene Coordination Centre. At on-scene coordination centre, the OPC will be in lead. The SmartRescue app will support him and the OSC to get an overview of the emergency situation. When the passengers and the crew act as publishers, the OPC and the OSC subscribe to receive data about the location and condition of the victims, the location of the crew, and the location and condition of the fire. Based on the available information and the ability of the app to predict fire, OPC and OSC can make better decisions.

5 Discussion and Conclusion

This paper tried to gather some of the most important challenges of mobile HCI in emergency management apps that might be overlooked by app developers. Two emergency management and crisis mapping tools was selected as a case study. By applying the two selected apps in an emergency scenario, the role of HCI is the design of the apps as discussed in Table 1 is more visible. As both apps are context-aware applications, they can sense their physical environment either by reading the sensors or by reporting using image or text. Both apps are easy to use, but still there can be some potential improvements. GDACSmobile has different UIs for its user groups, while SmartRescue has only one single UI. Both of these approaches can have pros and cons that can be discussed in future works. For having a deep understanding on the usability and goodness of the interfaces in these apps, there exist several usability test approaches, such as serious games, interviews, online surveys, and ISO 9241. As a future work, these methods will also be studied.

Acknowledgment. The research presented here has been partially funded by the research grant awarded to the SmartRescue project by Aust-Agder Utvikling- og Kompetansefond. Authors would like to thank Mr. Daniel Link and GDACSmobile group for their valuable cooperation and support.

References

1. Ushahidi. http://ushahidi.com/
2. Twitcident. http://twitcident.com/
3. LRA Crisis Tracker. http://www.lracrisistracker.com/
4. Bekker, W.: Apps for that-Tried and tested downloads for firefighters. http://www.firefightingincanada.com/equipment/apps-for-that-14885
5. FireRescue1. http://www.firerescue1.com/firefighter-iphone-apps/
6. Jerrard, J.: Smartphone Apps for the Fire Service. http://www.firefighternation.com/article/training-0/smartphone-apps-fire-service
7. Carver, L., Turoff, M.: Human-computer interaction: the human and computer as a team in emergency management information systems. Commun. ACM **50**(3), 33–38 (2007)
8. Love, S.: Understanding Mobile Human-Computer Interaction. Butterworth-Heinemann, Newton (2005)
9. Wang, L., Sajeev, A.: Roller interface for mobile device applications. Paper presented at the Proceedings of the Eight Australasian Conference on User Interface, vol. 64 (2007)
10. Wigdor, D., Wixon, D.: Brave NUI World: Designing Natural User Interfaces for Touch and Gesture. Elsevier, Amsterdam (2011)
11. Salazar, L.H.A., Lacerda, T., Nunes, J.V., von Wangenheim, C.G.: A systematic literature review on usability heuristics for mobile phones. Int. J. Mob Hum. Comput. Interact. (IJMHCI) **5**(2), 50–61 (2013)
12. Schleicher, R., Westermann, T., Reichmuth, R.: Mobile Human Computer–Interaction Quality of Experience, pp. 339–349. Springer, Heidelberg (2014)
13. Flentge, F., Weber, S.G., Behring, A., Ziegert, T.: Designing context-aware HCI for collaborative emergency management. Paper presented at the International Workshop on HCI for Emergencies in Conjunction with CHI (2008)

14. Paulheim, H., Döweling, S., Tso-Sutter, K.H., Probst, F., Ziegert, T.: Improving Usability of Integrated Emergency Response Systems: The SoKNOS Approach. Paper presented at the GI Jahrestagung (2009)
15. GDACSmobile. http://emm-labs.jrc.it/iOSEnterprise/GDACS/
16. SmartRescue. http://ciem.uia.no/project/smartrescue
17. Centre for Integrated Emergency Management. CIEM. http://ciem.uia.no/

An Exploration of Shape in Crowd Computer Interactions

Anthony Scavarelli$^{(\boxtimes)}$ and Ali Arya

School of Information Technology, Carleton University, Ottawa, Canada
{anthony.scavarelli,ali.arya}@carleton.ca

Abstract. In this paper we explore crowd-computer interactions using a crowd shape generated from participating crowd members, both simulated and non-simulated, in three main shape forms (blobby, precise, and a combination of the two) to explore whether such an interactive form, and which of the three forms, can be both a viable and interesting method of having many people collaboratively interacting with large public displays in public spaces.

Keywords: Crowd-computer interaction · Natural user interface · Crowd shape · Human computer interaction

1 Introduction

Due to the increasing power and flexibility of large projected and screen-based displays, as well as the many types of interaction now easily accessible to even moderately skilled programmers and designers, with frameworks such as Openframeworks, Cinder, and Processing [17], there has been a surge of public installation work in recent years within museums, concerts, classrooms, and public outdoor areas. Such installations frequently allow interaction of large group of users with the system.

Though touched on in some research, crowd-computer interaction, where a crowd of people whose combined actions interact with an interactive installation, remains elusive. Examples of prior work includes Baarkhuus et al's "Cheering Meter" where the culminated volume of a crowds' cheers determined the outcome of rap battles [1], Maynes-Aminzade et al's "Pong" where the combined movements of a large classroom move a virtual paddle [5], and O'Hara et al's "Red Nose Game" where crowds' movements moved a virtual ball [6].

In this paper, we propose a new way of visualizing and identifying crowd, and furthermore an interaction approach that uses "crowd shape" as a variable that can provide specific inputs and also be affected by system outputs. We investigate three methods (*blobby*/approximated, *precise*/people tracked, and a *combination* of those two) of displaying "crowd shape" and study the usability of these shapes as a means of interaction between large user groups and computers, and conversely as individuals interacting with large groups through natural computer interfaces. Through these experiments, we investigate cases where user is part of the crowd, or is interacting with a crowd. We believe such a "crowd shape" can be a helpful method for groups of users to coordinate their actions or for individuals and automated systems to monitor and

© Springer International Publishing Switzerland 2015
M. Kurosu (Ed.): Human-Computer Interaction, Part II, HCII 2015, LNCS 9170, pp. 775–786, 2015.
DOI: 10.1007/978-3-319-20916-6_71

react to crowds, especially if we can successfully associate certain crowd features such as mood or energy to the shape.

In our experiments we focus specifically on how the visual feedback and display of a crowd can effect participation effectiveness, pleasantness, ease-of-use and suitability through the use of three objective-based exercises grouped into two different experiment phases: *Ball-catch and Pattern-Match* for exploring multiple users collaborating together using crowd shapes, and *Swarm-Chase* for exploring how individuals view and react to a crowd shape. These exercises were built to be "continuously variable and socially familiar" [7] with a group-dependent nature to reduce the social embarrassment factor [2], while also utilizing Reality-Based Interaction themes such as "Naïve Physics" and "Body Awareness Skills" to greatly reduce the gulf of execution for participants [4]. Our results, though inherently noisy, suggest that there is a significant difference between the three different crowd shapes used, and furthermore that the difference is focused on crowd shapes that reflect some feedback as to the individuals positioning in both the Precise and Combined shapes.

In Sect. 2, some related work will be reviewed. Section 3 introduces our crowd visualization methods, and Sects. 4 and 5 will discuss the experiment design and results. Some concluding remarks will be presented in Sect. 6.

2 Related Work

In the literature of social psychology and collective behavior, a group or crowd can act as a unique entity. A great example of this comes from Baarkhuus et al's "Cheering Meter" where it was cited that "as soon as approximately 25 % of the audience is applauding, the applause quickly cascades to 100 %" [1]. In this section we will overview the research done thus far with a selection of projects that focus on crowd interaction. To remain identifiably different from the many types of interactive installations we will focus on projects where many individuals act as a "crowd" in which the group displays an "illusion of unanimity" [9] as they complete collaborative objectives.

2.1 Cheering Meter

Researchers Barkhuus and Jorgensen created a sound-monitoring system that was manually controlled to receive and measure the amplitude (volume) of the sound generated by a crowd of spectators for rap-battles. This is to determine which of the rap-battle performers received the loudest cheers, and thus arguably the victor of the rap-battle itself [1]. The audience as a crowd is significant as "many crowds are formed as audiences" [3].

By cheering with a large number of others there was no real opportunity for one to see their own or others' individual output; though individuals did express "joy over being part of the concert" [1]. It should be noted that this could also be a weakness in crowd-computer interactions – the difficulty of seeing your own contribution and receiving individual feedback. Also the cheering meter was lauded by its researchers for its ability to enhance the performance rather that detract from it [1].

2.2   Crowd Collaborative Collective Games

Dan Maynes-Aminzade, Randy Pausch, and Steve Seitz, inspired by a crowd-controlled game at SIGGRAPH in 1991, created: "Audience Movement Tracking", "Beach Ball Shadows", and "Laser Pointer Tracking." Audience Movement Tracking is a game that allowed a crowd to control a paddle's left and right movements in a Pong-type game by leaning left or right in concert. Beach Ball Shadows uses the shadow of a beach ball hit into the air by a crowd cast to deflect missiles from hitting the virtual cities on the ground in a Missile Command type game. Laser Pointing Tracking consists of several games that track many individual laser pointers in the crowd to interact with a projected image. Specific uses of this technology are a "scratching game" that tracks laser pointers to scratch and reveal a hidden image (like a scratch and win lotto card), a graffiti wall that allows multiple coloured lines to be drawn simultaneously, and a whack-a-mole type game that required laser pointers to "catch the moles" [5].

Over the eight months, they tested these games on crowds ranging from 150–600 students. Through observations and short surveys completed afterwards by the college-level students, the developed several principles of system design and social factors, such as "focus on the activity not the game, not required to sense every participant, make the control obvious, play to emotional sensibilities of the crowd, and facilitate collaboration between participants" [5].

Taking in the principles recorded by researchers Maynes-Aminzade, Pausch, and Seitz above, we start to see a crowd-computer interactional framework form, remarking that in crowd-computer interactions it is most important that everyone feels involved even if the technology does not always allow them to be.

2.3   Urban Screen Game

Within three UK cities, researchers Kenton O'Hara, Maxine Glancy, and Simon Robertshaw created a camera and projection based collaborative game called "The Red Nose Game" [6]. Each of the three "Big BBC Screens" high above a public space features a camera image of the area directly below it. Superimposed on the camera image are several red blobs. As people walk into the camera image on the projection their bodies are tracked and are able to push around the red blobs into each other so that they combine, ultimately all combining into one large blob. When all are combined together a point is scored and the game is then restarted [6].

Crowd computer interaction is difficult. In the Red Nose and Lecture Clicker studies researchers made sure that all participants could interact; whereas when the crowd became too large, in the case of the 600 persons classrooms of the Collaborative Games study, the Cheering Meter, and with the "large modes" of the Light beyond the Edges study, the interaction became much more subtle and was based upon the collective body as opposed to the culmination of each of the individuals interactions. Do all participants feel connected to the interaction when acting as a collective body? And if they do not, is it really that important as the interaction, as in the case of the cheering meter, is merely enhancing their experience of another event (the rap-battle in this case)? Also we must consider the use of technology in crowd-computer interactions. In this sense, we find that most researchers use cameras and image processing software such as computer vision tools to help remove the technology from the hands of the participants and instead rely on more "natural interaction modes" such as voice and the "body awareness skills" [4]. This would make sense as Natural Interfaces do lower the gulf of execution, "the gap between a user's goals for action and the means to execute those actions" [4].

3 Crowd Visualization

In both of our experiment phases, we explore three types of crowd visualization. Specifically the *Blobby* shape, the *Precise* shape, and the *Combined* shape, as shown in Fig. 1. While the Precise shape represents a typical view of the crowd with emphasis on individuals, the Blobby shape aims at visualizing the crowd as a single entity. Such visualization may potentially help viewers understand and interact with crowd as a single element instead of focusing on individual movements. Our primary research hypothesis is that using, or adding such visualization will help improve interaction when individual movements are less important than collective actions, and/or when a collective and overall shape can provide a better way of understanding and tracking movement.

Two different methods have been used to create these three types of visualization: using Kinect2 3D sensor, and using regular 2D webcams. The first method was more precise but could only be used for groups of up to six users, i.e. small crowd. This was the case in two of our research experiments that involved participants acting as a member of group. The second phase of experiments involved participants interacting with a large crowd "from outside" and the second method of creating visualization was utilized in that case.

The Precise shape represents the unique silhouettes of each participants, each coloured a different colour to better represent each individual. This is accomplished by tracking each individual participant using the Kinect2 for Windows 3D depth camera [17] which we found was much less noisy than using a web camera and computer vision libraries such as OpenCV [14]. For our Blobby shape we took all participant user silhouettes and combined them into a single texture we could then apply various per-pixel filters onto such as a blur, erode, dilate, and finally a threshold until we got a very rough

Fig. 1. The three shape types used within this experiment, as visualized during the Ball-Catch exercise. From left to right, Precise, Blobby, and precise/blobby (combined).

approximation of the participants. For the Combined shape, we layered the precise silhouettes onto the Blobby shape. This method was used in Ball-Catch and Pattern-Match experimental games where participants were part of a relatively small crowd.

For the second experiment phase involving the Swarm Chase game we used a slightly different method. As we wanted to simulate a much larger crowd of 30 participants we wanted to create an application that would more likely resemble the sort of application that would be used for actual crowd-computer interactions. Because of the six user tracking limit, and relatively short range, of the Kinect2 we decided to use a colour camera in this case – a PS3 Eye camera noted for its low cost and high quality image.

To track the participant we used an OpenCV face-tracking algorithm, smoothed with a Kalman filter for predictive tracking [14]. We decided that we only needed to track the face of a participant as we could assume they would be facing the screen (and thus also a well positioned camera). Experiments training our own head-tracking algorithm were far too slow to be used in real-time; and deemed unnecessary for one participant. For the Precise shape we merely displayed a green person graphic where the participants position was determined, and the crowd was a 2D point cloud that moved together using variations of Craig Reynolds steering behaviours [19]. Each point was displayed as a salmon-coloured person graphic. For the Blobby shape we took the crowd point cloud and connected each into triangles using Delaunay Triangulation [16] to form a polygon which we could then draw into an OpenGL framebuffer object and blur using pixel/fragment shaders. Again, for the Combined visualization, we layered the Precise shape onto the Blobby shape (please see Fig. 1, farthest right image).

4   Experiment Design

The fundamental idea behind this research was that visualization through appropriate crowd shape can improve the users' performance in systems with large number of concurrent users. In order to verify this hypothesis, we started by developing three possible crowd shapes as described in Sect. 3. These shapes represent two possible approaches to visualizing crowds: individual and collective. Our initial pilot tests showed that users can potentially be interested in both of these approaches so we introduced a third "combined" option that we hypothesized will be associated with the best performance.

Once the possible visualizations have been determined, we designed two sets of experiments that demonstrate possible forms of crowd interaction: participating as part of the crowd, and participating against a crowd. First, we explored how several participants work together as a group (in this case 5–6 participants), creating the "illusion of anonymity" [9], to interact with a large screen in two objective-based forms; and secondly an additional experiment that explores how an individual reacts to a crowd shape without the added noise of an actual crowd present – instead focusing on the shape itself, generated from a simulated crowd and crowd movement. Overall we ran three experiments, two for the first "group" phase (*Ball-Catch* and *Pattern-Match*) and one for the second "individual" phase (*Swarm-Chase*).

At the end of each experiment we gave each participant a questionnaire to fill out that asked them to rate on a *7-point Likert scale*, chosen for greater variance, how

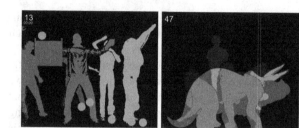

Fig. 2. The three "games" developed for testing the roles of shape in crowd-computer interactions. From left to right we have Ball-Catch where balls falling from the top had to bounced into a virtual basket within 30 s, Pattern-Match, where a score was displayed signifying how closely the participants crowd shape matched the stegosaurus silhouette, and Swarm-Chase where participants were asked to avoid a simulated crowd wandering.

strongly they felt about experience across four dimensions: *Effectiveness*, *Pleasantness*, *Ease-of-Use*, and *Suitability*. Our pilot studies very closely aligned with our final experiments; and helped to point out some bugs in the code as well as determine that in order to reduce learning bias towards trials ran after previous trials we had to run the experiments in different orders for each group/participant. We were also able to better focus our questionnaires with better descriptions, and even images in Swarm Chase, to help understanding.

Each program was developed using Cinder Frameworks [12], a C++ and OpenGL coding framework, running on a PC to be displayed on a large 54″ TV and using a Kinect2 for Windows depth camera and SDK [17] for the first two experiments; and a PS3 Eye camera and the OpenCV C-based library for live image processing and facial detection [14] for the last experiment, Swarm-Chase (Fig. 2).

And after each trial was completed, the score was noted (if appropriate), and each participant was asked to fill out the same 7-point Likert scale questionnaire that rated each crowd shape's effectiveness, pleasantness, ease-of-use, and suitability during the experiment, as well as any additional comments. The results of these tests can be found in Sect. 5.

Ball-Catch was developed to test a group's ability to work together to form an optimal shape for collecting falling circles into a basket on the screen. The shape that would provide a platform for the circles to collide and collect upon was the crowd shape itself; and each group was given 30 s to collect as many balls into the basket as possible.

For Ball-Catch each group of 5–6 members would stand in front of a large 54″ screen that displayed the crowd-shape and game, and a Kinect for Windows version 2 depth camera that allowed us to capture and track each users silhouette so that we could colour each uniquely for the Precise shape trial.

Pattern-Match was the second experiment of the multi-user phase that asked participants to use their crowd-shape displayed on the screen to match another shape displayed on the screen in front of them (the silhouette of a stegosaurus). Each group of 5–6 was given as much time as required to try and get the highest score possible for each of the three crowd-shape types (score is a number from 1–100 that reflects how closely the groups' crowd shape matches the stegosaurus shape, 1 being no intersection at all to 100 a perfect fit).

Swarm-Chase was developed as a mirror of the interactions we were studying in the first phase of experiments with groups of participants for Ball-Catch and Pattern-Match. Instead of studying how a group of people interact together, we created an application that allowed us to explore how an individual can react and relate to a crowd displayed on the screen as one of the three crowd-shapes. In this particular case, using flocking algorithms [15], we simulated the movement of a crowd of thirty salmon-coloured people moving around on a large projected display; and using facial detection to track the participant as a green-coloured person that could move around the display by moving side to side and up and down when facing towards the screen. In this sense we were hoping to capture the type of full body interaction we would expect in an actual crowd interaction.

Their objective was simply to avoid the crowd as they randomly moved together across the screen, which the researcher could subtly control by setting points of interest so that the crowd was always moving close and/or towards the participants avatar on the screen. For each trial we spent about 30 s having the participant actively avoid the crowd for each crowd-shape type presented.

5   Experimental Results

The first phase of experiments included 3 groups of 6-5-6 members, giving us 17 participants in total for "group" part. In the "individual" part, Swarm-Chase, we had 20 participants. For both phases we had approximately 67 % males and 33 % females, and most participants were in the process of, or completed, a post-secondary degree. Ages for the first phase were almost completely within the range of 18–24 (predominantly university students) while the second phase expanded to include most of its participants within the ages of 18–34 (predominantly university students and young secondary school teachers), with 22 % ages 35–54 and another 22 % 55+. Computer expertise was slightly higher in the lower age groups. It should be noted that in the Swarm-Chase two participants' data were removed as the questionnaires were filled incorrectly and their comments afterwards about "hoping they answered how the researchers would like" suggested a possible Hawthorne effect where they were not answering for themselves [18]. This brought down our sample total for Swarm-Chase from 20 to 18.

5.1   Quantitative Data

Table 1 shows the mean and standard deviation for responses on our evaluation criteria in three experiments.

As these results were obtained from Likert scale data (ranges 1–7) we can only assume that the data is both ordinal and non-normal leading us to analyze them using non-parametric statistical methods [11]. Since we used repeated testing procedures with the same participants to collect the data respective to each of the three crowd shapes (*Blobby*, *Precise*, and *Combined*) across four dimensions (*Effectiveness*, *Pleasantness*,

Table 1. Mean and standard deviation (in brackets) for all evaluation criteria

	Effectiveness	Pleasantness	Ease-of-Use	Suitability
Ball-Catch (n = 17)				
Blobby	4.47 (0.80)	4.71 (1.49)	4.29 (1.36)	4.29 (1.31)
Precise	5.12 (1.45)	5.59 (1.37)	5.12 (1.45)	5.00 (1.66)
Combined	4.94 (1.09)	5.29 (1.36)	5.12 (1.17)	5.41 (1.23)
Pattern-Match (n = 17)				
Blobby	4.35 (1.50)	4.24 (1.60)	4.18 (1.55)	3.71 (2.02)
Precise	5.41 (0.94)	5.82 (1.07)	5.29 (1.65)	5.47 (1.59)
Combined	5.12 (1.11)	5.53 (1.07)	5.29 (1.21)	4.88 (1.36)
Swarm-Chase (n = 18)				
Blobby	5.11 (1.18)	5.06 (1.55)	5.56 (1.38)	5.33 (1.24)
Precise	5.61 (1.14)	5.72 (0.89)	5.89 (0.96)	5.44 (1.25)
Combined	6.00 (1.08)	5.78 (1.06)	6.11 (0.96)	5.72 (1.27)

Table 2. All recorded Friedman P-Values at 0.05 alpha - asymptotic Sig. (2-tailed) with degrees of freedom of 2. Those highlighted represent where we see significant differences between the response data i.e. we reject the null hypothesis that the samples are the same.

	Effectiveness	Pleasantness	Ease-of-Use	Suitability
Ball-Catch (n = 17)	0.118	0.309	0.576	0.341
Pattern-Match (n = 17)	0.021	0.001	0.017	0.028
Swarm-Chase (n = 18)	0.003	0.027	0.05	0.285

Ease-of-Use, and *Suitability*), we used a Asymptotic Sig. (2-tailed) Friedman test to determine if there is significant variance between the crowd-shape response data [11]. The results are shown in Table 2.

After determining where there are differences between the three dependent groups of data we conducted further post hoc testing using the Wilcoxon signed-rank test to determine where the significant differences lie between each pair (*Blobby-Precise, Blobby-Combined*, and/or *Precise-Combined*) [11]. Please see Table 3 for each p-value calculated at alpha 0.05.

In Fig. 3 we can see two examples of the point estimates/pseudo-medians of both Pattern-Match and Swarm-Chases' graphed with their appropriate confidence intervals calculated in R.

Looking at the point estimates in Fig. 3 we can see that there should be some differences between responses and so Wilcoxon signed rank tests were performed on all sets that passed the Friedman test, using a Bonferroni adjustment of the p-value from 0.05 to 0.017 (0.05/3) to determine significance in Table 4.

Looking at our results we see that there are some perceived differences and patterns within the data. We can see that the Friedman test exposes some sample fluctuations in Pattern-Match and Swarm-Chase across all four dimensions, with the exception of suitability in Swarm-Chase.

Table 3. As the Friedman and Wilcoxon test medians this table presents all the point estimates (pseudo medians), consistent with the Wilconox test. We ignore Ball-Catch as there were no significant differences detected by the Friedman test.

	Effectiveness	Pleasantness	Ease-of-Use	Suitability
Pattern-Match (n = 17)				
Blobby	4.5	4.0	4.5	4.0
Precise	5.5	6.0	5.5	5.5
Combined	5.0	5.5	5.5	5.0
Swarm-Chase (n = 18)				
Blobby	5.0	5.0	5.5	5.5
Precise	5.5	5.5	6.0	6.0
Combined	6.0	6.0	6.0	6.0

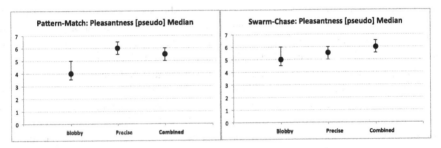

Fig. 3. Visualized here are the point estimates (pseudo medians) and confidence intervals consistent with the Wilcoxon signed-rank test that show possible differences between the Blobby, Precise, and Combined shapes for the pleasantness response for the Pattern-Match (left) and Swarm-Chase (right) experiments.

Table 4. All Wilcoxon signed-rank tests on data pairs for each game type (except Ball-Catch as no Friedman significance detected). If significant i.e. $p < 0.017$ (via Bonferroni adjustment) then the cell will be highlighted.

	Effectiveness	Pleasantness	Ease-of-Use	Suitability
Pattern-Match (n = 17)				
Blobby-Precise	0.042	0.003	0.03	0.014
Blobby-Combined	0.028	0.001	0.004	0.012
Precise-Combined	0.34	0.26	1	0.142
Swarm-Chase (n = 18)				
Blobby-Precise	0.075	0.085	0.222	0.642
Blobby-Combined	0.002	0.015	0.026	0.107
Precise-Combined	0.052	0.862	0.234	0.132

Within Pattern-Match we can see that after the Friedman tests expose differences within the samples, that using Wilcoxon post hoc tests, show the differences tend to lie between the Blobby and Combined shapes for both Pleasantness, Ease-of-Use, and Suitability. Interestingly the Combined shape is considered more pleasant, more easy-to-use, and more suitable than the Blobby shape in Pattern-Match. We can also see that the Precise shape is rated higher than Blobby in both Pleasantness and Suitability. We can see this result echoed in Swarm-Chase where the significant differences within the sample lie between the Blobby and Combined shapes in both Effectiveness and Pleasantness. In Swarm-Chase the Combined shape is deemed both more effective and pleasant.

5.2   Comment Data

Overall we observed that participants seem to enjoy themselves during the crowd-based games: Ball-catch and Pattern-Match. Ball-Catch did seem to incite more critiques about the technology in the comments where we found 7 unique mentions of lagginess or low framerate; and during play the "slowness" was often attributed as an issue to enjoyment and objective particularly when using the Combined shape.

Also, participants seem to generally prefer a shape that had the Precise or "people" shapes present, as there were positive reflections (comments that use wording such as "prefer", "liked", or "best") within the comment sections about both the Precise and Combined shapes; though interestingly none about the Blobby shape exclusively. Additionally, when looking through the data we do see references to participants enjoying the combined aspect, but critiquing its size, with comments such as it "was easier to get the approximate shape but the blob outline was too large", "method was pretty good but maybe make the Blobby shape a bit smaller", "Best. Would be nice to have a less wide shape", "Overall I found it best", and interestingly "favourite b/c I could see the 'people' and the boundaries …".

Participants also came across as quite interested in the interaction as many suggested possible changes to the shapes and to the game itself with 26 mentions of changes to make the game(s) better and 42 mentions of how to make the shapes better within the comments section, focusing on the Blobby shape in particular as a source of ambiguous visual design: In the comments we see sentiments of this where the Blobby shape was mentioned as showing "little information on what the blob represents", "not resembling much different human beings", needed "more stimuli to represent the crowd", and "hard to distinguish who is where". Fortunately, only 3 comments were made about how either the shape or exercise was confusing.

6   Discussion

Looking at the results, we can see that the Blobby Shape seems less effective, less pleasant, less easy-to-use and less suitable than the Combined shape in all areas we determine there is significance in Pattern-Match and Swarm-Chase. Additionally, we can see that the Precise shape is also determined to be more effective, pleasant, easy-to-use, and suitable than the Blobby shape as well. There is no significant difference detected between the Precise and Combined shapes, although the median graphs of the Combined and Precise shape seem to have differences that suggest the Combined shape is generally preferred; and the comments received also seem to suggest this same preference for the Combined shape. Future studies would likely best focus here with larger sample sizes.

This follows well that participants would better enjoy experiences where they are not presented with merely an abstract shape but a shape they can recognize as a group of persons. Wanting to see themselves in the shape is not too surprising as Snibbe et al. write of the power of shadows is user experiences [7] and one reality-based user interfaces main principles concerning "body awareness" [4]. Even in much larger groups our participants seemed much more comfortable with having some sort of visual feedback representing where they are, and where they are relative to others.

As for why Ball-Catch experiment showed no significant differences, we would likely hypothesize it is a combination of the difficulties in becoming more comfortable with the interaction as all three groups started the experiment with that interaction, as well as technological issues where many of the comments mentioned the low framerate, of the Combined shape particularly, being a deterrent to their enjoyment and usability of the experience.

7 Conclusion

In this paper, we have presented three potential methods for visualizing a crowd, and also the research results on their usability. We feel that these experiments help expose how important individual feedback still is, even in crowd interactions - that participants still strongly want to see how they contribute to the whole. Furthermore, though the results are not strong enough to conclusively state that the combined Precise and Blobby shape is the preferred shape of the three, for dynamic crowd-computer interactions we feel with further tests and larger sample sizes that this would likely be the case as individual feedback is important; but also is a more approximate or "blobby" understanding of the interaction of the entire crowd on its surrounding environment.

Acknowledgments. This research is supported by Social Science and Humanities Research Council of Canada through IMMERSE Research Network.

References

1. Barkhuus, L., Jorgensen, T.: Engaging the crowd – studies of audience-performer interaction. In: CHI 2008, pp 2925–2930 (2008)
2. Brignull, H., Rogers, Y.: Enticing people to interact with large public displays in public spaces. In: Proceedings of INTERACT 2003, Switzerland, pp. 17–24, 1–5 September 2003
3. Brown, B., O'Hara, K., Kindberg, T., Williams, A.: Crowd computer interaction. In: Proceedings of the 27th International Conference Extended Abstracts on Human Factors in Computing Systems, pp. 4755–4758. ACM, April 2009

4. Jacob, R.J.K., Girouard, A., Hirshfield, L.M., Horn, M.S., Shaer, O., Solovey, E.T., Zigelbaum, J.: Reality-based interaction: a framework for post-WIMP interfaces. In: Proceeding of the Twenty-Sixth Annual SIGCHI Conference on Human Factors in Computing Systems (CHI 2008), pp. 201–210. ACM, New York (2008)
5. Maynes-Aminzade, D., Pausch, R., Seitz, S.: Techniques for interactive audience participation. In: Proceedings of the 4th IEEE International Conference on Multimodal Interfaces, p. 15. IEEE Computer Society, October 2002
6. O'Hara, K., Glancy, M., Robertshaw, S.: Understanding collective play in an urban screen game. In: Proceedings of the 2008 ACM Conference on Computer Supported Cooperative Work ACM, pp. 67–76, November 2008
7. Snibbe, S.S., Raffle, H.S.: Social immersive media: pursuing best practices for multi-user interactive camera/projector exhibits. In: Proceedings of the 27th International Conference on Human Factors in Computing Systems, pp. 1447–1456. ACM, April 2009
8. Tang, A., Finke, M., Blackstock, Y., Leung, R., Deutscher, M., Lea, R.: Designing for bystanders: reflections on building a public digital forum. In: Proceeding of the Twenty-Sixth Annual SIGCHI Conference on Human Factors in Computing Systems, Florence, Italy, 05–10 April 2008
9. Turner, R., Killian, L.M.: Collective Behavior. Prentice Hall, NJ (1972)
10. Reynolds, C.W.: Steering behaviors for autonomous characters. In: Game Developers Conference 1999, pp. 763–782, March 1999
11. Gibbons, J.D., Chakraborti, S.: Nonparametric Statistical Inference, 5th edn. Chapman & Hall/CRC Press, Boca Raton. e Universe of Creative Coding, Explained in Five Minutes (2011). http://createdigitalmotion.com/2013/01/awesome-universe-of-creative-coding-explained-in-five-minutes-video/. Accessed 1 January 2015
12. Turner, R., Killian, L.M.: Collective Behavior, 2nd edn. Prentice- Hall, Englewood Cliffs (1972)
13. OpenCV (n.d.). http://opencv.org/. Accessed 1 January 2015
14. Reynolds, C.W.: Steering behaviors for autonomous characters. In: Game Developers Conference, vol. 1999, pp. 763–782, March 1999
15. Bourke, P.: Efficient triangulation algorithm suitable for terrain modelling. In: Pan Pacific Computer Conference, Beijing, China (1989)
16. Kinect for Windows (n.d.). http://www.microsoft.com/en-us/kinectforwindows/. Accessed 1 January 2015
17. McCarney, R., Warner, J., Iliffe, S., van Haselen, R., Griffin, M., Fisher, P.: The Hawthorne effect: a randomised, controlled trial. BMC Med. Res. Methodol. 7(1), 30 (2007)

COLUMN: Discovering the User Invented Behaviors Through the Interpersonal Coordination

Yasutaka Takeda, Shotaro Baba, P. Ravindra S. De Silva,
and Michio Okada[✉]

Interactions and Communication Design Lab,
Toyohashi University of Technology, Toyohashi 441-8580, Japan
{takeda,baba}@icd.cs.tut.ac.jp
{ravi,okada}@tut.jp
http://www.icd.cs.tut.ac.jp/en/profile.html

Abstract. We developed soccer ball-shaped interactive artifacts (COL-UMN) consisting of eight modules that are connected to twelve servomotors. Our motivation is to explore a variety of a robot's body configuration for rolling behaviors which are invented by three user's coordination. In the interaction, COLUMN becomes a social mediator to prompt the connectivity of the users. We explore how and what are the effects when a robot become a social mediator and investigate the conflict rates and interpersonal coordination of the users. Finally, we discover different body configuration patterns (sequences) from the user's connectivity in each group. Each sequence of body configurations are directed to extract essential parameters to the rolling behaviors.

Keywords: Social mediator · Interpersonal coordination · Visually-mediated connectedness · COLUMN

1 Introduction

We all had have the experience of seeing people walk on the street or playground with their dog as part of their daily exercise for both the person and the dog, and as a kind of companionship for the walker. During the walk, the dog often appears as the stimulus in initiating an experience with some unknown or known person who is willing to talk to the owner, as they mostly have to question how to initiate their conversation in an appropriate-way. In this context, their conversation mostly starts on the topic of their dogs and afterwards smoothly strengthens their relationship toward the topics. The above scenario can be convincing in showing that the dog plays a vital role as a social mediator to establish the conversation between the people. All of the above instances directed at an animal, people, object (e.g., TV), etc., can be turned into a social mediator to establish interactions among the people.

© Springer International Publishing Switzerland 2015
M. Kurosu (Ed.): Human-Computer Interaction, Part II, HCII 2015, LNCS 9170, pp. 787–796, 2015.
DOI: 10.1007/978-3-319-20916-6_72

Fig. 1. Appearance of the COLUMN

Following the above manners, HRI community has been exploring how robot can become social mediators for children with special needs (autism) to enhance their social interaction by investigating a variety of collaborative (with caregiver or teacher, parent ect) play [1,2]. The play scenarios were designed by centralizing the robot-based interaction which comport as social mediator to the context while grounding the communicative connective among the children, teacher/caregiver, and parent [3,4]. All of the above terminations indicate the usage of the robot as social mediator [5,6].

In contrast to the above approach, strategically we can utilize a robot as a social mediator to connect the users while establishing the co-action in order to extract patterns of dynamic connectives of the users [7,8]. Moreover, our motivation is to explore how a social mediator can be utilized to discover a variety of behavior patterns (Exploring the user's connectivities) with essential parameters of unique artifacts call COLUMN.

The COLUMN is a soccer ball-shaped interactive artifact consisting of eight modules that are connected to the twelve servomotors. We can transfer the COLUMN body shape by moving the actuators with modules, and these actuators can be controlled by a wireless communicator called a "COLUMN Gear". Each of the users (three participants) can control the 4 servo-motors of the COLUMN, and a user can swing the COLUMN gear to change its body shape (transfer its modules). In this study, three users have to move the COLUMN from the starting position to the end point by coordinating their interactions (changing the shape of the COLUMN) [9].

During the defined interaction, interesting encounters will emerge; how does a robot become a social mediator (through visual perception, verbal and non-verbal communication, etc.)? What are the reciprocal coordinations (interpersonal) between users, where the people start to coordinate their actions? etc., [10,11]. By answering a combination of the above questions, it might lead to determine the robust approach to generate the artifact's behaviors/motions.

Initially, users have to realize which channel or media (communicative) is mostly used to distribute the information to ground their joint efforts (coordination); visual information (shape of the robot), and kinematic information is used (by combining the perpetual information of swing acceleration and shape of the robot), etc. It might possible to employ both or either communicative channel or media. Even initially they do not have an idea how individuals do their actions (swing), how/when they need to coordinate with the partner, how individual adapt to the partner, and how/when the individual switches the coordination etc. [12].

In this case, all that might be represented is one's own action part ("ME"), the fact that someone will take care of another action part ("Y") required to achieve the joint goal, and the joint action goal (ME +Y) achieved by combining the individual action parts. Therefore, during this process each of them has to coordinate with each other while adapting to their own action (swing interaction) under real-time constraints [10,13]. In addition, when the user experiences with several interactive sessions, they can predict the partner's action (time constrain of the swing), who controls the shape (vertical, horizontal, etc.) of the COLUMN, and also when is the best time to afford one's own contribution, etc. We can define the above users' connection as an interpersonal coordination, and with experience in interactive sessions, the users enhance their action (swing interaction) synchronization toward obtaining the COLUMN's rolling behaviors. Therefore, the motivation of our study is to extract the patterns of user's interpersonal coordination when establishing the COLUMN as a social mediator. It is also interesting to explore how these patterns lead to imagine behavior for an artifact which has different degree of freedom of its body than the existing.

2 Designing Architecture of the COLUMN

The artifact becomes a cubic when servo-motors extend their motors with maximum intensity. The modules (eight) are situated at the corners of the cubic, and each module is designed for gibing with other modules. The cross-section of the module where other modules are fit is cut at a tilt for avoiding interfering with other modules. Because of absorbing the frame distortion by using the ball-shaped moving part of joint, the COLUMN is protected from damage. The modules are made of artificial wood (chemical wood) and are moderately hard but lightweight. We used AX-12+ for the servo-motors, which are small-scale but high-powered and used mainly for the self-produced robot. The electrical circuit of the COLUMN is specialized for controlling AX-12+. AX12+ servomotors connect to a ZigBee wireless communication module via a microcomputer. We can transfer the COLUMN body shape by moving the actuators with the modules, and these actuators can be controlled by a wireless communicator called a "Column Gear". The acceleration of swing (each of the users) map to change the degree of the servo motors; changing the body shape of the COLUMN is proportional to acceleration of the swing (Fig. 1). The COLUMN gear is a spherical-shape device that is 50 mm in diameter with a weight of 50 gms, and is comfortable to grasp by human hand. The exterior of the column gear is constructed by chemical wood, and it has translucent plastic for penetrating the light of the LED between the exteriors, which indicates the power of the swing.

In this study, three users have to move the COLUMN from a defined starting point to end point (goal). During the interaction, users have terminus to obtain the COLUMN's rolling motion while having to coordinate with others by their swing motion. Since people's coordination is gradually set-up with the desired goal of the users (COLUMN moving from start to end) which indicates that the COLUMN becomes a social mediator by connecting each other through the interactions.

3   Experiment

We have arranged the experiment setup as shown in Fig. 2. Three users have to proceed to the COLUMN from the starting point to goal point by using their swing interaction while coordinating with each other efforts. Within five minutes users have to reach the goal, otherwise, again they have to begin at the starting point. At least each of the groups has to participate in five trials, and the groups also have to undertake more trials if they cannot reach the goal at least once within five trials. The reason for the five-trial setup is that sometimes it is possible for a group to reach to goal with their random swings during the initial trials. Five groups (15 users, aged between 22-24 years old) participated in the experiment and were randomly assigned as members of a group. All of the users had no prior experience about controlling a robot. During the interactions, we gathered the user's swing acceleration, COLUMN degree of freedom, and videos (to obtain the states of rolling and behaviors).

Fig. 2. Image sequences show that during the interaction, one of the groups was rolling the COLUMN through their swing interactions.

4   Results

4.1   COLUMN as a Social Mediator

Initially, our motivation was to encounter any user's connection during the interactions. If we determined any user's connectivity, then the result could ensure the COLUMN became a social mediator for the interactive users.

Figure 3 shows the number of trials (x) against the rolling counts (y) for each group. The figure also indicates when the groups had experience with the interactive sessions (trials), the number of rolling converges between 5-15. In addition, there were fewer number of rolling counts when they successfully reached the final destination (goal-point) except during some trials of $G2$ and $G3$ groups. $G2$ and $G5$ reached the goal-point within 6-7 rolling counts, with an increase of rolling counts (more than 8) indicating that most of the time the COLUMN

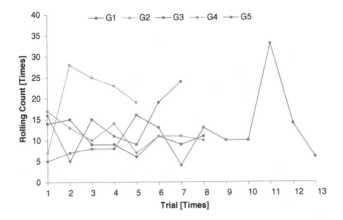

Fig. 3. Figure represents the rolling count in each trial to reach the goal point by considering each of the group. The x-axis represents the trial number and the y-axis represents the number of rolling counts.

moved away from the goal-point (rolling to different directions). $(G1, G4, G5)$ were able to reach the goal after having experience with more than five trials. $G2$ and $G3$ groups accomplished the goal within fewer number of trials, but their rolling counts were higher than those of $G1$, $G4$, and $G5$ groups. Overall the results indicated that when users had interactive experiences, the number of their rolling counts necessary to reach the goal point had decreased. This not have might happen without the establishment of interpersonal coordination among the interactive users.

4.2 Conflict Rates and Interpersonal Coordination

As pointed out, each of the users can control four servo-motors of the COLUMN and can change the shape of the COLUMN (either vertical, horizontal, and diagonal) by using their swing acceleration. According to the mechanism, if users established the smooth coordination for rolling behaviors, then each of the users have to equally contribute with their swing acceleration. If an interactive user increases the swing acceleration parallel to the partner's, then the conflict rate will be quite higher. Oppositely, if we have a lower conflict rate, then there is potential to having cooperation of the users. In our COLUMN mechanism, cooperation of interactions can be determined as interpersonal coordination of the users, because in order to obtain the rolling behaviors of the robot, each of the users has to coordinate their swings in the dynamic interactions.

Our next step is to explore conflict rate of the group by considering the pair of the users in each trial. To estimate the conflict rate of the users, we employed the swing acceleration to the following equation (Eq. 1, where $i, j = 1, 2, 3$) by considering each of the pairs.

$$Conflict_t^{u_i u_j} = Acceleration_t^{u_i} \times Acceleration_t^{u_j} \tag{1}$$

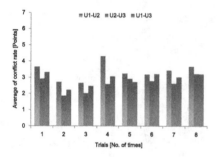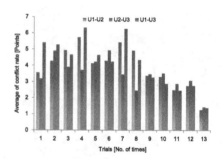

Fig. 4. Figure shows the average conflict rates of each user combinations in each trial for groups $G1$ and $G5$. Here the x-axis represents the trials and the y-axis represents the average conflict rate.

Figure 4 depicted the average conflict rate (x-axis) against the number of trials (y-axis) for group $G1$ and $G5$. In initial trials, every group has higher conflict rates than the later trials of the interactions. Also, the average conflict rate for every pair-combination of the users ($U1 - U2, U2 - U3$, and $U1 - U3$) became approximately equal in the later trials of the interactions. In addition, the conflict rates gradually converged to interval; e.g., in $G1$ it varied between 0-3, and between 0-2.5 for $G2$, etc., and the $G5$ group clearly showed a convergence in the conflict rate.

Table 1. Following table summarizes the user combinations of highest and lowest conflict rates (number of times) by considering the enter trials of the interactions. Here Gi and Uj represent the group number and the user's number, where $i = 1, 2, 3, 4, 5$ and $j = 1, 2, 3$.

Group	Higher conflict rate		Lower conflict rate	
	Combination	Number of times	Combination	Number of times
G1	U1-U2	7	U2-U3	6
G2	U2-U3	3	U1-U2	4
G3	U2-U3	3	U1-U3	4
G4	U1-U3	6	U1-U2	4
	U2-U3	6	U2-U3	4
G5	U1-U3	6	U2-U3	5

Table 1 summarized the higher (number of times within the trials) and lower conflict rates (number of times within the trials) according to the user combination by considering the enter trials for each group. These data showed which user combination had an interpersonal coordination (low conflict rate) in entering trials. Most of the time U1-U2 user combinations of G1 had a higher conflict rate than other user combinations, because the G1 group had eight trials to reach the goal-point, but during seven times U1-U2 had a higher conflict rates than the other groups. However, U2-U3 maintained the interpersonal coordination (lower conflict rate) during six times out of eight trials. These results indicate that during the interaction some users had an interpersonal coordination, while some of them did not possess an interpersonal coordination. A similar kind of interpersonal coordination was established in every group as depicted in Table 1. In the initial trials, most groups did not exhibit an interpersonal coordination among the each user's combinations; however, after having experience with a few trials, the results showed that some of the user's combinations were gradually starting to connect with each other. These kinds of interpersonal coordination disclose the variety of shape changes of the COLUMN to obtain the rolling behaviors.

4.3   Patterns of Body Configuration

We investigated all of the rolling patterns in each trial in each group. First, we explored the trials which had low rolling counts, less differences of acceleration between interactive users, and less conflict rates of each user's combinations. Most of the above conditions were satisfied when users experienced with a number of trials.

We have funded similar kinds of patterns for body configuration which satisfied the above conditions as shown in Fig. 5(left). Figure 5(left) depicted the time (x-axis) against the swing acceleration (y-axis) for $G1$ group at trial 8. Interactive users had an equal (approximately) swing acceleration between each other at the rolling point of the COLUMN, which implies less conflict among each user's combinations. In this pattern, we explored the statues of the machine (degrees of freedom) and swing acceleration of the users (Table 2). To obtain the rolling behaviors, users have to switch the COLUMN degrees of freedom as $100[deg]$, $135[deg]$, and $180[deg]$, and the swing acceleration as $(low, low, high)$, $(log, high, middle)$, and $(low, high, middle)$ at starting, rolling, and finish stages.

In the second stage, we explored a variety of body configurations when two users have higher conflict rates. The reason for the investigation is sometimes even when the user has higher conflict rates, it s still possible to obtain different body configurations of the robot to obtain the rolling behaviors. However, random users' connectivity might obtain these patterns, which would most likely

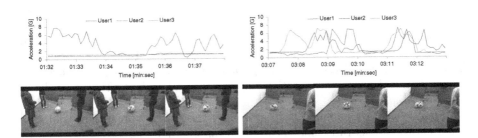

Fig. 5. Figure shows the discovered body configuration pattern in the 8th trial of group G1. All user combinations have a low-conflict rate at rolling behavior (Figure(left)). All user combinations having higher conflict rate at rolling behavior in trial 2 of group G5 (Figure(right)). Here the x-axis represented the time and y-axis represented conflict rate.

Table 2. Table depicts the switching sequences of COLUMN degree of freedom and swing acceleration in the discovered robot body configurations.

Group-Trial	Conflict	Time Features	Machine status	User	Acceleration
G1-T8	No conflict	Start	120[deg]	U1	Low
				U2	Low
				U3	Low
		Rolling	135[deg]	U1	High
				U2	Low
				U3	Low
		Finish	180[deg]	U1	Middle
				U2	Low
				U3	Low
G5-T1	U2-U3 conflicted	Start	100[deg]	U1	Low
				U2	Low
				U3	High
		Rolling	135[deg]	U1	Low
				U2	High
				U3	Middle
		Finish	180[deg]	U1	Low
				U2	High
				U3	Low
G5-T2	U1-U2-U3 conflicted	Start	110[deg]	U1	Low
				U2	Low
				U3	Middle
		Rolling	135[deg]	U1	Middle
				U2	Middle
				U3	Middle
		Finish	180[deg]	U1	High
				U2	Low
				U3	Low

occur during the initial trial of the interactions. After exploring the variety of patterns, we found that $G5$ at trial 1 has unique body configurations to obtain the robot's rolling behaviors (Table 2). As shown in Table 2, $U2$ and $U3$ have dissimilar swing accelerations which was affected by obtaining the conflict between users $U2$ and $U3$ at the statues of rolling, as shown in Table 2. According to Table 2, the degree of the body configuration shifted to 100[deg], 135[deg], and 180[deg], and the swing acceleration shifted to ($low, low, high$), ($low, high, low$), and ($low, high, low$).

Finally, we have explored the patterns of the body configuration trial that has different conflict rates among three users as shown in Fig. 5(right). Evidently, Fig. 5(right) shows that three users had considerable differences in their swing accelerations, which was effected by having the conflict rate between every user combinations. As shown in Table 2, the extracted body configuration patterns had

110[deg], 135[deg], and 180[deg] shifting degrees of freedom, and (low, low, low), (high, low, low), and (middle, low, low) switching accelerations between the users.

We have found the above three kinds of patterns of the body configuration of the COLUMN to obtain the rolling motions. Each of the patterns has different switching degree of freedom and swing accelerations. According to the results, less rolling counts, less swing acceleration differences, and less conflict rate conditions were directed by the smooth rolling patterns, and these kinds of patterns were obtained when the users had long term interactions. This might be obtained when a user became an expert in the task. But a user's unconscious (random) connectivity was also directed toward obtaining different patterns of the body configuration, with this pattern mostly obtained at the initial trial of the interactions, which can be posited as a weak connectivity of the users (beginners) with less experience on the task.

5   Discussion

The results showed that the defined interactive scenario was motivated by connecting the interactive users, which indicated the powerfulness of the COLUMN as a social mediator. However, initially most of the groups have spent considerable rolling counts to reach to the goal. The intended direction of the COLUMN rolling was away from the goal (random rolling); but after experience with several interactive sessions, the groups had fewer rolling counts. This might occur when the user understood the rolling mechanism of the COLUMN, and coordinated with each other, etc. The reduction of the rolling count provides some indication of the user connectivity around the COLUMN.

In reality, rolling behaviors can be obtained in two different circumstances: rolling behaviors can be obtained through the exact coordination of the users and sometimes through random user's connectivity. Therefore, the conflict rate is a suitable parameter to explore body configurations of the robot in each trial by considering the groups. To explore these patterns, we initially have to consider the trials which have less conflict rate among three users' combination (approximately zero), two user combination having conflict rate, and finally all of the user combinations having different conflict rates.

As depicted in Fig. 5 and Table 2, we found three kind of rolling patterns. However, when all user combinations have less conflict rates (all users were well connected), we found only one pattern of body configuration for rolling behaviors. But we found two kinds of body configuration patterns when at least one user combination had a significant conflict rate. The important summary of the beginning study is depicted in Table 2; however, Table 2 depicts the status of the COLUMN (degree of freedom) and swing acceleration for the extracted three patterns of the robot body configuration. The results indicate useful low-level features for a robot to obtain the rolling behaviors in different patterns of body configuration. Thus, we can consider these kinds of sequential switching for body configuration and swing acceleration (power of servo motors) to propose an automotive behavior generation mechanism by considering the above patterns and low-level features.

6 Conclusion and Future Works

In this study, we explored a variety of COLUMN body configurations which were invented by users. Those patterns were extracted by investigating the user's connectivity in the interactions. We can map the extracted body configuration into low-level features as degree of freedom and power of the servo motors. Therefore, our future work is to utilize the extracted body configuration patterns with low-level features to attain self-automation behaviors for COLUMN. Also, utilization of social mediator might be thoroughly beneficial to invent a variety of behaviors for this kind of unique artifact.

Acknowledgement. This research has been supported by both Grant-in-Aid for scientific research of KIBAN-B (26280102) and Grant-in-Aid for scientific research for HOUGA (24650053) from the Japan Society for the Promotion of Science (JSPS).

References

1. Papadopoulos, F., Dautenhahn, K., Ho, W.C.: Exploring the use of robots as social mediators in a remote human-human collaborative communication experiment. Paladyn **3**(1), 1–10 (2012)
2. Wong, A., Tan, Y.K., Tay, A., Wong, A., Limbu, D.K., Dung, T.A., Chua, Y., Yow, A.P.: A user trial study to understand play behaviors of autistic children using a social robot. In: Ge, S.S., Khatib, O., Cabibihan, J.-J., Simmons, R., Williams, M.-A. (eds.) ICSR 2012. LNCS, vol. 7621, pp. 76–85. Springer, Heidelberg (2012)
3. Wainer, J., Dautenhahn, K., Robins, B., Amirabdollahian, F.: Collaborating with kaspar: Using an autonomous humanoid robot to foster cooperative dyadic play among children with autism. In: Humanoids, pp. 631–638 (2010)
4. Scassellati, B., Admoni, H., Mataric, M.: Robots for use in autism research. Annu. Rev. Biomed. Eng **14**, 275–294 (2012)
5. Okada, M., Sakamoto, S., Suzuki, N.: Muu: artificial creatures as an embodied interface. In: ACM SIGGRAPH Conference Abstracts and Applications, p. 91 (2000)
6. Tahir, Y., Rasheed, U., Dauwels, S., Dauwels, J.: Perception of humanoid social mediator in two-person dialogs. In: HRI, pp. 300–301 (2014)
7. Marsh, K.L., Johnston, L., Richardson, M.J., Schmidt, R.C.: Toward a radically embodied, embedded social psychology. Eur. J. Soc. Psychol **39**, 1217–1225 (2009)
8. Sebanz, N., Bekkering, H., Knoblich, G.: Joint action: bodies and minds moving together. Trends Cogn. Sci. **10**(2), 70–76 (2006)
9. Takeda, Y., Yoshiike, Y., Silva, R.S.D., Okada, M.: Column: dynamic of interpersonal coordination. In: HRI, pp. 389–390 (2011)
10. Vesper, C., Wel, R., Knoblich, G., Sebanz, N.: Making oneself predictable: reduced temporal variability facilitates joint action coordination. Exp. Brain Res. **211**(3–4), 517–530 (2011)
11. Roberts, M.E., Goldstone, R.L.: Adaptive group coordination and role differentiation. PLoS ONE **6**(7), e22377, 07 (2011)
12. Clark, H.H.: Using Language. Cambridge University Press, Cambridge (1996)
13. Schelling, T.C.: The Strategy of Conflict. Harvard University Press, Cambridge (1996)

Multimodal Interaction Flow Representation for Ubiquitous Environments - MIF: A Case Study in Surgical Navigation Interface Design

Gul Tokdemir[1]([✉]), Gamze Altun[1], Nergiz E. Cagiltay[2],
H. Hakan Maras[1], and Alp Ozgun Borcek[3]

[1] Computer Engineering Department, Cankaya University, Ankara, Turkey
{gtokdemir,hhmaras}@cankaya.edu.tr,
c1371205@student.cankaya.edu.tr
[2] Software Engineering Department, Atilim University, Ankara, Turkey
necagiltay@atilim.edu.tr
[3] Department of Neurosurgery, Gazi University, Ankara, Turkey
alpborcek@gmail.com

Abstract. With the advent of technology, new interaction modalities became available which augmented the system interaction. Even though there are vast amount of applications for the ubiquitous devices like mobile agents, smart glasses and wearable technologies, many of them are hardly preferred by users. The success of those systems is highly dependent on the quality of the interaction design. Moreover, domain specific applications developed for these ubiquitous devices involve detailed domain knowledge which normally IT professionals do not have, which may involve a substantial lack of quality in the services provided. Hence, effective and high quality domain specific applications developed for these ubiquitous devices require significant collaboration of domain experts and IT professionals during the development process. Accordingly, tools to provide common communication medium between domain experts and IT professionals would provide necessary medium for communication. In this study, a new modelling tool for interaction design of ubiquitous devices like mobile agents, wearable devices is proposed which includes different interaction modalities. In order to better understand the effectiveness of this newly proposed design tool, an experimental study is conducted with 11 undergraduate students (novices) and 15 graduate students (experienced) of Computer Engineering Department for evaluating defect detection performance for the defects seeded into the interface design of a neuronavigation device. Results show that the defects were realized as more difficult for the novices and their performance was lower compared to experienced ones. Considering the defect types, wrong information and wrong button type of defects were recognized as more difficult. The results of this study aimed to provide insights for the system designers to better represent the interaction design details and to improve the communication level of IT professionals and the domain experts.

Keywords: Interaction design · Ubiquitous interfaces · Diagrammatic reasoning · Defect detection

© Springer International Publishing Switzerland 2015
M. Kurosu (Ed.): Human-Computer Interaction, Part II, HCII 2015, LNCS 9170, pp. 797–805, 2015.
DOI: 10.1007/978-3-319-20916-6_73

1 Introduction

As diagrams transfer, and leverage knowledge that is essential for solving problems, they can be more powerful than sentential representations depending on the usage [1]. Diagrams provide compressed information; hence, they are very effective in information systems for transferring information between stakeholders of the system.

The ubiquity and real time access feature of mobile agents, smart glasses and wearable technologies provide diverse interaction alternatives to people in different domains. The success of those systems is highly dependent on the quality of the interaction design. Moreover, domain specific applications developed for these ubiquitous devices involves detailed domain knowledge which normally IT professionals do not have, which may involve a substantial lack of quality in the services provided. Hence, effective and high quality domain specific applications developed for these ubiquitous devices require significant collaboration of domain experts and IT professionals during the development process. However, people from different domains have different mind sets and perceptions about the world which could create significant communication problems between them during the system development life cycle.

Hence, tools to provide common communication medium between domain experts and IT professionals would provide necessary medium for communication. There are such tools used for this purpose largely by IT professionals like UML representations which provide several graphical tools like activity, class, and sequence diagrams. They are vastly used by IT professionals for system design in which the main focus if action or the process. Therefore, a design represented by UML for a mobile application or a desktop application may result in the same design which would lack the different interaction modalities like gesture-based controls. To our knowledge, none of the available design diagrams host specific interaction characteristics of the ubiquitous devices.

Hence in this study, first a new modelling tool for interaction design of ubiquitous devices like mobile agents, wearable devices is proposed which includes different interaction modalities which is used to model interface of neuronavigation device interface that is quite critical since is used during the surgery, in operation rooms which imposes several constraints. In order to better understand the effectiveness of this newly proposed design tool, an experimental study is conducted with graduate and undergraduate students of Computer Engineering Department of Cankaya University to better understand the comprehension of the proposed tool. Background section below contains related studies found in the literature, Research Procedure section explains the experiment, Result section analyzes the experiment results and Discussion and Conclusion section talks about the insights gained through this study. The results of this study are expected to provide insights to the researchers, IT professionals and domain experts to improve interface design process of ubiquitous devices.

2 Background

There are several studies aim to improve representation languages which are commonly used in software engineering. Formal languages are a model for software requirements and its specifications but it is not adequate for particular design. On the basis of this idea, several studies have been performed on how representation languages can be used for this purpose. TERMOS [2] is a UML-based formal language that uses graphical scenarios and specifies these scenarios in test and verification activities. This is not a new approach, but the originality of this study is application of scenario-based verification in mobile computing system. TERMOS incorporates three elements that are spatial view, event view and communication events. It specifies properties that are subset of the spatial configuration nodes to taken into account spatial configuration and changes events. For this reason, several scenarios are considered that are: positive requirement, negative requirement and test purpose [2].

Vegard and Aagedal [3] define entity's change of location or possibility of its movement in a framework by extending UML class and activity diagrams. This approach is very close to Grassi et al. [4] modelling, but the big difference from their studies is to include vertical mobility. Also they performed a case study application based on the framework to validate their profile.

On the other hand, many researchers investigate their own representation methods instead of extending or improving existing languages. They revised commonly used GUI objects and presented new GUI notation due to limitation of existing UML and the other languages. These objects allow the designer to design interfaces for software development processes and interact with each other in a composite pattern. Jose and Paternò [6] develop a mobile framework based on jigsaw metaphor for the people who have not any knowledge of development process, to help implementing and executing their own application. Puzzle allows end users to easily explore the framework and create or change their own application according to their requirements. This study purposed that include end user in development process to increase possibility of combination to add innovative view of the applications. However, the aim of the study does intent to overcome existing languages' problems.

Concerning to healthcare software, usability problems have direct effect on patient safety [5] which is even critical for the software employed in operation room embodying several constraints. Therefore, it is important to include healthcare experts in the software development process to ensure usability, quality, effectiveness and efficiency. Effective systems can be established through collaboration of IT and healthcare professionals in development process to ensure the usability goals are met. But this reveals a new problem which is communication gap between expert judgment and IT professionals' knowledge. To overcome this problem there are various studies in IT field such as different modelling and representation guidelines. These methods do not adequately address specific domain and still need improvement. Erturan [7] presented new representation which is called MAFR. MAFR notation consists of composite representation elements. MAFR tool is used in a case study to investigate if the new approach is more preferable than UML representation for both IT and healthcare professionals [7].

Hence, in this study, MIF tool is proposed for modelling ubiquitous environment interaction, based on MAFR. Defects were seeded into the MIF diagram of neuro-navigation device interface design. Then, the defect detection process was analyzed to obtain insights about the cognitive processes of the novice and experienced participants. Mainly, three different types of defects, namely, wrong information (WI), wrong flow (WF) and wrong button (WB) have been seeded into the MIF representations.

The following research question is aimed to be answered is 'Which types of defects (WI, WF, or WB) are easy to detect in MIF representations? Is there a difference in success of defect detection process for novice and experienced participants?

3 Research Procedure

The MAFR tool [7] was proposed for mobile agent interface design to incorporate touch gesture interaction. This study extends MAFR by adding speech, eye and gesture modalities into the interface design.

We have interviewed 2 surgeons to gather their preferences of alternative interaction styles for neuronavigation device. They have stated they cannot use the device affectively during the operation as they couldn't use their hands and have to get the help of nurse to use the touch interface of the system. This causes misunderstandings and waste of time which may create critical situations during the surgery. The MIF representation elements were used to design interface of neuronavigation device interface by the surgeons' input through MIF elements. We have performed an experiment to observe and collect data for defect detection process of novice and experienced participants during MIF diagram review.

The experimental study is conducted with 11 undergraduate students (3rd and 4th year students) and 10 graduate students of Computer Engineering Department of Cankaya University. The MIF element explanations, neuronavigation system interface requirements and experiment design were provided to the participants prior to the experiment.

The interface was designed using MIF and 9 defects of wrong information (WI), wrong button (WB) and wrong flow (WF) were seeded to the diagram (Table 1). During the experiment, the participants were asked to find the defects and report them using the defect detection collection tool as given in Fig. 1.

Table 1. Defect types

ID	Defect in MIF
D01	Wrong information (WI)
D02	Wrong flow (WF)
D03	Wrong button (WB)
D04	Wrong flow (WF)
D05	Wrong flow (WF)
D06	Wrong information (WI)
D07	Wrong button (WB)
D08	Wrong information (WI)
D09	Wrong button (WB)

This tool is used to record the defect explanations, the duration and order of the defects found by participants.

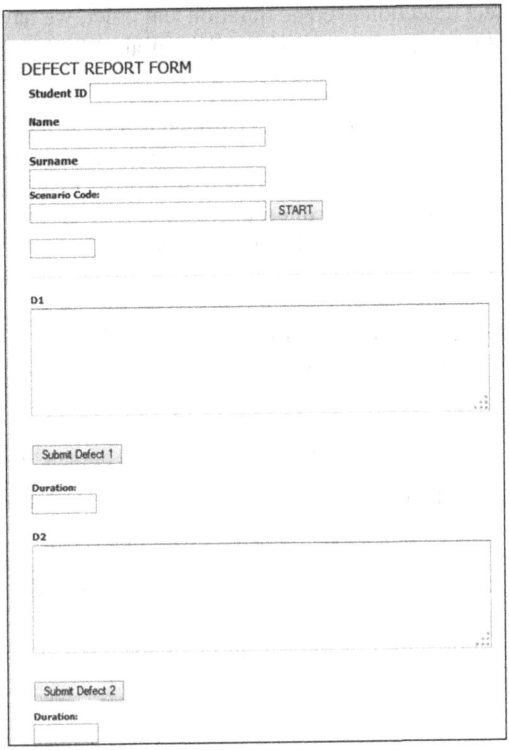

Fig. 1. Defect collection tool

Table 2 depicts the defects seeded into the MIF with their defect types. The defect locations seeded in the MIF diagram can be reached from http://www.cankaya.edu.tr/~gtokdemir/defectlocations.pdf.

Table 2. Defect explanations

Defect	Description	Defect type
D01	"Explanation for the action line to plan screen in Arayuz 1" is wrong	WI
D02	"Arayuz 1 to navigation screen flow direction" is wrong.	WF
D03	Button of Kayit tipi in Arayuz 1.1 is wrong (gesture based)	WB
D04	Flow direction of yontem 1 to Arayuz 2 is wrong	WF
D05	Flow direction of yontem 3 to arayuz 1.1 is wrong	WF
D06	Combobox button which shows the methods (yontemler) in arayuz 2 is wrong	WI
D07	The button of "3B model olustur" is wrong (gesture based)	WB
D08	"Symbol after particular process" between Arayuz 2 to Arayuz 3 is wrong	WI
D09	Button of Kayit tipi in Arayuz 3 is wrong (gesture based)	WB

Based on the defect detection average duration and order, we have calculated defect difficulty of each defect using formula of Cagiltay et al. [8].

$$DF_j = \frac{D_j \bullet O_j}{\dfrac{R_j}{m}}$$

DF_j: Defect detection difficulty level of the jth defect
D_j: Average duration spent by all participants for finding defect j
O_j: Average score of all participants for detecting j^{th} defect
R_j: Number of people who detected defect j
m: Total number of participants

Formula 1. Defect detection difficulty level formula [8].

After calculation of the defect detection difficulty, each participant's performance was calculated through Formula 2.

$$PP_i = \frac{\sum_{j=1}^{n} DF_j}{\sum_{k=1}^{s} DF_k}$$

PP_i: Defect Detection Performance of the ith participant

DF_j: Difficulty level of the jth defect calculated by formula 1

n: Total number of defects detected by participant i

s: Total number of defects seeded in the ERD

Formula 2. Participant's defect detection performance [8].

Additionally, questionnaire was applied to get perceptions of the participants[1].

4   Results

As seen in Table 3, two defects (D06 and D08) were not detected by any participant in the low-experienced group which were both WI type defects. Accordingly, as these defects were never detected, they are considered as hard to detect ones and the sum of D_{fi} values calculated for the other defects for this group (13075) is assigned for those. All defects were detected by the experienced group.

As it is seen from Table 3, average of D_{Fi} values for the experience group (2314) is lower than that of novices (4358) which indicate that, the defects were realized as more difficult for the novices.

There were 11 novice and 10 experienced participants involved in this study. When defect detection performance of the participants are analysed it is clearly seen that, mean value of the novices' performance (24) is lower than that of experienced ones (30) (Table 4).

When defect difficulty levels (D_{Fi}) are analysed according to the defect types, as seen from Table 5, wrong information and wrong button type of defects are recognized as more difficult to detect compared to the wrong flow type of defects.

In the questionnaire, most of the participants from both groups reported that detecting wrong button type of defect was the hardest one which is in parallel with the experimental results. Participants from both groups mostly declared that, using the

---

[1] Available at http://www.cankaya.edu.tr/~gtokdemir/questionnaire.pdf.

Table 3. Defect difficulty levels (D_{Fi})

Defect	Novice	Experienced
D08	13075	4842
D03	3245	3170
D05	1874	2958
D06	13075	2797
D02	189	1854
D09	3386	1824
D01	853	1686
D07	3179	1244
D04	350	450
Average	**4358**	**2314**

Table 4. Defect detection performances of the participants (Ppi)

	Novice	Experienced
	3	2
	7	6
	8	14
	10	18
	12	21
	13	24
	14	31
	29	31
	34	57
	47	96
	82	
Average	**24**	**30**

Table 5. Defect detection types, defect difficulty levels (D_{Fi}) and experience levels of participants.

Defect type	Novice	Experienced	Average
Wrong information	9001	3108	6055
Wrong flow	804	1641	1222
Wrong button	3270	4006	3638

symbols and descriptions about the experimental study helped them to detect the defects easily. They reported that, since the user interface documentation used in the experiment was complex one, recognizing the symbols and buttons was a hard process for them.

5   Discussions and Conclusion

This study proposes an interface design representation for ubiquitous computation including multimodal interactions. In this respect we have extended the MAFR representation [7] which was developed for mobile applications to include mobile agent interactions. The new representation is called "Multimodal Interaction Flow Representation for Ubiquitous Environments- MIF" which includes interactions through mobile agents, smart glasses and wearable technologies in ubiquitous environments.

A case study was performed to assess the comprehension of these diagrams by designing an interface of a neronavigation device through MIF elements used in operation room by collecting surgeons' requirements. This design is used in experimental study to assess defect detection process of participants in reviewing these diagrams. For this purpose interface description of the neuronavigation device, MIF element explanations, experiment setting description were prepared and sent to the participants prior to the experiment to let them get familiar with the context. 9 defects of type wrong information (WI), wrong flow (WF) and wrong button (WB) were seeded to MIF diagram and during the experiment, 21 students of Computer Engineering Department of Cankaya University were asked to review the given defected diagram and find the defects seeded by comparing it with the interface description. During the review process, participants were asked to report the defects they found to record their explanations, order and defect detection duration through a web based tool. Defect detection difficulty levels and participant performance values were calculated. At the end of the experiment, a questionnaire was applied to gather perceptions of the participants.

Results revealed that novice participants have never found 2 of WI type defects whereas experienced participants have found all of the defects. Overall, the defects were realized as more difficult for the novices. Additionally, novice participants' performance was lower compared to experienced ones. Considering the defect types, wrong information and wrong button type of defects were recognized as more difficult to detect compared to the wrong flow type of defects by both groups which was supported by the questionnaire answers. Moreover participants stated that using the symbols and descriptions about the experimental study helped them to detect the defects easily. The results of this study are expected to give insights to future research in ubiquitous computing interactions. As a future study we will compare the effectiveness and efficiency of the proposed MIF representation with the available languages like UML and repeat the experiment with surgeons to get their perceptions about the MIF elements.

Acknowledgements. This research is conducted for the Surgical Navigation Project (CAN) which is supported by TUBITAK (113S094). The research team would like to thank TUBITAK support for realizing this research study.

References

1. Larkin, J.H., Simon, H.A.: Why a diagram is (sometimes) worth ten thousand words. Cognit. Sci. **11**(1), 65–99 (1987)

2. Waeselynck, H., Micskei, Z., Rivière, N., Hamvas, Á., Nitu, I.: TERMOS: a formal language for scenarios in mobile computing systems. In: Sénac, P., Ott, M., Seneviratne, A. (eds.) MobiQuitous 2010. LNICST, vol. 73, pp. 285–296. Springer, Heidelberg (2012)

3. Dehlen, V., Aagedal, J.Ø.: A UML profile for modeling mobile information systems. In: Indulska, J., Raymond, K. (eds.) DAIS 2007. LNCS, vol. 4531, pp. 296–308. Springer, Heidelberg (2007)

4. Grassi, V., Mirandola, R., Sabetta, A.: A UML profile to model mobile systems. In: Baar, T., Strohmeier, A., Moreira, A., Mellor, S.J. (eds.) UML 2004. LNCS, vol. 3273, pp. 128–142. Springer, Heidelberg (2004)

5. Johnson, C.W.: Why did that happen? Exploring the proliferation of barely usable software in healthcare systems. Qual. Saf. Health Care **15**, 76–81 (2006)

6. Danado, J., Paternò, F.: Puzzle: a mobile application development environment using a jigsaw metaphor. J. Vis. Lang. Comput. **25**(4), 297–315 (2014)

7. Erturan, Y.N.: A method to improve the communication between information technology and healthcare professionals during mobile healthcare application development process. M.Sc thesis (2013)

8. Cagiltay, N.E., Tokdemir, G., Kilic, O., Topalli, D.: Performing and analyzing non-formal inspections of entity relationship diagram (ERD). J. Syst. Softw. **86**, 2184–2195 (2013)

Author Index

Printed in the United States
By Bookmasters